D0393888

RETIREMENT RX

RETIREMENT RX

The Retirement Docs' Proven Prescription for

Living a Happy, Fulfilling Rest of Your Life

FREDERICK T. FRAUNFELDER, M.D.

JAMES H. GILBAUGH JR., M.D.

AVERY ■ A MEMBER OF PENGUIN GROUP (USA) INC. ■ NEW YORK

AVERY

Published by the Penguin Group
Penguin Group (USA) Inc., 375 Hudson Street, New York, New York 10014, USA • Penguin Group
(Canada), 90 Eglinton Avenue East, Suite 700, Toronto, Ontario M4P 2Y3, Canada (a division of Pearson
Canada Inc.) • Penguin Books Ltd, 80 Strand, London WC2R 0RL, England • Penguin Ireland,
25 St Stephen's Green, Dublin 2, Ireland (a division of Penguin Books Ltd) • Penguin Group (Australia),
250 Camberwell Road, Camberwell, Victoria 3124, Australia (a division of Pearson Australia Group
Pty Ltd) • Penguin Books India Pvt Ltd, 11 Community Centre, Panchsheel Park, New Delhi–110 017,
India • Penguin Group (NZ), 67 Apollo Drive, Rosedale, North Shore 0632, New Zealand (a division
of Pearson New Zealand Ltd) • Penguin Books (South Africa) (Pty) Ltd, 24 Sturdee Avenue,
Rosebank, Johannesburg 2196, South Africa

Penguin Books Ltd, Registered Offices: 80 Strand, London WC2R 0RL, England

Most Avery books are available at special quantity discounts for bulk purchase for sales promotions, premiums,
fund-raising, and educational needs. Special books or book excerpts also can be created to fit specific needs. For details, write Penguin Group (USA) Inc. Special Markets, 375 Hudson Street, New York, NY 10014.

Library of Congress Cataloging-in-Publication Data

Fraunfelder, Frederick T.
Retirement Rx: the retirement docs' proven prescription for living a happy, fulfilling rest of your life /
Frederick T. Fraunfelder, James H. Gilbaugh Jr.
p.   cm.
ISBN 978-1-58333-311-2
1. Retirement—United States.   2. Retirement—United States—Planning.   3. Baby-boom generation—
United States.   I. Gilbaugh, James H.   II. Title.
HQ1063.2.U6F725   2008   2008009082
646.7'90973—dc22

Printed in the United States of America
1   3   5   7   9   10   8   6   4   2

BOOK DESIGN BY MEIGHAN CAVANAUGH

While the authors have made every effort to provide accurate telephone numbers and Internet addresses at the
time of publication, neither the publisher nor the authors assume any responsibility for errors, or for changes that
occur after publication. Further, the publisher does not have any control over and does not assume any responsibility for author or third-party websites or their content.

Neither the publisher nor the authors are engaged in rendering professional advice or services to the individual
reader. The ideas, procedures, and suggestions contained in this book are not intended as a substitute for consulting with your physician. All matters regarding your health require medical supervision. Neither the authors nor
the publisher shall be liable or responsible for any loss or damage allegedly arising from any information or suggestion in this book.

To our wives,

Yvonne and Marilyn,

Our families, our teachers, and our patients

ACKNOWLEDGMENTS

We have to acknowledge the game of golf! It was on the tee box of the ninth hole about six years ago that the moment of conception for our book took place. Dr. Fritz, aka "the planner," had taken a sabbatical from academic medicine. During that time he read everything he could on the nonfiscal side of retirement but wasn't satisfied with the information available to him. Dr. Jim, aka "the feeler," was semiretired, thinking about his future and loaded with ideas on how he wanted to live it. We shared our thoughts with wives, families, and friends—thus the book was born.

Early thoughts and brainstorming were done with Charlie Allis, Bill Countant, Tom Cummins, Dick Cunningham, David Duxbury and Nancy Fletcher, Jack Faust, Joe Ferguson, Betty and John Gray, Britt Hayes, Jackie and Jerry Inskeep, Dan Isaak, Jack Johnston, Jan and Bob Kalina, Meritt Linn, Jim Maletis, Ruth and Joe Matarazzo, Ron Mehl, Courtland Mumford, Margaret Beth Neal, Frank O'Conner, Jim and Shirley Rippey, George Saslow, Alice Scannell, Gary Stewart, Fred and Pat Stickel, Ken Swan, Ann and Bill Swindell, Lou Terkla, Joan and Fred Thompson, and Ted Vigeland.

Early encouragement from Ken Blanchard, Eric Bollinger, Joe Hayes, Ed Pittock, and Betsy Vierck was important to us.

Many helped proof the book and came up with excellent suggestions, including Sigrid Button, Clem Connolly, Michael Gourley, Joanne Henry, Steve Kelley, Howard Lincoln, Patricia Robertson, Mollie Suits, Richard U'ren, and Werner Zeller.

The staff at the Casey Eye Institute at Oregon Health & Sciences University in Portland, Oregon gave support—Stephanie Lyons, Kelly Medlar, Nancy Mitchell, Joan Randall, Jeannine Ransome, Joe Robertson, Bree Vetsch, and Dave Wilson. We can't forget about our golf partners, who had to hear about, get quizzed, and have ideas bounced off them between erratic shots: Ernest Blatner, Dennis Dahlin, Al Henry, Fred Nomura, Dick Newman, and George Wells.

Our patients who gave their heartfelt time, talent, and ideas filling out lengthy questionnaires that became the basis of this book get extra credit. We owe "big-time" to Marilyn Gilbaugh, who is the voice of this book and made it what it is.

Our thanks to Jean Naggar and Mollie Glick of the Jean V. Naggar Literary Agency Inc., New York, our agents, for their guidance, suggestions, and help. To Karen Kelly for her amazing organizational skills. She truly was our book doctor. And to Lucia Watson of Avery, Penguin Group USA, New York, for her understanding and expertise.

CONTENTS

PART THREE: THE EXIT CONSULTATION

RETIREMENT RX

INTRODUCTION: HURRY UP, YOUR LIFE IS WAITING

A
s doctors with subspecialties in geriatrics, we have seen many patients on the brink of, just starting, or deeply into their retirement years. Their widely varied responses to this time and its challenges are remarkable. Some rise to new heights, whereas others seem ready to heave a heavy sigh, sag into a rocking chair, and settle in for good. For instance, one patient, Joanne, a recently retired real estate agent, told us her post–work life remained the same as it was while she was selling property. The only real difference was the gift of time that retirement had given her. She was now able to indulge in a midmorning haircut or spa treatment, linger over lunch, spend extra time browsing in the library or bookstore, or take her grandchildren or just herself to an afternoon matinee, all activities that she previously had time only for in the evening or on weekends. She considered this luxury truly golden.

When we compared Joanne's outlook to that of another patient, Brian, a man who had enjoyed a successful advertising career, we saw a dramatic difference. He could find little to enjoy about his retirement and went so far as to say that he had lost much of the pleasure of living! Even leisure activities that, as a working person, he had enjoyed participating in with his wife now held little interest for him, including dinner parties, cribbage competitions, or simply discussing current events with his spouse. Some of his withdrawal, Brian admitted, came from his increasing forgetfulness, which both scared and embarrassed him. But what bothered him most of all was spending so much time by himself—a situation he had rarely found himself in when he worked. Still, he lacked the will and the gumption to get out and get on with his life. He felt lost and without direction.

What makes one person embrace the second half of life, while another seems only capable of withdrawing from it? Why did some of our patients manage to maintain the vitality that had marked their working years while others failed to make the transition? We wanted to find some information about happy retirees that would assist our patients who were finding retirement a rough go. Exploring bookstores, libraries, and the Internet, we were relentless in our search for retirement advice. Most books we found focused on financial planning, and those that didn't were anecdotal—filled with standard recommendations to eat well, get enough sleep, and exercise. Good suggestions but too general and unscientific for our needs.

The search continued in our own practices: we began to look at our patients to identify with clinical certainty the skills, habits, and characteristics associated with people who experienced what we observed to be productive, well-adjusted, or "successful" retirements, which we define as richly endowed with good health, loving relationships, outside interests, and, most important, the resilience and wisdom to graciously accept the inevitable, which is loss—of family, friends, loved ones, health, memory, and, ultimately, life.

We wanted to collect accurate data, so we created and conducted a professionally designed survey. More than fifteen hundred of our patients were asked to anonymously fill out what we had come to call The Retirement Docs' Survey. It was the first time that a survey such as this had centered on retired people and their insights. The questionnaire consisted of multiple choice and essay questions, which took anywhere from an hour to an hour and a half to complete. The return rate was an unheard-of 72 percent. Our respondents replied candidly and often at length—their essays running the gamut from succinctly matter-of-fact to lengthy and deeply emotional, from warmly positive to grimly negative.

As you can imagine, we had amassed a tremendous amount of original research and strong data. We used well-established, controlled research and analysis methods to study the results, including assistance from a local university's gerontology statistics department. After our first look at what we had gathered, we realized that retirement success is not related to gender, marital status, children, hobbies, or grandchildren. Highly successful retirees come from all walks of life, from stay-at-home moms to corporate leaders, from astronauts to cab drivers, from people forced to retire because of office politics or poor health to those who couldn't walk away from the nine-to-five treadmill.

From the initial sorting, the statisticians identified four distinct phases of retirement, and nearly eighty traits that successful retirees shared. Those findings were then further distilled, which led us to identify eight specific traits that had the greatest statistical significance and were shared by all of the top 20 percent respondents in the Retirement Docs' Survey.

The four phases and the eight traits of highly successful retirees are the backbone of *Retirement Rx*. Helping you identify and use the traits you already possess and showing you how to develop those you may lack is the purpose of this book. It's the kind of "retirement investment" that pays dividends socially, intellectually, and physically.

PART ONE

PUTTING THE REST OF YOUR LIFE IN PERSPECTIVE

Part One of *Retirement Rx* makes the case for why you need to care about your retirement, and summarizes the findings of our research. You will also find a simplified and much shorter version of the original Retirement Docs' Survey, which we call the Retirement Docs' Quiz. Complete it and find out where you rank in terms of realizing your own successful retirement. Along with the quiz, we provide a customized prescription so that you can achieve or fine-tune any of the particular eight traits that we go into in detail in Part Two of *Retirement Rx*. Sharpen your pencils and let's get on with the rest of your life.

1

A New Kind
of Retirement

Massive cultural change is about to happen. Older adults are poised to become trustees of civil life in America. As people live longer, healthier lives they are increasingly looking to give back to their communities and expand in new ways.

—Marc Freedman

Extended human longevity has rocked our world. In 1900, 4 percent of Americans were age sixty-five and older; 14 percent is the prediction for 2030. Currently, people eighty-five and older are the fastest-growing group in America. Consider this: In 1776 our life expectancy was just thirty-five years. In 1920 it had improved to where the healthiest among us could expect to live into our fifties. Today, we can look forward to living well into our seventies. If you are sixty and reading this, and free of heart disease or cancer, you could easily make it to your eighties or nineties. Medical breakthroughs and improvements in health care and lifestyle over the next two or three decades have led longevity forecasters to predict that men and women born in 2040 will have a general life expectancy of more than ninety!

More time on our hands means one thing: We better stop thinking of our post–employment life as an afterthought and start thinking of it as a second career—one that in all likelihood we'll spend as much if not more time involved in than our first! The reality is that we spend an average of twelve to sixteen years educating ourselves; twenty-five to forty years earning a living; and twenty-five to thirty-plus years in "retirement." If we play our cards right, and we can, those two or three extra decades can be a time to explore and enjoy a new set of intellectual, cultural, social, and even romantic possibilities.

We have a mutual friend named David. He is a with-it guy in his early sixties who is in comparatively good health. It occurred to him one day that after he left his job, he would have many remaining years to fill. He had to change a long-held and conventional belief that one life equaled one career. Both he and his wife, Nancy, who was nearing retirement, felt that their "second career" would allow them to freely pick where they wanted to live,

Check out the time line below. Do you notice anything interesting about it? These days, our retirement can easily equal and sometimes even surpass our wage-earning years. This represents a tremendous paradigm shift, one that changes the nature of retirement.

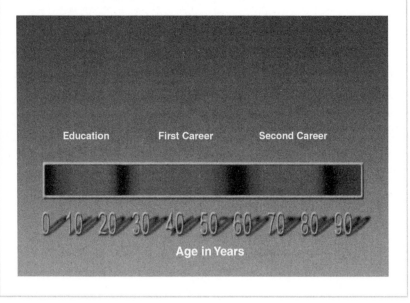

Life can be divided into three ages: the age of learning, the age of working, and the age of living.

—RETIREMENT DOCS' SURVEY

what they wanted to do, and who they wanted to be and with whom. The couple moved, pursued hobbies they had no time for previously, and took up new interests. Nancy said she, very wisely in our opinion, saw retirement as a chance to do a life makeover.

THE FOUR PHASES OF RETIREMENT

Our survey data showed that retirement is divided into four distinct phases:

PHASE ONE: PLANNING FOR RETIREMENT

In this stage, you're fully employed but preparing and planning for life beyond your income-earning years. Ideally, fiscal planning should start in your thirties and at the latest in your early forties. By the time you reach your mid- to late-fifties, you should be financially prepared for your future. This is also the time to get serious about your vision for the nonfiscal side of retirement. Keep in mind that you should give yourself at least five to ten years *before* your semi- or full retirement to start laying the groundwork for a successful retirement. Phase one is a great time to "field-test" some leisure activities that you enjoy and that you can continue to pursue through the next three phases. Fifty-eight was the average age of our phase-one survey respondents.

PHASE TWO: SHIFTING INTO SEMIRETIREMENT

Semiretirement basically means that we are working part-time in some capacity and being paid for it. Statistically, we found that our respondents with high incomes and/or high levels of education spent more time in this phase than in phases three and four, probably because they derived a great deal of satisfaction from their jobs and were not ready to entirely give up their work. Many also enjoyed the extra income part-time work provided. Spending as much time as possible during phase two is good for your emotional, financial, and physical health—studies show that seniors who don't do any work at all die sooner than their peers who labor on.

You can stay in phase two for a very long time, in fact so long that you may spend just a few years, months, or even days in phases three and four. Think of all the well-known people who have managed this: At ninety-four, fitness guru and entrepreneur Jack LaLanne is still in phase two; Hollywood director Vincent Sherman, who died at ninety-nine in 2006, worked well into the 1980s as a TV director; the revered "French Chef," Julia Child, who lived to be ninety-two, started a television career at fifty-one and continued working well into her eighties. And there are many other examples of people who made their mark *after* they reached "retirement age."

The secrets to staying in phase two for a long time are, first, to maintain your health so you *can* work, and, second, to stay focused on work you truly *enjoy* and feel passionate about. Rid yourself of drudgery or any task that bores you. One of our favorite responses was from a guy who had been a podiatrist in his first career. He had decided "Enough of feet!" long before he left his full-time occupation behind. In his retirement, he found a part-time job driving a florist's delivery van. "Everybody loves getting flowers," he told us. With no complaints, and aromatic bouquets delighting him, he genuinely enjoyed his retirement's second career. Our phase-two survey respondents had an average age of sixty-seven.

Our fathers and grandfathers looked forward to a full retirement. For one thing, it indicated to their community that they had "earned it." They had worked hard and saved wisely. Since they were financially solvent, full retirement was an achievement of pride. The pendulum has swung. We no longer throw around the "when I retire" phrase. I look forward to being productive for as long as I can.

—RETIREMENT DOCS' SURVEY

PHASE THREE: FULL RETIREMENT

These are those carefree no-responsibility years you knew would be yours one day—you just might not have expected them to arrive so quickly. You might think that you can't wait to reach full retirement, but for many it's a tough transition. While there can be a thrill in not heading to work each morning, you may soon start to wonder what you are going to do with all the hours, days, and years yet to be lived.

Along with the challenges of having to fill free time, you may start to feel some health effects related to aging, or you may have new caregiving responsibilities for a mate or an aged parent. But the good news is that you can do more in this phase—from pursuing travel to learning a new language to engaging in artistic interests—with more vitality than ever before. The world is your oyster! Phase-three survey respondents had an average age of seventy-two.

I am afraid to retire. There, I wrote it and I'm reading it back to myself. I am afraid of retirement because I am my job. My friends are my friends because of my job. My life is framed around my job, and it's been that way for thirty-four years. I love what I do, I love my friends, and I love my job. I have a wife and a family and I cherish them, but they will be around and my job won't. My company is a small operation, and my wife and I work there together, not in the same office but in the same facility. In fact, that's how we met. So now I'll retire and my wife won't. I feel like a part of me is dying and in fact it is. I don't want a watch; I don't want a party. I don't want to leave my job. I don't want to be retired.

—RETIREMENT DOCS' SURVEY

PHASE FOUR: RESTRICTED FULL RETIREMENT

When you hit the last phase of retirement, you may experience many more limitations due to health, age, and finances. Without a doubt, the most difficult period of retirement is phase four. In this phase, adversity can come at you in waves, often with little or no time to recover between assaults. Loss of loved ones, depression, chronic disease, and aging changes all have an impact. We found that women weather this period better than men do, and in fact, a few of our female respondents felt that this was their happiest, most-successful phase. And as we've already explained, these days both men and women can expect to live into their eighties, nineties, and beyond, so it is crucial to learn how to deal with the last phase of retirement because chances are good that it will be a part of most of our lives. Some people die at their desks, but most of us won't. The average age of our phase-four survey respondents was seventy-eight.

THE RETIREMENT PHASES ARE DYNAMIC

The majority of us will experience many loops, twists, and turns throughout our retirement's four phases, until restrictions set in and physical and mental limitations makes it impossible for us to be as flexible. The really good news is that our society is fluid enough to find a place for the changing lives and needs of older adults. As our numbers increase, the world will—must—become more and more amenable to those needs.

Most of the people we studied worked full-time during phase one and then entered phase two's semiretirement by either cutting back on the hours they devoted to their jobs or by leaving a first career and starting another less-demanding or less time-consuming one that was either similar to their previous work or completely different (the accountant who opens a weekend-only antique shop, for example).

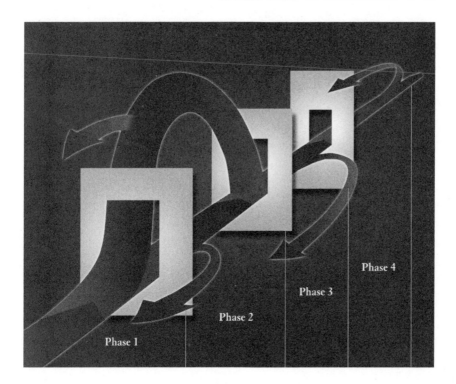

What is significant about the four phases is that they aren't necessarily progressive. Sometimes an opportunity comes along that won't take "no" for an answer, or a financial setback occurs, or just plain boredom sets in, and suddenly we go from phase two or three back to phase one's full employment. Or you may find yourself going directly from full employment right into phase three's full retirement. Then, just as suddenly, you find that you're back in phase two when you switch to a part-time job or engage in some paid consulting work.

Retirement success can also vary significantly between phases. For instance, many of our respondents reported that moving directly from full-time employment to full-time unemployment proved a most difficult adjustment. The majority of unhappy respondents were people who had been forced into mandatory and involuntary retirement owing to health issues, job loss, or an assortment of personal reasons. Retirement failure rates occurred most often in two areas: The first occurred among people who hopped directly from phase one's full-time employment into phase three's full-time unemployment. If you can transition into phase two's semiretirement and then taper off into a complete retirement, you're giving yourself an adjustment advantage. How long you spend tapering is highly individualized, so field-test various options before making life-changing decisions.

The second area of high failure rates arrives in phase four's restricted retirement. There is no doubt that phase four and the losses and life-altering changes it brings with it make the vast majority of us most vulnerable. But what was encouraging was that most people seemed able to get through the tough phases *if* they were able to make some attitude and behavior adjustments. Six to eighteen months after retirement most people become much more acclimated to their full retirement.

The Retirement Docs' Survey Says . . .

- 14 percent said retirement had changed their values and beliefs.
- 18 percent missed their old jobs.
- 21 percent had increased emotional problems related to aging.
- 20 percent experienced events that drastically affected their retirement plans.
- 20 percent were unhappy or were adjusting slowly to one or more of retirement's four phases.
- 26 percent thought retirement had changed their personalities.
- 30 percent needed considerable time to adapt. Some never fully adjusted to retirement.
- 80 percent could bounce back after experiencing a major setback.

HIGHLY SUCCESSFUL RETIREES POSSESS THE SAME EIGHT TRAITS

Along with the four phases that emerged from our study came eight traits that every one of the most highly successful, well-adjusted, and content retirees shared (the top 20 percent of respondents). The good news is that even if you do not have all of these traits today, you can learn and master them, even if you think you have a genetic or cultural predisposition against them. What's more, possessing these eight traits *guarantees* you a highly successful retirement.

1. Sowing Seeds—The Planner's Advantage

Of the eight traits, planning was statistically the most significant. Retirees who had a game plan for both the fiscal and the often-neglected nonfiscal aspects of retirement and who frequently revisited and updated that plan were the most satisfied with their lives during phases two, three, and four. Our most successful retirees were not primarily interested in money, but they had taken care of making sure they had enough of it to maintain their standard of living and sometimes even improve it.

2. Accentuate the Positive—It's All About Attitude

Your *perception* of your own health, financial well-being, age, and achievements matters more to your retirement success than your *actual* age, health, income, or position in life. Social scientists and psychologists (Martin Seligman at the University of Pennsylvania being one of the most prominent) say that while people are genetically wired to be either cheerful or grouchy, all of us can learn to be more optimistic by examining how we think about situations and consciously changing negative thoughts into positive ones.

3. Go with the Flow—Accept Change

As we age, physical and mental challenges increase. For many of us, fear plays a huge role in adjusting to a new life without the titles, labels, or acknowledgments that life before retirement provided. Each advancing phase brings with it new trials and traumas. People with the ability to accept change in their first careers will almost always carry the same ability right into their second careers. Those who successfully overcome major upheavals before retirement usually have the confidence to tackle new challenges. In all four phases, the abilities to adapt and to accept change are crucial to your success.

Our highly successful retirees considered retirement their life's bonus and emphasized these advantages:

■ Increased time devoted to leisure, social, and fitness-related activities.
■ The ability to develop and enjoy a positive attitude toward life and aging.
■ Involvement in meaningful and purpose-filled activities, including giving back to their society.
■ Freedom to do what they like.
■ The ability to live for the present, not for the past and not for the future. And many of them were doing so for the first time.
■ A chance to spend more quality time with their mate or best friend.

---

4. A Little Help from Your Friends (and Family)

Develop a wide and varied support group. Surround yourself with people your age as well as those who are older and younger. Your intimate support group should include your spouse, life partner, or best friend; your children; grandchildren; and other extended family members. In this day and age, with the definition of "family" ever broadening, it can also include a larger community made up of close friends, religious and social organizations, special-interest groups, and, yes, even a pet. Ongoing involvement with your support-group family is one of those eight traits you must master throughout your four phases to guarantee a highly successful retirement.

5. Kick Back—Enjoy Your Leisure Time

Though the kinds of interests you pursue will often vary in each retirement phase, it's important to choose and develop a wide variety of both mentally and physically challenging activities in three specific categories: those you commonly do with one other person (playing chess, seeing a movie, romantic activities); those you do in a group (golf, cards, dinner parties); and those you do by yourself (reading a book, taking a walk, shopping). Some activities, for example, seeing a play or taking a vacation, can be done in any of these three variations. These are not necessarily things that you are passionate about, but they should be enjoyable activities that free your mind and relax you. They help reduce stress by unwinding your brain. That is the essence of leisure.

6. Here's to Your Health

Seventy-two percent of the people we surveyed considered heredity the prime factor for long-lasting health and a long life. *Not true.* After age sixty it's not your genetics but your lifestyle that is the main ingredient for longevity. Most serious hereditary diseases expose themselves before age sixty; after sixty, it's not so much the hand you've been dealt as how you play it. Highly successful retirees take care of themselves: They have regular medical checkups, watch their diets, follow exercise programs, don't smoke, watch their alcohol intake, and control their weight. People with planned exercise programs had up to almost 70 percent less physical disability in the final year of their lives: yes, year is singular and it says 70 percent! That's quite a final bonus if we can learn to take care of ourselves.

7. Passion and a Purpose

In retirement, your identity no longer comes from a job title but from an overall view of yourself. The earlier you figure out what gives you a sense of fulfillment, the more successful you'll make your retirement. Engaging in an activity that makes time fly, an activity so intriguing or meaningful that you get lost in it, is a passion to hang on to. Stamp collecting, gardening, antiquing, training for and running a marathon, writing a screenplay, playing a musical instrument, and volunteering for a political or social cause are all examples of engaging and purposeful passions. And don't be afraid to make a mistake in the process of developing a new passion; they can be great learning tools. You have time to try a variety of activities and find those you really love.

8. Let the Spirit Move You

In retirement, having a belief in something "bigger" than we are can offer a major assist when we're faced with trauma. This is especially important in phases three and four, when setbacks occur more frequently, such as deteriorating physical and emotional health (in ourselves or a partner); the death of a partner, family member, or close friend; increased caregiving responsibilities; and/or major illness. Many of our respondents told us that spirituality offers them strength, solace, and hope. It's clear that facing the last stages of life without some form of spirituality is an enormous challenge.

There's a caveat to these eight traits: The 80 percent of respondents who did not make the highly successful mark (we've dubbed them the Not Yet Such Successful Retirees) lacked one or more of the eight traits. We found that every survey respondent who was missing *even one* was unable to meet the highly successful criteria. The same survey information also pinpointed that failure in, or omission of, any of the eight traits often caused failure within one or more of the four phases. That tells us that you can have all eight traits working for you in one phase, but if you fail at any one of them in another phase, you're not where you should be, and the warranty on our guarantee will run out.

We also noticed that the importance and weight of each trait varies depending on the phase, even though, for success, they are all required to one degree or another for every phase. For example, spirituality does not seem to be as important during phases one through three as it is in phase four, when it becomes crucial. Likewise, the ability to actively accept change is essential for success in phases one through three, but it becomes somewhat muted during phase four, when much of the change, except for the "final passage" may have already taken place in your life. As you read about the traits in-depth in part two, you will learn more about how and why the intensity of each trait changes throughout your life.

SO WHEN DO YOU KNOW
YOU SHOULD RETIRE?

There is no best or set time to retire. While it is usually an individual decision, sometimes, as we said earlier, retirement from a job can be forced upon people by circumstances beyond their control. If it is possible to take a sabbatical from your job (many companies actually offer this benefit), do so as a way of field-testing retirement. Or take all the vacation time you can in one fell swoop. If you hate it, well, keep working. If you loved lengthy time off, consider these guidelines as a way of helping you determine whether it is time to call it quits on your first career and get going on your second:

■ **Take a Serious Look at Your Financial Fitness:** If you can't maintain your preretirement standard of living, don't retire, or consider working part-time. Our data and the data of others suggest that not being able to live in the style to which you are accustomed is a significant factor of unhappiness for retirees.

■ **Location, Location, Location:** Happiness in retirement depends, for many of us, on one's ability to be in an environment in which we feel happy and in control. If you are fiscally fit and live in a place or can move to a place that you love, you're ready to roll.

■ **Go with Your Gut:** People know much more about themselves than they give themselves credit for. Take some quiet time and think about what you really want and what you are ready for. Most of us know when it's time to go into phase two or three, if we give it some serious thought. Make an appointment with yourself to think about your overall feelings about retirement, your health, your mate, your marriage or relationship, and whether you still like your job. These factors should also be taken into account before you make the decision to go from "business as usual" to no work at all.

ASSESS YOUR RETIREMENT READINESS

To further explore when and if it's time for you to retire and feel good doing so, ask yourself the following questions and then answer them using a scale of one to five:

1. Strongly disagree; 2. Disagree; 3. I'm neutral; 4. Agree; and 5. Strongly agree.

I have a gut feeling that it's time for me to slow down or quit work. _____

Only a small part of my self-worth comes from my work. _____

Generally, leisure time gives me more satisfaction than my work. _____

Most of my social life revolves around people outside of my work. _____

I don't have as strong a work ethic as I once did. _____

Financially I can maintain my standard of living if I don't work. _____

I look at retirement as a newfound freedom and a rebirth,
not an ending. _____

I have multiple interests outside of my work and have taken time
to develop leisure activities. _____

If I take time away from work, it does not cause me or my mate
stress. _____

I don't want a structured, routine life. _____

I look at retirement as a time to further explore happiness. _____

I have things in place that can fill the void both in time and the
self-image that my work provided. _____

Your Total Score: _____

Scoring:

48–60	You are ready to retire.
36–47	Consider semiretirement.
35 and under	Start planning before you stop working.

Now that you have a feel for when you should retire, it's time to turn your attention to what your chances are at this moment to be successful at retirement. Even if you don't have all the traits of a highly successful retiree now, you can work on developing them.

THE RETIREMENT
DOCS' QUIZ

Happy families are all alike, but each unhappy family is unhappy in its own way.

—*ANNA KARENINA*, LEO TOLSTOY

Likewise,

Highly successful retirees are all alike, but each unhappy retiree is unsuccessful in his or her own way.

—RETIREMENT DOCS' SURVEY

I f you're flipping through *Retirement Rx* and happen upon this page, STOP! Doing so could revolutionize your approach to your retirement. Give us ten minutes of your time and we'll give you back some information that will serve you well for the rest of your life. We have condensed the original survey questions from our large survey and created this more-streamlined version, the Retirement Docs' Quiz. Taking it is your big first step in guaranteeing a highly successful retirement. Your quiz results will accurately predict how well you can expect to do through all four phases of retirement. Even if you're already retired, the quiz will help you identify which areas you need to work on to improve and embrace the rest of your retirement. It's never too late to make changes.

The grading system results are accurate. In fact, in scientific lingo, our data have an alpha coefficient (reliability) of 0.75, and are highly predictive and acceptable for publication in peer-reviewed scientific journals. It's a real barometer, pointing to the kind of success you can expect from your retirement. You'll discover whether you need a tune-up in one or more of the eight traits. If you do, that's okay! Most of us do. Better to know now so that you can prepare yourself and get to work. The quiz will help you identify exactly where and/or what you're lacking. In part two we look at each trait in-depth and offer a prescription for developing and improving each one, if you find that you need work in one or more.

In order to get the most out of your retirement, retake the quiz whenever you enter or are about to enter a new phase. Each phase may require a different combination of skills and strengths, which often vary with the passage of time. Circle your response to each of the following questions, then enter that number in the "My Score" box in the column on the far right. After you've completed the quiz, total your score at the bottom. We recommend that you take this quiz whenever you have a major change in your life (use different-colored pencils so that you can note your progress over time). *Please* be honest in your answers! If you're not, we can't help you. You're only hurting yourself if you are not completely candid.

PLEASE RATE YOURSELF ON THE FOLLOWING:	POOR	FAIR	GOOD	VERY GOOD	EXCELLENT	MY SCORE
1. I can adapt or be flexible when events or circumstances in my life change.	0	2.5	5	7.5	10	

PLEASE RATE YOURSELF ON THE FOLLOWING:	POOR	FAIR	GOOD	VERY GOOD	EXCELLENT	MY SCORE
2. I am satisfied with the social support from my family and friends.	0	2.5	5	7.5	10	
3. I am satisfied with my financial planning for retirement.	0	2.5	5	7.5	10	
4. I am satisfied with my planning for the nonfinancial aspects of retirement.	0	2.5	5	7.5	10	
5. I will be able to maintain my standard of living after retirement.	0	2.5	5	7.5	10	
6. I have a positive mental outlook.	0	2.5	5	7.5	10	
7. I make an effort to control my weight.	0	2.5	5	7.5	10	

PLEASE RATE YOURSELF ON THE FOLLOWING:	POOR	FAIR	GOOD	VERY GOOD	EXCELLENT	MY SCORE
8. I have annual medical checkups.	0	2.5	5	7.5	10	
9. I am satisfied with my general health.	0	2.5	5	7.5	10	
10. Religion or spirituality positively influences my life.	0	2.5	5	7.5	10	
11. I have enough intellectual stimulation.	0	2.5	5	7.5	10	
12. I engage in and enjoy enough social and leisure activities.	0	2.5	5	7.5	10	
13. I am satisfied with my sex life.	0	2.5	5	7.5	10	
14. I get regular exercise and physical activity.	0	2.5	5	7.5	10	
15. I have a passion for multiple projects and/or subjects.	0	2.5	5	7.5	10	

PLEASE RATE YOURSELF ON THE FOLLOWING:	POOR	FAIR	GOOD	VERY GOOD	EXCELLENT	MY SCORE
16. I am involved in activities that make society better.	0	2.5	5	7.5	10	
17. I am satisfied with the variety in my leisure activities.	0	2.5	5	7.5	10	
18. I am happy with my life.	0	2.5	5	7.5	10	
19. I see myself as lucky or fortunate.	0	2.5	5	7.5	10	
20. Education level	Less than high school 0	High school 2.5	Some college 5	College degree 7.5	Postgraduate work or degree 10	
21. I smoke.	>1 pack 0	>½ pack 2.5	<½ pack 5	Quit 7.5	Never 10	
22. Alcohol consumption 1 drink = 12-oz. beer, 5-oz. wine, or 1.5-oz. liquor	>21 drinks/ week 0	14–21 drinks/ week 2.5	<14 drinks/ week 5	<7 drinks/ week 7.5	None/ occasionally 10	

Your Total Score: _____

Your Score and What It Means to You

IF YOU SCORED BETWEEN 185 AND 220:

Congratulations. You're with the top 20 percent of our Retirement Docs' Survey's respondents, our Highly Successful Retirees. Continue fine-tuning specific traits, particularly as you enter each new phase. You can guarantee yourself your own highly successful retirement if you maintain these eight traits.

IF YOU SCORED BETWEEN 150 AND 184:

Your score is in the top 40 percent, indicating that you're well on your way to a highly successful retirement but need some fine-tuning in specific traits. Which areas were you lacking in? For example, if you gave low scores to health-related questions (for example, you don't exercise), you will need to pay more attention to the health trait chapter. If you gave social questions low scores (for example, your circle of friends is very small), you need to pay attention to the support group, leisure activity, passions and purpose, and spirituality trait chapters.

IF YOU SCORED BETWEEN 120 AND 149:

Your score is in the middle of the pack, the average. Your future may be promising, but currently it's far from highly successful. You really need to focus on specific traits. Create a list of them *and make a conscious effort to improve them on a daily basis.* Mindfulness is really the key because you are so close to achieving a highly successful retirement. With a little effort and by paying close attention to the information provided for you in the following chapters, you can retake the test in six months and see a change for the better in your score.

IF YOU SCORED BETWEEN 85 AND 119:

Well, the bad news is that you've got lots of work to do. But the good news is that it is work you'll enjoy because it's all about you and your success. Your score is in the lowest 40 percent, so it's best to recognize and concentrate on the areas that indicate a need for additional attention. Whatever the phase, don't put it off: Get to work on those changes *now*. If you're not retired, commit to spending significant amounts of time working on the eight traits on your own, with a spouse or friend, or with a professional. You *can* become a highly successful retiree.

IF YOUR SCORE IS 84 OR LOWER:

It is definitely time to dig in. Your score falls in the lowest 20 percent of the Retirement Docs' Survey respondents. There is hope, especially since you've taken the time to pick up this book and take the quiz. We all have a chance to enjoy and benefit from retirement. Do a lot of checking back with *Retirement Rx* trait chapter guidelines, and retake the quiz while tracking when you change phases or when something major happens in your life.

No matter where you are on the scorecard, please take time to read about each trait more in-depth. For those who have work to do, start by setting small goals and following the advice at the end of each of the following trait sections.

PART TWO

A HIGHLY SUCCESSFUL RETIREMENT AND HOW TO MAKE IT YOUR OWN

The chapters in this section examine each of the important traits that make up all highly successful retirements. If you did well in a trait, meaning that you have a high score, don't neglect to read its corresponding chapter, as it will provide you with insights and ideas on how to maintain your strength in that area. If you are weak in one or more areas, then please pay special attention to the chapters that cover them for ideas on how to empower yourself and increase your chances of a highly successful retirement. Every trait chapter includes:

- a description and explanation of each trait.
- data and real-life anecdotes particular to the trait from the Retirement Docs' Survey and other individuals.
- the latest pertinent scientific research.
- a diagnosis so you can tell where you stand in terms of each trait.
- a prescription, including short- and long-term fine-tuning, to help you develop that trait more fully.

3

TRAIT ONE: SOWING
SEEDS—THE·PLANNER'S
ADVANTAGE

Someone to love, something to do,
and something to look forward to.

—ANCIENT CHINESE PROVERB

Highly successful retirees ranked planning as far and away the most important trait for achieving a positive retirement. Interestingly, nonfiscal planning slightly edged out the fiscal—it's not all about the money after all! It's not too much of a surprise because most of us intuitively know that in order to have a successful retirement we need to feel safe and secure. That's why many of us, very wisely, start planning for the fiscal side of retirement ahead of time, while still working full-time. Few people believe that a Social Security check alone will be sufficient for their needs. Our survey also revealed that while 92 percent of our respondents had done some financial retirement planning, only a third of them told us they'd given little to no thought to nonfiscal plans.

Transitioning from work to retirement is one of the hardest things I've ever done.
For me, the key to doing it successfully is ongoing planning.

—RETIREMENT DOCS' SURVEY

Like a savvy entrepreneur, you've got to do your research and develop a solid, realistic "business plan" when you are preparing for a second career. If you don't know how you'll spend your time, you won't enjoy a strong quality of life, and it doesn't really matter how many dollars you have in the bank. Highly successful retirees didn't scramble to put plans together weeks before they left their jobs. They started early, thinking, researching, and laying groundwork. The good news is that if you're reading this book, you've probably realized that you need to start planning for retirement. Even if you're already retired, the information in this book can help you enjoy retirement even more.

There are six categories that must be addressed if you hope to plan a highly successful retirement:

■ Your finances
■ Your work
■ Your life with your mate
■ Your professional and/or personal-growth goals
■ Your sense of identity
■ Your leisure time

As you work through the questions and ideas in this chapter, bear in mind that it's okay to approach planning in your own way. Maybe you're a person who likes to analyze data, making lists of the pros and cons of each decision you make; maybe you prefer thoughtful meditation or brainstorming with your friends; or maybe you'd rather register for a class. The questions we pose here will help you organize your thoughts. It doesn't matter how you come up with your retirement plan, just as long as you spend time making one. Speaking of spending time, be sure you spend some of it looking through our Retirement Resources at the back of the book for classes, support groups, and fields of study that are ready and waiting to assist you.

FINANCIAL SECURITY

Two-thirds of my retired clients who started to plan for retirement after age forty said that they should have started much sooner.

—RETIREMENT DOCS' SURVEY

It doesn't take a Wharton degree to know that the earlier you start formulating a financial plan for your retirement, the better. Our survey results revealed that the key to success isn't the total amount of assets accumulated—it's the ability to maintain your standard of living throughout the four phases. Ideally, you want to start setting some money aside in your late thirties or early forties. As doctors, we know when to refer out, and we'll leave specific investment advice up to the personal-finance experts.

A professional personal-finance manager will be able to help you determine whether you need to work during phase two, and how much money you need to make in order to fund phases three and four. As you begin to plan for the financial side of retirement, consider how soon you plan to retire, whether you will continue to pursue some paid work once you do scale back, and whether downsizing to a smaller, easier-to-maintain, and more conveniently located (to stores, entertainment, etc.) house makes sense for you. Retirees also should make contingency plans for the unforeseen complications of getting older, including illness and disabilities.

One potentially costly aspect of an active retirement, involving various leisure pursuits and travel, along with typical health-care and home maintenance costs, is an increase in spending—think sport activity fees; theater tickets; plane fare to faraway destinations; meals in restaurants; indulging in interests such as wine, rare books, antiques, or other collectible items; doctor visits; and home maintenance costs (as you get older, you often have to pay someone else to clean, maintain, and make basic home repairs). Almost all the respondents who indicated that they'd given some thought to their financial security ahead of time were able to cover the costs of their retirement.

If you have fiscal plans in place for retirement—a 401(k), pension, IRA, or savings account that you contribute to regularly, a diversified portfolio of stocks and bonds, and/or real estate investments, for example—you will likely be in the same position as our highly successful retirees find themselves: 65 percent of them indicated that their postretirement income remained the same as their preretirement income, 29 percent said it increased after retirement, and only 6 percent reported that it declined. Those who experienced a voluntary decrease in their income but kept their standard of living similar to what they had enjoyed in their working years fared well. However, those who experienced a forced or involuntary decrease in their standard of living felt significant stress and unhappiness.

Ask yourself the following two questions about financial planning. Your answers should help you and your financial planner get started on the appropriate strategy for your circumstance:

1. Do you project that you can maintain your current standard of living after you stop working full-time?
    ■ I believe that I am on the right track to maintaining my current standard of living in my retirement.
    ■ I don't know whether I can maintain my current standard of living when I am retired.
    ■ I don't think I will be able to maintain my current standard of living in my retirement.

2. If not, then have you thought about how to reduce spending (say, by cutting back or rearranging costs of social outings, reducing gift giving, or moving from a house you own to a smaller, less costly one or even a rental) so that you can maintain financial security and the freedom to pursue the activities that you love?
    ■ Some things that can reduce my spending when I am retired are:
        a.
        b.
        c.
        d.
        e.

NONFISCAL SECURITY

The difference between the moderately successful and the highly successful retirees in our survey was the amount of time and energy highly successful respondents devoted to nonfiscal planning. One of the most interesting findings of our study is that once you meet a certain threshold of financial security, your happiness in retirement isn't determined by how much money you have to spend—it's determined by how fulfilling you find postretirement work, relationships, well-being, and hobbies.

WORK

Postretirement work is certainly part of a larger financial picture, but we think it is more important to your emotional, psychological, and physical well-being than it is to your pocketbook. We discovered that the longer you work, the longer and happier your life will be. That's why we listed it first under nonfinancial retirement planning.

AARP's latest survey reports that 80 percent of Baby Boomers plan to do some work after retirement. Although most of us will stay in the same occupation, many of us will branch out or start businesses unrelated to our previous occupation, which may provide another bonus, retraining or education. And don't think it will be difficult for you to find a job once you've hit sixty or seventy. Depending on where you live and what you want to do, you may find employment riches waiting for you. Many economists predict that by 2030, the United States could experience a labor shortage of 35 million workers. Many businesses have responded to what they see as a coming labor crisis by seeking out older workers. There are also advantages for these companies in hiring older workers: Insurance costs are lower, since many senior citizens are enlisted in government health-care programs; older workers are more experienced and reliable than their younger counterparts; and senior citizens are a growing population that represents a large block of available and willing labor.

Consider the following factors when thinking about the kind and amount of work you want to do in your second career. Your answers will help you pinpoint the best job options for you:

- Why are you working?
- Do you work *primarily* for the income or for the activity?
- How much money do you have to make? Would there be a job you would not take because the pay was too little?
- What values, personality traits, and strengths influenced your choice of a first career? Have these values, traits and strengths changed over time? If so, what kinds of jobs would make best use of your current attributes?
- How much did your first career contribute to your sense of self or identity? Were there parts of your personality left untapped by your first career? If so, what kinds of jobs would allow you to explore these other aspects of yourself?
- Do you want to stay in your field? Would your current employer consider keeping you on part-time or as a consultant? Have you discussed this possibility with your company?
- Do you want to do something different?
- Do you want to reserve more recreational time during your active retirement years? How will this affect the kind of work you choose?
- How introverted or extroverted are you, and what level of social interaction would you like your second career to provide?
- Would a job that puts you in contact with people, such as part-time retail or restaurant work, or a customer-service role, be appealing, or would a more autonomous position that gives you a chance to learn new skills hold more interest (such as computer programming)?
- Is there a business you always wanted to start that uses your skills, talents, or interests—such as a book or antique store, craft, or carpentry? If so, how much capital would you need? Would you have to get a small-business loan? Is there a location near you that could

support such an enterprise, or could you combine the start of the business with a move to a location where you want to put down new roots?

■ How many hours a week do you plan to work?

■ Do you plan to work the same number of hours for the indefinite future, or do you plan to scale back further in the next few years?

Planning With Your Mate

Planning your second career is about you, but if you've got a life partner, then you won't be successful in putting your plans into action unless you consider your partner. Like a starry-eyed youth embarking on marriage for the first time, we've known newly retiring couples who imagine that their "new" life together will be blue skies, long walks hand in hand, sharing sunsets, and rekindling their early romance. Lovely, wonderful, and most certainly possible, but remember, we're living real life here. Retirement usually brings with it more "for better and for worse," and we all agree that life together is best when it's "for better."

When discussing your mutual retirement plans, talk about the lifestyle you'd both like to lead, where you both want to live, and who you both want to be close to. You may find that your visions differ on some or even many aspects of retirement. Think compromise. Settle on a plan that works for both of you. For example, you may have to put your dreams of living on a golf course in the sun on hold until your spouse is ready to retire and/or thinking the same way. If your lifelong ambition is to climb in the Himalayas and your mate hates heights, talk about climbing with a group of friends while your spouse realizes a life's dream doing what's high on his or her list. Retirement doesn't equal communal house arrest. You don't have to and you shouldn't do everything together. Chances are good that you haven't lived joined at the hip before retirement. Remember that a healthy relationship is built on independence and mutual respect, plus your togetherness.

(continued)

How much "together" time do you envision having on a daily basis? This is especially important if you both worked full-time in different businesses. Reducing work schedules or entirely eliminating them, then adjusting to a lack of structure, can be a shock to both of your emotional systems. "Who is this person?" you might ask yourself, if you spend an entire week at home with your spouse. If you find yourself irritated with a mate who is now home full-time, don't let your frustration fester— address your concerns and feelings honestly, compassionately, and right away. Figure out a way for each of you to spend time apart during the day—even if it is in separate rooms.

A retired couple we know, Sally and Ralph, prepared for constant togetherness by staying involved in their community. They downsized and bought a smaller house just a few blocks away from the one in the same town where they raised their family. They love riding bikes in the country, and three of their four children (and their offspring) live within fifty miles, so they visit them very often, alone or together. They have a variety of friends nearby as well. Ralph is involved in the local Rotary Club, and Sally is president of her town's garden club. In short, they have strong ties to the community. All of these social ties help alleviate any potential tension they may have when they find themselves at home, together, all the time. When they want to get away or really need a change of scenery, the couple can, together or individually, visit their fourth son, who lives with his wife and son about 120 miles away. And yes, their son and his family look forward to those visits.

Personal Growth and Self-Esteem

How do you want to be remembered? And how are you going to become that person? Many of us found our sense of identity and self-esteem in our first careers—whether we were involved in a successful occupation or supervised a successful household and family or both. If you're one of these people, where is your new self-image going to come from in retirement? For some of us, this might be an opportunity to reinvent our identities and leave a different or bigger legacy. Maybe you've worked in a corporate office and you're ready to give back to your community through volunteer work or by organizing or sponsoring a social interest group. Or maybe you want to mentor young people or someone starting out in your business. Perhaps you simply want to spend more time with family and friends because there was limited time with them while you were working. Whatever you decide is important, however, plan for your legacy not just in terms of leaving your money to a good cause. Your time and involvement while you're still around are just as important.

Your interests and skills will be best used in volunteer work that actually means something to you. If you're an animal lover, you could find yourself happier than you ever imagined working with those furry wonders—and it's on your own schedule. If you love art, becoming a docent at a museum or a member of a development committee are both wonderful ways to spend your time, are legacy-building, and help establish a solid and ongoing social structure.

Ann, one of our survey respondents, wrote that with just two and a half years left before she would retire at age sixty-five, she was busy planting the seeds for her happily anticipated free time and her legacy—literally. While Ann and her husband are still working, they use vacation time to visit successful community-garden projects all across the United States. Then, when retirement arrives, the first thing Ann plans to do, she told us, is to throw her own retirement party and invite all the people in her neighborhood to be her guests. Providing plenty of food and drink, she will conclude the celebration with a presentation on how she imagines the evolving community garden in her own area becoming even larger and more lush, with recommendations on how to involve people of all ages in its expansion and continuation.

Both of us know Bill, a man in his seventies, who has been married, divorced, and remarried. As a result, he has raised a combined family. Bill is accumulating grandchildren faster than he had ever anticipated. He has always been keenly interested in woodworking, and found that making a set of building blocks each from a different wood, for each grandchild's third birthday, held ongoing educational benefits for both his grandchildren and himself. In the process, Bill has become a recognized expert on woods both common and rare. His love of his grandchildren and his woodworking provides him with a positive self-image, a creative outlet (each set of blocks has a unique style of lettering and different images), and continuing family and community involvement.

Here are some questions that will help you identify your second career self-image and legacy-building aspirations, whether they be recognition from a world body, getting yourself a new body, or enjoying, for the first time, being more of a homebody. As you see it:

- How do you want to be remembered? What can you do to make it happen?
- What is a pressing matter facing society today? How can you address that need?
- What are the charities or interest groups or political candidates you have contributed to in the past, and which ones do you contribute time or money to now? Do any of them need the skills you can provide?
- Can any of your passions or interests be matched with a cause or nonprofit institution?

LEISURE

Research has shown that the leisure activities people pursue when they retire are the same as or similar to the ones they pursued before retirement. For instance, people who liked to do things in groups are not all of a sudden going to enjoy solo activities, and vice versa. However, this does *not* mean that you can engage only in activities you've enjoyed in the past. Far from it. It does mean that your essential self needs to be reflected in the activities you pursue. For instance, a person who has always loved reading cookbooks and cooking before retirement may now pursue cooking lessons, expanding techniques and in-depth knowledge of different cuisines with the possibility of combining travel, cultural study, and cuisine.

A soon-to-be-retired attorney we know, Mike, will combine his interest in certain leisure activities and personal passions with a plan to be close to his favorite niece, her husband, and their children, who live in Manhattan. Since he is long-divorced, single, and has no children, being close to Amanda and her family is important. But so is his love of people watching, walking, opera, music, and theater. Still living in New Jersey, he's already bought a seven-hundred-square-foot apartment in the city, which he sublets for the time being—the profit on rent he gets each month goes right into his "opera fund." The smaller place will be the perfect size for him when he stops working.

Enjoying a variety of leisure activities is actually one of the eight traits of all highly successful retirees. We've devoted an entire section to it (see page 17) so we won't spend too much time in this chapter going into it in great depth. However, here are a few questions to get you thinking and planning future leisure pursuits:

- What parts of retirement are you most excited about?
- How do you plan to realize these goals? Are you finally going to write that novel or perfect your golf swing, spend more time with grandkids or devote your time to a good cause?
- Can you make a list of six of your current leisure activities, and try to pinpoint which of them you'd like to devote more time to?
  1.
  2.
  3.
  4.
  5.
  6.

THE DIAGNOSIS

In first careers, we each have our individual styles. Some people like deadlines and structure, whereas others are procrastinators or prefer to fly by the seat of their pants. We're likely to approach our second careers similarly. There are many different ways to plan for retirement. For example, Dr. Fritz is an organized, deadline-oriented person. He started planning for the nonfiscal side of retirement way ahead of time.

My father, who lived to be ninety-four, was miserable in retirement. He was in show business, and when he left the stage, he had nothing to replace it. I witnessed his unhappiness and I didn't want it to happen to me.

Ten years before my projected retirement I took a sabbatical, and I read everything I could get my hands on and talked to anyone and everyone who knew anything about retirement. I then formulated my nonfiscal plan by field-testing various leisure activities. I took up golf for the first time at age fifty-five. I field-tested the art of bonsai but gave it up because my wife and I traveled a lot, and caring for the trees became stressful. I have always been a "planning kind of guy" and became obsessed with how to become highly successful in retirement.

—DR. FRITZ

In contrast, Dr. Jim is more spontaneous and intuitive. His retirement plan is likewise more spontaneous, but he has still laid the groundwork for a secure retirement.

My life has been patterned after what I learned from my extended family. I'm lucky enough to have lots of relatives, including down-and-outers and multimillionaires. Observing my family provided examples for me throughout my life. I saw firsthand that "the almighty dollar" was not my answer for living a successful life. Whatever my life's goals demanded, I always made time for leisure activities.

Early in my career I made a financial retirement plan but never thought about the need to plan for the nonfiscal. Along with a very full and satisfying ca-

reer, I maintained a wide social network and multiple hobbies. My wife calls me an emotional planner. Researching the materials for this book, mainly creating the Retirement Docs' Survey, and working with the data it provided has me fascinated with the knowledge that eight traits can guarantee my own successful retirement. If ever a doctor got a taste of his own medicine, this is it!

—DR. JIM

Whatever your style, the following questions should help you determine the planning you have ahead of you to ensure your successful retirement, and how much work it will entail.

1. What amount of time have you devoted to planning the nonfiscal side of retirement?
   ■ I have given as much time to the nonfiscal as to the fiscal.
   ■ I have spent some time planning for the nonfiscal aspects of my retirement.
   ■ I have given the nonfiscal little to no thought.

2. Have you talked with your mate about your retirement plans and mutual interests regarding retirement?
   ■ Yes.
   ■ No.

3. Have you investigated postretirement work options?
   ■ Yes.
   ■ No.
   List five that you are involved with now and/or would like to continue or explore when you're retired.
   a.
   b.
   c.
   d.
   e.

4. Have you found any activities that will allow you to contribute to your family or society, providing you with the same sense of fulfillment that your first career gave you?

■ Yes.

■ No.

5. Have you started pursuing a few more leisure activities—activities that specifically stimulate your mind—so that you'll have other interests should physical limitations dictate? Think about what is of interest to you—and remember, none of it is set in stone.

■ Yes.

■ I've given some thought to them.

■ No.

List five that might be of interest to you now—remember, these can change and should be updated at least once a year. Change is good!

a.

b.

c.

d.

e.

If you answered the preceding questions with positive responses and had no problems filling in the lists, you are a planner and on the right track to realizing a fulfilling retirement. If some of your answers or lack of them indicate that you have not given the time needed to ensure a successful head start, it's essential that you start focusing on the areas that need attention. When completed, it will put you on a par with our top 20 percent. We can guarantee you that your plans will prove to be an asset to you for the rest of your life.

THE RETIREMENT DOCS' PRESCRIPTION

Whatever your current phase of retirement, it's time to start transitioning from "making a living" to "making your life"—a great slogan for a T-shirt! Now is the time to start thinking about where you want to live; who you want to spend time with; how you want to spend your time; and, most important, who *you* want to be. If you're not naturally a planner, this might sound daunting, but it needn't be. You've taken the first steps by picking up this book, taking the retirement quiz, and pinpointing which of the eight traits you need to develop further. Now please continue reading about the other seven traits, and you'll find yourself well on your way to a fantastic rest of your life!

4

TRAIT TWO: ACCENTUATE
THE POSITIVE—IT'S ALL
ABOUT ATTITUDE

Any fact facing us is not as important as our attitude towards it,
for that determines our success or failure.

—NORMAN VINCENT PEALE

There is a subgroup within our highly successful retirees who are in poor physical health, but, because of strong positive attitudes along with their ability to accept change (and often a strong spirituality as well), they cope with any disabilities exceedingly well. In fact, our perception of our health or our attitude toward it seems to be as important as our actual health. For example, we know a guy named George, who is being treated for prostate cancer. Instead of wallowing in self-pity and viewing his diagnosis as a death sentence, he is treating his disease as an opportunity. He has started a sixty-plus support group at the hospital where he gets his chemo; he volunteers as a peer counselor to men who have just been diagnosed; and once a month he reads stories to the kids in the children's wing of the hospital. The caring obligations George has established may well make him live longer, and they will without a doubt give him a better mental quality of life.

It goes without saying that George will encounter some tough times, but by and large his optimistic behavior will get him through it.

Then there's Shirley—the arthritis in her shoulders and knees causes her pain a good deal of the time. You'd never know it, though. She's too busy knitting sweaters and blankets for her newest grandson, finding interesting yarns to use, and searching out novelty or vintage buttons to embellish them. So taken has the woman in the knitting store become with Shirley's efforts, she wants her to make some of her creations to sell in the shop! Who has time to "feel the pain" when there's so much to do?

A good attitude is not just of aid to those who are sick. Our friend Phillip has a ball throwing huge parties. He's never ruffled if the band arrives late or if the red wine doesn't show. Indeed, Phillip has an innate ability to turn negatives into positives, which we attribute to his flexible nature. Phillip just isn't rigid and certainly isn't into perfection. He innately knows that parties are supposed to be fun. He knows that the band *will* eventually turn up, and he's got enough cranberry juice for anybody desperate for something red to drink, which he labels Phillip's Folly, Vintage 2007, which will in the end make his party even more memorable.

Likewise, one of our wives works on call with her friend, Suzanne, who founded and runs a home-based company that creates and organizes indexes for books. Publishing companies often outsource indexing, and this fifty-something dynamo has all the work she can handle; yet she appears to remain minimally stressed as a project's deadline approaches. Nineteenth-century British statesman Benjamin Disraeli once said, "The secret of success is constancy to purpose." We suspect that that is just what is happening in Suzanne's case: She is positive that her projects will get done because she never lets a job overwhelm her. She calmly takes each aspect of indexing step-by-step, bit by bit, and her projects are always completed on schedule.

Eloise is a gracious grandmother of eleven. She is one of those timeless beauties, and although we would never ask her age, we guess her to be somewhere in her late seventies. She has an unflappable ability to have all of her grandchildren running around her house, if not actually hanging off her, as she throws open the doors of her home to a fund-raising event benefiting one of the many organizations with which she is involved. There she stands, greeting well over one hundred guests with ease and heartfelt warmth, with no attempt to rid herself of the children. She is so comfortable with herself, her guests, and those kids that guests can't help but be sucked into her world and her warmth.

The common thread that weaves these five stories together: George, Shirley, Phillip, Suzanne, and Eloise each have a positive attitude and a cheerful outlook on life. When we first noticed that our highly successful retirees all had similar positive attitudes, we wondered if the trait was learned or if our participants were born under a lucky star. As it turns out, the people we view as lucky—those who seem to sail through life with a smile, no matter the hardships they face—are not that way owing to happenstance. These people have subconsciously or consciously worked on developing a positive attitude toward life.

Research has found that happy people have a particular mind-set. They often have a history and track record of multiple successful past outcomes, but they aren't afraid to take risks or to fail. They have an expectation of continued success, so one setback is not viewed as a tragedy, just a bump in the road to maneuver around. Optimists are willing to experiment with different ways of doing things, and they take calculated risks if they think outcomes will be positive or fruitful. They tend to be gregarious, with an openness that allows them to accept constructive criticism, implement outside suggestions, and change their own behavior if they think it will change an outcome. The happy person gets more "hits" in life because he or she is purposefully positioned to come to bat more often, and is hopeful about striking the ball. Optimism is not associated with intelligence, academic achievement, or wealth. You're in control; you make the choice. *In other words, happiness is a skill you can learn.*

It's a good thing that you can train your brain to be happy because many scientists view a person's emotional state as one of the most important variables when predicting overall long-term good health. Researchers confirm that retirees with a positive attitude and optimism are healthier and live longer. One recent study found that people with positive attitudes lived an average of 7.5 years longer than people who had negative outlooks. This was true regardless of age, gender and socioeconomic status.

Esther Sternberg, M.D., author of *The Balance Within: The Science Connecting Health and Emotion,* says that the immune and nervous systems communicate with each other, creating a clear link between emotions and disease. In response to stressful or "negative" emotions such as anger or fear, the body secretes stress hormones, which make the heart and lungs work faster, tighten muscles, slow digestion, and elevate blood pressure. Pessimists are more likely to frequently excrete stress hormones, and, according to Sternberg, depression and physical illnesses are likely to follow prolonged negativity. On the other hand, positive emotions promote health and faster healing and recovery because positive emotions create immune system antibodies.

As Luck Would Have It

A classic joke goes this way: "LOST DOG: Right ear missing due to dogfight; left leg missing—caught in bear trap; lost right eye from thorn injury; lost tail in a lawn mower accident; and lost manhood jumping over a barbed-wire fence. Answers to the name of Lucky." Like the best humor, this story has more than a grain of truth to it: We all know people like Lucky who seem to have everything going for them, no matter what befalls them.

We admit that retraining your brain to be optimistic isn't easy. Formed by years of personal behavior patterns, our mind-set is deeply interconnected with many parts of our personality, and creates something called our *explanatory style.* University of Pennsylvania professor Martin Seligman, Ph.D., author of *Learned Optimism* and a leader in the field of positive psychology, defines explanatory style as a way of thinking about the cause of situations in our lives or how we explain why things happens to us the way they do. Explanatory styles can run the gamut from highly optimistic, the belief that the future holds promise, to pessimistic, the belief that the future will bring negative outcomes. Seligman argues that our explanatory style is formed during childhood, and unless deliberate steps are taken to change a negative style, it will last a lifetime, affecting the way we relate in the world.

In later life, we have essentially two choices. Either we can grow more conservative, more negative, more self-centered, more apprehensive, more narrow-minded, more opinionated, and more argumentative. Or we can reach out and be more helpful, more interested in others, more dedicated to helping and serving others, more tolerant, more forgiving, and more fun to be with. In other words, as I see it we have a choice. I realize that it takes effort but I know that there is a road to greater happiness and a feeling of self-worth and that's where I plan to travel.

—RETIREMENT DOCS' SURVEY

Here's an everyday extreme example of a pessimist and an optimist but one we can all relate to:

Joan, a pessimist, is in the grocery store and realizes she is in a very long line. She berates herself for being stupid enough to go to the grocery store at a busy time, knowing she will now be late for her next appointment. She feels trapped. Her day is ruined! Why does she always end up in the slowest lines? She directs her anger at the clerk, who seems to be purposely working as slowly as possible and engaging in inane prattle with customers. She's irritated at the people around her, shooting them angry looks. Mostly, though, Joan is mad at herself. In fact, she is so distraught by the time she gets to the clerk that she's close to tears. It takes her fifteen minutes of sitting in the parking lot to cool down and compose herself. She realizes that her two-fisted bangs on the steering wheel did nothing to aid in her angst. Now she's later than even she expected to her next meeting. When she finally arrives, Joan is completely flustered, unhappy, and disorganized.

There's also an optimist, Gail, stuck in the same line, right in back of Joan. She knows that there's probably a shorter line, and she should have looked around for it, but this is where she is, so she'll make the best of it. Gail uses the waiting time to make a to-do list, catch up on a couple of phone calls, and glance through *O,* Oprah's magazine, which is right there in the rack in front of her. By the time she's next in line, she has found a recipe she's been searching for; called her cousin in Cincinnati and a client in New York; and planned her weekend activities. The wait seemed to go by very quickly. Gail might be a few minutes late for her next appointment, but she's also called ahead to let them know she's running behind. They are, too, as it turns out! So everything has worked out perfectly.

While the grocery story scenario is a simplified example of how different explanatory styles can impact our lives, it's also a very real one. In short, how we tend to react to and resolve problems in general can be changed depending on how we look at a set of circumstances—whether it is a traumatic event or just an everyday irritation.

A positive attitude is not something that happens to you; it is a deliberate choice, which ultimately becomes habit. You are positive by deciding in advance that you will always choose the most resourceful response to any given set of circumstances . . . even if you are justified otherwise you will always take the high road . . . in a manner consistent with the goals you want to reach and the person you want to become.

—Success coach and author Tom Newberry

THE RESPONSE FACTOR

As geriatric doctors, we are often the bearer of life-changing, life-threatening, and/or fatal pronouncements. When we deliver news of a major illness, we find that after a patient's initial shock and normal short-term depression, the variability of responses is striking, depending on whether the person is a pessimist or an optimist. Optimists see situations as things caused outside of themselves, as temporary and owing to specific reasons. An optimistic patient may respond to bad news something like this: "Hey, I didn't expect to make it this far! I'm thankful to have any years left," or "I'm happy to take whatever time I can get." Pessimists, on the other hand, tend to feel that events are caused either by their behaviors or by outside forces beyond their control, which are working to destroy them. Pessimistic patients tend to give up, give in to depression and/or substance abuse, and respond something like "It figures. What's the point of living?"

Our estimation of recovery and survival rates for each of these two types of patients is very different. The optimist has a better chance of living better and longer than his pessimistic counterpart. Optimists will continue to take care of their health and seek out support from family and friends, whereas the depressed patient might "forget" to take important medicines, begin eating badly, and stop reaching out to family and friends. The extended longevity and better quality of life of the happy patient are precisely why having an optimistic outlook is so crucial as we age: The ability to accept and work through traumatic or stress-causing events, which happen more frequently as we age, and to treat them as temporary and specific, allows optimistic individuals to see their behaviors' positive effect on the outcome of their world. By compartmentalizing each component, we are able to behave in a proactive manner.

When someone generally believes that he or she is helpless and at the mercy of a cruel world, the occurrence of a traumatic event can appear to be daunting and of global proportion. The person reacts, thinking the bad outcome will last forever, and allows himself or herself to be ruled by thoughts of regret, as in "If only I'd done something different." Often completely overwhelmed, the person lacks the ability to actively participate in self-improvement and move through and past the event. If you are overwhelmed with feelings of hopelessness and loss, you tend to neglect physical as well as mental health.

A highly successful university baseball coach said he primarily recruited only high school players who came from strong, winning programs. He felt these kids only knew success, so would work extra hard to avoid failure.

—RETIREMENT DOCS' INTERVIEW

One of our patients, Maria, a stable and attractive seventy-two-year-old woman, is the mother of three successful grown children. Over the past five years we had watched her grow more and more depressed as a result of a series of events. It began with prolonged caregiving responsibilities involving her aged and senile mother. Her own chronic arthritic pain grew more severe with the passing years, and then the unexpected death of her mate took what little wind was left in her sails. Maria felt overwhelmed and helpless by the bad hand life had dealt her over the course of just a few years. With the help of her family and her doctors, she was able to see that life was still worth living—her children loved her and needed her. She had grandchildren who adored her. Maria's arthritis was treatable, and, in fact, with the right course of therapy she regained a lot of movement and dexterity in her hands. An appropriate prescription antidepressant also helped, as did developing a strong support system of friends. It became easier for her to realize how much better off she was than many of her peers and to regain her optimistic attitude.

Some good news for optimists (and for pessimists, too): Exposure to life's unavoidable traumas actually appears to prepare you for the feelings of helplessness that can come from old age. That is, major setbacks occurring anytime during a first career, which you are able to overcome, give you the confidence you need to meet traumatic events in retirement's phases two, three, and four. But if you can't find at least a glimmer of something positive that emerges from the traumatic event, chances are that your negative feelings will grow and you will only become more jaded as you age. That's why cultivating a positive attitude through your whole life is so important. It helps you find the hope and courage to move when you are faced with adversity. In retirement, it's even more important because it's inevitable that there will be more hurdles at this stage of your life. We want you to be able to jump over them!

Another one of our patients, Barbara, explained how her feelings about despair and moving on had changed through a life-altering experience. She had known a couple who had lost their sixteen-year-old son in a car accident. Both parents were understandably devastated, she explained. The father gave up his dental practice and moved to a small cabin in a remote area.

He just couldn't get on with his life. The boy's mother joined her husband for a while but at one point came to acknowledge that her son was gone, and though she would mourn his loss forever, she was still alive. Her husband was unable to come to terms with his grief.

Eventually the woman found it necessary to leave her husband and rebuild her life on her own. Barbara said that when her own son was killed in a similar accident, she remembered that couple and their different reactions and made a conscious decision to follow the path that the mother took, as opposed to the father. Yes, she was crushed by the death of her son, but because Barbara was naturally an optimist, she had the strength to continue living a productive life and, in doing so, honored the life of her son. "Little did that boy's mother know that her decisions, made long before my own, provided me with some insight to move on with my own life," she explained.

YOU HAVE THE POWER TO BE POSITIVE

Why choose to be optimistic? As we've discussed, there are sound scientific facts linking an optimistic outlook to a positive mood, a positive morale, perseverance, effective problem solving, excellent social skills, and good mental and physical health. Simply put, thinking good equals feeling good. Optimistic people take more risks, but that makes sense; they feel confident in their decisions—they believe they will succeed. But, most important, optimistic people remain open to all of life's possibilities, which is so important to successful aging and retirement. And as you age, this becomes more and more important. Too many of us seem willing to shut down and let our passion and interests slip away later in life. If you have a positive outlook, however, you'll find the courage to open your mind and take on new challenges and adventures—we've known seventy-somethings who've moved to Europe and the Caribbean, learned to ski, and written a play and had it produced. You can do whatever you can dream up—with the right attitude!

DIAGNOSIS

Listed below are some questions to help you discover where you lie on the optimistic-pessimistic spectrum. Think carefully about each of them and how they apply to you. Remember, these are building blocks, and they are all about you and your retirement success.

1. Did your parents value strong character, emotions, and happiness?
   - Yes
   - No
   - Somewhat

2. Do you feel that despite challenges, you will remain hopeful about your future?
   - Yes
   - No
   - Somewhat

3. Do you feel that you are a confident person?
   - Yes
   - No
   - Somewhat

4. Do you believe that your way of doing things will work out for the best?
   - Yes
   - No
   - Somewhat

5. Do you have a clear picture of what you want to happen in your future?
   - Yes
   - No
   - Somewhat

6. Do you know that you will succeed with the goals you set for yourself?
   ■ Yes
   ■ No
   ■ Somewhat

7. If you experience a bad outcome, can you focus on the next opportunity and plan to do better?
   ■ Yes
   ■ No
   ■ Somewhat

8. Did your grade school and high school teachers have lasting positive influences on your adult decision-making?
   ■ Yes
   ■ No
   ■ Somewhat

9. Did your teachers have any negative influence on your adult decision-making?
   ■ Yes
   ■ No
   ■ Somewhat

10. Have you recovered from a major trauma in your life and learned something beneficial during and from it?
    ■ Yes
    ■ No
    ■ Somewhat

11. When negative information comes your way, can you process it thoroughly and apply it to your goal-setting to make it a success?
    ■ Yes
    ■ No
    ■ Somewhat

12. Do you think that you are a creative and flexible person?
   - ■ Yes
   - ■ No
   - ■ Somewhat

If you answered most of the questions with "yes," you have a naturally optimistic explanatory style and will find it easier to maintain it as you age. If you circled mostly "no" and "somewhat" and just a few "yes" answers, you have to work hard to change what could well be a negative attitude. It won't be easy, but with mindfulness and concentration (see our suggestions and exercises later in the chapter), you can improve your disposition by at least 50 percent—this is significant! However, even if you have positive answers for all of the above questions, be aware that in all likelihood, you will experience multiple traumatic situations as you age that can leave you emotionally stretched and overloaded. When bad things happen when we are young, they usually don't happen frequently and we have the wherewithal to recover from them.

As we age, even starting as early as our fifties, traumas occur more frequently, starting with the loss of our job (even if it's voluntary), the loss of friends (whether because they move away or die), and our own increased propensity toward injury and illness, giving us less and less time to recover between events. The impact of those traumas can be reduced if you know that such things are bound to happen as an inevitable part of life and accept them as natural. If you can manage to develop such an attitude toward the rest of your life, we guarantee that you will enjoy it more, no matter what.

THE RETIREMENT DOCS' PRESCRIPTION

If you didn't respond positively to the diagnosis statements, there are simple things you can do to increase your positive attitude. But they take consistent daily practice and patience:

1. **Promise to be positive.** Each morning when you rise, look at yourself in the mirror and commit to being positive just for the day. If necessary, write down "I will be positive" on a piece of paper and tape it to your mirror so you see it everyday. This sounds pretty corny, but you will be surprised at how effective it is in reminding yourself to get the day off to a good start.

2. **Take a moment.** When something happens that you would normally react negatively to (a long line in the grocery store, a rude driver, a depressing phone call from a friend), don't judge it right away as a bad thing. Take a minute and stop yourself from having a bad thought. Changing negative beliefs or opinions into positive ones requires either challenging your pessimistic thoughts and disputing them or distracting yourself from them with a replacement positive thought or activity. Focus on something else or write down any negative thoughts and look back over them later.

3. **Congratulate yourself.** At the end of the day, review what happened and how you reacted. Pat yourself on the back for maintaining a positive outlook and be honest with yourself regarding less-than-positive reactions you may have had. How could you have changed them?

Your goal should be to get to the point where you do not have to actively pause and think about your explanatory style in every situation. But until then, practice the three steps above until reacting positively or at least nonjudgmentally becomes second nature. It may take a while, and you may have to practice the three exercises occasionally. In time, you will develop an ongoing optimistic point of view that will become habit.

We also recommend that you read Martin Seligman's book *Learned Optimism*. He describes the process as a simple look at your ABCs. *A* represents the Adversity we encounter. Perception of the adversity is not established on facts but rather on *B,* our Beliefs, which are based on our upbringing and our past experiences and which are usually habitual. These beliefs are directly linked to what we feel and eventually to how we will react, causing *C,* the Consequences. We can, with daily practice, learn to change our beliefs and, as a result, change our reactions and consequences.

Similar to our three simple exercises above, Seligman recommends that you consciously examine the links among Adversity, Belief, and Consequences and what they mean to the quality of your life. He urges people to look inward when faced with a positive or negative event and to analyze the effect they have on it and on their own frame of mind. For instance, when someone pays you an unexpected compliment, your whole day may improve just because the praise made you feel loved, wanted, and appreciated. Likewise, a criticism or thoughtless gesture might make you feel angry, depressed, or unworthy for an entire day. If we can recognize that it is not the external events that make our mood (such as pleasant or unpleasant comments) but our own reaction to them, we can learn to control our responses.

Your own explanatory style is so ingrained in your unconscious that there's a good chance you may not even notice that you are explaining events as permanent, pervasive, and personal. As you make a determined effort to notice your own beliefs and behaviors, you may discover pessimism of which you may not have been aware. If you can identify the cause of an adverse situation, recognize your beliefs regarding it, and then examine the consequences of your beliefs, you are identifying a means to a positive end. Doing so requires active *engagement,* which in turn results in a positive and dynamic approach to solving life's events.

THE GRATITUDE ATTITUDE

A positive outlook usually includes a sense of gratitude or thankfulness regardless of life's circumstances. In psychology, gratitude is thought of as an emotional state, while most religions regard it as a virtue. An attitude of gratitude may be one way we are able to turn a tragedy into some form of opportunity for spiritual growth. Think about mourning the loss of a family member, while at the same time experiencing a sense of gratitude for other family members still alive. Gratitude seems to be an essential element in holding a declining life together. You'll find the need to incorporate it in most religions and self-help organizations. Just look at Alcoholics Anonymous and its success. Like developing a positive outlook, we can increase our awareness of gratitude by practicing some simple techniques, which are taken from cognitive therapy:

1. Identify your nongrateful thoughts. Are they logical? Most of the time they aren't. ("No one loves me." "I've got nothing to do.")

2. Formulate gratitude-supportive thoughts. ("I have some very dear friends and healthy, happy children." "I have free time to pursue what I like.")

3. Substitute grateful thoughts for nongrateful ones.

4. Translate your inner feeling into outward actions. ("I have a few cherished friends" should translate into giving them a call, sending them a note, or making plans to see them. Recognizing that you have free time should result in making a plan to do something that you want to do—start or finish a craft project, read a book, see a movie, etc.)

Our research demonstrated just how important planning and goal orientation are in terms of developing or enhancing a positive attitude. Write to-do lists and stick to them, whether the goals are short- or long-term. Planning, exploration, and spontaneity are not mutually exclusive concepts. Running lists are a way of solidifying things you want to try to accomplish. There are many people who approach their futures with a sense of adventure and a desire to take on new challenges. Try it—it takes a positive attitude to regularly exercise your creativity and stay open to new ideas, new projects, and new stimuli. The payoff—an ever-enriching, involving, and evolving you—lasts right into a healthier, happier ripe old age.

It is always in season for old men to learn.

—AESCHYLUS

The psychologist and University of Chicago professor Mihaly Csikszentmihalyi wrote about remaining creative as we age in his excellent book *Creativity: Flow and the Psychology of Discovery and Invention.* Part of continuing to be creative, he writes, is in stretching ourselves by continually challenging our problem-solving skills with new questions and in attaining new, more difficult goals, even if they are ultimately unattainable. The more complex the problem, says Csikszentmihalyi, the better.

If you're always doing the "same old, same old," not only will you be bored but your brain muscles will atrophy. Some of the most significant artists and thinkers didn't even get started on exciting new ideas or achieve wide recognition until they were in their second stage of life—their positive attitude helped propel them to try out new ideas. The inventor Buckminster Fuller found fame and almost-cult status among young people in his seventies; the dog trainer Barbara Woodhouse famously said, "Life for me began at seventy," after becoming a TV celebrity; and Colonel Sanders founded his fried chicken empire in his sixties!

Use some of these Csikszentmihalyi-inspired tips to bring new adventures and challenges into your life:

1. **Stay curious.** Don't think you know all the answers. Creative people question the most obvious or seemingly obvious situations. Do not take refuge in the television, radio, newspaper, or pointless conversations. Seek out literature, people, and places that force you to ask questions and form opinions.

2. **Start each day with a specific goal, and end the day trying to come up with a more complex goal for the following day.** Before you retire for the night, think of one thing you want to do the next day. Make it something to look forward to—whether it be seeing a new movie, taking a new car for a test-drive, or researching a trip to a place you have never been before.

3. **Pay attention to what you are doing.** This sounds a lot easier than it actually is. When you engage in any activity, whether it is shopping for groceries, cleaning the house, or driving a car, *be present in the moment.* Focus just on what you are doing—and take in all that is around you. When you do this, you start to see the world differently, notice details that had escaped your attention before, and watch new ideas develop.

4. **Make a fantasy list, and then start checking it off.** Write down ten things you have never done before but would like to try—from the simple (shop at a new store, explore a new walking path) to the silly (ride a Ferris wheel, throw water balloons with your grandson, daughter, niece, or nephew) to the sublime (take a flying lesson, learn to play an instrument). Then, every week, do one of those things so that you can cross it off the list. When you are done with that list, make another one.

Finally, a positive attitude will, of course, help motivate you to develop and maintain all the other important traits for a highly successful retirement. We're not talking about being Pollyanna-happy and cheerful as much as we're talking about an attitude of hopefulness and possibility. It's essential if you want to develop highly successful retirement traits.

It is not the load that breaks you down, it is how you carry it.

—ANONYMOUS

5

TRAIT THREE:
GO WITH THE FLOW—
ACCEPT CHANGE

He who rejects change is the architect of decay. The only human institution which rejects progress is the cemetery.

—HAROLD WILSON, BRITISH POLITICIAN

At the age of twenty, Harriet Doerr interrupted her studies at Stanford University to get married. Forty-five years later, after she had raised two children as a stay-at-home mother, her husband died. Three years after that, her son Michael urged her to go back to college and complete her degree. She did. Doerr was old enough to be her fellow students' grandmother, but the difference in age did not stop her from easily befriending them. In fact, she became one of the gang, often joining her classmates for a beer or a burger after a long day. Her writing professor noticed that Doerr had a remarkable talent and challenged her to write a book, which she did.

Stones for Ibarra was the result, and it was published in 1984, when Doerr was seventy-three. The memoir won the National Book Award and became an international best seller—and Doerr became a literary sensation. Her second book, *Consider This, Señora,* was published in 1993 and also became a best seller. *The Tiger in the Grass,* a collection of stories and anecdotal pieces, was published in 1995, the year her son died of cancer. In her eighties, some devastating changes in her life took place: the loss of her beloved son and severe glaucoma that dramatically impaired her eyesight. Doerr shifted from writing to speaking, and continued to accept invitations to speak about her life and career. She died in 2002 at age ninety-two.

Doerr once remarked, "I operate from chaos," which to us signals a person who not only adapts to change but looks forward to it and embraces it. No wonder she was able to accomplish so much in the last twenty-five years of her life—more than most people accomplish in a lifetime. And this was after already living one life and raising a family!

We all know at least one survivor similar to Doerr, a person who responds to setbacks and change (the death of a spouse or a child) by adapting to the circumstances (going back to school as a senior citizen, mastering a skill like writing, speaking to others about her life experiences) and succeeding. Even those who live through a plethora of adversity—consider Abraham Lincoln, whose life was beset by tragedy and failure but who became one of our most revered presidents—seem to have been born with built-in endurance machines. But that's not the case. Social scientists label the capacity to cope with hindrances and challenges and to rise above them *resilience*.

Long-lived people as a group are strongly resilient; that characteristic is one of the reasons they make it to their eighties and nineties, or beyond. Resilient people can handle trauma and accept change. Our Retirement Docs' Survey data reaffirmed that accepting change becomes a priority particularly in retirement in phase two, when coping with the loss of full-time work and the professional and social satisfaction we derived from it can be and often is devastating, and in phases three and four, when the loss of loved ones and other major setbacks occur more frequently.

Fortunately, we can build up our resiliency and teach ourselves to deal with repeat upsets even if they happen in quick succession or simultaneously—for example, the loss of a job, workplace friends, regular income, and/or sense of purpose. Overall, self-confidence, decision-making ability, and a sense of independence are part of a resilient person's makeup. While many of these qualities are developed during childhood in secure and loving families led by caring and thoughtful parents, even people who had tough upbringings can learn to be resilient. If you think you are one of those people, and you're reading this book, our bet is that you are resilient and can become even more so.

PHASES TWO AND THREE— SURVIVING THE TRANSITION FROM JOB TO JOBLESS

Retiring from a job can be as heart-wrenching and shocking as being fired. One day you get up at 6:00 A.M. to get the 7:05 into the office, and the next you're up early wondering what to do with the next twelve hours. If you are not resilient, this is a scenario ripe for negative behavior and plummeting self-esteem. If you visualize yourself having a tough time going from working to wandering, you can make some preemptive strikes to soften the blow. As we discussed in chapter three, talk to your employer; see if it's possible to ease out of your workplace slowly—see if you can create a smooth transition for yourself from your company. There's a chance that with your expertise you can cut back on hours but stay on, doing something like keeping track of a project for a month or two—or as an on-call consultant or mentor. Make a list of ways you see yourself remaining valuable to your employer, whether you work for a huge company, in a small establishment, or for yourself.

RESILIENT PEOPLE HAVE CONTINGENCY PLANS

There will be a chance that your company doesn't have a place for you, and there may be a moment in between work and settling into a new routine or another job or business when you will find yourself facing a vacuum of time and autonomy. There is a solution for getting through this period. The advantageous difference between getting fired or laid off and retiring is that you know you are going to retire, and you usually know when. While some of us are thrilled to retire, others are not. If you are one of the latter, you can prepare and be ready to deal with and head off possible feelings of anger, shame, resentment, bitterness, and grief that can be a result of leaving a job or that may occur after the "honeymoon" period (those first few weeks or months after retirement), when you stop enjoying the sense of freedom you first felt when calling it quits. First of all, recognize that it is not unusual to experience resentment and hurt when you retire. We're not saying that you will have these feelings, but if you do, you are not alone. Many other fellow retirees feel the same way. Put a resiliency-building plan to work before you retire.

1. **Give yourself time to grieve.** You worked your whole life! Chances are good that you're going to feel bad about giving up a job and daily contact with individuals who mean a lot to you. Recognize that grieving is not the same as wallowing or feeling like a victim. Resilient people grieve for their loss; they don't blame their circumstance.

2. **Write and talk about it.** James Pennebaker, a psychologist at Southern Methodist University in Dallas and author of *Writing to Heal: A Guided Journal for Recovering from Trauma and Emotional Upheaval,* has found in numerous studies that people who confide their feelings, either to themselves in the form of a journal, or to a close friend or confidant, are better able to bounce back from trauma and have healthier immune systems.

3. **Create a new community.** You may be able to stay in touch with your former friends from work, but it won't be easy and it won't be the same, especially if you socialized with them only during your working hours. As the saying goes, "life goes on," and that's what's happening. The life they know marches forth and yours is no longer a part of that makeup. Attempting to hang on doesn't build resiliency. Have you seen the movie *About Schmidt,* in which Jack Nicholson plays the role of a new retiree? Disengage from your old job by seeking out a new bunch of "colleagues" to hang out with. One way of doing this is via social service and community volunteering. If you can't

or don't want to find a paying job, use your work skills to help society and create a new professional situation for yourself. Re-create the intrinsic qualities that made your first career meaningful.

4. **Ease out over time.** Do your skills translate into other jobs that can help you ease away from working altogether? One government researcher we know became a high school math teacher at a charter school for science and math in New Jersey after retiring from her Washington, D.C., job. Eventually, she retired from that, too, and lived happily ever after tutoring children in math after school, until she couldn't wait to not have to work at anything anymore. Now she travels, reads books, and simply enjoys the sunsets. She got over the need to work; she just took about fifteen years doing so.

PHASE FOUR—FACING THE CHALLENGES OF OLD AGE

It's a given, if we live long enough, that we will all face a series of major life-altering adversities, often with little or no recovery time in between. Advanced age brings with it a lot of baggage that needs to be recognized and managed. It's possible as elders that we could lose a spouse, deal with a sick loved one, become sick ourselves, and find it necessary to offer emotional support to a grown child who might have a crisis of his or her own, and all of this at the same time. Numerous changes can potentially overwhelm our basic resilience. Other major roadblocks that occur in phase four include our loss of independence, decreased stamina, decreased mobility, and the potential inability to care for ourselves by ourselves. Add to the lineup the developing major body changes linked directly to aging, chronic diseases, and decreased memory, hearing, and eyesight. Not our favorite list by far, but for each probable condition (every one of them a traumatic event), it's so important to be alert and ready with robust and ready resilience. Resilience rules! Resilience to the rescue! Tape that to your mirror too!

DIAGNOSIS

Here are some questions to ask yourself relating to the strength of your own resiliency factor, also known as the ability to accept change:

- Did a caring family raise you?
- Did your childhood incorporate religious, ethnic, and/or cultural beliefs?
- Overall, do you feel you've made positive decisions in your lifetime and have good problem-solving skills?
- Do you have a strong sense of spirituality?
- Do you have strong feelings of self-worth and confidence?
- Have you faced major traumas in your lifetime and generally recovered well?
- Are you able to accept change, even at the last minute?
- Are you merciful, as opposed to trying to get even?

This is just a glimpse at the complex characteristics of resiliency. If you answered yes to these questions, you are most likely a naturally resilient person. If you responded with negatives, you need to work hard at developing a resilient nature. If you want to do further resiliency-related research, an excellent book is *The Resilience Factor,* by Karen Reivich, Ph.D., and Andrew Shatte, Ph.D. In the meantime, our prescription for resilience, if practiced daily, should help you learn to bounce back and better. Take as needed.

THE RETIREMENT DOCS' PRESCRIPTION

Retirement and aging are inevitable. Understand that certain traumas are a part of the normal cycle of life. It is never too late to teach yourself to be a highly successful change survivor. Acknowledging that your life will change, coupled with a realistic attitude, leads to acceptance and ease of stress, which in turn add to basic resilience patterns. If you can develop a Harriet Doerr–like mind-set and embrace change and thrive on chaos, instead of running away from it or denying it, you can give yourself a "heads-up" advantage for coping.

Practice the following skills to shore up your resilience reserves. This is *not* a short-term process. You've got to keep at it. The ability to accept change is an ongoing, lifelong, ever-evolving skill.

1. **Develop and maintain an independent spirit.** Even if you have friends and family nearby, you still need a sense of self-determination and self-sufficiency. Resilient people can take care of themselves. They can do things on their own and enjoy it. Practice by solving a problem by yourself, taking in a movie or dining in a restaurant solo, or taking a trip on your own—and enjoying it. There will be many times when you will be alone after you retire—if you don't enjoy your own company, you're in trouble. Think again about Harriet Doerr and people like her whom you know—off she went to college at sixty-five, all by herself! Take responsibility for your actions. If physical disabilities linked to age create a loss of external controls, let them go. Transfer your energy into maintaining your internal reins. Resist letting other people do tasks for you if with a little extra effort you can accomplish them by yourself. Be in charge of your day-to-day life, and don't waste time on things that you can't control. And don't forget, blame only prolongs personal recovery processes.

2. **Cultivate insight.** This is the mental habit of asking yourself tough questions and answering them honestly. It entails moving away from being self-centered and toward being outwardly directed, trying to see the things from someone else's point of view. This can prevent you from falling into the "why me" and "everybody is against me" trap. Viewing the world as cruel or unjust may be simply growing old and feeling a frightening lessening of control, which in turn can create depression. No one we've ever met has liked feeling out of control, but again, it's a given. As you age, you're going to feel you're losing some

of your power. Becoming a senior citizen is not someone else's fault. It's real life marching you through your very own timetable.

3. **Get help.** Yes, we did just tell you to become independent. Yet independent people know when to ask for outside help—this is not the same thing as leaning on friends or family members for obligatory companionship or enforced "amuse-me" sessions. Resilient people participate in relationships, understand that they are a two-way street, and are willing to actively participate in the give-and-take necessary to make a relationship gratifying, not only for them but also for other people. Resilience researchers also say that strong, flexible people are not afraid to talk about obstacles or challenges with a professional, a confidant, a clergyperson, or a friend.

If I don't see one of my children every day, one or two of us will get in touch by phone. And now I'm e-mailing my grandchildren with thoughts on my long life. It makes me feel that I'm contributing emotional support, valuable memories of life's experiences, as well as keeping up with day-to-day involvements. I feel a real ongoing connection. I'm old, but I'm not unhappy. My family has become my life. They make me feel that they need me, and I know I sure need them.

—RETIREMENT DOCS' SURVEY

4. **Reframe your life and experiences.** Take a look at your life now and your history, and put them in perspective. You've survived this long—there has got to be a reason for it! If you can see why and how you "made it" this far, you can see your own strengths and achievements clearly. Basically, this is consciously taking a glass-half-full approach to life, as opposed to a glass-half-empty one. Make a list of your accomplishments—from bringing up happy children to making a contribution at your job to being a helpful neighbor—and see these things for what they are: the sum total of a brave and well-lived life. Make a list of "retirement advantages" so that you can visualize all the great things about not having to work anymore—everything from sleeping late during the week to traveling wherever and whenever

you like. An "advantages list" is a deceptively simple yet powerful way to reframe your situation.

5. **Create your life plan and refer to it often.** Getting a clear idea of who you are, how you want your life to operate, and how you see yourself in the future provides a fall-back strategy when you're faced with trauma or unexpected events. For example, plot out your responses to an illness in your family or to your own illness. Devise a scheme for when you want to move from where you are living. Be as concrete as possible, but also know that such plans can be revised. Respect yourself; capitalize on your own personal assets, your own uniqueness. Review your life plan on an ongoing basis, particularly following a stressful event. Does it provide the resilience and the psychological well-being you need to get back on track, or is it time to adjust and update? Comparing yourself to other people who have experienced adversities similar to yours will give you a sense of yourself, where you are now, and where you want to be. And remember, because this is your life plan, it's all about you—make it work for you.

I have noticed that some retired business leaders do not do well when faced with irreversible adversity. As captains of industry, they were able to correctly identify a problem. If they didn't know the answer, they consulted with others who would.

Now in retirement, their problems have no clear solutions, and these former leaders have more difficulty adjusting. They have lost control, as well as the knowledge of how to react.

—RETIREMENT DOCS' INTERVIEW

6. **Simplify.** In general, the older you get, the fewer balls you can keep in the air without dropping one or two of them. Why struggle to juggle? Unnecessary but stressful tasks, annoying chores, and irritating people, places, and things can erode your resiliency. This is the time to enjoy and spend time doing things you like. Retirement is all about eliminating tasks that you never enjoyed in the first place. What can you do to rid yourself of them? One consideration is maintaining "the

family home"—when most of the family has long vacated. The fact that your children (now most of them with their own kids) love making those memory-lane visits to "their house" or their life as it was is a great compliment to you, and we're not saying that you don't enjoy all the memories attached too. But what *was* isn't, and a good-sized home can easily become a drag as well as a big drain on you. Sell it! Free yourself from stress: moving to a location that requires less upkeep and provides a secure environment makes a lot of sense. Another stress reducer: eliminate annoying reading material, as well as radio and television programs if you know they will upset rather than inspire you. A liberal probably doesn't want to start the day listening to Rush Limbaugh. On the other hand, if controversy and politics excite you, that's not stress, that's positive energy! Make a conscious effort to distinguish which media are pleasurable for you to engage in and those that make you angry or unhappy so you know what to avoid. Likewise, if your cousin Millie's husband David makes you nuts, don't feel forced to spend time with him. Associate with the people you like and who make you feel great. The point is to be mindful about who and what makes you happy and put your energies and focus there.

From the beginning of time, the ability to adjust to change has been the basis for survival for all living things.

—RETIREMENT DOCS

6

Trait Four: A Little Help from Your Friends (and Family)—The Strong Support Group

Let us be grateful to people who make us happy; they are the charming gardeners who make our souls blossom.

—Marcel Proust

Human beings are not meant to live solitary lives. We are social creatures by nature, and maintaining close ties with family and friends becomes even more vital to our well-being after we retire. Our highly successful retirees overwhelmingly stated that close social and family relationships made their lives richer, happier, and more meaningful. But they also said they had to work at maintaining them. In the first half of our lives, up until our late forties and early fifties, family and social relationships are easy to maintain. They are truly a balance of give-and-take. Most of us live with or close to our immediate family, and our friends are easy to access at work and in the neighborhood. It's easy to blend personal and professional events and friendships. It's give-and-take in equal measure.

When we retire, there is a greater potential to fall into a social vacuum unless we strive to put ourselves in situations where we interact with family, old friends, and new faces. It requires extra effort on our part. It becomes more of a "give, give, give, and take" than a give-and-take scenario—to stay in touch with our kids, relatives, former friends/coworkers, and friends, who may move away or are just not as easy to reach as in the past, for any number of reasons (perhaps they still work and you don't). You need to watch and work on your social connections as carefully as you supervise your fiscal and health plans.

After my father died, I watched my mother become lonely and depressed. She was without any friends, and had an address book with most of the names crossed out. This made me supersensitive to gathering a wide and varied group of friends and to be emotionally close to my family. In my retirement, I track this much as I do my finances and my health.

—RETIREMENT DOCS' INTERVIEW

Along with a group of our lifelong friends, we all moved to a desert community and bought condos. It was a dream coming true; we had talked for years about retiring together and how perfect it would be. But before long, we found that no matter how close our friendships, some of us moved on to other areas, some developed other interests, some got sick, and, sadly, one in our tight-knit group has died.

My husband and I decided to expand and extend our social circle because we saw that unexpected and unplanned changes could leave us a future without close friends. We've met and formed new friendships with people in our community, and they have become important to us. We now feel that we can never have too many friends, especially at this time in our lives.

—RETIREMENT DOCS' INTERVIEW

Having friends is particularly good for your mental health: it's been known for some time that single and socially isolated people stand a greater chance of developing dementia, including Alzheimer's disease. A study conducted by Robert Wilson at Rush University Medical Center was the first to show a link between people who were lonely or disconnected and a higher risk of developing dementia later in life.

Friends also extend life: Australian researchers conducted a ten-year study of more than fifteen hundred people seventy and older, which concluded in 2002. They found that those who had regular contact, in person or on the phone, with at least five friends, had 22 percent fewer deaths in the following decade than those who had few friends and limited contact with them. According to the researchers, the friends of study participants provided them with a sense of intimacy, shared interests, and support during difficult times.

But as in real life, reality can bite—and the same was not always true of the Australian participants' family members, who often contributed to their stress. We also found this to be true in our research. As one of our respondents wrote:

> *Your support groups no longer have to be in your backyard, not with the caliber of support that you get from e-mails and the telephone. In fact, being geographically close to your kids may be a detriment when you retire. They interfere too much. They try to control your life, and then they try to make you feel guilty if you don't do things they want you to do. And heaven help you if you marry somebody that they don't like. They also interfere during holidays. Living a little ways away is not all bad.*
>
> —RETIREMENT DOCS' INTERVIEW

Despite the variety of emotions that family relationships often evoke, our mate, siblings, children, and other close relations remain the backbone of our support groups—most of us still rely on family for the give-and-take of emotional, physical, and financial support. Of course, perfect families, no matter what our generation, have always been the exception rather than the rule. But in what other setting can you make mistakes time after time and still be welcome? Where else can you talk openly with one another, even admit, "This family is dysfunctional!" and disagree, shout, laugh, cry, and (most of the time) hug and make up? Having a good family structure comes in shades of success, but a unified family increases all of your chances for happiness in your retirement years. If poor family relationships exist before retirement, they will usually continue after retirement. If this is the case in your family, and if you're getting our message, swallow your pride and at least make an effort to repair things.

Research has shown that a strong support group offers many benefits, including:

- Longer life
- Better mental and physical health
- A stronger immune system
- Quicker recovery from illness and surgery
- The need for fewer medications
- Lower blood pressure
- Fewer visits to doctors
- Feeling loved and highly regarded
- A connection to the community and the world
- Less smoking and alcohol intake
- Easier weight loss

CIRCLE AROUND TO YOUR CIRCLE OF SUPPORT

We like the idea of looking at your relationships as circles emanating around and out from us in an ever-changing and ongoing dynamic process: The people in our lives move from one ring and then back over time. The graphic here shows the entire circle of support, and each one of the four radiating rings is essential in supporting you. Some people will move back and forth among the four rings. But how you manage those circles and your relationship to and with them is central to your well-being.

CIRCLE OF SUPPORT

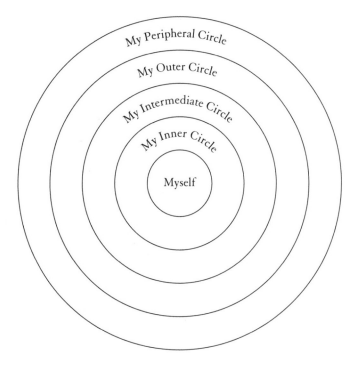

Inner Circle: Your first circle of support includes your intimate relation-ships, the people you feel so close to that your life without them is unimaginable. They often include your mate, your children and their mates, your grandchildren, your great-grandchildren, exceptionally close friends, and, sometimes, pets.

Intermediate Circle: This second circle of support includes dear friends, close relatives, and caregivers. After you retire, you have to make more of an effort to reach out to these people—and try to add new ones.

Outer Circle: The third circle of support fluctuates the most, starting when you enter phase two of retirement. It's made up of your basic support groups, people you enjoy being with but don't often see socially or on a regular basis. It may include acquaintances from re-ligious, social, volunteer, political, and community organizations, as well as new people you meet and become friendly with.

Peripheral Circle: This outermost circle is made up of people, animals, and plants that demand care from you or are a necessary part of your core maintenance but do not have as much emotional meaning to your lives. For example, your doctor, dentist, attorney, financial advisers, and clergy are in your peripheral circle. This ring may also include animals that don't belong to you but that you like, and plants that you nurture. Just think about the dog next door, always greeting you with a friendly bark and a lick on the hand, or the birds you see perched around your house or snacking at your feeder.

It's interesting to note that the number of people within each circle remains fairly stable before retirement, and throughout phase one and phase two of retirement. For example, if you have four people in a particular ring before you retire, in all probability there will be around four in phases one and two of retirement, and some of them will make it into phases three and four. You will, of course, see some decrease of those in your circles if you live a very long time—because of lapsed interest or involvement, illness or death—a good reason to continually add people to your circles.

Though it sounds somewhat calculating, maintaining and building friendships is really about planning ahead. When you have friends, along with acquaintances you can visualize as replacement friends waiting in the wings, you are building in future helpers for a time when you will really need them—phase three and especially phase four. Developing friendships is even important in phase two, since your spouse may not share every interest you have. Unless we die before our time, mentally and physically, old age asks for more than it's able to give. When our well-being demands active assistance, if we can have it delivered via a ready, willing, helpful, and caring support group, we're going to be a lot better off and a lot happier. Stop and think for a moment. Visualize yourself as old, really old. Shut your eyes and do it. Now, imagine yourself needing hands-on physical assistance with transportation as well as help with social interaction at a nephew's wedding; or day-to-day activities, like a trip to the bathroom; or your finances. How is the scenario looking?

Luckily, field-testing new support systems—also called exploring new friendships and associations—can be fun and will contribute to your zest for life. As you will see in the prescription section of this chapter, there are more options than ever available to meet people who share your interests, and an ever-growing number of clubs and organizations catering to the needs of adults.

After my wife and I married, my focus was limited to family involvement and my profession. I had little time to develop much more than my inner and intermediate circles of support. Over a five- to ten-year period before I entered phase two's semi-retirement with income, I ventured in and out of various potential support groups attempting to develop my outer circles. This was by design. I was preparing myself for decreased time on the job, and I was field-testing possible leisure-time pursuits. Then I fully entered phase two and worked on developing all four of my circles. The backbone of my inner circle remained my mate, our children and their mates, and our grandchildren. Making good friends outside the medical profession has been great fun, but the three major blessings I most enjoy are involvement with our children and our grandchildren, and spending more quality time with my wife.

—DR. FRITZ

I can't recall ever "planning" for a support group. They simply evolved as experiences with family, schooling, hobbies, and career development helped them naturally form. For example, early in my grade school education, a woodworking class attracted me. Learning as much as possible about woodworking led me to explore different disciplines, where I met more and more people as a result of our mutual interest. When I was ten, I started playing golf with neighborhood friends simply because there was a public golf course in our neighborhood. My interest continued through high school and college, and into my adult life. My family and I have been lucky enough to play on courses that in my childhood I only dreamed of. Golf has provided me with ongoing social support made up of both old and new friends. In fact, just last week I was in a foursome made up of those same pals from my childhood—we've never lost touch.

Medical school obviously produced new support groups with professors and colleagues, followed by patient-doctor relationships formed during the years of my practice. I have particularly valued what I learned from my patients.

My advice for finding your own support groups is to pay attention to what you love and share in it.

—DR. JIM

THE INNER CIRCLE: THE FAMILY UNIT AND ITS MANY FORMS

In common-sense terms, as you get older, your practical needs, both physical and emotional, markedly benefit from a loving and supportive family. A tolerant and somewhat supportive family is better than none at all. Even though cultural and economic factors have changed our idea of the traditional American family—currently only 24 percent of us who cohabitate are married, as compared to 1960, when 52 percent of us living together had tied the knot—most of us over sixty-five still rely primarily on the traditional family unit for support, as do Baby Boomers. The difference is that Boomers have added and expanded the definition of family to include a broader base of people, which can create a less-stable family unit.

Looking over the statistics in the previous paragraph, we realize it's no wonder that many people born between 1946 and 1964 are having a problem identifying their traditional roots.

MARRIAGE—AND HOW MEN AND WOMEN RETIRE

For better or for worse, retired couples spend more time with each other and about 40 percent less time with their friends than they do before they retire.

Like this famous historian, we all hope that we can feel as smitten by a special someone in our own later decades:

The love we have in our youth is superficial compared to the love that an old man has for his wife.

—WILL DURANT

But, often, couples find that they have different interests once they re-tire. In the beginning, negotiating these differences can be a trying time in some marriages. For example, you may be thrilled that you finally have the time to travel, but your spouse may want to spend his or her carefree days reading the books he or she never had time to enjoy.

In addition, research shows that men and women have different styles when it comes to cultivating outside relationships. Women tend to have an easier experience keeping a social network active when they retire than men typically do. They, like men, usually have at least one confidant but, unlike them, often a tight-knit group of best friends. They are by far much better than men at ongoing social networking, particularly under stressful conditions. More women go to support groups (whether medically or emotionally based). Women tend to group and men to scatter. As one of our survey respondents explained:

Some of my girlfriends feel closer to their girlfriends than they do to their hus-bands. Their husbands aren't interested in talking to them and, more important, listening to them. Their girlfriends are. I think that when a wife loses a husband, she may miss him with all her heart but still it seems that she fills her lonely times more easily than a man, usually with close friends. From what I've observed, more often than not, women have close friends and men have acquaintances.

—RETIREMENT DOCS' SURVEY

Many men often put their careers ahead of maintaining or making new friends, and as a consequence they lose the skills required to establish or keep ongoing friendships other than those that are work-related. It's no sur-prise that following retirement, about a third of men entering phases two and three spend significantly more time with their families. Fortunately, many men genuinely look forward to the amounts of time they find avail-able to involve themselves with their mates, children, and grandchildren. However, if they're doing so out of a new sense of excess time, many of those new retirees indeed feel lost and, temporarily, directionless.

Most men and their wives adjust to their new roles in time. A six- to eighteen-month adjustment period is the length of time you can expect to spend fine-tuning your "new" relationship. Occasionally you may feel as if you're growing apart, not closer, but if you survived a long-term union before retirement, research shows that there is little negative impact on matrimony owing to retirement, at least for most of us. David Ekerdt, a University of Kansas sociologist who studies retirement and aging, and Veterans Administration research sociologist Barbara Vinick found in a study of two hundred couples that retirement did not put relationships into a crisis mode, as was commonly thought. While some women complained that their husbands cramped their style to a certain extent, such as monitoring their daily routines or listening to their telephone conversations, husbands who were home took care of and shared in more jobs around the house, which made their wives very happy. And, after some discussion, most couples eased into the change in everyday routines comfortably.

A good marriage before retirement is generally a good marriage after. It may sound trite, but take time to remember those first "crazy in love" years of your marriage and get back to them. Time, talk, and a couple of tantrums will get you where you need to be to get on with the rest of your life.

One issue to be aware of—research shows that there is the possibility of a significant crossover effect of depression, health problems, and negative events from one partner to the other. This is especially true for the woman, since odds are that she is the more maternal of the two and, statistics show, probably in better health than her mate. It's important to find a balance. Concentrate on providing support and understanding to your spouse while taking care of your own physical and mental health.

Between the ages of sixty-five and seventy-four, 80 percent of men and 55 percent of women are married; after eighty-five, 50 percent of men and only 13 percent of women are married. Up to 60 percent of people over age sixty-five are living alone. With those kinds of statistics, it's important to recognize that either you or your spouse will probably die before the other one does—going out at the same time is not the norm. Make sure you both understand what you want to do and who you want to turn to, including your professional contacts—attorneys, accountants, money managers, insurance agents—and know the roles that they will perform for the surviving partner. This will help take some stress out of your life now as you ponder what the future holds.

TIME WITH GRANDCHILDREN

Of all the activities that couples enjoy doing together, our highly successful retirees ranked visiting grandchildren as number one. Both our own data and data from other studies found no correlation between the actual numbers of children or grandchildren and grandparent happiness. So if you have just one grandchild to lavish all of your attention on, or if you're one of the people jumping up calling out "Twenty-five! Twenty-five! Twenty-five!" when the "How Many Do You Have Now?" contest begins—hurrah for you both. You are equally happy with the most important part of all— they are yours! As grandparents, we can have a lot of influence, but, most important, we've got a lot of bonus playtime waiting to be had. *If you do not have a grandchild, get a pet, or develop a relationship with a niece, nephew, or a friend's child. Having friends of all ages is entertaining and educational.*

How could I not be crazy about my grandchild? My daughter recently sent me this e-mail she received from my three-year-old grandson's Baptist preschool teacher—"God loves me, Jesus loves me, and Grandma loves me." First, he got the order of importance right, and second, he's only three years old and he's already been published!

—RETIREMENT DOCS' SURVEY

For each grandchild's tenth birthday, my late wife and I made a practice of taking him or her individually almost anywhere he or she wanted to go for a three- to ten-day trip. Let me add that we have seen some amazing choices made: Cleveland? Not that we didn't fully enjoy our trip, but at the time it gave us pause. Cleveland versus the pyramids? One of our grandsons was a Cleveland Indians fan and a trip to their ballpark was a dream come true for him and, as it turned out, for us as well. His choice was one of the best of all our vacations, and I might add, Cleveland is a beautiful place to spend some time seeing. This individual bonding experience along with an annual all-family vacation has paid untold dividends for me throughout my life. I'm eighty-six years old, and some of my grandkids are old enough to have grandkids. The nice thing is, they still come and see me. I am in the more lonely late years of my life, and a visit from them sure makes my day.

—Retirement Docs' Survey

Close Friends

In demographic surveys of people born before 1946, respondants rank their mate as the most important source of support in their inner circle, followed by their children, grandchildren, and parents. Only a few included a very close friend. Enter the Baby Boomers, all 77 million of them, and though remaining traditionally reliant on spouses and children for their inner circle support, they more often include a close friend, and sometimes more than one, in their inner circle. Family relationships are, in part, bound by obligation and are virtually permanent. Friendships, on the other hand, are based on mutual consent. They can begin by chance, and they can end whenever the relationship is no longer rewarding.

Recent data suggest that we will live longer if we have very close friends and we are not dependent solely on our families for emotional support, particularly when we're old. It is ideal to have one or two very close friends and many acquaintances. Bleak as it sounds, as those close friends pass away, move, or have emotional or physical disorders associated with age, you need to have a reserve of other people you can depend upon. Just like the loss of a mate, it's not that we ever want to lose what we so much enjoy today, it's just a plain fact of life—it will happen. When you retire, the loss of your mate can be softened if you have an extremely close friend or friends. Digest this information, take a careful look, and do some thinking and planning for your future.

Since the majority of us over the age of sixty do not have a mate, the importance of developing close friendships becomes even more apparent. Take a cue from the single, the divorced, and the widowed; they know that gathering together plays a big part in their family-by-choice life support.

As we grow into retirement's phases three and four, we may relate more easily and more intimately to people who are of similar age and/or with similar infirmities. It's more difficult to talk to a family member about "plumbing problems" and all those other age-related diseases. A close friend or a group of similarly aged elders can understand and offer moral and emotional help—and sometimes even come up with a physical fix that actually works. After all, most of us have "been there, done that" after putting in many years.

INTERMEDIATE AND OUTER-CIRCLE SUPPORT

In the intermediate circle are individuals who are friends, a few of whom may have the potential to come into the inner circle. The outer circle is primarily organizations and/or acquaintances. These two circles also include more-distant friends and relatives.

Society is changing, and more and more leisure activities are becoming solitary: for example, watching television, working on the computer, playing computer games, and plugging in our iPods. No longer are we joiners; all national fraternal organizations and most religions have had a decrease in attendance. Adult athletic programs and bowling leagues are shrinking, and community involvement and almost all areas where you meet, greet, and develop new relationships are diminishing. Consequently, when the Boomers fully retire, many could find themselves with a feeling of not belonging anywhere or having no place to go.

I don't really miss work, but I do miss the people I worked with, the social interchange and feeling of community.

—RETIREMENT DOCS' SURVEY

As a retiree, it's very important to maintain these kinds of social connections. Specific suggestions appear later in this chapter.

PERIPHERAL CIRCLE

This circle includes anybody and anything that requires personal responsibility—for you or from you. This includes your support group of advisers, which your mate should be as familiar with as you are. It will allow a surviving spouse to keep the ongoing business of living intact. This circle also includes living things, such as animals other than your own pets and plants that depend upon your care and feeding. The responsibility and obligation that are parts of these peripheral relationships are actually crucial in keeping you alive and dynamic. They can become part of our "reason to live."

Maintaining a small garden you care about, seeing neighbors and enjoying casual chitchat with them, visiting your attorney or tax accountant or the woman at the bank with whom you discuss your personal business affairs are important simply in terms of continuing the varied nature of everyday life. Daily activities that include others are similar to keeping up with current events or taking in cultural activities. They simply add meaning and depth to life—and in a hands-on sense, going to the dentist, seeing your doctor for a checkup, and checking in with your investment adviser maintain your practical well-being. Losing interest in them is one of the first signs of depression!

Every few years my wife and I get together socially with our attorney, accountant, money manager, insurance agent, and pastor. We do it to stay involved with them in a friendly, not an all-business, relationship. We feel that if something were to happen to one of us, the other would feel comfortable and knowledgeable carrying on.

—RETIREMENT DOCS' SURVEY

THE DIAGNOSIS: HOW STRONG IS YOUR SUPPORT GROUP?

Read through the following list carefully and take time to answer each question. The more affirmative answers you give, the better off you are in terms of your circles of support. However, keep in mind that even if you have an active social life now, you have to continually maintain and add to it.

- Is my mate the most important person in my life?
- Do I have a close relationship with my children?
- Am I in contact with my grandchildren on a regular basis?
- Do I enjoy spending time with my children's mates?
- Do I enjoy helping other people?
- Do I attend church on a regular basis?
- Do I belong to a volunteer group or groups?
- Are there fish, birds, or other pets or animals that I care for?
- Do I have plants or other things that I care for and cultivate?
- Do I enjoy making new friends?
- Do I have at least one very close friend?
- Do I have friends or acquaintances who are both much younger and older than I am?

THE RETIREMENT DOCS' PRESCRIPTION: DEVELOPING AND MAINTAINING SUPPORT GROUPS

Relationships, like plants and pets, will wither and die if not looked after on a regular ongoing basis. Get your inner circle on a "care and feeding schedule" with the following simple tips. Look at your support groups as your own protective shield or your emotional safety-deposit box. Hopefully, you will never have to make demands on it, but if you live long enough, you more than likely will. Your groups are there for your emotional, physical, spiritual, and financial support. Just don't forget—your circles are ever-changing. Their maintenance requires time, effort, understanding, and that most noble of all virtues, forgiveness.

IT'S ALL ABOUT FAMILY

Not only will you be able to create a closer family support network by following the suggestions below, but you will also create a better you. Both are part of achieving a highly successful retirement.

- **Learn to forgive and forget!** Do you even remember how the feud between you and another family member began? Do you have strained relationships with your children or siblings that you need to address? *Now* is the time to act. Your mental health (and theirs) will benefit greatly. Keep in mind that grandchildren and nieces and nephews that you have a special affinity and love for can, by the nature of your relationship with them, become significantly unifying, often making it easier to bring quarreling family members to the same table.
- **Don't be judgmental.** If you are, stop. You'll be amazed at what a good time you can have with your family if you treat them with respect. Work to accept each of them as they are. There's a good chance that they will work just as hard when they see you making an effort to overlook their habits, quirks, and political opinions! You may find yourself receiving a lot of satisfaction by reaching out to a wayward child, grandchild, or other relative.
- **Expand your family circle.** Members outside one's immediate family are often untapped support resources. Aunts, uncles, cousins, in-laws, nieces, and nephews—these are all important relationships to nurture.
- **Be your family's guardian.** Offer your help to them in times of need, whether emotional, economic, or caregiving. If you're there for your

family before retirement, chances are they will be there for you when advanced age-related setbacks come calling.

■ **Gather the family together regularly to celebrate.** Salute birthdays, graduations, promotions, travel plans, and major holidays together. Get everyone involved in planning them—from who will bring the wine to who will make the pasta salad to who will bring the party hats.

■ **Take time away for family vacations.** Enjoy one another away from home. Often, being in a new, restful location eases tensions and helps everyone relax and enjoy one another's company.

MAINTAIN CLOSE FRIENDSHIPS

Friends provide support and understanding in nonjudgmental and unemotional ways that spouses or other family members often cannot—maybe you have a friend who shares your passion for the opera or reads history books with the same voraciousness. Or maybe they are just people you enjoy spending time with, sharing ideas and perspectives, and, most important, sharing a good laugh.

■ **Develop a small number of extremely close friends.** Too many close friends can actually take time away from maintaining closeness. Even one confidant is a major plus, and better than ten friendly acquaintances. It's hard to say exactly how to form close friendships because, like love relationships, close friendships often start with chemistry and go from there. Of course, to have a good friend, one must be a good friend. Once you stop working, the most likely way of finding people who have the potential to become good friends is to put yourself in situations where you will meet others who share your interests, values, and lifestyle. For example, if you like chess, join a chess club. If you love Italy, take an adult education course in Roman history. If you like kayaking, go kayaking with a group.

■ **If you are male and single, make friendships a big priority.** In our experience, men seem to find it much harder than women to make new friends and form close buddy relationships, especially once they stop working. We have found that many women have an easier time in retirement and are not as unhappy or lonely when their spouse dies as men are when they lose their wives. Men—you have got to force yourselves to forge new platonic relationships with other men and with women, especially if you plan a long life. Bond over sports, cards, cars, wine, or whatever. Meet people at groups that cater to your interest. Become a "regular" at the local coffee shop, or volunteer someplace where your skills come in handy. If you are open, interested in others, and friendly, of course, you can't help but meet and make new friends.

SPEND QUALITY TIME WITH YOUR GRANDCHILDREN

If you are lucky enough to have grandchildren, you can experience an enormous amount of joy in getting to know them and watching them mature. If not, and you want children in your life, you can involve yourself with friends' grandchildren or young nieces and nephews, or involve yourself with children's charities. We know one woman, who never married and has no children, who, despite these facts, loves children. She volunteers tirelessly at a shelter and day care for at-risk women and children. She has developed many mentoring, close relationships with children, many of whom she has seen grow up, go to college, and enter the workforce as successful people.

■ **Make it a priority to see your grandchildren regularly.** Research shows 56 percent of grandparents see one of their grandchildren at least once a week, and 60 percent of them babysit regularly.

■ **Spend some one-on-one time with each grandchild**—whether it's in person, by e-mail, or on the telephone. Make each one of them feel special.

■ **Find hobbies or activities you can enjoy together.** Do an art project, start a stamp collection, enjoy a sport, scrapbook or bake cookies together. Whatever it is, find a common interest. Do things that have meaning to just the two of you.

■ **Take trips.** Consider taking each grandchild on a "just the two (or three if you're including your mate) of us" vacation for a few hours or a few days, whatever works for you, when he or she is around age ten or there is a major event in their lives, such as a birthday or a graduation. You can go to the top of the Eiffel Tower or picnic by a river. It's not where you are but the quality of the time you're spending together. During an outing or any time you're together, remember to listen to, not talk *at*, your grandchild— or any child, for that matter. It makes for a delightful conversation and lifelong bonding.

■ **Adopt a pet.** Depending on your relationship with it, a pet may fall in your inner circle, not on the peripheral ring. An animal's unconditional love offers tremendous camaraderie. Some people have pets as an alternative to children, or as a substitute for or in addition to children, grandchildren, or close friends. Pets can give you a reason to greet the day—they provide a sense of responsibility, an exercise program, and a great opening for social interchange during walks with other pet owners.

Domestic animals are more popular than they have ever been before in the United States, and are at the top of many people's must-have list—just look at all the designer products and services that mimic our own needs and excesses. Here's what one of our survey respondents had to say on the importance of pets in her life:

I never wanted to have children. My life has been full without them. I have a wonderful mate, a career that I love, travel and fulfilling life experiences. I am lucky enough to have nieces and nephews that I am very close to and involved with; it must feel something like having grandchildren. I love being with them, but I don't have to raise them. My "child" is my dog. Besides my husband, of all the things that I've had and done, my one constant love is my dog. I can't imagine my life without her. She's there for me and I am there for her.

—RETIREMENT DOCS' SURVEY

YOUR INTERMEDIATE AND OUTER CIRCLES

When we retire, our social world usually narrows. We don't have the everyday relationships we once had at work, and we may find that we spend more time focused on our family and other members in our inner circle. Keeping a network of friends in our intermediate and outer circles can keep our perspective broadening and our interests expanding. Maybe you have a friend who shares your passion for the opera or basketball and you decide to get season tickets together? Or another friend introduced you to French films and now you're hooked.

- **Plan ahead.** Research shows group interaction decreases as we age. Start and maintain your new and ongoing relationships as much as possible in your retirement's phase one's planning for retirement, and phase two's semiretirement.
- **Be willing to take the time to develop new friendships and maintain current ones.** For many of us, this takes a recognized and planned effort on our parts: Don't skip that poker game or book club just because you've settled in. Get out of the house and off to that garden show. "It's raining," you say? Get an umbrella! All of those other people managed to get there.
- **Have a number of single friends.** When we're married, most of our friends tend to be involved in—we've all heard it many times—"a couple's world." Should you lose your spouse, you'll have a base of friends who won't have the time commitment that a partnership requires.

■ **If necessary, reeducate yourself: Make new friends.** Ask other people for input, make a list, read the local newspaper. Find things that are interesting to you and go there. Do you love to read? Volunteer for a couple of hours a week at your local library. Socialize in churches, hobby groups, volunteer groups, or schools, or take your dog to a local dog park; play cards, start going to the local ball games, join an exercise class; the list is endless. Involve yourself with a group of people who enjoy your hobby. Remember, friendships usually start via a common interest and over time develop by openly sharing thoughts, interests, and concerns. The key is not the activity; it's how you develop and use the activity as an opportunity to expand your support group.

■ **Get online.** An area of marked expansion for continuing senior social interaction has been the Internet. SeniorNet.com has led this movement along with many other dotcoms. The computer has given isolated retirees the opportunity to communicate with friends and potential friends, plus the ability to exchange information in a world of available and interesting topics, all the while providing excellent mental stimulation.

E-Friends

MySpace and Facebook, while not specifically geared to Baby Boomers (Facebook started as a site for college students), are welcoming to them. Both of these sites make it easy to create a page and connect with others who share your interests. In addition, a national organization called meetup.com helps people organize local, in-person meetings for all sorts of things—from singles events to garden clubs. It's a fantastic way to connect with people in your area who share your interest. Here is a list of some other online social networking Web sites, with their taglines, that are geared to Baby Boomers and their concerns.

(continued)

www.eons.com—Lovin' life: the flip side of 50

www.BOOMj.com—Boomer Nation Lifestyle Network

www.reZOOM.com—Redefining life for an ageless generation

www.BoomerTowne.com

www.BoomerGirl.com—Welcome to the Club

www.eldr.com—Celebrating aging

www.RedwoodAge.com—Think. Share. Act. Live.

www.BoomSpeak.com—Your whole life's in front of you

www.eGenerations.com—Connect. Learn. Explore.

www.itsBoomerTime.com—Having fun . . . while changing the
world

www.GrowingBolder.com—The Revolution Is Coming Soon

www.Boomer-Living.com— . . . Enhancing the lives of Active Baby
Boomers

www.tbd.com (TeeBeeDee)—Sharing Experiences to Thrive

www.LifeTwo.com— . . . Midlife Improvement

www.MyBoomerPlace.com—Like MySpace, but better . . . for
people over 40

www.MyPrimetime.com—Personal Trainer for Life

www.secondprime.com—Where people 50+ connect, create, and
contribute

www.MapleandLeek.com (United Kingdom)—Live it up at 50+.
Adventures start here

www.GrownUps.co.nz (New Zealand)—50+ Community

STAY INVOLVED WITH YOUR
PERIPHERAL CIRCLE

There are a number of people who may not be your close friends or colleagues, but who are crucial to your well-being and "life management."

■ **Know who they are.** In your second career, this circle is made up of the people who are necessary for keeping your life in order and functioning smoothly—people like your doctor, your accountant, your attorney, your banker, your insurance agent, your pastor, and anyone else you can think of who provides you with services you rely on. Both you and your spouse should become well acquainted with these professionals. If, and when, something happens to one of you, it will allow the other to feel comfortable continuing on with the business at hand.

■ **Make sure you are responsible for something living to tend to.** For example, a plant, a garden, an animal, a bunch of pigeons, or a pool of koi all give you a reason to get up in the morning, for without you your charges may not exist. Caregiving and caretaking are important to your overall well-being.

It is never, ever too late to make new friends. Make widening your social circle a top priority now if you feel that your circle will dwindle significantly once you fully retire. Friends who share your interests in sports, hobbies, crafts, or specific subjects will make wonderful companions when you begin pursuing leisure activities and passions, the two topics we discuss next.

7

TRAIT FIVE: KICK BACK—
ENJOY LEISURE TIME

*There is nothing more remarkable in the life of Socrates than that he found time
in his old age to learn to dance and play on instruments and thought it was time
well spent.*

—MONTAIGNE, RENAISSANCE SCHOLAR

Retirement, for many of us, represents the first time in our lives when
we are accountable only to ourselves. Our working lives probably left
many of us with little room for personal leisure. Then one day we finally have
time to transfer our energy from earning a living to the business of living life.
It's exchanging a paycheck for a payoff both in pleasure and retirement satisfaction. When all that time hits us in the face, we often become consumed
with our newfound freedom, and the activities and projects we've had on the
back burner for years finally come to life. Life is exciting! We accomplish our
goals in the first six to twelve months of our retirement, and then we're left
wondering: What in the world am I going to do with all that free time?

*To have a successful retirement, people need to begin the process of discovery
again. Though now as I face it, I wonder, is it possible to live a meaningful, ful-
filled life if work is no longer the center of it?*

—RETIREMENT DOCS' SURVEY

It seems to me that most of my life was spent living for tomorrow. In my retire-
ment, I am living for today. I find I want fewer and fewer material possessions
and more and more experiences.

—RETIREMENT DOCS' SURVEY

The answer to that question is found in phase one, before you retire. You should be cultivating as many leisure activities as you can at that time. As we've already explained, transitioning from work to retirement leisure will be easier for you if you have certain behaviors in place before you leave your job. Bear in mind that a partiality to certain leisure activities is usually not developed on short notice. For example, an interest in literature or appreciation for classical music usually takes many years to develop. It's also a good idea to develop and include a number of less-demanding interests and activities years before you are forced by age or physical limitations to do so.

If you're saying to yourself, "I've been too busy working to cultivate a lot of outside interests," don't also think it's too late to do anything about it. Everyone has at least one or two activities or areas that they are interested in, apart from (or even related to) the work they do. Whether you are about to retire, have just retired, or have been retired for a while, now is the time to start cultivating your interests and researching ways to get involved in them. You can begin developing interests by making a list of things you enjoy doing or think you would, could, or might enjoy (we give you plenty of opportunities to do so in this book). Even the act of *researching* an activity, *planning* a trip, *organizing* an outing, or *reading up* on a particular topic are in themselves ways to develop an interest.

Walter Kerr, author of *The Decline of Pleasure,* points out: "The twentieth century has relieved us of much labor without, at the same time, relieving us of the conviction that only labor is meaningful."

Our survey respondents were asked to rate their success as well as their partners' (if applicable), in developing and achieving satisfying leisure activities. We weren't surprised to find that our highly successful retirees had much commonality and positive support going for them. Couples felt that there was equal and adequate intellectual stimulation for them both, that they had ample social activities they did alone and together, and that each partner was or had been involved in planning and preparing for their retirement. Our respondents also said they watched television together 50 percent of the time, and surprise—they shared equally in handling the remote.

And, *aaah,* television and our dedication to it. Surveys show that just about 40 percent of our leisure time is spent watching TV. It is by far the number-one leisure activity from phase one right on through phase four, with viewing time increasing significantly as we age.

> *My wife is always after me to "turn that thing off and do something productive." She's an avid reader, and I've asked her what she thinks is the difference between watching programs that are interesting to me, and reading for hours on end the books she thinks are interesting. So far she hasn't answered. Maybe she's busy reading!*
>
> —RETIREMENT DOCS' SURVEY

There is no question that television watching can be intellectually stimulating, and watching sporting events or a thriller can increase your heart rate. TV is relaxing, and if you do live alone, it can provide a sense of "company." Our concern is moderation. Reclining in front of the tube five and a half hours a day, day in and day out, is the norm for many viewers over age sixty. That's excessive. Examine your viewing habits and make sure you're not glued in one place for far too long. And if you are going to stay tuned to television, at least come up with a few multitasking efforts during some of those viewing hours—knitting, crocheting, needlepoint, crosswords (during commercial breaks), organizing photos, etcetera.

This leads us to the key concept in spending free time well—leisure *doesn't* mean idleness. Controlled trials prove that mental and physical workouts, in the context of leisure activities, are major factors in keeping your mind alert and functioning. The best kind of leisure activities not only keep you entertained but also relax you, help you enjoy friends and family, and even connect you to potential passions and purposes (which we discuss in the next chapter). The great characteristic of leisure is that it does not need to be

Important with a capital *I*, or Meaningful with a capital *M*. Consequential activities are important. But in order to have a balanced life it is necessary to spend some of your time doing things simply because they are fun and not because they are vitally important to the greater significance of your life.

> *I retired at sixty and was very active. I golfed nearly every day. By seventy-six, medical problems and the loss of my wonderful wife took the wind out of my sails. But never count yourself finished until you are. At a class reunion, a chance meeting with a "girl" I hadn't seen for years led to my second marriage. I'm now eighty-four, don't golf anymore, but once or twice a week we get together with a group of friends and have savage putting competitions. We take great strolls, go on outings identifying and counting birds for our local Audubon Society, and in general enjoy life. I am much happier today than I have been in a long time.*
>
> —RETIREMENT DOCS' SURVEY

Leisure is about pleasure and unwinding: taking in a ridiculous but hilarious new comedy, reading a trashy espionage novel that you simply cannot put down, relaxing out on the deck with a really cold beer and a really good buddy, checking out fishing rods at the sporting goods store, or poking around antique shops on a Sunday afternoon. Or leisure can involve more physical projects, especially those long overdue, like renovating the bathroom, building a patio, or organizing the basement or closet (notice how enjoyable those things can be when you actually have time to do them?).

> *I don't like structure in retirement. I like going with the flow, though I have many interests, including my family, physical exercise (mainly running long distances, cross-country biking, and strenuous swimming), flying airplanes, golfing, reading, and gardening. While I make few plans in the main, when I wake up, depending on the weather, I will do two or three different activities that day. I randomly rotate them on a day-to-day basis. The core activity, however, is a daily hour to an hour and a half of one of my exercises. My goal is elevating my heart rate.*
>
> —RETIREMENT DOCS' SURVEY

A work ethic can be deeply ingrained in our psyches, and for many good reasons: It gives us an identity, self-esteem, and a psychological high for a job well done. This is why for many people, the perfect leisure activity is part-time employment, especially if it's of your own choosing, it's at your own pace, it isn't stressful, and it enhances your personal satisfaction. If your decision to "work till you drop" allows you to be of productive value to your employer and yourself—go for it. Just make sure you're not being a hanger-on. You need to continue to contribute wherever and however you find yourself involved.

It doesn't require a Herculean effort to begin shifting your perspective about yourself. Read your local newspaper events calendar. It will supply you with myriad interesting activities. That's just what we did and found listed, to name just a few, a model railroad club, square dancing with instructions, Meals on Wheels, a quilt guild, a toastmasters club, a runner's run (all abilities and ages welcome), a genealogical society meeting, an Apple computer users group meeting, an invitation to become involved in a food bank, a request for volunteer readers in area grade schools, an acting workshop, and a golf tournament. These all appeared on one page! As we mentioned in the support groups section, meetup.com is an online resource for meetings of all kinds of groups, including those interested in specific leisure pursuits. Your neighborhood may also have a block association with an online component that you can check for upcoming events.

I am a planner. I started field-testing various leisure activities ten years before my retirement. I made specific plans to use them if I became physically infirm as well as for the normal aging changes that would occur. I worked on developing activities I could do alone and with my mate, our friends, and my friends. I stopped working full-time seven years ago, but I have a work ethic mentality; that is, I have a need to stay productive. But I'm getting much better as time passes, and I feel that I've got my dilemmas under control. As I get older, my leisure activities are becoming more and more family-oriented. These are the best years of my life in large part because of a strong support group. For the first time in my adult life, I feel that I am in control of my time.

—Dr. Fritz

I've had so many outside interests in my life, other than medicine, that when I was forced to limit my surgery practice because of some visual problems, I hit the ground running. My strong family support group and wide circle of friends frequently allow just the two of us, my wife and me, only a few nights a week relaxing at home. While we value our time together, we also feel fortunate to have such a wide circle of support, and look forward to the stimulation that comes from our outings, be they with family, friends, or a new adventure. Since childhood, I have had so many interests, hobbies, and activities that I never feel that I have enough time for all of them.

I love sports, was a high school team player, loved working with my hands, and have always been in love with the arts. I have taken fine woodworking courses from some of the top craftsmen in our country. It's not that I wanted to be the world's best woodworker. Rather, I wanted to learn their techniques and enjoy their expertise. In fact, I'm just going to meet with a very talented guy who's going to teach me how to carve decoys. I guess I fell into the select group that had practiced the "retirement hop" without much conscious awareness of planning or preparation. However, as time goes on, I am working, as is Dr. Fritz, to fine-tune my eight traits. I feel that what lies ahead in phases three and four needs planning, particularly for a wide range of age-related fallback leisure activities.

—DR. JIM

And don't forget to include social support groups. There are card games (look at the popularity of poker and bridge), any kind of hobby club you can think of, book clubs, dinner groups, and rock and roll bands. We just read an article about the resurgence of the musicians among us dusting off those long-neglected instruments and gathering to enjoy some good times, jamming in their garages—and most of the participants were sixty or older!

I spent close to forty years doing the same work. My life was full of good fortune. I have an occupation that kept me, for the main part, fully engaged. I have a wife, children, and grandchildren who currently keep me balanced and on my toes. I have lots of friends, though I must admit that the majority of them were coworkers, and that part of my life has taken the biggest adjusting to. But I'm lucky—

the family grew up and my extended family is now a big part of where I look forward to spending my time. And though I miss the day-to-day structure and interaction of what I did for so long, I also now have the time to devote to my love of hiking and all the planning it involves. I recently began studying cartology, and that's opened up a whole new interest for me. I have plenty of family and friends (and some new hiking boots) who remain fit, able, and ready to go see the world.

—RETIREMENT DOCS' SURVEY

DIAGNOSIS

To find out if there are enough leisure activities in your life, answer the following questions. Don't hesitate to duplicate some activities within different categories. To get you thinking, how about golf, tennis, walking, birdwatching, gardening, family events, being with your grandchildren, cultural events, arts, movies, plays, reading, writing, painting, volunteering, elder hostels, community college classes, and church involvement? The sky's the limit. A keen interest in a specific hobby often creates an expert mentality and a feeling of accomplishment, but keep in mind the importance of having a variety of leisure activities. The point of these activities is to stimulate but also free your mind. Factor in activities that can be done when health problems, caregiving responsibilities, a change in economics, or age limitations occur.

Make sure you've included intellectual motivation and physical challenges in each of the categories below. They generate a sense of accomplishment and well-being. Just as muscles and bones remain healthy when exercised, our minds stay healthy when challenged. Remember, the more you can list, the better off you'll be.

■ List ten or more leisure activities that you do with your mate or mutual friends. For example, travel, play cards, golf, garden, go to the theater, volunteer, spend time with grandchildren and other family, and join various organizations—social, political, or spiritual. If there is a particular activity that you are deeply immersed in and it has several parts, it can count as three. For example, gardening could potentially count as planting, learning about horticulture, and caring for the landscape, and maybe even organizing the local garden club.

1. We enjoy . . .
2. We enjoy . . .
3. We enjoy . . .
4. We enjoy . . .
5. We enjoy . . .
6. We enjoy . . .
7. We enjoy . . .
8. We enjoy . . .
9. We enjoy . . .
10. We enjoy . . .

■ List ten or more leisure activities that you enjoy doing by yourself or with your own personal friends. Some examples are golf, tennis, attending sports events, exercising, reading, watching television, card games, gardening, social clubs, fishing, listening to music, visiting old friends, genealogy, woodworking, and spending time with grandchildren. As above, any multipart activity can count as more than one on the list.

1. I enjoy . . .
2. I enjoy . . .
3. I enjoy . . .
4. I enjoy . . .
5. I enjoy . . .
6. I enjoy . . .
7. I enjoy . . .
8. I enjoy . . .
9. I enjoy . . .
10. I enjoy . . .

■ List ten or more activities that make you feel good about yourself, things that make you feel as if you're helping others, affirming that you're still a player, or that there is a reason you are on this earth. Some examples are volunteering, writing, managing assets, teaching, lecturing, part-time employment, civic groups, and belonging to various local and national organizations. As above, any multipart activity can count as more than one on the list.

1. I am involved in . . .
2. I am involved in . . .
3. I am involved in . . .
4. I am involved in . . .
5. I am involved in . . .
6. I am involved in . . .
7. I am involved in . . .
8. I am involved in . . .
9. I am involved in . . .
10. I am involved in . . .

Both of us intend to be in phase two for as long as we're physically and mentally able to. We enjoy consulting with patients, speaking, writing, and doing research. This ongoing work gives us a feeling of self-worth and softens the loss of identity and self-esteem we received when practicing full-time medicine.

—JIM AND FRITZ, THE RETIREMENT DOCS

THE RETIREMENT DOCS' LEISURE PRESCRIPTION

When faced with excess time, the vast majority of retirees continue doing the same activities they did before their retirement, but they expand the amount of time they give to them. Our highly successful retirees were all expanders. They added to or field-tested relationships and involvement with new friends, hobbies, and activities to see which ones they wanted to pursue over the long term. Optimally, the process of planning and field-testing for filling in free time begins at least five to ten years *before* retirement, but very few of us are going to find ourselves in that position. Remember, several years before you retire, when you are retiring, or if you've been retired for some time, it's never too late to begin making a plan for good use of your leisure time. Just make sure it's a pleasure putting that plan into place!

To make good use of leisure time, keep these things in mind:

- Spend time with vibrant, stimulating, upbeat, and optimistic people.
- Increase activities, reading materials, and viewing materials that create positive feelings. Decrease those that create negative feelings.
- Include mental stimulation, physical exertion, and social contact throughout the four phases of your retirement.
- Select some interests that make you feel a sense of responsibility and give you a feeling of self-respect.
- Contribute to the well-being of other people.
- If retirement doesn't work, "un-retire." Full- or part-time employment is a great idea if it's enjoyable.
- The best leisure activities promote a healthy lifestyle.
- Look for ways to add spice to your life. Take risks and try new adventures.
- Retirement gives you the freedom to do what you want to do. Enjoy and protect it.
- The spirit of a leisure-time interest is as important as the activity. Eliminate anything mentally stressful, and spend your leisure time leisurely!
- Ideal leisure includes educational activities.
- Increase your social networking. Become involved in a variety of leisure activities that include people of all ages.
- Reach out and make your life meaningful. It usually won't happen unless you make the effort.

Success or failure in our second career will in great part be measured in terms of how we use or abuse the leisure time we have. The writer Freya Stark put it beautifully when she wrote something we can all think about, whatever our age and whatever our abilities:

> On the whole, age comes more gently to those who have some doorway into the abstract world—art or philosophy or learning—regions where the years are scarcely noticed and the young and the old can meet in a pale, truthful light.

Finally, we want you to remember that leisure is about pleasure. There is no better time to indulge in fun. Think of retirement as a sabbatical—this is the "someday" you've talked about for years, as in "Someday, I'm going to learn to sail, perfect the tango, or read *Moby-Dick*." The time has arrived— seize the day!

8

TRAIT SIX: HERE'S TO YOUR HEALTH

In health there is freedom. Health is the first of all liberties.

—HENRI-FRÉDÉRIC AMIEL, SWISS WRITER

Retirement Docs' Survey respondents rated a healthy lifestyle second most important after planning. Even so, we decided to name it trait six because we feel strongly that the psychological components of retirement are too often overlooked, and therefore more crucial to concentrate on first. Still, physical well-being is essential for a successful retirement, and our most highly successful retirees were also the most fit and active. In fact, these happy, healthy retirees are so dedicated to keeping fit and well that they consider exercise and healthy eating *nonnegotiable passions*. They know that the payoff for taking care of their bodies is increased energy, a better mood, and a greater overall satisfaction with life.

Clearly, given the choice (and you are given a choice), achieving and maintaining the best health we can is a real advantage to living longer and better. Can you remember how old you were when you realized that you and you alone, not your mother, spouse, or doctor, were responsible for your health and well-being? Years ago when we were in medical school, we were taught that a person's allotted lifetime, barring an untimely accidental death, was based heavily on genetic makeup. The conventional wisdom (which 70 percent of our respondents still believe) was that some of us were lucky with our ancestral pipelines, and some weren't. But now we know better. As the saying goes, it's not so much the cards you've been dealt but how you play them. We take that idea a step further: after age sixty, it's not so much about the genes you have been dealt, but it's how much help you're willing to give them.

Once you reach sixty, you have even more control of your health, your life satisfaction, and, to a great extent, your longevity than you did when you were younger. Michael F. Roizen, M.D., points out in *Real Age* that, "inherited genetics account for less than 30 percent of all aging effects, and the importance of genetic inheritance matters less and less the older your calendar age. By the age of eighty, behavioral choices account almost entirely for a person's overall health and longevity."

Of course, it's true that there is an occasional blip on the screen—we all know one or two people who seem to defy the odds by some genetically gifted providence, and go for decades abusing their bodies and living to see a healthy ninety-plus years. Think about Bette Davis turning up to spar with David Letterman, puffing away on a cancer stick well into her seventies. We've just celebrated one of our friend's century marks, which she greeted with martini and cigarette in hand. *However, be aware that this is far from the norm.* An article in that highly esteemed bible of medicine *The New England Journal of Medicine* stated that, "not only do persons with better health habits survive longer, but in such persons, disability is postponed and compressed into much fewer years at the end of life." And according to the World Health Organization, "Health isn't the absence of illness, but a presence of well-being, including your physical, mental and social wellness."

As we age, good health requires the full participation of the individual. I take care of myself because I know that I am my own responsibility. My best doctors are a balanced diet, regular exercise, mental stimulation, and moderation in diet.

—RETIREMENT DOCS' SURVEY

What follows is a rundown of the most important components of good health. We won't insult your intelligence by telling you that maintaining a healthy lifestyle is easy or can be done overnight, especially if you have not been paying attention to certain aspects of your health for a while. No matter—with a few small steps at a time (cutting out fried and processed foods, increasing the amount of vegetables and other whole foods you eat, talking a daily walk, etcetera), you can actually make very big health strides.

DIET AND WEIGHT: BALANCING THE SCALES

As much as any lifestyle characteristic, excess weight affects health and happiness. Today, more than at any time in our history, Americans are collectively fatter than ever. Our national obesity rates in the United States have doubled since 1980, and 25 percent of our population is obese compared to 7 percent of Europeans.

Excess weight can cause major cardiovascular problems, increased blood pressure, diabetes, and bone and joint problems, as well as an increased incidence of cancer and gout. The list goes on and on. The National Institutes of Health Consensus Development Conference states that in terms of suffering, the psychological burden of obesity alone may be its greatest adverse effect. It is estimated that obesity-related morbidity may account for almost 7 percent of the total health-care costs in the United States. A woman of average height (5 feet 6 inches) with a waistline measuring more than 36 inches has a dramatically increased chance of suffering a heart attack. The same is true for a man of average height (5 feet 10 inches) with a waistline of more than 40 inches.

Your Body Mass Index (BMI) is a fairly new term: it's the measurement of choice for many physicians and researchers when studying obesity. It's also the most accurate way to determine whether you have too few or too many pounds that could translate into health risks.

To calculate an adult BMI, use the following formula (alternatively, use one of the many easy BMI calculators available free on the Internet—use the keywords "BMI calculator" to find one).

■ Multiply your weight in pounds by 703.

■ Divide that number by your height in inches, squared (e.g., if you're 5'5", that's 65 inches. Your height squared—65 × 65—is 4225).

■ Round the first decimal point up if necessary. That is your BMI.

BMI Categories

■ Underweight = 18.5
■ Normal weight = 18.5–24.9
■ Overweight = 25–29.9
■ Obesity = 30 or higher

There are numerous Web sites that offer the BMI calculator. We used the National Heart, Lung, and Blood Institute site at www.NHLBISUPPORT .com. If you use the same organization, you'll find the Body Mass Index Calculator listed under Health Associated Tools. This NHLB site has an amazing array of health-related information. What a find! But back to our weight-related info.

What's your BMI? Get it into the normal weight category and positively below 30. Do your part to insure a healthy lifestyle.

A healthy diet and an ideal body weight may provide you with the health base that you need to add to a statistical life expectancy. On the other hand, the markedly obese, besides having weight-related aches and pains, could find themselves decreasing their lifespan by years. In extreme situations, there may be a swing either way of twenty-plus years. Healthy, you might give yourself another twenty-plus. Heavy, you could see a minus-twenty. Significant numbers, don't you think?

UCLA researchers reviewed thirty-one weight-loss studies and concluded that diet programs did not keep the pounds off. It's true that most people initially lose weight, but between a third and two-thirds of dieters regain that weight over a two- to five-year follow-up period. That's probably because in the past decade we have doubled or tripled our portion sizes. Recent research shows that almost 70 percent of us eat everything that we're served—and we get served huge portions at home and in restaurants. Men are three times more likely to eat everything on their plates than are women. A recent article in the *Journal of the American Medical Association* noted that decreasing serving portions by 20 percent extends your life. "Lick the platter clean" is history.

The National Weight Control Registry suggests that the best ways to keep lost pounds off are:

Eat breakfast. The morning meal does not have to be large, but you do need to eat it. A slice of whole-wheat toast with peanut butter or a cup of nonfat yogurt with fruit is enough to get your engine running.

Eat moderately and know what you're eating. Fill your plate with fiber-rich foods like whole grains (brown rice, cracked wheat), beans, deeply colored vegetables (leafy greens, sweet potatoes, tomatoes, carrots, beets), and fruit. Stay away from saturated fat (butter, steak) and stick to "good" fats, such as olive and canola oils, but use them in moderation. Eat lean protein (chicken breast, turkey, egg whites) but in moderation. Three-quarters of your plate should be filled with plant-based foods.

Weigh yourself daily. Make a chart and write down the date and your weight. If you're on a weight-loss program, keep a food journal and write down everything you eat. A free, easy-to-use online example is www.calorie-count.com.

Move everyday—at least thirty to sixty minutes.

Bonus tip: Drink wine and eat chocolate. We now believe that one or two glasses of red wine and a one-inch square of dark chocolate consumed each day may add to longevity and good health.

And one more—on us: Don't eat after dinner.

I'm at the age where food has taken the place of sex in my life. In fact, I've just had a mirror put over my kitchen table.

—RODNEY DANGERFIELD

What Mr. Dangerfield has to say about aging and eating is amusing. Should you find that you've gone ahead and installed the kitchen mirror, use it to take a good look at yourself! Think healthy, look healthy = be healthy.

Meditate on It

Meditation is good for your health. Meditation is simply the practice of sitting comfortably, with eyes closed, for fifteen to twenty minutes twice a day while mentally repeating a simple word or mantra (which can be anything from "yes" to "love"). This practice has drastically reduced medical costs in people aged sixty-five and over, according to a Canadian study. One hundred and sixty-three senior citizens from Quebec reduced visits to physicians by 70 percent during the five-year period after they started to meditate.

Om!

EXERCISE: THE REWARDS OF SWEAT EQUITY

Please note: When exercising, overdoing or pushing too hard, particularly as we get older, is a problem waiting to happen. Before starting any exercise program, consult with your doctor or health-care provider. Begin with something simple that you enjoy (you will never stick with something that you don't like doing), such as walking or riding a bike.

Getting your blood flowing improves your cardiovascular system and increases your lung capacity, your body's two most important systems. At the same time it's elevating your mood and aiding in your longevity. We have a good friend who is famous for shooting his age in most of his golf rounds. He claims his game is so good and so consistent because he never misses a ten-minute morning stretching routine and most days, an hour workout. By the way, he's eighty-four and a newlywed. A recent study by Dr. Teresa Seeman, professor of medicine and epidemiology at UCLA, found seventy- to ninety-year-olds functioned best and had the least psychological stress when they exercised regularly.

Further geriatric research indicates that it's a given—a diverse exercise program improves your perception of your health and aging. An ongoing, ever-adjusting variety of physical activities is ideal throughout the four phases of retirement. Consider walking with a group (keep the pace as fast as you can); joining a bird-watching club where participants go out seasonally on hikes and walks to count bird species; signing up for tap, line, square, or ballroom dancing; going for a hike; playing doubles tennis or golf; or anything that gets you up and out.

Exercise has always been important to me. I was able to transition from running marathons in my thirties to jogging several times a week in my sixties. Now that I'm in my eighties I thoroughly enjoy my walking group. Exercise has kept me active and energized for decades.

—RETIREMENT DOCS' SURVEY

We wanted to schedule a time to interview a friend of ours for this book. He's a psychiatrist who happens to be ninety-six. His receptionist said she would give him our message, adding, "As you know, he's in the office twice a week. Right now he's out with his personal trainer. I know about the book you two are working on, and it seems relevant that you know the doctor works out daily and meets with his trainer three times each week. He's remarkable." The fact that our friend's meetings with his trainer took precedence over the one we hoped to schedule was a good thing.

It's very hard to exercise alone, especially when you are just starting out! If you must, however, most cable television now offers a myriad of exercise programs, and one or two networks are devoted to fitness 24/7.

Based on one's ability, capability, and personality, individual exercise programs vary greatly throughout retirement's four phases. But continued consistency is paramount for overall health and feelings of well-being. This doesn't mean, mentioned earlier, that it's necessary to have a personal trainer or to attend an exercise class, though either is a smart choice, especially for someone who is getting back into exercise or embarking on a program for the first time. A certified fitness professional can help motivate you, and he or she can help you design, stick to, and implement the right program. The YMCA has personal trainers on staff, and membership is very affordable, especially for those who meet certain age requirements. Certified trainers are able to teach you to exercise properly for maximum benefit and minimum injury, and you meet other likeminded people at the gym.

Weight-bearing exercises are essential for bone strength and flexibility. According to a recent AARP study, people eighty and older who lifted weights were from 58 to 74 percent more optimistic than were people who didn't pump iron! Nothing fancy is required, but consistency is. If you miss a day, get back at it. One guy we know was twenty-four when he spotted a fifteen-pound steel rod in a trash bin. He's used it as his exercise weight daily for the past forty-four years.

People who think they have no time for exercise will sooner or later have more than enough time for illness

—JIM AND FRITZ, THE RETIREMENT DOCS

And for you "naysaying, just-won't-do-it" non-exercisers, please remember that even thirty minutes three times a week has obvious benefits if it gets your heart rate up. We once read that it takes twenty-eight days to make something a habit and three days to undo it. Exercise as you live: take the stairs instead of the elevator, garden, and park as far from the grocery store as you can to add additional steps to your day. Or grab a friend and commit to meeting three times a week for a power walk around the neighborhood. Making a commitment to another person makes us do what we should do, rather than thinking about what we should do and then not quite getting around to it. One woman we know took a daily walk with a friend who lived next door. It became a much-looked-forward-to evening ritual. It was "me time" for both of them, a time to unwind, review the day, and get some exercise.

A LAUGHING MATTER

Snicker, giggle, chuckle, and laugh until your sides hurt! Laughter is another important component of a healthy lifestyle. William Fry, M.D., professor of psychiatry at Stanford University Medical School, found that while kindergarten-aged children laugh about three hundred times a day, adults laugh only about seventeen times per day. Maybe we are growing older because we stop laughing! In an article by *Oregonian* columnist Margie Boulé, medical researchers specializing in laughter and the effect it has on our well-being found that laughing lowers blood pressure, reduces weight, strengthens hearts, boosts immune systems, and lowers stress hormones, and those are just some of the benefits.

Indeed, doctors all over the world are studying the effects of laughter on the immune and cardiovascular systems and finding amazing results. There is a now a field of medical study actually called "laughter therapy," which is designed to study the potential for laughter to promote healing and overall well-being. For instance, researchers at the UCLA Neuropsychiatric Research Institute and Hospital showed that patients undergoing painful medical procedures had significantly better pain tolerance while laughing at comedy shows during their private, individual procedures. The treatments went by faster for these patients, and they felt less afraid and less stressed. Dr. Jim's "doctor, heal thyself" prescription while recovering from recent major surgery was a daily dose of the Comedy Channel. He's fully recovered and, in part, found that laughter was indeed "the best medicine."

Medications: Too Easy to Swallow

Americans may well be the most overmedicated people in the world. Whether it's prescription medicine, over-the-counter drugs, or herbal products, many of us take too many medications. It seems to be our mentality that we should have something to take for each and every ailment we suffer, when the truth is that the tincture of time is most often the best cure for minor ailments. Do you realize that 98 percent of the time the potential interaction among any three medications that we may be ingesting is probably unknown?

Our highly successful retirees, with an average age of sixty-eight, while healthy, still take an average daily dose of two prescription drugs, two over-the-counter medications (such as vitamins, aspirin, and decongestants), and 0.5 herbal products. That adds up to a minimum of 4.5 pills a day, which is still about *half* the national average for sixty-eight-year-olds. That's a lot of swallowing. Women take more medications than men until age seventy, at which time men and women take the same amount. It's in your best interest to reevaluate many herbal and over-the-counter drugs. Herbal products often have significant variability in their ingredients and potency, as well as unknown interactions with other drugs.

While the exact content and potency are uniform in over-the-counter drugs, they are often used in excess and may interfere with prescription medication. Know what you are taking and why. Ask your physician if you can decrease the number and dosage of your prescription drugs. Data shows that the more "doctor-hopping" a person does, the more prescription medication he or she will take—and the more risk of combining drugs that should not be taken together.

In all probability, most of us are at least 40 percent overmedicated.

—*BRITISH JOURNAL OF GENERAL PRACTICE*

THE SMOKING GUN: CIGARETTES

I kicked most all of my bad habits by myself, but I needed professional help to stop smoking.

—Retirement Docs' Survey

The four leading causes of death in America are

- Heart disease
- Cancer
- Stroke
- Chronic obstructive pulmonary disease, including varying combinations of chronic bronchitis, asthma, and emphysema.

Half of all long-term smokers will face a severe—that's right, *severe*—form of one of these four diseases. However, if you're a smoker and can stop, quitting has shown a decrease in the incidence of tobacco-related diseases in as short a time as five months.

Here are some statistics that might make any of you smokers want to rethink lighting up. And those of you inhaling anyone else's smoke—change locations.

- Smoking from one to fourteen cigarettes daily will statistically decrease a life span by three years.
- Smokers lighting up fifteen to twenty-four cigarettes each day can subtract five years from their life expectancy.
- Smoke twenty-five or more cigarettes a day and expect to die eight years earlier than a nonsmoker.

And we haven't begun to talk about the decreased quality of life that smoking causes!

As for secondhand smoke:

- Secondhand smoke inhaled one hour per day decreases life expectancy by a year.
- One to three hours per day of direct exposure to secondhand smoke reduces life expectancy by two years.
- More than three hours per day of secondhand smoke inhalation shortens a life span by three years.

This is heavy statistical data. It is our hope that our children and their children will educate themselves regarding the perils of tobacco and then pass it on, snuffing this killer out for good.

THE SOBERING FACTS ABOUT ALCOHOL

There are love songs about its magic. We use it to toast special occasions, and there are pilgrimages to see it produced. We marvel at the multitude of beers, fine wines, and well-aged spirits. It relaxes us, it enables us, and it makes our aches and pains feel better. Its power is magical. Or is it? Just like anything that's out of balance with our body's needs, there are some very sobering facts about alcohol use and abuse.

A Gallup Poll survey has asked the same question annually since 1947. It is: "Has alcohol abuse caused problems in your family?" That first year, 15 percent of the respondents answered "yes." Recently it was 29 percent. In an *American Journal of Psychiatry* article, authors George Vaillant and Kenneth Mukamal placed the overuse of alcohol as one of six major predictive factors for overall failure in life. They wrote that "It's not only alcohol's toll on a person's health, but the destructive force it has on the alcohol abuser's support group. . . . The abuse destroys both health and happiness."

Some current literature recommends no more than two drinks of spirits per day for men and one for women. Moderation is the key. If you don't have a drinking problem, that is. If you aren't an alcoholic, there are some benefits from imbibing (there are *no* benefits to drinking for those who cannot control themselves around booze). Drinking alcohol in moderation is associated with an increased life expectancy of a year or more, though the added year isn't realized until a man reaches forty to fifty years old, and until women reach menopause or their late forties or early fifties. One four-ounce glass of wine or a one-ounce drink of spirits (such as gin or Scotch) may ease stress and relax aches and pains. Recent studies show that red wine contains compounds that may protect us from heart disease, diabetes, and even dementia. Plus, there's enjoyment many of us find in a glass of wine or a cocktail that pleasantly signals the end of our day.

Many, if not most, physicians feel that if you've never been a drinker, don't start. The older we get, the slower we metabolize. And our systems give alcohol the green light first, absorbing it into our bloodstream before anything else it happens to enter with. Add those two facts up and adjust accordingly: slower metabolizing and alcohol's digestive dominance.

Statistics show that many retirees consume more alcohol once they stop working. Less time on the job can often, for many reasons, equal more drinking, so that's something to keep in mind.

SNOOZE CONTROL

People who get a good, solid sleep are more alert, healthier, and happier—and even weigh less than those who do not get *at least* seven hours of sleep per night. An average night's sleep in 1910 was nine hours; currently it's less than seven and a half. The National Sleep Foundation and other sleep experts say that adults need anywhere from seven to nine hours of uninterrupted sleep.

Most of our survey respondents thought they got enough sleep, though a small number of them alluded to sleep problems but chose to more or less ignore them. That isn't surprising, since insomnia and sleep disorders can be common in older people. Some of the symptoms mentioned—and there were quite a few—were difficulty falling asleep, waking often, waking too early, an inability to get back to sleep, waking up tired, snoring, unpleasant feelings in the legs, and interrupted breathing (gasping). If you have any of the above symptoms and they are ongoing over a prolonged period of time (a few months or more), get professional help.

Changing sleep habits is preferable to taking pills. Your bedroom should be dedicated to sleeping and relaxing only. (Move the TV into the living room, and don't pay bills lying in bed—talk about nerve-wracking!) Avoid caffeine, alcohol, and extremely spicy meals late at night. Set and maintain regular sleep times. It's a known fact that senior citizens need seven hours per night of uninterrupted sleep.

And napping? If you happen to be a nap-taker, it's one of retirement's great pleasures, and there is good evidence that proves that it's good for you. Statistics have shown that a twenty- to thirty-minute nap every day decreases the incidence of heart attacks. In a good article on napping, *New York Times* reporter Mary Duenwald writes: "What sleep loss damages is thinking ability: learning, memory, concentration, and decision making. . . . The famously smart and productive—Leonardo da Vinci and Albert Einstein amongst them—have been some of the nap's biggest proponents. The director of the Sleep Research Centre at Loughborough University, England, commented, 'Sleep is by the brain and for the brain.' And a recent Harvard School of Public Health Study in Greece found that adults who took siestas at least three times a week for thirty minutes had a lower death rate from heart attacks."

We think Winston Churchill said it best: "Don't think you will be doing less work because you sleep during the day. That's a foolish notion held by people who have no imagination."

Driving: The Force Behind the Course

Driving is independence, it's the American way, and it's our right. We couldn't wait to get behind the wheel, and now we're determined to stay there, whatever our age. It's a fact: car accidents start to increase at age sixty and continue to rise with each decade. AARP offers a driving course for retirees that has decreased accidents so noticeably that most insurance companies give participants 10 to 20 percent percent off its premiums.

That's a terrific incentive because no one wants to give up his or her license or, worse yet, have someone else demand that it be relinquished. Count us among the automobile-able. If we could have our way, we would drive to our own memorial services.

So, out of consideration for all aging drivers, we've written about elderly driving issues in the third person, something for "the others among us" to keep in mind.

■ **Eliminate** night driving as soon as failing vision dictates.

■ **Avoid** driving during rush hour or to busy locations, if doing so causes a stressful trip. One can choose a less-traveled route during busy times or simply travel at less-crowded times of day (Tuesday and Wednesday afternoons, for example).

■ **Protect** the person behind the wheel and others by driving a heavier car with a bright exterior color.

■ **Observe and obey driving laws.** Speed limits are there for a reason. Decrease speed if necessary or step on it—driving too slowly causes accidents too. Go with the flow. On highways and freeways, the passing lane is there for that specific reason. How many drivers act as though the fast lane has been created just for them? Pass and return, right is right, and it's the law!

■ **Increase** the distance between the operator's car and other vehicles by at least a car length.

MENTAL HEALTH: THINK IT OVER

For my overall mental health, I identify the times that I'm the most content. Then I expand on those times and repeat them as much as possible. On the other hand, I try to identify the times I least enjoy and reduce or eliminate them as much as I can.

—RETIREMENT DOCS' SURVEY

Falling into depression, as we get older, is a real risk. The National Institutes of Health's Institute on Aging reports that severe depressive symptoms occur in about 15 percent of people sixty-five to seventy-nine years old, and in 23 percent of those eighty-five and older, yet often individuals and their family, friends, or primary caregivers don't recognize them. Temporary depression or sadness following a major traumatic event (loss of a job, death of a loved one) is normal. The good news is that the amount of mental stress we live with may not be as important as how we manage it. Depression is one of the most preventable and treatable diseases in all of medicine. If multiple symptoms (see the box opposite for a list) occur and last more than a few weeks, one should suspect major depression and immediately seek out professional counseling, support groups, and/or drug therapy. Current prescription antidepressants can be highly effective. However, it may take some time, in conjunction with your doctor, to find the right drug and the correct dose for you.

Before popping a pill, try some less-invasive techniques to fight the blues. Physical and mental health are closely associated—more than any time in modern medicine, we find the symbiosis between body and mind linked to overall health and happiness. In fact, many of the traits in this book, such as developing a positive attitude, and finding and pursuing a passion, have been shown to be effective weapons against depression. In addition, the "talking cure" and cognitive therapy have both been shown to be effective treatments for depression.

Depression is a biochemical illness, and willpower alone is not always the answer. Since it may not be perceived as "masculine," men don't seek professional treatment as often as women do. This may be in part why older Caucasian males have a 70 percent higher suicide rate than Caucasian women of the same age. Mild forms of memory loss can also become common as we mature. We can't emphasize enough the importance of stimulating your brain. In several controlled clinical trials, doing crossword puzzles, playing cards, and social intellectual interchange delayed brain degeneration. And forgetfulness can increase if we become anxious or experience stress. But keep in mind that misplacing your keys or glasses occasionally is a normal

TRAIT SIX: HERE'S TO YOUR HEALTH ■ 129

Classic signs of depression are

■ Apathy
■ Weight changes
■ Appetite changes
■ Sleep disturbances
■ Sluggishness
■ Guilt
■ Feelings of worthlessness
■ Poor concentration
■ Thoughts of death and suicide

part of aging, and though we may feel sensitive or let it upset us, it's not going to go away. We all do it. We have all, at one time or another, entered a room with a specific purpose in mind only to wonder why we're standing there. Memory usually returns under relaxed conditions. In reality, most of us aren't as forgetful as we think we are.

Normal aging does not necessarily result in a significant decline in intelligence, memory or learning ability.
—Nancy Hooyman and H. Asuman Kiyak, *Social Gerontology*

Tragically, however, for some people memory problems are a sign of dementia, the most common form being Alzheimer's disease. The National Institutes of Health and the drug industry are investing heavily in research into the various forms of this disease, and promising therapies are in the pipeline, but for the moment there are really no effective treatments or preventive medicines on the market.

We don't know why, but women up to age eighty are two to three times more likely to develop Alzheimer's than men. After reaching age eighty, there is no difference in the incidence between men and women. Alzheimer's disease is the ninth most important factor leading to death over age sixty-five. To date, some research suggests that an active, stimulated mind and a planned exercise program can deter the disease. Additional therapy for women also includes estrogen replacement, anti-inflammatory agents, and antioxidants—but so far none have been definitively proven to work.

SEX AND SEXUALITY: WHEN FOREVER MEANS FOREVER

Throughout our research for *Retirement Rx,* a good friend has provided us with valuable insights. One time, he advised that if we were serious about getting and keeping our male readers' attention, we should begin the first sentence of each new topic with "Sex . . . !"

There's a lot of good news about sex these days. Research shows that no matter how old you live to be, closeness counts—holding hands, hugging, kissing, words of endearment, good conversations, a flirtatious glance, and of course a good romp with someone you care about all contribute to good mental health. Feeling loved, feeling valued, and feeling sexy are positive attributes that we seek from early adulthood right on through our final winks. Thirty percent of American women between the ages of eighty and one hundred and two are still having sex. And it's 63 percent for men in that same age group. So, Baby Boomers, you *do* have something to look forward to! We are pleased to report that sex at sixty and long after, for both men and women, is alive and well.

These days, corporate America is aiming its advertising directly at us "senior citizens." Medications such as Viagra and Cialis have created a major niche in the prescription drug market, targeted mainly at a male audience—women, too, but mainly men. We can't avoid viewing the huge advertising dollars spent on television ads promising romance and intimacy, since they're placed right on target, where most of us can't miss them—all of our favorite sports programs. The manufacturers of these products have done their homework; the couple we watch is "of a certain age," good-looking but not too good-looking. We could be them. They are active, alive, all smiles, and looking forward to spending some intimate time together. Isn't it refreshing to know that sex and all the intimacy and vigor we radiate because of it aren't over until we are? For the 25 percent of men in our survey who experience erectile dysfunction, these drugs are truly wonderful!

So now we all know it—mature men and women think about, desire, and want to have sex. Here's more happy news from the AARP:

■ Sexual activity seems to have a protective effect on men's health. In the Caerphilly Cohort Study conducted in South Wales, United Kingdom, over a ten-year period, researchers Smith, Frankel, and Yarnell found a 50 percent lower death rate if the men had frequent orgasms (at least twice a week).

■ Men who had frequent orgasms cut down on the incidence of prostate cancer, according to a study reported by another group of researchers.

■ An AARP survey of women and sexuality found that:

■ 49 percent were satisfied with their sex life.

■ 60 percent agree or strongly agree that sexual activity is a critical part of a good relationship.

■ 84 percent disagree or strongly disagree that sex is only for younger people.

Man's desire for sex continues from the day he's born until three days after he dies! (And this goes for plenty of women too!)

However, there are a few more physical challenges—the reality is that testosterone and estrogen levels decrease as we age, and we're not as agile or energized as we were. These are facts of life. They all contribute to a more mature lovemaking, but they don't eliminate the urge for enjoying a sexual relationship.

If you are involved in a new relationship, recognize that sexually transmitted diseases, such as HIV, AIDS, gonorrhea, and syphilis, are still alive, active, and contractible, no matter what your age. Make sure that you and a new partner both agree to a Sexually Transmitted Disease (STD) test before you become sexually committed. According to the federal Centers for Disease Control and Prevention, one in four new diagnoses of HIV-AIDs between 2000 and 2003 was in the 45 and older age group. Know whom you go to bed with and remember that you are having sex with all the previous contacts of your sexual partner. Venereal disease has a long trail. Not the most romantic or passionate of thoughts but certainly the safest. First and foremost, be passionate about getting tested, and then get on with the fun.

Next, remember, whatever his age, a man's sperm is capable of impregnating a woman in her childbearing years. Those sperm may become more sluggish as the male ages but they're still able to make a baby.

THE DIAGNOSIS

We don't think we need to give you a quiz to find out if you are healthy or not—if you smoke, have more than one drink every day, and are sedentary, you've got work to do. Quit smoking, cut back on or eliminate liquor, start eating whole, fresh foods, and start an exercise program. If you are already paying attention to your health, congratulations. Keep focused on maintaining your healthy habits, and find new ones to add. Our prescription can act as an action plan to improve your health, no matter where you fall on the spectrum—from robust to at risk.

THE RETIREMENT DOCS' PRESCRIPTION

Small steps make a big difference over time. We cannot offer a game plan for recognizing illness or depression—those are highly individual issues that need the personal attention of a physician. We will make the assumption that you are visiting your doctor regularly and that both of you are keeping an eye on your overall health and addressing any health issues you are facing. In fact, before embarking on any of the suggestions below, check with your doctor. He or she will be absolutely thrilled that you're making an effort to exercise more, eat better, and keep your mind active!

If you ask me what the ten most important traits for a successful retirement are, I would say the first nine would be a healthy lifestyle.

—RETIREMENT DOCS' SURVEY

■ **Develop a weekly exercise game plan:**
What days can you definitely exercise?

_____

_____

_____

What times of day can you definitely exercise?

_____

_____

_____

What kinds of exercise can you do?

_____

_____

_____

Who among your friends can you enlist to join you?

_____

_____

_____

■ **Keep a food journal:** Use one of several free online food diary Web sites or create your own in a blank book. Even if you think you are a healthy eater, writing down what you consume each day makes you aware of how much you are putting in your mouth. You can also see, after just a week of record keeping, what times of day you "fall apart" and succumb to snacks or fattening foods (for many people it's midmorning and midafternoon). After a week or two, ask yourself:

- Which foods should I cut out? (French fries, steak)
- Which foods should I add? (More veggies, whole grains)
- What are my "fall-apart" foods and when do I eat them? (A bag of chips at 3:00 P.M.)
- What can I replace my "fall-apart" foods with? List five distraction activities (cleaning out a closet, surfing the Internet, reading, calling a friend . . .) and then list five foods that are more healthful alternatives than, say, potato chips, a bag of salt-free pretzels or vegetable chips (instead of a cookie, some dried fruit).
  1. _____
  2. _____
  3. _____
  4. _____
  5. _____

  1. _____
  2. _____
  3. _____
  4. _____
  5. _____

- **Train Your Brain:** It doesn't matter if you are working full-time or part-time or are completely retired—you have to exercise your brain in ways that are different and distinct from what you do at your job each day. Agility comes from a variety of tasks, and that's true both of physical movement and mental exercise. We urge you to plan three to five activities you can do to challenge your intellect and keep your memory sharp. For example, if you are an accountant, we recommend that you incorporate reading novels and poetry into your weekly routine. Bridge or a good game of poker provides a counterbalance for someone who is engaged in creative activities.

1. _____

2. _____

3. _____

4. _____

5. _____

Without good health, the world can be a narrow and inhospitable place for a retired person. A foundation of healthful practices like the ones we have discussed here will lay the groundwork for long-term vitality. Don't put off working on your well-being. Start today. Start now.

9

TRAIT SEVEN:
PASSION AND PURPOSE

Nothing is more dishonorable than an old man, heavy with years, who has no other evidence of having lived long except his age.

—SENECA, ROMAN PHILOSOPHER

The data from our Retirement Docs' Survey made it very clear that passion and purpose are fully intertwined and are crucial to a successful and meaningful retirement. In fact, we found that our highly successful retirees differed from our not-yet-so-highly successful retirees primarily in two key areas. The first was that *all* of our highly successful retirees had a driving passion to stay as physically fit as possible and saw it as an ongoing commitment. To delay and offset changes occurring in restricted retirement's phase four, it's so important that you develop long-lasting passions with purpose in phases one, two, and three, which are mentally *and* physically stimulating. Medical science has proven that keeping both an active mind and an active body will decrease and delay many of later life's disabilities.

The personal mosaic makes you the individual you are . . . reflects the sum total of your habits, your outlook on life, your frame of mind, your spiritual or religious beliefs, and the love you have for those around you.

—ISADORE ROSENFELD, M.D., FROM *LIVE NOW, AGE LATER*

The second area in which the passions of our highly successful retirees differed is that they felt a strong desire to give something back to society and be an active participant in making the world a better place. They devote a lot of their time to the causes they believe in—feeling strongly that the satisfaction they receive from the work outweighs any time commitment. Having a passion for some type of volunteer work cannot be underestimated; it bolsters your identity and has incredibly positive effects for your mental health.

We were put here on this earth for one purpose and that is to make it a better place. We should, therefore, be contributing members of society. And if the earth, as a result of our having been on it, is a better place than it was before we came, then we have achieved our destiny.

— GEN. JIMMY DOOLITTLE, WORLD WAR II THREE-STAR GENERAL

By *passion* we mean "intense, driving, or overmastering feeling or conviction," and by *purpose* we mean something "set up as an object or end to be attained." (Both of these definitions are from *Merriam-Webster's Collegiate Dictionary*, eleventh edition). These activities are different from leisure pursuits in terms of power, principle, and function. While leisure activities help us to get out of ourselves by entertaining us and allowing us to relax and unwind, passions with purpose involve intense emotion, which sparks compelling action, an energetic and unflagging activity that manifests a person's devotion to a cause or a goal.

Ideal passions are those that engage the body, the brain, and the soul. And the goal shouldn't be easily attainable—involving and engaging us instead in a long-term quest. The process of striving offers the greatest amount of challenge, interest, happiness, and feelings of success. Following a passion can involve stress—but it's a good stress. The best kinds of passions occur when a person's body or mind is stretched to its limits in a voluntary effort to accomplish something difficult and worthwhile. We just read an article about a skilled crossword puzzle whiz, a woman who became renowned in her social circle for her keen ability. Her ongoing passion for puzzles led her to push herself beyond her comfort zone and across the country to the American Crossword Puzzle Tournament. It wasn't about the outcome but rather about her passion to go after new experiences and achieve new heights. It's a great example.

As Mihaly Csikszentmihalyi says in his book *Flow: The Psychology of Optimal Experience* (an excellent book about pursuing passion as the key to happiness):

> *The best moments usually occur when a person's body or mind is stretched to its limits in a voluntary effort to accomplish something that is difficult and worthwhile. Optimal experience is something we make happen. . . . Such experiences are not necessarily pleasant at the time they occur. The swimmer's muscles might have ached during his most memorable race, his lungs might have felt like exploding, and he might be dizzy with fatigue—yet these could have been the best moments of his life. . . . In the long run, optimal experiences add up to a sense of mastery—or perhaps better, a sense of participation in determining the content of life—that comes as close to what is usually meant by happiness as anything else we can conceivably imagine.*

Csikszentmihalyi's description is also a good explanation of why it is impossible, and probably not even advisable, to continually pursue a passion seven days a week, twelve hours a day. Successful retirees, and people in general, need an active balance of both leisure and passion in their lives. The swimmer in the preceding example surely blows off steam by doing something fun but not particularly challenging after a major accomplishment.

> *My major passion was making a living. Now, in retirement, it is about making a life. I retired from work, not life.*
>
> —RETIREMENT DOCS' SURVEY

Most of us find life before retiring full of purposes and passions which revolve around marriage, family, building that first career, striving for a certain standard of living, educating our children, and working toward fiscal security. It's a good and busy fast track, but then what? What about the purposes and passions we'll need during our long-lived second careers, when great numbers of us will be around for a great many more years?

Having reached your goals, you will certainly miss one thing: the process of getting there.

—MARIE VON EBNER-ESCHENBAC

The best passions are those that evolve over time as we change. Make some selections with a specific goal of seeing you through the physical, mental, and social changes that aging brings with it. For example, let's say you've always been a jazz fan, a passion that is flexible enough to be enjoyed in many different ways through time. You studied the clarinet in high school, college, and after college; you played in a jazz quartet and even had some paying gigs. Your group disbanded owing to time constraints and the need for all of you to get "straight" jobs. You kept playing on the side and practicing, which kept your lungs in good shape. And you continued to listen to the pros play jazz both in live performances and on recordings. You enjoy discussing jazz with other like-minded people of all ages who share your passion, and you joined an Internet e-mail news group devoted to jazz. After retiring, you formed a band with some friends who also love to play—and got a regular gig at the little Italian restaurant downtown. You even convinced a pro to join you on trumpet once in a while. But then, as you grew even older and became disabled, you just didn't have the wind it took to play the clarinet. It was difficult to attend live jazz performances, but you still listened to jazz and you continued to share your knowledge through a lifetime of memories with your Internet news group.

Eva Zeisel, a ceramist and product designer born in 1906, has been making and designing beautiful utilitarian items for decades. She has said in many interviews and in her own book, *Eva Zeisel on Design,* which she wrote and published in 2004, that the only thing she could absolutely rely on in life was her design work and the goal of doing good and making a contribution to society. She has never stopped working, although for many years she has worked with young assistants who, because of her failing eyesight and inability to work clay and other materials with her own hands, carry out her ideas with their eyes and their hands. Her love of design and her passion to create have never been daunted by age, disability, or physical degeneration. As long as her spirit is willing, she finds a way to bring ideas to fruition.

It's great to have an interest that carries on throughout a lifetime, but it's just as important and never too late to pick up new ones:

I knew long before I retired that it was vital for me to have a number of interests, hobbies, and goals and to have them in place before I stepped down. Call it fear of the unknown or call it change; whatever it is, I know myself pretty well, so when I did retire, I immediately filled my newly found free time enjoying my projects. My advice is, don't retire and then look for something; retire while you still have your health, not when it's becoming a problem. To be on the safe side, I have some "just in case" passions I chose solely because they wouldn't require leaving my home.

—RETIREMENT DOCS' SURVEY

I never gave any thought about passions until writing this book. I worked backward to get to know my passions by first figuring out my life's themes and goals for my second career. My first goal was finding substitutes for the "highs" I got from practicing medicine; others were a spinoff from my first career. My passions, which I have taped over my desk at home, are

1. *Doing everything I can to keep my mate happy. This includes taking on some of the housework and expanding specific activities to do with her.*

2. *Being there for my family and our children's families both emotionally and fiscally. We are lucky because we were able, with expert financial advice, to set up trust funds for our grandchildren's college educations. It makes us feel like we can leave them with education, a part of us that we really care a lot about—and that makes us feel great.*

3. *Having a structured plan to work on the eight traits outlined in this book, especially a healthy lifestyle.*

4. *Doing multiple activities that are productive and related particularly to medicine; ongoing research, writing, updating previously published textbooks, and staying mentally challenged as long as possible.*

5. *Developing a passion for helping myself and other people have a successful second career.*

— DR. FRITZ

Because Retirement Rx was not available for me, as the years passed by, I did the things that seemed to be the right thing to do at the time. I think I did a pretty good job of selecting a wide range of passions and purposes that interested me at various stages of my life; I just didn't give them labels. There was no science to it, just a "feeling" of what I wanted to do. Many opportunities were offered— I accepted some and rejected others. My first marriage ended in divorce after twenty years, but those years produced three wonderful children. My second marriage is still going strong after twenty-five years—creating a blended family and offering me more understanding of all that life has to offer. My conclusion is that passion and purpose never stop, and that realization has made me a very happy man.

— DR. JIM

Many of us find purpose with passion at home with our family. Having time to engage with them after retirement allows us to become active participants in our children's, grandchildren's, and great-grandchildren's development. Others of us find passion in caregiving as we age—taking care of loved ones out of necessity and love can be deeply meaningful and satisfying for many people. But the added responsibilities of looking after another person as we age are accompanied by emotional and physical challenges. Finding and chasing your passion and purpose is about balance. It's important to find and follow passions that excite you, but take time for self-care if that passion involves looking after others.

As one of our respondents noted:

It dawned on me one day that many of my friends had become caregivers, giving their time and talents to their incapacitated mates. And every so often, those friends passed away before their loved ones. I think that administering this loving care as a primary purpose cheated my friends out of some of their prime time.

—RETIREMENT DOCS' SURVEY

DIAGNOSIS

If you want to make sure that you don't feel aimless after you stop working, serious contemplation is required before you retire. If you are a retiree, take a look at the rest of your life and how you want to spend it. Realize that it's never, ever, too late to answer the following questions and apply them to how you want to see yourself. Take time to write down the answers and revisit them from time to time. A retirement that can last thirty or forty years of pointlessly filling time not only leads to depression but is a missed opportunity to leave something behind—a legacy of wisdom, or charity, or actual physical creation. Your legacy need not receive notoriety beyond your own family to have deep and lasting meaning or impact. Those who remember your contributions will doubtless carry them on into the rest of their lives in one way or another.

■ Have you thought about *what* you want to achieve in retirement?

_____

_____

_____

■ Do you have purposeful goals for your second career?

_____

_____

_____

■ Have you thought about *who* you want to be and how you would best like to be remembered?

_____

_____

_____

▪ Do you know *how* you're going to accomplish your objectives?

_____

_____

_____

▪ How many things do you currently feel passionate about? Can you identify the purposes behind your passions?

_____

_____

_____

▪ What are the activities you do that you find completely absorbing? What things do you do that you get lost in—the kind of things that seem as if you've spent only a couple of hours at and it turns out that you're wondering where the day went?

_____

_____

_____

▪ Are your purposes easily attainable? Does it surprise you that they shouldn't be? You can't be passionate without an ongoing goal.

_____

_____

_____

▪ Can you list five, ten, or more purposeful undertakings that will serve you well from the present right on through your final farewell?

_____

_____

_____

▪ Do you have passions that make you available to people, as well as societal and environmental needs? Do you give more of yourself than you want in return?

_____

_____

_____

▪ Do you have passions that will continue to promote a healthy lifestyle?

_____

_____

_____

▪ Are you thinking ahead to second-career passions that will weather the storms of possible and probable age-related limitations or medical setbacks? Can you list them?

_____

_____

_____

I am lucky enough to have a ninety-four-year-old, bright and active grandmother who has a true passion for living. She told me that before she gets out of bed each morning, she makes a plan, or I guess it's more a question and an answer, anyway her kind of plan. She figures out what she can do that day to make someone else's life a little bit easier. She may send a note or card to a grandchild or do something for a neighbor like visiting or baking banana bread. These seem like small things, but their effect is great. The passion to show love to others could be the greatest purpose of all. That is what she does everyday. My grandmother remains a joy and an inspiration to our entire family.

—RETIREMENT DOCS' SURVEY

THE RETIREMENT DOCS' PRESCRIPTION

Take the answers from the previous set of questions and use them to identify the person you want to be, along with the goals you hope to accomplish and how you'll go about *being* and *doing* them. Then, make a list of pursuits that are engaging enough to become deeply involved in. This is not the same as making a commitment to taking care of your health or exercising on a regular basis. Those are activities we would classify as "maintenance behaviors." It's also not the same as leisure stuff you do for fun and relaxation. List the loves, interests, causes, ideas, and hobbies that you can lose yourself in. Make a note of when you can begin to act on each. Can you start right away (there's no time like the present)? Or is it something that requires more time, and you will begin it when you are fully retired? Knowing when you can start something makes planning for it easier, and the anticipation is more pleasurable.

Take a look at these specific suggestions gathered from highly successful retirees. They just might help you get on with or add to your own retirement.

- Learning about fresh, local, and seasonal ingredients from my local farmer's market. This is both in an effort to expand my culinary abilities and a way of getting to know local growers, and to become involved in the sustainability movement, which is important to me. Cooking with fresh whole foods also contributes to a healthy lifestyle.
- Learning to fish for "big game" in the ocean. Fly-fishing is fun, but I want to master offshore fishing and see if I can bag a marlin or tuna. I want to compete in tournaments. It's a sport that requires strength, concentration, and dexterity. It's also good exercise. And it's going to give me a chance to pursue another passion—travel. The best big-game fishing happens to take place in all the places I want to go but have never seen, like the coast of California, the eastern coastline of Australia, Hawaii, and South America.
- Volunteering my marketing and writing skills in the next presidential election. I want to work at a grassroots level and pass on my knowledge to young staffers. And I want to get my candidate elected!
- Start a skateboard business. I love sports and young people. Skateboarding is making a comeback. It's a good business to be in right now. I love the designs on skateboards, and I am actually designing my own board in my workshop, which I plan to sell in my shop. And I'm still young enough to do a few turns myself.
- Run for office. I am going to throw my hat in the mayoral ring in my town.

■ I have been reading mysteries for more than forty years and consider myself an expert at every murder technique, twist, and surprise ending. So now I am going to write one—actually I am going to write a series. I have a "continuing" character in mind and a setting. I have the first plot planned out. I may even have a first draft done before I retire completely.

■ I never finished college, so I am enrolling. My plan is to get a degree in art history. I have been volunteering at the local children's museum for several years, helping them plan fund-raisers and charity events. They have recently asked me to sit on their board of trustees. I feel it's my obligation to complete my studies so I can make a greater contribution to the institution.

■ Hike the entire Appalachian Trail before I can't walk anymore! I'm starting next month.

■ See Europe. I might even stay a while. I've always wanted to live in France. I might even be able to get a job there, since I understand that there is a labor shortage all over Western Europe.

■ There are a few things I'm interested in that center on wellness—hospice work, yoga, and meditation. I am already working toward yoga certification, and hope to teach classes and bring my knowledge to hospices, where I think it can do a lot of good.

■ Collect every Louis Armstrong recording ever made. I have amassed a pretty impressive collection, but there are still several sides I'm missing. I search on eBay, have joined 78-record auction lists, and scour record bins in antique stores wherever I am (they are usually in cardboard boxes under tables). Then I plan to catalog my finds, and compile them on my fourteen-year-old grandson's iPod (with his help). Hurrah for him, hurrah for me—he's showing an interest in the trumpet.

I feel it is very important to have a purpose in retirement like I had during my working years, a reason to get up in the morning.

—RETIREMENT DOCS' SURVEY

We hope you embrace finding your passions as a chance to learn about the subjects that have always intrigued you but that you never had time to pursue—an opportunity to explore the world in-depth, the luxury of time on your side working *for* you, not against you. What a chance we have to live optimally, enthusiastically, and with the wonder and curiosity of a child, but with the advantage of wisdom. Enjoy.

10

Trait Eight: Let the Spirit Move You— Spirituality and Religion

The human quest for spiritual understanding passes through multiple lenses of experience. To some it comes in Scripture; others find the message etched in nature. To some it is unfolded in endless variety. To some it is fostered by rule; to others it is being free. The spiritual quest, whatever the course, has elevated the human spirit. It has tapped genius, created music, inspired poetry, nurtured ethical systems, and become philosophy. Deep within each person is a spiritual longing. It is a thirst unquenched, a hunger unfulfilled, a vision only partly seen.

—Ralph Waldo Emerson

Highly successful retirees specifically pinpoint spirituality/religion as necessary for retirement success. In life's final chapter, we will all look back over a lifetime of what we did or what we didn't do and what we might have done differently. We said it before: as doctors we know when to refer out. We're a good team for ongoing dialogue. Dr. Fritz is searching for what spirituality means in his quest for a guaranteed retirement, and Dr. Jim is a cradle Catholic. Boy, have we had some great discussions!

What is spirituality? Dictionaries define it as relating to or having the nature of spirit; a state of being concerned with affecting the soul, which is neither tangible nor material. We've heard others describe it simply as anything outside yourself that gives you comfort or solace. The conventional expression of it is organized religion. However, as Ralph Waldo Emerson points out in the epigram that opens this chapter, spirituality can take many other forms.

Where two or more gather together in recognition of a power greater than themselves, to listen to the inner life—where music lives.

— George E. Valliant, author

According to two gerontology scholars, Nancy Hooyman and H. Asuman Kiyak, "Spirituality or spiritual well-being can be differentiated from organized religion and is defined as the following:

■ Self-determined wisdom in which the individual tries to achieve stability in his or her environment.
■ Self-transcendence or crossing a boundary beyond the self in which the individual adjusts to loss and rejects material security.
■ Achievement of meaning and purpose for one's continued existence.
■ Acceptance of the wholeness of life."

We questioned priests, preachers, and rabbis, listened to the Dalai Lama, interviewed agnostics and atheists, and talked with a range of people whose beliefs and spiritual needs are met through the sun, the moon, the earth, and the galaxies. We have even taken meditation classes. And we've concluded that until our lives are over, we can't give you any definitive answers about spirituality, and we certainly cannot tell you what religion or belief system is best for you in retirement. The one constant is that the afterlife is a mystery, and it's up to each of us to decide how to make sense of it. What we *can* do is share what we've learned about how spirituality specifically relates to retirement.

Sometimes, when I think about my life and my faith, I revert to childhood memories and how life does indeed come full circle. When I was a little girl, my teddy bear meant the world to me. There was nothing make-believe about the companionship, support, and security he provided. When my son was just a little guy, his blanket gave him the same stability. And most of my grandchildren had a similar need for sharing with a pretend friend. It occurred to me one day that now that I am older and my religion offers me such comfort and safety, I really have done nothing more than find my "grown-up" support. My life really has come full circle.

—RETIREMENT DOCS' SURVEY

Our Retirement Docs' Survey asked respondents to rate the importance of spirituality/religion in their lives by checking one of the following: extremely important, very important, important, somewhat important, or not very important. We then correlated and separately compared each of retirement's four phases against every respondent's answer. In the first three phases of our participants' retirements, there was no statistical difference in one group over the other regarding their responses to the faith question. In fact, it was the least important of the eight traits. It became clear that spirituality/religion religion tends to change only late in life.

We found that in phase four there was a statistically significant jump in faith-based involvement when we compared our top 20 percent against the rest of the group. When we analyzed our data, it was apparent that we had our hands on information that we had not seen reported before: In order to have a highly successful retirement you've got to have some form of spirituality in phase four. Some form of spirituality became a must-have trait for our highly successful retirees in the final stage of their retirements (and their lives).

Our top 20 percent reported that their faith provided them with a sense of inspiration and a source of hope outside of themselves, a happier, healthier lifestyle, a needed calm and inner strength, support for the normal process of aging, and for help in coping with chronic illness, death of loved ones, isolation, and overall depression. Approaching our life's final years, major adjustments, both physical and mental, will occur. Each and every one of us will see a shift in our priorities—all we know is that being born is fatal. Facing restricted retirement without the support spirituality provides can be an enormous challenge.

Have Faith in the Facts

According to a recent Gallup Poll:

■ 96 percent of Americans believe in God or a universal spirit.

■ 90 percent pray.

■ 85 percent say spirituality or religion is very or fairly important to them.

■ 41 percent attend religious services weekly.

■ 48 percent of eighteen- to twenty-nine-year-olds say religion is very important to them.

■ 73 percent of Americans older than age sixty-five say the same.

If you're feeling shaky at this point, reflecting back over your past history of sitting through sermons that seemed as if they would never end and going through the motions of a religion that may have turned you off to God when you were younger, relax. Psychologists and researchers have found that the positive effects of spirituality on mental health are not limited to participation in organized religions. Clinical studies have found that the benefits of a strong faith, in whatever form it takes, include improved self-esteem, a stronger immune system, lower blood pressure, better social skills, a greater will to live, a decrease in stress, and a positive image of aging. Many Boomers are searching for or using a more practical and individualistic rather than doctrinal approach. Eastern philosophies, Jungian psychology, self-help groups, and a long list of other alternatives are emerging among Boomers, who for whatever reason have turned away from their childhood religions, or are taking bits and pieces from each religion to form an individual spiritual philosophy.

When my husband died, I replaced his role in my life with spirituality. I continue to take daily walks, talking my problems over with the universe . . . this may or may not necessarily be God. Often it seems like it's just nature—the trees, the flowers, or the birds. But in my walks, I'm talking to somebody or something greater than myself. I kind of turn things over to an "extra spirit." By the time I get back home, I always feel better.

—RETIREMENT DOCS' SURVEY

MAYBE YOU SHOULD GET ORGANIZED

Organized religion enters many people's lives in some way around puberty, levels off, then becomes stronger in our late twenties or early thirties, coinciding with the time most of us start a family. During midlife, religion remains level unless adversity occurs. In our survey, there's another spike in religious involvement one more time in later life (phase four). And while we said earlier that it is not necessary to attend formal religious services on a weekly basis to get the health benefits of faith, there is a clear preference for organized religion among seniors (people over sixty-five).

More seniors belong to Christian churches or Jewish synagogues than all other community nonreligious organizations combined. This high percentage of believers indicates that formalized religion fills a human need for more of us than does any other spiritual expression or a lack of a faith. For many, belonging to an organized group offers the opportunity to find support among those who share a common set of traditions, beliefs, values, and practices. It also expresses a common way of life through liturgies, stories, and disciplines.

The pastor of a large congregation told us that he feels that the increase in the number of elderly women joining his church, compared to men of the same age (outside of mortality or disability rates), is because women spend more time thinking about the past. They have by nature a more spiritual conscience, and religion offers them an understanding of their lives as well as comfort. He felt that men more often reviewed their lives in much broader terms: "Did I lead a good life? Did I do more good than harm? Did I lead an honest life?" Affirmative answers to those questions offer comfort when facing adversity, and many senior males can outline their faith and their personal spirituality through them.

Lifelong religious conviction remained strong throughout retirement for people who had parochial school educations and for those who attended religious services on a regular basis during their working years. But it was often the people who lived with excess trauma, especially if they were able to successfully deal with their setbacks, who had the strongest faith later in their lives. Religious beliefs can become a formalized coping mechanism for these individuals.

Raised awareness of the inevitability of death and a search for life's meaning may well act as an important catalyst propelling adults toward thoughts about the end of life. It is a telling fact that for assistance with personal problems, more senior "believers" sought advice from their clergy than from their doctors. It's a time of self-reflection and self-analysis, looking back on life's accomplishments, disappointments, and transgressions. And it's a period when many unsolvable traumas occur, often with minimal time in between for recovery. We find ourselves wanting something or someone to believe in beyond ourselves, a system providing solace and comfort.

During my first ten years of marriage I think I unknowingly (or I choose to tell myself it was unknowingly) convinced myself that my wife and children were number one in my life when number one was really establishing my career. My wife told both herself and me that I was number one, whereas number one was really raising the family. Now in my later years, number one is honestly about us and looking together for answers to what our purpose is here on Earth. I guess it's a different kind of achieving at a different time of life.

—RETIREMENT DOCS' SURVEY

Yet another key role in organized religion is its ability to be responsive to the social needs of senior citizens. Up to a third of the senior population is severely depressed at some time during phase four's restricted retirement. Depression occurs in people with and without religious beliefs, but the support of a formal religious practice has multiple benefits. Religious seniors have less depression, fewer suicides, better subjective well-being, more satisfaction with life, and higher self-esteem.

Retirement has given me the opportunity to be more active in volunteering in my church and civic organizations. Reaching out to others, sharing ideas, meeting others with like ideas. My motto: Don't lose who you are and what you like to do. Be active and involved, and keep making friends.

— Retirement Docs' Survey

One of the people we turned to for research and insight as we were working on this chapter is a good friend, Father Howard Lincoln. A man of unquestioning faith, he is a real Catholic go-getter and gatherer of the followers. His parish is located in Palm Desert, California, and throughout the week he draws several thousand to hear what he's got to say. When we sent him a rough chapter outline, he recognized in one of our respondent's comments, copied below, the philosopher Blaise Pascal's idea that we might as well choose to believe that God exists because it might lead to eternal life and happiness; and if it turns out He doesn't exist, nothing would be lost. If we don't believe and we are wrong, we could be in trouble:

Someone once asked me if I believed in God. I've heard the answer I gave a few times before and it still makes perfect sense to me. You bet I do. Since I don't know what's waiting for me on the other side, why not have some faith? I have nothing to lose. If there is a God, I'm on the winning team, and if there isn't, well, my religion has offered me some great guidelines.

— Retirement Docs' Survey

Whatever else our survey respondent had in common with Pascal, we *do* know that the two of them thought alike on at least one thing—you might as well hedge your bets and start believing in something. The benefits of doing so in the here and now are tangible and quantifiable, and as far as the hereafter goes. . . .

DIAGNOSIS

So, how do you know if you are spiritual or religious? Is there a measuring stick? If you find one, please contact us and share it. Each of us makes this determination based on our philosophy, our own coping skills, adaptive skills, and stress-reducing mechanisms that we find outside ourselves. It's normal if your assessments fluctuate from month to month or even day to day.

THE RETIREMENT DOCS' PRESCRIPTION

I know the God who created me and because I do, I find it easier to be content with what I have and those I live with. I let God be in charge of my life and I'm not afraid to try anything. God will correct my progress if it needs correcting.

— Retirement Docs' Survey

Religious or spiritual growth arises for a wide range of practical reasons. Again, as medical doctors, we can't help you develop or find the type of spirituality the suits you, but we can review with you various prescriptions that have provided other people comfort.

If it hasn't been a part of your life before entering your second career, this spiritual trait is one of the most, if not *the* most, difficult to achieve. Unfortunately, if you didn't have a strong religious background during your childhood or in your first career, religion is often difficult to realize in your second. Some of the best prescriptions for finding and using religion that we can provide come from comments on our Retirement Docs' Survey from respondents. To the point and briefly, they told us how they felt about their lives and their spirituality. For example, one person succinctly described religion and aging with elegant perspective when he wrote, "Religious beliefs and common sense allow me to age gracefully, accepting inevitability. Katharine Hepburn told it like it was when she said, 'Growing old ain't for sissies.' I put my relationship with God first in all my plans. He directs me to what and where I am. Generally speaking, old age is not easy or comfortable, but with God leading the way, I know an inner peace."

Others felt that early morning spiritual reading, joining a community of fellow seekers, and regular prayer from the heart all helped them move closer to the source of spiritual inspiration in their lives. When nurtured, the source slowly strengthened over time and gave them a newfound sense of inner power. Still others felt that attending church provided them with a passion in life, and something meaningful to replace the hours they had spent at a job. "My church activities have provided that resource," one wrote.

Another said spirituality helped ease the stress of illness: "Needing to find joy in my life while living with illness proved a challenge. I was drawn to people and sought a compassionate community in which to share my struggles and gain spiritual support. The gifts of courage, trust, and wisdom came to me through people sharing their stories." One respondent told us that she used religion to clean out her soul. "I worked on getting rid of pettiness, forgiving myself and others, and clearing out negative baggage that I've been dragging around way too long. This spiritual release allows me to let go of my stress and makes more room for love. I'm far from success, but I keep at it."

I am highly spiritual: I have faith in my family, I have faith in nature, and I have faith in science.

— Retirement Docs' Interview

There is no standard, FDA-approved prescription for achieving your own spirituality. This is your own personal quest. The sooner it is in place and established, the greater chance for your success in protecting yourself later in life.

■ The essence of most religions are love, forgiveness, and the belief in and acceptance of God. This for most of us should be the backbone of spirituality. To the end, make peace with your family and friends. Use your love to give back to society. And, for the religious, try to find a meaningful place in your heart for God.

- There are no do-overs in life. Learn to accept the life that was handed you and the way you played the cards. Accept disappointments and move on. Do not dwell on your past mistakes—no one is perfect—learn to love and forgive yourself.

- Emphasize the good deeds or things (or whatever you want to call them) you have done in your life; take stock of them consciously and purposefully—it will give you comfort and inner peace as one ages. We should all have an instant-recall memory bank full of warm fuzzies—those acts of kindness or grace we bestowed on others and those that were directed by others to us. These fond memories can help warm up an otherwise bleak day.

- Take up a spiritual quest by reading, questioning, meditating, and exploring religion and various forms of spirituality.

- Review your life—hunt for that "spark" that gave your life meaning and expand on it. At various phases of life, there are transitory "sparks" that last a lifetime and affect your inner being/soul.

- Take on the role of "wise elder" in your family, keeper of family traditions, historian and counselor. This can be expanded to a similar role as advisor or consultant in volunteer efforts, community affairs, or group activities.

- Embrace your spirituality/religion so that it becomes more center-stage later in life, as material things become less so.

- For some, the form of spirituality that comes to you may not be as important as something outside yourself that gives you comfort and solace.

- For many at the late stages of life their greatest comfort comes from family, or extended family. Often, this is the "spark" in phases one, two, three, and four.

- Accept the natural process of all living things; birth, growth, maturity, aging, and death. To achieve an inner peace as we approach our own mortality, we are helped by the awareness that we are completing a natural life cycle; death is a normal part of that cycle. Acceptance of this notion is paramount, whether you also rely on religious beliefs of reincarnation or of heaven and hell.

■ Organized religion is the gold standard of spirituality for most. Baby Boomers seem to be leaning toward the philosophy of author Ken Kesey: "Take what you can, and leave the rest go." Some forms of spirituality may stand alone or be additive to religion.

Don't fret if you find it difficult to allow the spirit to move you. Awe of the universe or God comes with time. For now, a line taken from an old African-American spiritual offers good counsel: "I'm doing the best I can with what I've got." Do the best with whatever beliefs you have, and expand on them. If you are currently connected to a religion or spiritual movement, preretirement and retirement are the perfect time to become more deeply involved in it, particularly those activities that put you in contact with other attending members. The more deeply you become involved in your spiritual community now, the better off you will be later on—when the social and spiritual services it offers can provide support when you need it most, in the third and fourth phases of retirement.

PART THREE

THE EXIT CONSULTATION

Some wise person once said: *"Beautiful young people are creations of nature; beautiful old people create themselves."*

— ANONYMOUS

To which we add: *"Beautiful people in their retirement create themselves from the inside out."*

— RETIREMENT DOCS' SURVEY

As we said at the beginning of our journey, retirement offers you the opportunity to create your life as you want it to be, to define it as you wish, and to live it the way you want to. Don't miss out on this incredible opportunity. This is the essence of *Retirement Rx*. And just as we do when a patient is about to leave the doctor's office, we're going to briefly recap what we've done, and send you out with a few final words of advice about your future highly successful retirement.

11

INTO THE FUTURE

Age only matters when one is aging. Now that I have reached a great age, I might as well be twenty.

— PABLO PICASSO

I n the data we obtained from our Retirement Docs' Survey, the top 20 percent of our respondents, known as the highly successful retirees, taught us that if we paid attention to what they had to teach us, then practiced what they had to teach us, and then perfected what they had to teach us, we could be as they were—guaranteed highly successful retirements. Our information was groundbreaking, authentic, scientific data, and we found it awe-inspiring. From that information we were able to identify eight traits that made up the backbone of the guarantee, which are described in detail in the previous pages.

Each trait must be operational in order for you to achieve a highly successful retirement, though some of the traits serve more important roles at different times in the four phases. It's an absolute given that the eight traits are never stagnant but are evolving and interdependent in multifaceted ways. Weaving back and forth and into one another, they circle in and out at phase boundaries, as well as ebbing and flowing like tidal currents throughout our second careers. The traits necessary for a highly successful retirement are so interdependent that failure in just one of them can cause dysfunction in multiple areas. Success in a specific trait demands the support of anywhere from two to six of the others. Take, for example, the trait "go with the flow," or "the ability to accept change." In order for it to work, it requires the additional support of several of the traits, including planning, a strong support system, a healthy lifestyle, leisure, a positive attitude, and a good dose of spirituality. If any one of the six required is lacking you will have a tough time accepting change.

Stay vigilant in maintaining the traits. Unfortunately, a trait may be performing well and then, for any number of reasons, can weaken, and your retirement success will be in limbo until the trait is up and working again.

We recommend that you take the Retirement Docs' Quiz whenever you enter a new phase, or when something major in your life happens, to see how you're doing. It's especially important when you're entering a new phase. It's a quick way to identify the traits that might need your attention.

We found that most of our highly successful retirees who had life partners planned for their futures as a team, especially when moving into another phase. When we looked at the data collected from all of our survey respondents and then identified all of those with mates we found the following: in total 37 percent of them worked as a team planning and preparing both fiscal and nonfiscal aspects, 28 percent to a large extent, 15 percent to a moderate extent, 11 percent to some extent, and only 9 percent had very little joint involvement.

Besides taking the Retirement Docs' Quiz periodically, it's a good idea to get together with your mate and write down your short-term goals (one year from retirement); and your long-term goals for the next three to five years. It works best if you make your lists independently and then compare and discuss them. Some guidelines to consider are new leisure activities, employment, family relationships, travel plans, health issues, and how long you see yourselves as being really fit and what you want to achieve in that time. Make it an action plan for accomplishing what works for you.

We have had so many more years of good health than did our parents. We never expected or thought about all the things we could look forward to. My husband and I plan where we want to live, what we want to do, what we want to accomplish, and what we see as our goals and our legacy. It's a great time in our lives.

— RETIREMENT DOCS' SURVEY

Whether you're in phase one, approaching retirement, or fully into phase four, be aware of the great power you possess through the multitude of senior services available to you and yours. Peruse the Retirement Resources on pages 181–183. We've compiled a partial listing, partial because every day introduces new possibilities and a changing list. Look these over and be amazed at what is out there for us. When Goldie Hawn and Paul McCartney are featured in AARP's monthly magazine, we know we're "cutting-edge," baby! We've got the power—let's use it.

Writing this book helped us so much to age with grace, energy, love, and laughter. We've come to look at and accept that aging is a natural part of living. After all, we come into the world doing it, and as far as we know, it's not going to stop until we do.

The *Retirement Rx* exploration has led to a better understanding of ourselves, and it has made us better people, husbands, and fathers. We know the direction that we want our lives to take—and that will happen just as long as we keep working on and developing our own eight traits. We must admit that we're not quite at the guaranteed level yet, close but no gold stars (or should that read gold watches?). We both need more points on the Retirement Docs' Quiz, but by fine-tuning a couple of the traits and working especially on healthy lifestyle for Dr. Jim and spirituality for Dr. Fritz—hey, we're getting closer.

All of us want to make our track record equal a successful life's run. Identifying and adjusting any of the problems retirement can throw across your path and having the ability to choose correct solutions will keep you in the race and way ahead of most of the pack. We hope that *Retirement Rx* gives you the map to make your decision making easier, decrease problems along the way, and make your run a victorious one.

We are, as always, inspired by the ability of Ralph Waldo Emerson to put what we feel into just the right words. We quoted him earlier in the book and he's here again. We hope he was enjoying a highly successful retirement (he lived to be seventy-nine) when he wrote the following:

To laugh often and love much; to win the respect of intelligent persons and the affection of children; to earn the approbation of honest citizens and endure the betrayal of false friends; to appreciate beauty; to find the best in others; to give of one's self; to leave the world a bit better, whether by a healthy child, a garden patch or a redeemed social condition; to have played and laughed with enthusiasm and sung with exultation; to know that even one life has breathed easier because you have lived—this is to have succeeded.

We invite your stories and comments at www.theretirementdocs.com.

CONCLUSION

To know how to grow old is the masterwork of wisdom, and one of the most difficult chapters in the great art of living.

— HENRI-FRÉDÉRIC AMIEL

H ere is our favorite collection of wisdom gleaned from Retirement Docs' Survey respondents, the people who have walked the walk. At least 20 percent of them, those highly successful retirees, figured out how to get the most out of their retirement years. We set off their words or tips or suggestions here in the hope that you will photocopy the list and keep it in a place where you will see it—and read through it—every day.

- Make a "to-do" list each day, and cross off everything completed by the end of the day.
- Keep your sense of humor.
- Life is fragile, so live each day to its fullest, and treat it and yourself with respect.
- Enjoy yourself. You can learn to be your own best company.
- Plan for the unexpected along with the expected.
- Retire to something, not from something.
- It's better to have halitosis than no breath at all.

- Challenge your interests. Work part-time or volunteer your talents.
- Nurture friendships. To have a friend, you have to be a friend.
- Plan to live longer than you expect to.
- Compromise is the name of the game. Spousal agreement is the goal!
- Any morning that you can smell the coffee is a great morning.
- Try new things. If they don't suit you, try something else. You won't have any fun if you wait for someone to knock on your door.
- Be prepared for no days off!

SOURCES

CHAPTER ONE: A NEW KIND OF RETIREMENT

AARP. "New AARP study finds Boomers vary in their views of the future and their retirement years." (1998) www.aarp.org/press/1998/nr060298.html

Bolles R.N. *The Three Boxes of Life and How to Get Out of Them.* Berkeley: Ten Speed Press, 1978.

Buford, B. *Stuck in Half-Time: Reinvesting Your One and Only Life.* Grand Rapids: Zondervan Publishing House, 2001.

Cantor, D, and A. Thompson. *What Do You Want to Do When You Grow Up? Starting the Next Chapter of Your Life.* Boston: Little, Brown and Company, 2002.

Diamond, J. "Zebras, Unhappy Marriages, and the Anna Karenina Principle." *Guns, Germs, and Steel: The Fates of Human Societies.* New York: W. W. Norton & Company, 2001.

Freedman, Marc. *Prime Time: How Baby Boomers Will Revolutionize Retirement and Transform America.* New York: Public Affairs, 1999.

Fyock, C. D., and A. M. Dorton. *UnRetirement: A Career Guide for the Retired . . . the Soon-to-Be-Retired . . . the Never-Want-to-Be Retired.* New York: American Management Association, 1994.

Kaplan, L. J. *Retirement Right: Planning for Your Successful Retirement.* Garden City Park, New York: Avery Publishing Group Inc., 2003.

Olshansky, S. K., and B. A. Carnes. *The Quest for Immortality: Science at the Frontiers of Aging.* New York: W. W. Norton & Company, 2003.

Sheldon A., P. J. M. McEwan, and C. P. Ryser. *Retirement: Patterns and Predictions.* Rockville, Md.: National Institute of Mental Health, Section on Mental Health of the Aging, 1975.

Walker, J. W., D. C. Kimmel and K. F. Price. "Retirement Style and Retirement Satisfaction: Retirees Aren't All Alike." *International Aging and Human Development* 12(4): 267–80, 1980.

Weiss S. S., and E. H. Kaplan. "Inner Obstacles to Psychoanalysts' Retirement: Personal, Clinical and Theoretical Perspectives." *Bulletin of the Menninger Clinic* 64(4): 443–61, 2000.

CHAPTER TWO: THE RETIREMENT DOCS' QUIZ

CHAPTER THREE: TRAIT ONE: SOWING SEEDS— THE PLANNER'S ADVANTAGE

Bernstein, A., and J. Trauth. *Your Retirement, Your Way: Why it Takes More than Money to Live Your Dream.* Los Angeles: McGraw-Hill, 2006.

Fletcher, D. *Life After Work: Redefining Retirement—A Step-by-Step Guide to Balancing Your Life and Achieving Bliss in the Wisdom Years.* Bangor, Me.: Booklocker.com, 2007.

Helen, M., and S. Smith. *101 Secrets for a Great Retirement.* Los Angeles: McGraw-Hill, 2000.

Hudson, F. M. *The Adult Years: Mastering the Art of Self-Renewal.* San Francisco: Jossey-Bass Publishers, 1999.

Leibowitz, M. *Charting a Course in Rough Financial Seas. TIAA –CREF Participant* (May 2001), pp. 5–10.

Leider, R., and D. Shapiro. *Repacking Your Bags—Lighten Your Load for the Rest of Your Life,* 2nd ed. San Francisco: Berrett-Koehler, 1995.

Mark-Jarvis, Gail. *Saving for Retirement Without Living Like a Pauper or Winning the Lottery.* Upper Saddle River, N.J.: Pearson Education Inc., 2007.

Older American 2000: Key Indicators of Well-being. Federal Interagency Forum on Aging Related Statistics, 2000.

Stewart, L. *So What Are You Doing with Yourself These Days?* PaineWebber, 1993.

CHAPTER FOUR: TRAIT TWO: ACCENTUATE THE POSITIVE—IT'S ALL ABOUT ATTITUDE

Canning, D., and P. Canning. "Retired Life Fun: Retirement—Make It Your Golden Age." www.retiredlifefun.com/rlf3a.htm (accessed 6/27/2000).

Chang, E. C. *Optimism and Pessimism.* Washington D.C.: American Psychological Association, 2001.

Kimmell, D., K. Price, and J. Walker. "Retirement Choice and Retirement Satisfaction." *Journal of Gerontology* 33, no.4 (1978): 575–85.

Newberry, T. *Success Is Not an Accident.* Decatur, Ga.: Looking Glass Books, 2000.

Oskamp, Stewart, and P. Wesley Shultz. *Attitudes and Opinions.* Florence, Ky.: Lawrence Erlbaum, 2004.

Peterson, C., and M.E.P. Seligman. *Character Strengths and Virtues: A Handbook and Classification.* American Psychological Association, Oxford University Press, 2004.

Scheier, M., C. Carver, and M. Bridges. "Distinguishing Optimism from Neuroticism (and Trait Anxiety, Self-Mastery, and Self-Esteem): A Reevaluation of the Life Orientation Test." *Journal of Personality and Social Psychology* 67, no. 6 (1994): 1063–78.

Seligman, M.E.P., *Learned Optimism: How to Change Your Mind and Your Life.* New York: Simon and Schuster, 1998.

Snyder, C. R., and S. J. Lopez. "Optimistic Explanatory Style." *The Handbook of Positive Psychology.* London: Oxford University Press, 2002.

CHAPTER FIVE: TRAIT THREE: GO WITH THE FLOW— ACCEPT CHANGE

Baruth K. E., and J. J. Carroll. "A Formal Assessment of Resilience: The Baruth Protective Factors Inventory." *Journal of Individual Psychology,* 58, no. 3 (2002): 235–44.

Bergeman, C. S. and K. A. Wallace. "Resiliency in Later Life." *Life-Span Perspectives on Health and Illness.* T. L. Whitman, T. V. Merluzzi, and R. D. White, eds. Mahwah, N.J.: Lawrence Erlbaum, 1999, pp. 207–25.

Bonanno, G. A., J. T. Moskowitz, and A. Papa, et al. "Resilience to Loss in Bereaved Spouses, Bereaved Parents, and Bereaved Gay Men." *Journal of Personality and Social Psychology* 88, no. 5 (2005): 827–53.

Bonanno, G. A. and C. B. Wortman, et al. "Resilience to Loss and Chronic Grief: A Prospective Study from Preloss to 18-months Postloss," *Journal of Personality and Social Psychology* 83, no. 5 (2002): 1150–64.

Brzowsky, Sara. "How to Be Stress-Resilient." *Parade Magazine,* October 12, 2003, pp. 10–12.

Glover, R. J. "Perspectives on Aging: Issues Affecting the Latter Part of the Life Cycle." *Educational Gerontology* 24 (1998): 325–31.

Hooker, K. and D. Ventis. "Work Ethic, Daily Activities, and Retirement Satisfaction." *Journal of Gerontology* 39, no. 4 (1984): 478–84.

Langer, N. "The Importance of Spirituality in Later Life." *Gerontology and Geriatrics Education* 20, no. 3 (2000): 41–50.

Leider, R. J., and D. A. Shapiro. *Repacking Your Bags: Lighten Your Load for the Rest of Your Life,* 2nd ed. San Francisco: Berrett-Koehler, Inc., 1995.

Lopez, S. J., and C. R. Snyder. *Handbook of Positive Psychology.* New York: Oxford University Press, 2002.

Mahoney, S. "Ten Secrets of a Good Long Life." *AARP The Magazine.* (July/August 2005): 46–53.

Oddgeir, F., Dag Barlaug, and Monica Martinussen, et al. "Resilience in Relation to Personality and Intelligence." *International Journal of Methods in Psychiatric Research* 14, no. 1 (2005): 29–42.

Reivich, Karen and Andrew Shatté. *The Resilience Factor: 7 Essential Skills for Overcoming Life's Inevitable Obstacles.* New York: Broadway Books, 2002.

Smith, H., M. Smith, and S. Smith. *101 Secrets for a Great Retirement: Practical, Inspirational and Fun Ideas for the Best Years of Your Life.* Los Angeles: Lowell House, 2000.

Watson, D., B. Hubbard, and D. Wiese. "General Traits of Personality and Affectivity as Predictors of Satisfaction in Intimate Relationships: Evidence from Self- and Partner-ratings." *Journal of Personality* 68 (2000): 413–49.

Watson, D., D. Wiese, and J. Vaidya, et al. "The Two General Activation Systems of Affect: Structural Findings, Evolutionary Considerations, and Psychobiological Evidence." *Journal of Personality* 76 (1999): 820–38.

Chapter Six: Trait Four: A Little Help From Your Friends (and Family)—The Strong Support Group

Acitelli, L. and T. Antonucci. "Reciprocity of Social Support in Older Married Couples." *Journal of Personality and Social Psychology* 67 (1994): 688–98.

Antonucci, T., and H. Akiyama. "Social Relationships and Aging Well." *Generations* 15 (1991): 43–59.

Calasanti, T. "Gender and Life Satisfaction in Retirement: An Assessment of the Male Model." *Journal of Gerontology Series B: Psychological Sciences and Social Sciences* 51 (1996): 18–29.

Cutrona, C., D. Russell, and J. Rose. "Social Support and Adaptation to Stress by the Elderly." *Psychology and Aging* 1 (1986): 47–54.

Fletcher, W., and R. Hansson. "Assessing the Social Components of Retirement Anxiety." *Psychology and Aging* 6, no. 1 (1991): 76–85.

Gordimer, Nadine. *Get a Life.* New York: Penguin, 2006, pp. 68–110.

Helen, M., and S. Smith. *101 Secrets for a Great Retirement; Practical, Inspirational, and Fun Ideas for the Best Years of Your Life.* Blacklick, Ohio: McGraw-Hill Companies/NTC Contemporary Publishing Group, no date, pp. 101–8.

Hooyman, N., and A. Kiyak. *Social Gerontology: A Multidisciplinary Perspective.* Needham Heights, Mass.: Allyn & Bacon, 2004.

Howard, Julie G., "Marital Dyads and Crossover Effects in Retirement Adjustment and Well-Being." Ph.D. diss., Portland State University, 2005.

Larson, R., R. Mannell, and J. Zuzanek. "Daily Well-Being of Older Adults with Friends and Family." *Psychology and Aging* 1 (1986): 117–26.

Polston, B. *Loving Midlife Marriage: A Guide to Keeping Romance Alive from the Empty Nest through Retirement.* New York: John Wiley & Sons, 1999, pp. 214–22.

Ray, D. *The Forty Plus Handbook: The Fine Art of Growing Older.* Nashville: W Publishing Group, 1979, pp. 63–97.

Rowe, John W., and Robert L. Kahn. *Successful Aging.* New York: Dell Publishing, 1999, pp. 97–120; 152–66.

Uhlenberg, P. "Essays on Age Integration." *The Gerontologist* 40, no. 3 (2000): 261–308.

Vinick, B., and D. Ekerdt. "Retirement and the Family." *Generations: Journal of the American Society on Aging* 13 (1989): 53–56.

Zelinski, E. *How to Retire Happy, Wild, and Free: Retirement Wisdom That You Won't Get from Your Financial Advisor.* Berkeley: Ten Speed Press, 2004, pp. 141–64.

CHAPTER SEVEN: TRAIT FIVE: KICK BACK— ENJOY LEISURE TIME

Barnett, J. *How to Feel Good as You Age: A Voice of Experience.* Acton, Mass.: VanderWyk & Burnham, 2000.

Broderick T. and B. Glazer. "Leisure Participation and the Retirement Process." *American Journal of Occupational Therapy* 37, no. 1 (1983): 15–22.

Csikszentmihalyi, Mihaly. *Creativity: Flow and the Psychology of Discovery and Invention.* New York: HarperCollins, 1996.

Giffin J., and K. McKenna. "Influences on Leisure and Life Satisfaction of Elderly People." *Physical and Occupational Therapy in Geriatrics* 15, no. 4 (1998): 1–16.

Guinn B. "Leisure Behavior Motivation and the Life Satisfaction of Retired Persons." *Activities, Adaptation and Aging* 23, no. 4 (1999).

Hooyman, N., and A. Kiyak. *Social Gerontology: A Multidisciplinary Perspective.* Needham Heights, Mass.: Allyn & Bacon, 2004.

Kerr, Walter. *The Decline of Pleasure.* London: Touchstone, 1962.

Kujala, U. M., J. Kaprio, and S. Sarna, et al. "Relationship of Leisure Time Physical Activity and Mortality." *Journal of the American Medical Association* 279, no. 6 (1998): 438–43.

McGuire, F. A., F. D. Dottavio, and J. T. O'Leary. "The Relationship of Early Life Experiences to Later Life Leisure Involvement." *Leisure Sciences* 9, no. 4 (1987): 251–57.

Menec, V. H., and J. G. Chipperfield. "Remaining Active in Later Life: The Role of Locus of Control in Seniors' Leisure Activity Participation, Health and Life Satisfaction." *Journal of Aging and Health* 9, no. 1 (1997): 105–25.

Yamada, N. "The Relationship Between Leisure Activities, Psycho-Social Development and Life Satisfaction in Late Adulthood" [Japanese]. *Japanese Journal of Developmental Psychology* 11, no. 1 (2000): 34–44.

CHAPTER EIGHT: TRAIT SIX: HERE'S TO YOUR HEALTH

Boulé, Margie. "Go Ahead and Giggle: Laughter Really Is the Best (Ha-Ha) Medicine." *The Oregonian,* June 26, 2007.

Centers for Disease Control and Prevention. "Obesity and Overweight: Introduction," www.cdc.gov/nccdphp/dnpa/obesity/

Chang, Alicia. "Diets Fail in the Long Run, Study Says." The Associated Press, 2007.

Cronin-Stubbs, D. "Sick in Mind and Body." AARP Andrus Foundation. www.andrus.org/...l/latestresearch/ssi/healine4.html

Fabrigoule, C., L. Letenneur, and J. F. Dartigues, et al. "Social and Leisure Activities and Risk of Dementia: A Prospective Longitudinal Study." *Journal of the American Geriatrics Society* 43 (1995): 485–90.

Finch, C. E., and R. E. Tanzi. "Genetics of Aging." *Science* 278 (1997): 407–11.

"Gallup Poll, 2000." The Gallup Organization, www.gallup.com/poll/indicators/indalcohol.asp

Gilbaugh, J. H. *Men's Private Parts.* New York: Simon & Schuster, 2002.

Goldberg, Linn, and Diane L. Elliott. *The Healing Power of Exercise: Your Guide to*

Preventing and Treating Diabetes, Depression, Heart Disease, High Blood Pressure, Arthritis, and More. Hoboken, N.J.: John Wiley & Sons, Inc., 2000.

Goldberg, R. J., M. Larson, and D. Levy. "Factors Associated with Survival to 75 Years of Age in Middle-aged Men And Women." *Archives Internal Medicine* 156 (1996): 505–9.

Grant, W. "Incidence of Dementia and Alzheimer's Disease in Nigeria and the United States." *Journal of the American Medical Association* 285 (2001): 2448.

Johnson, S. *Who Moved My Cheese?* New York: G. P. Putnam's Sons, 1998.

Kolata, G. "Old But Not Frail: A Matter of Heart and Head." *The New York Times,* October 6, 2006, p. 1.

Larson, E. "Exercise Associates with Reduced Risk of Dementia in Older Adults." *Annals of Internal Medicine* 144 (2006):73–81.

Leitzmann, M., E. A. Platz, and J. S. Meir, et al. "Ejaculation Frequency and Subsequent Risk of Prostate Cancer." *Journal of the American Medical Association,* 291, 13 (2004): 1578–86.

Mann, T., A. J. Tomiyama, E. Lew, et al. "Medicare's Search for Effective Obesity Treatments: Diets are Not the Answer." *American Psychologist* 62, no. 3 (2007): 220–33.

Morris, M. "Consumption of Fish and Omega-3 Fatty Acids and Risk of Incident of Alzheimer's Disease." *Archives of Neurology* 60 (2003): 940–46.

Morris, M. "Dietary Fats and the Risk of Incident of Alzheimer's Disease." *Archives of Neurology* 60, no. 2 (2003): 194–200.

Morris, M. "Dietary Niacin and the Risk of Incident Alzheimer's Disease and of Cognitive Decline." *Journal of Neurology, Neurosurgery, and Psychiatry* 75, no. 8 (2004): 1093–99.

Paffenbarder, R. S., Jr., R. T. Hyde, and A. L. Wind, et al. "The Association of Changes in Physical Activity Level and Other Lifestyle Characteristics with Mortality Among Men." *New England Journal of Medicine* 328 (1993): 538–45.

Perls, Thomas, Margery Hutter Silver, and John F. Lauerman. *Living to 100: Lessons in Living to Your Maximum Potential at Any Age.* New York: Basic Books, 2000, pp. 155–210.

Reynolds, C. F., G. S. Alexopoulos, and I. R. Katz, et al. "Chronic Depression in the Elderly: Approaches for Prevention." *Drugs and Aging* 18, no. 7 (2001): 507–14.

Roizen, M. F. *Real Age: Are You as Young as You Can Be?* New York: Cliff Street Books, 1999.

Rosenfeld, I. *Live Now, Age Later: Proven Ways to Slow Down the Clock.* New York: Warner Books, 1999.

Ross, Emma. "Obese People Can Still Be Fit, Expert Says." *The Oregonian,* July 18, 2001, p. A9.

Rowe, John W. and Robert L. Kahn. *Successful Aging.* New York: Dell Publishing, 1999, pp. 97–120.

Smith, G. D., S. Frankel, and J. Yarnell. "Sex and Death: Are They Related? Findings from the Caerphilly Cohort Study." *British Medical Journal,* 315, no. 7123 (1997): 1641–44.

Sorlie, Paul D., Eric Backlund, and Jacob B. Keller. "U.S. Mortality by Economic, Demographic, and Social Characteristics: The National Longitudinal Mortality Study." *American Journal of Public Health* 85, no. 7 (1995): 949–56.

Spriegel, K., R. Leproult, and E. V. Cauter. "Impact of Sleep Debt on Metabolic and Endocrine Function." *The Lancet:* 354 (1999): 1435–39.

Takeuchi, J., and S. Groeneman. "'Stealing Time' Study: A Summary of Findings." Washington, D.C.: AARP Research Group, 1999.

Vaillant, G. E., and K. Mukarnal. "Successful Aging." *American Journal of Psychiatry:* 158 (2001): 839–47.

Weller, I., and P. Corey. "The Impact of Excluding Non-leisure Energy Expenditure on the Relation Between Physical Activity and Mortality in Women." *Epidemiology* 9 (1998): 632–35.

West, R. R. "Smoking: Its Influence on Survival and Cause of Death." *Journal of the Royal College of Physicians of London* 26, no. 4 (1992): 357–63.

CHAPTER NINE: TRAIT SEVEN: PASSION AND PURPOSE

Csikszentmihalyi, Mihaly. *Flow: The Psychology of Optimal Experience.* New York: Harper & Row, 1990.

Helen, M. and S. Smith. *101 Secrets for a Great Retirement.* Los Angeles: McGraw-Hill, 2000, pp. 1–157.

Hudson, F. M. *The Adult Years: Mastering the Art of Self-Renewal.* Revised edition. San Francisco: Jossey-Bass Publishers, 1999.

Leibowitz, M. "Charting a Course in Rough Financial Seas." TIAA-CREF Participant, May 2001, pp. 5–10.

Leider, Richard J., and David A. Shapiro. *Repacking Your Bags—Lighten Your Load for the Rest of Your Life.* San Francisco: Berrett-Koehler, 1995.

Older American 2000: Key Indicators of Well-Being. Federal Interagency Forum on Aging Related Statistics, 2000.

Stewart, Lisa. "So What Are You Doing with Yourself These Days?" NY., N.Y., PaineWebber, 1993.

CHAPTER TEN: TRAIT EIGHT: LET THE SPIRIT MOVE YOU—SPIRITUALITY AND RELIGION

Achenbaum, A., and S. Modell. "Joan and Erik Erikson and Sarah and Abraham: Parallel Awakenings in the Long Shadow of Wisdom and Faith." *Religion, Belief, and Spirituality in Late Life.* New York: Springer Publishing Company, 1999, pp. 13–24.

Birren, J., and K. Warner Schaie. *Handbook of the Psychology of Aging.* Oxford, U.K.: Elsevier Science, 2001.

Fowler, J. *Stages of Faith.* New York: Harper & Row. 1981, pp. 9–15.

"Gallup Poll, Religion." The Gallup Organization, 2006. www.galluppoll.com/content/default.aspx?ci=1690

Hooyman, N., and A. Kiyak. *Social Gerontology: A Multidisciplinary Perspective.* Needham Heights, Mass.: Allyn & Bacon, 2004.

James, William. *The Varieties of Religious Experience: A Study in Human Nature.* Centenary edition. London: Routledge, 2002.

Jewell, A. *Aging, Spirituality, and Well-Being.* London: Jessica Kingsley, 2003.

Koenig, H., L. George, and I. Siegler. "The Use of Religion and Other Emotion-Regulation Coping Strategies Among Older Adults." *Gerontologist* 28, no. 3 (June 1988): 303–10.

Levin, J. "Religion." *The Encyclopedia of Aging.* Second edition. New York: Springer Publishing Company, 1995, pp. 799–802.

Mitroff, I., and E. Denton. "A Study of Spirituality in the Workplace." *Sloan Management Review* (Summer 1999): 83–92.

Pascal, Blaise. www.oregonstate.edu/instruct/phl302/philosophers/pascal.html

Roof, W. C. *Spiritual Marketplace: Baby Boomers and the Remaking of American Religion.* Princeton, N.J.: Princeton University Press, 2001.

Thomas, L., and S. Eisenhandler. *Religion, Belief, and Spirituality in Late Life.* New York: Springer Publishing Company, 1999.

Tornstan, L. "Late-Life Transcendence: A New Developmental Perspective on Aging." *Religion, Belief, and Spirituality in Late Life.* New York: Springer Publishing Company, 1999.

Wink, P. "Addressing End-of-Life Issues: Spirituality and Inner Life." *Generations: Journal of the American Society on Aging* 23, no. 1 (Spring 1999). San Francisco: ASA Publications.

Wolfe, A. *The Transformation of American Religion: How We Actually Live Our Faith.* New York: Free Press, 2003.

Zinnbauer, B., K. Pargament, and B. Cole, et al. "Religion and Spirituality: Unfuzzying the Fuzzy." *Journal for the Scientific Study of Religion* 36, no. 4 (1997): 549–64.

CHAPTER ELEVEN: INTO THE FUTURE

Buford, Bob. *Game Plan—Winning Strategies for the Second Half of Your Life.* Grand Rapids: Zondervan Publishing House, 1999.

Carlson, B. "The New Rules of Retirement." *Bob Carlson's Retirement Watch,* Sep. 1–2, 2000.

Howard, Julie G. "Marital Dyads and Crossover Effects in Retirement Adjustment and Well-Being." Ph.D. diss., Portland State University, 2005.

Kolata, G. "Old But Not Frail: A Matter of Heart and Head." *The New York Times,* Oct. 6, 2006, p. 1.

Larsen, E. "The Occasional Volunteer." *AARP The Magazine,* January/February 2001, pp. 53–61.

Mahoney, Sara. "Ten Secrets of a Good Long Life." *AARP The Magazine,* July/August 2005, pp. 46–53.

Moen, P., W. A. Erickson, and M. Agarwal, et al. "Cornell Retirement and Well-Being Study Final Report." Ithaca, N.Y.: Bronfenbrenner Life Course Center, 2000.

Novelli, W. "Reinventing Retirement: Tell Us What You're Doing." *AARP The Magazine,* March 2002, p. 20.

RETIREMENT RESOURCES

HOUSING

Retire in Style: 60 Outstanding Places Across the USA and Canada by Warren R. Bland, Ph.D. (Chester, N.J.: Next Decade, Inc., 2002).

CAREGIVERS

American Medical Association Guide to Home Caregiving by the American Medical Association (New York: John Wiley & Sons, 2001).

The Caregiver's Essential Handbook: More than 1,200 Tips to Help You Care for and Comfort the Seniors in Your Life by Sasha Carr, M.S. (New York: McGraw-Hill, 2003).

The Comfort of Home: An Illustrated Step-by-Step Guide for Caregivers, 2nd Edition by Maria M. Meyer and Paula Derr, R.N. (Portland, Ore.: Care Trust Publications, 2002).

The Complete Eldercare Planner: Where to Start, Which Questions to Ask, and How to Find Help, 2nd Edition by Joy Loverde (New York: Three Rivers Press, 2000).

MENTAL HEALTH

The Healing Journey Through Retirement by Phil Rich, Ed.D., MSW, D. M. Sampson, and D. S. Fetherling. (New York: John Wiley & Sons, 1999). *Transitions: Making Sense of Life's Changes* by William Bridges, (New York: Da Capo Press, 2004).

EDUCATION AND COMPUTERS

It's Never Too Late to Love a Computer: The Fearless Guide for Seniors by Abby Stokes (New York: Workman Publishing, 2005). *Senior's Guide to Easy Computing: PC Basics, Internet, and E-mail* by Rebecca Sharp Colmer (Chelsea, Mich.: Eklektika Press, 2004).

VOLUNTEERING

The Power of Purpose: Living Well by Doing Good by Peter S. Temes (New York: Three Rivers Press, 2007). *Volunteering: The Selfish Benefits: Achieve Deep-Down Satisfaction and Create That Desire in Others* by Charles A. Bennett (Oak View, Calif.: Committee Communications, 2001).

TRAVEL

Complete Guide to Full-Time RVing: Life on the Open Road by Bill and Jan Moeller (Ventura, Calif.: Trailer Life Books, 1998). *Have Grandchildren, Will Travel: The Hows and Wheres of a Glorious Vacation With Your Children's Children* by Virginia Spurlock (New York: Pilot Books, 1997).

HEALTH AND FITNESS

Fitter After 50: Forever Changing Our Beliefs About Aging by Edwin Mayhew (Bloomington, Ind.: 1st Books Library, 2002).

STATISTICS

DESCRIPTION OF DATA ANALYSIS FOR RETIREMENT STUDY

All survey data were input and analyzed using the Statistical Package for the Social Sciences software. Chi-square analyses were conducted to identify group differences in categorical variables. For continuous variables, independent sample t-tests were used to identify differences between men and women, and between homemakers and working/retired women. To identify differences by group/stage/phase of work-retirement (the four groups), one-way analysis of variance and Scheffé post hoc comparisons were conducted.

The Retirement Quotient (RQ) was constructed using a combination of literature review and inductive and empirical methods. Possible indicators of perceived success in retirement were identified through a review of the literature and through the judgment of the investigators. Correlation analyses of each of these indicators with perceived retirement success were then conducted. Also, inter-item correlation analyses were conducted to determine indicators that were so highly correlated as to be essentially duplicative of each other. The resulting 22 indicators are those that constitute the RQ, with an alpha coefficient (reliability) of .75.

Multivariate analyses were also conducted. Specifically, using multiple linear regression, the 22 RQ indicators were entered into the equation simultaneously to determine which ones contributed the most to predicting perceived success in retirement.

This work was conducted by Margaret Beth Neal, Ph.D., director of the Institute on Aging, Portland State University.

INDEX

oigo, *I hear;* **doy,** *I give*   **naciones,** *nations*
bou, *(Catalonian mode of fishing)*   **cuota,** *quota*
triunfo, *triumph*   **cuita,** *grief*

a. No diphthong, but two distinct syllables, will be the result, (1) when two strong vowels come together, as in **Saavedra** (a proper name), **faena,** *task,* **caoba,** *mahogany,* etc.; (2) when the accent falls on a weak vowel adjacent to a strong vowel, as in **traído,** *brought,* **oído,** *heard,* etc.; or (3) when two adjoining weak vowels are pronounced separately, as in **flúido,** *fluid;* **huída,** *flight;* **construído,** *constructed.* In the last two cases the accent is always written on the stressed vowel.

6. Triphthongs. — There are but four of these; they are formed when a stressed strong vowel stands between two weak vowels. Final **i** of a word is written **y.** The combinations are

    iai, as in **principiáis,** *you begin*
    iei, as in **principiéis,** *may you begin*
    uai (uay), as in **averiguáis,** *you ascertain;* **guay,** *woe*
    uei (uey), as in **continuéis,** *may you continue;* **buey,** *ox*

CONSONANTS

7. Of the consonants, **f, m,** and **p** may be said to have practically the same values as in English. **Ch** has the sound of English *ch* in *church.* **H** is silent : **hora,** *hour;* but **h** from **f** was pronounced as late as the sixteenth century : **hacer** (from *fazer*). **K** has the English sound and occurs only in foreign words. **Q** never occurs except with a following **u,** and the two together mean **k;** moreover they can appear only before **e** or **i,** as in **aquel,** *that,* **quitar,** *to take away.* **W** is found only in foreign words and has the foreign value; the sound of the English *w,* as in *well,* etc., is possessed by the Spanish unaccented **u** in hiatus before another vowel, as in **cuestión,** *question,* **cuando,** *when,* etc. The other consonants need special consideration.

8. B, v. — These have one and the same value which is usually that of a bilabial spirant. It is given to neither of them in English, and is produced by bringing the lips quite close to each other and allowing the air to pass out constantly between them; there is no stoppage of the air as in the case of the English *b*. The sound of the English *v* does not exist in Spanish. In a measure the Spanish sound in question may be realized by trying to utter *b* and *v* in the same breath: cf. **cuba,** *vat,* **uva,** *grape.* Initial **b** or **v** more nearly resembles English *b,* as in **basta,** *enough,* **brazo,** *arm,* etc. After **m** or **n** (within a word or at the end of a preceding word), both **b** and **v** acquire the full value of the English *b,* as in **también,** *also,* **en verdad,** *in truth,* **envidia,** *envy.* (In these cases the **n** becomes **m** in pronunciation.)

9. C, z. — **C** has two values. Before **a, o,** or **u,** or before a consonant (except in **ch**) it is pronounced *k,* as in **calle,** *street,* **codo,** *elbow,* etc. Before **e** or **i** it has approximately the value of *th* in English *thin,* as in **cena,** *supper,* **cinco,** *five.* But in Spanish America and in parts of Spain (especially southern Spain) the **c** before **e** or **i** is pronounced like the English *ss.*

Z has in all positions the value of *th;* in the regions in which **c** has the sibilant value, it, too, is pronounced like *ss.*

10. D, t, l, n. — These differ from the English sounds in that they are produced farther forward in the mouth: when making them, the tongue touches the upper teeth, or at least the roots of the upper teeth.

In most positions, **d** is practically a spirant, and its sound somewhat resembles that of English *th* in *father.* It may be compared to a prolonged English *d,* but pronounced with the tongue farther forward: cf. **todo,** *all,* **madre,** *mother.* Initial **d** more nearly resembles English *d,* as in **dámelo,** *give it to me.* After **l** and **n** Spanish **d** acquires the full value of English *d:* cf. **espalda,** *back,* **tienda,** *shop.* At the end of a word **d** is sometimes pronounced like the *th* of *thin,* or is omitted altogether, but neither course is sanctioned by the best usage. There is a tendency for it to disappear in pronunciation between vowels, especially in the ending –ado.

Aside from the fact that they should be produced well to the front in the mouth, t, l, and n are not unlike the English sounds.

11. Ll, ñ. — These are palatalized modifications of l and **n.** The sign ll does not mean double l at all; it simply denotes an l pronounced in that part of the mouth in which a y is regularly produced. In the endeavor to make an l the tongue is arched toward the palate (near which a y has its place of enunciation); hence it is a palatalized l. The sound, as in Spanish **millón,** is rendered in a measure by that in English *million.* In Spanish America, as in certain parts of Spain, the ll has become simply a y in pronunciation (which shows how strong the y element is in the ll), so that **caballo,** *horse,* is pronounced **cabayo.**

The ñ is, similarly, a palatalized variety of **n,** that is, an **n** produced in the y place in the mouth: the *ny* in the English *canyon* is an approximate rendering of the ñ in the Spanish **cañón.** The mark over the ñ is called a **tilde** (a word derived ultimately from the Latin "titulus," *title, sign*).

12. G, j. — Before **a, o,** or **u** and before a consonant **g** has the so-called "hard" sound, as in **gota,** *drop,* **grande,** *big.* Before **e** or **i** this sound is rendered by **gu** (in which the **u** has no pronounceable value of its own), as in **guerra,** *war,* **guisar,** *to cook.* Intervocalic "hard" **g** tends to become an indistinct spirant, as in **hago,** *I make,* **sigue,** *he follows.* **G** followed immediately by **e** or **i,** and **j,** wherever it occurs, have the "velar" sound given to *ch* in the Scotch-English "loch" or in the German "noch," as in **gente,** *people,* **jardín,** *garden.* While the sound indicated is the correct Castilian one, many Spanish speakers pronounce this **g** like a strong form of the *h* in English *hat.*

a. A diæresis is placed over **u** when it is pronounced in **gue–** or **gui–,** as in **lingüístico,** *linguistic.*

13. R, rr. — Wherever it occurs, the Spanish **r** is carefully pronounced with an unmistakable trill of the tongue. It has a well defined utterance, which resembles that of a carefully enunciated English *r*, as in **caro,** *dear,* **grande,** *large,* **amar,** *to love.* When initial in a word, when it immediately follows **l** or **n,** and when written **rr** between vowels, it has a re-enforced value of this sound, as in **roto,** *broken,* **Enrique,** *Henry,* **alrededor,** *about,* **perro,** *dog.*

14. S. — In most cases of its occurrence, between vowels and elsewhere, the Spanish **s** has the voiceless sound of the English *ss,* but it is hissed less: cf. **ser,** *to be,* **casa,** *house,* **más,** *more.* It should not receive between vowels the *z* sound which it often has in English. Nowadays, however, there is a tendency to voice it, that is, pronounce it like English *z,* before a voiced consonant (**b, d, g, l, r, m, n**), and many speakers aspirate it or fail to pronounce it at all before a consonant or at the end of a word. The better rule for foreigners is to pronounce it like English *ss* wherever it occurs.

15. X. — This is a sound of infrequent occurrence in Spanish. Between vowels it has ordinarily the English value. Before consonants it may be pronounced like the English *x* (that is, as *ks*) or as *s*; both **sexto** and **sesto** are found as spellings for the word meaning *sixth.*

16. Y. — This sound has been treated in part under the heading **Vowels.** At the beginning of a word or syllable it has a value comparable to that of the English *y.* However, when it is initial in a word, it is uttered strongly, and, in dialectal Spanish in Spain and rather generally in Spanish America, it acquires the sound of the English *j,* so that **yo,** *I,* becomes **jo** and **ya,** *already,* becomes **ja.** For Castilian a forcible **y** pronunciation suffices.

17. Double letters. — When Spanish letters, with the exception of **ll** and **rr,** are written double, each is pronounced separately. Of the vowels, **a**, **e**, and **o** may appear as doubled; and of these double **e** is the commonest, as in **leer**, *to read*, **creer**, *to believe*. Of the consonants doubled in writing only two are pronounced separately; these are **cc** and **nn**. **Cc** can occur only before **e** or **i**, and then the first **c** is *k* in sound and the second is the spirant *th*, as in **acceder**, *to accede*, **acción**, *action*. Careless speakers are prone to neglect the first **c** in such cases. Double **n** is found only where the first **n** belongs to a prefix, as in **innoble**, *ignoble*.

ACCENTUATION

18. Most Spanish words reveal the place of their accent by their very form; for a considerable number, however, a written accent is thought necessary. The leading rules are these:

1. Words ending in a vowel, or in the consonants **n** or **s**, stress regularly the next to the last syllable and require no written accent, as in

> **habla**, *he speaks*   **examen**, *examination*
> **dulce**, *sweet*   **paraguas**, *umbrella*
> **especie**, *species*

a. S and n are often inflectional endings or a part of inflectional endings. Usually their presence does not vary the accent which the particular word would have without them; thus,

> **carta**, *letter;* **cartas**, *letters*
> **ama**, *he loves;* **amas**, *thou lovest;* **aman**, *they love*

2. Words ending in a consonant except **n** or **s** stress regularly the last syllable and take no written accent, as in

> **libertad**, *liberty*   **amar**, *to love*

a. For accentual purposes final **y** is treated as a consonant.

3. A written accent is required for words not obeying the two rules just given and for all words whose stress comes more than two syllables from their end. (This means that **a** written accent is needed by all words ending in a vowel

and stressing it, by words ending in **n** or **s** and stressing the last syllable, by all those ending in a consonant — except **n** or **s** — and not stressing their last syllable, and by all words not stressed on either the last or the next to the last syllable). Examples:

papá, *papa*	**lápiz,** *lead pencil*
sofá, *sofa*	**mármol,** *marble*
razón, *reason*	**ejército,** *army*
interés, *interest*	**telégrafo,** *telegraph*

a. The addition of the plural sign –**es** sometimes involves the use of a written accent not needed in the singular; thus, **crimen,** *crime,* but **crímenes;** on the other hand, it may mean the omission of an accent required in the singular, as in **razón,** *reason,* **razones.**

b. In general, the addition of a plural sign has no effect upon the place of accent in the particular word; however, two words advance one syllable toward the end the place of stress; these are **carácter,** *character,* **caracteres** (for which word no written accent is necessary), and **régimen,** *rule of conduct,* **regímenes** (for which the written accent is still necessary, as it occurs more than two syllables from the end of the word).

19. Accents are also used merely to indicate different parts of speech. Certain monosyllables (which, of course, need no written accent to indicate the place of stress), and certain demonstrative, interrogative, and exclamative words require an accent to distinguish them from other words spelled and pronounced like them. Compare:

mí, *me, myself*	**mi,** *my*
sí, *himself,* etc.; *yes*	**si,** *if*
más, *more*	**mas,** *but*
éste, *this one* (pron.)	**este,** *this* (adj.)
ése, *that one* (pron.)	**ese,** *that* (adj.)
aquél, *that one* (pron.)	**aquel,** *that* (adj.)
qué, *what, which* (interrog. and exclam.)	**que,** *who, whom, which* (rel.)
quién, *who, whom* (interrog. and exclam.)	**quien,** *who, whom* (rel.)

a. A recent ruling of the Spanish Academy makes it no longer necessary to write the accent on **a,** *to, at,* **e,** *and,* **u,** *or,* and **o,** *or* (except on **o** between Arabic numerals, as in **2 ó 3**).

b. The written accent of a verb form must not be omitted even though, by the addition of an object pronoun to it, the place of the accent is clear enough, thus, **hablé,** *I spoke,* **habléle,** *I spoke to him.* A verb form which does not take an accent when it stands alone may require one, if the addition of object pronouns to it throws the stress of the compounded form on a syllable preceding the next to the last; thus, **diciendo,** *saying,* **diciéndomelo,** *saying it to me;* **traer,** *to bring,* **traértelo,** *to bring it to thee;* **escriba Vd.,** *write,* **escríbalo Vd.,** *write it.*

SYLLABIFICATION

20. — 1. A single consonantal character and the digraphs **ch, ll, rr** (these three being inseparable combinations) are, in a syllabic division, passed over to the following vowel; so, also, are most combinations of a consonant with an ensuing **l** or **r** (except **rl, sl, tl,** and **sr,** which are separable):

la-bio, *lip*	cu-brir, *to cover*	no-ble, *noble*
ja-ca, *pony*	su-frir, *to suffer*	mo-fle-tu-do, *chubby-cheeked*
la-do, *side*	re-pri-mir, *to repress*	su-plir, *to supply*
ne-xo, *knot*	la-cre, *sealing-wax*	te-cla, *key*
mu-cho, *much*	ma-gro, *meager*	si-glo, *century*
bu-llir, *to boil*	ma-dre, *mother*	
pa-rra, *vine*	cua-tro, *four*	

Cf. **mer-lu-za,** *cod* .   **es-la-bón,** *link*
At-lán-ti-co, *Atlantic*   **Is-ra-e-li-ta,** *Israelite*

2. With the exception of the inseparable combinations mentioned in the foregoing rule, two consonants between vowels are so divided that one remains with the preceding, the other goes to the following vowel:

ap-to, *fit*   **más-til,** *mast*   **in-no-ble,** *ignoble,* etc.
cor-te, *court*   **ac-ci-den-te,** *accident*

3. Where the combination of consonants between vowels is of more than two, there is a tendency to pass over to the second vowel only a single consonant or one of the inseparable combinations mentioned above in 1; e.g.:

par-che, *plaster*   **cons-truc-ción,** *construction*
pers-pi-ca-cia, *perspicacity*

4. Prefixes felt as such are usually kept intact, contrary to the rules given above in 1; e.g.:

> **des-es-pe-rar,** *to despair* (cf. **esperar,** *to hope*)
> **sub-le-var-se,** *to rebel* (cf. **levar,** *to raise*).
> **ab-ro-ga-ción,** *abrogation* (cf. **rogar,** *to ask*).

PUNCTUATION

21. The only notable points here are: (1) the double use of question marks and exclamation points, which not only end their clause, but in an inverted form usually precede it (e.g. **¿Cómo está Vd.?** *How are you?* **¡Qué hermosa mujer!** *What a beautiful woman!*); (2) the frequency of suspension points (. . .) in narrative or dramatic style; and (3), in dialogue, the use of a dash (—) to indicate a change of speaker.

CAPITALIZATION

22. Capitals are less commonly used in Spanish than in English. Unless they begin a sentence, a line of verse, or a quotation, proper adjectives and the pronoun **yo,** *I*, are not capitalized. National or other locative adjectives used as nouns may take a capital when they denote persons (although usage varies in this respect); when they denote languages, they usually take no capital, even though used substantively: **los franceses** (or **Franceses**) **hablan francés,** *Frenchmen speak French.*

In the titles of books and in the headings of chapters, paragraphs, etc., it is customary in Spanish either to use capital letters (**emplear letra mayúscula**) exclusively, or to capitalize only the first letter of the title or heading and use small letters (**letra minúscula**) elsewhere, as in **RESUMEN GRAMATICAL** or **Resumen gramatical, GÉNERO DE LOS NOMBRES** or **Género de los nombres,** etc.

Atención de la Unión Panamericana

LA EMBAJADA NORTEAMERICANA EN SANTIAGO DE CHILE
The American Embassy is one of the many stately buildings in the Chilean capital.

UNA CLASE DE NIÑOS

Interior of a classroom in a school in Buenos Aires.

LESSON I

(Lección Primera)

23. Gender of Nouns. — All Spanish nouns are either masculine or feminine. There are no neuter nouns.

libro, *m.*, book   pluma, *f.*, pen

24.   Indefinite Article

MASCULINE   FEMININE

un, a, an   una, a, an

un libro, a book   una pluma, a pen

25. Un is used with masculine nouns and **una** with feminine nouns.

26.   yo tengo, I have   usted tiene, you have

EXERCISES

un lápiz, a pencil   una pluma, a pen
un libro, a book   y, and
papel, *m.*, paper

A. 1. Yo tengo papel. 2. Usted tiene papel. 3. Yo tengo un lápiz. 4. Usted tiene un lápiz. 5. Yo tengo una pluma. 6. Usted tiene una pluma. 7. Yo tengo un libro. 8. Usted tiene un libro. 9. Yo tengo papel y lápiz. 10. Usted tiene papel y lápiz. 11. Yo tengo un lápiz y una pluma. 12. Usted tiene un lápiz y una pluma.

B. *Escríbase en español.* 1. You have a book. 2. I have a book. 3. You have a pencil. 4. I have a pencil. 5. You have paper. 6. I have paper. 7. You have paper and a pencil. 8. I have paper and a pencil. 9. You have a pen and a pencil. 10. I have a pen and a pencil. 11. You have a book and a pencil. 12. I have a book and a pen.

RESUMEN GRAMATICAL

Al Profesor: Sería conveniente que los alumnos dedujeran de los ejemplos precedentes las reglas que siguen, y así sucesivamente con todas las reglas de las lecciones siguientes.

23. Género de los nombres. — Todos los nombres en español son o masculinos o femeninos. No hay nombres neutros.

24–25. El artículo indeterminado (o indefinido). — **Un** se usa con los nombres masculinos y **una** con los femeninos.

LESSON II
(Lección Segunda)

27. Gender of Nouns.—1. Nouns ending in –o are usually masculine.

     un libro, a book   **un ejercicio,** an exercise

2. Nouns ending in –a are usually feminine.

     una pluma, a pen   **tinta,** *f.,* ink

3. If nouns do not end in –o or –a, it is usually best to learn the gender of each noun separately.

28. Interrogative Sentences. — An inverted interrogation mark is placed at the beginning of a question.

     ¿Tengo yo? have I?   **¿Tiene usted?** have you?

29.   **yo escribo,** I write.   **¿escribo yo?** do I write?
      usted escribe, you write.   **¿escribe usted?** do you write?

Note that the English auxiliary verb *do* is not expressed in Spanish.

EXERCISES

     con, with   **en,** in, on
     un ejercicio, an exercise   **tinta,** *f.,* ink

A. 1. ¿Tiene usted un lápiz? 2. Yo tengo papel y un lápiz. 3. ¿Escribe usted en papel con lápiz? [1] 4. Yo escribo en papel con pluma y tinta. 5. ¿Escribe usted un ejercicio

[1] Note the omission of **un,** *a.*

con lápiz?   6. Yo escribo un ejercicio con pluma y tinta.
7. ¿Escribe usted en un libro?   8. Yo escribo en un libro.

B. *Contéstese afirmativamente a las siguientes preguntas.*
1. ¿Tiene usted un lápiz? (*Respuesta:* Yo tengo un lápiz.)
2. ¿Escribe usted con lápiz?   3. ¿Tiene usted pluma y tinta?
4. ¿Escribe usted con pluma y tinta?   5. ¿Tiene usted papel?
6. ¿Escribe usted en papel?   7. ¿Escribe usted en papel con
lápiz?   8. ¿Escribe usted en papel con pluma y tinta?
9. ¿Escribo yo un ejercicio? (*Respuesta:* Usted escribe un
ejercicio.)   10. ¿Escribo yo en papel?   11. ¿Escribo yo con
lápiz?   12. ¿Escribo yo con pluma y tinta?

C. 1. I have a pencil. 2. You have a pen. 3. I write with [a][1]
pencil. 4. You write with [a] pen. 5. I write on paper. 6. I write
on paper with [a] pencil. 7. You write with pen and ink. 8. Have
you a book? 9. Do you write in a book? 10. Do you write with
[a] pencil? 11. Do you write with pen and ink? 12. Have I a pen?
13. Do I write with pen and ink? 14. Do I write on paper?

D. *Escríbase.* 1. I write on paper. 2. Do you write with
[a] pencil? 3. I write with pen and ink. 4. Have you a pen?
5. I have a pen and a pencil. 6. Do you write an exercise with [a]
pencil? 7. I write an exercise with pen and ink. 8. I write with
[a] pencil. 9. You write with pen and ink. 10. Do I write in a
book? 11. You write in a book with [a] pencil. 12. I write in a
book with pen and ink.

RESUMEN GRAMATICAL

27. Género de los nombres. — 1. Los nombres que terminan
en −o son, por regla general, masculinos. 2. Los nombres que
terminan en −a son, por regla general, femeninos. 3. En cuanto a
los nombres que no terminan ni en −o ni en −a, el género de cada
uno debe aprenderse por separado.

28. Frases interrogativas. — En español las preguntas van pre-
cedidas por un signo de interrogación invertido.

Nótese que el verbo auxiliar *do* no se expresa en español.

[1] English words in brackets [ ] are to be omitted in Spanish.

LESSON III

(Lección Tercera)

30. Plural of Nouns. — 1. Nouns ending in a vowel add
–s to form the plural.

libro, book	**pluma,** pen
libros, books	**plumas,** pens

2. Nouns ending in a consonant add –es to form the plural.

papel, paper	**lección,** lesson
papeles, papers	**lecciones,** lessons

Note that **lecciones** does not have the accent mark. The
plural of **lápiz** is **lápices.**

31.   Definite Article

Singular		Plural
Masculine	**el**	**los** ⎫ the
Feminine	**la**	**las** ⎭

el libro, the book	**los libros,** the books
la pluma, the pen	**las plumas,** the pens

(See also §§ 96, 98)

32. In Spanish the definite article is usually repeated before each noun to which it refers.

La pluma y la tinta.   The pen and (the) ink.

33.   yo tengo, I have
          usted tiene, you have
          el alumno tiene, the student has

          yo enseño, I teach
          usted enseña, you teach
          el profesor enseña, the teacher teaches

          yo escribo, I write
          usted escribe, you write
          el alumno escribe, the student writes

The same form of the verb is used when **usted** is the subject that is
used when the subject is a singular noun. This is true of all verbs.

EXERCISES

la **alumna,** the student, *f.*	¿**quién?** who?
el **alumno,** the student, *m.*[1]	**señor,** sir
la **lección,** the lesson	**señora** ⎫ madam, ma'am [4]
la **pizarra,** the blackboard	**señorita** ⎭
(*of slate*) [2]	**sí,** yes
el **profesor,** the teacher, *m.*[3]	la **tiza,** the chalk
la **profesora,** the teacher, *f.*	

yo estudio, I study; **usted estudia,** you study

A. 1. ¿Tiene usted los libros? 2. Sí, señor (señora *o* señorita); yo tengo los libros y estudio las lecciones. 3. ¿Escribe usted los ejercicios en papel? 4. Sí, señor; yo escribo los ejercicios con pluma y tinta. 5. ¿Estudia el alumno (*o* la alumna) las lecciones? 6. Sí, señor; el alumno (*o* la alumna) estudia las lecciones. 7. ¿Quién enseña las lecciones? 8. El profesor (*o* la profesora) enseña las lecciones. 9. ¿Quién escribe los ejercicios? 10. El alumno escribe los ejercicios en la pizarra. 11. ¿Escribe el alumno con tiza? 12. Sí, señor; el alumno escribe con tiza en la pizarra.

B. *Contéstese afirmativamente a las siguientes preguntas, empezando cada respuesta con las palabras* **sí señor** (**señora,** *o* **señorita**). *Úsense en la respuesta tantas palabras de la pregunta como sea posible.*
1. ¿Estudia usted las lecciones? 2. ¿Escribe usted los ejercicios en la pizarra? 3. ¿Escribe usted los ejercicios con tiza?

[1] In an elementary school a *pupil* is **discípulo;** in a university a *student* or *undergraduate* is **estudiante. Alumno** may be used for all grades.

[2] **Pizarra** means *slate.* In Spain and in some Spanish American countries a *blackboard* made of slate is also called **pizarra,** while in Mexico and some other countries it is called **pizarrón.** A *blackboard* made of waxed and painted cloth is called **encerado,** and one of painted boards is called **tablero.**

[3] In a high school or academy, in which each teacher gives instruction in only one subject, the *teacher* should be called **profesor, –ora.** In an elementary school, *teacher* is **maestro, –a.** A university *professor* is called **catedrático.**

[4] **Señorita** is used in addressing a young unmarried teacher. In addressing an older woman, whether she be married or single, **señora** is considered more respectful.

4. ¿Estudia el alumno (o la alumna) las lecciones? 5. ¿Escribe el alumno los ejercicios? 6. ¿Escribe el alumno con lápiz? 7. ¿Escribe la alumna los ejercicios? 8. ¿Escribe la alumna con pluma y tinta? 9. ¿Enseña el profesor (o la profesora) las lecciones?

Contéstese, empleando como sujeto del verbo **el alumno** *o* **la alumna, el profesor** *o* **la profesora.** 10. ¿Quién tiene los libros? 11. ¿Quién estudia las lecciones? 12. ¿Quién escribe los ejercicios en la pizarra? 13. ¿Quién enseña las lecciones?

C. *Tradúzcase y repítase después, poniendo todos los nombres en plural.* 1. I have the book. (**Yo tengo el libro. Yo tengo los libros.**) 2. I study the lesson. 3. I have the pencil and the pen. 4. I write the exercise. 5. You teach the lesson. 6. Who has the book? 7. Who studies the lesson? 8. Who has the pencil and the pen? 9. Who writes the exercise? 10. Who teaches the lesson?

Tradúzcase y repítase después en forma interrogativa. 11. The student has the book. 12. The student studies the lessons. 13. The student writes the exercises. 14. The student writes on the blackboard. 15. The student writes with chalk. 16. The teacher teaches the lesson.

D. *Escríbase.* 1. I study the lessons. 2. Do you write the exercises? 3. Yes, sir; I write the exercises on the blackboard. 4. Does the student write with pen and ink? 5. Yes, sir; the student writes the exercises with pen and ink. 6. Does the teacher teach the lessons? 7. Yes, sir; the teacher teaches the lessons. 8. Who studies the lessons? 9. The student studies the lessons. 10. I write the exercises on the blackboard with chalk. 11. You write the exercises on paper with pen and ink. 12. The student studies the lessons and writes the exercises.

RESUMEN GRAMATICAL

30. Plural de los nombres. — 1. Los nombres que terminan en vocal forman su plural añadiendo una –s.

2. Los nombres que terminan en consonante forman su plural añadiendo –es.

Obsérvese que el plural de **lección** (**lecciones**) no lleva el acento. El plural de **lápiz** es **lápices**.

32. Por regla general, se repite el artículo determinado (o definido) delante de cada uno de los nombres a que se refiere.

33. La misma forma de verbo se usa cuando el sujeto de la frase (u oración) es **usted** que cuando el sujeto es un nombre en singular. Esta regla conviene a todos los verbos.

LESSON IV
(Lección Cuarta[1])

34. Position of Adjectives. — 1. In Spanish, descriptive adjectives usually follow their noun.

Una lección fácil.	An easy lesson.
Un ejercicio difícil.	A difficult exercise.

2. Limiting adjectives (articles, possessives, demonstratives, numerals, etc.) usually precede their noun.

Un libro, muchos libros.	A book, many books.

35. Inflection of Adjectives. — 1. An adjective that ends in **-o** in the masculine singular has four forms, thus:

	SINGULAR	PLURAL	
Masculine	**rojo**	**rojos**	red
Feminine	**roja**	**rojas**	

El libro rojo.	The red book.
La casa roja.	The red house.
Los libros rojos.	The red books.
Las casas rojas.	The red houses.

2. Other adjectives have, as a rule, only two forms of the ending, one for the singular and one for the plural.

[1] In titles a numeral often follows its noun, as here, but usually one would say **la cuarta lección.**

	Singular	Plural	
Masculine and feminine {	inteligente	inteligentes	intelligent
	fácil	fáciles	easy

El alumno inteligente.   The intelligent student, *m.*
La alumna inteligente.   The intelligent student, *f.*
Los alumnos inteligentes.   The intelligent students, *m.*
Las alumnas inteligentes.   The intelligent students, *f.*

     El ejercicio fácil.   The easy exercise.
     La lección fácil.   The easy lesson.
     Los ejercicios fáciles.   The easy exercises.
     Las lecciones fáciles.   The easy lessons.

36. The plural of adjectives is formed like that of nouns.

37. Agreement of Adjectives. — An adjective, no matter where it stands in the sentence, agrees with its noun or pronoun in gender and number.

EXERCISES

aplicado, –a, industrious, diligent   mucho, *adv.*, much, a great
blanco, –a, white   deal
la casa, the house   muy, very
difícil, difficult   negro, –a, black
fácil, easy   rojo, –a, red
mucho, –a, much   también, also, too
muchos, –as, many   todo, –a, all

    es, is; son, are; es aplicado, (he) is a hard worker

A. 1. Yo tengo tinta negra y una pluma. 2. ¿Tiene usted papel blanco también? 3. Sí, señor (señora *o* señorita); yo escribo los ejercicios en papel blanco. 4. ¿Son difíciles los ejercicios? [1] 5. Sí, señor; toda la lección es muy difícil. 6. ¿Escribe el alumno muchos ejercicios en la pizarra? 7. El alumno escribe todos los ejercicios en la pizarra.

[1] Note that a single predicate adjective usually precedes a noun subject in an interrogative sentence. But in D. 7, the two predicate adjectives may well follow the noun.

8. ¿Es aplicado el alumno (o aplicada la alumna)? 9. Sí, señor; el alumno (o la alumna) estudia mucho todas las lecciones. 10. Los alumnos son todos muy aplicados. 11. ¿Tiene usted muchas casas? 12. Yo tengo una casa roja y una blanca (a white one) también.

B. *Contéstese afirmativamente a las siguientes preguntas.* 1. ¿Tiene usted papel blanco? 2. ¿Tiene usted tinta negra? 3. ¿Tiene usted muchos libros rojos? 4. ¿Tiene usted lecciones muy difíciles? 5. ¿Tiene usted una casa roja? 6. ¿Tiene usted una blanca también? 7. ¿Estudia mucho el alumno? 8. ¿Escribe el alumno muchos ejercicios? 9. ¿Es fácil la lección? 10. ¿Son fáciles los ejercicios? 11. ¿Es aplicado el alumno? 12. ¿Son aplicados todos los alumnos?

C. *Tradúzcase y repítase después en plural.* 1. The lesson is difficult. 2. The exercise is easy. 3. The student (m.) is [a] hard worker. 4. The student (f.) is [a] hard worker. 5. The book is red. 6. The house is white. 7. The pencil is black.

Tradúzcase y repítase después en forma interrogativa. 8. The lessons are difficult (*véase* A. 4). 9. The student studies a great deal (*véase* B. 7). 10. The student writes many exercises. 11. All the students are hard workers. 12. The teacher teaches many lessons.

D. *Escríbase.* 1. Do you study the lessons a great deal? (*véase* A. 9). 2. I study all the lessons and write all the exercises. 3. Are the lessons difficult? 4. Many exercises are very difficult. 5. Do you write the exercises with [a] pencil? 6. I write all the exercises with pen and ink. 7. Is the ink black? 8. The ink is black and the paper is white. 9. All the students are very hard workers. 10. The teacher teaches many lessons. 11. Have you a white house? 12. I have a white house and a red one (*véase* A. 12) too.

RESUMEN GRAMATICAL

34. Colocación de los adjetivos. — 1. En español, por regla general, los adjetivos descriptivos (o calificativos) siguen al nombre.

2. Los adjetivos determinantes (artículos, adjetivos posesivos, demostrativos, numerales, etc.), por regla general, preceden al nombre.

35. Inflexión de los adjetivos. — 1. El adjetivo masculino singular que termina en –o tiene cuatro formas: –o, –a, –os, –as.

2. Los demás adjetivos solamente tienen, por regla general, dos formas, una para el singular y otra para el plural.

36. El plural de los adjetivos se forma del mismo modo que el de los nombres.

37. Concordancia de los adjetivos. — El adjetivo, cualquiera que sea el lugar que ocupe en la frase, concuerda en género y número con el nombre o pronombre a que se refiere.

LESSON V

(Lección Quinta)

38. Agreement of Adjectives. — 1. An adjective that modifies two or more masculine nouns or pronouns is in the masculine plural.

El papel y el sobre son blancos.   The paper and the envelope are white.

2. An adjective that modifies two or more feminine nouns or pronouns is in the feminine plural.

La casa y la escuela son blancas.   The house and the school are white.

3. An adjective that modifies both a masculine and a feminine noun or pronoun is usually in the masculine plural.

La tiza y el papel son blancos.   The chalk and the paper are white.

39. Similarly a noun or pronoun in the masculine plural may refer to both men and women.

    Los profesores   The teachers (*men and women*)
    Los alumnos   The students (*boys and girls*)

40. Negative Sentences. — In negative sentences, **no,** *not*, is placed before the verb.

    Usted no estudia.   You do not study.
    ¿No estudia usted?   Do you not study?

EXERCISES

la **carta**,[1] letter	**inglés**, English
la **clase**, class	**no**, no, not
la **dirección**, address	**o**, or
la **escuela**, school	¿**qué**? what?
español, Spanish	el **sobre**, envelope

hay, there is, there are; **no hay**, there is not, there are not

A. 1. ¿Qué estudia usted en el libro? 2. Yo estudio lecciones y ejercicios muy difíciles. 3. ¿Es usted (*véase* § 33) muy aplicado?[2] 4. No, señor; yo no estudio mucho las lecciones. 5. ¿Hay muchos alumnos en la escuela? 6. Sí, señor; hay muchos alumnos y muchos profesores en la escuela. 7. ¿Son muy aplicados todos los alumnos? 8. No, señor; los alumnos no son todos muy aplicados. 9. ¿Escribe el alumno (*o la alumna*) muchas cartas en inglés y en español? 10. El alumno (*o la alumna*) no escribe muchas cartas en español. 11. Escribe (*He, o She, writes*) la carta y la dirección con pluma y tinta. 12. La tinta y el lápiz son negros: el papel y el sobre son blancos.

B. *Contéstese negativamente a las siguientes preguntas.* 1. ¿Escribe usted cartas con lápiz? (*Respuesta:* No, señor; yo no escribo cartas con lápiz.) 2. ¿Escribe usted cartas en papel rojo? 3. ¿Escribe el alumno muchas cartas en español? 4. ¿Son fáciles las lecciones y los ejercicios? 5. ¿Son aplicados todos los alumnos? 6. ¿Hay muchos profesores en la clase?

Contéstese según el sentido. 7. ¿En qué escribe usted la carta? 8. ¿En qué escribe usted la dirección? 9. ¿Con qué escribe usted la carta y la dirección? 10. ¿Con qué escribo yo en la pizarra? 11. ¿Son blancos o negros el papel y el sobre? 12. ¿Son blancas o negras la pizarra y la tinta?

---

[1] Hereafter the English definite article will be omitted from the special vocabularies.

[2] In addressing a woman, one would say: ¿**Es usted muy aplicada?**

C. 1. The chalk is white. 2. The paper is white. 3. The chalk and the paper are white. 4. The ink is black. 5. The pencil is black. 6. The ink and the pencil are black.

Tradúzcase y repítase después negativamente. 7. The lesson is easy. 8. The exercise is easy. 9. The lesson and the exercise are easy. 10. The student (*m.*) is [a] hard worker. 11. The student (*f.*) is [a] hard worker. 12. The students are hard workers.

D. *Escríbase.* 1. Are the paper and the ink white or black? (*véase* B. 11). 2. The paper is white and the ink is black. 3. Are not the pencil and the chalk white? [1] 4. The chalk is white; the pencil is black. 5. Does not the teacher teach many lessons? 6. Are the lessons easy or difficult? [1] 7. The exercises are not very difficult. 8. Does the student write many letters? 9. [He] writes many letters in English: [he] does not write letters in Spanish. 10. I write letters in English and in Spanish too. 11. What does the student write on the envelope? 12. [He] writes the address with pen and ink.

RESUMEN GRAMATICAL

38. Concordancia de los adjetivos. — 1. Un adjetivo que modifica a dos o más nombres o pronombres masculinos debe ponerse en masculino plural.

2. Un adjetivo que modifica a dos o más nombres o pronombres femeninos debe ponerse en femenino plural.

3. Un adjetivo que modifica a la vez a dos nombres o pronombres, uno masculino y otro femenino, debe ponerse, por regla general, en masculino plural.

39. Igualmente un nombre en masculino y número plural puede referirse a hombres y mujeres.

40. Frases negativas. — En las frases (u oraciones) negativas el adverbio de negación **no** se coloca delante del verbo.

---

[1] See the footnote to IV, Exercises, A, 4.

LESSON VI
(Lección Sexta)

41. Present Indicative of Tener, *to have*.

SINGULAR	PLURAL
yo tengo, I have	nosotros / nosotras } tenemos, we have
tú tienes, thou hast	vosotros / vosotras } tenéis, ye have
usted tiene, you have	ustedes tienen, you have
él / ella } tiene, he / she } has	ellos / ellas } tienen, they have

42. Pronouns. — 1. **Tú,** *thou,* is used in familiar speech, as between the members of a family or between intimate friends and when speaking to small children and animals (the dog, the horse, etc.). It is also used in poetry and in prayers to the Deity. The plural of **tú** is **vosotros, –as.**

2. **Usted,** *you,* is required in more formal speech. In addressing a stranger or mere acquaintance, **usted** must be used. The plural of **usted** is **ustedes.**

Usted is used with the third person singular of the verb, and **ustedes** with the third person plural.

Usted and **ustedes** are abbreviated to **Vd.** and **Vds.**, and also to **Ud.** and **Uds.** or **V.** and **VV.**

3. **Nosotros, –as,** *we,* **vosotros, –as,** *ye,* and **ellos, –as,** *they,* have both masculine and feminine forms. **Nosotros, –as** is the plural of **yo, ellos** is the plural of **él,** and **ellas** is the plural of **ella.**

Él, *he,* is distinguished by the accent mark from **el,** *the.*

43. Tener que means *to have to, must.*

Yo tengo que estudiar.	I have to, *or* I must, study.
¿Tiene Vd. una lección que estudiar?	Have you a lesson to study?

44.   Some Infinitives

enseñar, to teach   **escribir,** to write
estudiar, to study

EXERCISES

alto, –a, high   **para,** for, in order to (*with an*
ancho, –a, wide, broad   *infinitive*)
el **asiento,** seat   la **clase,** classroom[2]
la **mesa,** table, desk[1]   la **silla,** chair
                       la **ventana,** window

A. *Continúese, usando como sujetos de los verbos todos los pronombres personales, tanto masculinos como femeninos en el número plural. Si lo prefiere el profesor,* **tú** *y* **vosotros, –as,** *y las formas correspondientes de los verbos pueden omitirse por ahora.* 1. Yo tengo muchos libros (tú tienes muchos libros), usted tiene . . ., él tiene . . ., *etc.* 2. Yo tengo que estudiar mucho. 3. Yo tengo que escribir cartas. 4. Yo tengo ejercicios que escribir.

B. 1. La clase tiene ventanas anchas y altas. 2. Hay muchos asientos. 3. Hay también una mesa (un escritorio) para el profesor (*o* la profesora). 4. Todos los alumnos tienen asientos. 5. Los profesores tienen sillas y mesas. 6. ¿Qué tienen que estudiar los alumnos? 7. Los alumnos tienen que estudiar las lecciones y escribir los ejercicios. 8. Tienen (*They have*) libros para estudiar las lecciones. 9. Tienen papel para escribir los ejercicios. 10. Los profesores tienen muchas lecciones que enseñar. 11. Yo tengo papel para escribir una carta. 12. ¿Tiene Vd. un sobre para la carta?

C. *Contéstese afirmativamente.* 1. ¿Tienen Vds. libros para estudiar la lección? 2. ¿Tienen Vds. papel para escribir los ejercicios? 3. ¿Tienen Vds. pluma y tinta para escribir? 4. ¿Tienen Vds. cartas que escribir? 5. ¿Tienen Vds. sobres

[1] If the teacher's desk resembles a table, it is called **la mesa del profesor**; if it is a writing desk, it is more properly called **el escritorio.**

[2] A lecture room in a university is called **sala de conferencias** or **aula.**

para las cartas? 6. ¿Tienen Vds. tiza para escribir en
la pizarra? 7. ¿Tiene la clase ventanas altas y anchas?
8. ¿Tienen asientos los alumnos? 9. ¿Tiene una mesa el
profesor (o la profesora)? 10. ¿Tienen que estudiar mucho
los alumnos? 11. ¿Tienen los alumnos muchos ejercicios
que escribir? 12. ¿Tiene el profesor muchas lecciones que
enseñar?

D. *Tradúzcase, y repítase después en plural omitiendo los artículos
indeterminados. En este ejercicio y en los siguientes tradúzcase* you
por usted *o* ustedes, *a menos que se indiquen* tú *y* vosotros, -as.
1. I have a broad desk. (**Yo tengo una mesa ancha. Nosotros
tenemos mesas anchas.**) 2. I must (*or* have to) study a lesson.
3. You have a difficult exercise. 4. You have a lesson to study.
5. You have a letter to write. 6. You must write with [a] pen.
7. He has an exercise to write. 8. He must write a letter too.
9. She hasn't a book. 10. She hasn't a chair.

E. *Escríbase.* 1. We have to study and to write a great deal.
2. We have lessons to study and exercises to write. 3. We
must (*or* have to) write the exercises in Spanish. 4. Have you
also letters to write in Spanish? 5. Yes, sir (*or* madam); we have
many letters to write in Spanish and in English too. 6. The
students in the classroom have seats. 7. The teacher has a chair
and a broad desk. 8. [He] writes (**Escribe**) many letters on
the desk. 9. In the classroom all the windows are wide and
high. 10. What must the students write on the blackboard?
11. They have to write all the exercises in Spanish. 12. They
must study much in order to write the exercises.

RESUMEN GRAMATICAL

41. Presente de indicativo del verbo *tener* (primera persona,
segunda persona, tercera persona del singular, etc.).

42. Pronombres. — 1. El pronombre **tú** se usa en la conversación
familiar, entre los diferentes miembros de una familia, entre amigos
íntimos, y cuando se dirige uno a niños pequeños y a los animales
(el perro, el caballo, etc.). También se usa en la poesía y en las
oraciones a la Divinidad. El plural de **tú** es **vosotros, -as.**

2. El pronombre **usted** es de rigor en la conversación formal. Cuando habla uno con un extraño o simple conocido debe emplear **usted**. El plural de **usted** es **ustedes**.

Usted se usa con la tercera persona del singular del verbo y **ustedes** con la tercera persona del plural.

Usted y **ustedes** se abrevian **Vd.** y **Vds.**, y también **Ud.** y **Uds.**, o **V.** y **VV.**

3. **Nosotros**, plural de **yo**, **vosotros**, plural de **tú**, y **ellos**, plural de **él**, tienen las formas femeninas **nosotras**, **vosotras** y **ellas**.

El pronombre **él** se distingue del artículo **el** por el acento escrito.

43. **Tener que** significa *to have to, must.*

44. Algunos infinitivos: . . .

LESSON VII

(Lección Séptima)

45. Genitive Case.[1] — Possession is denoted by the preposition **de**, *of.*

El libro de Juan   John's book.

Spanish nouns have one form for the singular and one for the plural; they have no ending that corresponds to the English 's.

46. De + el is contracted to **del**; but **de la, de los,** and **de las** are not contracted.

Los libros del alumno.   The student's books.
Los libros de los alumnos.   The students' books.

47. Present Indicative of Ser, *to be.*

SINGULAR

yo soy, I am

tú eres, thou art

usted es, you are

él } es, he } is
ella }   she } is

PLURAL

nosotros } somos, we are
nosotras }

vosotros } sois, ye are
vosotras }

ustedes son, you are

ellos } son, they are
ellas }

[1] Or Possessive Case.

CAMINO MILITAR ENTRE SAN JUAN Y PONCE, PUERTO RICO
An old military road in Porto Rico, built by the Spaniards.

Escuela Presidente Roca
A public school building in Buenos Aires.

EXERCISES

ahora, now
la aritmética, arithmetic
la geografía, geography
la gramática, grammar
Juan, John
la lectura, reading
María, Mary

la ortografía, spelling, orthography
perezoso, -a, lazy [1]
pero, but
poco, -a, little
pocos, -as, few
poco, adv., little

clase [2] de español, Spanish class; ejercicio de español, Spanish exercise; lección de gramática, grammar lesson or lesson in grammar; libro de lectura, reader.

A. *Continúese.* 1. Yo soy aplicado.[3] 2. Yo no soy perezoso. 3. Yo no soy el profesor. 4. Yo tengo que estudiar ahora.

B. 1. ¿Tiene Vd. el libro de lectura de Juan? 2. No, señor (o señora); yo tengo el libro de María. 3. Juan y María son alumnos de la escuela. 4. ¿Son ellos aplicados o perezosos? 5. Juan es un poco perezoso, pero María es aplicada. 6. Juan tiene pocos libros, pero María tiene muchos. 7. Juan, ¿qué estudia Vd. ahora? 8. Yo estudio la lección de ortografía. 9. ¿Es la lección fácil o difícil? 10. Es (*It is*) fácil, pero la lección de aritmética es muy difícil. 11. María, ¿es difícil la lección de geografía? 12. Sí, señor; es difícil, y la lección de gramática es difícil también.

C. *Contéstese afirmativamente.* 1. ¿Tiene Juan el libro de María? 2. ¿Estudia él la lección de español? 3. ¿Es fácil la lección de español? 4. ¿Tiene María el libro de Juan? 5. ¿Estudia ella la lección de gramática? 6. ¿Es difícil

[1] Some teachers would call *a lazy student* un alumno flojo. When thus used, flojo is a harsher term than perezoso.

[2] Note that clase means both *class* and *classroom*.

[3] If there are young women in the class, they should early form the habit of using the feminine form of a predicate adjective or noun with yo soy, as well as the feminine form of the personal pronoun, first person plural, thus: yo soy aplicada, nosotras somos aplicadas.

la lección de gramática? 7. ¿Hay muchos alumnos en la escuela? 8. ¿Son aplicados todos los alumnos? 9. ¿Son Vds. alumnos de la escuela? 10. ¿Tienen Vds. muchos libros? 11. ¿Tienen Vds. libros de lectura? 12. ¿Tienen Vds. ejercicios que escribir?

D. *Tradúzcase, y repítase después en plural.* 1. She is not [a] hard worker. (**Ella no es aplicada. Ellas no son aplicadas.**) 2. He is very lazy. 3. I have the student's book. 4. I have a reader. 5. I have to study the lesson. 6. You are the teacher. 7. Is the grammar lesson easy? 8. Is the Spanish exercise difficult?

E. *Escríbase.* 1. John has the teacher's book and is writing (**escribe**) the exercise. 2. John, is the Spanish lesson difficult? 3. The exercise is easy, but the grammar lesson is very difficult. 4. Mary, what are you studying (**¿qué estudia Vd.**) now? 5. I am studying (**Yo estudio**) the lessons in arithmetic and geography. 6. Have you (*pl.*) many books in English and in Spanish? 7. We have many books in English, but [we] have few books in Spanish. 8. Are the students industrious (**aplicados**) or lazy? 9. Few are lazy; many are industrious. 10. All the students in the Spanish class are hard workers. 11. We have difficult lessons and exercises to study. 12. [We] must study a great deal in order to write the Spanish exercises.

RESUMEN GRAMATICAL

45. Caso genitivo. — La idea de posesión se expresa mediante la preposición **de.**

Los nombres en español tienen una terminación para el singular y otra para el plural; carecen de una terminación análoga a la inglesa *'s.*

46. La preposición **de** y el artículo **el** se contraen en la forma **del,** pero **de la, de los,** y **de las** no se contraen.

LESSON VIII
(Lección Octava)

48. The Regular Conjugations. — Spanish verbs are divided into three conjugations, according to the infinitive endings −ar, −er, −ir:

I	II	III
Hablar, *to speak*	**Aprender,** *to learn*	**Vivir,** *to live*

Like these are inflected all regular verbs with corresponding infinitive endings.

49. The inflectional endings of the Present Indicative are:

I: −o, −as, −a, −amos, −áis, −an
II: −o, −es, −e, −emos, −éis, −en
III: −o, −es, −e, −imos, −ís, −en

50.

Present Indicative
Hablar, *to speak*

SINGULAR

habl-o, I speak, do speak, am speaking
habl-as, thou speakest, dost speak, art speaking
habl-a { you speak, do speak, are speaking
{ he, she *or* it speaks, does speak, is speaking

PLURAL

habl-amos, we speak, do speak, are speaking
habl-áis, ye speak, do speak, are speaking
habl-an, you *or* they speak, do speak, are speaking

Aprender, *to learn*		Vivir, *to live*	
I learn, do learn, am learning; etc.		*I live, do live, am living;* etc.	
SINGULAR	PLURAL	SINGULAR	PLURAL
aprend-o	aprend-emos	viv-o	viv-imos
aprend-es	aprend-éis	viv-es	viv-ís
aprend-e	aprend-en	viv-e	viv-en

a. Each of the verb forms given above may be translated in either one of three ways, thus: **aprendo,** *I learn, I do learn,* or *I am learning.* But **no aprendo** is usually to be translated in only two ways: *I do not learn* or *I am not learning.*

b. Note the accent on the ending of the second person plural in the present indicative of all three conjugations (**habláis, aprendéis, vivís**).

51. Omission of the Subject Personal Pronoun. — In Spanish the subject pronoun is usually omitted.

tengo, I have   **aprendemos,** we learn

a. Sometimes the subject pronoun is needed for emphasis or to make the meaning clear.

Él estudia, pero ella no estudia.   He studies, but she does not study.

b. It is usually more polite to express **usted** or **ustedes,** but this pronoun need not be repeated within a sentence.

EXERCISES

el **borrador,**[1] eraser	la **falta,** mistake
borrar, to erase	**pasar,** to pass, go (*to the*
correctamente, correctly	*blackboard*)
el **cuaderno,** notebook, exercise book	**señalar,** to point out, call attention to
la **dificultad,** difficulty	**si,** if
entonces, then	**subrayar,** to underline
explicar, to explain	

A. *Continúese, usando primero los pronombres sujetos de los verbos, y repitiendo después las mismas frases sin los pronombres.* 1. (Yo) señalo las faltas. 2. (Yo) aprendo la lección. 3. (Yo) no escribo correctamente. 4. (Yo) hablo español.

B. 1. Escribimos los ejercicios de español en los cuadernos. 2. Si escribimos correctamente, no hay faltas. 3. Pero si no escribimos correctamente, el profesor subraya las faltas con tinta roja. 4. En la clase de español pasamos a la pizarra. 5. Escribimos todo el ejercicio en la pizarra con tiza. 6. El profesor señala todas las faltas. 7. También explica todas las dificultades. 8. Entonces borramos el ejercicio con el borrador. 9. Los alumnos tienen que estudiar mucho para aprender las lecciones. 10. También estudian mucho para escribir correctamente los ejercicios. 11. ¿Es (*Is it*) difícil escribir correctamente un ejercicio de español? 12. Sí, señor; es muy difícil; pero el profesor explica las dificultades.

---

[1] Also called **cepillo.**

C. *Contéstese afirmativamente, omitiendo los pronombres sujetos de los verbos.* 1. ¿Escribe Vd. el ejercicio en un cuaderno? 2. ¿Escribe Vd. con tinta negra? 3. ¿Señala las faltas el profesor? 4. ¿Subraya las faltas con tinta roja? 5. ¿Explica todas las dificultades? 6. ¿Pasan Vds. a la pizarra? 7. ¿Escriben Vds. el ejercicio en la pizarra? 8. ¿Escriben Vds. con tiza? 9. ¿Borran Vds. el ejercicio con el borrador? 10. ¿Aprenden Vds. todas las lecciones? 11. ¿Escriben Vds. todos los ejercicios? 12. ¿Es difícil escribir correctamente los ejercicios?

D. *Tradúzcase, y repítase después usando las formas plurales de los sujetos y de los verbos.* 1. I live in a white house. 2. [I] study a great deal. 3. You learn the Spanish lesson. 4. You write the exercises. 5. He points out the mistakes. 6. She explains the difficulties. 7. You go to the blackboard. 8. You erase with the eraser. 9. The student writes the exercises. 10. The teacher calls attention to the mistakes.

E. *Escríbase.* 1. We do not speak Spanish, but we are learning to (a) speak. 2. If we study much, we learn much. 3. We write all the exercises in exercise books. 4. The teacher points out the mistakes and explains the difficulties. 5. He underlines all the mistakes with red ink. 6. [It] is very difficult to write correctly all the exercises. 7. Do you (*pl.*) go to the blackboard in order to write the exercises? 8. Yes, sir; we write with chalk and erase with the eraser. 9. The industrious (**aplicados**) students study much: the lazy [ones] study little. 10. All must study a great deal in order to learn the lessons. 11. There are many difficulties in Spanish. 12. But there are also many difficulties in English.

RESUMEN GRAMATICAL

48. Las conjugaciones regulares. — En español las conjugaciones de los verbos se dividen en tres, correspondiendo a las terminaciones del infinitivo, a saber: –ar, –er, –ir. Todos los verbos regulares se conjugan como **hablar, aprender,** o **vivir.**

49. Las terminaciones del presente de indicativo son: . . .

50. *a.* La forma verbal del presente de indicativo español corresponde a tres formas inglesas; por ejemplo, **aprendo** puede traducirse *I learn, I do learn* o *I am learning;* pero la forma negativa del mismo tiempo sólo equivale a dos formas inglesas, por ejemplo, **no aprendo** sólo puede traducirse por *I do not learn* o *I am not learning.*

b. Nótese el acento escrito que lleva la terminación de la segunda persona del plural del presente de indicativo en las tres conjugaciones: **habláis, aprendéis, vivís.**

51. Supresión del pronombre personal que sirve de sujeto. —En español se suprime, por regla general, el pronombre que sirve de sujeto al verbo.

a. Algunas veces se necesita el pronombre sujeto del verbo para dar mayor énfasis a la expresión o para darle mayor claridad.

b. La expresión resulta más correcta y cortés con el empleo del pronombre **usted** o **ustedes,** pero no es necesaria la repetición del pronombre en la frase.

LESSON IX

(Lección Novena)

52. Possessives

SINGULAR

mío, –a, –os, –as	or **mi, mis**	my (mine)
tuyo, –a, –os, –as	or **tu, tus**	thy (thine)
suyo, –a, –os, –as	or **su, sus**	your (yours), his, her (hers), its

PLURAL

nuestro, –a, –os, –as		our (ours)
vuestro, –a, –os, –as		your (yours)
suyo, –a, –os, –as	or **su, sus**	your (yours), their (theirs)

53. The short forms, **mi (mis), tu (tus), su (sus),** are used when they precede their nouns.

Mi madre. My mother. **Mis libros.** My books.
But, **¡Madre mía!** [1] My mother! **Los libros son míos.** The books are mine.

[1] An inverted exclamation point (**signo de admiración invertido**) is placed at the beginning of an exclamatory sentence.

54. Suyo (su) may mean *your, his, her, its,* or *their.*

¿Tiene Vd. sus libros?	Have you your books?
Juan tiene sus libros.	John has his books.
María tiene sus libros.	Mary has her books.
Juan y María tienen sus libros.	John and Mary have their books.

a. *Your (yours)* is often best expressed by **de usted.**

¿Es de Vd. este libro?   Is this book yours?

55. Agreement of Possessives. — Possessives agree in gender and number with the thing possessed, not with the possessor.

a. Possessive adjectives are usually repeated before each noun to which they refer.

Mi padre y mi madre.   My father and mother.

56. Interrogative *whose* is **de quién** or **de quiénes.**

¿De quién es el libro que Vd. tiene?   Whose book have you? (*lit.,* Whose is the book that you have?)

Note that the plural of **quién** is **quiénes.**

57.   Past Participles

    I. **Hablar:** **hablado,** spoken   III. **Vivir: vivido,** lived.
   II. **Aprender: aprendido,** learned

Like these are formed the past participles of all regular verbs.

a. **Escribir** has an irregular past participle: **escrito,** *written.*

58.   Present Perfect Indicative of Hablar

I have spoken; etc.

Singular	Plural
he hablado	hemos hablado
has hablado	habéis hablado
ha hablado	han hablado

Like **he hablado,** etc., is formed the present perfect indicative of all Spanish verbs.

34 FIRST SPANISH COURSE

EXERCISES

bien, well
hallar, to find
el hermano, brother; la hermana, sister
la madre, mother
la música, music
el padre, father; los padres, parents [1]
escuela municipal, municipal or city school;
trabajamos mucho, we work hard

el piano, piano
tocar, to play (a musical instrument)
todavía, yet
tomar, to take
trabajar, to work

A. *Continúese.* 1. Yo toco el piano. 2. Yo tengo mis libros (tú tienes tus libros, *etc.*). 3. Yo tengo mis plumas. 4. El piano es mío (tuyo, *etc.*). 5. La casa es mía. 6. He estudiado la lección. 7. He vivido en Chile.

B. 1. Tengo un hermano y una hermana. 2. Ellos son alumnos de una escuela municipal. 3. Estudian la gramática, la ortografía, la aritmética y la geografía.[2] 4. Mi hermana toca muy bien el piano. 5. Mi hermano no ha tomado lecciones de música. 6. Mis hermanos [1] toman lecciones de español. 7. Trabajan mucho, pero todavía no hablan español. 8. Hallan difíciles las lecciones de gramática. 9. Pero son aplicados y escriben todos los ejercicios. 10. Mi padre y mi madre (*o*, Mis padres) no hablan español. 11. Pero estudian todas las lecciones con mis hermanos.

C. *Contéstese.* 1. ¿Tiene Vd. su gramática? 2. ¿Tiene él su aritmética? 3. ¿Tiene ella su geografía? 4. ¿Tienen Vds. sus libros? 5. ¿Tienen ellos sus plumas? 6. ¿Tengo yo mi lápiz? 7. ¿Toca ella el piano? 8. ¿Ha tomado él [3] lecciones de música? 9. ¿Ha tomado Vd. lecciones de español? 10. ¿Han estudiado Vds. las lecciones? 11. ¿Trabajan Vds. mucho? 12. ¿Son Vds. aplicados? 13. ¿Es nuestra la casa? 14. ¿Son nuestros los libros? 15. ¿Es de

[1] See §39. [2] Note the use of the article.
[3] Note the position of the subject pronoun in **¿Ha tomado él?** etc. See §135.

Vd. el lápiz? 16. ¿Es de Vd. la pluma? 17. ¿De quién es el libro que Vd. tiene?

D. *Tradúzcase y repítase después en plural.* 1. The house is mine. (**La casa es mía. Las casas son mías.**) 2. My house is white. 3. The book is mine. 4. My book is red. 5. The pencil is yours. 6. Your pencil is black. 7. The pen is his. 8. I have his pen. 9. The letter is hers. 10. I have her letter. 11. Whose book have you? 12. Whose pen have I?

E. *Escríbase.* 1. Does your brother play the piano? 2. Yes, sir; but he does not play very well. 3. I have not (**Yo no he**) taken music lessons. 4. We are students in (**de**) a city school. 5. We take lessons in (**de**) grammar, arithmetic, geography, and Spanish.[1] 6. My brother and I have had to (**hemos tenido que**) work hard. 7. But our parents also work hard. 8. We do not speak Spanish yet. 9. Our parents have studied the lessons too. 10. But they do not speak Spanish yet. 11. I have your book. Whose book have you? 12. I have my sister's book, and I have written the exercise.

RESUMEN GRAMATICAL

52. Posesivos: . . .

53. Las formas apocopadas **mi** (**mis**), **tu** (**tus**), **su** (**sus**) se usan cuando preceden al nombre.

54. Suyo (**su**) puede significar *your, his, her, its,* o *their.*

a. Con frecuencia *your* (*yours*) se traduce más acertadamente por **de usted.**

55. Concordancia de los posesivos. — Los posesivos concuerdan en género y número con la cosa poseída y no con el poseedor.

a. Los adjetivos posesivos, por regla general, se repiten ante cada nombre a que se refieren.

57. Participios pasados (o pasivos). — Como **hablado, aprendido** y **vivido,** se forman los participios pasados (pasivos) de todos los verbos regulares.

a. **Escrito,** el participio pasado de **escribir,** es irregular.

58. El perfecto. — Como **he** (**has,** etc.) **hablado,** se conjuga el perfecto de indicativo de todos los verbos españoles.

[1] Do not use the article here after **de.**

LESSON X

(Lección Décima)

59.   Demonstrative Adjectives

este, –a, –os, –as, this, these

ese, –a, –os, –as
aquel, aquella, –os, –as } that, those

60. Ese usually denotes that which is near or which refers to the person addressed. **Aquel** denotes that which is more remote.

a. A demonstrative adjective is repeated before each noun to which it refers.

Este hombre y esta mujer.   This man and (this) woman.

61.   Demonstrative Pronouns

éste, –a, –os, –as, this (one), these   **esto,** this

ése, –a, –os, –as
aquél, aquélla, –os, –as } that (one), those   **eso**
aquello } that

62. Esto, eso, and **aquello** are neuter. They are used to denote a thing not mentioned by name or a mere idea. They can not represent a noun, since there are no neuter nouns in Spanish.

¿Qué es esto?   What is this?
¡Eso es!   That's it! That is right!

a. Note that the masculine and feminine demonstrative pronouns are distinguished by the accent mark from the demonstrative adjectives. The neuter demonstratives are never used as adjectives and therefore the neuter demonstrative pronouns do not need the accent mark.

63.   Cardinal Numerals

un(o), **–a,** one	**nueve,** nine
dos, two	**diez,** ten
tres, three	**once,** eleven
cuatro, four	**doce,** twelve
cinco, five	**trece,** thirteen
seis, six	**catorce,** fourteen
siete, seven	**quince,** fifteen
ocho, eight	**diez y seis,** sixteen

64. — 1. **Uno** loses the final **o** of the masculine singular when it precedes its noun.

2. **Un(o)**, **-a** has both a masculine and a feminine form, but the other numerals given above have only one form each for both genders.

Un lápiz.	One pencil.	**Una pluma.**	One pen.
Dos lápices.	Two pencils.	**Dos plumas.**	Two pens.

a. Note that **un lápiz** may mean either *one pencil* or *a pencil*, and **una pluma** may mean either *one pen* or *a pen*.

EXERCISES

el **abuelo**, grandfather; la **abuela**, grandmother; los **abuelos**, grandparents

anciano, **-a**, aged, old

fuerte, strong

el **hijo**, son; la **hija**, daughter; los **hijos**, children (= *sons and daughters*)

el **hombre**, man

leer, to read (*past part.*: **leído**)

mismo, **-a**, same

la **mujer**, woman

muy . . . para, too . . . to

que, *rel. pron.*,[1] who, which, that

rico, **-a**, rich

ya no viven, they are not living now

A. *Continúese.* 1. No he leído este libro. 2. No he vivido en aquella casa. 3. He aprendido la primera lección. 4. Hallo fácil esta lección. 5. He escrito muchas cartas.

B. 1. Este hombre y esta mujer viven en aquella casa blanca. 2. Tienen dos hijos, Juan y María. 3. Estos hijos tienen dos abuelos. 4. Los abuelos viven en la misma casa. 5. El abuelo es anciano, pero es un hombre muy fuerte. 6. La abuela también es anciana; no es una mujer fuerte. 7. Los abuelos no son ricos y han tenido que trabajar mucho. 8. Ahora son muy ancianos para trabajar mucho. 9. Juan, ¿qué lee Vd. en ese libro? 10. En este libro yo estudio la lección de español. 11. Hallo difícil la lección. 12. ¿Y qué estudia su hermana en aquel libro rojo? 13. Ella aprende la lección de aritmética. 14. También halla difícil la lección.

[1] Note that interrogative **qué** is distinguished by the accent from relative **que**.

C. *Contéstese.* 1. ¿Viven este hombre y esta mujer en aquella casa? 2. ¿Tienen ellos dos o tres hijos? 3. ¿Tienen dos abuelos Juan y María? 4. ¿Son ancianos los abuelos? 5. ¿Son ricos? 6. ¿Han tenido que trabajar mucho? 7. ¿Son muy ancianos para trabajar mucho? 8. ¿Es el abuelo un hombre fuerte? 9. ¿Es la abuela una mujer fuerte? 10. ¿Viven los abuelos en la misma casa? 11. ¿Qué lee Juan en aquel libro? 12. ¿Halla la lección fácil o difícil? 13. ¿Y qué estudia su hermana en el libro rojo? 14. ¿Halla difícil la lección de aritmética?

D. *Tradúzcase, y repítase después omitiendo los nombres y usando* **aquél** *por* that. 1. You have lived in that house. 2. I have read these letters. 3. We have written this exercise. 4. She has studied this lesson. 5. This student is [a] hard worker. 6. That student is lazy. 7. These men are rich. 8. Those women are not rich.

E. 1. Two, four, six, eight, ten. 2. One, three, five, seven, nine. 3. Fifteen, fourteen, thirteen, twelve, eleven. 4. Two and two are four. 5. Three and three are six. 6. Four and five are nine. 7. Five and ten are fifteen. 8. Six and seven are thirteen.

F. *Escríbase.* 1. Mary, what are you studying in that book? 2. I am reading the grammar lesson in this book. 3. What is John reading in that red book? 4. He is studying the first Spanish lesson. 5. Do your grandparents live with you (**Vds.**)? 6. Yes, sir; they live in the same white house. 7. Is your grandfather very old? 8. Yes, sir; he is old and he has worked hard. 9. He is too old to work much. 10. Our grandmother reads and writes a great deal. 11. Our father is the son of our grandparents. 12. The parents of our mother are not living now.

RESUMEN GRAMATICAL

59. Adjetivos demostrativos: . . .

60. El adjetivo demostrativo **ese** se refiere, por regla general, a la persona o cosa que está cerca de la persona a quien se habla. **Aquel** se refiere a la persona o cosa que está más distante.

a. El adjetivo demostrativo se repite, por regla general, delante de cada nombre a que se refiere.

61. Pronombres demostrativos: . . .

62. Esto, eso y **aquello** son neutros. Se usan para indicar una cosa que no se menciona por su nombre o una idea. No pueden representar nombres, puesto que no hay nombres neutros en español.

a. Nótese que los pronombres demostrativos masculinos y femeninos se distinguen de los adjetivos demostrativos por llevar el acento escrito. Los pronombres demostrativos neutros nunca se usan como adjetivos y en consecuencia no necesitan el acento.

63. Numerales cardinales: . . .

64. — 1. Uno pierde la –o final del masculino singular cuando precede al nombre.

2. **Uno** admite la forma femenina **una,** pero los demás adjetivos numerales citados sólo tienen una forma para ambos géneros.

a. **Un lápiz** puede traducirse *one pencil* o *a pencil* y **una pluma** puede traducirse *one pen* o *a pen.*

LESSON XI [1]

Radical-Changing Verbs

65. Many verbs of the three conjugations change the radical vowel e to **ie,** or the radical vowel o to **ue,** whenever the stress falls on the root.

Present Indicative

I. Cerrar, *to close*		Contar, *to count*	
SINGULAR	PLURAL	SINGULAR	PLURAL
cierro	cerramos	cuento	contamos
cierras	cerráis	cuentas	contáis
cierra	cierran	cuenta	cuentan

[1] In referring to the *lesson, exercise, page* (**página**), etc., either ordinal numerals or cardinal numerals may be used after **décimo,** *tenth,* but the cardinal numerals are more commonly used; thus: **la undécima lección** or, more commonly, **la lección once.** Observe that a cardinal numeral thus used follows its noun.

II. Entender, *to understand*		Volver, *to return*	
SINGULAR	PLURAL	SINGULAR	PLURAL
entiendo	entendemos	vuelvo	volvemos
entiendes	entendéis	vuelves	volvéis
entiende	entienden	vuelve	vuelven

III. Sentir, *to feel*		Dormir, *to sleep*	
SINGULAR	PLURAL	SINGULAR	PLURAL
siento	sentimos	duermo	dormimos
sientes	sentís	duermes	dormís
siente	sienten	duerme	duermen

66. Some verbs of the third conjugation change the radical vowel **e** to **i** whenever the stress falls on the root.

Pedir, *to ask, ask for*

SINGULAR	PLURAL
pido	pedimos
pides	pedís
pide	piden

a. Note that in the present indicative of radical-changing verbs the radical vowel does not change in the first and the second persons plural, since in these forms the stress falls on the inflectional ending and not on the root.

b. With the exception of the regularly recurring changes in the radical vowels, the radical-changing verbs are inflected like regular verbs.

c. There is no rule by which all radical-changing verbs can be recognized (but see §254). Whenever a verb is radical-changing, this fact will be indicated in the vocabularies, thus: **sentir (ie), pedir (i), dormir (ue).** See also the list of verbs in § 282.

EXERCISES

Ana, Anna
bajo, –a, low
el **baño,** bath, bathtub [1]

la **biblioteca,** library
la **cocina,** kitchen
el **comedor,** dining room

[1] *Bathtub* is also called **tina del baño** (as in Mexico) and sometimes **bañadera** (as in Argentina).

el **criado,** servant, *m.*; la **criada,** servant, *f.*

¿cuál, cuáles?, which?

don,[1] Mr.; **doña,** Mrs. (*used before given names only*)

el **dormitorio,** bedroom [2]

el **esposo,** husband; la **esposa,** wife

la **familia,** family

Fernando, Ferdinand

la **pieza,** room (*in general*)

el **piso,** story, floor

el **primo,** cousin, *m.*; la **prima,** cousin, *f.*

querer (ie),[3] to wish, want

la **sala,** drawing room

el **sobrino,** nephew; la **sobrina,** niece

el **tío,** uncle; la **tía,** aunt

cuarto de baño, bathroom; **piso alto,** upper story *or* floor; **piso bajo** ground floor

A. *Continúese.* 1. Aprendo la lección. 2. No entiendo la lección. 3. Toco el piano. 4. Cuento las sillas. 5. Pido una pluma. 6. He dormido poco.

B. 1. En la familia de mi tío Fernando hay cuatro personas. 2. Éstas son: don Fernando; doña Ana, su esposa; un hijo, Juan; y una hija, María. 3. Mis tíos (§ 39) tienen también una criada. 4. Viven en una casa de ocho piezas. 5. Éstas son la sala, la biblioteca, el comedor y la cocina en el piso bajo. 6. Y el cuarto de baño y tres dormitorios (alcobas) en el piso alto. 7. Todos duermen en el piso alto. 8. No quieren dormir en el piso bajo. 9. En la biblioteca hay muchos libros en inglés y en español. 10. Nuestro tío Fernando es hermano de nuestra madre. 11. Juan y María son nuestros primos. 12. Ellos son sobrinos de nuestros padres.

C. *Contéstese según el contexto de B.* 1. ¿Quiénes son don Fernando y doña Ana? (Don Fernando y doña Ana son nuestros tíos.) 2–3. ¿Quién es el hijo (¿Quién es la hija) de don Fernando y doña Ana? 4. ¿Tienen un criado o

---

[1] **Don** and **doña** are much used in Spanish as terms of respect when addressing or referring to a relative or friend. It is often best not to translate **don** or **doña** into English.

[2] A *bedroom* is also called **alcoba** (as often in Spain), or **recámara** (as in Mexico).

[3] Irregular in some tenses (see §271).

una criada? 5. ¿Viven en una casa de ocho piezas?
6. ¿Duermen todos en el piso alto? 7. ¿No quieren dormir
en el piso bajo? 8–9. ¿Cuáles son las piezas del piso bajo
(del piso alto)? 10. ¿Hay muchos libros en la biblioteca?
11. ¿Son Vds. sobrinos de don Fernando y doña Ana?
12. ¿Son Vds. primos de Juan y María?

D. *Tradúzcase y repítase después con* **ustedes** *como sujeto del*
verbo. 1. We close the window. (**Nosotros cerramos la ventana.**
Vds. cierran la ventana.) 2. We teach the lesson. 3. We ask for
chalk. 4. We learn the lesson. 5. We understand the lesson.
6. We erase the exercise. 7. We count the books. 8. We work
hard. 9. We sleep little. 10. We do not wish to study.

E. 1. My parents, my two brothers, and I live (**vivimos**) in a
white house. 2. [It] is a two-story house (**casa de dos pisos**).
3. [It] has four rooms on the ground floor and five on the upper
floor. 4. The rooms of the ground floor are the library, the drawing room, the dining room, and the kitchen. 5. On the upper floor
we have four bedrooms and a bathroom. 6. We sleep on the upper
floor. 7. We do not wish to sleep on the ground floor. 8. There
are five persons in our family. 9. We have one servant, but she
does not sleep in our house. 10. My brothers and I have (**tenemos**)
two cousins, John and Mary. 11. Their father Ferdinand is our
mother's brother. 12. I am [a] nephew of my uncle Ferdinand
and of my aunt Anna.

RESUMEN GRAMATICAL

65. Muchos verbos de las tres conjugaciones cambian la vocal
radical **e** en **ie,** o la **o** en **ue,** siempre que el acento prosódico recaiga
sobre la raíz.

66. Algunos verbos de la tercera conjugación cambian la vocal
radical **e** en **i,** siempre que el acento prosódico recaiga sobre la
raíz.

a. Obsérvese que en la primera y segunda persona del plural del
presente de indicativo la vocal radical no cambia, debido a que el acento
prosódico no recae sobre la raíz sino sobre la terminación.

La Ciudad de México

Mexico City, looking northeast from the Cathedral.

La Torre del Oro y la Catedral con la Giralda, Sevilla

An unusual view of Seville from the Guadalquivir River, showing the Golden Tower at the left, and the Cathedral with the famous Giralda Tower.

b. Con excepción de los cambios constantes en la vocal radical, estos verbos se conjugan lo mismo que los verbos regulares.

c. No hay regla absoluta para conocer los verbos que cambian su vocal radical. Siempre que un verbo sufra esta alteración, se indicará en los vocabularios del modo siguiente: **sentir (ie), pedir (i), dormir(ue).** Véase igualmente la lista de verbos en el§ 282.

LESSON XII

67. Dative Case.—The indirect object[1] requires the preposition **a,** *to.*

¿A quién da ella el libro?	To whom does she give the book?
Ella da el libro a Juan	{ She gives the book to John, *or* { She gives John the book.

Note that the preposition *to* may be omitted in English if the indirect object precedes the direct object. The Spanish preposition **a** cannot be thus omitted before a noun.

68. Accusative Case. — The direct object does not, as a rule, require a preposition, but the preposition **a** is required before the direct object, if the object is a proper noun, or any noun or pronoun[1] that denotes a definite person or personified thing.[2]

Busco mi libro.	I am looking for my book.
But: **Busco a mi padre.**	I am looking for my father.
Quiero ver a Madrid.	I wish to see Madrid.

a. The preposition **a** is sometimes placed before the direct object merely to distinguish the latter from the subject of the verb.

El adjetivo modifica al nombre.[3]	The adjective modifies the noun.
A la guerra sigue la paz.	Peace follows war.

[1] Except the relative pronoun **que** (dir. obj.), and a personal pronoun that is the object (dir. or indir.) of a verb and is placed immediately before or after it.

[2] Including intelligent animals such as a dog or horse.

[3] Since in Spanish the subject often follows the verb, the omission of **a** in this sentence might cause ambiguity.

44 FIRST SPANISH COURSE

b. The preposition **a** is usually omitted after **tener**; and **querer a** means *to be fond of, to like* (a person), and not *to wish* or *want*.

Vd. tiene dos primos.	You have two cousins.
¿Quiere Vd. a sus primos?	Do you like your cousins?

69. **A + el** is contracted to **al.**

Buscamos al profesor.	We are looking for the teacher.

70. The following adjectives lose the final −o of the masculine singular when they immediately precede their noun.

buen(o), −a, good	**un(o), −a,** one
mal(o), −a, bad	**algun(o), −a,** some[1]
primer(o), −a, first	**ningun(o), −a,** none
tercer(o), −a, third	

El tercer ejercicio.	The third exercise.
But: **El tercero.**	The third (one).

EXERCISES

el **amigo,** friend, *m.*; la **amiga,** friend, *f.*

el **aparador,** sideboard

buscar, to seek, look for

el **cuadro,** picture

eléctrico, −a, electric

la **luz** (*pl.*, **luces**), light

el **mes,** month

el **mueble,** piece of furniture; los **muebles,** furniture

pensar (ie), to think, intend

poder (ue),[2] can, to be able

recibir, to receive

el **sillón** (*pl.*, **sillones**), armchair

el **sofá,** sofa

visitar, to visit, call on

da, gives; **dado,** given

A. *Continúese.* 1. Busco mi libro. 2. Busco a mi padre. 3. Quiero papel. 4. Quiero mucho a mi madre. 5. No puedo cerrar la ventana.

B. 1. Mi tío Fernando es anciano, pero trabaja mucho. 2. Su esposa doña Ana no puede trabajar. 3. Ellos no son ricos, pero viven bien. 4. Los muebles de su sala son un piano, una mesa, un sofá, sillas y sillones, y muchos cuadros.

[1] **Algún** and **ningún** require the accent mark.

[2] Irregular in some tenses (§270).

5. Reciben a sus amigos en la sala. 6. En la biblioteca hay una mesa, un escritorio, dos sillas, algunos sillones y todos sus libros. 7. Mis tíos tienen muchos libros en inglés pero muy pocos en español. 8. En el comedor hay un aparador, una mesa, sillas y también algunos cuadros. 9. Tienen luz eléctrica en toda la casa. 10. Nosotros tenemos luz eléctrica en nuestra casa también. 11. Pienso visitar a mis tíos y pasar un mes con ellos (*them*). 12. Quiero mucho a mis primos Juan y María que son muy buenos.

C. *Contéstese según el contexto de B.* 1. ¿Es anciano don Fernando? 2. ¿Trabaja mucho don Fernando? 3. ¿Puede trabajar doña Ana? 4. ¿Son ricos los tíos? 5. ¿Viven bien los tíos? 6. ¿Cuáles son los muebles de su sala? 7. ¿Reciben a sus amigos en la sala? 8. ¿Cuáles son los muebles de la biblioteca? 9. ¿Tienen los tíos muchos libros en inglés? 10. ¿Tienen muchos libros en español? 11. ¿Cuáles son los muebles del comedor? 12. ¿Tienen los tíos luz eléctrica en toda la casa? 13. ¿Tienen Vds. también luz eléctrica en su casa? 14. ¿Piensan Vds. visitar a sus tíos? 15. ¿Quieren Vds. a sus primos?

D. *Tradúzcase y repítase después con los verbos en plural.* 1. I have looked for my books. (**He buscado mis libros. Hemos buscado nuestros libros.**) 2. I have looked for my parents. 3. I intend to visit Madrid. 4. I intend to visit my cousins. 5. Do you wish the book? 6. Do you like your uncle Ferdinand? 7. He wishes to speak Spanish. 8. He is writing the first exercise. 9. He is writing the first [one]. 10. Does the adjective modify the noun? 11. She receives many letters in Spanish. 12. She receives her friends in the drawing room. 13. Have you electric light in your house? 14. Have you many cousins? 15. Do you intend to spend a month with your uncle and aunt (§39)? 16. I have little furniture (= few pieces of furniture).

E. 1. In my parents' house there is electric light in all the rooms. 2. My uncle and aunt have electric light in their house

too. 3. We can read very well with the electric light in the library.
4. Our library has armchairs, a writing desk, and many good books.
5. The drawing room has many pictures and many chairs, a piano,
a sofa, and two tables. 6. My mother receives all her friends (*f*.)
in the drawing room. 7. My brothers and I receive (**recibimos**)
our friends in the library. 8. Our dining room has a table and
chairs, a sideboard, and some pictures. 9. We have little furniture, but it-is (**son**) good. 10. There is much furniture in my
uncle Ferdinand's house. 11. I intend to spend a month with
my cousins John and Mary. 12. My parents are very fond of
(**quieren mucho**) their nephew and niece (§39). 13. John and
Mary like my parents too. 14. My father has given my cousins
many good books.

RESUMEN GRAMATICAL

67. El complemento indirecto (caso dativo) requiere la preposición a (excepto delante de los pronombres me, te, etc.).

En inglés puede suprimirse la preposición *to* del complemento indirecto
si éste precede al complemento directo. En español no puede hacerse
esta supresión delante del nombre.

68. El complemento directo (caso acusativo), por regla general,
no requiere preposición. Pero se emplea la preposición a con el
complemento directo si éste es un nombre propio, o cualquier nombre
o pronombre (excepto que y me, te, etc.) que exprese una persona
determinada o cosa personificada.

a. Algunas veces la preposición a precede al complemento directo
solamente para distinguir a éste del sujeto del verbo.

b. La preposición a se suprime generalmente después del verbo
tener; y querer a significa *to be fond of, to like,* y no *to wish* o *want.*

69. La preposición a y el artículo el se contraen en la forma al.

70. Los siguientes adjetivos pierden la –o final del masculino singular cuando preceden inmediatamente al nombre que
califican: . . .

offer of goods and services more quickly, you may even be ready to give the telemarketer a piece of your mind for interrupting the evening's meal.

This example of the telephone ring is to begin our conversation about the first of the seven Taxi Terry tenets: *Set high expectations and then exceed them.*

I notice out of the corner of my eye that my cab is approaching. The driver halts his vehicle in front of me and then, much to my surprise, springs out of his cab, points his index finger in my direction, and practically shouts at me: "Are *you* ready for the *best* cab ride of your *life?*"

I've often thought about the first words Taxi Terry said to me and how they contrasted with what every other cab driver in the line that evening said to his or her customers upon pickup from the queue.

What do you imagine were the first words that the other taxi operators said to their soon-to-be passengers?

Here are a few of the opening lines I heard that evening from the other cab drivers:

- "How ya' doing tonight?"

- "Where you heading this evening?"

- "Ready to go?"

  (I really did hear that one. I wanted the traveler to whom the comment was directed to respond, "No. I haven't spent nearly enough time standing in line yet. Make a couple laps, then come back to get me." As the comedian Bill Engvall would say, "Here's your sign.")

- "You in a hurry?"

- "I don't take credit cards."

- "I can take four; any more than that, you'll need a second cab."

Now, stop for a moment and consider some of the opening lines you encounter at various establishments when you are the customer. Have you ever heard any of these?

- Can I help you?

- What brings you in today?

- Hi! How are you doing?

- Good morning/afternoon/evening (then nothing else).

- Hey, how's it going?

- Welcome to (name of business) (Again nothing else).

This list doesn't even contain the all-time absolutely worst opening of the bunch. That's the one you get when you enter a place of business and *absolutely nothing* is said to you at all.

The tenet of "set high expectations and then exceed them" suggests that the opening comment simultaneously initiates two highly valuable facets of the coming transaction for every customer:

1. It creates a first impression.

2. It sets the tone—or the expectation—for what the customer is about to encounter.

As we examine these two facets, consider how Taxi Terry's initial words to me established a foundation to achieve his goals of creating distinction for his business and developing a customer for life.

Creating a First Impression

Part of the challenge we encounter in creating Ultimate Customer Experiences stems from the fact that we have three terms that should have different definitions yet are traditionally used interchangeably. How many times have you heard about these topics?

1. Customer satisfaction

2. Customer service

3. Customer experience

My bet is that when you notice these terms being used, there is very little distinction made between them.

Until we understand these three are very dissimilar, especially when we examine them from the *customer's* point of view, it will be extraordinarily difficult to develop and execute the strategies necessary to create Ultimate Customer Experiences (UCEs). In other words, if we cannot define what we are doing, how in the world can we accomplish it?

As we proceed, you will learn how these are fundamentally different aspects of our relationship with the customer. Later in this book, you will learn the three distinct levels on which we interact with all of our customers and why that affects the critical difference between satisfaction, service, and experience.

However, let's begin at a pretty obvious place: the beginning. Consider this story:

While I was dining with my wife this past Valentine's Day, the waiter approached our table in the crowded restaurant. "I'm Jason; I'll be serving you tonight," he stated curtly. He was sweating profusely and scowling. "I'd better get your drink order now, because I'm really slammed. If you know what you want to eat, just go ahead and tell me that now, too."

Wow! That approach really enhanced the romantic atmosphere I was hoping to create.

The problem for Jason and his restaurant was that no matter what happened next, the experience of the evening was a bit soiled. We wanted to have a nice romantic Valentine's Day dinner, but instead our first impression is that it's going to be a challenging night with a difficult server.

Don't get me wrong. I'm sorry that Jason was slammed, but what did he expect on Valentine's Day evening? And did he really think his problems should be transmitted to the people in charge of the table's postmeal tipping decision? The problem is that Jason didn't stop to think about the importance of setting expectations and the power of first impressions.

As I am writing this, I am sitting on a United Airlines flight from Indianapolis to Denver. My shoes are shined, I'm wearing my best dark suit, and my shirt is pressed. I'm doing my best to create a professional and powerful image because when I arrive, I will be creating something very powerful: *an impression.*

My mother back home in tiny Crothersville, Indiana, isn't an expert when it comes to business, but neither the march of time nor advances in technology have made one of her parental clichés outmoded:

You never get a second chance to make a first impression.

However, it is not just first impressions that count. Every time you communicate with an internal or external customer, you're making an impression. Just about every office I've visited, plant I have been to, and team I have encountered has "that guy" who is grumpy in the morning or "that gal" who rolls her eyes whenever someone makes a statement. Each time they make that impression of being grumpy toward or dismissive of their internal customers, the respect and credibility they have is damaged a bit.

If that's the case, why do many professionals fail to understand its impact?

For example, human resources executives tell me—and my personal experience supports it—that during the interview process, prospective employees often kill their chances by focusing their communication on what *they want* from the job rather than what they can *contribute to the organization* where they are applying for a position.

Certainly, part of the interviewing process has to contain details about your experience and education. However, what every organization seeks in an interview is for you to display a passion for performance directed toward the company at which you seek employment. (Who would want to hire a future internal customer who cares only about himself or desires only to advance himself and not the team?)

GradView.com lists some pretty awful approaches taken by some interviewees[1]:

- Applicant stretched out on the floor to fill out the job application.

- Applicant brought her large dog to the interview.

- Applicant chewed bubble gum and constantly blew bubbles.

- Balding applicant abruptly excused himself and returned to the office a few minutes later, wearing a hairpiece.

- Applicant challenged the interviewer to arm wrestle.

- Applicant asked to see the interviewer's résumé to see if the personnel executive was qualified to interview him.

- Applicant announced she hadn't had lunch and proceeded to eat a hamburger and French fries during the interview.

- Applicant wore a jogging suit to interview for the position of financial vice president.

- Applicant said if he were hired, he would demonstrate his loyalty by having the corporate logo tattooed on his forearm.

- Applicant interrupted to phone his therapist for advice on answering specific interview questions.

- Applicant refused to get out of his chair until interviewer agreed to hire him. Interviewer had to call the police to have him removed.

- A telephone call came in for the job applicant. His side of the conversation went as follows: "Which company? When do I start? What's the salary?" When the interviewer said he assumed the applicant was not interested in completing the interview, he promptly responded, "I am as long as you'll pay me more." The interviewer did not hire him and later found out there was no other job offer; it was a scam to get a better offer.

- Applicant said he didn't really want to get a job, but the unemployment office needed proof he was looking for one.

These are funny lines, of course, but what do they have to do with customer experiences? The most terrifying aspect is that these people are working somewhere. What types of customer experiences do you suppose they are creating for the internal and external customers they encounter?

More important, however, is the lack of knowledge about how to create a positive professional impression. Let's face it: the impressions we create in our professional lives follow the same patterns as the impressions in our personal lives.

How do you create a positive impression? Center your thinking on these three points:

1. Everything matters.

2. Focus on the other.

3. Be your best self.

First, everything matters. The more important the impression is, the greater your focus should be on everything.

Legend has it that Henry Ford was interviewing a prospective executive over breakfast for a major management position with his rapidly growing company. When the candidate took the shaker and salted the eggs he had yet to taste, the cantankerous Ford said, "This interview is *over*."

When asked to explain by the stunned executive, Ford reportedly replied, "If you'll salt eggs you have yet to taste without knowing whether or not they need it, you'll spend my money without knowing whether or not the investment will bring results."

Thankfully, not every customer is as persnickety as Ford was as an interviewer, if the legend is accurate. However, for all of us evaluating an impression, everything—no matter how small—matters.

Second, focus on the other, as in the *other person:* from the internal customer to the blind date across the table.

If you center your communication on yourself, you run the risk of appearing vain, arrogant, or insecure. If you channel your strengths to have an impact on the other person's needs, wants, and concerns, you appear confident and the kind of person we all want as a colleague or customer or a companion for a social evening.

Third, be your best self. Usually, this is the point at which someone says that you should just be yourself. However, that's not what makes the best impression.

Being myself could include the self that smokes too many cigars at a local steakhouse or gets too rowdy at football games. My best self is the one who is attuned to the challenges and needs of others, who seeks to identify solutions rather than problems, and who projects strength through humility. I would suggest that that is your best self too.

Consider two short telephone inquiries and what the results each might generate could mean to your organization:

First example:

Receptionist: XYZ Rentals. How can I help you?

Customer: I need to rent a party tent.

Receptionist: Okay, what size tent?

Second example:

Receptionist: Thank you for calling XYZ Rentals. This is Shelley. How may I help you?

Customer: I need to rent a party tent.

Receptionist: Great. I will be happy to help you with that. May I get your name, please?

These differences are major, not minor. The positive impression and personal interest created by the simple effort taken by the receptionist in the second example can have a significant impact on the customer.

At Peterson's Restaurant in suburban Indianapolis, the hostess stand you see on first entering the establishment has a terrific sign. It says DIRECTOR OF FIRST IMPRESSIONS. I love that idea. It should be on the desk of every receptionist and on the minds of every sales professional and customer service agent in the country. It would serve to impress on all of us the importance of the impressions we are creating for customers every time we have a conversation with them.

Now, recall my encounter with Taxi Terry. The initial impression he created was *incredible*.

Taxi Terry set the stage for an Ultimate Customer Experience: "Are *you* ready for the *best* cab ride of your *life*?" he asked. If we surveyed your customers about the initial impression they had of you, what would their answers be? Are you a Taxi Terry or the grumpy guy or eye-rolling gal we mentioned earlier?

Had Taxi Terry had a bad day on the particular date I was riding in his cab? Honestly, I don't know. He made the trip all about *my* needs and wants, not his. Unlike Jason, the waiter from the restaurant example, Terry put his effort and focus on the other—*the customer*—instead of on himself.

My friend and a famed motivational speaker, the late Zig Ziglar, is often quoted as having said, "You can have everything in life that you want—if you just give enough other people what *they* want."

Jason the waiter wasn't too concerned about what we wanted. He was slammed and preferred to get our ordering and dining over with as quickly as possible to serve his need to turn the table and make more money. We never returned to that restaurant because of the terrible experience, for which the tone was firmly set by the first impression.

However, as another great motivational speaker, the late Jim Rohn, used to say, "That which is easy to do is also easy *not* to do. Which explains why most people won't do it!"

In other words, it's *easy* to answer the phone in the manner of the second example above. It is so easy, in fact, that many people fail to do it that way. It's almost too simple. It doesn't require the expenditure of any funds and costs only a tiny bit of effort and discipline, yet it makes such an extraordinary difference.

How many cab drivers could have said, "Are *you* ready for the *best* cab ride of your *life*?" The answer is, of course: all of them!

Yet until my encounter with Taxi Terry, how many had said that to me? None of them!

Naturally, you can do better, and the way to begin to create Ultimate Customer Experiences is to start with an ultimate first impression.

Setting the Level of Expectations

The second reason the initial comments made to a customer are so critical is that they set the tone—or the expectation—for what the customer is about to encounter.

The tenet clearly says "set high expectations," which implies that you have the ability to set or establish to a significant degree the level of eagerness that the customer will have about proceeding with his or her encounter with you and your organization.

It's a well-established fact that the expectations we have play a significant role in the outcomes that we create for ourselves and that we consciously and subconsciously encourage in others.

For example, *Fathering* magazine reported in its March 22, 2005, issue that the degree of involvement that the mother of a child expected the father to have in raising their offspring had a direct relationship to the time the man actually spent doing parental activities.[2]

A study from the insurance industry found that doctors were frequently dissatisfied clients of their insurance companies, most often because the insurance company had failed to set expectations for its customers and was unfamiliar with what its doctor-clients really expected. This meant that it was practically impossible for the insurance company to deliver a satisfactory level of service because its success would be measured by a standard of performance of which it was unaware.[3]

It's pretty hard to exceed the expectations of your customers if you haven't set those expectations or don't know what they are.

In an April 2005 article by Steven Phelan,[4] the *New England Journal of Entrepreneurship* went so far as to suggest that one of the primary purposes of business is the setting and managing of expectations for internal and external customers.

"Entrepreneurial profits flow from differences in expectations between buyers and sellers regarding the future value of resources," the article stated. In other words, the smart business—and the intelligent person working for that organization—creates the expectation that the customer will receive more in value than he or she invests in the cost of the product or service.

"Expectations management may be conceived as any attempt to change opinions about the value of a resource," the article continued.

This begs the question: What opinion do you suppose your customers and prospects had about your product or service before encountering you?

We each bring our own personal set of expectations to every business— and businessperson—we encounter. When I walk into a McDonald's, there is a level of service I anticipate that varies greatly from what I would expect if I were entering a Morton's Steakhouse. Arriving at the lobby of a Hilton, I bring a different set of expectations than I do striding up to check in at a Motel 6.

Often, we encourage the expectations we have to be satisfied both con-sciously and subconsciously. I don't intend to be shorter in conversation with the clerk at the fast-food restaurant than I am to the server at the steakhouse, yet I must admit that often I am. I shouldn't treat the check-in clerk at the budget hotel with less courtesy than the front desk manager at the resort, but perhaps I do.

This expectations phenomenon in which we encourage what we expect has long been labeled the Pygmalion effect, and you've probably heard of or read about it. This effect, in which we create a new result by changing our expectation of what the outcome will be, has been thoroughly researched, and its validity established.

The name is derived from a story historically ascribed to the Roman poet Ovid. "Pygmalion is a sculptor who falls in love with a statue he has created. George Bernard Shaw borrowed the theme for his play 'Pygmalion'—later turned into the musical 'My Fair Lady'—in which Professor Henry Higgins makes over the Cockney flower girl Eliza Doolittle, becoming besotted with her even as he teaches her how to speak proper English ('The rain in Spain stays mainly in the plain . . . ')."[5]

This suggests, for example, that if you want your kids to get better grades in school, you begin by clearly displaying to them that you know they already possess the intelligence and drive to do so instead of constantly telling them that if they don't get their homework done, everyone will think they are stupid.

"If people define situations as real, they are real in their consequences. Experiments have shown that students who believed that they were working with intelligent animals liked them better and found them more pleasant. They unknowingly communicated high expectations to them, as they sincerely believed in the distinction, though there was none. Better performance resulting from high expectations leads us to like someone more, the reverse being true for the low expectations," according to the *Indian Journal of Industrial Relations*.[6]

We know that "raising supervisory expectations regarding workplace productivity would help determine subordinate performance."[7] In other words, if your manager expected a higher level of performance from you, the chances are pretty good that you would deliver better results.

This does not mean that your supervisor should be domineering and increase the pressure to demand that you get more done; instead, it is a matter of confidence and belief that your capacity is higher than you currently assume that it is. We're not seeking to understand ultimatums; we're examining expectations.

The golem effect is the other side of the coin: it suggests that when we expect inferior results, people find a way to deliver them. *Golem* is a Hebrew word that implies an "idiot" or, as the Merriam-Webster dictionary states, is a synonym of the term *blockhead*.[8] Unfortunately, some blockheads fail to realize that if they set low expectations or negatively influence their internal customers, they are encouraging inferior results.

It's easy to understand that if I enter the budget hotel anticipating that its rooms are nothing more than a commodity and that I'll be treated like cattle, everything from the language I use with the front desk clerk, to my facial expressions, to my body language will express my low expectations.

In addition, if that front desk clerk fails to understand the critical principle we are discussing here and merely responds to my expressions rather than establishing a higher expectation for my visit, guess what happens next? Everything that will transpire will confirm the idea that I'm just cattle or a commodity, and it's practically impossible to deliver an Ultimate Customer Experience to someone who has chosen to feel like that.

Let's return to the waiting line for taxis at the Jacksonville airport. As I'm standing and waiting for my ride, what do you suppose my expectations are for the experience that I am about to have?

Here's a partial list:

- I hope the car is clean, but I'm not certain that it will be.

- I hope the cab driver speaks fluent English; however, I'm not convinced that will be the case.

- I hope the driver is friendly, but at this time of night and in light of my previous experiences, I have my doubts.

- I hope the driver doesn't take an inordinately long route and overcharge me, yet I've had exactly that happen before.

- I hope the line moves briskly and I can get this over with as quickly as possible.

Remember what the first group of cab drivers said in their impersonal and mechanical opening lines to customers?

- "How ya doing tonight?"

- "Where you heading this evening?"

- "Ready to go?"

Note that these initial statements from other taxi drivers not only created inferior first impressions but also served to *reinforce the low expectations* I anticipated of the experience I was about to have.

As a professional, it is important for you to take control and help the customer set a higher level of expectation because the customer's take on the situation frequently is completely wrong.

For example, in today's world of instant gratification, it often seems it has reached the point where it's no longer "what have you done for me lately?" but "what are you doing for me *now*?" Perhaps there is no better example of this phenomenon than the field of sports, in which fans—the customers of the team—commonly have such a strong desire for victory that their expectations become so lofty as to be unreasonable.

I'm reminded of the coach who was brought to a premier college sports program to win a championship. After *13* years on the job, his best result was third place in a regional tournament. In the three subsequent years, his record was 16–10, 16–9, and 14–12. Not losing seasons, obviously, but his results were not exactly setting the world on fire. Many of the alumni wanted him ousted; remember, they had championship aspirations for their team, and after 15 years, this guy had won exactly zero titles.

Would you have believed this record over a decade and a half was all the evidence you'd need to prove this guy would *never* meet the championship expectations of his employer? Would you have pulled the trigger and moved in another direction? Taken a chance on a flashier leader? Believed more in your expectations than in the coach's ability?

If so, you've just fired John Wooden from UCLA.

Over the next 12 years, Wooden won *10* NCAA championships, a record that will probably never be equaled. During those dozen years, his teams lost a total of 22 contests while winning *335* games!

My point is this: just as the expectations of many of the alumni of UCLA were incorrect regarding the ultimate performance of John Wooden, many of the external and internal customers you encounter will erroneously assume that the probability of your delivering something extraordinary to them is slight.

Your job is to do for them exactly what John Wooden did to those who criticized him earlier in his career: prove them wrong.

Taxi Terry arrives in front of me. He is about to prove that what I have believed about taxicabs and their drivers is incorrect, at least when it comes to *his* business. Terry initiates my experience with that extraordinary phrase: "Are *you* ready for the *best* cab ride of your *life*?"

Consider this: the statement works for Terry on several levels, not the least of which are these three:

1. It is possible to have the best cab ride of your life.

2. It implies that Taxi Terry is the one who is able to provide it.

3. It is about to happen right now . . . to *me*.

Now, that's setting up a positive expectation. (He's a Pygmalion, not a golem.)

You should examine carefully and think thoroughly about the initial impression and expectation-setting ritual when a customer first approaches you or your business. Yes, *ritual* is the correct word.

When you enter that store in the mall and all the clerks ignore you at first and then with a snooty tone and a snide approach ask, "May I help you?" they are performing an organizational ritual. How do you know? I bet it happens at that store just about every time regardless of the specific individual employee you encounter.

Remember the classic scene in the hit movie *Pretty Woman* in which Julia Roberts, dressed down and very casual, is ignored by the sales clerks in a store on Rodeo Drive? Recall what a great moment it was later in the film when, now decked out in stylish designer dress, hat, and shoes, Roberts reenters the same store and makes certain they know what a "big mistake" it was not to be of assistance on her previous visit.

Why were those scenes so wonderful? Part of it is the perfection of Roberts's performance. However, the additional aspect is that to some degree we have all been there. Sure, maybe not on Rodeo Drive, but we've all wanted to put it in the faces of those who fail to make a great impression and set a high expectation for us when we are the customer.

Here's your new goal: don't be the person you would want to embarrass if the tables were turned and you were the customer.

This leads us to the next important aspect of this first tenet: it is not just about setting high expectations; it's about *exceeding* them.

The audience was a group of highly successful financial advisors, and the setting was the exclusive Beverly Hills Hotel. As I was in my hotel room, getting dressed to give my presentation to that august group in that sterling setting, I was shocked to discover that I had forgotten to pack a tie, which is pretty much a required part of the uniform at a meeting such as this.

I made my way from my hotel room to the meeting room, got my computer set up, and did a sound check with the audiovisual technician to prepare for my speech. Now I had to purchase a tie—*fast*. Previously, I had noticed a display in the lobby about a men's clothing store in the hotel owned by a designer named Amir. I was hoping I could find a tie in his boutique.

Dashing in, I was assisted by a friendly, efficient saleswoman who looked at my suit and selected the perfect tie. However, when she told me the price, I swallowed hard. It was more than I paid for a suit when I started in the speaking business many years ago. However, what could I do? There were no alternatives: I *had* to purchase the tie.

I rushed back upstairs to give my presentation. After the meeting concluded, several members of the audience told me that they not only loved my speech, they loved my tie.

When I told my wife, who had accompanied me on the trip, what had happened and how much my new tie had cost, she said—the first time in recorded history anyone has ever uttered these words—"Too bad you didn't have time to go to Rodeo Drive. You could've saved some money!"

She then informed me that she had to visit a store that could charge that much for a tie if for no other reason than a tourist's curiosity.

The next day, dressed very casually, I took her to Amir's. This time the greeting came from Amir himself, as we were coincidentally fortunate enough to visit when he was in the store. Amir is the absolute model of charm and charisma. To say he is a gracious gentleman is a supreme understatement. He asked me sincerely why I had needed a tie in such short order and was fascinated by both my previous problem and my profession.

Amir started discussing some of the people who had been his customers and sported his creations, and what a list he shared. He told me that Bill Clinton delivered two of his State of the Union speeches dressed by Amir. Other world leaders, including Mikhail Gorbachev, have been clients. We discovered that Amir's introduction to the Hollywood elite came via his first celebrity client, the legendary Cary Grant.

Then, however, Amir deftly changed the conversation to the importance of image and packaging and how that related to my profession. "One's look," he stated, "becomes one's image and brand in the world." He couldn't have said it better, and he was absolutely right.

I set an appointment with Amir to have a more in-depth dialogue about image, and I became a customer for his suits and more. You see, Amir doesn't just sell you a suit. He sets a high expectation and then exceeds it.

He talks with you from his wealth of experience with style. He makes suggestions about what you need to do to project a more polished, authoritative, and commanding image. Then he designs a look for you that surpasses your wildest expectations.

Everything was perfect about the experience with Amir from the look of the store (every color is designed to draw your attention to the clothes, not the fixtures), to fresh flowers for a great look and aroma, to the terrific team he has assembled. Amir provides his customers with an experience that is compelling, differentiated, and everything they really want.

Here are three of the ways he does it:

1. He models what he wants his customers to become. His look is so polished and sophisticated that his customers naturally want to raise their appearance to his level.

2. He is sincerely interested in his clients. He made me feel that I was as important to him and his business as the presidents and premiers he has attired.

3. He gives of himself and his spirit. I later learned Amir is involved in numerous charities. Paying it forward is part of his character.

When my wife happened to mention that we were staying an extra day in the hotel to celebrate my birthday, Amir reached over, grabbed another of the glorious and expensive ties, handed it to me with a smile and a handshake, and warmly said, "Then allow me to also wish you a happy birthday!" *That's* exceeding a customer's expectations.

The reason I'm sharing my experience with Amir is not to brag about the nicest suit (far and away) I've ever owned. It's to establish that the tenet of "set high expectations and exceed them" works anywhere from taxicabs in a midsize city to high-end clothes in one of the most opulent locations in the nation.

In other words, no matter what you do or where you do it, this tenet is critical to your success. Your role in this process is absolutely critical, and that's recognized by no less of an authority than the billionaire Richard Branson.

In his regular column in *Entrepreneur* magazine, Branson noted in July 2012, "The key is to set realistic customer expectations, and then not to just meet them, but to exceed them—preferably in unexpected and helpful ways. Setting customer expectations at a level that is aligned with consistently deliverable levels of customer service requires that your whole staff, from product development to marketing, works in harmony."[9]

Branson's comments suggest the three steps to exceeding expectations:

1. Know what the customer expects.

2. Develop a strategy to deliver on those expectations.

3. Find unexpected and helpful ways to go the extra mile.

Know What the Customer Expects

At meetings around the world, I've heard managers from a myriad of organizations state a commitment to exceed customer expectations. Yet many times when I ask them to specifically say what those expectations are, they stop talking. In other words, most businesses state that they seek to exceed expectations but haven't a clue what those expectations are and the specific steps they need to take to perform at that level.

You cannot meet, set, or exceed an expectation of which you are not aware.

As I'm sitting here reading the latest issue of *Golf* magazine, it strikes me that every month I am searching for—and the publication provides— information on hitting a golf ball longer and straighter.

It's kind of funny in a way, isn't it? I subscribe to a magazine that I receive a dozen times a year, and the entirety of what I am seeking from any and all of the myriad articles, pictures, advertisements, and instructional tips is how to hit the ball *long* and *straight*. In fact, this month's edition has an article on "easy ways to find the fairway and blast it past your buddies." Well, what else could I possibly want?

Not only *Golf* magazine but every manufacturer of golf clubs, golf balls, training aids, and any other product associated with the game understands that there are millions of people just like me who are trying to hit a golf ball longer and straighter.

If you truly want to achieve distinction, the research clearly shows that it's not additional features that you need to add to sell more customers and serve them better—it's really all about simplicity.

What about your customers? If you boil it down to the true essence of what they really wanted, could you make it as clear and precise as these golf companies have made longer and straighter?

Develop a Strategy to Meet Those Expectations

If we were going to make a movie, I seriously doubt that we would round up the cast, crew, and equipment; secure the necessary financing; and then say, "Okay, now what?" We would never proceed past the initial discussions about making a movie unless we had a script that we wanted to produce.

Yet many organizations and the professionals who work for them put enormous resources into stores and offices, make remarkable investments in hiring professional staff, and drop lots of cash into marketing and advertising without a specific strategy for how they will engage the lifeblood of their business: customers.

If you're in a leadership position in your organization, you need to begin immediately to develop a specific game plan—a script, if you will—for what happens every time a customer comes in contact with your organization.

If your job is working directly with external customers or even if your focus is on internal customers, imagine yourself as an actor in a film or on the Broadway stage. You wouldn't walk in front of the camera or the audience without knowing your lines. Plan specifically what you're going to say to create a compelling impression and set high expectations.

One way to build your strategy is to play the "and *then* what?" game. You start the game at the beginning of the specific customer situation you want to improve. For example, a customer walks into your retail store. Now ask: "And *then* what?"

Be very specific with your answer. Exactly how long will you let the customer browse before you approach him or her? Thirty seconds? Two minutes? Be precise.

Let's say you decide the best answer for your situation is that you'll give the customer one minute. Okay, "and *then* what?" How do you approach the customer? At Les Schwab Tire Centers in the Pacific Northwest, they bolt out the door and sprint to the customer's car. However, at my favorite restaurant, they wait a bit before bringing the menu to make a statement that they aren't trying to rush your dining experience. What's right for you? "And *then* what?"

What are the first words you say to a customer? Carefully plan the way you will open the interaction with the customer. Then continue to ask "and *then* what?" for every situation you can anticipate you might encounter with every customer or prospect.

If you don't know precisely how you're going to initiate the contact with the customer, you really don't have a strategy of any kind. Instead, you're just hoping for the best and playing the lottery.

Do you think you'd be reading this book right now if Taxi Terry had pulled up and mumbled, "Uh . . . hello"?

Find Unexpected and Helpful Ways to Go the Extra Mile

It's an interesting combination of concepts. *Unexpected* obviously means something that the customer hasn't anticipated, and *helpful* implies an aspect that is of personal, not just generic, value. To achieve both, there has to be an activity that is something we find appealing and that it didn't occur to us you were actually going to deliver.

For example, for the supermarket to bag my groceries and put them back in a shopping cart, making it easier for me to roll my purchase out to the car to be unloaded, is helpful. For the bagger to actually shepherd the cart to my car and do it for me is highly unexpected and connects with me at a significantly higher level. If the bagger takes my groceries out to the car and hands me an umbrella so that I don't get wet during a rain shower, I know I'm doing business someplace special.

Don't get me wrong. To be merely helpful is very important and is appreciated by the customer. However, when you find ways to combine helpful with unexpected, you are on the pathway to creating Ultimate Customer Experiences.

During my ride with Taxi Terry, there were several steps he took to be both helpful and surprising, and they form the basis for some of the tenets we will discuss later in the book.

With his opening line, "Are *you* ready for the *best* cab ride of your *life*?" Taxi Terry set a high expectation. Then he set about to exceed it. How he did that leads us to the next of the seven tenets.

Taxi Terry Takeaway

The expectations that you set for customers are obviously extremely powerful—as are the expectations they have of your ability to fulfill their needs and desires.

- How do you currently ascertain the expectations that customers have of you? How could you do a better job of discovering what they really want?

- Take a look at one specific aspect of the interaction that you have with a customer (regardless of whether it is an internal or external one). Now, try the "and *then* what" approach and develop two ideas of steps you could take that would enhance the connection you have with the customer in that situation.

- If you, too, are the "director of first impressions," specifically describe the impression that you are delivering. How could you enhance it to create an even more powerful impact upon the customer's expectations?

THE SECOND TENET

Delivering What Helps the Customer Helps You.

CHAPTER **3**

I believe that every job has features that the person in that position isn't excited about doing. You may absolutely love your career, but I bet there is some part of it that you tolerate only so that you can accomplish all the other aspects you enjoy.

As crazy as it may sound, the part of my work that I merely endure is flying. I love my work as a professional speaker: the time on the stage, the work I do with all of the wonderful professionals I encounter, the time I spend writing books. Everything about my work appeals to me except flying to and from the meetings, consulting conferences, or personal appearances. In fact, *USA Today* did a major story on my reluctance to fly titled "A Job Can Mean Flying in Spite of Your Fear."[1]

I have to admit that I'm a bit reluctant to share this fact about myself with you. I know that many people have parts of their jobs that are much worse than what I have to deal with, and so I realize that I don't have room to complain. As I told *USA Today*, when I think about all the things my dad—who worked in a factory, then as a butcher in the little grocery store he owned, and later as a truck driver—did for a living, if this fear of flying is the worst aspect of my job that I have to deal with, then I am the luckiest guy in the world.[2]

As the article mentioned, I do travel internationally, usually in business class or first class. That's not because I like to spend the big bucks on luxurious travel; it's exactly the opposite. However, I have so many frequent flier miles and so much travel status because of the consistency of my trips and the number of my miles that the airline typically bumps me up front for free in an attempt to secure my loyalty.

On every flight on a domestic U.S. carrier with first class, they will take my suit jacket, hang it up, and then return it to me at the end of the flight. It's part of the final approach ritual, the passing out of the coats. There's no doubt that it's a nice touch. Many times, I'm proceeding directly from the airport to a meeting, and so having a wrinkle-free blazer is definitely an advantage.

Something slightly different occurred on Singapore Airlines when I had the opportunity to travel on that airline for the first time. The flight attendant didn't return my jacket until after the flight had landed. She waited until I had stood up from my seat, and then she positioned herself behind me and helped me put on the jacket. Other flight attendants did the same thing for every other passenger with a jacket.

It was a small gesture, yet it made a big impact. Isn't it interesting, however, that *that* is the primary aspect I've chosen to share about Singapore Airlines?

After all, according to its website,[3] Singapore Airlines flies on six continents and is responsible for several firsts among global airlines:

- First to offer free headsets, a choice of meals, and free drinks in economy class

- First to introduce satellite-based in-flight telephones

- First to involve a comprehensive panel of world-renowned chefs in developing in-flight meals

- First to offer audio and video on-demand capabilities in all classes of travel

- First to operate the world's longest nonstop commercial flight—between Singapore and Los Angeles—and then surpassing the record (in terms of distance) later that year with nonstop service to New York (Newark)

Obviously, Singapore Airlines is also an employer of thousands of people and is in possession of billions of dollars' worth of airplanes.

In spite of its size and scope and the number of firsts for which it is responsible in its industry, what I want to tell you about the airline is that they helped me put on my coat.

If you were an executive at Singapore Airlines, wouldn't that drive you crazy? Would you think, "Here we are with so much investment in airplanes, an enormous commitment to a huge staff, working every single day getting planes and people to their destination despite the weather and other factors, and with all of that, this guy is writing about putting on his jacket? Come on!"

In fact, that's probably what the executives at any number of other airlines might be hearing in their heads, but not those at Singapore Airlines. They understand the second of the Taxi Terry tenets: Delivering what helps the customer helps you.

It's important to state early in our discussion about this tenet that I'm not offering this as a way to manipulate the customer's behavior. This approach certainly isn't about trying to scheme and conspire to acquire something for ourselves by using a conniving methodology to influence someone to do what we wanted him or her to do in the first place.

Instead, I'm suggesting what I believe to be a more enlightened approach. It's somewhat akin to business karma.

The philosophy of karma states that basically we reap what we sow. If you take loving, good actions in your life, you will receive respect, admiration, and kindness. If, in contrast, your actions are selfish and rude, you will receive negativity and undesirable circumstances.

Don't we often see that phenomenon in business? Companies focused on their customers' needs tend to enhance their business, whereas those just trying to hawk their products can't expand their profitability. Managers who try to encourage their team usually end up with high performers, but those so-called leaders who are on an ego trip frequently build resentment and disloyalty among their colleagues.

I'm always impressed by *Fortune* magazine's list of the top 100 companies to work for, especially in relation to the profitability and success of those organizations. The top five for 2013 were Google, SAP (one of my favorite clients), CHG Healthcare Services, Boston Consulting Group, and Wegman's Food Markets.[4] I don't think it's a coincidence that they are also leaders in their respective industries and have loyal, engaged customers. In other words, being responsive to their colleagues—and helping their customers—has helped make each of them an extraordinary organization. That's what I mean by business karma.

"Where we heading tonight, Mr. McKain?" Taxi Terry asks.

"The Marriott downtown," I reply.

"Great!" he exclaims, "Let's check out the weather!"

Weather? It hasn't even crossed my mind at midnight what tomorrow's weather is going to be, and frankly, in my tired and grouchy state of mind, I don't even care on this late night in Jacksonville if there is weather. However, when Taxi Terry touches the dashboard of his cab, it seems to light up. Embedded in the dash in a very elaborate bracket is an old PDA—a pocket PC—with a magnifying glass over the screen; I can clearly read it from the backseat. He has it directed to Weather.com for Jacksonville, and I can clearly observe each second ticking away there on the screen. I now have the "up-to-the-minute" weather forecast for my visit!

"I hope you play golf, Mr. McKain," he says, "because you are going to have a beautiful stay in Jacksonville!"

My best guess is that nowhere in the taxi driver training manual—if there is one—does it state that it is incumbent upon a cabbie to be a source of meteorological information for his or her passengers.

Yet Taxi Terry gave me up-to-the-instant information on the weather for my stay in his city. That's interesting and valuable—and helpful.

How can you determine what would be helpful for your customers? Here are four ideas:

1. What would you want to know?

2. Where would you need help?

3. How would someone different from you desire assistance?

4. Sweat the small stuff.

What Would You Want to Know?

Most people are so busy *doing* what they do that they never make the time to *think* about what they do.

Most taxi drivers are so busy moving their riders from one place to another and then finding someone else who will pay a fare, they fail to think about something as simple and basic as "If I were a passenger in a taxi in an unfamiliar location, what would I want to know about?"

For example, if I were traveling into the Jacksonville, Florida, area, which is well known for its terrific assortment of golf courses, stretching from Amelia Island to St. Augustine, the chances are that I really *would* want to know what the weather was going to be for my visit.

Notice as well that Taxi Terry could reasonably assume I was not a local resident: he picked me up at the airport and was driving me to a downtown hotel.

What if you were a real estate agent showing houses to a young couple? There are some points that are fairly obvious, such as the quality and location of area schools. However, there are some that are not so apparent: shortcuts on city streets that might help a busy wife get to work more quickly than fighting expressway traffic during rush hour, for instance.

The first step in helping your customer is simply to take a sheet of paper and pen and ask yourself, "If I were in the customer's situation, what would I want and need to know?"

Where Would You Need Help?

I've never been a gym rat, someone who spends a lot of time in a health club or gymnasium, working out or playing a competitive sport. Unfortunately, as the years have passed, my physical fitness isn't what it should be. I know it's time to start to take better care of myself.

I joined a health club. It's strange. As I was parking my car, I noticed that my hands were sweating a little. I talk with audiences around the world about dealing with organizational and professional change, and now it was time to take a dose of my own medicine and get outside my comfort zone.

Doing anything unfamiliar tends to be a bit uncomfortable. I pictured every male in the health club looking like Dwayne "The Rock" Johnson and every female having a similar appearance to the contestants at the Miss America pageant. Needless to say, I don't look like that, and I was concerned that my somewhat out-of-shape, overweight physique would make me a subject of quiet derision from the members of the gym.

If you worked at that health club and saw me walking in the door, what would you do to deliver an Ultimate Customer Experience?

For one thing, you could show me the routine. In other words, you could walk me through what I should do every time I enter the club. You could take me to the lockers, put me through a short workout, walk me back through the facility, make me feel comfortable. You could do this with such excellence that I would look forward to coming back instead of having sweaty palms in the parking lot.

This is a bit different from the first point because the initial idea there centered on *information* that would assist me that you could impart. Here, however, we're focusing on the *example* that you could provide to make a difference.

If I'm your customer—let's say I'm a young man in a clothing store purchasing my first tie—you can give me the brochure with the arrows and diagrams on how to create the proper knot, and you will have delivered what I need to know. The chances are, though, that I'm going to need something more than that to make me feel comfortable.

What's really needed is for you to stand with me in front of a mirror and show me how it's done.

Apple has become a highly overused illustration in an overwhelming number of business books; however, it is a superb example of this point. Its great products and innovative approaches are well documented. Another aspect to its success, conversely, is found in its in-store classes that show customers how certain aspects of its equipment or software work so that customers can get more out of the purchases they have already made.

Guess what happens next. Those customers return and purchase more, in part because they've lost the fear that they won't be able to use the computer or software they've acquired.

"Stepping into an Apple Store is a cross between attending a seminar led by graduate students and hanging out at Starbucks," as the *Oakland Tribune* described it.[5]

One aspect you quickly notice is that Apple Stores are often filled with customers not currently purchasing a product. While that might seem like anathema to most retailers, Apple conducts frequent training sessions in the store, so that customers will learn how to more effectively use the products that they've purchased. Frequently, the result is that these now more skillful owners will upgrade both hardware and software—meaning a "win" for Apple retail. Apple has always promoted a simpler operating system and products. The problem is that many people still need to be shown how to use those tools regardless of how user-friendly the engineers and designers believe they are. A cornerstone of the success of the Apple Stores is centered on showing—not merely telling—their customers what they need to know.

How Would Someone Different from You Desire Assistance?

When we make our list of the information that we would desire or the examples that we would prefer to be shown and the lessons we need to be taught, we naturally answer from our personal perspective. However, it should go without saying that not everyone thinks the way you think, sees the way you see, and believes in the way you believe.

Obviously, this means that you usually will not develop a diverse list unless you begin to think differently.

At a recent banking industry program where I was speaking, I had the privilege of listening to the other main stage presenter, Kelly McDonald. Her book *How to Market to People Not Like You: "Know It or Blow It" Rules for Reaching Diverse Customers* (Wiley, 2011) is a terrific challenge to our traditional way of thinking about our changing customer base.

During her talk, Kelly related the story of a wireless telephone company that wanted to make a marketing push for its services in a major American city. In an effort to appeal to the Hispanic segment, the company ran a "Cinco de Mayo sale." However, as Kelly humorously related, the problem was that the city in question was Miami, and the predominantly Cuban population there considers the Mexican holiday of Cinco de Mayo as relevant to them as we felt about Bastille Day on my Indiana farm.

If I'm Taxi Terry, I'm not only going to ask myself what *I* would like to know. I need to ask, for example, how I could be of greater assistance to a physically challenged passenger. Specifically, with your position at your organization, how could you be of greater help to someone with a background different from yours? It could be a physical challenge that you don't have or a cultural or religious difference from your experience.

One of the very interesting aspects to this is in the way it stretches and broadens your perception. In an absorbing article in *Forbes*,[6] Katherine Phillips, associate professor of management and organizations and cochair of the Center on the Science of Diversity at the Kellogg School of Management at Northwestern University, discussed research that she had published with

Katie Liljenquist of Brigham Young University's Marriott School of Management and Margaret Neale of the Stanford Graduate School of Business. In their study, they found that "members of a social majority are more likely to voice unique perspectives and critically review task-relevant information when there is more social diversity present than when there is not. Our research suggests that the mere presence of social diversity makes people with independent points of view more willing to voice those points of view, and others more willing to listen."

What I find fascinating about their study is that the persons who are bringing diversity to the group do not have to present positions that are distinctive from those of anyone else. Simply having diversity in the group, the research clearly demonstrates, makes everyone think more about alternative viewpoints and has the added effect of encouraging people to become better listeners to everyone else's insights.

The fundamental question then becomes: Are you willing to make the effort required to be of greater assistance to all external or internal customers with whom you come in contact?

If you want to be inspired by human potential—and personal resilience—look no further than my friend Roger Crawford. He is undoubtedly successful: a member of the Professional Speakers Hall of Fame, a colleague of mine in the exclusive Speakers Roundtable, a bestselling author, and a person whose programs are in high demand for meetings everywhere. He was recently honored at the International Tennis Hall of Fame Legends Banquet held during the U.S. Open.

Roger received the 2013 ITA Achievement Award presented by the International Tennis Hall of Fame and Rolex Watch USA. A legendary Wimbledon and U.S. Open tennis champion, Stan Smith, made the presentation.

But here's something you might not know: Roger has a physical challenge—a birth defect—that has affected all four of his limbs. He could have used that as his excuse to keep his life mired in self-pity. Instead, he became a hall of fame athlete.

Here's an important distinction: He's *not* recognized as a disabled athlete; he's an award-winning, hall of fame NCAA Division I athlete who competed in standard collegiate tennis who just happens to have physical challenges. *Sports Illustrated* has recognized Roger as "one of the most accomplished physically challenged athletes in the world."[7]

You think you have to deal with change? Every two years or so Roger has a *body part*—a prosthetic leg—replaced. How would you deal with a new limb every couple of years?

I promise you that Roger Crawford is the type of person every organization of any type would love to have as a customer. I don't think it is asking you to stretch too much to take a few moments and ask yourself on behalf of all people who have something about them that isn't quite the same as your situation, "How could we be of greater help and service to him or her?"

Sweat the Small Stuff

Ironically, one of Roger's close friends in life was Dr. Richard Carlson, author of the book, *Don't Sweat the Small Stuff . . . and It's All Small Stuff* (Hyperion, 1996). Tragically, Carlson passed away in December 2006, at the age of 45.

With great respect, I would suggest an alternative viewpoint to Dr. Carlson's. There are some things—personal health is a critical one in our personal lives; customer engagement is primary in our professional world—that make up the stuff over which we truly do need to sweat.

If Taxi Terry had taken a wrong turn and delayed me on that evening even further after my earlier problem with the airline, he could have said, "Hey, don't sweat the small stuff." However, to his customer, an additional delay would have been huge.

Delta Airlines could say, "We fly 15,000 flights every day; one single flight is small stuff." However, if they cancel the flight I'm traveling on to get home to my family after many days on the road, to me that isn't small.

You might be late delivering a report to one of your internal customers. You could rationalize, "It's only a couple of days late; don't sweat the small stuff." However, if the delayed report means that she will lose an account that was awaiting the information, it's an enormous setback for her.

In other words, what's small stuff to you may be enormous to someone else.

I love people and organizations that sweat the details. It reminds me of the legendary speaker Joel Weldon, who will ask his audiences to participate by answering two simple questions. The first is, "How many of you here in our group today have ever been bitten by an elephant?" Naturally, none of the people in the crowd raise their hands.

Then Weldon poses his second query: "Now, how many of you here have ever been bitten by a mosquito?" Unsurprisingly, *every* person in the crowd will raise a hand.

The master speaker pauses for effect, then delivers the knockout punch line: "See? It's the *little things* that always get you!"

Joel Weldon is absolutely correct. It's the little things—the small stuff— where so many professionals get tripped up. As Perry Paxton said, "Excellence is in the details. Give attention to the details and excellence will come."[8]

Here's a three-step plan for sweating the small stuff.

Step 1: Is Everything Exactly Right?

I realize that when you read that first step, you may be inclined to say, "You don't understand how things are where I work, Scott. Nothing ever goes *exactly* right." That certainly may be the case.

However, if we fail to ask what it would be like if everything went exactly right, we diminish the likelihood that we are detail-oriented enough to meet every need of our customers.

Are you that concentrated on getting everything *perfect*?

A few years ago, I mentioned this point to an organization of chiro-practors that had booked me for a speaking engagement. After their meeting, I received an e-mail from one doctor in attendance who noted that because of my comment, he had walked around the exterior of his office building to be certain its appearance was exactly right. He mentioned that to his surprise, he observed that weeds were growing around the steps to his office. Rushing to the office every morning with his mind on his practice, he had never noticed them before. Realizing that it wasn't exactly right for his patients if they had to see or step over weeds to get inside, he had them pulled and had the area landscaped.

The shocking aspect for this chiropractor was that for the next couple of days, every patient mentioned it to him. Unfortunately, some even said, "I wondered how good of a doctor you could be when you couldn't even take care of your front steps."

Consider for a moment what this means: if you work in an office, becoming a Taxi Terry can start with making your workspace more inviting for the internal customers you serve. If you travel in a sales position, it means that your car is spotless. After all, if prospects or customers see that you can't take care of your vehicle, they'll wonder how you'll take care of their accounts. If you are a bank teller, loan officer, retail store clerk—anyone with frontline responsibilities—you make certain that your area—and *you*—present as perfect an appearance as you possibly can.

How would you feel if the bank teller counted out your cash and you noticed that his fingernails were dirty? Although you might not change banks because of this, there's no denying that it makes the experience less than exactly right. There's no need to look as though you were personally dressed by Amir; however, there's no excuse for failing to maintain a professional appearance.

Presenting a polished and professional image is *your* responsibility, not your employer's. I've observed employees at a wide array of national chains who present a wildly varied image, and I bet you have too. You can walk into a McDonald's or pick up a car from Hertz and easily observe some employees with their uniform shirts tucked in and their hair neatly done, presenting an image of complete competence and service. Then, sometimes even at the same location, you will see people with half of their shirts out and their pants sagging, exuding tension and anxiety, and presenting as if they wanted to divert their trauma over to you.

It's pretty easy to ascertain that it's not about the uniform. It's all about the person wearing it. And when I'm your customer, that person is you.

Remember in Chapter 2 when we stated that one of the elements of making a good impression is that everything matters? The same thing is true in this tenet. You can't overlook anything and still hope to get it exactly right.

Start by imagining a single situation in which you have contact with an external or internal customer. Take a piece of paper and write down step by step how that communication would transpire if everything went exactly right.

Obviously, you'll want to temper this with a dose of realism. I've had program participants write for their example that a colleague threw her arms around the employee and said, "You should be our CEO!" Although that might constitute exactly right from the employee's perspective, I seriously doubt that it's quite the way the colleague would perceive perfection in communication. Remember, it's exactly right from the internal or external customer's point of view.

Step 2: What Action Steps Do I Need to Take to Deliver Exactly Right?

After you've developed your list of what exactly right looks and sounds like, you come to the next logical question: What specifically do I/we need to do in order to deliver?

You may have heard that employees at Starbucks are forbidden to wear cologne or perfume at work because it would interfere with the aroma of the coffee. When you discover how focused Starbucks has been over the years on getting everything exactly right and then taking the action steps required to deliver on that standard, you begin to more deeply understand their extraordinary success.

Break down the action steps at Starbucks for a moment. They have decided exactly right means that when a customer enters, the aroma of the coffee is so enticing that it creates a more compelling experience. The question then becomes, "How do we deliver that for our customers?"

Starbucks certainly wouldn't want a customer saying to a barista, "Wow, your Tommy Girl perfume smells wonderful!" They certainly would, however, want a customer to remark, "That Sumatra has a fantastic scent; I'd better upgrade to a Venti!" (That's perfect for both the customer and Starbucks, and that customer may leave a bigger tip. Remember, what helps the customer helps you.)

Two Hotels in Hawaii.   Both resorts are in Hawaii: one on the island of Kauai and the other on Maui. Both are pretty close to the definition of paradise. When my wife and I visited several years ago, both properties could have used some freshening. Each looked a little dated: the carpets worn, the furniture scuffed, the hallways dinged.

At the hotel in Maui, a room service tray evidently from the previous occupants of our room sat in the hall for two days. Part of the shower was broken. A lightbulb in the bathroom was out and was never replaced. The THIS ELEVATOR UP sign at one station in the lobby was broken and had what appeared to be exposed wiring. Our bed was made each day, but the room wasn't really cared for: the ironing board remained out, and trash remained in the can.

After I accidentally left my key in the room, I went to the front desk with my ID to ask for another. I gently reminded the desk clerk to be certain that I also had access to the club on the twenty-second floor, for which I qualified as a frequent guest of that hotel chain.

"No, you don't," she stated. "It's nowhere on your record that you have access." I softly explained that I had the gold sticker on my key and that my wife and I had previously been to the club on this trip.

"No, you haven't," she argued. "It is nowhere in my records here that you qualify."

"Well," I asked as politely as I could, "then how do I know about the gold sticker on the key?"

"You must have seen someone else's."

When I returned to my room, I found my old key with the sticker and for the heck of it went back to the front desk and said, "I wanted you to see this so you would know I was telling you the truth."

Believe it or not, her response was, "Well, I have no idea how you got *that*."

I took laundry to the bell desk my first morning at the Maui hotel only to be told by another woman there, "We normally come and pick that up."

"Oh," I responded with a smile. "Well, I saved you the trip!"

Her response? "Hmmmmph." No "thank you" or "you shouldn't have" or "I'm calling security on you." Nothing but "Hmmmmph."

At the Maui resort, the not too subtle attitude is "We have a great view of the ocean. We even have penguins in the damn lobby. If you want service, go someplace else. We don't have to work too hard with real estate like this."

Meanwhile, at the Princeville Hotel in Kauai, the bellman apologized for the hotel's wear and tear and vowed, "We are going to make sure you have a *fabulous* stay!" (It reminded me of Taxi Terry asking if I was ready for the "best cab ride of my life.")

He engaged us in conversation. He asked several questions: How long had we been married? Was this a honeymoon? How many times had we been to Hawaii? His sincere and engaging manner did not make his inquiries feel intrusive; rather, he seemed truly interested in us as people, not merely customers from whom he sought a tip.

He then told us the story of how he had come to Hawaii for vacation and never returned to Pennsylvania.

Later that day, as we checked in for the hotel's luau, the professional behind the registration table, a man named Doug, welcomed us enthusiastically and sincerely. He, too, engaged us in conversation, asking in-depth questions about our initial impressions of the property.

The next morning, after working out in the hotel gym, Tammy and I went to the bar to order a smoothie, only to notice that Doug was working behind the bar. Immediately he smiled and said, "Hey! Good morning to the McKains!"

Are you kidding me? He remembered our names?

The following morning it was "Good morning, Scott! Good morning, Tammy!" He told us the hotel was going to be undergoing renovation and moving up to the St. Regis brand after all the remodeling work had been done. His enthusiasm for the future of the resort made an impact.

Obviously, neither of these Hawaiian hotels was going to go bankrupt without our business. Both were pretty full on the February week when we were guests. I realize that their future was not dependent on our choice to stay with them.

However, at the end of the day, it's not about your location; it's primarily about the assistance you deliver. It's about making everything exactly right for the people you're doing business with because you realize that that is a reflection of your character. It is being a Taxi Terry regardless of where you work or what you do. It is delivering the Ultimate Customer Experience.

I wouldn't return to the Maui hotel even for a much cheaper rate. However, we're saving up for a return trip to see the St. Regis in Princeville even though it's probably going to cost us more for our next trip.

In Kauai, although the sign on the front and the decor had yet to be upgraded to read "St. Regis," the hotel already had elite-caliber people such as Doug and the bellman working at the resort who are committed to taking the action steps required to make it exactly right for my wife and me.

In Maui, the hotel isn't the only thing that needs refreshing.

Both properties were a little worn at the time we were guests. However, the *people* created the terrific experience in Kauai—they became Taxi Terrys—because they took the action steps required to help us. By doing that, they earned repeat business, recommendations and referrals, more money (through larger gratuities), and a greater sense of personal reward for a job extraordinarily well done.

In other words, by helping us, they helped themselves.

On the same sheet of paper you used in step 1, write down the precise action steps you'll need to take to deliver exactly right. My experience has been that the longer you contemplate the steps, the more vast and excellent your list will become. This isn't easy work; you'll probably be amazed at how much is involved in making something exactly right.

However, it is worth the effort for your customers and for yourself.

Step 3: What Policies, Procedures, and Activities Should I/We Stop Doing?

One of my best friends on the planet is Larry Winget. You may know him from his frequent appearances on FOX News, or perhaps you've seen him as a guest on *Dr. Phil* and other top-rated television shows or read one of his many bestselling books, which include *Grow a Pair: How to Stop Being a Victim and Take Back Your Life, Your Business, and Your Sanity* (Gotham, 2013).

Larry sometimes asks his audiences, "Do you know the two phrases that customers hate to hear more than anything else?"

He believes—and I tend to agree—that the answers are

1. We can't do that. It's against company policy.

2. We've never done it that way before.

Let's consider each of those two statements and see if there is a way that we can be of greater assistance to our customers.

We Can't Do That. It's Against Company Policy.

Have you ever seen those jokes on the Internet about the differences between what men and women say and what they hear on a date?

For example, when a man says, "How about pizza tonight?" the woman hears, "I'm cheap." When a woman says, "Let's just be friends," the man hears, "You are never touching me again."

Many of these jokes are amusing (admittedly, some aren't; they're just sexist and rude) and point out a common communication phenomenon: there is frequently a significant difference between what is said and the meaning that is conveyed.

When you say, "That's not company policy," what you may mean is the following:

- That's against the rules my supervisor has explained to me.

- I can't take responsibility for doing something outside our standard practices or my level of training.

- I could lose my job if I did what you're asking me to do.

However, what the customer frequently hears is the following:

- You're not important enough to make an exception.

- We're going to do it our way, and if you don't like it, tough.

- I'm too lazy to see if I can do what it takes to serve you.

An aspect of communication we will explore in greater depth in Chapter 4 is that the listener acts on his or her perception of what you say, not what you actually say. If you fear for your job because you would be breaking the rules yet what I'm hearing is that you're too lazy to help me, guess how I will respond?

However, there's another critical aspect involved here. Cynthia Wihardja, a business coach in Indonesia, writes, "Most of the time, when your staff says those words to a customer like me, I believe it's not because the policy is poorly made, but it's usually because the policy is poorly communicated. Someone in management made the policy and possibly just sent the memo down the stream—without teaching the team how to communicate it to clients and how to overcome objections."[9]

Therefore, if you're in management:

- It's important to constantly reevaluate your policies to be certain they primarily have the customer's—not the company's—best interests in mind.

- Get rid of outdated and outmoded policies that serve neither your contemporary needs nor the customer's desires.

- Communicate your policies and procedures thoroughly and provide the training and education required for your team to provide the help and engagement that customers deserve.

If you're not in management:

- It's critical to communicate with your managers about the policies that customers are most frequently questioning.

- Constantly seek superior solutions so that you can be of greater service.

I've been amazed how many times in my consulting practice I will ask for the specific reasons a particular policy is in place, and the answer is one of the following:

1. You know . . . I can't remember.

2. We've always done it that way.

We've Never Done It That Way Before.
Speaker and author George Torok has developed a top 10 list of the real meanings of "but we've always done it this way"[10] that is highly insightful. Here are three of my favorites:

- How dare you question the wisdom of your predecessors? It was good enough for them; why isn't it good enough for you? Have you no blind respect and subservience to those who were here before you?

- Perhaps you believe that you have the right to ask questions, but you're wrong. Shut up and go with the flow.

- It's working the way it is. Leave it alone. Can we go now?

In Larry Winget's classic story about being told by a retail store manager, "We've never done it that way," Larry's brilliant comeback is, "Well, congratulations! Because today you're going to get to try a *new way!*"

No customer should ever be told under any circumstances, "We've never done it that way." In the history of business, there has never been a customer who heard that phrase and instantly felt that the way she or he was being treated was exactly right.

Just as you worked on the phrasing required to create a positive initial impression and set high expectations with the first tenet, the same effort is required here to discover a better way of communicating with a customer. Your goal, as this book has stated many times previously, is to find every avenue possible to help your customer because ultimately, when you help your customer, you help yourself.

To summarize the first part of this chapter, the three steps for sweating the small stuff are as follows:

- Step 1: Is everything exactly right?

- Step 2: What action steps do I need to take to deliver exactly right?

- Step 3: What policies, procedures, and activities should I/we stop doing?

In Chapter 2, I mentioned the compelling and classic phrase from the late Zig Ziglar: "You can have everything in life that you want if you just help enough other people in life get what they want." Here is a story about the acclaimed motivational speaker.

Zig Ziglar was born in 1926 as the tenth of 12 children. His family moved early in his life from Alabama to Yazoo City, Mississippi, where his father had taken a new job. Tragically, when Zig was only six, his father died unexpectedly. His younger sister died two days later. Later in life, Zig and his wife, Jean (known from his speeches as the Redhead), lost one of their children in 1995.

Ten years later, when I lost my wife, Sheri, to ovarian cancer, I walked to the mailbox and found a four-page handwritten letter of sympathy and insight from Zig. The fact is that although Zig and I were acquainted through our common bond as speakers, had met a few times, had once had dinner together, and were both members of the National Speakers Association, we were not close friends by any means.

Yet he took the time to write me about his experiences dealing with the loss of a loved one and even offered to personally help me in any way he could.

I have men and women in my life I consider very close friends who didn't make the effort in my time of grief that Zig did.

When Zig passed away in 2012 at the age of 86, I related that story to my friends and via a YouTube video to others for the first time. What I discovered was that there were countless other people who had their own stories about how Zig had personally reached out to them and helped in any way he could.

The reason for sharing this story is not to impress you but to impress *upon* you two critical points:

1. What Zig said was absolutely correct. His life is a perfect example that you can have all you could ever want by helping enough people get what they want.

2. Unlike some of the charlatans or blowhards who merely talk a good game, Zig Ziglar actually lived what he advised. When you practice what you preach, you not only help others, you help yourself.

As Jennifer Powell wrote in the *Boston Herald*, "The bottom line is that doing good can be good for business, if it's done right."[11]

I would amplify her statement and state that it's great for business *only* if it's done exactly right. That's why every item we've discussed in regard to this second tenet is critical to your success and moves *you* closer to being a Taxi Terry.

Taxi Terry Takeaway

As this chapter states, doing what helps the customer will help you, in the long run.

- Name three things you are doing for your customer to be of assistance to them above and beyond what would be an industry standard or expected in the normal course of business.

- If you easily named three, try to think of two more—and if you failed to come up with three answers, guess where you need to start working?

- Select one specific aspect of your interaction with customers and then develop a short list of steps you could take that would enhance your business karma.

THE THIRD TENET

Customers Are People, So Personalize Their Experience.

CHAPTER **4**

Here's a trivia question for you: Who said words to the effect of "It's not personal; it's just business"?

The answer is: well, a *lot* of people. If you answered Michael Corleone in *The Godfather*, you'd be right. If you named any major character in any film or TV drama about the Mafia since then, you'd probably be accurate, too.

Donald Trump uses the phrase occasionally on his television show. It was billionaire investor Carl Icahn's description of the reasoning behind his massive investment in Herbalife.[1] Gordon Gekko, the Michael Douglas character in the movie *Wall Street*, had his own version of it that he used to dismiss Charlie Sheen's Bud Fox. It's even in the Tom Hanks romantic comedy *You've Got Mail*.

In other words, the phrase is pretty much everywhere, from the mob and business on the screen, to investors on television, to a line that you may have personally heard or used.

Quite simply, here's the problem with "it's not personal; it's just business": if there isn't someone who *is* taking it personally, there is no need for the statement in the first place.

"It's fashionable to see business as an impersonal activity," writes Adrian Savage, the author of *Slow Leadership: Civilizing the Organization* (Pusch Ridge Publishing, 2006). "It's not like that. Not at all."

"At the heart of all business transactions are two intensely personal relationships," Savage continues. "The simplest can be summed up in four words: *You sell, I buy.* That *is* business. Without buying and selling, there can be no profit, no investment, no reason to produce anything beyond what each individual needs to survive."[2]

My friend Dr. Joseph Michelli, the author of many bestselling business books, including *The Starbucks Experience: 5 Principles for Turning Ordinary into Extraordinary* (McGraw-Hill, 2006), posted on his blog, "In most of my books, I find myself touching on a theme that sounds something like '*all business is personal.*'"

"I think I am attracted to this message," Michelli suggests, "because well-intentioned business leaders can get drawn into tasks, products, and profits and lose sight of the basic importance of personal care for staff and customers."[3]

"I hope you play golf, Mr. McKain," Taxi Terry says, "because you are going to have a beautiful stay in Jacksonville!"

"Tell me, sir," he continues, seeking to make a more personal connection, "if you don't mind my asking, why are you here?"

"I'm in town to give a speech at the hotel to a group of professionals about customer service," I respond.

"Customer service!" he exclaims. "I am so *into* that!"

I think, "No kidding. It shows."

Taxi Terry displayed on our cab ride the same principle that Michelli and Savage were writing about: the importance of creating personal experiences for your customers. He saw that I was not a revenue unit being transported. I was—and am every time I climb into a taxi—a guy who needs to go from one place to another.

What Taxi Terry understood so well is that customers are people. Even if you work for a business that does B2B (business-to-business) transactions and are not marketing to individual consumers or clients, you still are dealing with human beings who are working for their organizations, just as you are working for yours.

This third tenet, "customers are people, so personalize their experience," works regardless of your industry. From heavy equipment sales to high-tech security, from medicine to manufacturing, from retail to real estate, everyone wants a personal experience.

My wife and I were considering a move to Las Vegas. I had previously lived there and loved it; however, she had never resided outside our common home state of Indiana. I thought it might be a reasonable approach to rent a house for a year to see if she liked the area as well as to determine whether she felt good about the relocation. By renting instead of owning, we would be able to try another location after only a year if Tammy didn't enjoy residing in Nevada.

After finding an ad for a house in an area that I know and like, we got an appointment to see the place. The owner provided directions, and we drove to the property.

"Nice place," my wife said as we pulled up. "But," she cautioned, "let's not jump on the first thing we see."

Then Craig, the owner, arrived. He welcomed us enthusiastically; he asked us many questions about where we were currently living, why we were considering a rental home in the Vegas area, and what we were looking for in the way of both living space and lifestyle. Then he started to describe his house with passion and personality, and we became captivated. His complete willingness to provide what we were seeking was totally engaging.

So much so, in fact, that Tammy whispered to me, "We can't do better than this!"

Result? We now have a home in the Vegas area. (And my wife is very happy.)

Don't get me wrong: I realize it is easy to read this and assume we were sold by a slick talker. That is simply not the case. Craig is a passionate presenter but is not slick; he's totally professional in his communication.

Actually, we had already done a significant degree of due diligence by looking at literally hundreds of listings online. In addition, I already was very familiar with the area. We knew what we wanted, and this house more than provided it.

What moved us to immediate action, however, wasn't the property; it was the *person*.

That, I believe, is the aspect that many businesses—and the professionals who work for those organizations—frequently forget. They erroneously believe that the product sells itself. They think an order taker is sufficient and therefore scrimp on training and education for the sales and marketing teams.

Often, they wrongly assume that this saves the organization money. Instead, it is an *expense* in the long run in terms of sales and the retention of customers—and keeping the best employees.

It always ends up being about the people. I would suggest that a person like my landlord (and friend) Craig—or Taxi Terry—is exactly the kind of people-centered professional every business needs.

It doesn't take much of a shift in thinking to realize that all business is personal, as we've discussed previously. A customer is a person first and foremost; that is why it is logical that customers want a personalized experience. The real question is, How do we do it?

Here are five primary steps to creating a highly personal, ultimate customer experience:

1. Know and use the customer's name.

2. Ask great questions.

3. Collect information about the customer that personalizes his or her experience.

4. Don't get uncomfortably personal.

5. Display interest in the customer's interests.

Know and Use the Customer's Name

Benjamin Franklin once said, "The sweetest sound in any language is a man's own name." I'd suggest that in today's world of business, one of the sweetest sounds that any customer can hear is when she is called by her name.

Perhaps you're old enough to remember or have seen on reruns of episodes of one of the true classic situation comedies in the history of television, *Cheers*. For 11 seasons we were both entertained by and engaged in the lives and antics of the patrons and staff of a Boston bar. Certainly, the performances of the terrific cast, which included Ted Danson, Shelley Long, George Wendt, Rhea Perlman, John Ratzenberger, Woody Harrelson, Kirstie Alley, and Kelsey Grammer, were at the core of the reasons why millions of people loved the show. Yet in addition, part of the very foundation of the show's success was that *Cheers* represented a place where every employee of the establishment knew your name. Don't we all want to have a place where we can go and feel just the way Norm did when he walked into the bar?

When you know your customers' names, they feel that you have their best interests in mind and that they have value to you. Also, knowing the customers' names tends to inspire them to return.

Here's a personal example. Be forewarned: I can't imagine how many people they see on a daily basis; that is why the experience was so amazing and made such an impression on me.

On a recent speaking trip to India, I stayed first at the Taj Palace Hotel in New Delhi, arriving on a Thursday night. On Sunday morning, I departed for three days to make a presentation in Srinagar in the troubled state of Kashmir, near the border with Pakistan. Finally, on Tuesday afternoon, I returned to my original hotel to freshen up and get ready for the 27-hour flight home.

After landing again in Delhi, nearing the end of my trip, I was tired as the hot, tiny cab with a driver nothing like Taxi Terry pulled into the driveway of the Taj Palace for me to check in again. Even with a temperature at the astronomical 115 degrees that's considered normal there at that time of year, a greeting awaited me from a sentry with a perfect uniform and a smile to match.

"It is a good day at Taj Palace, for our Mr. Scott has returned!"

Between the heat and my fatigue, I wasn't certain what I had heard. I wish I could honestly report that I turned to him from the backseat of the dusty cab and sounded like the debonair Cary Grant saying, "Pardon me, old chap; I didn't quite catch your remark."

What I really said was, "Huh?"

The doorman had a white beard that perfectly offset his black uniform and dark skin, and his smile gleamed as he repeated, "I said, sir, it is a good day at the Taj Palace. For, you see, our Mr. Scott has returned!"

I thought that along with my suitcase, they were going to have to load me onto a luggage cart after that. I know and appreciate the little trick played at many Ritz-Carlton and Four Seasons hotels in which the bell captain tells the front desk by radio the name of the incoming guest so that when the guest approaches to check in, the desk clerk can say, "Welcome back to the Ritz-Carlton, Mr. Smith."

Here, however, this man was the very first person from the hotel whom I saw on this visit. In other words, he had memorized and remembered my name.

Because of its location in the middle of several of the world's embassies to India, security is quite high (and appreciated) at the Taj Palace. With the painful knowledge that it was their sister hotel in Mumbai that was the target of a terrorist attack several years ago, they are quite thorough. Every guest must go through an airport-like search of baggage and body (done electronically, not a pat-down) to enter the hotel.

However, waiting at the front was a woman I recognized from the front desk during my earlier visit. "So good of you to return, Mr. McKain." (Again someone called me by my name.) She walked me in the hotel and personally handled my check-in. I usually carry my own bags, but the bellman was taking them for me this time, as I had injured my back a bit and was in a little pain.

When my luggage arrived, I was asked by the bellman if I needed anything else. "Ice would be very helpful," I replied.

"How about a drink to go with that, as my treat?" he responded.

"No, that won't be necessary," I said. "I screwed up my lower back, and it will help to put some ice on it. Thanks anyway."

He was off like a flash and returned with a small tub of ice and a hot water bottle to put the ice in. "And, Mr. Scott [again my name], just take it with you. It's a long, long flight home, and it may help your journey." I've never received a gift from a hotel that was more appreciated.

When I checked out at 10 p.m. to head to Delhi's international airport, the hotel's assistant manager surprised me yet again. "We have appreciated your two stays with us, Mr. McKain. And as we know that you will return to India, we would be honored for you to visit us again. Please accept this gift to remind you of your friends at Taj Palace."

I waited until I arrived home to open the gift. It was a small sculpture of the Taj Mahal. It is still sitting on my desk as a constant reminder of the importance of knowing a customer's name and delivering an Ultimate Customer Experience.

Here are some questions for you:

- Where will I insist on staying when I'm back in Delhi?

There is no doubt.

In fact, on the ride back to the airport, we passed a new JW Marriott under construction, and I thought, Well, there is one I won't be staying in. I am now loyal to the Taj Palace.

- What did it cost them financially to do what they did?

In terms of items they had to purchase, it was a hot water bottle and a small gift in a box. In turn, they acquired a customer for life.

You see, it's not what they spent on the customer in the way of gifts or discounts; it's what they invested in the relationship—learning my name, making me feel appreciated and special—that mattered.

It makes me wonder if airlines would be better managed if they saved a little money by delaying the purchase of a new plane and instead educated their flight attendants to remember customers' names and go the extra mile. Rather than flying the new ultimate Boeing 787 on United, I would prefer an Ultimate Customer Experience from that airline any day. (Why, we might ask, would it be impossible to do both? I believe they could do it if they decided it was worth the effort and it became the priority of the company.)

Something else: it astounds me that the people at the Taj Palace, where I've visited just two times in my life, remembers my name, yet the employees at my bank in Henderson, Nevada, where I'm in the branch two or three times every week and where I have both my business and my personal accounts, do not.

Yet every week I get mail from the people at the bank about some product—mortgage, credit card, CD—that they want to sell me.

Why do they think I would want more products from a place that doesn't know me?

Don't they get it that I am willing to change banks not because there's a better checking account at a competitor but because my current bank hasn't personally connected with me in a meaningful manner? Obviously not.

However, I will not be changing hotels in New Delhi, India. The Taj Palace is the only place for me.

Have you ever wondered what would happen if just one simple thing such as knowing the customer's name was added to the mix of the way you communicate?

The real-world problem, however, is this: What does it take to remember someone's name?

In Chapter 3, I mentioned how the motivational great Zig Ziglar was a person who walked his talk throughout his life. Therefore, as I aspire to emulate his example, I need to admit here that remembering names is one characteristic of professionalism that I'm working on. I'm not a memory expert by any means and am still practicing these techniques, but my ability to remember names has improved because of these six simple steps:

1. Decide it's worth the effort.

2. Focus on the person's name when introduced.

3. Say the person's name immediately after the introduction.

4. Create a word-picture association.

5. Introduce a spouse, friend, or colleague.

6. Admit it when you can't remember.

Decide It's Worth the Effort

If you don't understand the impact and importance of remembering and using a customer's name, you won't do what it takes to be able to recall it. As simplistic as it sounds, the first step I had to take was simply making the decision that the effort I was going to put into remembering names more effectively was going to be worth the trouble it was going to take.

Focus on the Person's Name When Introduced

A problem that I realized I had was that often when I was introduced to someone, other things were going on. In other words, I was at a meeting with many people, or a party, or with music playing and other people talking. Unfortunately, I allowed those distractions to take my focus away from concentrating on the name of the person I was meeting. Even if I have to strain to do so, I listen very intently when someone offers her name. If the noise around us prevents me from hearing it, I always ask her to repeat it to make certain I get it right.

Create a Word-Picture Association

A web search will help you find many articles and books on how to create effective word-picture associations. The one question that helped me understand this principle is this: Have you ever walked up to someone and said, "I remember your name, but your face escapes me." Of course not. We remember the picture, the face, but we have more difficulty with the words that accompany it. In other words, our brains have evolved to remember images more effectively than words.

Therefore, finding some kind of word association so that you create a picture can help tie the two together in your memory.

Introduce a Spouse, Friend, or Colleague

This technique works on two levels. First, if you can immediately introduce someone else to the person you've just met, it means that you are using that person's name immediately in conversation, which will reinforce your memory.

Second, if you run into someone and can't remember his name, simply say, "I'd like for you to meet my colleague Bill Smith." At that point, the person whose name you can't remember will probably say something like, "Hi, Bill; my name is Pamela." Or your colleague may say, "Great to meet you. And *you* are?"

Admit It When You Can't Remember

Okay, in the real world the fact is that you're probably not going to remember everyone's name like the memory expert who can meet the entire audience and identify every person at the end of the show.

As much as I hate to admit it, I would try to fake it when I couldn't remember someone's name. The more I worked on being better at names, the more I realized that it was eventually more comfortable for both of us if I just said, "Good grief, I can't believe this, but I'm drawing a blank on your name. I'm really sorry."

In addition, if I could describe where I met the person, what we talked about, or some characteristic that would clearly display that I remembered him but just could not pull his name out of my memory bank, it would ease the awkward feeling for both of us.

Those steps have certainly helped and continue to help in my effort to become better at remembering names. I hope you'll join me in a commitment to improve.

Ask Great Questions

Why are great questions so important in connecting with customers? Think about it. . . you've just experienced an example.

Here's what I mean: By asking you a question, as I just did in the previous paragraph, I've enhanced my ability to personalize the experience for you in two significant ways.

First, I will receive an answer from you that may assist me in personalizing the experience for you in the future. Questions provide an opportunity to obtain important information.

Second, it compelled you to start thinking, and you were pondering the topic that I wanted you to consider. Questions present an opportunity to get the customer thinking about the topic on which you would like to acquire that important information.

The importance of asking good questions naturally causes us to inquire: What makes for good questions? We probably all have heard the basic questions: Who? What? When? Where? Why? Those are the five starting points. However, our goal is to become someone of service asking questions so that we can be of greater assistance, not sound like an interrogator from *Law & Order*.

For over a decade I had the coolest part-time job on the planet. I was a movie reviewer, and my comments on entertainment were syndicated to about 80 television stations across the United States. Because of that, I had the opportunity to interview some of the biggest movie stars in the world: Tom Hanks, Arnold Schwarzenegger (who booked me for a speech), John Travolta,

Meryl Streep, Bruce Willis, and many, many more. Because these celebrities were being interviewed by hundreds of journalists, I knew that I had to learn how to ask questions that would receive something more than a rote response. I didn't want them answering my questions with the same answer they were giving everyone else both because that would mean my viewers could see a practically identical interview elsewhere and because my competitive nature made me want to learn something about these superstars that was exclusive to my interview, that no one else had uncovered.

This meant I had to get pretty good at asking interesting questions. Here are the five methods of questioning that served me well:

1. Ask open-ended questions that require creative thinking.

2. Ask what they don't expect.

3. Ask again; follow up.

4. Ask and then listen.

5. Ask about their beliefs.

Ask Open-Ended Questions That Require Creative Thinking

As you probably know, open-ended questions are ones that cannot be answered with a mere yes or no. As you also are aware, that type of question warrants a longer answer; therefore, we assume we are learning more because we are receiving more information from the other party. However, that assumption may not be accurate.

For example, let's say that I work for a dealership that sells boats. A prospective customer enters, and I begin a conversation with him.

A closed-ended question would be: "Are you here to buy a boat?"

This question is closed-ended because the answer would be either a yes or a no unless I was tempted while looking out over a showroom filled with various vessels and hearing such a stupid question to respond, "Boat? I was looking for a truck."

We know that open-ended questions are better, but they're often almost as lousy: "How may I help you?" This question may make the checklist in certain training programs, but in real life it's a query that we tune out because it is so bland.

The goal should be to ask open-ended questions that require creative thinking both on our part to originate such a question and on their part to react to it.

"Before we get started," I might ask, "would you mind telling me what part of boating you like the best?"

This is important for a couple of reasons. First, by focusing the customer's thoughts on what she likes best about something, I'm attempting to create positive emotions from the very beginning of the conversation. Second, I'm gaining very valuable information. If the response is "Spending relaxing time with the family," I'm not going to show him a superfast cigarette powerboat. However, if the response is, "I get goose bumps when I'm shooting rapidly across open water," we are going to stay away from the pontoon boat section of the store.

Sometimes, however, seeking negative emotions can work just as well.

If I enter a bank and meet with a representative about establishing a checking account, I probably will hear a question something like "And where is your current checking account located?" The answer really tells the banker nothing except where my money is currently parked. It provides zero insight into why I am moving from one bank to another.

What would happen, however, if the banker inquired, "Before we talk about our different types of checking accounts, I just have to ask something. Would you please tell me about your absolutely worst banking experience?"

My response would probably be to vent about how the place where I'm banking now screwed up my account, or after five years of banking there they still didn't know my name, or there is a teller at the branch who is rude, or some other bit of potentially valuable information. This would give the banker the opportunity to both insist that such a transgression would never happen at her branch and set the stage for how her bank's products and services will be positively positioned.

The important point is that it's not enough to simply ask open-ended questions. The key is to ask open-ended questions that are creative and require the person answering them to do a bit of creative thinking in order to properly respond.

Ask What They Don't Expect

Let's not get carried away here. If I'm in a business meeting about an important company project, I don't expect to be asked if my wife is still faithful to me. Not only do I not expect it, it is not appropriate. Asking what they don't expect does not mean asking a question just for shock value. It means asking a question that demands a different or higher level of thinking.

Sometimes it doesn't take that much of a shift in questioning to accomplish this if you know the principle.

I learned in my interviews that if I wanted better responses, I had to ask questions in a manner that wasn't expected. For example, every interviewer would ask Tom Hanks a question like "Why did you decide to make this movie?" And as he had done many times before, Hanks, an exceedingly nice guy, would politely answer that he wanted to work with this director, the story was interesting, he loved his costars, and he thought it would be a film that people would want to see.

Instead, I would ask: "When you read the script for the first time, what was so inspiring about it that it made you decide you'd invest a year of your life to make the movie?"

When you ask, "Why did you do this?" the answer tends to be a checklist of reasons and rationales. When you inquire with the unexpected, such as "What inspired you to do this?" the response is often much more emotional— and revealing.

By shifting the question to one that is emotion-based, I'm asking something that is frequently found by the other party to be unexpected and more engaging.

Questions such as "What *inspired* you?" "What *motivated* you?" "What *encouraged* you?" "What *discouraged* you?" "What *instigated your decision* to?"

and "What *stimulated your thinking* about?" are the ones I've found most successful.

At a meeting in the office, I could start the session by asking my colleagues the expected question: "What results are we seeking as an outcome of this project?" Or I could ask something less anticipated, such as "When we successfully complete this project that we are about to undertake, what will our customers feel about doing business with us at that point that they're not feeling now?"

If I begin with that type of question, the group starts thinking about how customers are going to feel about quicker response times, for example, rather than just providing a litany of the steps required to achieve our goal. When we begin to ask questions in this manner—How will our internal or external customer *feel* about the difference?—we begin to initiate more creative thinking. Perhaps we wouldn't just suggest how we could respond more promptly; we might also develop an idea like Southwest Airlines' practice of having a humorous audio play when customers are placed on hold.

Let me be clear: at some point in the process, we will have to develop a list of action steps. However, if I can begin with a question that requires creative thought to answer, my personal experience is that I'll also receive more creative—and successful—action steps to achieve the results we all desire.

Ask Again; Follow Up

I've studied interviewers on television for about three decades, and it seems to me that what separates the amazing, legendary interviewers from the good ones is not found in the first question they ask. To be successful to the point where you're asking questions for network or national cable television and interviewing global leaders and celebrities for a living, you have to possess a high degree of skill.

As we know, there are some who have attained legendary status among both the public and their peers. For example, George Stephanopoulos and Katie Couric are excellent broadcasters, whereas Larry King and Mike Wallace are legendary interviewers. What has made the difference, and, how can we learn from the legends so that we can connect at a higher level with our customers and be more like Taxi Terry?

When you examine the work of the extraordinary interviewers, you find that most of the time their initial questions are not very different from those of everyone else. It's the *follow-up* questions that make all the difference.

Let's try a hypothetical example. Let's imagine that the typical news network correspondent has gone back in time and is interviewing John Adams, the second president of the United States. It might go something like this:

Reporter: Before you became president, you served in a number of other capacities, correct?

Adams: Yes, I was a member of the First Continental Congress with Washington, Franklin, Jefferson, and others and served as the first vice president of the United States under George Washington.

Reporter: What were your specific duties as our first vice president?

Interesting, no doubt. History geeks like me would love to hear what Adams's responsibilities were as the first vice president so that we could compare and contrast them with the current situation. Note, however, that this follow-up question, which I'm putting unfairly into someone else's mouth, is basically asking Adams to give us a list of his duties. It's practically asking him to recite his job description.

Here, in contrast, is how I picture Larry King handling the same interview:

King: Before you became president, you served in a number of other capacities, correct?

Adams: Yes, I was a member of the First Continental Congress with Washington, Franklin, Jefferson, and others and served as the first vice president of the United States under George Washington.

King: Interesting. George Washington . . . nice guy?

Now, that's moving from interesting to *fascinating*. Would you rather Adams tell you what his duties were or provide insight into what Washington was really like?

In other words, ordinary interviewers tend to ask follow-up questions like a prosecuting attorney, starting with the big question and using the follow-up to narrow the information and focus.

Q: Where were you on the night of November 4?

A: I was having dinner in a restaurant with my wife.

Follow-up Q: And exactly *where* were you dining with your wife on the night in question?

Legendary interviewers, in contrast, turn the funnel upside down to open up the questioning, and by doing so they often gain a higher degree of trust from the subject of their inquiries.

Q: Where were you on the night of November 4?

A: I was having dinner in a restaurant with my wife.

Follow-up Q: Great! Was it a special occasion? Were you celebrating something?

At this point, you might be saying, "Wait a minute, Scott. I'm no Larry King or Mike Wallace, and I'm certainly not going to be asking questions of movie stars, politicians, or criminals." Of course you're right, but the same principle will help you personalize the customer experience to a much higher degree.

If you have prepared great opening questions to initiate the customer experience—"Are you ready for the best cab ride of your life?"—your next step is simply to plan for what the next, follow-up question will be.

Our earlier example was: "Before we get started, would you mind telling me what part of boating you like the very best?" If you have experience in talking with customers, you already know enough to make a list of the usual responses. Previously, we cited two: one customer loved the speed; the other enjoyed time with family. Knowing that, we could develop two follow-up questions that give us more information that we can use to personalize the experience.

For example, if the customer says, "Spending relaxing time with the family," I might follow up with, "I agree; that's great. If you were going to describe the perfect day on the water, what would that be like?"

After my office team answered my first question ("What will our customers feel about doing business with us at that point that they're not feeling now?"), I might follow up with something like "You said those were ways that the customer might feel differently. Could you describe to us where you were doing business the last time *you* felt that way and what they did to encourage those feelings?"

Naturally, common sense is critical here. If the customer says, "I want to buy a blue suit," it is perhaps not a proper response to say, "What inspired you to seek a blue suit?"

However, you could say, "Before we take a look, may I just ask: Is this going to be a suit for work, a special occasion, or any other specific purpose?" This follow-up would compel the customer to provide very useful information. I'm assuming that you'd want to treat a customer shopping for an awesome suit because he's flying to Vegas this weekend to get married just a little differently from the way you'd treat someone who states that he has had a death in the family and needs a new suit for the funeral in a couple of days.

The two critical points on follow-up questions are as follows:

1. Every question should be prepared with follow-up options in mind.

2. The best initial follow-ups open the customer's mind and spirit to provide more information, not to narrow the conversation.

Ask and Then Listen

Earlier, I mentioned that as a kid I worked at a local radio station. When I learned in my early teens to be a disc jockey, I was taught the craft by watching a station employee named Ray Hickman. My first week of training consisted of just sitting in the studio, watching Ray run the board.

At larger stations, the on-air personality frequently has an engineer or producer or both who get the commercials ready to play, maintain the station log (so that the sponsors have an affidavit that the commercials—called spots— that they've paid for are played at the proper time), answer the phones for the call-in segments, and handle all the other technical aspects that have to be taken care of to put the show on the air. However, at smaller stations like the one where Ray and I worked, the announcer does all those tasks himself or herself. Sitting behind a control board as you talk on the radio and perform all those functions is called running the board.

When you begin, there are so many things to simultaneously keep track of—how long the song you are playing is, what the next song is going to be, timing the song so that it will end precisely at the time you need it to, what the next commercials are, whether there are competitors' commercials running at the same time, whether you are following the format clock pertaining to when you play new songs versus old songs, and about a hundred more—that it is easy for a new employee to be trying to do so many things at once that the song ends and the announcer isn't prepared. When that happens, the radio goes silent; the industry term for that is *dead air*.

Dead air is welcomed in broadcasting with about the same level of enthusiasm as the Black Plague was in fourteenth-century Europe. I don't remember everything that Ray Hickman told me during my week of training, but I can still hear him saying, "Screwing up gets you yelled at. Dead air gets you fired."

Fast-forward several years, and now I'm interviewing celebrities, with time constraints that demand that I keep my time with them strictly within their parameters. Keeping my earlier training in mind, I would ask a question, an answer would barely be completed, and I would jump in with the next question, terrified that I would let a second of dead air get between us.

Later I noticed that other reporters were receiving more thoughtful, interesting answers from the same stars I was interviewing. I discovered the difference was that they were asking questions and then allowing the celebrity to think about the answer. In addition, they didn't jump in with another question until there was a moment's pause.

You see, the celebrities, just like the rest of us, had been trained too.

The world we live in bombards us with constant entertainment and information and very, very little dead air. Because we have become infinitely less accustomed to silence, our natural tendency is to fill it. Therefore, sometimes the best information comes to us when we just listen and give the person we are talking to permission to continue.

When I ask about the boat and get the response that the customer loves time with the family, if I jump in immediately, that's all the information I'll receive from that query. However, if I'm willing to wait a beat or two, the customer, in her desire to fill the dead air, may tell me that her brother lives on the other side of the lake and she wants a pontoon boat just like her sibling's so that they can tie up together and have fun.

The lesson is: dead air is bad for disc jockeys but can be very valuable when you're asking questions in business.

Ask About Their Beliefs

No, I'm not suggesting that you ask about the customer's political or religious beliefs unless, of course, you are campaigning for your favorite candidate or work at a church, synagogue, mosque, or other religious institution. Sometimes, however, it's best to establish the playing field before the game begins. By that, I mean that frequently people may have differing beliefs that may cause perceptual problems in their communication.

If you believe that no matter what, the company I work for is going to screw you over while I believe that the organization that employs me behaves honorably, you may view my questions with suspicion, and I may easily misinterpret your responses. Neither of these assessments will be of assistance to you, the customer, or me, the company's representative.

In my business, we frequently have conversations with people who presume that all professional speakers are motivational speakers and hold with that the image of a fire and brimstone, get down on both knees and rip out chest hair, swing from the chandelier loudmouth with tons of enthusiasm and zero content.

I understand; I can't stand those guys, either.

However, if our conversation begins with my perception that my programs have high content and our prospective customer has that aforementioned negative impression of all speakers, we have to handle the prospect's belief system before we can ever get to a resolution that is positive for my business and the prospect's meeting.

If we don't ask questions about it at some point, we will never recognize the problem.

The important point here is to constantly be aware of differences in belief systems and assumptions in all conversations with external and internal customers.

When you apply these five principles, you can become an expert in asking great questions.

Collect Information About the Customer That Personalizes His or Her Experience

One of my best and favorite clients is Cisco. I've had the privilege of working with that company and its partners on several occasions. One of several reasons why I admire them so much is the amount of research they do into the concepts that matter to the clients they serve.

One research project conducted for them produced this fascinating fact: "Customers are willing to exchange private information to receive more personalized service."[4]

Yet the same study said that, for example, only 45 percent of banking customers believed the bank knew enough about them to offer services with any degree of personalization.[5]

What good would it do to gather all that information by asking great questions and then do nothing of lasting value with it?

Although the information collection and retention methods vary from business to business, almost every organization I've ever worked with understands the importance of customer data. It's usually collected in software or through a process called CRM (customer relationship management).

Yet many of them do it, in my opinion, exactly wrong. It appears that the Cisco research supports my contention.

For example, because you're reading this book, you probably know that my name is Scott McKain. However, according to the CRM data of many companies, it's not.

You see, my full given name is Dallas Scott McKain, but everyone I've ever known, from my parents, to schoolteachers, to business associates, to best friends, has always called me Scott.

The small-town doctor who delivered me suggested my name. However, Dr. Frank Bard always liked names that had an initial first, with a full name second. One of his favorite authors was F. Scott Fitzgerald.

The leader of the FBI, J. Edgar Hoover, was enormously respected—at least at that time. There were sports legends such as H. Lou Gehrig, rich industrialists such as J. Paul Getty, authors such as W. Somerset Maugham, presidents of the United States such as T. Woodrow Wilson, and first ladies such as A. Eleanor Roosevelt, and they all used their middle names as their given names. No problem, right?

In today's world, consider W. Brad Pitt, C. Ashton Kutcher, A. Kelsey Grammar, O. Marie Osmond, F. Murray Abraham, L. Reese Witherspoon, H. Ross Perot, G. Gordon Liddy, S. Truett Cathy (Chick-fil-A), T. Boone Pickens, the author T. Coraghessan Boyle, the systems theorist R. Buckminster Fuller, and the astronaut M. Scott Carpenter. No list like this would be complete without L. Ron Hubbard, the founder of Scientology; the legendary lawyer F. Lee Bailey; the civil rights activist H. Rap Brown; E. Howard Hunt of Watergate fame; the mutual fund founder T. Rowe Price; and many more.

However, many CRM programs require a full first name and then provide space only for a single middle initial.

It is one of the reasons I believe the name of these types of systems is totally wrong. It shouldn't be CRM but CIM: customer *information* management. Most CRM is in actuality DUM: data under management. It's not about relationships. It's almost always about data: How much did they buy in the past? What is the address required to invoice them? Where do we call if there is a collection problem?

Everyone who knows me calls me Scott, yet Delta Airlines, for example, will often answer the phone saying, "How may I assist you, Dallas?"

I'm one of Delta's best customers on the planet, as exemplified by my Diamond Medallion SkyMiles frequent flier status, yet they don't know my name or at least can't get my name right. How can you have a relationship with someone if you don't know the name he always goes by?

If you want to truly be distinctive, develop fields in your CRM system for the things that really matter to your customers. Don't have just the customer's name; include the names of the customer's partners and children, how they drink their coffee, what their favorite sports teams are, the charitable organizations they are committed to, and more.

What if you and a small team came up with a list of the aspects you should really know about your customers to build and enhance relationships with them? What would happen if you built your CRM system so that it included that type of information?

Every person with whom I have a true relationship knows these things. So why do many of the organizations where I do business not know enough to call me by the name my mom put on my birth certificate and has always called me?

It's in part because their CRM is DUM. Don't merely amass information. Instead, collect the information from your customers that will assist you in creating a more personalized relationship with them.

Here's an idea for a new type of software: plug in all the information about your family—birthdays, anniversaries, names of your kids' teachers, likes and dislikes of each member of your clan—hit "Save," and let the software do the rest.

You also can get a virtual assistant in another country who will be notified by the software when a birthday comes around, and he or she will take care of obtaining and delivering the gift. Don't worry about your spouse; this program will make certain he or she feels totally loved and desired.

The software can be programmed to do periodic follow-up with the teachers at your child's school, sending letters from a template at each grading period, along with insights that are mail-merged from your database. You'll have none of the usual needless ongoing concern for your kids' education; this program will ensure that you are a part of it.

It's perfect. You can appear to be engaged, which is what you really want. By that, I mean you crave the appearance of being connected without the investment of energy and time that it takes to be a contributing, involved part of a family.

How does that sound?

Well, for many of us, it's ridiculous. To think that software could create and maintain compelling relationships within our families or that we could pull away and just farm it out to a virtual assistant and a program is borderline offensive.

So why do we seem to believe it will work just fine for *customers?*

The "R" in CRM stands for "relationship." Although I certainly advocate that all of us be better organized, keep track of details, and be timely— activities in which software can be of great assistance—it's ludicrous to believe for a moment that we can abdicate the relationship aspects of our business and transfer them to a software program.

If you wouldn't outsource your personal relationships, why would you believe that could work for your professional ones?

If you want customers to know they matter to you, show it by being interested in what matters to them.

Don't Get Uncomfortably Personal

In our attempt to personalize the experience for our customers, it is assumed that we recognize that there is a line of formality that we should not cross. We never want to become so personal that it becomes uncomfortable—not to mention inappropriate—for anyone with whom we do business.

But in these changing times, what is the standard? Where do we draw the line?

When I was starting as a professional speaker, the criterion I set for myself with platform material many years ago was "If I can't say it on television, I'm not going to say it in front of an audience." Well, that benchmark would certainly not be acceptable today, would it? Not only do pay services such as HBO and Showtime push the envelope, the constant use of the double entendre and innuendo on network shows is something that I would never use before a corporate audience.

There is such a wide variance between what some people find acceptable and what others find totally offensive that there's only one yardstick I can offer: If in doubt, leave it out.

If there is any question in your mind whatsoever that you might be asking something that is inappropriate or might cause discomfort, don't ask it.

Naturally, a caveat here is that if you are in the healthcare industry, for example, you may be required as a medical professional to ask your customers—patients—questions that they may not be comfortable responding to. Yet you must do so for their own good.

If you are in the financial services industry, I may not feel comfortable answering your questions about my income and credit history, yet I know I must answer them for you to do your job and for me to receive my mortgage.

However, intensely intimate inquiries outside our professional need to know do nothing but alienate the very people we are seeking to serve more effectively. If you are uncertain whether the question you are about to ask is too personal, remember our mantra: if in doubt, leave it out.

Many times the same question—when asked by different individuals in different circumstances—can make us respond with enthusiasm or make us feel uncomfortable.

My first wife, Sheri, was a marketing and intellectual licensing professional until her untimely passing. Because of her position, she often traveled to conferences and conventions. We often talked about how one man could be talking with her and bragging about how much he loved his wife and showing her pictures of his kids and then say, "Are you married? Do you have children?" and it was a great part of the conversation.

A few minutes later, another man, this time a guy with his shirt unbuttoned a little too much and wearing what Sheri used to call the "Mr. T starter kit"—a single thick gaudy gold chain around his neck—would approach. In practically a single breath, he would ask if he could buy her a drink and say, "Are you married? Do you have children?"

She would laugh about how the very same inquiry that could be engaging in one situation could be absolutely repulsive in another.

However, what if a customer asks you a question that is uncomfortably personal? Naturally, you don't want to offend that person with your response, but you have every right to draw the line between your professional life and your personal one.

The "Job Doc" in the *Boston Herald*—his real name is Paul Hellman—had a highly interesting column on October 5, 2012, titled "When the Question Is Too Personal."[6] Hellman begins by discussing a question that comedian Jerry Seinfeld asked his longtime friend Larry David about his underwear. We make an interesting assumption: we expect not only an answer but in addition a humorous retort because we are listening to these two close pals who are obviously having a good time.

In contrast, in a different situation, Seinfeld was asked by a radio interviewer to tell him the number of expensive Porsche sports cars he owns.

As Hellman writes, "Seinfeld has a sizable collection, but he refused to answer. He told the interviewer, basically, 'You're a man of stature and reputation, and I hold you to a higher standard than that question.'"

"Good answer," Hellman continues. "Tip: When asked a question, you've got options. One is to decline [to answer]."

That's great advice. Not only when it comes to the questions we ask our customers but also when they ask us a question we find overly personal, when in doubt, leave it out.

Display Interest in the Customer's Interests

It was the fund-raising drive for the band at Crothersville Junior Senior High School. We needed new uniforms, and I, as the fifth-chair trumpet player from the seventh grade, wanted to make certain I was candy sales champion to impress both our director and the high school musicians ahead of me.

Dashing into a store while my mom waited in the car, I found that the owner wasn't there. I proceeded to tell an employee of the store all the important reasons they would want band candy at their checkout counter and how they could play an important role in community pride as our band, resplendent in our new uniforms, would represent Crothersville in the finest possible manner.

As I jumped back into the car, Mom asked how it went with the store's owner. I explained the situation, Mom thought for a moment and then asked: "Scott, do you feel the man who is the employee you just talked to is as interested in the band as you are?"

Naturally, as young people approaching or in their teens have a predisposition to do, I thought Mom had lost her mind.

"Of course not," I answered. "He's not in the band; I am!"

"Exactly," Mom replied. "So why did you trust him to become your salesman?"

I didn't understand.

"Look," Mom explained. "You didn't tell the person who could make the decision about the band candy; you told his clerk. Now that employee has to tell the store's owner about band candy. Do you think he will be as enthusiastic as you? Will it mean as much to him as it does to you?"

I hung my head. I got the point.

"Be very careful," Mom said in a teachable moment, "who you trust or who you transfer the authority to become a salesperson on your behalf."

If you don't consider yourself a salesperson, you may be wondering: How does the lesson of this story apply to me?

Simply this: if you're communicating with a customer (internal or external) about something about which you feel great passion, you can't assume that she will advance your ideas or concepts until you connect it with something that she is ardent about. The store employee was never going to relay the information about band candy to the owner with the obsessive pride with which I had presented it to him because he didn't care about new band uniforms one way or the other.

In sales, you will always be more concerned that someone buy your product than the customer will feel an obligation to purchase it. An office manager will usually be more concentrated on productivity than will the other people on the team. How do you get others to be more interested in what's important to you or the organization?

Always remember that if we aren't interested in their interests, the connection we establish won't have enough depth to create true engagement.

Therefore, when we are interested in what the customer is interested in, we can personalize the experience for that customer to a significant degree.

When Taxi Terry said, "Customer service? I am so *into* that!" I immediately felt that we had a great deal in common. Terry had displayed an interest in what interested his customer.

If you are executing the previous five steps—know and use the customer's name, ask great questions, collect information about the customer that personalizes his or her experience, and don't get uncomfortably personal—this fifth step is merely the culmination and application of what we've discussed in this chapter.

It would have done Terry no good to know my name, ask me great questions, collect information, maintain his professionalism in conversation, and then do absolutely nothing to display an interest in me, especially given all that he did to amass that body of knowledge.

The old cliché that knowledge is power is completely, totally wrong. Knowledge that is unused, unapplied, and unemployed for a productive purpose has zero impact.

Knowledge has an influence or an effect on an issue only when it is applied. If you have executed the previous steps and then keep that knowledge to yourself, it has the same consequence as if you didn't do it at all.

Your challenge is to personally express that you are interested in their interests.

I have a friend who is definitely not a football fan, yet I just received an e-mail from him asking if I'm excited that the Indianapolis Colts will be kicking off their new season in just a few days. I feel more connected to him simply because I know that he must value our friendship because he's expressed an interest in *my* interests.

After talking casually with a financial service professional at a charity function, I received a clipping of a *Far Side* cartoon from him. He remembered that I had mentioned in conversation that I found Gary Larson's strange sense of humor to be hysterically funny. My wife and I later bought life insurance policies from him. Our relationship had grown not because he tried to sell me something but because he displayed an interest in my interests. (That was an important decision because my wife, as I mentioned earlier, later tragically passed away from cancer.)

Make a list of all the methods you can use to display interest and you will probably develop an extraordinarily long directory. From sending gifts to writing personal cards, from a promotional product to a telephone call, there are almost an infinite number of ways to use the information you've collected in a manner that connects with the customer and enhances your business.

When you can sincerely say to a customer, just as Taxi Terry said to me, that you are "so into" what is important to him or her, you've created an important bond.

Taxi Terry Takeaway

This chapter discusses the importance of personalization; however, it has little traction for you and your business until you take action with specific customers to enhance your relationships.

- Write down the names of five important customers.

- Next, think of a question you could ask each customer that would provide you information that could help you enhance the personalization you provide to him or her.

- Finally, name an interest of each of these customers, and develop one action step that would display to them that you are interested in what is important to them. If you don't know their interests, now you have a great question to ask them.

THE FOURTH TENET

Think Logically and Then Act Creatively and Consistently.

Dr. Charles Jarvis was often called "America's Painless Dentist," and with good reason. After about 12 years building his practice, he decided to forgo his work on molars and dentures in San Marcos, Texas, and become a humorist. For three decades he enthralled audiences across the nation with his special brand of insight.[1]

As a young man, I attended one of his talks. I'll never forget Jarvis asking members of the crowd to "raise your hand if you believe you possess common sense." Dutifully, like just about everyone else in the crowd, I held my hand aloft.

"Of course you do!" he exclaimed. "There is lots of common sense in this crowd, in this state, in this nation. And, do you know why there is so much common sense around? Because people don't *use* much of it!" All of us in the audience started to laugh.

Dr. Jarvis was on a roll. "Yep," he said in his Texas twang, "you see it all the time. You'll ask yourself, 'Now, why did I do something stupid like that?' Here's the reason why—evidently you're afraid that if you use your common sense . . . why, sooner or later, you might just *run out of it*!"

I'll wager that you see it all the time: customers, whether external or internal, have a way of doing and saying things that often leave us scratching our heads in disbelief.

There are several websites that collect stories of some of the ridiculous and illogical things that customers say. My favorite is Notalwaysright.com, obviously so named because they believe the customer is not always right.

For example, here's one of my favorites: a call to the reservations center of a major airline:

Caller: I want to book a flight from here to LA.

Me: From where?

Caller: From here.

Me: What city are you in?

Caller: Same as you.

Me: I'm in Baltimore. Is that where you are?

Caller: No. Can't you tell?

Me: I have no way of knowing. Just tell me what city you'd like to depart; I can look up flights.

Caller: If you don't know where I am, what good are you? *Click*[2]

Chances are that if you spend much time with external customers, you have plenty of stories about your industry that are similar to that one.

Those examples of illogical behavior aren't limited solely to customers who are external to the organization, are they? Occasionally, we wonder what the people with whom we work—our internal customers—are thinking.

I liked this one from StupidCoWorkers.com:

Coworker on phone: Hold on a minute. [Presses "hold," then says to Team Leader], John is on the phone and needs to talk to you.

Team Leader: Tell him I'm at lunch.

Coworker: [back on phone] Hi, he says to tell you that he's at lunch.

Team Leader: [rage in eyes]

Coworker: Whaaaat?[3]

As you read this next Taxi Terry tenet, which requires logical thinking, you may be saying to yourself, "I understand why this is important, and I do think logically. It's those knuckleheads I have to deal with who are causing all the trouble."

You may be right. However, one of the most fascinating aspects to me when it comes to this topic of logical thinking and acting with common sense is this: almost every person I've asked—out of the million or so who have attended one of my programs over the years—says that he or she thinks and behaves rationally.

In other words, it seems to always be the other guy—or the other organization—not thinking straight.

Here is an important point: People almost always behave logically—from their point of view.

My wife will come home loaded down with shopping bags from purchases at the mall. I go crazy. "How could you spend all that money?" I ask desperately.

She smiles sweetly, holds the bags higher, and announces, "I saved us *so* much money today."

"How?" I ask, perplexed.

Of course, she replies confidently, "I bought all of this *on sale!*"

Now for the critical question: Which one of us is right?

When I ask this question at seminars, men typically shout, "*You* are!" Women jump to their feet to declare, "*She* is!"

The answer is that we *both* are from our own individual, respective, logical points of view.

As the person in our family in charge of the budget, I am logical and correct to be highly concerned about expenditures. As the person with most of the responsibility for buying clothes and school supplies for the children, she naturally looks for savings on her purchases.

For me, it is entirely correct to get emotional about how much she is spending. For her, it is entirely correct to get emotional about how much she is saving.

In other words, for one of us to appear irrational to the other is totally logical.

Therefore, I'd like to suggest a slight amendment in the way you understand this tenet, which states, "Think logically and then act creatively and consistently." You will be better served if you consider it in this manner:

Think logically *from the customer's point of view*; then act creatively and consistently *to deliver what is of value from the customer's perspective.*

There is a three-step process to accomplish the goal expressed in the tenet, and my bet is that it will seem very familiar to you. It's the same way in which you connect with individuals of significance in your personal life. Perhaps you haven't thought of it in this manner: you didn't clinically break down the process of getting acquainted and dating someone who became a significant other, life partner, or spouse into three steps, for example.

However, it's always important to keep reminding ourselves that as we have discussed in this book, customers are people just like us. Therefore, the behaviors and emotions we have noticed others display in our personal lives are identical to the behaviors and emotions we will see them display in our professional relationships.

The three steps are

1. Align

2. Engage

3. Commit

Align

Why would customers do business with you? There has to be a fundamental reason or they would be staying at home or at least spending their money elsewhere. What need drives them to look at your organization as an option? What motivates them to make the effort to engage with you?

Once you know the answer to those questions, you can begin the process of alignment.

I've often heard it said that in people's personal lives opposites attract. Over my years of observing as well as being involved in personal relationships, my conclusion is that although opposites may attract, such relationships often have a difficult time enduring.

We tend to associate most with people we perceive to be like us. Personal relationships flourish when there are common areas of interest. Don't get me wrong: I'm not saying you have to enjoy everything your partner appreciates or vice versa. It's that our common interests, values, and desires pull us together.

When you align your thinking with another person's, you begin to appreciate and understand that person more deeply. I am not suggesting that you have to adopt the other person's choices or beliefs; instead, I am strongly recommending that to connect emotionally with another person, you must at least temporarily be able to approximately think as that person thinks, choose as he or she chooses, and feel as he or she feels.

It would not be overreaching to suggest that this simple act is at the basis of many of the world's problems and has been for centuries. Because of our unwillingness or inability to even temporarily align our thinking with those of another religion, ethnic background, culture, or national diversity, we act and communicate in a way others with different experiences fail to comprehend.

This reinforces our earlier and critical point: people rarely behave illogically. People almost always behave logically—from their point of view.

The fundamentally important aspect here is illustrated in the story of my wife's shopping trip: if she seeks to influence my logic and my emotions, she must first align with my point of view and communicate with me on that basis. Simply insisting that she saved us money because the items she purchased were discounted won't persuade me.

However, once she begins to communicate from my logical perspective— "Honey, I know you are worried about our finances. These are items you have been thorough enough to have already considered, and I was able to spend less than we anticipated for items we were going to need to acquire anyway."—she has won the day.

It doesn't mean she has to change her beliefs. It just means that to be effective at the next stage—engage—she needs to align her thinking to a point where I feel we are connected.

Engage

Note that my wife won the day when she aligned and then engaged. What good would it do for her to align—to make the effort to understand my logic—and then just keep it all to herself?

Engaging without aligning wouldn't have accomplished what she desired.

If she had said, "You don't understand. The sale was 50 percent off! It's half of what it normally would have been," it would not have engaged me, because we wouldn't have been aligned. The problem is that without the alignment, I would have been hearing, "You don't understand. Because it was on sale, I spent money I didn't need to spend, and because it was half off, I bought twice as much."

In today's world of marketing, there is a significant amount of discussion about the term *customer engagement:* what it means and how to measure it. For our purpose here in learning the tenets of Taxi Terry and creating an Ultimate Customer Experience for our external and internal customers, the word *engagement* has a precise meaning: the effort you are making to initiate and sustain an aligned interaction with customers.

People respond more enthusiastically and productively when they are engaged. According to an article in the June 2007 issue of *CFO* magazine, the electronic retailer Best Buy initiated research that revealed that "where employee engagement increases by 0.1 [on a 5-point scale], [the store] experiences a $100,000 increase in annual sales."[4]

If you can increase sales by enhancing the engagement of your internal customers, why aren't you working right now to create a team of Taxi Terrys to deliver Ultimate Internal Customer Experiences so that they in turn create Ultimate External Customer Experiences, enhancing sales, retention, and referrals and growing your organization?

Commit

Let's say you coach young kids on a team in a local sports league. You align with them because you understand a bit about the challenges they are facing as they learn a sport and compete with other teams. You engage them as you call each one by his or her name, share a smile and some encouragement, and attempt to keep their spirits high.

Every young person on the team is pretty terrific. However, one of the kids is your daughter. To you, which person on the team is the most special?

Pretty obvious, right? Although you are aligned and engaged with every young person, you have a commitment to your own child that runs deeper than words can describe. That commitment makes all the difference.

To be blunt, there is no way you will ever possess a commitment to a customer as strong as your bond with your offspring (nor should you). However, this example should illustrate that when there is true commitment, there is additional—and significant—emotional intensity.

In our personal lives, we have acquaintances, friends, and true commitments. With individuals with whom we have shared commitments—whether romantic or platonic—we develop a higher level of concentration on making certain we are contributing to their well-being in a positive, productive manner.

It's a similar phenomenon when we exhibit a commitment to our customers. We simply develop and display a higher level of concentration and intensity in regard to creating an experience that contributes to their personal and professional success.

If you are willing to align your thinking with your customers' logical point of view, engage them in a dialogue regarding their perspective, and commit to deal with them by intensely focusing on their needs, you've met the first standard of this tenet.

However, as with many aspects of business and life, there are exceptions.

There is nothing here about aligning with another's point of view that should make you believe that you have to sacrifice your own beliefs. F. Scott Fitzgerald famously wrote, "The test of a first-rate intelligence is the ability to hold two opposed ideas in the mind at the same time, and still retain the ability to function."[5] You don't have to change your beliefs; just use your first-rate intelligence to hold the customer's point of view in your mind.

Along a similar line, there is nothing in this material about engaging and committing that should imply that any conversation with any customer is ever permitted to cross a line of ethical behavior and good manners. Taxi Terry is a perfect example to me of the Ultimate Customer Experience, yet I promise that if a customer in his backseat crossed the line of reasonable behavior, Terry would have the offender's butt out of the taxi and on the sidewalk even after promising the best cab ride of his or her life. The fact that you're engaging at a higher level with the customer doesn't mean that you have to put up with anything that makes you feel uncomfortable.

Now that we have repositioned our logical thinking to the perspective of the customer through the process of align, engage, commit, we have to deliver to the customer what he or she desires in a creative and consistent manner to attain the goals of this tenet. Let's examine how we can become both unique and uniquely reliable.

Act Creatively

If you've read my previous books, either *Collapse of Distinction* or its revised edition, *Create Distinction*, you are aware that I devoted major sections of those works to a study of how businesses must develop the strategies required to enhance their creative output. To get you up to speed if you haven't read them and as a review for those who have, here are some ideas on the importance of acting creatively. For our purposes here, as opposed to the target readers of those books, let's focus our attention on expanding our creativity for internal and external customers.

What makes you different? Obviously, if we're going to act creatively, that implies that we cannot do exactly the same things for our external customers that our competitors do or that our internal customers are accustomed to seeing all the time.

After I chatted with the person sitting next to me on a recent flight, she gave me her business card at the end of our conversation.

I was interested in her organization because she was involved in a business very similar to the one my late wife, Sheri, worked in for many years. Going online to the website that was on her business card, I noted something very striking: The page touted the headline "What Makes Us Different."

Naturally, as I'm fascinated by what makes one company or department stand out from the competition, I read the bullet points detailing what they believed separated them from the others in their industry. Here are their four points and my commentary after each one:

1. *Experience* (Is the competition totally staffed with rookies who have no background?)

2. *Depth of knowledge* (You're asserting that the competition is dumber than you are, right?)

3. *A company founded by innovative entrepreneurs* (Since by definition the competition had to be founded by entrepreneurs, too, I guess those organizations must have been started by *traditional* entrepreneurs?)

4. *Depth in multiple market segments* (As my wife said the same thing about the company where she worked in the late 1990s, I promise you this is nothing new.)

None of these points would be interpreted by savvy prospects or clients to suggest that the company was creative or different in any manner. These points would be required, however, to make that company relevant in the hypercompetitive industry in which it plays.

However, from a client's or prospect's perspective, there is absolutely nothing here that is creative enough that it would truly qualify to be listed under the heading "What Makes Us Different." In other words, the company has clearly displayed that it doesn't know what would make its customers perceive it as one that acts creatively and delivers service that is superior to that of the competition. If you don't understand that, why wouldn't a prospect also surmise that you might not get other salient aspects of doing business together?

This obviously raises the question: What should my seat mate's company do?

As you might imagine, I would suggest that they can advance their cause to a significant degree with this tenet—as we've stated, one should start by thinking logically from the customer's perspective—and then really get creative.

Noncreative, nondistinctive organizations and professionals frequently find themselves in difficulties that are challenging to resolve, as proved by one of my favorite television programs, *Restaurant Impossible* on the Food Network. The show is hosted by the extraordinarily charismatic chef Robert Irvine, and its premise is that this highly successful restaurateur has two days and just $10,000 to totally revamp a restaurant that is on the verge of failure.

Every episode I've seen, although it follows a format that is easy to identify after a couple viewings, has been totally compelling.

It begins with Robert describing a bit about the restaurant and then arriving on-site to meet with the owners. Oddly, in many episodes the owners have a difficult time admitting that there is anything wrong with the menu and the management even though they're losing money, are about to go under, and have even requested Irvine's assistance. Robert confronts them with the facts about their impending failure.

Lesson 1: Denying the Problem Never Solves It

I've talked with everyone from CEOs to store managers who are blind to the challenges they face. They fail to think about how things appear from the customer's point of view and shy away from creative solutions and approaches. I've talked to some who honestly believe that the only solution is to cut the price.

The problem with these responses is that each of them denies the critical problem: they aren't creating experiences that are creative and compelling enough that customers naturally want to do business with them, and therefore they will never find the solution.

Next, Robert has the staff bring him the dishes that the restaurant normally serves to its customers, which he usually rips to shreds. Often, the restaurant owners are using frozen or canned food because it's easier to prepare, thus delivering an inferior product to the customers and simultaneously driving up the costs and overhead. In addition, on several episodes, the kitchen crew and owners have lacked the daily discipline to keep the kitchen clean and sanitary.

Lesson 2: Taking the Easy, Noncreative Way Out Can Drive Away Customers and Escalate the Cost of Production

Sure, price matching so that customers know they'll get the same price from you that they get from another retailer is one way to address a problem in sales. But what will that do to your margins? Could it mean that all you become is a showroom? In other words, if price matching is all you're known for, could a customer desiring assistance presume that qualified help won't be available from you?

Many times, the quickest, most traditional way to solve the problem ends up creating additional problems.

Robert then approaches the servers, seeking to create accountability and standards of performance. In several of the episodes, the wait staff will argue with Robert about their abilities. They frequently see themselves as being much better at their jobs than the reality of the situation and the finances of the business make blatantly obvious to the viewer.

Lesson 3: Often, Some People on Your Team Will Overvalue Their Creativity and Contribution and Undervalue the Negative Impact They Have on Customers

I'll wager that right now you have team members who have fantastic product knowledge that they cannot wait to elaborate on for your prospects and customers—and that they believe this information makes them extraordinarily special members of your organization.

I will also bet that some of them are driving the customers absolutely bonkers.

Those team members are delivering what they value and know but *not* what many of today's customers desire. Every employee becomes the chief executive officer of the Ultimate Customer Experience to the prospects and customers he or she connects with at your store. Are you certain they are delivering in a creative manner what the customer really wants? Do they— and you—truly realize the impact we all have on customer acquisition and retention?

Each episode of *Restaurant Impossible* concludes with the owners being brought into their newly designed restaurant, and they (and we) are stunned by what Robert's team has done with an investment of just $10,000. A large crowd waits outside to be thrilled by the new menu Robert has planned, and it appears that the owners have had their business revitalized and are on their way to success.

Lesson 4: You Can Make Creative Improvements with a Smaller Financial Investment Than You Might Imagine If You Do It Smartly

Being creative and delivering the Ultimate Customer Experience doesn't mean that you have to break the bank. In fact, it probably does not require as large an investment as you may think.

When you search the Internet for what happens to these restaurants after Robert leaves, you'll find a few websites complaining that some of them close and go out of business after his departure. If you dig a little deeper into the subject, however, you'll find that in many cases the owners who fail have simply gone back to their bad, noncreative habits once the expert has departed.

Lesson 5: Over the Long Haul, It Won't Help to Bring in an Expert to Grow Your Business and Enhance Creativity and Then Go Back to Doing What You've Always Done

If you're going to become a Taxi Terry, you're going to have to do a few things differently. That doesn't mean you are just shuffling or rearranging; it means you are changing your approach and being more creative to establish the true connection with customers that you may have been lacking.

However, a problem I've noticed with many people is that when I start talking about acting creatively in their engagement with customers, they flinch a bit and say something like "That might be a great approach, but you see, I'm not very creative."

Especially in today's world—with 24/7 news channels, constant entertainment options via online companies such as Netflix and Hulu, movies available for instant download from your cable company and Apple TV, and a video about anything you can imagine available at any time on YouTube—we are surrounded as never before by creativity. Perhaps we assume that raises the pressure on folks like you and me to be just as excellent when we attempt to deliver innovative solutions for our customers. Nothing could be further from the truth.

Unlike our personal situation when we watch television or movies, our customers today, along with the vast majority of us, are facing a dearth of creative encounters. In fact, we are fairly bored with the way many companies treat us as we offer them our hard-earned money—organizationally and individually—in return for their goods or services. As I wrote in my book *Create Distinction: What to Do When "Great" Isn't Good Enough to Grow Your Business*:

> Over the past several years we have seen the homogenization of practically everything. The box I drive probably looks a lot like yours, no matter the nameplate. The big store where I shop almost certainly appears and feels a lot like yours, no matter the logo on the door, no matter the community where it is located.
>
> If you cannot find it within you to become emotional, committed, engaged, and . . . yes . . . FERVENT about creating distinction, then you had better be prepared to take your place among that vast throng of the mediocre who are judged by their customers solely on the basis of *price*. As mentioned earlier, it is the singularly *worst* place to be in all of business. If you aren't willing to create distinction for yourself in your profession—and for your organization in the marketplace—then prepare to take your seat there in the back, with the substantial swarm of the similar, where tedium reigns supreme.

You can't stand out if you are the same as everyone else. You can't become a Taxi Terry by driving your cab the same way that all the other cabbies in town do. You can't create distinction without thinking—and *acting*—creatively.

How can you act more creatively?

Many years ago, when I first set a goal to become an author of business books, I knew that I was going to have to become more creative to succeed. I discovered that there are many terrific books on the subject of enhancing your creativity, such as my personal favorite, *A Whack on the Side of the Head* by Roger von Oech (Creative Think Publishers, 1983). I strongly encourage you to discover your own favorites.

In addition, let me share four of the action steps that I take to enhance my ability to deliver creative solutions to my customers:

1. Get it down—now.

2. Ask, "What if . . . ?"

3. Have fun.

4. Pretend you are someone else.

Get It Down—Now

For many of us, it's not that we don't think creatively; it's that when an idea springs into our thoughts, we don't capture it. Therefore, we often catch ourselves saying, "Now what was that idea I had yesterday?" Perhaps this explains why we'll point at the television or to a magazine when a new product is promoted and silently think, "Hey, *I* thought of that!" This also emphasizes an important point: to gain the reward, you have to take action on your creativity, not just think creatively.

I keep a notepad and pen by the bed so that if I wake up with a good idea, I can write it down and return to sleep knowing that I won't have to worry about forgetting it in the morning. Every iPhone and Android device can easily record your thoughts and ideas. Use that function on your smartphone to be certain that the good ideas don't get away.

Ask, "What if . . . ?"

My good friend and Speakers Roundtable colleague Mike Rayburn has an entire program based on that question. Mike employs his extraordinary talent as a guitar virtuoso (he's played several times at Carnegie Hall) to dramatically display the potential impact from asking the simple question "what if?" An example would be "*What if* . . . the illustrious rock band AC/DC performed the words of Dr. Seuss's legendary *Green Eggs and Ham*?"

Although that may sound outlandish at first, consider that, for example, Enterprise Rent-A-Car is now the largest company in its industry. That success is really based on one simple question: "*What if*. . . instead of making the customers come to us to acquire their rental vehicles, we picked them up?"

Herb Kelleher and Rollin King basically asked, "*What if*. . . we let people choose their own seats on the plane, told jokes, and had fun instead of doing it the way it has been done by the major airlines?" The end result, of course, was the creation of Southwest Airlines.

It won't come naturally at first; however, if you practice asking yourself that question, it will most likely enhance your creative abilities.

You'd probably be amazed how many major breakthroughs in every industry and within specific departments and activities in every organization came about because someone asked those two critical words that stimulate our creativity: "*What if*. . . ?"

Have Fun

It's difficult to be creative when you feel beaten down, broke, tired, sick, and ugly. We have all had those days, haven't we? My guess is that there are more of them in store as well. However, if you want to be more creative, you can't allow those days to dominate your existence; instead, you've got to have some fun.

By fun, I do not mean being frivolous. While we shouldn't be solemn in our approach, we do need to be serious about the customer experiences we are creating.

However, undertaking enjoyable activities builds creativity in two major ways. First, the disconnection from the day-to-day commotion we normally endure frees us to consider more than just making certain that our to-do list gets completed.

Second, because our brains tend to seek patterns in our activity, a new undertaking may open our minds to thoughts we wouldn't contemplate otherwise. For example, taking a cooking class may cause us to wonder what ingredients it would take to achieve a higher level of customer interaction. Or we might ask, How could we sweeten the experience of our internal customers so that our employee retention is enhanced? Maybe we will ruminate on how we can add some spice to the office environment so that it is not so drab.

Having fun encourages the mind to skip barefoot through new pastures of thought and makes us more productive as a result.

Pretend You Are Someone Else

Jim Cathcart, a legendary motivator, sales trainer, and professional speaker, has a great line in his programs: "Ask yourself this question," Jim encourages the audience. "How would the person I'd *like to become* handle the situation I'm currently facing?" Isn't that brilliant? All of a sudden, you start making decisions that are based on what's important instead of what's urgent. You begin to respond to situations in a much more thoughtful and mature manner as a result of Jim's question.

When it comes to creativity, there is a variation that will assist us. Ask yourself "How would" and then insert the name of someone you admire, your manager, or someone else you respect in the business world before finishing with "creatively enhance this situation?"

You may find yourself asking, for example, "How would Steve Jobs have handled our product development problem?" or "How would Steve Martin make our people more committed to this project?" Then make a list of some of the steps you think they would take if they were the ones facing your current challenge.

I have friends who envision a dialogue between two famous people and imagine they are debating each other on a particular issue. For example, if you own a dry cleaner and want to expand your business, imagining how Steve Jobs and Bill Gates would have argued with each other about the proper course to take may stimulate some original thinking from you on the subject.

While you may not want to ask yourself how Tony Soprano would've handled a problem employee, putting yourself into the mindset of a leader who you admire is a terrific tool to help you fuel your creativity.

These four approaches can help you think more creatively. However, as we mentioned earlier, it's not enough to just think creatively; you must act creatively as well. Don't invalidate your innovative ideas with inaction.

Nike has never said, "Just think about it." The key is to "just do it."

There are many examples of artists who disparage consistent performance. For example, Oscar Wilde wrote, "Consistency is the last refuge of the unimaginative."[6]

Taxi Terry is a wonderfully creative example.

However, his business would fail if I and his hundreds of other clients could not be certain that he would be at the airport for the pickup. The world is filled with stories of creative types who were so woefully disorganized and unable to consistently apply their ideas that they went belly up.

I prefer a more contemporary example: that of one of my favorite comedians, Louis C.K. "I've learned from experience that if you work harder at it, and apply more energy and time to it, and more consistency," he wrote, "you get a better result."[7]

Even in the highly creative field of show business, creativity alone won't make you a success.

On a hectic road trip filled with major presentations, I had a Sunday afternoon all to myself, alone in Manhattan. Taking a walk down one of the multitude of busy streets in the Broadway area, I passed the marquee of the Gerald Schoenfeld Theatre. It had the name of an actor I had always dreamed of seeing in person but never imagined the opportunity would be realized: Al Pacino.

Not only was Pacino playing in that very theater on that very afternoon, he was also starring in one of my favorite plays: David Mamet's brilliant *Glengarry Glen Ross*.

Walking up to the box office window, I naturally assumed that this and every other performance was sold out. However, an opportunity like this probably would not come my way again, and so I had to inquire. Standing behind two couples at the ticket window, I waited my turn. Seeing their discouragement as they turned to walk away, shaking their heads, I didn't figure the odds were in my favor.

"Excuse me, sir," I began. "I just had to inquire if there were any tickets available for this afternoon's matinee."

Peering over reading glasses, the old man gruffly asked, "You want *one?*"

"Yes, sir," I responded. "Just me."

"You're in luck. I have one ticket."

I would have been happy with any ticket; imagine my thrill upon receiving a tenth-row-center seat for the performance.

Alfredo James Pacino is quite obviously an acting legend. In addition to an Oscar for best actor, he's won two Tony awards, two Emmy awards, and four Golden Globes.[8] One solitary performance on a single Sunday afternoon to the audience in a small theater would not affect his reputation in the slightest.

Yet from the opening scene until the moment the curtain closed while the audience loudly cheered, Pacino's performance was electric. I watched in awe at his remarkable delivery and marveled at his extraordinary consistency.

Pacino delivered that exceptional level of performance throughout the production—every show, every time. If you were sitting in the audience, would you want him to perform at any other level? As another Tony winner, Sir Jim Dale, said about the craft, "Good acting is consistency of performance."

What if after you had stood in line and were breathlessly awaiting the opportunity to see such a master, Pacino sauntered onto the stage, took a deep breath, and said in his unique style, "Folks . . . I ain't *feelin'* it tonight! Sorry. Just gonna say the lines, man. Just *sayin'* the lines."

Would you jump up and cheer? Would you shout, "No prob there, Al. You've earned it!" No! You would be stunned and thoroughly disappointed.

That is the point: when *we* are the customer, we expect and demand a reliable performance after we've invested our time, money, and effort. You can even be an incomparable artist such as Al Pacino, and we still expect you to hit the mark and consistently deliver excellence.

The same principle is true for you. This tenet states that you have to act creatively and *consistently*.

To attain a higher level of consistency, here are six steps you can take:

1. Set a goal.

2. Decide about the required amount of investment.

3. Develop a calendar.

4. Select an accountability partner.

5. Create momentum.

6. Reward yourself.

Set a Goal

It's really difficult to consistently perform when there are no clear objectives regarding the standards or requirements of your performance. Perhaps this is the primary reason some people aren't consistent: they don't know what's expected or the repetition with no goal line in sight becomes excruciatingly boring, and so their performance erodes.

Goals have three critical properties. They should be

- Specific

- Realistic

- Written

Specific

It's impossible to be consistent when your goal is nonspecific. For example, I believe it's not a good plan to have a goal to be happy. Happiness is the residual benefit of a continual progression toward a worthy goal.

The more precise you can make your goal, the greater the probability that you'll achieve it. For example, I set a goal to write the book you're reading right now. That's pretty specific; I'll know I've attained the goal when I complete this manuscript. However, just setting the specific goal isn't nearly enough; next, I have to be specific about other aspects, such as the length of the book and the date of completion and whether my publisher approves its content.

Unlike the open-ended questions we discussed in Chapter 4, the key ingredient here is to be able to ask yourself if you know exactly when you will have attained the entire goal or some of the steps associated with it. If you can answer yes or no at each point, you have a specific goal.

Realistic

Unlike some motivational speakers, I don't believe that you can do anything as long as you want it badly enough. No matter how much I channel a burning desire to be the starting center for the Indiana Pacers or the winning jockey at the Kentucky Derby, neither will become an element in my future.

In the long run, an unrealistic goal will neither motivate you nor inspire you toward highly consistent behavior. Instead, sooner or later you'll become frustrated.

However, as I have been teaching audiences for many years, most of us do not set unrealistic goals. Instead, we establish unrealistic time frames.

In our world of instant gratification, it seems that we want everything to be resolved immediately. Perhaps part of this springs from all the years we've watched everything from murder mysteries to world wars successfully summarized and resolved in only an hour on television. When we've observed that for decades, why should we have to work hard and deliver a consistent performance over an extended period to please our internal and external customers?

If you want to enhance your consistent performance, give your specific goal a realistic time frame for achievement.

Written

If you keep your goals locked in your head, then by our definition here, you do not have a goal. Instead, you have a wish or a dream.

A written goal is your contract with yourself for consistent performance and higher achievement. It's not something that you are required to share with others, although that's a personal choice and you certainly can if you want to. Transcribing your goal is a strategic decision to put it in writing because for some reason, when we write it down, a goal seems more definite.

Decide about the Required Amount of Investment

If you want to be more consistent in your performance, you have to make investments. I'm not suggesting that you have to spend money, although you may decide to invest in tools or technology that improves your personal efficiency. You will, however, be required to invest time, effort, intellect, and more.

Depending on the goal and on your professional and personal preferences, you are going to have to decide about your investment level. What you may find to be an acceptable level of investment, I may decide is too demanding.

You will be consistent over an extended period only when you are investing at a level to which you are willing to commit. If you've ever felt that an organization or an individual was taking advantage of you, it probably involved making a consistent contribution at a level you weren't prepared to invest.

You're better off at a comfortable level of investment for a longer period—as we covered in the segment on setting your goals—than you are trying to consistently maintain an uncomfortable effort, even if it takes a little less time.

Develop a Calendar

One uncomplicated method to enhance your consistency is to get a calendar and schedule your activities.

For our company, one area in which this activity has really helped is improving our efforts on social media. With the advent of Twitter, Facebook, YouTube, Foursquare, LinkedIn, blogging, and more, we were very irregular in the way we were using new media to connect with our clients and develop new contacts and friends. Developing a social media calendar has greatly enhanced our consistency—and results.

All we needed to do was create a calendar that said, for example, "We'll do a weekly YouTube video every Monday, which means that Scott needs to shoot the content on the preceding Thursday to allow for editing."

Here's another example: "We want to post five original tweets daily as well as five retweets of items we find interesting and want to share with our tens of thousands of followers." With the help of HootSuite, a web-based program that allows the user to schedule the postings around the timing the user determines in advance, we're able to consistently achieve our goals.

Notice as well how this synchronizes with our point about goal setting. We are specific in what we want to accomplish, we're realistic in terms of how much we're going to achieve as a result, and not only have we written the goal, we also write the specific action steps on our calendar. Whatever your desired outcome, this approach will work for you, too.

Select an Accountability Partner

Here is a step where I cannot cite research behind the principle explaining why it works; however, I can assure you that it does. Having a person who requires that you report on your activities to him or her will help you maintain consistent performance. You'll find that you will hold yourself more accountable if someone is going to be asking if you kept your word.

Here are three suggestions for selecting an accountability partner:

Have Specific, Predetermined Times to Touch Base

If you both agree that you'll speak, for example, every Tuesday at 3 p.m., it will become a ritual that you'll both schedule and uphold. If you are lackadaisical about your timing in contacting each other for some reason, you'll soon find that you're inconsistent in your efforts.

Challenge Each Other but Don't Condemn

Your commitment to each other is to hold each other accountable and to reassure and challenge each other to achieve higher levels of consistency and performance. It's not to overly criticize or condemn your accountability partner. Be certain to keep your comments uplifting and encouraging. You can help your partner do a better job if you give him or her in advance insights on how he or she might inspire you to higher levels.

One financial service professional related to me that his accountability partner provided the challenge necessary by getting him to agree that if he didn't make 25 prospecting calls, he would contribute $250 to Hillary Clinton's campaign. The financial advisor then said, "I do not like her politics or policies. That was motivation enough to move me to make all the calls!"

Be Willing to Give as Well as Receive

It's not just about accountability; it's also about partnership.

When you select an accountability partner, make certain that you've chosen someone from whom you can receive encouragement and that you can provide it for that person as well. There is a reciprocal nature to accountability; it does not flow in a single direction. You've got to be just as willing to hold someone accountable as you are willing to look for someone to keep you consistent in your performance.

Create Momentum

As a rabid sports fan, I can tell you that the expression "the Big Mo" has been around for ages. Play-by-play broadcasters as long as I can remember have loved describing what happens on the field or court when one team is able to change the momentum in a game from their opponents to themselves. This is important for a critical reason: having momentum evidently increases the likelihood of success. If it didn't, it would not be so important for the announcers to describe or for the team to try to seize.

Although I believe that sports analogies are frequently overused in business, this is an area where there is relevant application. Momentum is basically the force and power gained from movement. A train sitting still on the track won't affect a thing. When the train gets rolling, however, picking up speed and moving rapidly—gaining and growing in force and power—imagine the impact it would have if it collided with another object.

As you strive for greater consistency, you'll find much the same thing. Building momentum is critical. If you have it, you'll find it easier to maintain consistency in customer relationships, and customers will tell their friends, do more business with you, and improve their engagement with you. As a result, your business grows and your momentum is enhanced even further. If you don't have momentum, it is admittedly difficult to initiate. (Try to envision the concentrated effort it takes to get that train started and moving down the track.)

This is not to imply that you haven't been working hard. However, for many of us, a lack of consistency is not the result of a lack of effort but of a lack of focus. To get the train moving, concentration is centered on the track: the specific target the train seeks to advance upon. If you don't have goals—from our previous point—that are precise and provide direction and focus, you're what Zig Ziglar used to call a "wandering generality instead of a meaningful specific."

You probably had a similar experience to mine: a boring class in school in which a teacher droned, "An object in motion tends to stay in motion and an object at rest tends to stay at rest." I never realized in my school years how significant a role that law of physics would play in business success and personal achievement.

If you procrastinate and delay, you'll never connect with customers. You can't be a Taxi Terry if you keep the car in the garage. As trite as it may sound, the key to creating momentum is simply to change from being at rest to being in motion. Once you get going, however, you'll realize that momentum builds upon itself: that's why it's easier to lead it than it is to launch it. Creating momentum can become a critical key in connecting with customers in the Taxi Terry manner.

Reward Yourself

One of my favorite business books of all time is my friend Dr. Michael LeBoeuf's *The Greatest Management Principle in the World* (Putnam, 1985).

Here's the principle that Dr. LeBoeuf says is the greatest in the world: "behavior rewarded is behavior repeated." Pretty simple, right? We get what we reward.

However, upon further examination, that's a lot more profound than it might first appear. For one thing, it means that we don't get what we *want;* rather, we get what we *reward*. This, of course, implies that we had better be very careful about what we reward with our customers, our colleagues, our kids, and ourselves.

Many times, I've seen people make extraordinary efforts to improve their consistency and performance—make headway toward their goals—and then almost inexplicably lose their momentum. I've realized that one of the major reasons is that they have failed to reward themselves for the success they are beginning to attain. Frequently, they'll reward their colleagues on their teams or make their customers feel like a million bucks but withhold any kind of personal compensation or incentive.

The facet that will hold the previous five points together is this: reward yourself for improvements in consistent performance, because behavior rewarded *is* behavior repeated.

Taxi Terry created the best cab ride of my life, in part because he approached his business—and my needs as a customer—very logically. Simultaneously, he created distinction from everyone else in the marketplace by delivering his service with extraordinary creativity and remarkable consistency.

Follow this approach and you too—no matter your position in the organization or industry in which you work—can deliver at Terry's level.

Taxi Terry Takeaway

Being both creative and consistent are critical factors in delivering an Ultimate Customer Experience.

- Think of a specific internal or external customer with whom you may have a communications problem. Write a specific action plan on how you will attempt to first align, and then engage, and finally commit to improving the situation.

- Take just two minutes to consider some of the challenges you may be experiencing. Ask the question for each challenge, "Could a part of the problem be rooted in my denial to see the real issues here?" Then, answer why or why not.

- After you've selected your accountability partner, ask him or her to help you evaluate whether or not you have the "Big Mo" working in your favor—and how to initiate or maintain it.

THE FIFTH TENET

Make Your Customer the Star of the Show.

In Chapter 5, we learned that behavior rewarded is behavior repeated. Obviously, that important principle not only applies to our efforts to become more consistent but also can pertain to acquiring and retaining our customers, whether they are internal colleagues or external spenders.

How can we reward our customers for their contributions to our success and then leverage that reward to create even more momentum? If a customer is rewarded for doing business with us in a compelling manner, it stands to reason that he or she will want to repeat that process, doesn't it?

Taxi Terry pulled in front of the hotel, ran to the trunk of his car, removed my bag, and held it as if it were a family member. He walked briskly to the hotel employee standing as a sentry at the front door, gently handed the bag to the waiting bellman, and announced he was "Presenting Mr. McKain . . . and his luggage!"

It struck me that in my entire life I had never been "presented" to anyone before. Taxi Terry had driven me to the Marriott, yet he made me feel like a movie star, walking the red carpet at the premiere of a film in which I was the main attraction. That's quite a feat.

Taxi Terry made me feel like the star of the show. Naturally, that is a feeling that I want to experience repeatedly, and it is a critical quality you can deliver to your customers as well.

If you're going to make the customer the star of your organization's show, it begins with learning a principle that I started speaking to audiences about in the 1980s and then examined in my first business book in 2002, *All Business Is Show Business*.

Any form of entertainment—whether a movie, television show, or play—only truly succeeds when it establishes an emotional connection with the audience. The more profound the connection with the audience, the greater the success of the production. It's a great example of what you need to do in business to become a Taxi Terry. You must establish a passionate linkage with your customers and colleagues to create the type of loyal relationship we all seek with our most important targets.

I realize that when I suggest you should "make your customer the star of the show" that some will consider this akin to suggesting frivolity, song, and dance. That's not the case.

When you seriously examine the entertainment industry, you come to realize that for some products the desired audience response is amusement. However, you would never assume that a sense of light-hearted fun or slapstick mirth was the purpose of movies like *Twelve Years a Slave* or *Captain Phillips*—both highly successful products of the entertainment industry.

You—and your organization—must maintain that same emotional flexibility. For some businesses, creating and enhancing a connection with your audience—our external and internal customers—will be found through increased humor and fun. Others, like a pharmacy for example, will establish their emotional bond through an enhanced sense of caring and concern transmitted to customers. Regardless of the outcome, however, your business *is* show business.

If you are skeptical about the correlation, please remember: they don't call it show *art* but show *business*, and for very good reasons. The bottom line is that your internal and external customers are going to have an emotional experience because of their contact with you whether you like it or not. Your responsibility—and challenge—is to provide them with the kind of emotional connection that will inspire productivity and loyalty.

Let's break this down into specific steps that will work for you. First we'll discuss *why* the customer should be the star of your show, and then we will examine *how* you make it happen.

"All business is show business" is based on a simple philosophy of mine. Whether it is the latest television hit or a classic movie that we stream from Netflix, Howard Stern on Sirius/XM or Rush Limbaugh on your car radio, Fallon or Letterman, the entertainment industry surrounds us. The position that I developed is that show business has inundated us so thoroughly that it has literally altered the way we buy and the manner in which we work.

A stark realization of this phenomenon was driven home to me when I was requested to return to my small hometown of Crothersville, Indiana.

I was asked to travel back home and visit my old school the day before the current student body arrived to begin the school year. My job was to present a program to the school's teachers for a kickoff meeting being held to help create some momentum as the fall semester was about to begin.

I began my presentation with a very basic question that many speakers and authors ask to begin a lecture. "Let's start by having you tell me," I said, "what your biggest problem is. That way we will make certain we touch upon your most significant challenges." I thought I had prepared the answers to the issues that I anticipated the teachers were going to raise: student discipline, lack of parental involvement, a changing curriculum, and lack of government funding for educational programs.

Imagine my surprise when a former teacher of mine raised her hand and declared, "Scott, I believe education's biggest problem today is *Sesame Street*."

My response to her answer was immediate and profound: "Huh?"

My former educator then asked me, "Scott, who taught you your ABCs?"

"Well, my mother and my grandmother."

"Of course," she said. "However, for the last several decades, young people have been taught the alphabet by Big Bird and Bert and Ernie. This means that they arrive on the steps of this school for their very first day of formal instruction expecting to be entertained as they are educated."

My elementary school teacher was still teaching me.

For decades—at the most basic level—we have taught everyone in this culture that education, as well as everything else that is supposed to happen in life, is going to be wrapped in an experience that we can expect to be entertaining. Whether we approve of this phenomenon isn't the issue; the fact remains that it is reality. Entertainment is an integral part of our learning and training from an early age, and so it certainly behooves us to understand exactly what entertainment does.

As we've already said, entertainment doesn't just make us laugh.

It is not just about fun, and it is certainly not superficial. Instead, entertainment is about establishing and communicating an emotional connection with a designated audience. As I stated earlier, the more powerful the connection, the greater the success.

Your organization may be investing millions of dollars and thousands of hours to train you and your colleagues in the skills needed to perform the tasks required by your product or service and to engage customers at the desired level of performance. However, no amount of money or employee time is enough to overcome the behavior ingrained by our immersion in media.

"Americans consumed 1.27 trillion hours of media in 2008, says a study by researchers at the University of California, San Diego. A trillion not doing it for you? In that same period, 10.85 quadrillion words were consumed. In this evaluation of the nation's media consumption, the sheer totals are astounding," NBC News reported.[1]

A huge chunk of the average American's day is spent watching television. Forty-one percent of our time is watching some form of television—and we consume about 36 million hours of it just on our mobile devices every month, according to the University of California.[2] Remember, the study was analyzing data from 2008; it's logical to assume that mobile device viewing with the explosion in growth of iOS and Android platforms means that we're watching our tablets and smartphones at a significantly higher rate than we did just those relatively few years ago.

Therefore, I suggest that it stands to reason that you aren't going to connect with customers unless you use a method similar to what they experience when they are connected. It's all about establishing a powerful connection with your audience: the internal and external customers so important to you and your organization.

In a previous book, I discussed how all organizations have a recruitment strategy for finding new employees but significantly fewer have a retention strategy for keeping and growing the employees they've brought on board. Now I'm suggesting to you that the same principle applies to the manner in which many businesses deal with customers.

As the late Dr. Kenneth McFarland, one of the early professional business speakers in the United States, often suggested, when you think about it, the only thing any advertisement really represents is an *invitation* to go through the sponsor's front door. You'll see countless ads from businesses on billboards, newspapers, and television that want you—their prospect—to come inside. These companies often have not a clue how to develop the *experiences* that engender loyalty from the customers they've just acquired. It's like the old line about the dog chasing cars: he wouldn't know what to do if he caught one.

What if you were invited to a party only to arrive and discover that there were no snacks, drinks, music, or anything else to encourage you and the other guests to have a good time? You'd probably believe that you had been intentionally misled. Some employees and customers feel the same way about the experience they encounter after the invitation they receive to do business with the organization where they are working or purchasing.

Because many businesses center their activities on acquisition instead of retention, on prospecting instead of loyalty, and on transactions instead of experiences, they create a huge disconnect between what customers are truly seeking and what the organization is offering. They don't know how to create a compelling emotional connection once they have your attention.

Have you ever watched the previews for a film and become excited about seeing that movie upon its release? Then have you stood in line at the cinema, paid your money, and discovered that the actual movie was nothing like the trailer that promoted it to you? Feels pretty lousy, doesn't it? Unfortunately, that's the same emotion that organizations create for their colleagues and customers when they fail to connect with them and when they promise an experience that they can't deliver.

By inundating us with entertainment, our culture has thoroughly trained us to expect an experience. When we cannot or do not deliver according to those expectations, we alienate the very individuals and groups we seek to influence. When we fail to grasp that all business is show business, we become like an ordinary cab company that is about to be left in the dust by a Taxi Terry.

This is more important than ever before in the history of business because according to a study by Forrester Research that was commissioned by the digital marketing solutions provider Silverpop, "Customers now control the buying process far more than today's vendors control the selling process." The report continues by suggesting that if you do not have a "customer-obsessed approach" as well as an "in-depth understanding of customers' behaviors and needs" and a customer-engagement strategy "that is calibrated to those behaviors and needs," you are in serious trouble.[3]

"That's all well and good," you may be thinking, "but I'm not in management. What does this have to do with me?" Simply this: regardless of your specific responsibilities, this revolution in which customers of all types expect an experience and have greater control than ever before is affecting your organization and therefore your job.

You can sit back, not make a meaningful contribution, and merely hope for the best. Or you can become a Taxi Terry.

You can decide that regardless of whether you're driving a cab or working in retail, running a small enterprise or working in middle management at a multinational, you will create compelling experiences for the internal and external customers who cross your path.

I loved the opening line of a news story written by Joyce Smith of McClatchy Newspapers: "It's not only the Grinch who stole Christmas. Some grouchy salesclerks do, too."

The article states that up to 40 percent of revenues for a retailer can come from sales during the December holidays. Yet I would suggest that at precisely the moment when they should be displaying their best efforts to build a customer relationship, many businesses put poorly trained employees on the front lines.

The article continued: "A study this year by American Express found that nearly 80 percent of Americans have ditched intended purchases because of poor service. But on the flip side, consumers said they would spend an average of 13 percent more with companies that provided excellent service."[4]

In other words, if you are a frontline clerk, you have a massive impact on your organization's success at obtaining and retaining external customers, the lifeblood of any business. Every member of the team has a significant contribution to make, and every member of the team can become a Taxi Terry.

That's *why* it is so important to make the customer the star of the show. Now let's examine *how* you can do that.

Treat Your Customer Like a Celebrity

How do you believe celebrities are treated?

In my movie reviewing experience, I had the opportunity to be around many movie stars and observe what it's like firsthand. Here are the four major characteristics I noticed.

Everyone Knows Their Names

This is something we discussed earlier in this book. You can't be a star if people don't know your name. If an actor is walking the red carpet and the paparazzi are saying, "Who is *that* guy?" that actor has yet to attain true celebrity status.

From the Taj Palace to Taxi Terry, when a business knows and repeatedly uses the customer's name, it is making the customer feel special. A study by

RightNow Technologies stated that "51 percent [of customers] said companies are impersonal."[5] Simply stated, if all you do is remember and use a customer's name, you may already be in the upper half of all of that customer's experiences.

They Are Constantly Being Thanked and Praised

In an interview I did with Tom Hanks to promote the release of the film *Forrest Gump*, he remarked to me that fame does "bad things to you before it does good things for you."

When I asked him to elaborate, we began a discussion of how difficult it is to handle the constant praise and attention while maintaining the proper perspective. That attitude and humility are essential ingredients in the success and longevity of Hanks's career. However, most "normal" people never have to deal with this kind of lavish admiration and constant compliments. It might get a little irritating for celebrities to be unable to go to the grocery store without everyone knowing who they are and praising their work; however, for the rest of us it feels pretty good on occasion.

Earlier, we discussed the importance of the first words customers hear from you and your business. Now for a moment, consider the *last* words they receive when they depart. I'm constantly amazed at how many times I spend money—both personally as I'm shopping and professionally in my role with my business—and fail to receive a sincere thank you.

"When was the last time you wrote or received a handwritten note of thanks or even a thank-you e-mail?" Joanna Krotz asked on a Microsoft forum for small and midsize companies. "Strictly in gratitude, mind you, not as prelude to asking for something else. Customers and suppliers notice such gestures. Depending on your business, the note can vary from no-frills to fancy."

Krotz also cites a comment by Joseph Ungoco of Brand Wrangler, a boutique New York public relations agency specializing in the fashion business, who suggests that "thank-you notes in his industry are key to maintaining the personal relationships that support business ones."[6]

Research indicates that 33 percent of customers will decide to do business with your organization because it has a brand with a good reputation. However, *73 percent* of customers will do business with your organization because it has "friendly employees or customer service representatives."[7]

If you fail to thank a customer and proactively take care of that customer's needs and concerns, you are responsible for your organization losing that customer's business.

That's a tough statement, to be certain, but research clearly shows it to be accurate. Remember: the number one reason for losing a customer is "dissatisfaction with customer service."[8]

If you are in management, doesn't this bring up the question: How much time, resources, and effort are you spending on *branding* versus the time, resources, and effort you spend on *customer service education* for your team?

Although it may be easy to remember to thank external customers after they've spent money with you or internal customers after they've successfully completed an assignment, there are at least five occasions when, just as a celebrity is constantly praised, we should thank our customers to ensure that they know they are the stars of our show:

1. Thank customers when they say no.

2. Thank customers when they provide insight.

3. Thank customers when they are nice to you.

4. Thank customers when they refer you.

5. Thank customers for no specific reason.

Thank Customers When They Say No

Although this may sound a bit daft at first—"Hey, they told me no! Why should I thank them for a rejection?"—you should always remember that even though external customers may have chosen not to spend money, they did invest their time and attention.

Thanking them for that investment—especially when you consider that one can always earn more money but no one can create more time—keeps the communication flowing. If you've treated me indifferently or, worse, after I've decided to take part of my business elsewhere, why would I want to repeat that experience with you for other business in the future?

It's a lesson I learned at a young age. I was in my teens and was working for our local radio station when the manager decided that he wanted to eliminate part-time employees. He figured that this would permit him to have air personalities who were totally committed to the station, with few outside obligations. Naturally, as a high school student, I had some additional commitments that were preventing me from becoming a full-time member of the staff.

When I was told I was being let go, I took it really hard. I had been devoted to my job, had great ratings when I was on the air, did all the extras I could to be a valued employee—even taking out the trash every night—and I was being fired?

Returning home practically in tears, I told my father what had happened. Rather than sharing my anger at the manager, Dad suggested that I contact the station's owner. Bill Vogel of Murfreesboro, Tennessee, had acquired several small-town radio stations and had been extremely nice to me during visits to his Indiana broadcasting company.

"Yeah," I told my dad, "I'll let Mr. Vogel know how the manager is screwing up the station."

"I don't think that's the message you need to give him," my father counseled. He reminded me that I was only sixteen years old and that Mr. Vogel had invested many thousands of dollars in the business in which I was an employee. Dad said, "And there were many times that you were there alone, on the air, the only person with responsibility at a place that he had put major funds into. He trusted you with a lot at just sixteen."

After a moment, I realized that Dad was absolutely right.

When I phoned his office in Tennessee, Vogel took my call. I told him that the manager had dismissed me from employment, and I could sense that he was uncomfortable because he was assuming I was calling to complain. Instead I said, "Although I would love to continue as an employee, I just wanted to thank you for the opportunity you have given me. I really appreciate it."

A few months later, the station manager I worked for was gone and his replacement called me. "Scott," he said, "Mr. Vogel suggested that I call you and that you're the type of person we want to have working for us." I was back on the air and very appreciative not only for Mr. Vogel but also that my father had taught me the lesson of saying thanks even when things don't go as you'd hoped.

That new radio station manager was the one who introduced me to the Oak Ridge Boys, as I described in the introduction of this book. It's amazing what can happen when you express thanks, even when someone tells you no.

Thank Customers When They Provide Insight

Although you are probably an expert on the products or services that you and your organization provide, the customers receiving them feel exactly the same way. Customers perceive that they have a unique perspective on what you sell, and they do. They are using it in the field to meet their needs and wants, and they properly believe that they have the right to tell you what they think.

I'm guilty of this phenomenon. Although the automotive company that manufactured the model that I motor around in has a team of highly trained engineers and talented designers, I assume that I'm an expert on the car as well. After all, I sit in one and drive it every day. "Why," I say to myself, "how could they refuse to listen to my expert ideas on how to make one of these models better?" Never mind that I know practically nothing about design or engineering.

When a customer takes the time to offer his or her advice, evaluation, or insight, the initial step we should always take is to thank the customer for making the effort even if we disagree with the suggestion.

The problem for many of us is that thanks to social media, we're now receiving more feedback than we ever imagined possible. It seems as though if you post where you're having lunch, you'll receive replies and tweets from folks who think they have a better location to offer.

I wrote online about a negative experience I had in the emergency room of a local hospital and received literally dozens of responses, ranging from patients who had a similar disappointing experience to others who were astonished because their encounters there had been exactly the opposite.

The best response, however, came from the hospital. First, they thanked me for sharing the experience even though, they acknowledged, it was not the kind of report they enjoyed reading.

Next, they explained every point where there had been a miscommunication and, more important, described what they were doing about the problem. Then, when they suggested a couple of points where I had been perhaps a bit unfair in the intensity of my critique, I did not perceive them as being defensive and had to admit that they were probably right.

Finally, they offered to review anything I would write to help them resolve the issue, or have a telephone conversation, or meet with them in person. I chose the latter.

Here's the important point from the hospital's perspective: I hope I don't need the services of emergency room physicians again; however, if I do, I will go back to that hospital. I'm convinced, in part because they sincerely seemed to appreciate my feedback, that they are making enormous efforts in patient care and satisfaction.

Am I suggesting that you respond to every communication from a customer: every Tweet, every post online, every Facebook mention?

Yes—within reason.

If you walked up to me at a party, extended your hand, and introduced yourself and my response was merely to turn and walk away, what would your opinion of me be? Rightly, it would be highly negative. "What an insensitive jerk!" you might think, and you would be justified in feeling that if those were my actions.

The problem is, social media is merely a digital expansion of that party; that's why it's called *social* media. If you refuse to be social—if a customer can post about you and receive no thanks and zero response—you've broken the rules of proper professional behavior.

There is exception to this rule: ignore the haters.

There are some people who, thanks to the anonymity of the Internet, seem to have set as their primary goal and exclusive task to upset, damage, berate, rebuke, and harangue anyone and everyone who is attempting to achieve anything of purpose. As I can tell you from personal experience, it is hurtful to be on the receiving end of the lies, exaggerations, and blatant disregard of personal feelings that these purveyors of venom unleash.

I can advise you from experience that your first reaction is probably incorrect. If you're like me, you think, "If they just knew the truth, they wouldn't think that way about me." You then try to justify your position, which is just throwing fuel on the hater's fire. They aren't attempting to shine a light on what is right and true; they're purely focused on drawing attention to themselves regardless of the emotional pain they inflict on others.

Responding to their vitriol is merely giving them what they want. When you respond, it makes them feel as though they have control over you, especially if you provide an emotional retort. That's why the superior solution is to ignore them. It's the one response they can't stand: that feeling of insignificance and irrelevance.

One part of going through the process of dealing with a hater that amazed me was that when I told author friends and professional speaking colleagues about it, I found out that a significant number of them had endured a similar experience. That's unfortunate; however, it also means that the impact of the haters is rapidly diminishing. People are realizing that the hater—at his or her core—only seeks to gain attention by denigrating others, rather than taking action that is positive and substantial. The credibility of the hateful post or Tweet is rapidly collapsing under its own weight.

Thank Customers When They Are Nice to You

Remember that important phrase "behavior rewarded is behavior repeated"? It applies here as well. When customers are nice to you, thank them for it. It helps assure that they'll behave the same way the next time.

I was standing in line at the airport when I overheard the Delta Airlines ticket agent saying to the passenger in front of me at the counter, "Sir, I have to tell you, *thanks*. You have been the very nicest person I have talked to all day. I really appreciate you."

The guy started smiling all over. Barely able to contain his enthusiasm, he thanked her, saw me standing next in line, and said to me, "You're going to love having her take care of you. She's great!"

At that instant, what was that customer's opinion of Delta? Here's a company with 80,000 employees and more than 700 expensive and highly technical aircraft, coordinating flights to 330 destinations in 65 countries on six continents.[9] And this guy's opinion is that they are fantastic because one employee thanked him for behaving in the manner that she would have preferred that he behave anyway.

There's a residual effect you'll receive from thanking nice customers as well. As I am a somewhat competitive guy, what was now my goal? I wanted to be the new "very nicest person" she'd talked to all day.

When I made it through the TSA checkpoint and arrived at my gate, the same gentleman was talking to another Delta representative. He was now the friendliest traveler you could imagine—another case of "behavior rewarded, behavior repeated." If you take notice when customers are nice to you, they will return the favor.

Thank Customers When They Refer You

The best thing a customer can do is do business with you.

The second best thing a customer can do is to tell (and bring) their friends and colleagues to do business with you.

When a customer is kind enough to refer you, find an extraordinary way to display your profound appreciation. We've long heard that word-of-mouth advertising is the best kind of promotion a business can receive. It's obviously important, then, that you support and enhance positive customer recommendations.

I'm not a big fan of promotions that say, "Bring us a friend and we'll give you $20!" If I don't believe in your services, 20 bucks is not an incentive to get me to throw a friend under the bus. If I do believe in what you do, 20 bucks is not compensation enough for how I can help both you and my friends. Also, I infer from your statement that the value you place on friendship is about 20 bucks.

Here's what I do like: keeping me in the loop. If I refer a friend, send me a short e-mail saying something like this:

> Again, Scott—thanks for the kind referral of your friend, Jane Doe. I reached out to Jane with the attached message and suggested that she expect a call from me on Wednesday morning. Please let me know if there is anything else I should be doing for her—and for you! In addition, I'm sending you a gift card for dinner at your favorite restaurant. Thanks again—I truly appreciate your kind recommendation!

How does he know my favorite restaurant? Well, you did read the earlier tenets, right? To get my business and make such an impression that I'm going to spread the word of your excellence to my friends, it's one of those things you should know.

I was remarking to a colleague that I'd just sent my best client a bottle of his favorite wine—Duckhorn Cabernet Sauvignon—to thank him for a recommendation he had provided. My associate said, "If I had someone give me a recommendation like that, I would learn his favorite wine, too."

I told him that he had it exactly backward. Part of the reason he felt comfortable providing such an important reference for me was that I knew so much about those things. In other words, I didn't learn his favorite wine because of the recommendation; instead, I got the recommendation because I knew things such as his favorite wine.

Thank your customers in a manner that has significance for them when they provide you with a genuine referral.

Thank Customers for No Specific Reason

Why does there have to be a specific motive for saying thank you to a customer? Sometimes the best time to express your appreciation and the time it makes the greatest impact is when it appears to the customer to be totally spontaneous.

Frankly, when I'm the customer—and you're probably very similar—I *expect* a thank you when I purchase a product or service from you. I have a right to anticipate a thank you if I refer a friend to spend his or her money with you, too. I appreciate a thank you of recognition when I care enough to let you know how you might serve me better or improve your products and services. And although I don't await for a thanks when I've been nice, it's another case of the customer doing something first and then receiving thanks.

That's why it can be so impactful when we let customers know out of the blue how much we appreciate their business. Your appreciation in this example is not a response to my behavior as the customer; it is your expression of sincere gratitude for my patronage.

With an external customer, a handwritten note, a call, or an e-mail that is sincere and personal—not a form message sent as a blast to everyone—is highly valued. For your colleagues—the internal customers—why not stop by the office, poke your head in the door, and express thanks for the hard work and dedication they've brought to your team effort?

"Three out of four customers say they have spent more with a company because of positive experiences," according to Salesforce.com.[10] How can it be a positive experience for customers and how can they feel that they are the stars of your show if they aren't thanked and praised for doing business with you?

This leads to the next aspect of how we assume that celebrities are treated.

They Receive Special and Preferential Treatment

A Rasmussen Reports poll says that 78 percent of us believe that star athletes and 72 percent believe that entertainment celebrities receive special treatment when they break the law.[11]

While I realize that some of us aren't fond of the frequent handling of celebrities that often seems overly privileged, I'd suggest that most of us want it both ways. Although, for example, we don't want celebrities to receive favored treatment from a justice system that is supposed to be blind to status, we cannot get enough of the latest news and gossip about the luxury and privilege in the lives of movie stars. It seems as though we would all love to be behind the ropes. Let's face it: if nobody wanted to see the pictures, the paparazzi would be out of work.

When I did a Google search on "celebrities receive special treatment," over 345,000 results were returned in less than a half second. Most of the responses were stories or blog posts complaining about star treatment in the justice system, at rehab centers, and even in the line at the Apple Store.

Yet at the top of the page—in the space that Google sells to advertisers— was this very enticing offer: "Get Celebrity Treatment: Universal Studios Hollywood!" After the URL for the website that would enable you to connect with Universal, I saw the bonus tagline: "Experience the Real Hollywood with Our VIP Tour. Live Like a Star!"

Six years after publication of my *All Business Is Show Business,* another colleague in the professional speaking industry, Donna Cutting, released her book *The Celebrity Experience: Insider Secrets to Delivering Red Carpet Customer Service* (Wiley, 2008). The point Cutting makes is an essential one, the same one expressed by the ads from Universal Studios: it's important to deliver special and exclusive treatment that makes your customers feel like stars.

"But Scott," you may be thinking, "if all of us are special, in actuality none of us are." That's a great point.

A great analogy to this point is found in the loyalty programs used by several retailers, especially the frequent flier programs offered by most airlines.

Only one flight segment permits me to join Delta Airlines' SkyMiles program. I can start accruing benefits immediately that not only build and enhance my loyalty to the airline but also can assist Delta in determining specifically what special benefits and exclusivity I should receive.

If I fly more frequently and become a better customer, I can receive benefits such as waived fees for checking baggage and a shorter priority line for check-in and boarding as I advance through tiers labeled as Silver, Gold, and Platinum. By the time a Delta customer reaches the highest level— Diamond Medallion—he or she receives frequent free upgrades to first class, a

125 percent bonus on miles flown to reach awards for free tickets more rapidly, and more.

However, one of the aspects that I like best is that almost every time I board a Delta flight, I hear someone from the airline saying words like "Mr. McKain, we thank you for your loyalty. Customers like you are why I have a job, and I want you to know that I truly appreciate it." Not only is Delta making their best customers feel like stars, they're providing the preferential treatment that we all desire.

Also, you should recognize three objectives important to your organization that they've achieved in the process:

- Identify your customers and make all of them feel that they belong.

- Recognize and reward your customers for their loyalty.

- Provide the most exclusive rewards, recognition, and preferential treatment to your best customers.

In other words, Delta can't treat every flier like a Diamond Medallion. Also, if you're on the front line for your company, you need to devote most of your attention—and provide the most preferential treatment—to your most valuable customers. Some will disagree; however, I feel that you should treat your best customers differently from the rest.

Remember our earlier example? Let's say you're coaching a youth softball team and your daughter is one of the players. My assumption is that you're going to treat her a little bit differently simply because of the stronger mutual commitment you have to each other. You may say, "I treat all my players exactly alike," but I don't believe it. Either you're going to treat her better because you love her and know that the lessons she learns will affect her and your family for decades to come, or you're going to overcompensate and treat her worse than the others, attempting so hard to play no favorites that you're tougher on your own daughter than you are on anyone else's.

Most customers expect that we are going to treat those who spend the most with a little more exclusivity than we treat a first-time buyer. (Those who do not understand that principle are probably not going to become good customers, anyway.)

When my wife and I dine at our favorite restaurant in Indianapolis—Sullivan's Steakhouse—the manager, John Stanley, meets us at the front door. Others on the management team, such as Kimberly, Hal, and Stephanie, stop by and say hello. We get a nice table, and the servers are wonderful to us. They're friends as well as folks with an establishment where we enjoy dining, and we are in there a lot.

Did they treat us that way the first time we dined there? Of course not. We did receive superior service, which, combined with the great food, inspired several return trips. However, the extraordinary level of engagement between us and the team at Sullivan's grew as we became more dedicated and loyal customers.

It also helps drive our business to Sullivan's. When we are considering our dining choices, my wife and I often ask, "Why go somewhere that we would be a stranger when we can get a personal experience at Sullivan's?"

Although all customers need to receive superior treatment, the Ultimate Customer Experience is so important it should be reserved for your best.

The fourth way that celebrities are treated is as follows.

Stars Are Frequently Asked What They Think, and Many Are Interested in What They Believe

Even after years of broadcasting movie reviews and interviewing the biggest movie stars in the world, I am amazed at how many times those celebrities were asked what they thought about every subject known to humankind. Entertainment reporters from all over the globe would assemble in Hollywood to ask the likes of John Travolta for his opinion on his latest film as well as on politics, religion, economics, and world affairs.

For some reason, there are millions of us who are fascinated by what these celebrities think, and there are thousands employed to ask them and pass along that information to the public.

In addition, our purchase decisions in a wide variety of areas can be influenced by the endorsement of someone with celebrity status.

"The history of celebrity endorsements is over 100 years old, dating back to at least the late 19th century when acclaimed stage actress Lillie Langtry began appearing on packages of Pear's Soap," says Anthony Rufo, an attorney with law firm Foley Hoag, writing for *JD Supra Law News*.[12]

Celebrities also have a history of political endorsements. "Some historians credit Republican President Warren G. Harding with running the first campaign that made liberal use of celebrity endorsement. When Harding ran in 1920, film was still just a fledgling industry. Harding, who invented the word 'normalcy,' was backed by conservative silent film stars like Lillian Russell, Douglas Fairbanks, Mary Pickford and Al Jolson, evidently as part of a well-orchestrated campaign by ad agency Lord & Thomas," according to an article by Linda Rodriguez McRobbie on the website MentalFloss.com.[13]

Even celebrities who are no longer living influence our decisions through the products with which their images and endorsements are associated. Based in my hometown of Indianapolis, CMG Worldwide is a globally respected leader in the representation of celebrity estates. Under the leadership of my friend Mark Roesler, CMG licenses and controls the images of idols such as James Dean, Jackie Robinson, Ingrid Bergman, Malcolm X, and Buddy Holly. The multi-million-dollar enterprise leverages the enormous recognition and goodwill built by these extraordinary individuals for the benefit of CMG's clients.

This extraordinary influence possessed by celebrities generates five "what ifs?" for you to consider:

1. What if we were as inquisitive about the customers of our organization as the press is about celebrities?

2. What if we asked external customers for their opinions more frequently than we cashed their checks?

3. What if we more actively sought the opinions of external and internal customers rather than waiting for them to tell us about a problem?

4. What if we went beyond a suggestion box or impersonal requests for employee ideas and asked in a highly personal manner how we could help our internal customers do their jobs more effectively?

5. What if we had our own version of a celebrity magazine or website that featured our internal and external customers, highlighting their answers to our questions and their thoughts regarding professional and industry issues?

Perhaps if we asked as many questions of our customers—both internal and external—and listened as intently as the general public does to celebrities, we would make them truly feel like stars. We would be fulfilling the goal of this tenet, delivering an Ultimate Customer Experience, and attaining the level of engagement of a Taxi Terry.

Make your customers the star of your show and they'll return for the sequel. This leads us to the next tenet: "Help your customer come back for more."

Taxi Terry Takeaway

Here are some ideas to help you make your customer the star of the show:

• Somewhere at your business, there is probably a place that employees can access—but customers cannot. Create a "Hall of Fame" wall with pictures of your best customers there, so that all of your employees can see who is doing business with you most frequently. This also helps your newest team members learn quickly who the most valuable customers are to your organization.

- Record an interview with your best customers, external and internal, and upload the video to your website. Not only will it make your current customers feel like a star, it is a great marketing tool to convince your prospects why you are a superior choice.

- Send a handwritten thank-you note to your best customers—for no reason at all, other than to let them know how much you appreciate their business.

THE SIXTH TENET

Help Your Customers Come Back for More.

CHAPTER 7

Let's envision for a moment that you are a member of the Broccoli family.

No, I don't mean that you are a cousin of the larger cabbage clan or a healthy vegetable with a big, flowery edible head.

Instead, I mean you should imagine that you are one of the descendants of Albert "Cubby" Broccoli.

The younger of two children, Cubby Broccoli was born in Queens, New York, in 1909. Later, his family moved to a farm on Long Island. (The family claimed that its ancestors brought the first broccoli seeds to the United States in the 1870s.) When young Cubby was ready to strike out on his own, he decided to go to London and find a way to break into the film business. After forming a small company and successfully producing several films with a partner, Broccoli became interested in a relatively new series of moderately successful novels and sought to obtain the film rights to produce those books in what he hoped would be popular movies.[1]

In 1962, he made it happen. Along with a new partner—the Canadian producer Harry Saltzman, who Broccoli learned had already acquired the film rights from the author of the novels—he was able to bring the first movie based on the books to the screen.

The film was *Dr. No*, and it was the first time the world became enthralled by the cinematic adventures of 007, the British spy James Bond.

Before he died in 1996 at age 87, Broccoli had obtained sole control of the franchise and passed the production over to his daughter, Barbara Broccoli, and stepson, Michael G. Wilson.

Picture now that you are part of their family, making decisions about the future of the most successful series in the history of motion pictures. What are your desires for the future?

Your initial answer might be, "I want lots of people to come back and see the next James Bond movie we make." That's not a bad first step. However, if you stop and really consider the question, you'll find it goes much, much deeper than that.

As I mentioned over a decade ago in my book *All Business Is Show Business*, the desire of every business and each professional should be to earn an encore and a standing ovation from his or her customers. Yet countless businesses leave money on the table and many of the employees of those organizations unknowingly or carelessly fail to maximize the profitability and productivity available from every customer simply by making it difficult for the customer to come back and do more business with them.

My experience over many years working with the leading corporations of the world has taught me that the most successful organizations are the ones that make it easy to do business with them and even easier to come back for more. They understand that there are many avenues to create additional business and exploit those opportunities for the good of both the customer and the company.

Then Taxi Terry turns to me without a card or paper or form in his hand and says, "Mr. McKain, I realize you are going to need a receipt to document the trip for your business purposes, and someone brought you here, so someone is going to have to take you back to the airport, and I hope that's me!"

Part of what can help your customer come back is to understand a little about what makes *you* tick. My guess is that because you've been exposed to the story of Taxi Terry, you may want to ride with him if you're in Jacksonville. Knowing a bit about him and his business creates an experience that you want to repeat.

Picking me up at the Minneapolis–St. Paul airport on a cold Monday morning in February, my new client and friend from 3M asked if I had any preference for a lunch location.

"Something familiar," he asked, "or some local color?" Naturally, I opted for the local place, somewhere more distinctive than the national chains.

That's how I ended up at St. Paul's unique Obb's Sports Bar & Grill.

Obb's doesn't look all that different from a thousand other local places. You go inside and feel as if you've been transported back a few decades. Obb's first opened as a licensed bar shortly after the repeal of Prohibition.

We sat down after a very friendly greeting from a nice server, and I began to scan the menu. There I saw it: the story of Obb's.

As I read the story, my host from 3M suggested that I turn and take a look behind me. There was a gray-haired senior citizen working with enthusiasm, serving diners, and talking with everyone. Pointing to the menu, my client focused on a picture, nodded, and whispered to me, "That's Rosie!"

Rosie Johnson—the widow of Bob, who spent his life owning and working at Obb's, and the mother of the current owner—is still working and waiting on customers even though she's in her nineties (she could easily pass for being in her seventies).

As amazing as that might be, there is an additional reason I'm telling you the story of Obb's: it's because they tell you their story on their menu. It's easier for me as a thrilled customer to share the story of this wonderful bar and grill because they tell their own story.

Think about the flip side of the coin, however. If I came home uninformed, possessing no knowledge of Obb's and the story of Rosie, and told friends and family I had a 90-year-old waitress at lunch in St. Paul, what would their typical reaction to my dining experience be? My guess is that, for a number of reasons, they might assume I did not have the unique and extraordinarily wonderful experience that I enjoyed. Telling the story helps me come back and refer Obb's to my family and friends.

Consider this aspect: it's one thing to wonder what the history of the place might be; however, it bonds you and creates emotional connections when you learn the real story of where you are doing business.

Whether you are the frontline person, speaking directly with an external customer, or the CEO of a large company, your goal of helping your customers do more business with you can be accomplished if you focus on five basic aspects of the experience that you are creating for them organizationally and individually.

Those five characteristics are as follows:

1. Target the experience.

2. Repeat the experience.

3. Upgrade the experience.

4. Expand the experience.

5. Extend the experience.

Let's briefly examine each of them to better understand how you can get your customers to become more engaged with your business and more excited about the future, just as we became (and remained) more engaged with the series of movies about 007.

Target the Experience

Try the following thought experiment:

- Imagine that you are staging a play that is highly irreverent, erotic, and controversial only to discover that your audience is a group of clergy.

- Imagine the characters in *SpongeBob* performing inside a maximum-security correctional facility.

Obviously, these examples are absurd. However, they illustrate the point that if you do not know your audience, your chances of success are drastically reduced.

Successful entertainment companies are focusing their products and services with more precision than ever before. Variety-type shows intended for a generic audience—the old *Ed Sullivan Show*, for example—are basically a thing of the past.

I remember sitting as a child in the living room of my family's home in southern Indiana on Sunday evenings as we watched *The Ed Sullivan Show* together. One memory I will always retain is my mother and father shaking their heads at those outrageous four lads from Liverpool as I sat there, a little boy, thrilled to hear "I Want to Hold Your Hand."

If you didn't like the Beatles on *The Ed Sullivan Show*, however, you wouldn't have to wait long until the little Italian puppet mouse Topo Gigio or a comedian such as Joan Rivers or Rodney Dangerfield would appear. Even opera singers and Broadway performers frequented Sullivan's guest list. At that time in broadcasting, the key to Sullivan's success was in part that there was something for everyone.

That aspect was critical in a period when most houses received only three or four stations that were viewed on the family's one television set, which usually was the centerpiece of the home's living room. Even the name of the medium—*broad*casting—showcased the desire of the networks to deliver to their viewers a lineup of programs that were universally acceptable.

All you have to do is look at today's channel lineup from your cable or satellite television provider to realize the dramatic upheaval that has occurred. Although we still use the term *broadcasting* to describe the function, in actuality what we are now in is the age of *narrow*casting. In other words, entertainment companies now target us with tight accuracy. ESPN does not worry too much about the viewing habits of homemakers. The Food Network isn't going to be concerned if football fans bypass it when they are zapping through channels.

This has a powerful impact in all business situations. Remember, all business is show business. A great example is cited in the book *The Inside Advantage: The Strategy that Unlocks the Hidden Growth in Your Business*[2] by the advertising giant Publicis Worldwide's CEO, Robert H. Bloom, and the business writer Dave Conti. According to the authors, Procter & Gamble was having global success with its Swiffer Wet Mop because the product provided customers with abundant convenience except, for some reason, in Italy. There the product was faltering even as sales in the rest of the world were rapidly expanding. The company needed to find out why, and fast.

As their subsequent research discovered, the Italian market valued *strength* in cleaning products significantly more than *convenience*. After P&G targeted a precise message in Italy for the specific desires of that unique marketplace, Swiffer became a huge success there as well.

How does this affect you? Examine every aspect of your engagement with your customers and evaluate how you have targeted the experience they receive specifically to their needs, desires, and requirements.

If you are in retail and an elderly person enters your store, how will you assist him? And how will that approach be targeted in a manner slightly (or perhaps even greatly) different from the experience that a college-age prospective customer will receive? Although the student may appreciate a system in which she can order your product from her iPhone and have it delivered directly to her doorstep, an older customer may prefer personal instruction on how to use your product so that he feels assured that he is making a good purchase.

The Inside Advantage outlines a four-step plan to assist you in targeting your audience.[3] To paraphrase, the approach is basically as follows:

1. Decide *who* your target audience is for this specific product, service, or approach.

2. Determine *what* you can do that will be unique regarding how you interact with them.

3. Define *how* your strategy will persuade targeted customers to do more business with you.

4. *Own it*—take imaginative initiatives that enhance and expand your distinctive approach so that you become indispensable to your customers.

If you haven't considered all your potential alternatives, you may not be connecting with your customers the way Taxi Terry does.

For example, some occasional travelers may discover that arriving at an unfamiliar airport and trying to find the proper location to meet a limo driver is stressful. Terry has targeted those who aren't road warriors and helps them with a video on his website that literally walks you through the airport to the precise spot where he will meet you for "the best cab ride of your life." By the time you've arrived in Jacksonville, you feel as if you have been there before, because Terry has targeted you and delivered a solution that helps you do business with him.

Repeat the Experience

Although these two points may not initially seem to logically progress from one to the next, remember that the more I feel personally connected to an experience, the more likely I am to want to repeat it. By targeting the audience, you become better equipped to ensure repeat engagement. Naturally, this works with both external customers returning to purchase more of your products or services and internal customers striving to maintain or enhance a level of performance to experience a successful project, engagement, or effort again.

The reason that *Titanic* became one of the biggest box office hits of all time is the number of repeat customers it secured. Even though the movie lasts well over three hours, people wanted to view it again and again. The producer-director, James Cameron, then created the production that topped his own movie for the box office record, *Avatar*.

A movie like *Titanic* or *Avatar* is called by the film industry one that has legs because it is a movie that has a longer than usual life at the box office. It is the kind of movie that attracts repeat business. It brings people in to see the movie not just once but again and again.

Isn't that aspect also true in your business? A key to higher profitability is the repeat customer. If you are an accountant, for example, your lifeblood is not found in a person for whom you prepare taxes once and never see again; it is built upon advising, consulting, and preparing taxes for the same clients year after year after year. If you're a waitress, having regulars, who usually tip more than a one-time customer, is an essential part of how much money that you take home.

For everyone in every business, a critical question is this: Is the experience that you are delivering to your customers so compelling that they will want to repeat it?

Upgrade the Experience

As I'm writing this, my desk is a drop-down tray table on a Southwest Airlines flight from Las Vegas to Austin, Texas. As I was standing in the gate area, about to board this flight, I heard an announcement that for a nominal charge I could upgrade my ticket to "a 1–15 boarding," meaning I would have the ability to be one of the first passengers to board the plane, which ensures a better seat selection. Although I did not choose to partake, I noticed a couple of travelers who took advantage of the offer to upgrade the experience.

If Southwest charges $40 for the upgrade, it has made $80 more on this flight than it would have without the offer. Although that may not sound like much to such a big airline, consider the multiples. If they achieve those mere two upgrades on just 10 percent of their 3,700 daily departures, including AirTran,[4] that's an extra $29,600 they've made today, with practically zero expense. That adds up to almost *$11 million* a year of extra profit dropping directly to the bottom line just for asking customers if they want to upgrade the experience.

While playing a golf simulation game on my iPad, I was prompted by a message that asked if I wanted to add some courses to the program. I can now pretend I'm golfing at even more of the world's most exclusive courses for just a minimal cost to upgrade. Although it costs only $3.95 for me to upgrade, it can have an enormous impact on the profitability of the company that created the game.

McDonald's and other fast-food giants have made millions simply by encouraging customers at the drive-through to upgrade their orders from regular to supersize.

Movie buffs will spend more on the 3D or IMAX version of a major release. A significant percentage of the box office records constantly being set, seemingly with each passing year, for blockbuster movies is the result of average ticket prices growing higher because a significant portion of the audience chooses to upgrade their experience.

What does this mean to you? No matter what you do for your organization, you need to be seeking avenues for your customers to upgrade their experience. It will take a bit of creativity and perhaps a lot of effort; however, as you can see from these examples, it can become highly rewarding to your business—and you.

Expand the Experience

Although it is very similar to upgrading, there are a few subtle differences when a customer expands the experience.

To continue with the movie example, if I'm upgrading the experience, I'm taking something that I'm already doing at that moment—seeing the movie— and bumping it up a bit by watching it on an IMAX screen or paying a bit more to watch the 3D version instead of the regular flat-screen presentation.

If I expand the experience, I'm now going out after I've watched the film and purchasing the DVD of the movie to watch the director's cut, view deleted scenes that didn't make the version I watched, or listen in to the stars of the movie having a conversation about some of the scenes in the film.

In other words, upgrading focuses on the question, "How can we move the customer to spend more during this experience?" Expanding, in contrast, focuses on the question, "How can we deliver additional compelling features for the customer, based on this experience?"

In some cases, this may be an example of a concept called brand extension. For example, moving me from purchasing a regular bottle of Scope mouthwash to purchasing a larger bottle is getting me to upgrade my purchase. Expanding it means that I not only purchase the mouthwash, I also buy a tube of Crest Complete Whitening toothpaste with Scope. In both situations, I'm purchasing more Scope. However, in the former example, I'm spending more on the existing product at the time of purchase, whereas in the latter, I'm purchasing something additional that allows a broader use of the existing product.

I'd suggest that one of the requirements for expanding the experience is that highly similar product lines or service commitments should be involved to make the concept work most effectively.

Toothpaste and mouthwash go together, as do seeing a movie in the theater and watching that film on a DVD at home. These are approaches of taking the same product, whether it is mouthwash or a movie, and creating additional uses of that product by the customer.

Another way to expand the experience is through related products or services that leverage the emotional connection and goodwill built from the core purchase.

It's fun to go to eBay.com to look at old music or movie memorabilia and recognize the extraordinary marketing efforts that a number of rock bands and film projects have made in this respect. For example, recently on eBay I saw a large number of offers for widely varied designs of Beatles lunch boxes. Obviously, for many young people in the 1960s, a way to expland the Beatles experience beyond buying their records was to pack a lunch in a container adorned by the image of their favorite musicians.

Naturally, every organization has to be certain that the expanded experience is congruent with its product or service. Scope mouthwash added to my toothpaste is brand extention that succeeds; if they infused it into shampoo, I'd probably pass.

The company that makes Zippo lighters markets a perfume for women as well as a men's cologne. Their product is packaged in what appears to be a metal container almost exactly like the distinctive Zippo lighter. My question, of course, is, Why? My father used to carry a Zippo and swore it was the best lighter ever made, yet at no point did anyone in our family ever say, "And it smells great, too, Dad."

Bic—the company that makes the famed disposable ink pens, razors, and lighters—once attempted to market, believe it or not, disposable underwear.[5] Shaving for a few days and then pitching my cheap razor is one thing; I don't want to even think about applying that formula to boxers or panties.

A lunch box works for the Beatles because the same young girls and boys who were clamoring for their records would carry the pail to school. Scope in toothpaste works because the same customers use that product at practically the same time they are rinsing with the mouthwash. When it is appropriate and congruent, there is significant potential in expanding the experience for you as well.

It begins with these two questions:

1. How else could our customers use our products or services in addition to the way in which they are used now?

2. What else could we deliver, make, or license that would expand the experience we are currently creating for the benefit of our customers?

If you can discover useful and innovative approaches to answer that question, you can help your customer and your organization by expanding the customer's experience.

Extend the Experience

When I was reviewing movies for national syndication, one of the films I really enjoyed was the first *Lethal Weapon*. Starring Mel Gibson as Martin Riggs and Danny Glover as Roger Murtaugh and directed by Richard Donner, this 1987 film was one of the better action movies I had seen.

The film's producers certainly had *targeted* the experience for an audience just like me. Because of their success at both making the movie and targeting the audience, not only did I enjoy the film, *I repeated* the experience, watching it twice in the theater. I even *upgraded* the experience, because the second time I went to see the movie, I took my wife and chose a better theater with fantastic sound and great seats—and a higher ticket price. I *expanded* the experience by purchasing the VHS videotape of the film.

However, the greatest profit that I, as a customer, generated for the studio that produced the film was when I *extended* the experience by following the same steps with the second, third, and fourth *Lethal Weapon* sequels. Why did I extend my *Lethal Weapon* experience? Naturally, I wanted to see what happened next in the story of Riggs and Murtaugh.

Expanding the experience with your products or services means that I'm so impressed with my previous experiences, I want to deepen my engagement with you.

For example, I was an Apple fan long before it became cool to be one. I owned a Mac 512K and just about every version since. I would travel with my PowerBook 170, later making my briefcase lighter with the PowerBook Duo. As a writer and creative type, I certainly fell within Apple's target market. I obviously repeated my experience by purchasing additional computers from them. (What I would give if I still owned them and they were in pristine condition!) I upgraded my Macs with additional memory and hard drive space. I extended the experience with peripherals such as a LaserWriter printer and other products to make my Macintosh more productive and enjoyable.

However, I expanded my experience when I got in line and bought my first iPod, again when I stood in the queue for an iPhone, and yet again when I waited patiently for an iPad. In other words, because I was so engaged with Apple—from target to repeat, upgrade, and extend—it only makes sense that I would want to expand my acquisition of products and services from them.

Often, however, it's highly difficult for organizations and their teams to arrive at the expansion point because taking this step frequently requires that they alter the way they think about themselves.

If the *Lethal Weapon* franchise didn't move the story forward, we wouldn't want to see the sequel. In fact, many film franchises fail because the audience perceives that they're seeing a rerun of a previous movie rather than the next step.

The same might be true for you regardless of your corporate responsibilities. Sometimes new leadership brings a remarkable perspective to any team. Perhaps a new coworker has a way of serving the customer that revitalizes your approach. A new product or service may reinvigorate an entire sales team. If these results are possible for you internally within the organization, why wouldn't it work for your customers as well?

In my book *Create Distinction* I outlined the destroyers of differentiation, and one of a trio of factors was that "familiarity breeds complacency." If your product line is static, if your level of service is never changing, if there's no updating or innovation, why would any customer expand the relationship he or she has with you?

At this point, occasionally someone will mention to me the possibility that "customers will expand and grow the relationship if we have the cheapest price and they want more of an item." Perhaps that is the case; however, consider this: Are they expanding the relationship with you, or are they displaying loyalty to the lowest price? Would you lose the business if you were not the rock-bottom cheapest? If that is the case, chances are that you don't have much of a relationship with that customer anyway.

However, discovering congruent ways in which your customers can expand their experience with you means that you've helped them come back for more.

It's quite possible that you may have to change the way you think to help customers do more business with you. As we will discuss in greater detail in Chapter 9, Taxi Terry had to think about his small enterprise differently to help customers do more business with him. If he had limited himself to the taxi business, some of the growth you will learn that he later experienced would not have been possible. Changing his concept from taxis to transportation resulted in some incredible opportunities. He refused to be "just a . . . ," as we discussed in the Introduction.

If Apple and Steve Jobs remained rigid about the perspective that manufacturing computers was their solitary reason for existence, they never would have created the "insanely great" products that stimulated their monumental success. As you probably know, those new products—the iPod and the iPhone—created a halo effect around Apple that increased the sales of its computer business exponentially.

One of the critical changes in thinking is revealed by my friend Jeffrey Summers of the Summers Hospitality Group, a major firm in the restaurant industry that helps stimulate innovation. Jeffrey says that to grow your business and improve customer relationships, it's essential to "realize that you have to think long term continually and not short term constantly."[6]

I love that quote. So many organizations are so focused on thinking short term—from one quarter to the next—that they fail to recognize that true distinction in the marketplace will occur only when they, as Jeffrey says, "think long term continually."

Too many employees are just trying to make it through the day or get through this shift and seldom, as Stephen Covey often said, "begin with the end in mind." Even if you're a frontline employee, you need to be thinking long term: understanding the value and importance of every customer and recognizing the enduring impact that you make through your performance. Your productivity today is important; however, thinking about how your entire team can be more productive in the future is monumental.

Notice how this returns us to the phrase that every customer hates to hear: "We've always done it that way." When we limit our thinking, we restrict our service, and when we restrict our service, we enhance the difficulty and reduce the desire that a customer has to come back for more.

A former British prime minister, the late Harold Wilson, said, "He who rejects change is an architect of decay. The only human institution which rejects progress is the cemetery."[7] Changing the way you think may enhance the progress you make in helping the customer return to do additional business with you and your organization.

Here are three additional ideas of steps you can take to help your customer come back for more.

Be Consistent

If I'm comfortable as a customer because I know the drill, I'm more likely to come back. Southwest Airlines makes it easy because its consistency assures me that there won't be additional charges to check my bag and that I can always get an aisle seat if I check in early enough to get in the "A" boarding group (or I can pay the $40 if they have space left in the previously mentioned upgrade program). On Delta, I know that I'll receive a bit of special treatment because my level in their SkyMiles program will afford me early boarding and other perks. At McDonald's I'll probably get my food quickly, whereas at Sullivan's Steakhouse I'll receive an extraordinary filet.

The more consistent and reliable that I find the delivery of your performance, the greater the likelihood that I'll feel comfortable in returning for a repeat experience.

Here's an area where asking customers for their opinions can provide vital information. Although you may have data that establishes that you are reliable and consistent, if the gut feeling of the customer is that you're unreliable and inconsistent, you have major problems that need to be addressed.

Talking with your customers and promoting your consistency increases their comfort factor, resulting in repeat business. If you aren't dependable, why should the customer be expected to return to endure additional inconsistency?

Keep in Touch

With today's social media, not to mention e-mail and texts, there is no good reason for failing to maintain contact with your customers.

Naturally, none of us wants to be spammed or contacted so frequently that it becomes intrusive. However, it's hard to enhance a relationship when there isn't ongoing contact. As the cliché goes, out of sight, out of mind.

What is the best way to stay in touch with our customers? *Ask them.* Customers will generally appreciate that you're willing to customize your approach to fit their preferences, and they can be highly irritated if you don't.

There is a national chain of health spas with therapeutic massage that has experienced substantial growth over the last few years; however, they have one practice that drives me bonkers. They love to call to remind their customers that they haven't been in for an appointment for 30 days. Not realizing why they were collecting the information, I unfortunately provided them with my cell phone number. The problem is that the 9 a.m. call from Indianapolis may awaken me because it is 6 a.m. if I'm in Las Vegas or because I took a red-eye back to the Midwest from California and arrived in Indianapolis at 5 a.m. Yet when I asked if they would just send me an occasional e-mail reminder, well, I was informed that they've "never done it that way."

They're on the verge of losing a customer, because the manner in which they stay in touch isn't in sync with that of the person they want to return with his business.

What's so difficult about asking the customer and letting him or her determine the preferred method of contact? If she wants to stay connected via e-mail, send her attention-grabbing innovative messages in that format. If he hates sifting through tons of messages on his laptop, give him a call and leave a voice mail. How can customers ever be convinced that you'll consistently provide what they want if you aren't willing to communicate with them in the manner they desire?

Always Follow Up

A critical element of keeping in touch is following up both to ensure that the customer is satisfied with the product and to be available to answer any questions customers may have about your service. Unfortunately, sometimes customers, both internal and external, will not understand how they are supposed to use a product or get the most from your service and fail to share their lack of knowledge with the very people who could assist them. By being proactive and keeping in touch with your customers, you can alleviate potential dissatisfaction and open the channel for additional opportunities to serve their needs.

I've previously written about the great team at H.H. Gregg appliances in my hometown of Indianapolis. However, when my wife and I purchased a new washer and dryer, we were astounded. Gregg followed up by having the delivery technician conduct an on-the-spot seminar for us on all the features of our new laundry appliances.

Although at the beginning of his presentation I thought, "You gotta be kidding. How hard can it be to run the washer?" I softened my tone quickly upon learning about the multitude of features this technological marvel possessed. Following up with more than we expected and ensuring that we thoroughly understood all the features of the product dramatically enhanced the likelihood that we will return to H.H. Gregg the next time we're looking for appliances or electronics.

If you simply follow up at the precise time you have indicated, you will move to the front of the class as far as most customers are concerned. Why would a customer give you future business if you won't follow up on the transaction you've already completed?

It's important to note here that we can frequently assign following up as an activity required for sales professionals and not emphasize it enough for every member of the team. When we modify our thinking so that we view our colleagues as internal customers, it may help us recognize that prompt and thorough follow-up is a critical activity for every professional.

Follow-up contributes to helping the customer do more business with us because it does the following:

1. Clearly demonstrates that we care about the outcome for the customer.

2. Establishes our professionalism and shows that we're on top of our game.

3. Shows that we have shared goals; we both want to see the customer succeed.

4. Proves that we are accountable and can be relied on.

5. Expands and enhances the dialogue with the customer, providing an opportunity to discuss additional business without appearing to be pushy.

Do you notice any of these five that you would not desire for your business? Are there any of them that you would reject if you were the customer? Me either.

On November 9, 2012, I joined the line at my nearby cinema to purchase a ticket, enter the theater, and watch the latest installment in the series of James Bond movies; this one was titled *Skyfall*.

Consider what had happened over the last few years with the Bond franchise: a new, grittier actor portraying 007 in Daniel Craig; a reboot of the entire series via the storyline of *Casino Royale*; and a reframing of Bond's character from the more campy portrayal by Roger Moore, through the suave Pierce Brosnan, to the more steely and confident performance of Craig, which was perhaps more reminiscent of the original movie Bond, Sean Connery.

In other words, the descendants of Cubby Broccoli displayed that they were—by their willingness to think differently about their business, target the experience, and help their audience upgrade, expand, repeat, and extend—focused on taking the creative steps necessary to motivate their customers to do more business with them.

The results were quite astonishing. *Skyfall* became the most successful James Bond film in the history of the franchise. It became the first Bond film to earn over $1 billion at the box office. It earned the spot (as of this writing) as the eighth highest-grossing film in the history of motion pictures. Even when adjusted for inflation—as, obviously, ticket prices were cheaper in the mid-1960s and the dollar was worth significantly less—*Skyfall* became the third biggest Bond film of all time, behind only two Sean Connery classics, *Thunderball* and *Goldfinger*.[8]

The first Bond film that Cubby Broccoli produced, *Dr. No*, was released in May 1963. *Skyfall*'s success meant that Broccoli and his family had kept their customers interested, engaged, and coming back for half a century. That's remarkable in any industry, but it's positively shocking in the fickle world of show business.

What would you do next if you actually were a member of this legendary show business family, as I asked you at the start of this chapter? My suggestion is that you continue to do what you've done for the last 50 years and what is making Taxi Terry and others so successful right now:

Help your customers come back for more.

Taxi Terry Takeaway

One of the most overlooked aspects of business by all employees at every level is the value of the repeat customer. That's why taking action on these steps is critical to your future success!

- Select two of your current customers, then make a list for each of them that details how you could target, upgrade, repeat, expand, and extend their experience with you more effectively.

- Create a long-term thinking list that outlines where you want your business or department to be five years from now—and where *you* would like to be, in a professional sense, at that same point in time.

- Just as my wife and I received great instruction on how to operate our new washer and dryer, your customers want to be assured they know how to do business with you in a manner that maximizes the value of the relationship. How would you evaluate your efforts to assist the customer in understanding how to best use the product or service that you provide? What could you do to improve?

THE SEVENTH TENET

CHAPTER 8

Creating Joy for Your Customer Will Make Your Work—and Life—More Joyful.

Throughout history, the number 7 has been considered the most powerful and magical of all numerals.

There are seven days to the week, and the musical scale has seven major notes. In ancient days the Egyptians had seven original gods, and in the Bible God created the world in six days, only to rest on the seventh to review and appreciate his work.

There were Seven Wonders of the Ancient World, and the highest level of nirvana is often referred to as Seventh Heaven. Hitting a jackpot on a slot machine often means that three sevens have lined up for you. Major League Baseball, the National Hockey League, and the National Basketball Association have the World Series, Stanley Cup, and NBA Finals, respectively, to determine the season's championship. They are all decided in a best-of-seven playoff series.

Sailors embark upon journeys on the Seven Seas, and explorers sought to tame the seven continents. On dice, the opposing sides always add up to seven, and there are seven colors in a rainbow.

The late author Stephen R. Covey schooled us on the "7 Habits of Highly Effective Leaders," and countless fictional works have revolved around the seven deadly sins.

It stands to reason, then, that the seventh tenet of Taxi Terry is going to be pretty important, and it is. It's one that can make a critical difference for both your customer and you.

"Creating joy for your customer" is the first part of the tenet that we will examine; then, later in this chapter, we'll explore why this approach can have such a powerful impact on others and dramatically influence your performance and everything about your life.

Check out the shelves at any bookstore or search any online book retailer and you will discover that there is a plethora of business literature on sales and service. It's not difficult to locate an abundance of advice on management and marketing.

When I went to Amazon.com and searched for a book on "management," it returned *855,576* results. For "customer service," there were over *90,000* options to choose from.

However, when I scoured Amazon's site for a book on "customer joy," among the millions of titles in their collection, there were only 271 responses. The top one on the list was *The Joy of Checks: How to Succeed in Business by Getting Paid* by a New York attorney, W. Adam Mandelbaum, which might be a terrific read—although the subtitle also made me wonder how you could succeed in business by *not* getting paid—however, this book doesn't address exactly what I meant by joy for the customer.

We profusely discuss how to serve our customers and manage our organizations, but we seldom talk about the steps we should be taking to really, truly make our internal and external customers thrilled, amazed, happy—*joyful*—because they've connected with us.

When I exited the cab that night in Jacksonville, Florida, after my ride with Taxi Terry, I was grinning from ear to ear. Entering the Taj in Delhi after my name had been recalled, I was smiling like the proverbial Cheshire Cat. I would guess that you also have had experiences in other establishments when you were a customer that brought you great joy. If you haven't, you need to find better places to do business.

Note, however, that a joyful experience as a customer is not dependent on the level of quality of the merchandise or the perceived "class" of the establishment. Certainly, one could argue that there is more pressure on the Louis Vuitton store marketing its affluent merchandise in a very upscale shopping area to create a high level of customer experience than there is on a Walmart selling a handbag by Parinda for less than 30 bucks.

However, I respectfully disagree.

The steps that Taxi Terry took to create joy for his customer were not prohibitively expensive measures by any means. I've been treated better on many Southwest Airlines flights than I have been on competitive carriers even when the latter have bumped me up into a first-class seat.

Instead of a commitment of cash, creating customer joy requires dedication to distinctive engagement. It means that you individually make a pledge that you are going to enhance the interaction between the customer and yourself. This is an important point: organizations cannot make that promise or demand it from their employees as an obligation. It occurs only when individuals take personal responsibility to make the experience a customer has a joyful one.

Whether it is an internal or an external customer, why would a customer remain loyal to any organization if it's drudgery to work or purchase there? We only have to look at television and the declining loyalty to both networks and to individual programs to see a pattern. A terrific column by Dave Morgan, CEO of Simulmedia, on OnlineSpin from MediaPost.com, outlines the three major contributors to this phenomenon.[1]

So Many Good Choices

There are lots of great TV programs, and you have lots of worthy competitors in your business as well. This sheer explosion of options means that customers can be like kids in a candy store in just about any industry, including yours. The Internet only exacerbates this issue. Now your competition may be in India as well as Indiana.

Here's an example. It provides what my wife calls TMI—too much information—but here goes. She hates it that I snore. This is not curtain-flapping, wall-contracting, log-sawing snoring and, thankfully, not sleep apnea, which is a serious medical condition. Evidently (I'm taking her word for it, because I'm obviously sleeping at the time), I sometimes snore just enough to disturb her sleep, and I feel guilty about it. She decided to pick up some earplugs at the local drug store and found that CVS offered two or three types, none of which fit her small ears quite as comfortably as she would have liked.

We Googled the word *earplugs* and were amazed at the number of responses. At the top of the list was The Ear Plug Superstore and its website, http://EarPlugStore.com. This website is, in the words of that great American philosopher Peter Griffin, "freakin' sweet." You won't believe how many options there are for earplugs. There are industrial earplugs, ones crafted especially for musicians, ones that are custom fitted for your individual ears, ones that are reusable and others that are for a single use, special ones for hunting and shooting, others for swimming and diving, tiny ones to protect a child's hearing, others especially for concertgoers, some with built-in metal detection devices for tracking, ones that block almost all sound, and others that let a designated amount of noise in for safety purposes. To my wife's delight, there were also ones labeled "snoring relief hearing protection."

The Sleep-Eze In-Ear White Noise Machine (2013 Model) is, according to the Ear Plug Superstore website, "a tiny device built using hearing aid technology that fits inside your ear emitting the soothing sound of pure white noise while it isolates you from outside noises that disturb your precious sleep."[2] It's priced at $319 for the pair, along with a free memory-foam ear pillow.

I was hoping for something a little less expensive, and so I bought my wife the SilentEar Reusable Ear Plugs—Orange Body with Clear Flange set for $9.95. She's now sleeping fine despite the racket that I might make at night.

Consider in all seriousness, however, that range of good choices among products as innocuous as earplugs. Varieties were available—within a specific specialty subset of a product we might agree is a bit out of the mainstream—ranging from about $320 to $10.

However, if you are the Ear Plug Superstore, here's the issue of primary importance: your competitors probably have just as many varieties of earplugs. Even though my purchase is from a dollars and cents standpoint small, why should I choose to do business with you?

If you aren't creating joy for customers and colleagues, why shouldn't they look elsewhere?

One element that I really appreciate is that the Ear Plug Superstore has terrific descriptions of each of its products. Frankly, I had no idea how much variance there could be between one type of earplug and another. Also, the owners have posted a page on why and how they got started in the business, why hearing safety means so much to them, and why it is a joy for them to create joy for their customers.

Poor Information and Navigation

Morgan's column suggests that for broadcasting, this means, "There are no tools available today that can easily inform viewers in a timely way about all the available programming that they might enjoy." For your business and career, it might mean that customers and prospects are underinformed or misinformed and therefore cannot make decisions that would break your way. How can a deluded or ignorant customer be one who is simultaneously experiencing joy? "Ignorance is bliss" is only part of the quote. The English poet Thomas Gray, perhaps paraphrasing Sophocles, actually wrote in 1742, "Where ignorance is bliss, 'tis folly to be wise." In today's world of technology and hypercompetition, no one could seriously argue that it is folly—madness, in other words—to be a wise person.

Get a friend—one who doesn't work with you—to try to buy something on your website and see how easy and friendly it is for that person. How easily can your friend navigate your site?

Naturally, if there are problems—and there frequently are—the design team will usually first attempt to defend why things are the way they are. It's human nature. However, if there are navigation challenges for someone, that person is not going to have your team with him or her to explain them. Your job is to make it as easy as possible for customers with no previous knowledge to obtain information and make purchases.

Listen in as they call your office and ask for you. Sure, your team is probably nice when *you* call in, but how do they speak to people they don't know?

I have a great friend and longtime colleague who works with an assistant who is terrible on the phone. She's rude and condescending, arrogant and unhelpful. She has provided my office with erroneous information. She's damaging his business. Yet when I had a conversation with him about it, he couldn't believe it. "Why, she's always great when she talks with me," he said.

Make certain your team and your colleagues are creating joy for your customers, internal and external, not just kissing up to the few who control their compensation.

Changing Loyalties

Dave Morgan suggests that for TV this means that viewers are now loyal to "their TVs, to the days and times when they turn them on, and to favorite genres of programming. Most are no longer loyal to specific programs or networks." Today's technology also means that if you can't be home watching *Family Guy* on Sunday night, it's no problem. A few years ago it meant you would miss the program altogether, but now you just record it on your DVR and watch it at home when you desire or go to Hulu.com and view it on your laptop.

For your business, it means that loyalty could be to a product, a particular location, or even an individual employee.

When Nordstrom first opened many years ago in Indianapolis, I decided to see what all the frenzy regarding its supposedly extraordinary level of customer service was about.

Standing in the men's department, I was ready to play the just-looking game that happens so often in retail. To me, that's when a clerk approaches and says, "May I help you?" I immediately respond, "No, just looking." Then they leave me alone.

As I'm getting ready to say my line, a woman approaches, thrusts out her hand, and brightly says, "Good morning! My name is Lori; what's yours?" To which I respond, "Just looking! Oh . . . no. Wait—my name is Scott."

"Hi, Scott!" Lori exclaims. Then, surveying the entire store with her eyes, she finally focuses on me and says, "Look at this new store! Isn't it great?" I have to agree. Lori then proceeded to deliver an Ultimate Customer Experience to me that was a total joy. Because of that, just about every stitch of clothing I purchased from there on was from . . .

Were you expecting the next word in the preceding sentence to be *Nordstrom*? Well, it's not. I bought my clothes from Lori. If she had changed her employment to Saks, I would have gone there. Nordstrom benefited immensely from my loyalty to Lori.

In business today, many times the customer is fickle and fails to retain the loyalty we desire. However, sometimes the loyalty is deep; it's just not directed where we may believe. Lori has now retired from Nordstrom, and I have to admit I haven't been as loyal as I previously was to the store. My guess is that Nordstrom would probably assume that my loyalty has waned. In terms of dollars spent at their business, they'd be right. However, what really happened is that when Lori retired, perhaps they didn't understand *why* my loyalty might change. I'm still waiting for a new Lori to make it a joy for me to buy men's clothing from him or her.

Each of these three challenges is significant. Collectively, they present monumental problems and opportunities. How can you and your team address them to create joyful customers? Note: the question is not "How can your company improve?" It is "What can you and your team *do*?"

At a seminar in Amsterdam, I was asked after the session to come up with three questions the organization I was working with could ask internally that would help it understand what is needed to deal with the challenge of customer loyalty.

Tough challenge, right? I admit that I had to work on it a bit. Here are the three questions that I came up with on the spot. Consider them and see if you can develop better and more precise ones for your organization.

Do Customers Want It?

Gourmet quality lattes are certainly wonderful, but would it add to the customers' experience to serve them if you're running a funeral home? How about a sporting goods store? I doubt it. There are other aspects that would probably be more desired by those patronizing your business.

This isn't to suggest that we shouldn't be innovative in what we deliver; however, if there is a disconnect between our idea for the experience and our core purpose, it's not going to enhance the loyalty we desire from our customers.

Can We Provide It?

This isn't necessarily a matter of whether we can provide it with our current team or our current structure. However, we do have to ask ourselves if we have the bandwidth to do what it takes to provide the experience that will generate loyalty and create customer joy. If we don't have it immediately available, we should start thinking about the specific steps that we will need to execute to make it happen in the future.

Is It Worth It?

In my first book, I wrote: "The purpose of any business is to profitably create experiences so compelling to customers that their loyalty becomes assured."

Although it's reasonable to focus on the importance of the word *experience*, it is also easy to overlook the critical term *profitably*.

There are a number of aspects your organization must confront on a daily basis. This is simply a matter of asking, "Is it worth doing this *instead of* other projects?" You have only a finite amount of time and scarce resources. The question also insists that you project how the effort you're making will enhance the profitability of your organization in the future.

Take note, however, that creating an Ultimate Customer Experience certainly affected the profitability of Southwest Airlines, Apple, and numerous other companies we have discussed in this book. Overlooking the importance of it is one of the elements that destroyed the profits of Circuit City, Blockbuster, and countless other companies.

Just because it won't drive immediate income, however, that doesn't mean it isn't immensely important.

If you confront these three questions, you're taking the right steps to develop what customers really want in today's hypercompetitive market so that you can grow your business, enhance the experience of your customers, and begin to deliver on the challenge of creating customer joy.

Here is a critical aspect that is frequently ignored: *companies cannot improve.* It's impossible for an organization to improve. What happens instead is that the *people* in an organization get better and lift the entire enterprise because of their efforts.

Therefore, if you want your business to get better, the first step is for *you* to get better regardless of your position or degree of influence at your job.

The vast majority of employees and entrepreneurs do not have the ability to completely control the price of their goods and services in the marketplace. Even the CEO of General Motors is not likely to wake up one morning and decide that a Chevy should cost $100,000 . . . or $100. However, what all of us have the power to do is to decide on the focus and intensity of our personal efforts. What this seventh tenet states is that we should make the decision to concentrate passionately on elating our customers.

Ajay Aggarwal, the chief customer experience officer for Klisma of India, a mobile- and web-based service that brings consumers and retailers together to get group discounts and provides loyalty benefits for shopping with its merchants, wrote in an article titled "Customer Joy—Not Sales—Key to Retail Success," "While no brand can provide a problem-free shopping experience, their ability to solve customer problems quickly is what the customer values."

Aggarwal's belief is that just because the number of complaints you receive is low, it doesn't ensure that your customers are happy. The reason is because many customers won't take the time to voice a complaint—they'll just give up on you, and take their business elsewhere.

"By improving their customer experience," Aggarwal stated, "[retailers] will drastically improve their bottom line."[3]

You don't have to be in retail for this insight to be applicable. Create joy and improve the experience and the bottom line will improve.

"For some companies this is a radical notion," writes Shawn Murphy, managing director of organizational development at KAI Partners.[4] "I can hear executives bristle with agitation, dismissing such a shift as idealistic, clinging to protect the familiar hierarchy of the 20th century."

Murphy makes a great point: a primary reason we haven't focused on creating joy for our internal and external customers is simply (ready for this?) that "we've never done it that way before." Again, that tired old excuse isn't good enough for today's marketplace, or customer.

If we're going to deliver it, we had better define it. What *is* customer joy?

Obviously, it consists of many aspects, and it will vary with the customer's specific needs, wants, and desires and your products and services in the marketplace.

What's important and joy-creating for one customer of yours may not provide the same level of amazement and enjoyment for another. However, it's very difficult to precisely define. You're probably familiar with Supreme Court Justice Potter Stewart's famed comment in the case *Jacobellis v. Ohio* in 1964 in which he remarked that obscenity is something that "I know it when I see it."

Joy is almost as difficult to describe. However, we do know it when we see it in our customers and colleagues.

"Joy is an outcome of doing something that makes you happy. Joy is contagious. It has a force of energy that moves people forward with optimism" is the definition that Shawn Murphy gives.[5]

Happiness, I would submit, is more event-driven and transitory. If I've been arguing with you about a disputed charge on my bill and you finally agree to remove it from my account, I'm momentarily happy that you've done so. However, the fact that I've had to engage in an argument with you to achieve the outcome I desired probably won't make me joyful about doing business with you.

From my perspective, joy is a state of being. It's more of a persistent internal delight, whereas happiness is a momentary feeling of pleasure or satisfaction. Don't get me wrong; I want my customers to be happy. However, that isn't a standard that is high enough to make an enduring difference. I want them to be so consistently happy in doing business with our organization that it becomes joy-inspiring.

You only have to look as far as the myriad of lottery winners who end up in bankruptcy to understand that even a monumental event that brought phenomenal happiness wasn't enough to inspire a life of enduring joy. However, there are just as many examples of people without great financial means who are living lives of extraordinary significance through their professional and personal engagements and are experiencing enormous joy and satisfaction. Happiness can be created by mere luck; joy, in contrast, has deeper roots.

Landing in Las Vegas right after Apple's presentation to its Worldwide Developers Conference, I quickly called the Apple Store at the Forum Shops. I had flown to Las Vegas on Delta, and with its Gogo Wi-Fi service on the plane, I had been following all the company's interesting announcements in San Francisco that morning as I traveled. Apple's relatively new (at that time) CEO, Tim Cook, had announced a new MacBook Pro with Retina display, and I wanted to know if it was already in stock. It was time for me to upgrade my computer, and it sounded like exactly what I had been waiting for.

A very nice guy on the phone said no; however, he stated that he would know more about the availability of the new MacBook Pro Retina the next day. He asked for my name, took my number, and suggested that I call back and "be sure to ask for Josh."

Josh also stated that if he didn't hear from me, he would get in touch as soon as he had information. I gave him my name and told him to expect my call.

The following morning, I had finished my speech at Caesars Palace and was near the Apple Store at the Forum Shops anyway, so I figured: Why call when I can just walk in? An employee at the front welcomed me and then, pressing her finger to her ear, seemed to hear something over her earpiece. She asked, "Excuse me, are you Mr. McKain?"

More than a little surprised, I responded that I was, but how in the world did she know? She smiled and said, "Josh just told me over the radio."

A young guy who I am guessing was of college age walked up and introduced himself. "Hi, Mr. McKain," he said. "I'm Josh." (From my earlier stories about remembering names, you've probably already guessed that he had my attention.)

"After we hung up from our conversation yesterday," Josh told me, "I Googled your name and saw your website and YouTube videos. You see, I really want to know my potential customers." Josh even told me that he went on YouTube and watched my story about Taxi Terry.

Ponder these three questions based on my experience with Josh that I asked myself for a moment:

1. Do you and your colleagues care so much about creating joy for potential customers that you research them even before you have an opportunity to make a sale?

2. If you knew prospective customers better, would they become more convinced that you are there to help them instead of merely sell to them?

3. Could this be an initial step toward ensuring that your customers are joyful when they consider doing business with you?

Josh informed me that they had just received *one* of the new Retina display MacBook Pros to put in stock. "If you want it, Mr. McKain," Josh said, "it's yours." Here are two more questions:

1. Do you think that at this point I tried to negotiate a lower price?

2. Could you imagine that I said that I would have to think about it and let Josh know later?

Of course not. I had to make that new Apple laptop mine.

Josh brought the box out of the back and placed it on the table in front of me as if he were carrying the crown jewels. He removed the cellophane wrapping from the package and then stood back and looked at me. "Your turn, Mr. McKain," he said.

I later learned that this approach is mandatory at Apple: the customer receives the thrill of opening his or her package and celebrating the experience of ownership. It's one of those little things and really is an essential element in the progression toward creating customer joy.

Here's an additional question about the Josh experience for you:

* Have you examined each step in the way you deal with customers and asked, "What could we do at this point to make it more of a joy to do business with us?"

Here's another unreal aspect of this uniquely joyful experience. As I was leaving the Apple Store with my new purchase, someone announced, "We have just sold the very first of the new MacBook Pros! A round of applause to the customer giving it a new home!"

The store employees, most lined up by the door, started clapping for me as I walked out. Some customers cheered as well, probably wondering what was happening. (Fortunately for the Apple employees and customers, I was a little embarrassed and befuddled by the attention, and merely departed the store. Usually, when I hear applause, I stand up and give a speech!)

Here's one more question:

* Do you think Best Buy or Fry's has a chance when it comes time to buy my next computer?

No way; I'm going back to the Apple Store. Certainly, I understand that there's a premium you pay for Apple and many other products or services of distinction, but I think that it's worth it for the magical mix of technology and experience that is creating so much joy for customers on a global basis.

How do you put a price tag on joy, anyway? Ask new parents what having a newborn is worth, and they aren't going to say, "Evidently about $3,500, because that's what the hospital charged us." The ecstasy of the event creates an emotion that transcends the transaction.

If I go see the latest blockbuster comedy movie and the theater is dirty and the projector's bulb is dim and old, the experience is soiled no matter how momentarily happy the film on the screen makes me. Why would a concert promoter or venue, for example, permit a situation in which security is rude, getting to concessions and restrooms requires the patience of the Dalai Lama, and everything from parking to drinks costs a fortune regardless of how happy I am to see the act onstage?

Why would your business think it's any different when your employees talk to one another but not to customers, when you offer better deals to new customers than to existing ones, or when you can't answer my questions and act as if you don't care regardless of what you're selling?

Why would any business think it's any different when you've cut staff to the point where you can't meet deadlines, when your services deliver less than you've promised, and when you stop showing me care and consideration right after I sign a contract?

In show business, the artist gets the applause, not the fans. What if the experience—from cinema to clubs to coliseums—was set up to make the audience feel connected and appreciated instead of gouged? What if at your business your customers felt engaged and became advocates for your efforts instead of feeling merely processed through your system?

Maybe, just as they do with Apple, your audience would spend more, more frequently. Perhaps they would feel as joyful about doing business with you as I felt about the experience I received from Josh.

Although creating customer joy involves a number of steps specific to your industry and particular to your organization, there are three critical aspects that are important for every company and every customer:

1. Be distinctive.

2. Let each person shine while working on the team.

3. Create an Ultimate Customer Experience for your audience.

I learned about these three characteristics from a highly unusual source.

When I was about 16 years old, the new manager of the small-town radio station I worked for that I've previously mentioned told me that we were going to be emceeing the concert of a gospel quartet from Nashville. As you can imagine, to a teen unfamiliar with the group we were going to hear and not a fan of gospel music, the prospect did not sound extraordinarily appealing.

All that changed, however, the first time I heard the Oak Ridge Boys.

Recently, I had the chance to see them once again, and I was struck by three major points that we could—and *should*—learn from them. You may be wondering how in today's high-tech, hypercompetitive business world one could learn anything from a past-their-hit-making-prime quartet made up of older men who sing country music. I'd suggest to you that success—whether in your business or in theirs—leaves clues that can be applied across a wide spectrum. Here are the three points.

Be Distinctive

Today, many have forgotten that when the Oak Ridge Boys expanded their audience and repertoire to country music, the Statler Brothers were already hugely famous. Some in radio and the music industry assumed that the Oaks were going to merely be a pale imitation of the Statlers, hoping to siphon off a bit of that quartet's established success.

The Oak Ridge Boys understood from the onset that to create enduring success, you have to create distinction. Whereas the Statlers dressed alike, each of the Oaks had his own individual style. The Statlers' stage presence most frequently involved singing to a microphone firmly planted on a stand; the Oaks moved dynamically all over the stage. The Statlers were known for their comedy; the Oak Ridge Boys became known for their energy. In other words, though the Oaks were respectful and appreciative of others in their field, they were not willing to settle for becoming a copy of anyone else.

It would have been easy for the Oaks to merely imitate the Statler Brothers and try to score a few hits. Instead, they created distinction and built an enduring career. If you want to create joy for your customers, you should do the same thing.

Let Each Person Shine While Working on the Team

When you think of the Oak Ridge Boys, you probably first think of their amazing harmony. When you see one of their concerts, a primary element of what is truly incredible is the level of talent of each member of the group.

Consider this point, however: the only way you know that Joe, Duane, William Lee, and Richard are singularly talented is that each of them has a chance to shine as an individual during the performance.

I've seen basketball teams that have one outstanding player, but because he takes all the shots (and the credit), the team becomes dysfunctional and loses games that it shouldn't. I've seen businesses that have a team leader who seeks the glory and doesn't allow his colleagues to be recognized, and the group fails to achieve its objectives.

Working as a team is critical, but you cannot achieve your goals and create joy for your customers over the long haul unless you provide each member of your team with his or her individual time in the spotlight.

Create an Ultimate Customer Experience for Your Audience

I watched backstage that night before the Oaks took the stage as they hosted a meet-and-greet with many fans before taking the stage. They had performed the night before near Reno and taken a flight to Vegas a few hours later on the morning of the concert at which I saw them. As they were on stage for their show that night, all of them knew that they had to meet their ride to the airport the following morning at 4:45 a.m. for a 7 a.m. flight back home to Nashville.

Before their performance, however, there they stood for an extended period welcoming their fans and getting pictures taken. For the moment that each fan had their attention, they made every person feel as though he or she were the center of the universe.

Then they gave their all during their concert, ending with a rousing standing ovation, and since it was Easter Sunday, they pulled out an old gospel song ("Because He Lives") that they had not performed for three decades on stage. Every fan, every audience member, went home thrilled by the show. The Oak Ridge Boys had created joy for their customers.

Why are the Oaks still filling auditoriums when lots of other groups, some with just as many hits, have disbanded because they can't sell tickets? Simply because the Oak Ridge Boys create a joyous experience their customers want to repeat and share with their friends to the point of bringing them along. They don't just spread happiness; they infuse their audiences with joy with all that they do.

As you look at your business, is your performance so compelling that your customers want to repeat the experience and not only tell their friends but bring them when they come back for more?

Forty years ago, these four men inspired me by their hard work, talent, dedication, and distinction. And guess what. They still do.

These four men—Joe Bonsall, Duane Allen, William Lee Golden, and Richard Sterban—have been performing together for *40 years*. They don't have to meet fans before every show or put themselves through such a grueling concert schedule. So why do they continue to do it?

Just as it will do for you, bringing joy to their customers is what brings joy to them.

When I asked Joe Bonsall if the Oaks ever thought about retiring, he asked me, "Scott, did you ever hear how Willie Nelson answered that question when someone inquired when he was going to retire? Willie said, 'All I know how to do is golf and sing. Which one of those two would you want me to give up?'"

Then Joe added the kicker to the story: "None of us even know how to play golf! It's been joyful for many years, and we're not giving that up!" Nor should they.

However, this principle applies to more than entertainment. Do you believe Southwest flight attendants have a more joyful workplace than those at other airlines with poor reputations for the customer's experience? I do, and those I've talked with from Southwest heartily agree.

Do you believe employees at the Apple Store have a more joyful experience than do those working at other electronics retailers? I do, and those I've talked with from the Apple Store concur.

As customers, we can't help but notice when the individuals with whom we are dealing from your organization are joyful and help us become more that way ourselves. Ever notice someone who is really passionate about his or her work? In my small hometown of Crothersville, Indiana, the owner of our solitary funeral home is Mark Adams. Now, I realize that joy may be an unconventional word to use in describing a funeral home director; however, having used his services for the funerals of my father and grandmother, and a memorial service for my late wife, I can attest that he delivers joy to his customers.

He's so passionate about his job and makes so certain that a sad situation is handled with the utmost compassion and integrity, it is a joy to be his customer. In every situation, regardless of your business, you have the opportunity to create joy for customers.

However, Mark and his wife, Leslie, who is also a licensed funeral director, are extremely joyful people to be around as well. To illuminate the second component of this critical tenet, by creating joy for others, they have enhanced the delight in their own lives.

If it sounds appealing that you can enhance your life by creating joy for customers, what's the formula for making that approach work for you? It starts with a single simple act.

The late author and broadcaster Earl Nightingale frequently said that "success is like a person and a wood stove." If you want heat, you have to put wood in the stove and set it ablaze. It would never occur to you to say to the stove, "If you first give me heat, then I will put in some wood."

Yet, as Nightingale wisely observed, that is exactly how most people behave when it comes to their personal satisfaction and success. We seem to say, for example, "If customers were nicer to me, I would treat them better" or "No one else here cares for customers; why should I go first?" That attitude, in essence, is saying, "give me heat *before* I put in the wood."

It doesn't work with stoves, your car won't give you transportation and let you put in the gasoline after you arrive at your destination, and it doesn't work in creating joy for your customers. *You* have to go first.

But then something amazing begins to happen: you begin to make it a joy for a customer to be engaged with you. It's the result of your actions in making these seven tenets a reality for your customers.

One of the greatest lessons in life is to realize that our lives mirror our actions. In other words, the way people usually treat you is a reflection of the way they perceive you are treating them. The level of success you have attained in your career is approximately equal to the relative effort and commitment you have invested in it.

When you execute these seven tenets and become a joy for customers to work and deal with, their joy will reflect back to you. Then your life and your job will become infinitely more rewarding in ways you never previously imagined.

Here's the catch: *you* have to go first.

Does it work every time? No, of course not. What does? Even a baseball player making $25 million a year gets a hit only about 3 out of every 10 times at bat. Michael Jordan missed more shots than he made. Great chefs have made inedible dishes. No one, regardless of his or her level of expertise, knowledge, and ability, can make something work every single time.

The key is the phrase *more often than not*. Whereas another hitter might strike out in a pressure situation, more often than not the superstar will deliver. That's why he gets $25 million and the other batter, though a terrific player, earns much less. The chef may occasionally make a bad dish, but more often than not you are going to want to dine at her restaurant.

You may have a favorite movie star; for me, it is Robert Duvall. Your favorite, like mine, has undoubtedly made some bad movies. However, more often than not you know that whatever he or she is in is going to be spectacular. That's why they have become our favorites.

Delivering the Ultimate Customer Experience means that *significantly* more often than not customers are going to be thrilled to do business with you and will share that joy with their friends (meaning you have more customers and your business does better) and with you (meaning work and life become more rewarding).

It's the mirror effect: the joy you create for your customers—internal and external—becomes the joy you enhance for yourself.

As I wrote those words, I can almost hear some readers saying, "Come on, you can't be serious! If you think work can be fun—even joyous—you've never worked where I do!"

You're probably right about one aspect: I've almost certainly never worked where you do, as this book will go to literally thousands of companies.

However, I would ask you to consider this point: by saying what I've just imagined coming from some of you—"Work can't be fun or joyous where I work"—you are doing exactly what we discussed previously about personal responsibility. It's not your company's mission to make your job enjoyable. It's *your* responsibility.

My dad was a butcher who would go to farms in the middle of the winter and work for farmers, butchering their cattle. The conditions in the cold and with his job were worse than I could endure. Yet my father loved it because he chose to. His enthusiasm was contagious, and his customers reflected it back to him, making his work a joy to him.

If my father could find a way to make butchering cattle in snow and subzero temperatures joyous, it's hard for me to believe that you cannot find a little more impact and meaning in your work.

But it is your choice. You have to go first.

If you do, the joy you will provide to your customers and the gift that you are giving to yourself can become truly remarkable.

That's the last of the seven tenets. Now let's tie a ribbon around the package and see what happened to Taxi Terry.

Taxi Terry Takeaway

As mentioned, while joy is a difficult term to define, we certainly know it when we see it.

- With that in mind, write down the name of the most joyful colleague— or the most engaging customer—who you encounter. What are three specific things that he or she does that convinces you of his or her joy?

- Examine those three attributes. Then, write down how you could use each of them in your own life to make your customers and yourself more joyful.

- When was the last time that you experienced joy as a customer? What specifically occurred that generated this feeling? How can you take a similar approach to deliver a similar experience to your customers?

I'M NOT DONE YET

CHAPTER **9**

It had been several years since my initial ride with Taxi Terry, and I was heading back to the Jacksonville area. Naturally, I called his number and made arrangements for him to pick me up and take me to the hotel in Amelia Island, Florida, where I was speaking. Interestingly, Terry didn't answer the phone; he now had a dispatcher who was scheduling his trips.

The dispatcher found it interesting that I specifically requested and insisted on Terry, and she mentioned that they had several terrific drivers. When I gave my name, however, it was obvious that she too had watched the YouTube video of me describing my trip with him. She assured me that Terry himself would be waiting on me upon my arrival.

As I walked out to the pickup area after arriving at the Jacksonville airport, there he was. Guess what his first words were to me?

"Scott! Are you ready for the best cab ride of your life?"

I jumped in the front seat with Terry, and we were off to Amelia Island.

After a few pleasantries, Terry said, "When you rode with me that first time, Scott, it was just me and my car. One taxi, one driver. That's all. Now I have multiple cabs and several drivers!"

Thrilled by his good fortune, I said, "Terry, congratulations! What remarkable success."

He immediately responded, "I'm not done yet."

"Some people," Terry continued, "want the cheapest ride they can get from the airport to their hotel. They'll put up with a stop or two along the way in order to save a few dollars. So I bought a couple of vans, and I now own E-Z Airport Shuttle Service. We move vans full of people from the airport to their hotels and back practically all around the clock."

"Wow," I exclaimed. "Terry, that is absolutely fantastic!"

"I'm not done yet," Terry persisted.

"It was on my bucket list to someday have a big, long, shiny black limo. And now . . . I've got it! I now have a business I call Terry Transportation that provides upscale limo service throughout the area."

"Good grief, that's great."

"A few months ago, the Clinton Global Initiative was held at the Ritz-Carlton on Amelia Island. And guess who was selected to drive the former president of the United States, Bill Clinton?" Terry then produced a picture—one that is now also on his website—of him and the former president.

Thrilled and moved by his great success, I then uttered what may have been the dumbest question to ever spring from my lips.

"So, Terry," I stupidly asked, "what did you say to Bill Clinton?"

After a bit of a pause for effect and perhaps a bit of rolling his eyes, Terry exclaimed, "I said, 'Mr. President, are you ready for the best limo ride of your life?'"

Turning to me and shrugging his shoulders just a bit, he then teased me. "What else *would* I say?"

Indeed. What else would Taxi Terry open with even to the former president of the United States? And I bet that it *was* the best limo ride Bill Clinton has ever had.

Taxi Terry's business has grown from that initial ride I had with him because every day he delivers on the seven tenets we've been discussing in this book. Although there are no guarantees of anything in life except the proverbial death and taxes, the fact remains that your likelihood of expanding your business, engaging your customers, and enjoying your work can be increased if you deliver on those tenets too.

A final time, the seven tenets are:

1. Set high expectations and then exceed them.

2. Delivering what helps the customer helps you.

3. Customers are people, so personalize their experience.

4. Think logically and then act creatively and consistently.

5. Make the customer the star of the show.

6. Help your customers come back for more.

7. Creating joy for your customer will make your work—and life—more joyful.

Now it's your challenge to go out there and deliver the greatest—whatever it is that *you* do—that your customers and colleagues have ever had in their lives.

NOTES

INTRODUCTION

1. Greco, Jamie, "Children's Theatre Turns Back Time with 'Schoolhouse Rock.'" *Daily Herald* (Arlington Heights, IL). Paddock Publications, 2010. Retrieved August 29, 2013, from HighBeam Research: http://www.highbeam.com/doc/1G1–240149673.html.

2. Bohn, Kevin, "'I'm Just a Bill': Schoolhouse Rock, 40 Years Later, Still Teaches Generations," CNN. Retrieved August 29, 2013, from http://www.cnn.com/2013/01/14/politics/schoolhouse-rock-40.

3. Elsmer, Mark, Elsmer Cove Forums. Retrieved August 30, 2013, from http://www.elsmer.com.

CHAPTER 2

1. "How Not to Act in a Job Interview: Real Examples of Hilariously Bad Behavior Reported by Interviewers," GradView.com. Accessed August 30, 2013, from http://www.gradview.com/articles/careers/big_mistake.html.

2. Cook, Jerry L., Randall Jones, Andrew Dick, and Archana Singh, "Revisiting Men's Role in Father Involvement: The Importance of Personal Expectations," *Fathering*. Men's Studies Press, 2005. Retrieved August 30, 2013, from HighBeam Research: http://www.highbeam.com/doc/1G1–133977961.html.

3. Moore, Mel T., "Provider Satisfaction: An Analysis Based on Expectation," *Physician Executive*. American College of Physician Executives, 1993. Retrieved August 30, 2013, from HighBeam Research: http://www.highbeam.com/doc/1G1–13240441.html.

4. Phelan, Steven E., "Entrepreneurship as Expectations Management," *New England Journal of Entrepreneurship*. College of Business, Sacred Heart University, 2005. Retrieved August 30, 2013, from HighBeam Research: http://www.highbeam.com/doc/1P3–982183211.html.

5. Priyabhashini, Alpana, and Venkat Krishnan, "Transformational Leadership and Follower's Career Advancement: Role of Pygmalion Effect," *Indian Journal of Industrial Relations*.

Shri Ram Centre for Industrial Relations and Human Resources, 2005. Retrieved August 29, 2013, from HighBeam Research: http://www.highbeam.com/doc/1G1–189653426 .html.

6. Ibid.

7. Reynolds, Dennis, "The Good, the Bad, and the Ugly of Incorporating 'My Fair Lady' in the Workplace," *SAM Advanced Management Journal.* Society for the Advancement of Management, 2002. Retrieved August 30, 2013, from HighBeam Research: http://www .highbeam.com/doc/1G1–90334364.html.

8. Merriam-Webster online dictionary. Accessed August 30, 2013, from http://www .merriam-webster.com/dictionary/golem.

9. Branson, Richard, "The Secret to Exceeding Customer Expectations," *Entrepreneur*, July 15, 2012. Retrieved August 31, 2013, from http://www.entrepreneur.com/ article/223969.

CHAPTER 3

1. Jones, Charisse, "A Job Can Mean Flying in Spite of Your Fear," *USA Today*, September 28, 2012. Retrieved August 31, 2013, from http://www.usatoday.com/story/travel/ flights/2012/09/28/dealing-with-fear-of-flying/1599711/.

2. Ibid.

3. Singapore Airlines website. Accessed August 31, 2013, from http://www.singaporeair .com/en_UK/about-us/.

4. "The 100 Best Companies to Work For," *Fortune.* Retrieved August 31, 2013, from http://money.cnn.com/magazines/fortune/best-companies/.

5. Boudreau, John, "'Personal Training' Creates Bonding Experience for Apple Customers," *Oakland Tribune.* Alameda Newspaper Group, 2008. Retrieved August 31, 2013, from HighBeam Research: http://www.highbeam.com/doc/1P2–15481142.html.

6. Phillips, Katherine, "Diversity Helps Your Business—But Not the Way You Think," *Forbes*, June 2, 2009. Retrieved August 31, 2013, from http://www.forbes.com/2009/06/02/ diversity-collaboration-teams-leadership-managing-creativity.html.

7. Cited at http://RogerCrawford.com. Retrieved August 31, 2013.

8. Paxton, Perry, quote retrieved from SearchQuotes.com on August 31, 2013: http://www .searchquotes.com/quotation/Excellence_is_in_the_details._Give_attention_to_the_ details_and_excellence_will_come./224685/.

9. Wihardja, Cynthia, "Sorry, but It's 'Company Policy': What Not to Say in Business," *Jakarta Globe*, September 13, 2012. Retrieved September 1, 2013, from http://www .thejakartaglobe.com/archive/sorry-but-its-company-policy-what-not-to-say-in-business/.

10. Torok, George, "But We've Always Done It This Way: Top Ten List," http://www.Torok .com. Retrieved September 1, 2013, from http://www.torok.com/articles/creativity/ ButWe.html.

11. Powell, Jennifer Heldt, "Doing Good Can Be Good for Business: Charity Gives Customers Incentive to Buy," *Boston Herald*. Herald Media, 2010. Retrieved August 31, 2013, from HighBeam Research: http://www.highbeam.com/doc/1G1–217331638.html.

CHAPTER 4

1. La Roche, Julia, "Icahn: My Herbalife Stake Is About Making Money, It's Not Personal." BusinessInsider.com, February 15, 2013. Retrieved September 2, 2013, from http://www .businessinsider.com/carl-icahn-is-on-cnbc-2013–2#ixzz2dmKZ16XC.

2. Savage, Adrian, "All Business Is Personal." Lifehack. Retrieved September 2, 2013, from http://www.lifehack.org/articles/featured/all-business-is-personal.html.

3. Michelli, Joseph, "Listen—All Business Is Personal," http://JosephMichelli.com; posted on January 6, 2011. Retrieved September 2, 2013, from http://josephmichelli.com/ blog/?p=738.

4. Cisco Systems, "Customer Experience." Retrieved September 4, 2013, from http://www .cisco.com/en/US/solutions/ns1168/customer_experience.html.

5. Ibid.

6. Hellman, Paul, "When the Question Is Too Personal," *Boston Herald*, October 5, 2012. Retrieved September 3, 2013, from http://www.boston.com/jobs/news/jobdoc/2012/10/ when_the_question_is_too_perso.html.

CHAPTER 5

1. "On Humor: Dr. Charles W. Jarvis," Squaresail.com. Retrieved September 4, 2013, from http://www.squaresail.com/drjarvis.html.

2. "No Vocation For Location, Part 5," London, NotAlwaysRight.com. Retrieved September 5, 2013, from http://notalwaysright.com/no-vocation-for-location-part-5/ 27421.

3. Posted by "Hard Worker," StupidCoWorkers.com; Originally posted May 22, 2012. Retrieved on September 5, 2013, from http://www.stupidcoworkers.com/index.php? startpos=12.

4. Leibs, Scott, "Measuring Up: Many Companies Still Struggle to Use Metrics Effectively: It May Be That Fresh Thinking Is What Really Counts," *CFO*, June 1, 2007. Retrieved September 4, 2013, from http://cfo.com/printable/article .cfm/9214066/c_9277557.

5. Fitzgerald, F. Scott, "The Crack-Up: One of the Greats Confronts the Pressures of Fame in a Most Public Forum," *Esquire*, March 1936. Retrieved September 4, 2013, from http://www.esquire.com/features/the-crack-up.

6. Wilde, Oscar. Quote retrieved September 4, 2013, from http://www.brainyquote.com /quotes/keywords/consistency.html#Dh22hlFgMybSP0b4.99.

7. Louis, C.K. Quote retrieved September 4, 2013, from http://www.brainyquote.com /quotes/quotes/1/louisck452787.html.

8. Retrieved from Wikipedia.org, September 4, 2013: http://en.wikipedia.org/wiki/ Al_Pacino.

CHAPTER 6

1. Coldewey, Devin, "America's Media Consumption So High It's Measured in Zettabytes," NBC News, August 17, 2012. Retrieved September 6, 2013, from http://www.nbcnews.com/technology/americas-media-consumption-so-high-its-measured-zettabytes-950292.

2. Ramsey, Doug, "How Much Information Do We Consume?" University of California, San Diego, December 9, 2009. Retrieved September 6, 2013, from http://www .universityofcalifornia.edu/news/article/22528.

3. White paper commissioned by Silverpop, "Use Behavioral Marketing to Up the Ante in the Age of the Customer," Forrester Research, May 2013. Retrieved September 6, 2013, from http://www.silverpop.com/marketing-resources/white-papers/all/2013/Up-the-Ante-in-the-Year-of-the-Customer/.

4. Smith, Joyce, "Good Service Is Key to Keeping Shoppers Happy," McClatchy Newspapers, December 27, 2011. Retrieved September 6, 2013, from http://www .indystar.com/article/20111227/BUSINESS/112270341.

5. RightNow Technologies, "Customer Experience Impact Report: Getting to the Heart of the Consumer and Brand Relationship," RightNow Technologies, 2011. Retrieved September 6, 2013, from http://www.rightnow.com/files/analyst-reports/RightNow_ Customer_Experience_Impact_Report_North_America_2011.pdf.

6. Krotz, Joanna L., "The Power of Saying Thank You," Microsoft.com. Retrieved September 7, 2013, from http://www.microsoft.com/business/en-us/resources/marketing/ customer-service-acquisition/the-power-of-saying-thank-you.aspx?fbid=ySYsYACqQBP#.

7. Ibid.

8. Salesforce.com, "10 Ways to Find True Love with Customers," Desk.com, a division of Salesforce.com. Retrieved September 6, 2013, from http://www.desk.com/customer-service/training-tips.

9. Facts about Delta Airlines, Inc., retrieved September 7, 2013, from http://news.delta .com/index.php?s=18&cat=47.

10. Ibid.

11. ChatAfrik Publisher, "72% Say Celebrities Get Special Treatment When They Break the Law," AfrikPoll.com, March 13, 2011. Retrieved September 7, 2013, from http:// afrikpoll.com/poll-news/item/42-72-say-celebrities-get-special-treatment-when-they-break-the-law.html.

12. Rufo, Anthony, "Celebrity Trademark Watch: Elizabeth Taylor, Godmother of Celebrity Branding, Is This Year's Highest Earning Dead Celebrity," *JD Supra Law News*,

December 3, 2012. Retrieved September 7, 2013, from http://www.jdsupra.com/legalnews/celebrity-trademark-watch-elizabeth-tay-37420/.

13. Rodriguez McRobbie, Linda, "Wilt Chamberlain Was a Nixon Man: A History of Celebrity Political Endorsements," MentalFloss.com, December 12, 2007. Retrieved September 7, 2013, from http://mentalfloss.com/article/17577/wilt-chamberlain-was-nixon-man-brief-history-celebrity-political-endorsements.

CHAPTER 7

1. Biography: Broccoli, Albert R., IMDb.com. Retrieved September 22, 2013, from http://www.imdb.com/name/nm0110482/bio?ref_=nm_ov_bio_sm.

2. Bloom, Robert H., and Dave Conti, *The Inside Advantage: The Strategy That Unlocks the Hidden Growth in Your Business*, McGraw-Hill, September 26, 2007.

3. Ibid.

4. "Daily Departures," Southwest Airlines fact sheet. Retrieved September 26, 2013, from http://swamedia.com/channels/Corporate-Fact-Sheet/pages/corporate-fact-sheet#daily-departures.

5. "Number 10: Bic Underwear," *Daily Finance*. Retrieved September 26, 2013, from http://www.dailyfinance.com/photos/top-25-biggest-product-flops-of-all-time/?photo=2#!fullscreen&slide=982935.

6. Summers, Jeffrey, "How We See It," Summers Hospitality Group. Retrieved September 26, 2013, from http://shgww.com/strategic-thinking-for-restaurant-operators/.

7. Wilson, Harold, QuoteGarden.com. Retrieved September 26, 2013, from http://www.quotegarden.com/change.html.

8. "James Bond Movies at the Box Office," Box Office Mojo, Retrieved September 26, 2013, from http://www.boxofficemojo.com/franchises/chart/?id=jamesbond.htm.

CHAPTER 8

1. Morgan, Dave, "Most TV Viewers Don't Know What to Watch," Online Spin from MediaPost.com, December 17, 2009. Retrieved September 26, 2013, from http://www.mediapost.com/publications/article/119335/most-tv-viewers-dont-know-what-to-watch.html#axzz2gFOkgCf9.

2. "Snoring Relief," Ear Plug Superstore. Retrieved September 30, 2013, from http://www.earplugstore.com/snoring-relief.html?_s_icmp=HOMEBAR3_SNORING.

3. Aggarwal, Ajay, "Customer Joy—Not Sales—Key to Retail Success," *DNA News of India*, January 4, 2012. Retrieved September 26, 2013, from http://www.dnaindia.com/money/1633095/report-customer-joy-not-sales-key-to-retail-success.

4. Murphy, Shawn, "On Creating Joy at Work," Switch and Shift: Human Side of Business. July 18, 2012. Retrieved September 26, 2013, from http://switchandshift.com/on-creating-joy-at-work.

5. Ibid.

INDEX

LESSON XIII

71.   Present Indicative of Estar, *to be*

SINGULAR	PLURAL
estoy	estamos
estás	estáis
está	están

72. Estar, *to be*, is used instead of **ser**, *to be:*

1. To express position.

2. To express an accidental or temporary condition.[1]

1. **Mi padre está en Chile.**   My father is in Chile.
   Madrid está en España.   Madrid is in Spain.

2. **Juan está cansado.**   John is tired.
   María está enferma.   Mary is ill.
   Las sábanas están limpias.   The sheets are clean.

73. Some adjectives have one meaning when used with **ser**, and another meaning when used with **estar**.

ser bueno, to be good   **ser malo,** to be bad
estar bueno, to be well   **estar malo,** to be ill

74. Omission of the Indefinite Article. — 1. The indefinite article is usually omitted before an unqualified predicate noun.

Mi padre es médico.   My father is a physician.
Mi tío es abogado.   My uncle is a lawyer.
Nuestro amigo es español.   Our friend is a Spaniard.

2. The indefinite article is not used with **otro**, *other, another*.

otro libro, another book   **el otro libro,** the other book

---

[1] This rule has many apparent exceptions, thus: **él es joven**, *he is young*. Youth is, in a sense, temporary, but it is after all relatively permanent as compared with illness or fatigue.

EXERCISES

el **abogado**, lawyer	el **espejo**, mirror, looking-glass
la **almohada**, pillow	la **frazada**,[2] blanket
la **cama**, bed	la **funda de almohada**, pillowcase
cansado, –a, tired	la **lana**, wool; **de lana**, woollen
la **cómoda**, chest of drawers,	**limpio**, –a, clean
"chiffonier"	el **médico**, physician, doctor
cuando (*interrog.*, **cuándo**),	la **pared**, wall
when	la **sábana**, sheet
el **cuarto**, room[1]	el **tocador**, dressing table, "dresser"
enfermo, –a, ill, sick	la **verdad**, truth

en casa, at home; **en casa de un amigo**, at a friend's; **¿no es verdad?**
o **¿verdad?** is it not true? isn't it so?

A. *Continúese.* 1. No soy joven. 2. No soy médico.
3. Estoy en casa. 4. Estoy cansado, –a. 5. No soy malo, –a.
6. No tengo otra cama.

B. 1. Mi primo Juan tiene una buena (*fine*) cama en su
cuarto. 2. Las fundas de almohada y las sábanas están
limpias y blancas. 3. Las frazadas (mantas) son de lana.
4. Juan duerme muy bien en esta cama cuando está cansado. 5. Los otros muebles de su cuarto son un tocador con
un buen espejo, una cómoda, una mesa y algunas sillas.
6. Hay también algunos cuadros en las paredes. 7. Juan
no está ahora en casa. 8. Está en casa de un amigo que
está enfermo. 9. Este amigo es abogado. 10. Cuando el
abogado está bueno, trabaja mucho. 11. Pero cuando está
enfermo, no puede trabajar. 12. Juan quiere mucho a su
amigo el abogado.

C. *Contéstese según el contexto de B.* 1. ¿Tiene Juan una
buena cama? 2. ¿Están limpias y blancas las sábanas?
3. ¿Están limpias y blancas las fundas de almohada? 4. ¿Son
de lana las frazadas (mantas)? 5. Juan duerme bien en
esta cama, ¿no es verdad? 6. ¿Cuáles son los otros muebles

---

[1] Note the many words for *room*.   [2] Or **manta (de cama).**

del cuarto? 7. ¿Tiene el tocador un buen espejo? 8. ¿Está Juan ahora en casa? 9. Está en casa de un amigo, ¿verdad? 10. ¿Está bueno o malo el amigo de Juan? 11. ¿Es este amigo médico o abogado? 12. Juan quiere mucho a su amigo, ¿no es verdad?

D. 1. Is John lazy? 2. Is John ill? 3. Mary is good. 4. Mary is well, is she not? (¿no es verdad?) 5. The blankets are red. 6. Are the blankets woolen? 7. Are the blankets clean? 8. My uncle is old. 9. My uncle is not well. 10. His father is a physician, isn't he? 11. No, sir; he is a lawyer. 12. Haven't you another pillow? 13. This pillowcase is not clean. 14. I have another pillowcase.

E. 1. I have one friend who is a physician and another who is a lawyer. 2. The physician is an Englishman and the lawyer is a Spaniard. 3. My brother likes the lawyer, but he does not like the physician. 4. When my brother is ill, he does not want that (ese) physician. 5. My brother is not now at home; he is at the lawyer's (house). 6. Our bedroom is on the upper floor of the house. 7. We have two fine beds with clean, white sheets (= with sheets clean and white). 8. The pillowcases are also clean and white, but the woolen blankets are red. 9. When we are tired, we sleep well in these beds. 10. Our dressing table has a good mirror. 11. We have two chests of drawers (" chiffoniers ") also and some fine pictures on the walls. 12. There are also some books and a writing desk in our room.

RESUMEN GRAMATICAL

72. Estar y ser. — El verbo **estar** se usa en lugar de **ser**:

1. Para expresar situación.

2. Para expresar una condición accidental o temporal.

73. Algunos adjetivos cambian de significado según sean usados con el verbo **ser** o con **estar**.

74. Supresión del artículo indeterminado. — 1. Por regla general se suprime el artículo indeterminado delante del nombre predicado (o atributo) no calificado.

2. El artículo indeterminado no se usa con **otro**.

LESSON XIV

75. Personal Pronouns. — The following personal pronouns are used as objects of verbs:

Singular	Plural
me, me, to me	**nos,** us, to us
te, thee, to thee	**os,** you, to you

Te corresponds to **tú** and **os** to **vosotros, –as.**

76. The personal pronoun objects usually precede their verb (but see §194).

Me busca.	He seeks me.
Me da el libro.	{ He gives me the book, *or* { He gives the book to me.

77. Reflexive Verbs. — 1. The pronouns given above may also be used as reflexives. The reflexive pronoun of the third person, singular or plural, is **se.**

yo me engaño, I deceive myself
tú te engañas, thou deceivest thyself

usted ⎫
él ⎬ se engaña { you deceive yourself
ella ⎭ { he deceives himself
{ she deceives herself

nosotros (–as) **nos engañamos,** we deceive ourselves
vosotros (–as) **os engañáis,** ye deceive yourselves

ustedes ⎫
ellos ⎬ se engañan { you deceive yourselves
ellas ⎭ { they deceive themselves

2. Many verbs are used reflexively in Spanish, but not in English:

Me acuesto, I go to bed.	**Me desayuno,** I (have) breakfast.
Me levanto, I get up, rise.	**Me equivoco,** I am mistaken.

All the verbs given above are in the first conjugation.

3. If the subject is inanimate, the reflexive construction is generally preferred in Spanish to the passive voice.

La casa se calienta por vapor.	The house is warmed by steam.
Aquí se habla español.	Spanish is spoken here.

78.   Hours of the Day

Es la una, it is one (o'clock).

A la una, at one (o'clock).

Son las dos, it is two (o'clock).

A las tres y media, at half-past three (o'clock).

A las cuatro y cuarto, at a quarter past four (o'clock).

A las cinco menos cuarto, at a quarter to five (o'clock).[1]

A las doce y diez (minutos), at ten minutes past twelve (o'clock), **at** twelve ten.

A las ocho de la mañana, at eight (o'clock) in the morning (*or*, A.M.).

A las tres de la tarde, at three (o'clock) in the afternoon (*or*, P.M.).

A las once de la noche, at eleven (o'clock) at night (*or*, P.M.).

¿Qué hora es? what time is it? what o'clock is it?

a. **La una** agrees with **hora** understood, and **las dos, las tres,** etc., agree with **horas.** **Media** (*half*) is an adjective and agrees with **hora,** while **cuarto** (*quarter, fourth*) is a noun and therefore does not agree.

EXERCISES

el **aire,** air

  almorzar (ue), to lunch [2]

  aquí, here

  calentar (ie), to warm, heat

  caliente, warm, hot

el **calor,** warmth, heat

el **calorífero central,** furnace [3]

el **carbón de piedra,**[4] coal

  cenar, to sup, have supper

  comer, to eat, dine

el **día,**[5] day

la **hora,** hour

la **mañana,** morning

la **noche,** night

  producir, to produce, create

  quemar, to burn

el **sótano,** basement

la **tarde,** afternoon

el **vapor,** steam

A. *Continúese.* 1. Yo me levanto a las seis. 2. Yo me desayuno a las siete y media. 3. Yo almuerzo a la una.

[1] One hears also: **a un cuarto para las cinco,** or **a las cuatro y tres cuartos.**

[2] In Spain and Spanish America, it is customary to have a light breakfast (**desayunarse**) in the morning, to dine (**comer**) at noon, and have supper (**cenar**) in the evening. But in the large cities it is now becoming customary to lunch (**almorzar**) at noon and to dine (**comer**) in the evening.

[3] Or **estufa central.**

[4] Literally *stone coal.* It is also called **carbón mineral.** *Bituminous or soft coal* is **hulla.** *Charcoal* is **carbón vegetal** or **carbón de leña.**

[5] **Día,** *day,* though ending in –a, is masculine.

4. Yo como a las siete.   5. Yo me acuesto a las diez.   6. Yo me equivoco.

B. 1. Mi tío Fernando tiene un calorífero central en el sótano de su casa.   2. En este calorífero se quema carbón de piedra.   3. Con el calor que se produce se calienta toda la casa.   4. La casa se calienta por vapor.   5. También se calienta por vapor la casa de otro tío mío (*of mine*), si no me equivoco.   6. Se equivoca Vd.; la casa se calienta por aire caliente.   7. En nuestra casa nos levantamos todos a las siete de la mañana.   8. Nos desayunamos a las ocho.   9. A las doce y media almorzamos, y comemos a las seis y media.   10. Pero mis tíos y mis primos comen a las doce y cenan a las seis.   11. Nos acostamos a las once de la noche.   12. Nos acostamos a las diez si estamos cansados.

C. *Contéstese según el contexto de B.*   1. ¿Qué tiene don Fernando en el sótano de su casa?   2. ¿Qué se quema en el calorífero?   3. ¿Se produce mucho calor?   4. ¿Se calienta toda la casa?   5. ¿Se calienta por vapor?   6. ¿Se calienta por aire caliente?   7. ¿No se equivoca Vd.?   8. ¿A qué hora se acuestan Vds.?   9. ¿A qué hora se levantan Vds.?   10. ¿A qué hora se desayunan Vds.?   11. ¿A qué hora almuerzan Vds.?   12. ¿A qué hora comen Vds.?   13. ¿Almuerzan o comen los tíos a la una?   14. ¿Comen o cenan a las seis?

D. *Tradúzcase, y repítase después negativamente.*   1. He teaches me. (**Él me enseña. Él no me enseña.**)   2. They like me.   3. She seeks us.   4. Spanish is spoken here.[1]   5. English is spoken here.[1]   6. You are mistaken.   7. Coal is burned.[1]   8. Heat is created.[1]   9. The house is warmed.[1]   10. I rise at five o'clock.   11. We go to bed at eight.   12. It is twelve o'clock.

E. 1. I go to bed at nine o'clock and get up at six.   2. My father goes to bed at ten o'clock and gets up at half-past six.

[1] Place the subject after the verb. Note how often the subject may follow the verb in Spanish even in an affirmative sentence.

3. We breakfast at seven o'clock or at a quarter past seven. 4. We lunch at half-past twelve and dine at half-past six. 5. When we are at the table, we speak Spanish. 6. My cousins dine at twelve o'clock and have supper at six. 7. There is a good furnace in the basement of my father's house. 8. Coal is burned in the furnace. 9. The house is warmed by steam. 10. My uncle Ferdinand's house is warmed with (por) air. 11. I cannot study when the air is (está) very warm. 12. I cannot sleep well if the air of my bedroom is warm.

RESUMEN GRAMATICAL

75. Pronombres personales. — Los siguientes pronombres personales se usan como complementos (objetos) de verbo: **me, te, nos, os.**

76. Los pronombres personales usados como complementos, por regla general preceden al verbo (pero véase el § 194).

77. Verbos reflexivos. — 1. Los pronombres citados arriba se usan también como reflexivos. El pronombre reflexivo de tercera persona, singular o plural, es **se.**

2. Muchos verbos que en español son reflexivos no lo son en inglés.

3. Cuando el sujeto de la oración es un ser inanimado se prefiere en español la forma reflexiva a la pasiva.

78. Horas del día: . . .

a. **La una** concuerda con la palabra **hora** sobrentendida, y **las dos, las tres,** etc., concuerdan con **horas. Media** es adjetivo y concuerda con **hora,** mientras que **cuarto** es substantivo y por consiguiente no concuerda.

LESSON XV

79. Personal Pronouns. — 1. The personal pronouns of the third person used as objects of verbs are:

DIRECT OBJECT		INDIRECT OBJECT	
Sing.	le, him		⎧ him, to him
	la, her, it	le	⎨ her, to her
	lo, it [1]		⎩ it, to it
Pl.	los ⎫ them las ⎭		les, them, to them

Busco la carta.	I seek the letter.
La busco.	I seek it.
Busco las cartas.	I seek the letters.
Las busco.	I seek them.
Busco el libro.	I seek the book.
Lo busco.	I seek it.
Busco los libros.	I seek the books.
Los busco.	I seek them.
Busco al profesor.	I seek the teacher.
Le busco.	I seek him.

Note that **la, las,** and **los** are used both as articles and as object pronouns, but that the article **el** differs in form from the corresponding object pronouns **le** and **lo.**

2. All the pronouns given above serve also as the object pronouns corresponding to **usted** and **ustedes.**

Le busco.	I seek him *or* you, *m. sing.*
La busco.	I seek her *or* you, *f. sing.*
Los busco.	I seek them *or* you, *m. pl.*
Las busco.	I seek them *or* you, *f. pl.*
Le da el libro.	He gives him, her, *or* you the book.
Les da el libro.	He gives them *or* you the book.

[1] **Lo** is also used with the meaning of *him* or *you* (*m.*), but **le** is generally considered preferable.

3. English *it* (*dir. obj.*) is expressed in Spanish by **la** when it refers to a feminine noun, and by **lo** when it refers either to a masculine noun or to a mere idea or statement.

Tengo la pluma.	I have the pen.
La tengo.	I have it.
Tengo el libro.	I have the book.
Lo tengo.	I have it.
Creo eso.	I believe that.
Lo creo.	I believe it.

EXERCISES

asar, to roast
la batería de cocina,[1] kitchen utensils
la carne, meat
la cazuela, pan
cocer (ue), to bake, boil (*food*)
la cocina económica,[2] kitchen stove, range
el cocinero, *o* la cocinera, cook
la comida, food, meal, dinner

creer, to believe
fregar (ie), to scour
guisar,[3] to cook
el horno, oven
la olla, pot
el pan, bread
preparar, to prepare
sabroso, –a, savory; ser (estar) sabroso, to taste good

hay . . . que, there is (are) to; **eso no me gusta,** I do not like that *or* that does not please me; **nos gustan estos cuadros,** we like these pictures *or* these pictures please us.

A. *Continúese.* 1. No me (te, le, *etc.*) gusta esta casa. 2. No me gustan los muebles. 3. Don Juan me enseña. 4. Me da lecciones de español. 5. Mi (tu, su, *etc.*) tío me (te, le, *etc.*) busca. 6. Yo no guiso la comida.

B. 1. Nuestra cocinera guisa la comida en la cocina económica. 2. La comida que guisa es muy sabrosa.

[1] Or **trastos de cocina.**

[2] A modern, iron *cooking stove* or *range* is usually called a **cocina económica** or merely an **económica.** In some places it is also called **estufa.** Many Spaniards and Spanish Americans still cook over openings in the top of stone benches or shelves, in which charcoal is burned, or over open fireplaces. Either one is usually called **fogón.**

[3] Also **cocinar.**

3. El pan que cuece en el horno es muy bueno. 4. Y me gusta mucho la carne que asa en el horno o que cuece en una olla. 5. Esta mujer tiene que trabajar mucho en la cocina. 6. Tiene que preparar las comidas y fregar la batería de cocina. 7. Hay ollas y cazuelas que fregar. 8. Creo que le gusta trabajar en la cocina. 9. Le gusta guisar; no le gusta fregar las ollas y las cazuelas. 10. Pero no es perezosa y la batería de cocina está siempre muy limpia.

C. *Contéstese según el contexto de* B. 1. ¿Quién prepara las comidas? 2. ¿En qué se guisa la comida? 3. ¿En qué se cuece el pan? 4. ¿En qué se asa la carne? 5. ¿En qué se cuece la carne? 6. ¿Quién friega la batería de cocina? 7. ¿Qué friega la mujer? 8. ¿Trabaja mucho la cocinera? 9. ¿Le gusta guisar la comida? 10. ¿Le gusta fregar las ollas? 11. ¿Le gusta a Vd. (*Do you like*) guisar? 12. ¿Le gusta a Vd. fregar las ollas y las cazuelas?

D. *Tradúzcase, y repítase después, usando el pronombre personal que corresponda en lugar del último nombre de cada frase* 1. We prepare the meals. (**Preparamos las comidas. Las preparamos.**) 2. We roast the meat. 3. We bake the bread. 4. We scour the pans. 5. I am looking-for John. 6. I am looking-for Mary. 7. He gives the chair to John. 8. He gives the books to Mary. 9. He gives the letters to the men. 10. I do not like Doña Ana. (**No me gusta doña Ana. Ella no me gusta.**) 11. Do you like Don Fernando? 12. We like the teachers.

E. 1. Doña Ana's cook is a little lazy, and her pots and pans are not always clean. 2. She likes to cook the food, but she does not like to scour the kitchen utensils. 3. And in a kitchen there are many utensils (**trastos**) to scour. 4. The cook has to work hard in order to prepare three meals. 5. She bakes the bread in the oven of the stove. 6. She roasts the meat in the oven, or she boils it in a pot. 7. The food that she cooks always tastes good. 8. Do you like to bake bread and roast meat? 9. No, sir; I do not like to cook; but I am very fond of reading (**me gusta mucho leer**) books. 10. I like the library of our house, but I do not like the kitchen. 11. You like the dining room of your house, do you not? (¿no es verdad?) 12. Yes, I do like [it], but I do not like to prepare the meals.

RESUMEN GRAMATICAL

79. Pronombres personales. — 1. Los pronombres personales de la tercera persona usados como complementos verbales son: **le, la, lo, los** y **las** para el complemento directo (o caso acusativo) y **le** y **les** para el complemento indirecto (o caso dativo).

Nótese que las formas **la, las** y **los** se usan como artículos y también como pronombres complementarios; en cuanto al artículo **el** es de forma diferente de los pronombres complementarios correspondientes **le** y **lo**.

2. Todos los pronombres citados arriba hacen las veces de pronombres complementarios correspondientes a **usted** y **ustedes**.

3. El pronombre inglés *it* (complemento directo) se expresa en español por **la** cuando se refiere a un nombre del género femenino, y por **lo** cuando se refiere a un nombre del género masculino o a una idea o manifestación.

LESSON XVI

80. Personal Pronouns. — 1. When a verb has two personal pronoun objects, the indirect object precedes the direct.

Me lo da.	He gives it to me.
Te los da.	He gives them to thee.
Nos la da.	He gives it to us.
Os las da.	He gives them to you.

2. If both pronouns are in the third person, **se** is used as the indirect object instead of **le** or **les**. Although alike in form, this **se** and the reflexive **se** are different words.

Se lo da.	He gives it to him, her, it, them, *or* you.

Note that in this sentence **se** has all possible meanings of both **le** (*ind. obj.*) and **les**.

81. Prepositional Forms of the Personal Pronouns. ⟶
The personal pronouns governed by a preposition are the
same in form as the subject pronouns, except that **mí** and **ti**
are used instead of **yo** and **tú.** **Sí** is the prepositional form
of **se.**

para mí,	for me		para nosotros, –as,	for us
" ti,	" thee		" vosotros, –as,	" you
" usted,	" you		" ustedes,	" you
" él,	" him, it	}	" ellos, –as,	" them
" ella,	" her, it			

para sí, for himself, herself, *etc.*

a. **Mí,** *me,* is distinguished from **mi,** *my,* and the reflexive **sí** is
distinguished from **si,** *if,* by the accent mark.

82. When a personal pronoun is the object of a verb, the
meaning may be made clear or emphatic by adding **a mí,
a ti,** etc.

Me gusta a mí.	I like it.
Le gusta a ella.	She likes it.
Se lo da a él.	He gives it to him.
Se lo da a Vd.	He gives it to you.

a. One may say with still more emphasis on the pronoun: **A mí me
gusta,** etc.

b. With a noun the corresponding personal pronoun object is often
used thus even though it is not required to make the meaning clear or
emphatic: **le gusta a Juan,** John likes it; **se lo da a María,** he gives it
to Mary.

83. The definite article with **de él, de ella,** etc., may be
used instead of **su,** to make the meaning clear or emphatic.

Su libro, o el libro de él.	His book.
Su casa, o la casa de ella.	Her house.
Su cuarto, o el cuarto de Vd.	Your room.
Su padre, o el padre de ellos.	Their father.

a. With these expressions, compare **el libro de Juan,** *John's book;*
la casa de María, *Mary's house.*

ESTACIÓN DE FERROCARRILES
A part of the railway station in Buenos Aires.

LA CATEDRAL DE LIMA

UN RESTAURANT ARGENTINO

EXERCISES

el **almuerzo,** lunch, heavy breakfast

el **café,** coffee

el **campo,** country (*as distinguished from the city*); los **campos,** fields

la **cena,** supper

la **ciudad,** city, large town

¿**cuánto?** how much? ¿**cuántos?** how many?

cultivar, to cultivate

el **chocolate,** chocolate

el **desayuno,** (light) breakfast

después de, *prep.*, after

España, *f.*, Spain

el **ganadero,** cattle raiser

el **habitante,** inhabitant

el **hacendado,** planter

el **labrador,** farm laborer [1]

la **leche,** milk

la **mantequilla,** butter [2]

la **ópera,** opera

el **teatro,** theater

una vez, once; **dos veces,** twice; **tres veces,** three times; **algunas veces,** sometimes; **en vez de,** instead of; **al día,** daily

A. *Continúese.* 1. Me enseña la lección. 2. Me la enseña. 3. A mí me da el libro. 4. Me lo da a mí. 5. A mí no me gusta el campo. 6. Hay una carta para mí. 7. El profesor tiene mi cuaderno. 8. Mi hermano tiene mi gramática.

B. 1. En España los habitantes de las ciudades hacen (*have*) tres comidas al día: el desayuno, el almuerzo, y la comida o la cena. 2. Se desayunan a las ocho de la mañana, y toman a esta hora café con leche,[3] pan y mantequilla (manteca). 3. Muchos toman chocolate en vez de café. 4. Almuerzan a la una y comen a las siete o las siete y media. 5. Algunas veces cenan después del teatro o la ópera. 6. Los hacendados y los ganaderos comen a las doce o la una y cenan a las seis o las siete. 7. Los labradores tienen que trabajar mucho para cultivar los campos. 8. Se levantan a las cinco de la mañana y se acuestan a las ocho

---

[1] A *plantation* is **una hacienda** or, in Argentina, **una estancia.** In Mexico *farm* and *farmer* are **rancho** and **ranchero** and *a laborer* is **un jornalero.**

[2] In Spanish America *butter* is **mantequilla** and *lard* is **manteca.** In most of Spain, however, *butter* is **manteca (de vaca)** and *lard* is **manteca de cerdo.**

[3] **Café con leche,** a mixture of coffee and hot milk.

o a las nueve de la noche. 9. A mí me gusta mucho el
campo, pero a mi hermano no le gusta. 10. ¿Le gusta a
Vd. el campo? 11. — Sí, señor; me gusta mucho.

C. *Contéstese según el contexto de* B. 1. ¿Cuántas comidas al
día hacen los habitantes de las ciudades? 2. ¿Cuáles son
estas comidas? 3. ¿A qué hora se desayunan? 4. ¿Qué
toman a esta hora? 5. ¿A qué hora almuerzan? 6. ¿A
qué hora comen? 7. ¿Cuándo cenan? 8. ¿Trabajan mucho
los labradores? 9. ¿A qué hora se levantan? 10. ¿A qué
hora comen? 11. ¿A qué hora cenan? 12. ¿A qué hora se
acuestan? 13. ¿Le gusta a Vd. el campo? 14. ¿Le gusta a
su hermano?

D. 1. He has her book. 2. She has his book. 3. I have your
grammar. 4. Have you my grammar? 5. We have lunch (= We
lunch) at half-past twelve. 6. We have dinner (= We dine) at seven
o'clock. 7. We go to bed at ten. 8. We get up at seven. 9. He
gives the paper to me: he gives it to me. 10. He does not give
the chairs to you: he does not give them to you. 11. She teaches
me arithmetic: she teaches me it. 12. She prepares for me (**me
prepara**) a good lunch. 13. I like the country, but you do not
like it. 14. Mary likes the country, but John does not like it.

E. 1. Ferdinand, is your father a planter? 2. No, sir; he is a
lawyer and lives in this city. 3. Does your father like the country?
4. Yes, sir; he likes the country, and he likes the city too. 5. Do
the cattle raisers and the planters have to work hard? 6. The farm
laborers must work hard in order to cultivate the fields. 7. When
(**¿A qué hora**) do the planters have dinner? 8. They have dinner
at twelve o'clock and supper at six in the evening. 9. In the city
we have dinner at seven o'clock at night. 10. Sometimes we have
supper after the opera or theater. 11. If we take supper, we have
(**hacemos**) four meals. 12. For breakfast (**Para el desayuno**) we
take coffee and milk and bread and butter. 13. In Spain many
people (**personas**) take chocolate instead of coffee. 14. In our
family we all like (**a todos nos gusta**) to take coffee if it is not very
strong (**cargado**).

RESUMEN GRAMATICAL

80. Pronombres personales. — 1. Cuando el verbo tiene dos complementos pronominales, el pronombre complemento indirecto precede al pronombre complemento directo.

2. Si ambos pronombres son de la tercera persona, se usa el pronombre **se** en lugar de los complementos indirectos **le** o **les**. Aunque este **se** tiene la misma forma que el pronombre reflexivo **se**, son dos palabras distintas.

81. Formas preposicionales (o terminales) de los pronombres personales. — Cuando los pronombres personales van regidos de una preposición tienen la misma forma que cuando son sujetos del verbo, exceptuando las formas **mí** y **ti** que se usan en vez de **yo** y **tú**. **Sí** es la forma preposicional de **se**.

a. **Mí,** pronombre personal, se distingue de **mi,** adjetivo posesivo, y la forma reflexiva **sí** se distingue de la conjunción **si,** por el acento escrito que llevan.

82. Cuando un pronombre personal es complemento verbal, su significado puede aclararse o hacerse enfático añadiendo las expresiones **a mí, a ti,** etc.

a. La expresión es aun más enfática si **a mí, a ti,** etc., preceden al verbo.

b. Con un nombre, el pronombre personal complementario correspondiente se usa a menudo de esta manera, aunque no se requiera para aclarar o hacer enfático el significado.

83. En lugar del adjetivo posesivo **su,** se puede emplear el artículo determinado y las expresiones **de él, de ella,** etc., lo que da mayor claridad y énfasis a la frase.

LESSON XVII

84. Commands. — 1. To express a direct command with **usted** or **ustedes** as subject, the following forms of the regular verbs are used:

	SINGULAR	PLURAL	
I. Hablar:	hable Vd.	hablen Vds.	speak
II. Aprender:	aprenda Vd.	aprendan Vds.	learn
III. Vivir:	viva Vd.	vivan Vds.	live

2. Radical-changing verbs change **e** to **ie** or **i**, and **o** to **ue**, as in the third person of the present indicative.

	SINGULAR	PLURAL	
Cerrar:	cierre Vd.	cierren Vds.	close
Pedir:	pida Vd.	pidan Vds.	ask (for)
Volver:	vuelva Vd.	vuelvan Vds.	return

3. Some irregular verbs:

	SINGULAR	PLURAL	
Dar:	dé [1] Vd.	den Vds.	give
Hacer:	haga Vd.	hagan Vds.	do
Tener:	tenga Vd.	tengan Vds.	have
Traer:	traiga Vd.	traigan Vds.	bring

a. Usted or ustedes is usually expressed once in a command as in the examples given above, but not repeated.

Preparen Vds. la segunda lección y repasen la primera. — Prepare the second lesson and review the first.

85. — 1. Personal pronoun objects precede the verb in a negative command, according to the general rule for the position of these pronouns (§194).

No me dé Vd. ese libro. — Do not give me that book.
No me lo dé Vd. — Do not give it to me.

2. In an affirmative command the personal pronoun objects follow the verb and are attached to it so that the verb and the pronoun or pronouns form one word.

Déme Vd. ese libro. — Give me that book.
Démelo Vd. — Give it to me.

[1] Note the accent which distinguishes this word from the preposition **de**.

a. When a pronoun is thus attached to one of these verb forms having two or more syllables, the verb requires the accent mark. Compare **traiga**, *bring*, with **tráigame**, *bring me*.

86. — 1. **Vamos** (from **ir**, *to go*), used in commands, means *let us go.*

Vamos a la escuela.	Let us go to school.
Vamos a trabajar.	Let us go to work.

2. When followed by an infinitive, **vamos a** often means no more than *let us.*

Vamos a hablar con él.	Let us speak with him.
Vamos a estudiar la lección.	Let us study the lesson.

87.   Cardinal Numerals

diez y siete, seventeen	**veintidós,** twenty-two
diez y ocho, eighteen	**veintitrés,** twenty-three
diez y nueve, nineteen	**veinticuatro,** twenty-four
veinte, twenty	**veinticinco,** twenty-five
veintiun(o), –a,[1] twenty-one	

EXERCISES

la **cuchara,** spoon	el **mozo,** waiter[3]
el **cuchillo,** knife	**nuevo, –a,** new
donde (*interrog.* **dónde**), where	el **plato,** plate
en seguida, then (= next)	**repasar,** to review
entrar en,[2] to enter, go in(to), come in(to)	**repetir** (i), to repeat
escuchar, to listen (to)	el **restaurant,**[4] restaurant
hoy, to-day	**sentar** (ie), to seat; **me siento,** I seat myself, sit (down)
la **lista,** list, bill of fare	la **servilleta,** napkin
el **mantel,** tablecloth	**sobre,** on, upon
mañana, *adv.*, to-morrow	el **tenedor,** fork
mientras, while	el **vaso,** (drinking-)glass

hágame Vd. el favor de estudiar, please study;[5] **prestar atención,** to pay attention

[1] See page 209, footnote 1.   [2] **Entrar a** is also in common use.

[3] The *waiter* is sometimes called **camarero.** **Mozo** is also used to designate a *servant boy,* a *street porter,* etc.

[4] As **restaurant** is a French word, the final *t* is not pronounced.

[5] **Hágame Vd. el favor** is more emphatic than the English *please* and is used less often.

A. 1. El profesor dice (*says*) a los alumnos: Escuchen Vds. bien. 2. Esta lección es muy difícil. 3. Fernando, Vd. no presta atención. Cierre su libro. 4. Pasen Vds. a la pizarra y escriban el ejercicio diez y siete. 5. Juan, lea Vd. la primera frase del ejercicio. 6. No le entiendo a Vd.: repítala. 7. ¡Está bien! Borre Vd. la frase y siéntese. 8. Borren Vds. el ejercicio y siéntense. 9. Preparen para mañana la lección diez y ocho. 10. Y repasen también la lección de hoy. 11. Háganme Vds. el favor de aprender bien la nueva lección.

B. 1. Mi amigo y yo entramos en el restaurant y nos sentamos a una mesa. 2. El mozo nos da la lista. 3. Mientras leemos la lista, el mozo pone (*puts*) sobre la mesa un mantel blanco. 4. Nos trae en seguida platos, vasos, cuchillos, tenedores y cucharas. 5. Mozo, le digo (*say*), tráiganos Vd. dos servilletas también.

C. *Contéstese según el contexto de* A *y* B. 1. ¿Qué les dice el profesor a los alumnos (§82, *b*)? 2. ¿Qué le dice a Fernando? 3. ¿Qué les dice en seguida a todos los alumnos? 4. ¿Qué le dice a Juan? 5. A todos los alumnos, ¿qué les dice? 6. ¿Qué lección tienen que preparar los alumnos para mañana? 7. ¿Qué lección tienen que repasar? 8. ¿Quiénes entran en el restaurant? 9. ¿Dónde se sientan Vds? 10. ¿Quién les da a Vds. la lista? 11. ¿Leen Vds. la lista? 12. ¿Qué pone el mozo sobre la mesa? 13. ¿Qué les trae a Vds. en seguida? 14. ¿Qué dice Vd. al mozo?

D. 1. Let us repeat the lesson. 2. Let us prepare the new lesson. 3. Let us write the twentieth exercise.

Tradúzcase y repítase después negativamente. 4. Ferdinand, go to the blackboard. 5. Write the exercise. 6. Write it with chalk. 7. Now erase it. 8. Prepare (*pl.*) the twenty-first lesson (**la lección veintiuna**). 9. Prepare it for to-morrow. 10. Please prepare this lesson (*neg.*: **Háganme Vds. el favor de no preparar,** *etc.*).

Repítase, con el pronombre personal correspondiente en vez del nombre. 11. He enters (into) the restaurant. 12. He says to the waiter: Give me the bill of fare. 13. Bring me a napkin. 14. Do not bring me the napkin to-morrow.

E. 1. Please (*pl.*) close your books and listen. 2. John and Ferdinand, [please] go to the blackboard and write to-day's exercise. 3. Write all the sentences and then read them to the class. 4. John, repeat your sentences; you do not read well. 5. Now underline (*pl.*) the mistakes and take your seats (= sit down). 6. Prepare for to-morrow the twenty-first lesson with the twenty-first exercise. 7. Please prepare well all the new lesson. 8. Let us dine in this restaurant. 9. Very well! I like this restaurant. 10. Here they cook the meals well (*say:* well the meals) always. 11. The tablecloths, the napkins, and the plates are always clean. 12. Waiter, give us the bill of fare. 13. Please bring us the bill of fare. 14. While we are reading it, the waiter brings us glasses, knives, forks, and spoons.

RESUMEN GRAMATICAL

84. Expresiones de mando. — 1. Las formas de los verbos regulares empleadas en expresiones de mando con **usted** y **ustedes** son: . . .

2. Los verbos que sufren cambios constantes en su raíz cambian la vocal radical **e** en **ie** o **i,** y **o** en **ue,** como lo hacen en la tercera persona del presente de indicativo.

a. El pronombre **usted** o **ustedes** se expresa una sola vez, por regla general, en una expresión de mando, y no se repite.

85. — 1. Los pronombres personales complementarios preceden al verbo en las frases prohibitivas, según la regla general para la colocación de estos pronombres (§194).

2. En las expresiones de mando afirmativas los pronombres personales complementarios siguen al verbo al cual están unidos, formando así una sola palabra.

a. Cuando al verbo de dos o más sílabas se añade un pronombre, el verbo requiere el acento escrito.

86. — 1. **Vamos** (del verbo **ir**) en expresiones de mando se traduce al inglés por *let us go.*

2. Cuando la expresión **vamos a** va seguida de un infinitivo, muchas veces no significa más que *let us.*

LESSON XVIII

88. Infinitives. — 1. Some verbs require a preposition before a subordinate infinitive, but many do not.

Juan aprende a leer.	John is learning to read.
Empieza a escribir.	He is beginning to write.
Me enseña a hablar español.	He teaches me to speak Spanish.
Tratamos de estudiar.	We try to study.
No pienso entrar.	I do not intend to go in.
No quiero almorzar.	I do not wish to breakfast.
¿Prefiere Vd. tomar café?	Do you prefer to take coffee?
¿Puede Vd. hacerlo?	Can you do it?

For a list of these verbs, see §283.

2. Personal pronoun objects follow an infinitive and are attached to it, so that the verb and the pronoun or pronouns form one word. If there are two pronoun objects, the final syllable of the infinitive requires the accent mark.

Sentarse.	To seat oneself, sit down.
¿Quiere Vd. dármelo?	Are you willing to (*or,* Will you) give it to me?

3. After a preposition the infinitive is regularly used in Spanish instead of the present participle (gerund).

Antes de (Después de) comer.	Before (After) eating.
Estoy cansado de estudiar esta lección.	I am tired of studying this lesson.

4. Spanish **al** + infinitive is equivalent to English *on* + present participle (gerund).

Al entrar en el restaurant.	On going into the restaurant.
Al leer la carta.	On reading the letter.

89. Present Indicative of:

Ir, *to go*		Venir, *to come*	
I go, do go, am going; etc.		*I come, do come, am coming; etc.*	
SINGULAR	PLURAL	SINGULAR	PLURAL
voy	vamos	vengo	venimos
vas	vais [1]	vienes	venís
va	van	viene	vienen

Dar, *to give*

I give, do give, am giving; etc.

SINGULAR	PLURAL
doy	damos
das	dais [1]
da	dan

90. Forms of Ir, Venir, and Dar Used in Commands.

vaya Vd. } go	venga Vd. } come	dé Vd. } give
vayan Vds. }	vengan Vds. }	den Vds. }

91.   Idiomatic Expressions

Acaba de hablar.	He has just spoken.
Vuelve a hablar.	He is speaking again.
Vaya Vd. a buscarlo.	Go and get it, go after it.
Venga Vd. a verme.	Come and see me.

EXERCISES

acabar, to finish
antes de, *prep.*, before
el apetito, appetite
la botella, bottle
la carne, meat; carne de vaca,[2] beef
como, as
empezar (ie), to begin
la ensalada, salad
las frutas, *pl.*, fruit
la papa o patata, potato [3]
el pescado, fish

poder (ue),[4] to be able, can
los postres, *pl.*, dessert
preferir (ie), to prefer
la propina, tip
el queso, cheese
servir (i), to serve
la sopa, soup
la taza, cup
tratar, to try
la vaca, cow
el vino, wine

[1] Since **vais** and **dais** are monosyllables, they do not take the accent.

[2] In some countries called **carne de res.**

[3] Called **patata** in most of Spain.

[4] Radical-changing verb in the present tenses, but irregular in some other tenses. See §270.

A. *Continúese.* 1. Acabo de leer el libro. 2. Vuelvo a leerlo. 3. Voy a buscarlo. 4. Aprendo a hablar español. 5. Trato de estudiar. 6. Pienso trabajar mucho. 7. Yo no puedo hacerlo. 8. Yo empiezo a escribir la carta.

B. 1. Como me desayuno a las ocho, tengo buen apetito a la una. 2. Los primeros platos que pedimos son sopa y pescado. 3. Empezamos a comerlos con buen apetito. 4. Después de comer el pescado, pedimos ensalada, carne y papas (patatas). 5. La ensalada que sirven en este restaurant es buena y la carne es sabrosa. 6. Como todos los españoles toman vino en las comidas, pedimos una botella. 7. Nuestros postres son queso y frutas. 8. Después de acabar el almuerzo, tomamos una taza de café. 9. En el desayuno prefiero tomar una taza de café con leche. 10. Pero en el almuerzo y la comida no tomo leche. 11. Antes de levantarnos de la mesa, damos una propina al mozo (al camarero). 12. A mi amigo y a mí nos gustan mucho los almuerzos que sirven en este restaurant.

C. *Contéstese según el contexto.* 1. ¿Al entrar en el restaurant, se sientan Vds. a una mesa? 2. ¿Viene el mozo (el camarero) a la mesa? 3. ¿Va a buscar la lista? 4. ¿Les da a Vds. la lista? 5. ¿Leen Vds. la lista? 6. ¿Cuáles son los primeros platos que piden Vds.? 7. ¿Empiezan Vds. a comerlos con buen apetito? 8. Después de comer el pescado, ¿qué piden Vds.? 9. ¿Cuáles son los postres? 10. Después de acabar el almuerzo, ¿qué toman Vds.? 11. ¿Prefiere Vd. tomar café con leche en el almuerzo? 12. Antes de levantarse de la mesa, ¿qué dan Vds. al mozo (al camarero)? 13. ¿Les gusta a Vd. y a su amigo almorzar en este restaurant?

D. 1. Waiter, come to this table. 2. I am coming (**Allá voy**), sir. 3. What does the gentleman wish? (**¿Qué manda el señor?**) 4. Go and get me another glass. 5. This [one] is not clean.

6. Bring me also a plate of soup. 7. After the soup I wish fish.
8. Bring me a plate of the good salad that you (**Vds.**) serve in this
restaurant. 9. And bring me also a cup of coffee. 10. Do you
always give a tip to the waiter? 11. Yes, sir; I have just given him
a tip. 12. Do you give it to him before or after (**antes o después
de**) rising from the table? 13. Always before rising from the table.
14. I do not give tips to the waiters.

E. 1. Do you like the meals that they serve in this restaurant?
2. I like the soup, the salad, and the coffee which they serve here,
but I do not like the meat. 3. The tablecloth, the plates, the spoons,
the knives, and (the) forks are clean. 4. Sometimes the glasses are
not clean. 5. Let us (§86, 2) sit down at this table. 6. Will you
(**¿Quiere Vd.**) dine with us? 7. No, thank you (**gracias**), I have
just dined. 8. I do not wish to dine again (**volver a comer**).
9. But we can talk while you are eating. 10. As I have lunch
(**Como almuerzo**) at half-past twelve, I have [a] good appetite
for (the) dinner. 11. Will you take a cup of coffee? 12. No,
thank you; I have just taken one cup of coffee. 13. The waiter
that is serving us is very good. 14. Before rising from the table,
let us give him a tip.

RESUMEN GRAMATICAL

88. Infinitivos. — 1. Algunos verbos rigen a otros en el infinitivo
mediante preposición, pero muchos efectúan este régimen sin preposición.

2. Los pronombres personales complementarios siguen al infinitivo y se añaden a él formando una sola palabra.

3. En español se usa el infinitivo después de una preposición en
lugar del participio presente (o gerundio).

4. La expresión castellana **al** con el infinitivo corresponde a la
inglesa *on* con el gerundio.

91.   Expresiones idiomáticas: . . .

LESSON XIX

92. Imperfect and Preterite Indicative. — 1. Spanish has in the indicative mood two simple past tenses where English has one. These Spanish tenses are the Imperfect (or Past Descriptive) and the Preterite (or Past Absolute).

2. The inflectional endings of these tenses are:

IMPERF. $\begin{cases} \text{I} \ . \ . \ . \ . : \text{–aba, –abas, –aba, –ábamos, –abais, –aban} \\ \text{II and III: –ía, –ías, –ía, –íamos, –íais, –ían} \end{cases}$

PRET. $\begin{cases} \text{I} \ . \ . \ . \ . : \text{–é, –aste, –ó, –amos, –asteis, –aron} \\ \text{II and III: –í, –iste, –ió, –imos, –isteis, –ieron} \end{cases}$

3.

Hablar: Imperfect		Aprender: Imperfect	
I spoke, did speak, was speaking; etc.		*I learned, did learn, was learning; etc.*	
SINGULAR	PLURAL	SINGULAR	PLURAL
hablaba	hablábamos	aprendía	aprendíamos
hablabas	hablabais	aprendías	aprendíais
hablaba	hablaban	aprendía	aprendían

Preterite		Preterite	
I spoke, did speak; etc.		*I learned, did learn; etc.*	
SINGULAR	PLURAL	SINGULAR	PLURAL
hablé	hablamos	aprendí	aprendimos
hablaste	hablasteis	aprendiste	aprendisteis
habló	hablaron	aprendió	aprendieron

The imperfect (past descriptive) and the preterite (past absolute) tenses have the same inflectional endings in the third conjugation that they have in the second. All regular verbs are inflected in these tenses like **hablar** and **aprender**.

Note carefully the position of the accent marks.

93. **The Irregular Verb Ser**

Imperfect		Preterite	
I was; etc.		*I was; etc.*	
SINGULAR	PLURAL	SINGULAR	PLURAL
era	éramos	fuí	fuimos
eras	erais	fuiste	fuisteis
era	eran	fué	fueron

94. Uses of the Imperfect and Preterite. — 1. When the English simple past tense expresses an action or state as of indefinite duration, it is equivalent to the Spanish imperfect.

When it expresses an action or state as definitely past, it is equivalent to the Spanish preterite.

Era verdad.   It was true (*it may have been true long before and it may still be true*).

Fué verdad.   It was true (*it was true at the time to which the speaker refers*).

2. In narrations, the Spanish imperfect is used to describe the conditions or circumstances which prevailed when something happened, while the preterite is used to tell what happened.

Llovía cuando llegamos.   It was raining when we arrived.

a. In this use the imperfect is best translated by *was*, etc., + the present participle, as in the sentence above.

3. The Spanish imperfect is also used to tell what was customary or habitual.

Cuando yo era alumno de esta escuela, estudiaba mucho.   When I was a student in this school, I studied (used to study, would study) much.

a. In this use the imperfect is often best translated by *used to* or *would* + the infinitive, as in the sentence above.

EXERCISES

América, America
el árabe, Arab
ayer, yesterday
la compañía, company
descubrir, to discover
durar, to last, endure
encontrar (ue), to meet
la enfermedad, illness
los Estados Unidos, the United States
el indio, Indian

llegar, to arrive
llover (ue), to rain
morir (ue), to die
el mundo, world
nunca, never
el presidente, president
que, *conj.*, that
el siglo, century
varios, –as, several
el viaje, voyage, trip

¿cuántos años tiene Vd.? (*lit.*, how many years have you?), how old are you? tengo veinte años, I am twenty years old; le falta, he lacks (*lit.*, there is lacking to him)

A. 1. Cristóbal Colón (*Christopher Columbus*) descubrió el Nuevo Mundo el día 12 (**doce**) de octubre (*October*) de 1492 (**mil cuatrocientos noventa y dos**). **2.** Hizo (*pret. de* **hacer**) cuatro viajes al Nuevo Mundo. **3.** Tenía cincuenta (*fifty*) y seis años cuando hizo el **cuarto** viaje; le faltaba el vigor de la juventud (*youth*) y en el Nuevo Mundo tenía muchos enemigos (*enemies*). **4.** Muy enfermo volvió a España y pasó a Valladolid donde estaba la Corte (*Court*), y donde murió (*pret. de* **morir**) poco después (*afterward*).

" Por Castilla (*Castile*) y por León
Nuevo Mundo halló Colón."

B. 1. ¿Quién descubrió a América? **2.** ¿Cuándo descubrió a América? **3.** ¿Cuántos viajes hizo Colón al Nuevo Mundo? **4.** ¿Cuántos años tenía cuando hizo el cuarto viaje? **5.** ¿Le faltaba el vigor de la juventud? **6.** ¿Tenía muchos enemigos en el Nuevo Mundo? **7.** ¿Estaba enfermo Colón cuando volvió a España? **8.** ¿A dónde pasó? **9.** ¿Dónde estaba la Corte? **10.** ¿Dónde murió Colón?

C. *Tradúzcase, y dígase por qué el verbo está en el imperfecto o en el pretérito.*

1. La enfermedad duró varios meses.
2. Ella tenía veinticinco años cuando murió.
3. Juan escribía todas las cartas de la compañía.
4. Ayer escribió una carta a su padre.
5. Fernando no habló a mi padre cuando le encontró esta mañana.
6. Nunca hablaba Fernando a mi padre cuando le encontraba.
7. No hallé el libro que buscaba.
8. Yo escribía una carta cuando mi amigo entró.
9. Era la una de la noche cuando llegaron.
10. Cuando mis amigos llegaron a casa eran las dos y llovía.

11. Wáshington fué el primer Presidente de los Estados Unidos.
12. Los indios vivían en América.
13. Los árabes vivieron muchos siglos en España.

D. 1. When John was (**estaba**) in (the) school, he did not study much. 2. But he spoke Spanish every day (**todos los días**). 3. And he did learn to speak Spanish. 4. He used to write all the Spanish letters (**cartas en español**). 5. Yesterday he wrote a Spanish letter to his aunt Mary. 6. Did you find the letter that you were looking for? 7. No, sir; I did not find it. 8. I thought (**creí**) that you found it. 9. What time was it when they arrived? 10. It was ten o'clock at night when they arrived at the house, and it was raining. 11. Doña María was ill when she arrived. 12. Did the illness last long (**mucho tiempo**)? 13. No, sir; it did not last long.

RESUMEN GRAMATICAL

92. Imperfecto y pretérito de indicativo. — 1. El castellano tiene en el modo indicativo dos tiempos pasados simples mientras que el inglés sólo tiene uno. Estos tiempos castellanos son el imperfecto (o pasado descriptivo) y el pretérito (o pasado absoluto).

3. . . . Los tiempos imperfecto y pretérito tienen las mismas terminaciones para los verbos de la tercera conjugación que para los de la segunda; en consecuencia todos los verbos regulares se conjugan en estos dos tiempos como los verbos **hablar** y **aprender.**

Debe observarse cuidadosamente el lugar que le corresponde al acento gráfico.

94. Uso de los tiempos imperfecto y pretérito. — 1. Cuando en inglés el tiempo pasado simple expresa una acción o estado de duración indefinida, se traduce al español por el imperfecto.

Cuando expresa una acción o estado en tiempo completamente pasado, se traduce al español por el pretérito.

2. En español se usa en la narración el imperfecto para describir las condiciones o circunstancias que prevalecían cuando algún

hecho se verificaba, pero el hecho mismo se expresa mediante el pretérito.

a. En este caso el imperfecto español se traduce al inglés mediante *was*, etc., más el participio presente del verbo principal.

3. El imperfecto se usa también para expresar hechos habituales.

a. En este caso el imperfecto español puede traducirse al inglés por *used to* o *would* más el infinitivo del verbo principal.

LESSON XX

95. Imperfect and Preterite of Radical-Changing Verbs. — In the imperfect (past descriptive) and preterite (past absolute) indicative, radical-changing verbs are inflected like regular verbs, without change in the radical vowel, except in the preterite of the third conjugation. Here the radical vowels **e** and **o** are changed to **i** and **u,** respectively, in the third person singular and plural.

Preterite

Sentir: *I felt, did feel; etc.*		**Pedir:** *I asked, did ask; etc.*	
SINGULAR	PLURAL	SINGULAR	PLURAL
sentí	sentimos	pedí	pedimos
sentiste	sentisteis	pediste	pedisteis
sintió	sintieron	pidió	pidieron

Dormir: *I slept, did sleep; etc.*	
SINGULAR	PLURAL
dormí	dormimos
dormiste	dormisteis
durmió	durmieron

96. The Feminine Article el (*Review* §31). — Before a feminine noun with initial **a–** (or **ha–**) and with the stress on the first syllable, **el** is used instead of **la.**

El agua.	The water.
El hacha.	The axe.

But: **las aguas,** *the waters;* **las hachas,** *the axes.*

LA SUPUESTA TUMBA DE CRISTÓBAL COLÓN

This monument, erected in the ancient cathedral of Santo Domingo,
has been designated by the Dominican Republic as the actual
resting-place of the great Discoverer.

LA CATEDRAL DE MÉXICO
The cathedral in Mexico City.

97. The Neuter Gender. — There are no neuter nouns in Spanish; but pronouns and adjectives are called neuter when they do not refer to masculine or feminine nouns.

>Eso es bueno. That is good.

98. The Neuter Article lo. — The article lo is required before the masculine form of an adjective when the adjective is used substantively with the force of an abstract noun. **Lo** can not be used with a noun.

>Lo bueno. The good (= that which is good).
>Lo infinito. The infinite.

EXERCISES

aceptar, to accept
afectuosamente, affectionately
el alma, *f.*, soul
bañarse, to bathe, take a bath
la calle, street
el cielo, sky
¿cómo? how?
componerse [1] de, to be composed of
despedirse (i) de, to take leave of
dirigirse a, to make one's way to, go to

dormirse (ue), to go to sleep
frío, −a, cold
inmortal, immortal
la invitación, invitation
invitar, to invite
lleno, −a, full
nublado, −a, cloudy, overcast
el número, number
Pablo, Paul
salir [1] a, to go out into
vestirse (i), to dress oneself
ya, already

ya acabé, I have finished, I'm done; se acabó, it is finished, it's done; con mucho gusto, with great pleasure; llegué hace ocho (quince) días, o hace ocho (quince) días que llegué, I arrived a week (fortnight) ago.

A. *Continúese.* 1. Me bañé y me vestí. 2. Ya acabé. 3. Acepté con mucho gusto. 4. Lo sentí mucho. 5. Llegué hace ocho días. 6. Hace quince días que me despedí de ellos.

B. 1. Ayer me levanté a las siete, me bañé y me vestí. 2. Después de desayunarme, salí a la calle. 3. El cielo

---

[1] Irregular in some tenses (see **poner** §265, and **salir** §274).

estaba nublado, pero no llovía. 4. Las calles estaban llenas de hombres y mujeres. 5. Me dirigí a casa de mi amigo don Pablo. 6. Este amigo vive en la calle de Atocha, número 20. 7. Me recibió afectuosamente, y me invitó a pasar el día con él y su familia. 8. Acepté la invitación con mucho gusto. 9. La familia se compone de don Pablo, su esposa y tres hijos. 10. Después de comer me despedí de mis amigos. 11. Volví a casa (*home*) y me acosté. 12. Como estaba muy cansado, me dormí en seguida.

C. 1. ¿A qué hora se levantó Vd.? 2. Después de levantarse, ¿qué hizo Vd.? 3. Cuando Vd. salió a la calle, ¿estaba nublado el cielo? 4. Cuando Vd. salió, ¿llovía? 5. ¿Estaban las calles llenas de hombres y mujeres? 6. ¿A dónde se dirigió Vd.? 7. ¿Dónde vive el amigo de Vd.? 8. ¿Cómo le recibió a Vd.? 9. ¿Le invitó a Vd. a pasar el día con él? 10. ¿Aceptó Vd. la invitación? 11. ¿De quiénes se compone la familia de don Pablo? 12. ¿Después de la comida se despidió Vd. de sus amigos? 13. ¿Volvió Vd. a casa? 14. ¿Estaba Vd. cansado (cansada)? 15. ¿Se acostó Vd.? 16. ¿Se durmió Vd. en seguida?

D. *Léase* B, *cambiando a la tercera persona del singular todos los verbos y pronombres que están en la primera persona, y usando* **mi padre** *como sujeto de los verbos, verbigracia:* "Ayer mi padre se levantó," *etc.*

E. 1. *Conjúguense en el imperfecto y pretérito los siguientes verbos:* cerrar, contar, entender, volver, sentir, dormirse, y despedirse.

2. *¿Cuántas y cuáles son las formas del artículo determinado?*

Tradúzcase: 3. We prefer the good to the bad in this world. 4. The water is (**está**) cold. 5. The waters are cold. 6. The soul is immortal. 7. The souls of men (**de los hombres**) are immortal.

F. 1. When I lived [1] in Atocha Street, I rose at seven. 2. I took a bath, dressed, and had breakfast at eight. 3. Then I would

[1] The meaning is *I used to live, I used to rise*, etc.

go out into the street. 4. If it was not raining the streets were full of men and women. 5. I used to visit my friend Paul (**don Pablo**) who received me affectionately. 6. He would always invite me to spend the day with him. 7. After dinner I used to return home. 8. At ten o'clock I would go to bed. 9. —[1] Does your friend live in Atocha Street now? 10. — No. He doesn't live in Madrid. 11. A week ago I went to the house in which he used to live. 12. My friend was not there to (**para**) receive me, and I returned home.

RESUMEN GRAMATICAL

95. En los tiempos imperfecto (pasado descriptivo) y pretérito (pasado absoluto) de indicativo, los verbos que cambian la vocal de la raíz se conjugan lo mismo que los verbos regulares, es decir, sin cambiar la vocal radical, exceptuándose el pretérito de la tercera conjugación donde las vocales radicales **e** y **o** se cambian en **i** y **u** respectivamente, en las terceras personas del singular y plural.

96. El artículo **el** se emplea con nombres femeninos que empiezan por **a** o **ha** siempre que esta sílaba lleve el acento prosódico.

97. En castellano no hay nombres del género neutro; pero se consideran del género neutro aquellos pronombres y adjetivos que no se refieren a nombres masculinos o femeninos.

98. El artículo **lo** se usa con la forma masculina del adjetivo cuando éste hace las veces de substantivo abstracto. No puede emplearse con el nombre.

LESSON XXI

99. Inflection of Adjectives (*Review* §§35, 36). — By exception, the following adjectives ending in consonants add –**a** to form the feminine:

1. Adjectives ending in –**án,** –**ón,** and –**or** (not including comparatives in –**or**).

<table>
<tr><td>Un muchacho haragán, burlón y hablador.</td><td>An idle, roguish, talkative boy.</td></tr>
<tr><td>Una muchacha haragana, burlona y habladora.</td><td>An idle, roguish, talkative girl.</td></tr>
</table>

[1] In written Spanish a change of speaker is indicated by a dash.

2. Adjectives of nationality.

Un muchacho español.	A Spanish boy.
Una muchacha española.	A Spanish girl.

100. When an adjective of nationality denotes the language, it is masculine and usually takes the definite article.

El español no es fácil.	Spanish is not easy.
Estudiamos el español.	We are studying Spanish.

a. But the article may be omitted when the name of a language immediately follows **hablar,** or is used with **en.**

¿**Habla usted español** (o **caste-** **llano**)?	Do you speak Spanish?
Está escrito en español (o **en** **castellano**).	It is written in Spanish.

Note also such idiomatic expressions as **una lección de francés,** *a French lesson;* **un ejercicio de español,** *a Spanish exercise.*

b. The term **castellano** (*Castilian*) is considered preferable to **español** in certain expressions, such as **la gramática castellana,** *Spanish grammar;* and in some Spanish-American countries the Spanish language is more commonly called **el castellano.**

101. Most verbs classified as irregular form the imperfect indicative regularly. Thus, this tense is regular in the irregular verbs **estar, tener, poder,** and **querer.**

102. Preterite

SINGULAR	PLURAL		SINGULAR	PLURAL
Estar: *I was; etc.*		**Tener:** *I had,* or *did have; etc.*		
estuve	estuvimos		tuve	tuvimos
estuviste	estuvisteis		tuviste	tuvisteis
estuvo	estuvieron		tuvo	tuvieron

Poder: *I could,* or *was able; etc.* **Querer:** *I wished,* or *did wish; etc.*

pude	pudimos	quise	quisimos
pudiste	pudisteis	quisiste	quisisteis
pudo	pudieron	quiso	quisieron

Note that these irregular preterites have a change of stem, and do not have the accent on the endings of the first and third persons singular.

EXERCISES

Carlos, Charles
casi, almost
cortés, polite, courteous
la duda, doubt
Emilia, Emily
Felipe, Philip
fonético, –a, phonetic
francés, –esa, French
hermoso, –a, handsome
igualmente, equally
Isabel, Elizabeth
la lengua, language

más, more, most
el muchacho, boy; la muchacha, girl; los muchachos, children.
perfectamente, perfectly
que, than
romance, Romance (derived from Latin)
traidor, –ora, treacherous
trigueño, –a, dark-complexioned

al contrario, on the contrary; me llamo (lit., I call myself), my name is; ¿cómo se llama Vd.? what is your name?

A. Continúese. 1. No soy español (española). 2. Yo no hablaba español. 3. Yo quería aprender el castellano. 4. No pude hallar el libro. 5. Me llamo Felipe (Isabel).

B. 1. Don Felipe y su esposa doña Isabel eran españoles. 2. Tenían dos hijos, Carlos y Emilia. 3. Carlos tenía diez y seis años y Emilia doce. 4. Los dos muchachos eran trigueños, hermosos y corteses. 5. Como eran españoles, hablaban casi perfectamente el castellano. 6. Querían aprender a hablar y escribir el inglés también. 7. Yo les daba lecciones de inglés casi todos los días. 8. Creían que el inglés era más difícil que el castellano. 9. Yo creía, al contrario, que el castellano era más difícil. 10. La verdad es que las dos lenguas son difíciles. 11. Para aprender a hablar y escribir correctamente una lengua, tiene uno que (one has to) estudiar mucho. 12. No hay duda de que la ortografía inglesa es más difícil. 13. La ortografía castellana es más fonética que la inglesa. 14. Pero la gramática castellana y la gramática inglesa son igualmente difíciles.

C. Contéstese. 1. ¿Cómo se llamaba la esposa de don Felipe? 2. ¿Cómo se llamaba su hijo? 3. ¿Cómo se llamaba

su hija? 4. ¿Cuántos años tenía Carlos? 5. ¿Cuántos años
tenía Emilia? 6. ¿Eran españoles o ingleses? 7. ¿Hablaban
español o inglés? 8. ¿Querían aprender el inglés también?
9. ¿Les daba Vd. lecciones de inglés? 10. ¿Creían ellos que el
inglés era más difícil que el castellano? 11. ¿Creía Vd. que
el inglés era más difícil? 12. ¿Son difíciles las dos lenguas?
13. ¿Tiene uno que estudiar mucho para aprender una
lengua? 14. ¿Es más difícil la ortografía inglesa? 15. ¿Es
más fonética la ortografía castellana?

D. 1. *¿Cuáles son las formas masculina y femenina, singular y
plural, de* **blanco, fuerte, cortés, inglés, traidor, inferior?**

Tradúzcase. 2. This woman is handsome and strong. 3. This
man is talkative; this woman is not talkative. 4. This girl is
French; she is polite. 5. She does not speak Spanish. 6. She is
studying Spanish. 7. Spanish is not easy. 8. The English language
also is difficult. 9. This book is written in French. 10. French is a
Romance language.

E. 1. Spanish and French are Romance languages. 2. (The)
French grammar and (the) Spanish are equally difficult. 3. But
(the) Spanish spelling is more phonetic than (the) French. 4. When
I lived in Madrid, Don Felipe taught me Spanish. 5. I did not
speak Spanish correctly. 6. I wished to learn to speak it and write
it perfectly. 7. In order to learn Spanish I took lessons nearly every
day. 8. Doña Isabel, Don Felipe's wife, was handsome and very
courteous. 9. The two children (**hijos**), Emily and Charles, were
dark-complexioned. 10. They spoke Spanish and French, and
they wished to learn English. 11. When I talked English with them
they were glad (**contentos**). 12. I was able to give them lessons
nearly every day. 13. One day it rained, and I could not give them
an English lesson. 14. But they learned the lesson and wrote the
exercise.

RESUMEN GRAMATICAL

99. Inflexión de los adjetivos. — Por excepción los siguientes
adjetivos terminados en consonante forman su femenino añadiendo

una **a:** 1. los adjetivos terminados en –**án,–ón** y –**or** (sin incluir los comparativos terminados en –**or**) ; 2. los adjetivos que denotan nacionalidad.

100. Cuando el adjetivo de nacionalidad denota el idioma, toma el género masculino y va generalmente precedido del artículo determinado.

a. Se puede suprimir el artículo cuando el nombre de la lengua sigue inmediatamente al verbo **hablar,** o cuando se usa con la preposición **en.**

b. En ciertas expresiones se prefiere el término **castellano** al de **español,** por ejemplo, la **gramática castellana**; y en algunos países hispanoamericanos llaman comúnmente a la lengua nacional **el castellano.**

101. La mayor parte de los verbos irregulares forman su imperfecto de indicativo regularmente. Así, pues, este tiempo es regular en los verbos irregulares **estar, tener, poder,** y **querer.**

102. . . . Hay que notar que estos pretéritos irregulares sufren un cambio en su radical y no llevan el acento en las personas primera y tercera del singular.

LESSON XXII

103. The Definite Article is Required. — 1. Before a noun used in a general sense to denote all of the thing or kind it names.

Las mujeres aman a los niños.	Women (*as a rule*) love children (*generally speaking*).
But, **Compramos flores.**	We are buying (some) flowers.

2. Before a proper noun modified by a title or a descriptive adjective, except in direct address.

El señor García.	Mr. García.
La pequeña Isabel.	Little Elizabeth.
But, **Buenos días, señor García.**	Good day, Mr. García.

a. **Don** and **doña** (used before given names only) are exceptions in that they never require the definite article: **doña Emilia no está en casa,** *Doña Emilia is not at home.*

b. Note the meanings of **señor, señora, señorito,** and **señorita.**

señor, — Mr., sir, gentleman; **señores,** Messrs., sirs, gentlemen, Mr. and Mrs.

señora, — Mrs., madam (ma'am), lady.
señorito, — Master, young gentleman.
señorita, — Miss, young lady.

104. Present Indicative

Decir, *to say, tell*   **Ver,** *to see*

I say (tell), do say (tell), am saying (telling); etc.   *I see, do see, am seeing; etc.*

Singular	Plural	Singular	Plural
digo	decimos	veo	vemos
dices	decís	ves	veis
dice	dicen	ve	ven

105. Imperfect Indicative

Ir, *to go*   **Ver,** *to see*

I went, did go, was going; etc.   *I saw, did see, was seeing; etc.*

Singular	Plural	Singular	Plural
iba	íbamos	veía	veíamos
ibas	ibais	veías	veíais
iba	iban	veía	veían

The imperfect indicative of **decir** and **venir** is formed regularly.

106. Preterite

Decir   **Ver**

I said (told), did say (tell); etc.   *I saw, did see; etc.*

Singular	Plural	Singular	Plural
dije	dijimos	vi	vimos
dijiste	dijisteis	viste	visteis
dijo	dijeron	vió	vieron

Ir   **Venir**

I went, did go; etc.   *I came, did come; etc.*

Singular	Plural	Singular	Plural
fuí	fuimos	vine	vinimos
fuiste	fuisteis	viniste	vinisteis
fué	fueron	vino	vinieron

a. **Ir,** *to go,* and **ser,** *to be,* have the same preterite. This is because **ir** has lost its own preterite and has borrowed that of **ser.** Compare with the colloquial English expression: *I was to town yesterday.*

EXERCISES

amar, to love
el **apellido,** surname, family name
el **bautismo,** baptism; **nombre de bautismo,** baptismal *or* given name
casado, –a, married
comprar, to buy
conocer, to know (= be acquainted with), meet
conservar, to retain
cordialmente, cordially
enseñar, to show, teach
entregar, to hand, deliver
la **flor,** flower

el **hierro,** iron
el **marido,** husband
mortal, mortal
el **oro,** gold
pequeño, –a, little, small
preguntar, to ask (*a question*)
el **significado,** meaning, significance
la **tarjeta,** card; **tarjeta de visita,** visiting card
usar, to use, wear
útil, useful
la **visita,** visit

A. *Continúese.* 1. Fuí a verlos. 2. Los vi. 3. Vine a ver a Vd. 4. Le dije la verdad. 5. Conocí al señor García.

B. 1. En Granada conocí a los señores de García (al señor García y su señora esposa). 2. La familia se componía de don Fernando el marido, doña Emilia la esposa, y la pequeña Isabel su hija. 3. Don Fernando me invitó a hacerles una visita. 4. Fuí a verlos y me recibieron cordialmente. 5. Un día don Fernando vino a verme. 6. La criada me entregó la tarjeta de visita del señor. 7. En la tarjeta leí: "Fernando García y Morales." 8. Cuando conocí bien a este señor, le pregunté el significado de estos nombres. 9. Me dijo que Fernando era su nombre de bautismo (*o* de pila).[1] 10. Dijo también que García era el apellido de su padre y Morales el apellido de su madre. 11. Me explicó que muchos españoles usan los dos apellidos. 12. Me enseñó una tarjeta de visita de doña Emilia. 13. En esta tarjeta

---

[1] **Pila** is the baptismal font.

84 FIRST SPANISH COURSE

leí: "Emilia González de García." 14. Me explicó que en España las mujeres casadas conservan el apellido del padre. 15. González era el apellido del padre de doña Emilia. 16. Me dijo también que el nombre y los apellidos de la pequeña Isabel eran: Isabel García y González.

C. *Contéstese. Sería conveniente que el profesor, antes de hacer estas preguntas, escribiera en la pizarra los nombres de bautismo (o de pila) y los apellidos de la familia García.* 1. Cuando Vd. estuvo en Granada ¿a quiénes conoció? 2. ¿De cuántas personas se componía esa familia? 3–5. ¿Cómo se llamaba el marido? la esposa? la hija? 6. ¿Le invitó a Vd. don Fernando a hacerles una visita? 7. ¿Fué Vd. a verlos? 8. ¿Cómo le recibieron a Vd.? 9. ¿Vino don Fernando a hacerle a Vd. una visita? 10. ¿Qué le entregó a Vd. la criada? 11 ¿Qué nombres estaban escritos en la tarjeta? 12. ¿Le preguntó Vd. al señor el significado de esos nombres? 13–15. ¿Cuál era el nombre de bautismo del marido? de la esposa? de la hija? 16–18. ¿Cuáles eran los apellidos del marido? de la esposa? de la hija? 19. ¿En España conservan las mujeres casadas el apellido del padre? 20. Los hijos usan el apellido de la madre también, ¿no es verdad?

D. 1. Man is mortal. 2. Men are mortal. 3. Iron is useful. 4. Iron is more useful than gold. 5. He is buying iron with gold. 6. Do you like flowers? 7. Yes, sir; I like flowers. 8. I am buying flowers for my mother. 9. Mr. García is a Spaniard. 10. Mrs. García (**La señora de García**) is Spanish. 11. I met Mr. and Mrs. García in Granada. 12. I met Miss García also. 13. What are your given names? 14. What is your surname?

E. 1. Mr. García y Morales was the father of little Elizabeth. 2. Mrs. González de García was her mother. 3. The surname of Elizabeth was García y González. 4. Elizabeth was a handsome, dark-complexioned [girl]. 5. Like (**Como**) all Spanish girls she loved flowers. 6. She liked books and pictures, but she preferred flowers. 7. She used to buy flowers every day. 8. Mr. García did not like flowers. 9. He would say that coal and iron are more useful than flowers. 10. One day he bought coal to warm the house. 11. He said that he could not warm the house with flowers (*¿por qué no se usa el artículo?*). 12. Visiting cards are useful. 13. When Don Fernando came to see me, the maidservant handed me this gentleman's card. 14. I read on the card his given name and his family names. 15. I asked (to) Don Fernando the meaning of these names and he explained them to me.

RESUMEN GRAMATICAL

103. El artículo determinado se usa: 1. delante de un nombre usado en sentido colectivo y que se refiere a toda la clase o especie; 2. delante de un nombre propio modificado por un título o adjetivo descriptivo, exceptuándose el vocativo.

a. Los términos **don** y **doña** (delante de nombres de bautismo) deben considerarse como excepciones en el sentido de que no requieren el artículo determinado.

b. No se olvide cuáles son los significados de las voces **señor, señora, señorito,** y **señorita.**

106. — *a.* **Ir** y **ser** tienen el mismo pretérito. Esto se debe a que el verbo **ir** ha perdido su pretérito y ha tomado el del verbo **ser.**

LESSON XXIII

107. Definite Article for Possessive. — 1. When speaking of parts of the body or articles of clothing, the definite article is generally used instead of the possessive adjective.

Los niños abrieron los ojos.	The children opened their eyes.
Perdí el sombrero.	I lost my hat.

2. To avoid ambiguity, an indirect object pronoun may be used also.

Me corté el dedo.	I cut my finger.
Me puse el sombrero.	I put on my hat.

a. But the possessive is generally used before the subject of a sentence: **su sombrero es nuevo,** *his hat is new.*

b. Note the following use of **tener** + the name of a part of the body.

Tengo los ojos cansados.	My eyes are tired.
Tiene las manos muy frías.	His hands are very cold.

108. Distributive Construction. — When speaking of similar objects one of which belongs to each member of a group, the singular is generally used in Spanish.

Los niños se lavaron la cara y las manos. — The children washed their faces and hands.

(**Cara** *is singular since each child has one, while* **manos** *is plural since each child has two.*)

Se limpiaron los dientes con cepillo y polvos. — They cleaned their teeth with brushes and powder.

109. Present Indicative

Hacer, *to make, do*
I make (do), do make (do), am making (doing); etc.

SINGULAR	PLURAL
hago	hacemos
haces	hacéis
hace	hacen

Poner, *to put*
I put, do put, am putting; etc.

SINGULAR	PLURAL
pongo	ponemos
pones	ponéis
pone	ponen

Dar, *to give*
I give, do give, am giving; etc.

SINGULAR	PLURAL
doy	damos
das	dais
da	dan

110. Preterite

Hacer
I made (did), did make (did do); etc.

SINGULAR	PLURAL
hice	hicimos
hiciste	hicisteis
hizo	hicieron

Poner
I put, did put; etc.

SINGULAR	PLURAL
puse	pusimos
pusiste	pusisteis
puso	pusieron

Dar

I gave, did give; etc.

SINGULAR	PLURAL
di	dimos
diste	disteis
dió	dieron

a. The imperfect of **hacer, poner,** and **dar** is formed regularly.

111.   Present Indicative

Conocer, *to know, be acquainted with*

I know, do know, am knowing; etc.

SINGULAR	PLURAL
conozco	conocemos
conoces	conocéis
conoce	conocen

a. The imperfect and the preterite of **conocer** are formed regularly.

112. Most verbs ending in –cer or –cir preceded by a vowel are inflected like **conocer** (thus **nacer,** *to be born;* **lucir,** *to shine;* etc.). These are usually called Inceptive Verbs.

EXERCISES

abrir, to open
apresurarse (a), to make haste (to)
los **cabellos,**[1] hair (*of the head*)
la **cara,** face
cepillar, to brush
el **cepillo,** brush; **cepillo de dientes,** toothbrush
despertarse (ie), to wake up, awaken
el **diente,** tooth
el **jabón,** soap
lavar, to wash
limpiar, to clean

la **mano,** hand
el **niño,** small boy, child; la **niña,** small girl, child; los **niños,** children
el **ojo,** eye
peinar, to comb
los **polvos dentífricos,**[2] toothpowder
porque, because, for; **¿por qué?** why?
responder, to answer
saltar, to jump (out)
secar, to dry
la **toalla,** towel

en este momento, at this moment; **es hora de,** it is time to *or* for; **hace frío,** it is cold; **tengo frío,** I am cold; **tengo hambre,** I am hungry.

[1] Or **el pelo.**   [2] Or **polvos para los dientes.**

A. *Continúese.* 1. Abrí los ojos. 2. Me lavé la cara y las manos. 3. Me cepillé los cabellos (el pelo). 4. Yo tenía hambre. 5. No lo hice. 6. Yo conozco al señor Morales. 7. Me puse el sombrero. 8. Le di el libro.

B. 1. Los dos niños se despertaron y abrieron los ojos. 2. Saltaron de la cama porque ya eran las siete. 3. ¡La familia se desayunaba a las siete y media! 4. Los niños se lavaron la cara y las manos con agua y jabón. 5. Y se las secaron con una toalla. 6. En seguida se limpiaron los dientes con cepillo y polvos. 7. Se peinaron y se cepillaron los cabellos (o el pelo). 8. En este momento entró en el cuarto la madre de los niños. 9. Buenos días, mamá, dijeron los niños. 10. Buenos días, hijos míos, respondió la madre. 11. Ya es hora del desayuno. Vamos al comedor. 12. Los niños se apresuraron a vestirse. 13. Porque hacía frío en el cuarto y tenían hambre.

C. 1. ¿A qué hora se desayunaba la familia? 2. ¿A qué hora se despertaron los niños? 3. ¿Abrieron los ojos los niños? 4. ¿Saltaron de la cama? 5. ¿Con qué se lavaron la cara y las manos? 6. ¿Con qué se las secaron? 7. ¿Con qué se limpiaron los dientes? 8. ¿Se peinaron y se cepillaron los cabellos (el pelo)? 9. En este momento ¿quién entró en el cuarto? 10. ¿Qué le dijeron los niños? 11. ¿Qué respondió la madre? 12. ¿Qué hicieron los niños en seguida? 13. ¿Por qué?

D. *Tradúzcase, y repítase con los sujetos de los verbos en plural.* 1. The child opened his eyes. (**El niño abrió los ojos. Los niños abrieron los ojos.**) 2. The child washed his face and hands. 3. I cleaned my teeth with [a] toothbrush. 4. I combed my hair.[1] 5. I brushed my hair. 6. You made haste to dress. 7. You were hungry. 8. I was born in the United States.

---

[1] Omit. **Me peiné** is sufficient (but in 5 the noun is required).

E. 1. Good day, my children, said the mother on entering (§88, 4) the room. 2. Good day, mamma, said the children. 3. The children jumped out of bed, for it was half-past seven o'clock. 4. And they had-breakfast (*imperf.*) at eight! 5. They made haste to wash their faces and hands with soap and water. 6. Then they brushed their hair and cleaned their teeth. 7. To (**Para**) clean their teeth they made use of (**se sirvieron de**) toothbrushes and tooth powder. 8. They made haste to dress because it was breakfast-time. (*véase* B, 11). 9. They were cold and hungry. 10. When children are cold, they wish to warm themselves. 11. When they are hungry, they wish to eat. 12. Children always have [a] good appetite. 13. I knew these children and their parents. 14. They were all born (= All were born) in Spain.

RESUMEN GRAMATICAL

107. Empleo del artículo determinado en vez del posesivo. — 1. Para referirse a las diferentes partes del cuerpo humano o a las diversas prendas de vestir se emplea el artículo determinado en vez del adjetivo posesivo.

2. Para evitar ambigüedad se puede emplear un complemento indirecto pronominal.

a. En cambio se hace uso del adjetivo posesivo cuando se trata del sujeto de la frase.

b. Hay que notar el empleo del verbo **tener** con el nombre de las partes del cuerpo humano.

108. Uso distributivo. — Cuando se habla de objetos semejantes de los cuales uno corresponde a cada individuo del grupo, en español se emplea por regla general el singular.

110. — *a.* El imperfecto de indicativo de los verbos **hacer, poner** y **dar** se forma regularmente.

111. — *a.* El imperfecto y el pretérito de **conocer** se forman regularmente también.

112. La mayor parte de los verbos terminados en –**cer** o –**cir** después de vocal se conjugan como **conocer** (tales como **nacer, lucir,** etc.). Estos verbos llevan el nombre genérico de Incipientes.

LESSON XXIV

113.　　　　Negative Pronouns and Adverbs

1. **nadie,** no one, nobody　　　　**ni,** nor; **ni . . . ni,** neither . . .
   nada, nothing　　　　　　　　　　nor
   ninguno (ningún), –a, no, none　　**tampoco,** neither; **ni . . . tam-**
   nunca, never　　　　　　　　　　　**poco,** nor . . . either

　　¿Quién vino? — **Nadie.**　　　　Who came?　No one.
　　Nadie vino.　　　　　　　　　　No one came.
　　Nada tengo.　　　　　　　　　　I have nothing, *or* I haven't any-
　　　　　　　　　　　　　　　　　　　　　thing.

2. When such negatives follow the verb, **no** must precede it. This means that then they are really affirmative in force.

　　No conozco a (§68) nadie en　　I know no one, *or* I do not know
　　　Burgos.　　　　　　　　　　　anyone, in Burgos.
　　No tengo nada.　　　　　　　　I have nothing, *or* I haven't any-
　　　　　　　　　　　　　　　　　　　　thing.
　　No tengo ni pluma ni papel.　　I have neither pen nor paper, *or*
　　　　　　　　　　　　　　　　　　　　I haven't either pen or paper.

114. Changes in Spelling. — According to the Spanish system of orthography, it is sometimes necessary to change the spelling of the stem of an inflected word, to show that the pronunciation does not change.

1. The rules for the more common changes are:

To express the sound of:	k	hard g	gw	jota	zeta
Before –a or –o, or final, write:	c	g	gu	j	z
Before –e or –i, write:	qu	gu	gü	g	c

　　Sacar: saco, I take out; **saqué,** I took out.
　　Llegar: llego, I arrive; **llegué,** I arrived.
　　Coger: cojo, I catch; **coges,** you catch.
　　Empezar: empecé, I began; **empezaste,** you began.　**Luz,** light;
luces, lights.

EL ACUEDUCTO ROMANO DE SEGOVIA

This old Roman aqueduct is one of the finest in Spain.

EL PATIO DE LOS LEONES EN LA ALHAMBRA
The Court of the Lions in the beautiful Moorish palace
at Granada, Spain.

a. But verbs in –**jar** keep the **j** throughout: **trabajar: trabajo,** *I work;* **trabajé,** *I worked.*

2. When the stem of a verb of the second or the third conjugation ends in **a, e,** or **o,** its preterite is written as follows:

Singular	Plural
creí	creímos
creíste	creísteis
creyó	creyeron

a. Note the unusual accent-marks in the second person singular and the first and second persons plural, and the change of –ió and –ie– to –yó and –ye– in the third person. This is because stressed **i,** standing next to **a, e,** or **o,** requires the written accent; and **y** takes the place of unstressed **i** between vowels.

115. To express an act or state that continues from the past into the present, the present tense is used in Spanish, while in English the present perfect is used.

Hace veinticuatro horas que este libro *está* **sobre la mesa.**	This book has been on the desk for twenty-four hours.
Hace dos años que *vivimos* **en Madrid.**	We have lived, *or* we have been living, in Madrid for two years *(and we are still there, hence the present tense).*
Compare, *Hemos vivido* dos **años en Madrid.**	We have lived in Madrid for two years *(we are not there now, hence the perfect tense).*

a. Similarly, if the act or state continues from one period in the past into another less remote, the imperfect tense is used in Spanish, while in English the pluperfect is used.

Cuando mi padre murió, hacía dos años que *vivíamos* **en Madrid.**	When my father died we **had been living** in Madrid for two years.

EXERCISES

aguardar, to await, wait for
la americana, coat (*of a man's business suit*) [1]
la blusa, blouse
el bolsillo, pocket [2]
el calcetín, sock, half-hose
la corbata, necktie, cravat
el cortaplumas, penknife
corto, –a, short
el chaleco, waistcoat, vest
la chaqueta, (boy's) coat, jacket
largo, –a, long
la levita, frock coat

llevar, to carry
la media, stocking, hose
mirar, to look at
los pantalones, trousers [3]
la prenda de vestir, article of clothing
el reloj (de bolsillo), watch; reloj (de pared o de mesa), clock [4]
la ropa, clothes; ropa interior, underclothes
el zapato, shoe

creo que no, I believe not; digo que sí, I say yes; yo no, not I; acababa [5] de hablar, he had just spoken; acabó de hablar, he finished speaking.

A. *Continúese.* 1. Dije que sí. 2. Empecé a vestirme. 3. Acabé de vestirme. 4. No conozco a nadie en Caracas. 5. No pido nunca nada a nadie. 6. Hace un año que vivo aquí. 7. Hace un mes que estudio el español.

Escríbase. 8. *Presente de indicativo de* corregir (i), *to correct;* vencer, *to conquer;* nacer, *to be born.* 9. *Pretérito de* leer, *to read;* oír, *to hear;* pagar, *to pay;* sacar, *to take out;* rezar, *to pray.*

B. 1. Después de lavarse la cara y las manos los niños empezaron a vestirse. 2. Se pusieron la ropa interior y las medias (o los calcetines). 3. En seguida se pusieron los pantalones, la blusa y la corbata. 4. Como estos niños tenían

---

[1] Also called saco in some Spanish-American countries.

[2] Also called bolsa (*as in Mexico*).

[3] Also used in the singular: el pantalón, *trousers.*

[4] It is usually not necessary to express de bolsillo, de pared or de mesa.

[5] Only the present and the imperfect of acabar are used for English *have just* and *had just.*

el uno siete años y el otro nueve, no usaban pantalones largos. 5. Para ponerse los zapatos se sentaron en la cama. 6. Los hombres usan levita o americana (saco) y chaleco. 7. Los niños usan chaqueta pero no usan chaleco. 8. Estos niños llevaban en el bolsillo cortaplumas nuevos que su padre acababa de darles. 9. Ni el uno ni el otro tenía reloj. 10. Mientras se vestían, miraban la hora (*the time*) en el reloj de pared. 11. A las siete y media acabaron de vestirse. 12. Y se dirigieron al comedor donde los aguardaban sus padres.

C. 1. ¿Cuáles son las prendas de vestir de un niño de siete años? 2. ¿Usa pantalones cortos o largos? 3. ¿Usa chaqueta o levita? 4. ¿Usa chaleco? 5. ¿En dónde se sentaron estos niños para ponerse los zapatos? 6. Mientras se vestían, ¿en qué miraban la hora? 7. ¿A qué hora acabaron de vestirse? 8. ¿A dónde se dirigieron en seguida? 9. ¿Quiénes los aguardaban en el comedor? 10. ¿Qué llevaban los niños en el bolsillo? 11. ¿Quién acababa de darles los cortaplumas? 12. ¿Tenían ellos relojes?

D. (*Debe tenerse presente que* not any *es igual a* no one *o* none; not anything *a* nothing; *etc.*) 1. Haven't you anything to write with [= with which (**que**) to write]? 2. Not I. I have neither pen nor ink. 3. Nor I either. 4. I haven't anything. 5. I never have anything. 6. Haven't you any friends? 7. Yes, sir; I have some friends. 8. I haven't any. 9. We have not studied the lesson. 10. We have studied the lesson [for] two hours.

E. 1. Do boys ten years old (= of ten years) wear long trousers? 2. I believe not. Boys ten years old wear short trousers. 3. They never wear long trousers. 4. Men wear long trousers and coats and waistcoats (vests). 5. The two children of whom (**de quienes**) we were speaking made haste to dress. 6. It was cold in the room and they were hungry. 7. They put on their underclothes, their stockings and their shoes. 8. They put on their blouses and neckties, and then their coats. 9. They would look often at the clock

to see the time. 10. They did not carry watches in their pockets.
11. Before entering the dining room, they combed [their hair]
again (*úsese* **volver**). 12. At a quarter past eight o'clock they
finished dressing and entered the dining room. 13. Their parents
had just sat down at the table. 14. They had been waiting fifteen
minutes. 15. All began (the) breakfast with [a] good appetite.

RESUMEN GRAMATICAL

113. **Pronombres y adverbios negativos:** 1: . . .

2. Cuando estos vocablos negativos siguen al verbo, el adverbio
no debe precederle, lo cual quiere decir que dichos vocablos son
realmente afirmativos.

114. **Cambios ortográficos.** — De acuerdo con el sistema prosódico castellano, con objeto de conservar el sonido del radical de
una palabra, es necesario a veces cambiar su ortografía.

1. Cambios ortográficos que son necesarios para conservar el
sonido de las consonantes **c, g, gü, j, z:** . . .

a. El verbo cuyo infinitivo termina en **–jar,** conserva la **j.**

2. Cuando el radical de un verbo de la segunda o tercera conjugación termina en **a, e, u o,** su pretérito se forma de la manera
siguiente: . . .

a. Obsérvense los acentos gráficos excepcionales sobre la segunda
persona del singular y primera y segunda del plural, y el cambio de las
terminaciones **–ió** y **–ie–** en **–yó** y **–ye–** en la tercera persona. Esto
se debe a que la **i** acentuada junto a las vocales **a, e, o** requiere el
acento escrito; pero la **y** substituye a la **i** no acentuada cuando va
entre vocales.

115. Para expresar una acción o estado que continúa del pasado
al presente, en español se hace uso del tiempo presente gramatical
mientras que en inglés se requiere el presente perfecto.

a. Igualmente, si la acción o estado continuó desde un período de
tiempo pasado hasta otro menos remoto, en español se expresa la idea
mediante el tiempo imperfecto mientras que en inglés se usa el pluscuamperfecto.

LESSON XXV

116. Future and Conditional. — The future and the conditional (or past future) indicative of all regular verbs are formed by adding the following endings to the infinitives:

Future: –é, –ás, –á, –emos, –éis, –án
Conditional: –ía, –ías, –ía, –íamos, –íais, –ían [1]

117. Future		Conditional	
SINGULAR	PLURAL	SINGULAR	PLURAL

I. *I shall speak, shall be speaking; etc.* — *I should speak, should be speaking; etc.*

hablaré	hablaremos	hablaría	hablaríamos
hablarás	hablaréis	hablarías	hablaríais
hablará	hablarán	hablaría	hablarían

II. *I shall learn, shall be learning; etc.* — *I should learn, should be learning; etc.*

aprenderé	aprenderemos	aprendería	aprenderíamos
aprenderás	aprenderéis	aprenderías	aprenderíais
aprenderá	aprenderán	aprendería	aprenderían

III. *I shall live, shall be living; etc.* — *I should live, should be living; etc.*

viviré	viviremos	viviría	viviríamos
vivirás	viviréis	vivirías	viviríais
vivirá	vivirán	viviría	vivirían

118. All radical-changing verbs and many irregular verbs form the future and conditional indicative regularly.

Thus, the irregular verbs **ser, estar,** and **ir** form these tenses regularly.

---

[1] The Spanish indicative future tense is formed by postfixing to the infinitive the indicative present tense of **haber,** the conditional by postfixing the imperfect tense.

hablar(h)é	hablar(h)emos	hablar(hab)ía	hablar(hab)íamos
hablar(h)ás	hablar(hab)éis	hablar(hab)ías	hablar(hab)íais
hablar(h)á	hablar(h)án	hablar(hab)ía	hablar(hab)ían

Note the disappearance of **hab–**.

119. Names of the Months of the Year: enero, febrero, marzo, abril, mayo, junio, julio, agosto, septiembre, octubre, noviembre, diciembre.

All are of the masculine gender.

120. Days of the Month. — The cardinal numbers are used to express the days of the month, with the one exception of **primero,** *first.*

> **El primero (o el uno), el dos,** The first, the second, the third,
> **el tres,** etc. **de enero.** etc., of January.

EXERCISES

el **caballo,** horse	la **semana,** week
los **demás,** the rest, others	el **sitio,** place, site
el **jardín,** flower garden	**sólo,** *adv.,* only
el **lago,** lake	**tarde,** *adv.,* late
nadar, to swim	**temprano,** *adv.,* early
necesario, –a, necessary	**treinta,** thirty; **treinta y uno,**
partir de, to leave, depart from	**–a,** thirty-one
pescar, to fish	**último, –a,** last
la **población,**[1] town	el **verano,** summer
el **río,** river	

hace buen (mal) tiempo, the weather is fine (bad); **montar a caballo,** to ride on horseback.

A. *Continúese.* 1. Partiré el primero de julio. 2. Volveré el quince de agosto. 3. Montaré a caballo. 4. No me gustaría montar a caballo. 5. Me equivoqué. 6. Hace ocho días que llegué. 7. Hace quince días que estoy aquí.

B. 1. Este verano pasaremos algunas semanas en el campo. 2. Partiremos de la población el primero (el uno) o el dos de julio. 3. Y volveremos el último día de agosto. 4. Buscaremos una casa en un sitio hermoso. 5. No será difícil encontrar una casa con jardín. 6. En la población me levanto tarde. 7. En el campo me levantaré temprano. 8. Me

---

[1] Also **pueblo,** or, if small, **pueblecito** or **pueblito.**

acostaré temprano también. 9. Llevaremos con nosotros varios libros. 10. Si llueve, leeremos los libros. 11. Si hace buen tiempo, mi hermana montará a caballo. 12. Yo pescaré o nadaré en las aguas de algún lago o río. 13. Creí que sería necesario pasar el verano en la población, pero me equivoqué. 14. No me gustaría pasar los meses de julio y agosto en esta población.

C. 1. ¿Dónde pasarán Vds. el verano? 2. ¿Cuándo partirán Vds. de la población? 3. ¿Cuándo volverán Vds.? 4. ¿Qué buscarán Vds. en el campo? 5. ¿En la población se levanta Vd. temprano o tarde? 6. ¿En el campo se levantará Vd. temprano? 7. ¿Se acostará Vd. temprano también? 8. Si llueve, ¿qué leerá Vd.? 9. Si hace buen tiempo ¿montará a caballo su hermana de Vd.? 10–11. Si hace buen tiempo ¿en dónde pescará (nadará) Vd.? 12. ¿Creyó Vd. que sería necesario pasar el verano en la población? 13. ¿Se equivocó Vd.? 14. ¿Le gustaría a Vd. pasar los meses de julio y agosto en esta población?

C. *Apréndase de memoria:*

> Treinta días trae noviembre,
> Con abril, junio y septiembre;
> De veintiocho sólo hay uno;
> Los demás de treinta y uno.

D. *Tradúzcanse al español las seis primeras frases y después formúlense las respuestas.* 1–4. How many days has the month of January (February, March, April)? 5. How many days are there in a week? 6. How many weeks are there in a month? 7–9. The first (second, third) of May. 10. Shall you spend the summer in (the) town? 11. Shall you go to the country? 12. Will he work this summer? 13. Will he swim in the lake? 14. Will they fish in the river? 15. I have just arrived (§91). 16. John arrived two days ago.[1] 17. Mary has been here [for] ten days (§115).

[1] See vocabulary of Exercise XX.

98 FIRST SPANISH COURSE

E. 1. The month of January has thirty-one days. 2. The month of February has twenty-eight days. 3. January has three days more than February. 4. February has four weeks: January has four weeks and three days. 5. We shall not spend this summer in (the) town. 6. We shall go to the country the twentieth of June. 7. And we shall return to (the) town the tenth of September. 8. We shall try to find a house with [a] garden. 9. If the weather is fine, my brothers will ride on horseback. 10. I prefer to fish in the waters of some river or lake. 11. If [it] rains, I shall read books or write letters. 12. In the country we shall get up and go to bed early. 13. Sometimes in the city [it] would be necessary for-us-to-go-to-bed (**acostarnos**) late. 14. I should like to live in the country all the year.

RESUMEN GRAMATICAL

116. **El futuro y el condicional** (o futuro pasado) **de indicativo** se forman añadiendo al infinitivo de los verbos las siguientes desinencias: . . .

118. Todos los verbos que sufren cambios constantes en su raíz así como muchos verbos irregulares forman su futuro y condicional de una manera regular. Así los verbos irregulares **ser, estar** e **ir** forman estos tiempos de una manera regular.

119. **Los nombres de los meses del año** son del género masculino.

120. **Los días del mes.** Para indicar los días del mes se hace uso de los números cardinales, con excepción de **primero,** que es ordinal.

NOTE TO THE INSTRUCTOR

If the instructor wishes at this point to begin the reading of Spanish novels or short stories, the following program is suggested:

Study (1) §145, §151, 2, §152, §155, §156, §158, 1; (2) §159, §160, 1, §161, §165, §166, 1.

Resume the regular Lessons.

LESSON XXVI

121. The following verbs are among those that form the future and conditional indicative irregularly:

Future	Conditional
Querer: querr-é, –ás, etc.	querr-ía, –ías, etc.
Poder: podr-é, –ás, etc.	podr-ía, –ías, etc.
Tener: tendr-é, –ás, etc.	tendr-ía, –ías, etc.
Poner: pondr-é, –ás, etc.	pondr-ía, –ías, etc.
Venir: vendr-é, –ás, etc.	vendr-ía, –ías, etc.
Decir: dir-é, –ás, etc.	dir-ía, –ías, etc.
Hacer: har-é, –ás, etc.	har-ía, –ías, etc.

122. Future and Conditional of Probability. — The future indicative is often used to denote probability or conjecture in present time, and the conditional to denote probability or conjecture in past time.

¿Qué hora es? — Será la una.	What time is it? — It is probably about one o'clock.
¿Qué hora era? — Sería la una.	What time was it? — It was probably about one o'clock.
¡Será posible!	Is it, *or* can it be, possible!

123. The definite article is required before expressions of time modified by **próximo,** *next,* **pasado,** *past, last (= past),* and the like.[1]

El lunes próximo.	Next Monday.
La semana pasada.	Last week.
El mes que viene (que entra).	Next month.

124. Names of the Days of the Week: **domingo, lunes, martes, miércoles, jueves, viernes, sábado.** All are of the masculine gender. They usually take the definite article

[1] There are many expressions for *next* when referring to time. Thus *next month* may be translated by **el mes que viene, que entra,** etc. In referring to a specific date **próximo** may be used, but **próximo** really means *nearest,* either in the past or in the future. Note **el mes próximo pasado,** *the last month past.*

if **próximo** or **pasado** be expressed or understood, or if used in a general sense (*see* §103, 1). Those that end in –es have the same form in the plural as in the singular.

Llegó el martes.	He arrived on Tuesday.
Yo trabajo los sábados.	I work on Saturdays.

EXERCISES

acordarse (ue) **de,** to remember	la **hoja,** leaf
aparecer, to appear	el **invierno,** winter
el **árbol,** tree	el **otoño,** autumn, fall
cuarenta, forty	la **primavera,** spring
el **director,** principal, director	**principiar,** to begin
durante, during	**recitar,** to recite
la **estación,** season	**terminar,** to end, terminate
excepto, except	**viejo, –a,** old
la **fecha,** date	

por, o **en, la mañana,**[1] in the morning; **por,** o **en, la tarde,** in the afternoon, *or* in the early evening; **por,** o **en, la noche,** in the evening (*after dark*) *or* at night; **el curso,** school year; **el día de descanso,** day of rest; **el día de trabajo,** work day; **el tiempo de las vacaciones,** vacation time; **a** (**en**) **la escuela,** to (at *or* in) school; **a** (**en**) **la iglesia,** to (at *or* in) church.

A. *Continúese.* 1. No lo haré. 2. Le diría la verdad. 3. Vendré a las diez. 4. No podría venir. 5. Me pondré el sombrero. 6. No me acuerdo de la fecha.

B. 1. La (§ 103, 1) primavera es la primera estación del año. 2. En la primavera aparecerán las primeras flores en nuestros jardines. 3. Y los árboles se vestirán de (*with*) hojas. 4. El verano es la estación del calor. 5. Es también el tiempo de las vacaciones. 6. Ustedes no tendrán lecciones que aprender ni ejercicios que escribir. 7. El otoño es la estación de las frutas. 8. En el otoño principiará el nuevo curso. 9. Entonces irán Vds. a la escuela todos los días excepto los sábados y los domingos. 10. Estos días serán

---

[1] The time is more specific when **en** is used.

días de descanso, pero los demás serán días de trabajo.
11. Por la noche Vds. prepararán las lecciones. 12. Por la
mañana y por la tarde las recitarán. 13. El domingo por la
mañana Vds. irán a la iglesia. 14. ¿Cuántos años tiene el
director de la escuela? 15. — No es viejo: tendrá treinta
y cinco o cuarenta años. 16. ¿Cuándo terminó el curso
pasado? 17. — No me acuerdo de la fecha: terminaría el
cuatro o seis de junio.

C. 1–4. ¿Cuál es la primera (segunda, tercera, última)
estación del año? 5. En la primavera ¿qué aparecerá en
nuestros jardines? 6. ¿De qué se vestirán los árboles?
7–8. El verano (El otoño) ¿de qué es la estación? 9. ¿Cuál
es el tiempo de las vacaciones? 10. ¿Tendrá Vd. lecciones
que aprender en el verano? 11. ¿En qué estación principiará
el nuevo curso? 12–13. Durante la semana ¿cuáles serán los
días de descanso (de trabajo)? 14. ¿Cuándo preparará Vd.
las lecciones? 15. ¿Cuándo las recitará Vd.? 16. ¿A dónde
irá Vd. los domingos? 17. ¿Cuántos años tiene el director
de la escuela? 18. ¿Cuándo terminó el curso pasado?

D. *En las respuestas úsese el futuro o condicional de probabilidad.* 1. ¿Qué hora es? 2. ¿Qué hora era cuando Vd.
partió de Madrid? 3. ¿Qué hora era cuando Vd. llegó a
Barcelona? 4. ¿Cuántos años tiene Felipe? 5. ¿Cuántos años tenía Carlos cuando murió? 6. ¿Dónde estará
mi sombrero? (*tradúzcase: It is probably in your room.*)
7. ¿Dónde estarán mis libros? (*tradúzcase: They are probably
on the table.*)

E. 1. I studied (*pret.*) Spanish last year. 2. Next year I
shall study French. 3. The school year ended last month.
4. The new school year will begin next month. 5. Our vacations are not long. 6. My friends arrived last Tuesday.
7. They will leave next Friday. 8. Sunday (§ 103, 1) is [a]
rest day. 9. Monday is [a] work day. 10. Summer is the
warm season (*véase* B. 4). 11. Winter is the cold season.

102 FIRST SPANISH COURSE

12. Autumn is the season of fruits. 13. Spring is the season of flowers.

F. 1. Last year I studied Spanish. 2. Next year I shall study Spanish again (§91). 3. The second year will be more difficult than the first year, will it not? (¿no es verdad?). 4. The new school year will begin the fifteenth of September. 5. The last school year ended the sixteenth of June. 6. The summer vacations (= vacations of summer) will last three months. 7. These will be months of rest. 8. I shall be able to fish or swim every day. 9. [On] Sundays I shall go to church. 10. In the autumn I shall go to school Mondays, Tuesdays, Wednesdays, Thursdays, and Fridays.[1] 11. The Saturdays and Sundays [1] will be rest days. 12. But [on] the Saturdays I shall study my lessons at night. 13. The principal of our school will be forty years old next month. 14. How old are you? — I shan't tell you how old I am. 15. Shall you come to see me this afternoon? 16. I shall come to see you if I can. 17. What time is [it]? — [It] is probably about eleven o'clock. 18. I haven't my watch. [It] is probably on the table in (de) my room.

RESUMEN GRAMATICAL

121. Los verbos que siguen son de los que forman de una manera irregular su futuro y condicional (o futuro pasado): . . .

122. Futuro y condicional de probabilidad. — El futuro de indicativo se usa a menudo para denotar probabilidad o suposición en tiempo presente, y el condicional para denotar probabilidad o suposición en tiempo pasado.

123. Es indispensable el uso del artículo determinado delante de las expresiones de tiempo modificadas por las palabras **próximo, pasado,** etc.

124. Los nombres de los días de la semana son masculinos, y generalmente van precedidos del artículo determinado si se expresan las palabras **próximo** o **pasado** o si se sobrentienden, o si los nombres de los días se usan en sentido general. Los que terminan en **–es** tienen la misma forma para el plural que para el singular.

[1] **Los lunes, martes,** etc. Do not repeat the article.

LESSON XXVII

125. Past Participles. — If the infinitive of a verb ends in –ar, the past participle ends in –**ado**; if the infinitive ends in –er or –ir, the past participle ends in –**ido**.

Hablar: hablado, spoken.	Estar: estado, been.
Aprender: aprendido, learned.	Ser: sido, been.
Vivir: vivido, lived.	Ir: ido, gone.

126. The following verbs are among those that have irregular past participles:

1. Otherwise regular verbs:

Abrir: abierto, opened, open.	Cubrir: cubierto, covered.
Escribir: escrito, written.	

2. Radical-changing verbs:

Morir: muerto, died, dead,[1] killed.	Volver: vuelto, returned, turned.

3. Irregular verbs:

Decir: dicho, said.	Poner: puesto, put, set.
Hacer: hecho, done, made.	Ver: visto, seen.

4. When the stem of a verb of the second or third conjugation ends in a vowel, –**ido** receives the accent mark.

Creer: creído, believed.	Oír: oído, heard.

127. A past participle used as an adjective is inflected like an adjective.

Un libro bien escrito.	A well written book.
Una carta bien escrita.	A well written letter.

[1] **Morir** means *to die;* but the past participle, **muerto,** means either *died* or *killed*, according to the context, when it refers to persons.

128. When used with **estar,** a past participle has the force of an adjective and simply denotes a resultant state, rather than the passive voice.

La carta está escrita en castellano.	The letter is written in Spanish.
Don Pablo estaba muerto.	Don Pablo was dead.

129. The past participle is used with **ser** to form the tenses of the passive voice. The participle agrees in gender and number with the subject.

La carta será escrita por don Juan.	The letter will be written by Don Juan.
Don Pablo fué muerto por un ladrón.	Don Pablo was killed by a thief.

130. With passive verbs, *by* is usually expressed by **por;** but it may be expressed by **de** (instead of **por**) after some verbs that denote mental action.

La puerta fué abierta por el criado.	The door was opened by the servant.
Él es amado de todos.	He is loved by all (beloved of all).

a. For the use of the reflexive instead of the passive, see §77, **3.** But the use of *to be* in English really indicates the passive voice in Spanish when an agent is expressed, and then **ser** must be used.

EXERCISES

el **arquitecto,** architect
la **clase,** class, kind
  colocar, to place
  cómodo, –a, comfortable
  construir, to build, construct
  cubrir, to cover
la **escalera,** stairs, stairway
el **gas,** gas

  grande, large, big
el **ladrillo,** brick
la **puerta,** door
  subir, to go up, ascend
el **techo,**[1] roof
el **tejamaní,** (wooden) shingle
el **teléfono,** telephone

la **sala (de recibo),** reception room, drawing-room.

A. *Continúese.* 1. Fuí enseñado por mi padre. 2. Yo estaba cansado. 3. Me equivocaba. 4. Quiero ser amado de todos.

---

[1] A *roof of tiles* (**tejas**) is called **tejado.**

B. 1. Nuestra casa fué construída por un buen arquitecto.
2. No es grande, pero es hermosa y cómoda. 3. Las paredes
están construídas de ladrillos. 4. El techo está cubierto con
pizarra (con tejamaníes). 5. En el piso bajo están la sala (de
recibo), la biblioteca, el comedor y la cocina. 6. Cuando
subimos por la escalera al piso alto, hallamos cuatro dormitorios (o alcobas) y el cuarto de baño. 7. Prefiero la biblioteca a todas las demás piezas porque tiene libros de
todas clases. 8. Hay también un teléfono en la biblioteca.
9. Tenemos una buena cocina económica. 10. Se quema
carbón de piedra en ella (it) cuando se preparan las comidas. 11. En invierno la casa se calienta por vapor. 12. El
calor se produce en un calorífero central colocado en el
sótano. 13. En todas las piezas hay luz eléctrica que preferimos al gas.

C. 1. ¿Por quién fué construída la casa de Vds.? 2. ¿De
qué están construídas las paredes? 3. ¿Con qué está cubierto
el techo? 4–5. ¿Qué piezas están en el piso bajo (alto)?
6. ¿Cuál es la pieza que Vd. prefiere a las demás? 7. ¿Por
qué? 8. ¿Dónde está el teléfono? 9. ¿Dónde se preparan
las comidas? 10. ¿Cómo se calienta la casa en invierno?
11. ¿En dónde se produce el calor? 12. ¿Dónde está colocado el calorífero? 13. ¿Tiene la casa luz eléctrica o de gas?

D. 1. The door closed (se cerró). 2. The door was closed by
the servant. 3. The door was (estaba) closed. 4. The window
opened (se abrió). 5. The window was opened by Mary. 6. The
window was already open. 7. The book was written in English.
8. It was written by my brother. 9. This cooking-stove was made
by Pereda and Company (Compañía). 10. It is very well made.
11. It is said (Se dice) that Spanish is spoken here. 12. The house
was well built. 13. It was built by a good architect. 14. The
roof is covered with shingles. 15. The house is warmed with (por)
steam. 16. Coal is burned in the furnace. 17. Don Felipe is
loved by all.

E. 1. My uncle has just bought an eight-room house (= a house of eight rooms). 2. It is not large, but it is very comfortable. 3. All the rooms in (de) the house are warmed with steam. 4. And there is electric light in all the rooms. 5. There are four rooms on the first floor: the reception room, the library, the dining room, and the kitchen. 6. On the upper floor are four bedrooms and the bathroom. 7. The roof of the house is covered with slate. 8. The walls are built of brick (*véase* B. 3). 9. The house was built by an architect who lives in Chicago. 10. The cooking-stove and the furnace were made by Ayer and Company, and they are well made. 11. Yesterday I went to see my uncle's new house. 12. The door was opened by my cousin who received me affectionately. 13. My uncle and aunt were not at home, but my cousin showed me (**me enseñó**) all the rooms. 14. He prefers the library to the other rooms, because he likes books (§103, 1).

RESUMEN GRAMATICAL

125. Participios pasados (o pasivos). — Si el infinitivo del verbo termina en –**ar**, su participio pasado termina en –**ado**; si el infinitivo termina en –**er** o –**ir**, el participio pasado termina en –**ido**.

126. Los verbos que siguen son de los que forman irregularmente su participio pasado: 1. Verbos regulares en todas las demás formas: . . . 2. Verbos que sufren cambios constantes en su raíz: . . . 3. Verbos irregulares en varias formas: . . . 4. Cuando el radical del verbo de la segunda o tercera conjugación termina en **a, e, u o**, la terminación –**ido** del participio pasado recibe el acento gráfico.

127. Cuando el participio pasado se usa como adjetivo, sufre las alteraciones gramaticales propias de estos últimos.

128. Cuando el participio pasado acompaña al verbo **estar**, adquiere el carácter de verdadero adjetivo denotando un simple estado resultante y no la voz pasiva.

129. El participio pasado se usa con el verbo **ser** para formar la voz pasiva. El participio concuerda en género y número con el sujeto.

EL VALLE DE ARÁN

Bird's eye view of a cultivated valley in Northern Spain.

PATIO DE UNA CASA
A corner of an open court.

130. Con los verbos en pasiva *by* se traduce por la palabra **por**; pero puede expresarse por **de** (en lugar de **por**) después de algunos verbos que expresan acción mental.

a. En cuanto al uso de la forma reflexiva en vez de la pasiva, véase el §77, 3. Pero el empleo de *to be* en inglés indica la voz pasiva en español cuando se expresa el agente, y entonces debe emplearse el verbo **ser.**

LESSON XXVIII

131. Tener and Haber. — Spanish has two verbs meaning *to have:* **tener** and **haber.** *To have,* meaning *to possess,* is expressed by **tener.** As an auxiliary verb to form perfect tenses, *to have* is **haber.**

132. Perfect Tenses. — The perfect tenses are formed by combining the auxiliary verb **haber,** *to have,* with the past participle. When used with **haber,** the past participle is invariable in form.

133.   Hablar

Present Perfect   Pluperfect [1]

I have spoken, have been speaking; etc.   *I had spoken, had been speaking; etc.*

SINGULAR	PLURAL	SINGULAR	PLURAL
he hablado	hemos hablado	había hablado	habíamos hablado
has hablado	habéis hablado	habías hablado	habíais hablado
ha hablado	han hablado	había hablado	habían hablado

Preterite Perfect [2]

(when) I had spoken; etc.

SINGULAR	PLURAL
(cuando) hube hablado	(cuando) hubimos hablado
" hubiste hablado	" hubisteis hablado
" hubo hablado	" hubieron hablado

[1] Or Past Perfect.   [2] Or Second Past Perfect.

Future Perfect		**Conditional Perfect**[1]	
I shall have spoken, shall have been speaking; etc.		*I should have spoken, should have been speaking; etc.*	
SINGULAR	PLURAL	SINGULAR	PLURAL
habré hablado	habremos hablado	habría hablado	habríamos hablado
habrás hablado	habréis hablado	habrías hablado	habríais hablado
habrá hablado	habrán hablado	habría hablado	habrían hablado

The perfect tenses of all verbs are formed like those of **hablar.**

134. — 1. *I had (you had,* etc.*) spoken* is usually expressed in Spanish by **había (habías,** etc.**) hablado.**

Él no había venido.	He had not come.
Yo no lo había hecho.	I had not done it.

2. **Hube (hubiste,** etc.**) hablado** is used after the temporal conjunctions **cuando,** *when,* **luego que,** *as soon as,* and the like. But with these conjunctions the simple preterite indicative is the more common in colloquial Spanish.

Luego que hubo venido, le dije la verdad.	As soon as he had come, I told him the truth.

(Or, more commonly: **luego que vino, le dije la verdad,** *as soon as he came, I told him the truth.*)

a. Note the following idiom: **llegado que hubo,** *as soon as he had arrived.*

135. In Spanish it is usually best not to place the subject or an adverb between the auxiliary and the past participle of a perfect tense.

¿Ha venido Juan?	Has John come?
¿Le ha hablado Vd.?	Have you spoken to him?
Lo he preferido siempre.	I have always preferred it.

---

[1] Or Past Future Perfect.

EXERCISES

alumbrar, to light
la azotea, flat roof.
el brasero, brasier
cada (*invariable*), each
el centro, center
el clima, climate
el cobre, copper
crecer (§112), to grow
la chimenea, fireplace
la galería, gallery, veranda
el lado, side

la lámpara, lamp
luego que, as soon as
la lumbre, fire
el patio, (inner) courtyard
el petróleo, coal oil, petroleum
la piedra, stone
principal, main, principal
la tienda, shop, store
tropical, tropical
la vela, candle
el zaguán, vestibule, passageway [1]

dar a, to face; no más que, only, no more than; había, there was, there were

A. *Continúese.* 1. He vivido en Málaga. · 2. Hace seis meses que vivo en Málaga. 3. Hace seis meses que llegué. 4. Yo no había vuelto. 5. Yo lo habré hecho.

B. 1. Hemos pasado este invierno en Málaga. 2. La casa en que vivíamos estaba construída de piedra y tenía azotea. 3. En el centro de la casa había un patio donde crecían flores tropicales. 4. Entrábamos en el patio por el zaguán. 5. En el piso bajo había una tienda en cada lado del zaguán y algunos cuartos para los criados. 6. En el piso principal [2] estaban la sala de recibo, el comedor, la cocina y el cuarto de baño. 7. En el segundo piso no había más que alcobas que daban a la calle o a las galerías del patio. 8. Se alumbraba la casa con velas y lámparas de petróleo. 9. Y

---

[1] Leading from the street to the inner courtyard.

[2] In the larger houses of Spanish and Spanish-American cities, the *first floor* is called the piso bajo or cuarto bajo, the *second floor* the piso principal or primer piso, the *third floor* the segundo piso, etc. If there is an entresuelo (a floor between the piso bajo and the piso principal, with low ceilings, and usually occupied by the janitors and other servants), the *third floor* is called the piso principal, the *fourth floor* the segundo piso, etc.

se calentaba la casa por la lumbre de las chimeneas o de los braseros de cobre. 10. Para guisar (*o* cocinar) había en la cocina fogones[1] en que se quemaba carbón de leña. 11. El clima de Málaga durante el invierno ha sido casi perfecto.

C. 1. ¿Dónde han pasado Vds. este invierno? 2. ¿De qué estaba construída la casa en que vivían Vds.? 3. ¿Qué clase de techo tenía la casa? 4. ¿Dónde estaba el patio? 5. ¿Qué crecía en el patio? 6. ¿Cómo entraban Vds. en el patio? 7–9. ¿Qué había en el piso bajo? (piso principal? segundo piso?) 10. ¿Cómo se alumbraba la casa? 11. ¿Cómo se calentaba? 12. ¿Qué se quemaba en los fogones? 13. ¿Cómo ha sido el clima de Málaga durante el invierno?

D. 1. Has your friend arrived? 2. Yes, sir; he has just (§91) arrived. 3. Has Mr. Pereda come? 4. He had not come this morning. 5. Has the letter been (**sido**) written by John or by Charles? 6. It has not been written by Charles. 7. Charles has not written it. 8. As soon as he had finished it, I read it. 9. This house has been built by a good architect. 10. We have lived (§115) in this house [for] three years. 11. It (= *the weather*) has not been cold this winter.

E. 1. I have lived in Burgos and the other towns of the north (**del norte**) where the courtyards are covered. 2. And I have spent two winters in Granada and Málaga where many courtyards are (**están**) open (**descubiertos**). 3. I have always preferred the houses with courtyards open and full of flowers. 4. I like to sit on the veranda of the main floor and look at the flowers. 5. Last winter the window of my bedroom faced the street. 6. Some rooms (**piezas**) in (**de**) the house had no windows. 7. But each one of these rooms had a large door that faced the courtyard. 8. I had an oil lamp (*véase* B. 8) to (**para**) light my bedroom. 9. In some bedrooms there were only candles. 10. I had a fireplace in my

[1] See XV, Exercises, footnote 2.

room (**cuarto**) to warm me when it (= *the weather*) was cold.   11. I
have never liked the Spanish brasiers in which charcoal is burned.

RESUMEN GRAMATICAL

131. Tener y haber. — El verbo *to have* se traduce de dos
modos al español: por **tener** o por **haber**; el primero en el sentido
de " poseer " y el segundo para formar los tiempos perfectos.

132. Tiempos perfectos. — Para formar los tiempos perfectos
de los verbos se hace uso de los tiempos simples del verbo auxiliar
haber y se les agrega el participio pasado del verbo que se conjuga.
El participio pasado es invariable en su forma cuando se emplea
con el verbo **haber.**

133. En el modo indicativo los tiempos perfectos son: presente
perfecto; pluscuamperfecto; pretérito perfecto; futuro perfecto;
condicional perfecto.

134. — 1. *I had (you had*, etc.) *spoken*, por regla general, se
traduce al español por **había (habías,** etc.) **hablado.**

2. **Hube (hubiste,** etc.) **hablado** se usa después de las conjunciones temporales **cuando, luego que,** y otras semejantes. Pero con
estas conjunciones se prefiere usar el pretérito simple en el lenguaje
corriente.

135. En español, por regla general, no se debe colocar el sujeto
o el adverbio entre el participio pasado y el verbo auxiliar.

LESSON XXIX

136. Some Uses of Haber

1 Haber de + infinitive.

Él ha de tener hambre.	He must be hungry.
Ella ha de cantar esta noche.	She is to (*or*, she will) sing to-night.

Compare, **Tiene que hacerlo.** He has (got) to do it.

2. Impersonal **haber**.

hay, there is (are)	**habrá,** there will be
había, there was (were)	**habría,** there would be
hubo, there was (were)	**ha habido,** there has (have) been etc.

Note that the present indicative of impersonal **haber** is **hay** and not **ha**.

a. The noun or pronoun used with impersonal **haber** is the object of the verb.

¿**Hay buenas tiendas en esta población?**	Are there (some) good shops in this town?
Sí, señor; las hay muy buenas.	Yes, sir; there are (some) very good ones.

3. Hay . . . que and hay que + infinitive.

Hay mucho que estudiar.	There is much to study.
Hay que estudiar mucho.	One has to study much.

137. Saber, *to know*

Present Indicative

I know, do know, am knowing; etc.

SINGULAR	PLURAL
sé	sabemos
sabes	sabéis
sabe	saben

Preterite

I knew, did know; etc.

SINGULAR	PLURAL
supe	supimos
supiste	supisteis
supo	supieron

138.—1. The imperfect indicative of **saber** is regular.

2. The future and the conditional of **saber** are irregular:

sabré, –ás, etc.
sabría, –ías, etc.

139. Meaning of Saber and Conocer

1. **Saber** means *to know, know how, can* (= *know how*).

¿Sabe Vd. la lección?	Do you know the lesson?
¿Sabe Vd. nadar?	Do you know how to (Can you) swim?

2. **Conocer** means *to know* (= *be acquainted with*), *meet* (= *become acquainted with*).

¿Conoce Vd. al señor Ortiz?	Do you know Mr. Ortiz?

EXERCISES

el **aroma,**[1] perfume, aroma
cantar, to sing
ciego, –a, blind
el **gusto,** taste
la **importancia,** importance
menos, less, least
mudo, –a, dumb, mute
la **nariz,** nose
el **oído,** (inner) ear,[2] hearing

el **olfato,** sense of smell
el **olor,** odor, smell
el **órgano,** organ
la **palabra,** word, speech
percibir, to perceive
sin, without
sordo, –a, deaf
la **vista,** sight

esta noche, to-night

[1] Or **el perfume,** *perfume.* Note that **aroma** is masculine (see §174, 3).
[2] The outer, or visible, *ear* is called **oreja.**

A. *Continúese.* 1. Yo he de cantar esta noche.¹ 2. No conozco al señor Ortiz. 3. No sé nadar. 4. No supe la lección. 5. Tengo que estudiar mucho.

B. 1. El hombre tiene ojos para ver. 2. En este mundo hay mucho que ver. 3. El hombre tiene oídos para oír. 4. Mi hermano cree que la vista es de más importancia que el oído. 5. Pero yo preferiría el oído a la vista. 6. A mí me gusta mucho la música. 7. La nariz sirve para percibir los olores. 8. El olfato es de menos importancia que la vista o el oído. 9. Pero ¿a quién no le gusta el aroma de las flores? 10. La lengua es el órgano principal del gusto y de la palabra. 11. Sin la lengua no podríamos hablar: seríamos mudos. 12. Sin la vista no podríamos ver: seríamos ciegos. 13. Sin el oído no podríamos oír: seríamos sordos. 14. Y sin la nariz no podríamos percibir los olores.

C. *Contéstese.* 1–2. Para ver (Para oír) ¿qué tiene el hombre? 3. ¿Qué sirve para percibir los olores? 4. ¿Cuál es el órgano principal del gusto? 5. ¿Cuál prefiere Vd., la vista o el oído? 6. ¿Le gusta a Vd. la música? 7. ¿Cuál es de menos importancia, la vista o el olfato? 8. ¿Le gusta a Vd. el aroma de las flores?

Complétense las siguientes frases. 9–11. Sin la vista (Sin el oído, la lengua) no podríamos ——. 12–14. Sin la vista (Sin el oído, la lengua) seríamos ——.

D. 1. Do you know Miss Ortiz? 2. She is to sing to-night. 3. And I am to read. 4. Did you know the lesson? 5. I had been studying it three hours (§115, *a*). 6. But I did not know it. 7. Does this boy know how to read? (¿Sabe leer este niño?). 8. He can read a little. 9. But he can not write. 10. Was there much to do? 11. There were several lessons to study. 12. One had to study hard (mucho) in order to learn them.

¹ In colloquial Spanish yo voy a cantar (or yo canto) esta noche, would be commoner expressions.

E. 1. We have eyes in order to see and ears in order to hear. 2. Without eyes we could (**podríamos**) not see and without ears we could not hear. 3. I know a man who is blind. 4. He can not see, but he can hear very well. 5. Without a (**la**) tongue man could not speak. 6. The tongue is the principal organ of speech (*véase* B. 10). 7. I used to know a girl who was deaf and dumb.[1] 8. That girl could (**podía**) not learn to speak because she could not hear. 9. Now the deaf learn to speak. 10. Which is of more importance, sight or hearing? 11. My sister would prefer hearing because she likes music. 12. Without a (**la**) nose man could not smell (**percibir los olores**). 13. Which should you prefer, taste or the sense of smell? 14. I like perfumes, but I should prefer taste to the sense of smell.

RESUMEN GRAMATICAL

136. Algunos usos del verbo *haber.* — 1. **Haber de más el** infinitivo.

2. Uso impersonal del verbo **haber.**

Su presente de indicativo es **hay** y no **ha.**

a. El nombre o pronombre usado con el verbo impersonal **haber** resulta su complemento.

3. **Hay que** más el infinitivo.

138. — 1. Es regular el imperfecto de **saber.**

2. Son irregulares el futuro y el condicional de **saber.**

139. Significado de saber y conocer. — 1. Saber significa *to know, know how, can.*

2. **Conocer** significa *to be* o *become acquainted with.*

---

[1] **Sorda y muda,** or **una sordo-muda** (*a deaf mute*).

LESSON XXX

140.   **Present Participles**

1. Regular verbs:

Hablar: hablando, speaking   **Vivir: viviendo,** living
Aprender: aprendiendo, learning

2. Radical-changing verbs of the third conjugation:

Sentir: sintiendo, feeling   **Dormir: durmiendo,** sleeping
Pedir: pidiendo, asking

Note that the radical vowels **e** and **o** are changed to **i** and **u** respectively.

The present participles of radical-changing verbs of the first and second conjugations are regular.

3. Some irregular verbs:

Decir: diciendo, saying   **Venir: viniendo,** coming
Poder: pudiendo, being able   **Ver: viendo,** seeing
Ser: siendo, being

But many irregular verbs form their present participles regularly.

4. **Change in Spelling.** — If the stem of a verb of the second or the third conjugation ends in a vowel, −**iendo** becomes −**yendo** (but see §253).

Leer: leyendo, reading   **Oír: oyendo,** hearing

141. Agreement. The present participle is invariable in form.

Ví a un muchacho (a una mu-   I saw a boy (a girl) reading a
chacha) leyendo un libro.   book.

Review §88, 3 and 4.

142. Progressive Forms of Verbs. — English *to be* + present participle often equals Spanish **estar** or **ir** + present participle. **Ir** is used to denote motion or change of condition.

Estoy estudiando.	I am studying.
Estábamos trabajando.	We were working.
Va corriendo.	He is running, *or* he goes on the run.
El niño iba creciendo.	The child was growing.
Se fué [1] poniendo pálida.	She was turning pale.

a. The progressive forms are used to express an act or state as in progress at the time to which the speaker refers. They are used less often and are more emphatic in Spanish than in English.

b. **Estar** is not used with the present participles of **estar** and **haber** to form progressive tenses.

143. Personal pronoun objects follow a present participle and are attached to it so that the verb and object or objects form one word. The participle then requires the accent mark.

Mirándome.   Looking at me.

But in compound progressive tenses the pronoun object usually precedes the auxiliary verb: **me estaba mirando,** *he was looking at me.*

EXERCISES

la **acogida,** reception
adiós, goodbye, farewell
anunciar, to announce
besar, to kiss
la **bondad,** goodness, kindness
el **caballero,** [2] gentleman; ¡**caballero!** Sir!
celebrar, to rejoice at, be very glad to have
correr, to run, hurry
dispensar, to give, grant; to excuse, pardon
gracias, thanks, thank you
el **guante,** glove
inclinarse, to bow
íntimo, –a, intimate
llamar, to call, knock, ring (*a doorbell*)
la **ocasión,** occasion, opportunity
el **pie** (*pl.*, **pies**), foot
presentar, to present
quitar, to take off
la **reverencia,** bow
seguir (i), to continue, go on, keep on
el **sobretodo,** overcoat

hasta luego, farewell for a while, goodbye till we meet again; **otra vez,** again; **ponerse pálido,** to turn pale, grow pale.

A. *Continúese.* 1. Voy corriendo. 2. Estoy escribiendo. 3. Yo iba creciendo. 4. Yo estaba estudiando. 5. Me fuí

---

[1] **Fué** is here the preterite of **ir,** not of **ser.**

[2] **Caballero** is more formal than **señor.** There is no feminine form of **caballero.**

poniendo pálido, –a. 6. ¿A quién he de anunciar? 7. El
gusto era mío.

B. 1. Llamé a la puerta. 2. El criado me abrió la puerta,
y yo entré en la casa. 3. Le pregunté al criado: ¿Está [1] el
señor González? 4. El criado respondió: Sí, el señor está
en casa. 5. ¿Tendrá Vd. la bondad de decirme su nombre?
6. ¿A quién he de anunciar? 7. Quitándome el sombrero,
los guantes y el sobretodo, entré en la sala (de recibo).
8. Don Felipe me recibió cordialmente, y me dijo: ¿Cómo
está Vd., caballero? 9. Le respondí: Muy bien, gracias,
¿y Vd.? 10. Me presentó a su esposa, doña Carolina
Herrera de González. 11. Yo me incliné y dije: Ce-
lebro la ocasión de conocer a Vd., señora. 12. Después
el señor González *me presentó a su hijo, don Carlos.
13. Inclinándome otra vez, yo le dije: Caballero, tengo mucho gusto en conocer a Vd. 14. Don Carlos respondió: El
gusto es mío, caballero. 15. Al despedirme de la familia,
yo di gracias por (*for*) la buena acogida que me había dis-
pensado. 16. Haciendo una reverencia dije: A los pies de
Vd., señora. 17. Beso a Vds. la mano, caballeros. 18. Que
Vds. lo pasen bien (*May you all keep well*). 19. Cuando me
despido de un amigo íntimo, le digo: Adiós, o Hasta luego.

C. *Contéstese.* 1. ¿Quién abrió la puerta cuando Vd.
llamó? 2. ¿Qué le preguntó Vd. al criado? 3. ¿Qué le
respondió a Vd. el criado? 4. ¿Qué se quitó Vd. antes de
entrar en la sala? 5. ¿Cómo le recibió a Vd. don Felipe?
6. ¿Cuál era el apellido de don Felipe? 7. ¿A quién le presentó a Vd. este caballero? 8. Al inclinarse Vd., ¿qué le
dijo a doña Carolina? 9. ¿Cuál era el apellido de la señora? 10. Después ¿a quién le presentó a Vd. don Felipe?
11. ¿Qué le dijo Vd. a don Carlos? 12. ¿Qué le respondió
a Vd. este señor? 13. Al despedirse de la familia, ¿qué

[1] Note this common omission of **en casa.**

dijo Vd.?   14. Al despedirse de un amigo íntimo, ¿qué le dice Vd.?

D. *Repítase* B., *usando* **don Pablo** *como sujeto en lugar de* **yo.** (Don Pablo llamó á la puerta. El criado le abrió la puerta y don Pablo entró en la casa; etc.)

E. 1. Open (*pl.*) your books.   2. Ferdinand, read the first page. 3. Go on reading.   4. Close (*pl.*) your books.   5. Were you (*pl.*) working?   6. I was writing a letter.   7. My brother was studying. 8. Your brother studies all the time.   9. He is growing pale. 10. John, run and (a) get (**buscar**) the doctor.   11. Hurry! 12. John is running.   13. Mary is reading a book.   14. He was taking off his overcoat.   15. He was making a bow.   16. He was taking leave.   17. Excuse me.   18. Have the kindness to excuse me.

RESUMEN GRAMATICAL

140. Participio presente (gerundio): — 1. Verbos regulares: **hablar, hablando; aprender, aprendiendo; vivir, viviendo.**

2. Verbos de la tercera conjugación que sufren cambios constantes de su vocal radical: **sentir, sintiendo; pedir, pidiendo; dormir, durmiendo.**

Obsérvese que las vocales radicales **e** y **o** se cambian en **i** y **u** respectivamente. El participio presente es regular en los verbos de la 1ª y 2ª conjugación que cambian su vocal radical.

3. Algunos verbos irregulares: **poder, pudiendo; ser, siendo; ver, viendo; decir, diciendo; venir, viniendo.**

Muchos verbos irregulares forman su participio presente de una manera regular.

4. Cambios ortográficos. — Si el radical de un verbo de la 2ª o 3ª conjugación termina en vocal, la terminación –**iendo** del participio presente se cambia en –**yendo**: **leer, leyendo; oír, oyendo.**

141. Concordancia. — El participio presente es invariable.

142. Formas progresivas de los verbos. — La expresión inglesa *to be* con el participio presente equivale a menudo a la española formada con los verbos **estar** o **ir** y el participio presente. El verbo **ir** denota movimiento o cambio de condición.

a. Las formas progresivas se usan para expresar un acto o estado en ejecución en el momento a que se refiere el sujeto de la oración. Estas formas se usan menos y son más enfáticas en español que en inglés.

b. El verbo **estar** no se construye con el participio presente de los verbos **estar** y **haber**.

143. Los pronombres personales complementarios siguen al participio presente y toman el carácter de enclíticos, es decir que van unidos a él formando una sola palabra. En este caso el participio presente lleva el acento gráfico.

LESSON XXXI

144. Imperative Mood

	Singular	Plural	
I. Hablar:	habla (tú),	hablad (vosotros, –as),	(you) speak
II. Aprender:	aprende (tú),	aprended (vosotros, –as),	(you) learn
III. Vivir:	vive (tú),	vivid (vosotros, –as),	(you) live

The imperative mood is used only affirmatively. In negative commands the subjunctive is used.

145. Subjunctive Mood. — Present Tense:

I. — Hablar

Singular	Plural
hable	hablemos
hables	habléis
hable	hablen

II. — Aprender

Singular	Plural
aprenda	aprendamos
aprendas	aprendáis
aprenda	aprendan

III. — Vivir

Singular	Plural
viva	vivamos
vivas	viváis
viva	vivan

146. **The Present Subjunctive** (1) may be used to express a direct command or wish; or (2) it may be used in subordinate clauses.

147. Forms of Hablar Used to Express a Direct Command or Wish.

AFFIRMATIVE   NEGATIVE

SINGULAR

habla (tú) ⎫
hable Vd. ⎬ speak

(que) hable él,[1] let him speak

no hables (tú) ⎫
no hable Vd. ⎬ do not speak

(que) no hable él, let him not speak

PLURAL

hablemos, let us speak
hablad (vosotros, –as), ⎫
hablen Vds., ⎬ speak

(que) hablen ellos, let them speak

no hablemos, let us not speak
no habléis (vosotros, –as), ⎫ do not
no hablen Vds. ⎬ speak

(que) no hablen ellos, let them not speak •

All regular verbs of the first conjugation are thus inflected. Regular verbs of the second and third conjugations use similarly the forms of **aprender** and **vivir** given in §§144, 145.

a. In the third person, the **que** may sometimes be omitted. Without **que** the command is more direct.

148. The Spanish present subjunctive used in direct commands is generally to be expressed in English by *let* and the infinitive, if the subject is not in the second person. See above.

a. But if *let* means *allow* or *permit*, it is to be translated by **dejar** or **permitir**: **déjeme Vd. entrar,** *let me go in;* **permita Vd. que Juan hable,** *let John speak, permit John to speak* (lit., *permit that John speak*).

b. In the first person plural one may say either **estudiemos** or **vamos a estudiar,** *let us study. Let us not study* is **no estudiemos.**

[1] Or que él hable, que ellos hablen, etc.

149. — 1. The final −d of the plural imperative is lost before the object pronoun **os,** *you, yourselves:* **sentaos** (for **sentad-os**), *seat yourselves;* except **idos,** *go away,* from **irse,** *to go away.*

2. The final −s of the first person plural of the present subjunctive is omitted before the object pronoun **nos,** *us, ourselves:* **sentémonos** (for **sentemos-nos**), *let us seat ourselves.*

150. For the position of the personal pronoun objects of a verb used to express a command or wish, see §85.

a. But if the verb is introduced by **que,** a personal pronoun object precedes the verb: **que lo traiga ella desde luego,** *let her bring it at once.*

b. The present subjunctive, second person, with or without **que,** may also express a mere wish: **que seas feliz,** *may you be happy;* **¡viva el rey!** *long live the king!*

EXERCISES

agitar, to shake	la **dosis,** dose
amargo, −a, bitter	**feliz,** happy
apetecer, to have an appetite for, wish	la **fiebre,** fever
	la **medicina,** medicine
el **automóvil,** motor car, automobile	**observar,** to observe
beber, to drink	la **píldora,** pill
la **cucharadita,** teaspoonful	el **pulso,** pulse
deber, must, to be (expected) to	el **remedio,** remedy
débil, weak	el **resfriado,** cold (*a disease*)
la **dieta,** diet	el **rey,** king
el **dolor,** pain, sorrow; **dolor de cabeza,** headache	**telefonear,** to telephone

A. *Repítase con el verbo en plural.* 1. Habla más alto. 2. Hable Vd. más alto. 3. Hable él más alto. 4. Aprende la lección. 5. Aprenda Vd. la lección. 6. Que ella la aprenda.

Repítase negativamente. 7. Telefonea al médico. 8. Come todo lo que apetezcas (*anything you wish*). 9. Tómela Vd. 10. Agítela Vd. 11. Sentaos. 12. Sentémonos.

B. 1. Carlos, telefonea al médico que estoy enfermo. 2. —Sí, señor; le telefonearé desde luego. 3. Ya telefoneé al

LOPE FELIX DE VEGA CARPIO (1562–1635)
Lope de Vega was a great dramatist of the "Golden Age" of
Spanish Literature.

MIGUEL DE CERVANTES SAAVEDRA (1547-1616)

A portrait of Cervantes, the author of *Don Quixote* and other important works, which is now in the possession of the Royal Spanish Academy in Madrid.

doctor Heredia. 4. Dice que vendrá desde luego. 5. Aquí
viene él en su automóvil. 6. — Buenos días, señor doctor.
Estoy muy enfermo. 7. — Vamos a ver la lengua y a tomar
el pulso. 8. ¿Se siente Vd. (*Do you feel*) débil? 9. — Sí,
señor; me siento muy débil. 10. Tengo dolor de cabeza
y no tengo apetito. 11. Creo que tengo fiebre. 12. — Vd.
no tiene más que un fuerte (*bad*) resfriado. 13. Aquí tiene
Vd. algunas píldoras. 14. Tome Vd. dos cada (*every*) cinco
horas. 15. Y aquí tiene Vd. una medicina muy amarga.
16. Tome Vd. una cucharadita después de cada comida.
17. Agítese la botella (*Let the bottle be shaken*) antes
de tomar la medicina. 18. — ¿Qué dieta debo observar?
19. — Coma Vd. todo lo que apetezca. 20. — Adiós, señor
doctor. — Hasta luego, amigo mío: que lo pase bien.

C. *Contéstese.* 1. ¿A quién telefoneó Carlos? 2. ¿En qué
vino el médico? 3. ¿Quiso ver la lengua del enfermo (*patient*)? 4. ¿Quiso tomar el pulso? 5. ¿Tenía el enfermo
dolor de cabeza? 6. ¿Tenía buen apetito? 7. ¿Tenía un
fuerte resfriado? 8. ¿Qué remedios le dió el médico al enfermo? 9. ¿Cuántas píldoras debía tomar el enfermo cada
cinco horas? 10. ¿Era amarga la medicina de la botella?
11. ¿Debía agitarse la botella antes de tomar la medicina?
12. ¿Cuál era la dosis de esta medicina?

D. 1. Did you telephone to Dr. Heredia? 2. — Yes, sir; I telephoned to him. 3. He will come at once. 4. — Have you fever?
5. — No, sir; but I have a headache. 6. — You must have a
cold. 7. — Yes, sir; I have a bad cold. 8. — Here is (**Aquí tiene
Vd.**) a bottle of medicine. 9. — Is the medicine bitter? 10. I
do not like bitter medicine (§103, 1). 11. — Shake the bottle.
12. Let the bottle be shaken. 13. Take a teaspoonful every two
hours. 14. Here are some pills. 15. Take one pill before each meal.
16. Do not take the pill after the meal. 17. — I do not like pills
(§103, 1). 18. — Do not eat much. 19. — I shan't eat much.
20. I haven't [any] appetite.

124 FIRST SPANISH COURSE

E. 1. When I was ill, Charles telephoned to Dr. Heredia. 2. The latter (**Éste**) came to my house in his motor car. 3. Charles opened the door for-him (**le**). 4. Taking off his hat, his gloves, and his overcoat, he came into (**entró en**) my room. 5. I said to him: Good day, doctor; I am very ill. 6. He answered: Let (§148, *a*) me see your (**la**) tongue and take your (**el**) pulse. 7. You have a cold, but you are not very ill. 8. But, I answered, I have [a] headache, and I haven't [any] appetite. 9. You haven't [any] fever, said the good physician. 10. I took your (**el**) pulse and your temperature (**la temperatura**). 11. Here are twelve white pills. 12. Take one every two hours, and drink a great deal of water. 13. And here is a bottle of medicine. 14. Take a teaspoonful fifteen minutes before each meal. 15. In the morning you may (**puede**) eat anything you wish. 16. Do not eat much at (**de**) night.

RESUMEN GRAMATICAL

144. Modo imperativo. — El modo imperativo sólo se usa en la forma afirmativa. En expresiones de mando negativas se emplea el subjuntivo.

145. Modo subjuntivo.

146. El presente de subjuntivo (1) se emplea para expresar una orden o deseo directo; o (2) puede usarse en cláusulas subordinadas.

147. Formas del verbo *hablar* **en expresiones de mando o deseo:** . . .

Todos los verbos regulares de la primera conjugación se conjugan como el verbo **hablar.** Los verbos regulares de las segunda y tercera conjugaciones se conjugan igualmente como los verbos **aprender** y **vivir** (*véanse los* §§144, 145).

1. El vocablo **que** se suprime algunas veces en la tercera persona. Sin **que,** la idea de mando resulta más directa.

148. El presente de subjuntivo, en expresiones de mando directas, se traduce generalmente al inglés mediante el vocablo *let* y el infinitivo, con tal que el sujeto no sea de la segunda persona.

a. Pero si *let* significa **dejar** o **permitir,** debe traducirse por estos verbos.

b. En la primera persona plural se puede decir **estudiemos** o **vamos a estudiar,** *let us study. Let us not study* equivale a **no estudiemos.**

149. — 1. La **–d** final de la segunda persona plural del imperativo se pierde delante del pronombre complementario **os.**

2. La **–s** final de la primera persona plural del presente de subjuntivo se omite delante del pronombre complementario **nos.**

150. Para la colocación del pronombre personal complemento de un verbo en expresiones de mando o deseo, véase el §85.

a. Pero si el verbo va precedido de la voz **que,** el pronombre personal complementario precede al verbo.

b. El presente de subjuntivo, segunda persona, con la voz **que** o sin ella, puede también expresar un simple deseo.

LESSON XXXII

151. Radical-Changing Verbs. — 1. Imperative Mood:

> Cerrar: cierra, cerrad, close
> Contar: cuenta, contad, count
> Entender: entiende, entended, understand
> Volver: vuelve, volved, return
> Sentir: siente, sentid, feel
> Dormir: duerme, dormid, sleep
> Pedir: pide, pedid, ask (for)

2.   Present Subjunctive

Cerrar, *to close*

Singular	Plural
cierre	cerremos
cierres	cerréis
cierre	cierren

Contar, *to count*

Singular	Plural
cuente	contemos
cuentes	contéis
cuente	cuenten

Entender, *to understand*

Singular	Plural
entienda	entendamos
entiendas	entendáis
entienda	entiendan

Volver, *to return*

Singular	Plural
vuelva	volvamos
vuelvas	volváis
vuelva	vuelvan

Sentir, *to feel*   Dormir, *to sleep*

SINGULAR	PLURAL	SINGULAR	PLURAL
sienta	sintamos	duerma	durmamos
sientas	sintáis	duermas	durmáis
sienta	sientan	duerma	duerman

Pedir, *to ask*

SINGULAR	PLURAL
pida	pidamos
pidas	pidáis
pida	pidan

Note that in the imperative and in the present subjunctive, as in the present indicative, the radical vowel e changes to ie or i, and the radical vowel o changes to ue, when the root is stressed.

In the third conjugation (but not in the first or second), the radical vowel e changes to i, and the radical vowel o changes to u, in the first and second persons plural of the present subjunctive.

152. Subjunctive in Substantive Clauses.[1] — The present subjunctive may be used to express a direct command or wish (§§146, 147). It is also used to express an indirect command or wish, after **mandar,** *to command, order;* **pedir** (i), *to ask;* **querer** (ie), *to wish;* **preferir** (ie), *to prefer;* **aconsejar,** *to advise;* **dejar,** *to let, allow;* **prohibir,** *to forbid,* and the like.

Él manda que yo cierre la puerta.	He orders me to close (that I shall close) the door.
Quiero que tú seas feliz.	I wish you to be (that you may be) happy.
Preferimos que la escriba él.	We prefer that he write (that he should write) it.
Prohibo que tú entres en aquella casa.	I forbid your entering (that you should enter) that house.

Note that in these sentences the Spanish subjunctive is expressed in English by: (1) the simple subjunctive (as in *that he write*); (2) *shall,*

[1] A clause that is the subject or the object of a verb is called a substantive clause.

should, or *may* and the infinitive; (3) the infinitive alone; (4) the present participle (or gerund).

a. **Decir, escribir,** and the like, may be used as verbs of command: **me escribe que vuelva en seguida,** *he writes me to return immediately.*

153. If the principal and the subordinate verbs of a sentence have the same subject, the infinitive is used in Spanish instead of the subjunctive.

Quiero ser feliz.	I wish to be happy.
Preferimos escribirla.	We prefer to write it.

a. The infinitive is often used in English even when the principal and the subordinate verbs have different subjects (see §152). In Spanish the infinitive may be thus used only after a few verbs, such as **mandar, dejar,** and the like, chiefly when the logical subject of **an** affirmative subordinate verb is an unstressed personal pronoun.

Me mandó venir.	He ordered me to come.
No le dejamos entrar.	We do not let him come in.

EXERCISES

caro, –a, dear, expensive
la **casa editorial,** publishing house
clásico, –a, classic
completo, –a, complete
el **dependiente,** clerk
desear, to desire
la **edición,** edition
el **ejemplar,** copy (*of a book, etc.*)
encuadernar, to bind (*a book*)
escoger, to choose, select
ilustrar, to illustrate
importante, important
la **librería,** bookstore

la **literatura,** literature
el **lujo,** luxury; **de lujo,** de luxe, elegant
mandar, to command, send
mejor, better, best
necesitar, to need
la **obra,** work (*of art, literature, music*)
el **peso,** dollar
la **poesía,** poetry, poem
publicar, to publish
valer,[1] to be worth
el **volumen,** volume

A. 1. ¿Dónde está la librería de Victoriano Sánchez? 2. — Aquí está. ¿Quiere Vd. que entremos en ella?

---

[1] Irregular in some tenses (§273).

3. — Sí, señor; mi padre desea que le compre las poesías de Espronceda. 4. — Yo también necesito comprar varios libros. 5. En mi biblioteca ya tengo muchas obras clásicas. 6. Tengo las *Obras completas* de Calderón de la Barca y las *Obras escogidas* de Lope de Vega. 7. El profesor de castellano me aconseja que busque (§114) una buena edición del *Quijote*. 8. Me dice que es la obra más importante de la literatura castellana. 9. — Aquí tiene Vd. un buen ejemplar, ilustrado y bien encuadernado. 10. — Voy a pedirle al dependiente que me enseñe otra edición mejor que ésta. 11. — Aquí tiene Vd. una que acaba de publicar (§91) la mejor casa editorial de Madrid. 12. Es una edición de lujo encuadernada en doce volúmenes. 13. — ¿Cuánto vale la edición? — Vale veinticinco pesos. 14. — Es cara; pero la tomo. 15. — ¿Quiere Vd. que la mande a su casa? 16. — Sí; hágame Vd. el favor de mandármela a casa.

B. *Contéstese.* 1. ¿Quiere Vd. que entremos en la librería? 2. ¿Qué quiere su padre que le compre Vd.? 3. ¿Ya tiene Vd. muchas obras en su biblioteca? 4. ¿Tiene Vd. las *Obras completas* de Calderón de la Barca? 5. ¿Tiene Vd. las *Obras escogidas* de Lope de Vega? 6. ¿Cuál es la obra más importante de la literatura castellana? 7. ¿Quién escribió el *Quijote?* (Miguel de Cervantes Saavedra.) 8. ¿Quién le aconseja a Vd. que busque una edición del *Quijote?* 9. ¿Compró Vd. una buena edición del *Quijote?* 10. ¿Cuántos volúmenes tiene? 11. ¿Cuánto vale la edición? 12. ¿La mandó el dependiente a la casa de Vd.? 13. ¿Ha leído Vd. esta obra importante? 14. ¿Desea Vd. leerla?

C. *Repítase, usando* usted *como sujeto de los verbos subordinados.* 1. Deseo dormir bien. (Deseo que Vd. duerma bien.) 2. Carlos desea cerrar la puerta. 3. Ana prefiere escribirla. 4. Preferimos comprar otra edición. 5. Quiere mandarla a casa. 6. Te aconsejo que no entres en esa casa. (Le aconsejo a Vd. que no entre, *etc.*) 7. Prohibimos que tú

entres en ella. 8. No te dejamos entrar. (No le dejamos a
Vd. entrar.) 9. Tu padre te pide que no entres. 10. El
profesor me escribe que lo compre. 11. A ti te dice que no
lo compres (A Vd. le dice, *etc.*). 12. El padre de Juan le
manda que vuelva en seguida (Su padre le manda a Vd.
que, *etc.*).

D. 1. Have you in your library a good copy of *Don Quixote*
(del *Quijote*)? 2. Yes, sir; I have a handsome copy very well
bound. 3. Where did you buy it? 4. I found it in a Madrid bookstore (**librería de Madrid**). 5. My teacher wishes me to buy a
good edition. 6. He advises me to look for an illustrated edition of
this classic work. 7. He prefers that I should read *Don Quixote*
in Spanish. 8. He says (that) he will not permit me to read it in
English. 9. Why do you not ask your teacher (**a su profesor**) to
select (§152) the edition? 10. I shall ask him to select it and buy
it for me (**y me la compre**). 11. Are there many important works
in (the) Spanish literature? 12. Yes, sir; the works of Cervantes,
Calderón, Lope de Vega, and many others (**otros muchos**) are very
important. 13. I have not read the poems of Espronceda, Zorrilla, and Bécquer, but I intend to read them. 14. It is not worth
while to (**No vale la pena de**) read all the poems of Zorrilla.
15. He wrote some poems that I do not like. 16. Which is the
best edition of Bécquer's works? 17. The one which (**La que**) Victoriano Sánchez has just published. 18. Ask the clerk (**Pida Vd.
al dependiente**) to show it [to] you. 19. I will take it (**La tomo**);
but I desire you to send it to my house (*véase* A. 16).

RESUMEN GRAMATICAL

**151. Verbos que sufren cambios constantes en su vocal
radical.** — 1. **Modo imperativo.** 2. **Presente de subjuntivo.**

, Adviértase que en el imperativo y en el presente de subjuntivo, como
en el presente de indicativo, la vocal radical **e** se cambia en **ie** o **i,** y la
vocal **o** se cambia en **ue,** cuando sobre la raíz cae el acento prosódico.

En la tercera conjugación (y no en la primera o segunda), la vocal
radical **e** se cambia en **i,** y la vocal radical **o** se cambia en **u,** en las personas
primera y segunda del plural del presente de subjuntivo.

152. Subjuntivo en cláusulas substantivadas. — El presente
de subjuntivo puede usarse para expresar una orden o deseo directo
(§§146, 147). También se usa para expresar una orden o deseo
indirecto después de los verbos **mandar, pedir, querer, preferir,
aconsejar, dejar, prohibir,** y otros semejantes.

Obsérvese que en estas frases el subjuntivo español se traduce al
inglés por (1) el simple subjuntivo, (2) *shall, should* o *may* y el infinitivo, (3) el infinitivo solo, y (4) el gerundio.

a. **Decir, escribir,** y otros verbos semejantes, pueden usarse como
verbos de mando.

153. Si el verbo principal así como el subordinado en una
frase tienen un mismo sujeto, en español se usa el infinitivo en vez
del subjuntivo.

a. En inglés se usa a menudo el infinitivo aunque el verbo principal y el subordinado tengan diferentes sujetos (§152). En este caso,
en español sólo se usa el infinitivo después de determinados verbos,
tales como **mandar, dejar,** y algunos otros, especialmente cuando el
sujeto lógico de un verbo subordinado afirmativo es un pronombre
personal no acentuado.

LESSON XXXIII

154.   Some Irregular Imperatives

Decir: di, decid, say (tell)	**Venir: ven, venid,** come
Hacer: haz, haced, do (make)	**Ir: ve, id,** go
Poner: pon, poned, put (place)	**Ser: sé, sed,** be
Tener: ten, tened, have	

155. Stem of the Present Subjunctive. — 1. The present
subjunctive has, as a rule, the same stem as that of the first
person singular of the present indicative.

Pres. Ind. 1st Pers. Sing.	Present Subjunctive
Conocer: conozc-o;	conozc-a, –as, –a, –amos, –áis, –an
Decir: dig-o;	dig-a, –as, –a, –amos, –áis, –an
Hacer: hag-o;	hag-a, –as, –a, –amos, –áis, –an
Tener: teng-o;	teng-a, –as, –a, –amos, –áis, –an
Venir: veng-o;	veng-a, –as, –a, –amos, –áis, –an

2. The exceptions to this general rule are the six verbs whose present indicative, first person singular, does not end in –o.

	Pres. Ind. 1st Pers. Sing.	Present Subjunctive
Dar:	doy;	d-é, –es, –é, –emos, –eis, –en
Estar:	estoy;	est-é, –és, –é, –emos, –éis, –én
Ir:	voy;	vay-a, –as, –a, –amos, –áis, –an
Ser:	soy;	se-a, –as, –a, –amos, –áis, –an
Haber:	he;	hay-a, –as, –a, –amos, –áis, –an
Saber:	sé;	sep-a, –as, –a, –amos, –áis, –an

3. **Poder** (ue) and **querer** (ie) are inflected in the present subjunctive like radical-changing verbs of the second conjugation.

156. Subjunctive in Substantive Clauses, Continued. — 1. The subjunctive is required after expressions of feeling or emotion, such as **temer,** *to fear;* **esperar,**[1] *to hope;* **alegrarse de,** *to be glad of;* **sentir** (ie), *to regret, be sorry;* **ser lástima,** *to be a pity, be too bad,* and the like.

Tememos que él no llegue a tiempo.	We fear that he will not arrive in time.
Siento que Vd. esté enfermo.	I am sorry that you are ill.
Es lástima que Juan no estudie más.	It is a pity that John does not study more.
But (§153),	
Tememos no llegar a tiempo.	We fear that we shall not arrive in time.
Siento estar enfermo.	I am sorry to be ill (that I am ill).

a. A preposition is usually retained before a substantive clause in Spanish, but omitted in English: **me alegro de eso,** *I am glad of that;* **me alegro de que Vd. no lo crea,** *I am glad that you do not believe it.*

---

[1] The future indicative may be used after **esperar** and **temer** if certainty is implied. See XXXVI, Exercises, E. 15.

2. The subjunctive is required after expressions of *doubting* or *denying*, such as **dudar,** *to doubt,* and **negar (ie),** *to deny.*

Dudo que sea feliz.	I doubt that (whether) he is (*or* he will be) happy.
Niega que sea verdad.	He denies that it is true.

157. Expressions of believing or saying, such as **creer,** *to believe,* **decir,** *to say,* **estar seguro de,** *to be sure of,* and the like, usually take the indicative; but when they are negative or interrogative they may express doubt or denial, in which case they take the subjunctive.

Creo que es feliz.	I believe that he is happy.
But, **No creo que sea feliz.**	I do not believe that he is happy.
¿Cree Vd. que sea feliz?	Do you believe that he is happy? (*The speaker implies that* **he** *is in doubt.*)

a. Similarly, **no dudo, no niego,** and the like, may take the indicative to stress a fact: **no dudo que es feliz,** *I do not doubt that he is happy;* **no niega que es verdad,** *he does not deny that it is true.*

b. Note that the Spanish present subjunctive may express either present or future time, and that it is sometimes best translated into English by the present or the future indicative.

EXERCISES

apenas, scarcely, hardly
el **buzón,** mail box, letter box
el **centavo,** cent
cerca, near
certificar, to register (*a letter, package, etc.*)
el **correo,** mail, post office [1]
costar (ue), to cost
echar, to throw, put
enviar, to send

extranjero, –a, foreign
el **giro,** money order, draft
muchísimo, very much
el **país,** country
parecer, to appear, seem
el **porte,** postage
salir,[2] to go out, leave
el **sello,** stamp; **sello de correo,** *o* **sello postal,** postage stamp [3]

creo que sí (que no), I think so (not); **esperamos que sí (que no),** we hope so (not).

---

[1] *Post office* is also **casa de correos.**

[2] **Salir** is irregular in some tenses (see §274).

[3] Also called **estampilla de correo** in some countries.

PALACIO DEL CONGRESO NACIONAL
The Argentine Capitol or House of Parliament.

PLAZA DE MAYO Y MUNICIPALIDAD
A view of the Plaza de Mayo and the City Hall in Buenos Aires.

Un Museo de Bellas Artes

El interior de la Catedral de Santiago de Chile

A. 1. Acabo de escribir algunas cartas a mis amigos en los Estados Unidos de América. 2. Tengo sobres, pero no tengo sellos de correo (*o* sellos postales). 3. Siento muchísimo no tener sellos. 4. — ¿Quiere Vd. que vaya a buscarlos? 5. — Sí; tenga Vd. la bondad de ir a buscar diez sellos de cinco centavos cada uno. 6. Éste es el porte de una carta a un país extranjero. 7. — ¿Quiere Vd. que lleve las cartas al correo? 8. — Sí; el correo de la mañana sale a las nueve. 9. Temo que Vd. no llegue a tiempo. 10. Dudo que pueda llegar antes de las nueve. 11. — ¿Quiere Vd. que certifique las cartas? 12. — Apenas puedo creer que haya[1] tiempo para eso. 13. Ponga Vd. los sellos y eche las cartas en el buzón. 14. Es lástima que no tengamos sellos de correo en casa. 15. Pero me alegro de que esté cerca el correo. 16. ¿Cree Vd. poder llegar al correo antes de las nueve? 17. — Sí, señor; creo que sí. 18. — Yo espero que sí; pero no estoy seguro de que pueda hacerlo. 19. No me parece probable que llegue antes de las nueve. 20. Hágame Vd. el favor de traerme diez tarjetas postales de dos centavos cada una. 21. Mañana enviaré un giro postal de cuarenta pesos a una casa editorial de Bogotá. 22. Dudo que tengamos tiempo para hacerlo hoy.

B. *Contéstese.* 1. ¿A quiénes he escrito yo? 2. ¿Dónde viven mis amigos? 3. ¿Tenemos en casa sellos de correo (*o* sellos postales)? 4–5. ¿Cuál es el porte de una carta (de una tarjeta postal) a un país extranjero? 6. ¿A qué hora sale el correo de la mañana? 7. ¿Cree Vd. que yo pueda llegar al correo antes de las nueve? (*respuesta:* Sí, señor; creo que puede, *etc.*; *o*, No, señor; no creo que pueda, *etc.*). 8. ¿Le parece a Vd. probable que pueda llegar a esa hora? 9. ¿Está Vd. seguro de que no pueda llegar? 10. ¿Qué enviaré yo mañana a una casa editorial de Bogotá? 11. ¿Cree Vd. que tenga tiempo para hacerlo hoy?

[1] **Haya** is here the present subjunctive corresponding to **hay.**

C. *Repítase, usando* **usted** *como sujeto del verbo subordinado.*
1. Temo no llegar a tiempo. (Temo que Vd. no llegue a tiempo.) 2. Siento muchísimo estar enfermo hoy. 3. Espero poder hacerlo. 4. Me alegro de poder hacerlo. 5. Él está seguro de poder llegar a tiempo. 6. ¿Está él seguro de poder llegar a tiempo? 7. Ella niega haberlo hecho.

Repítase con **yo** *sobrentendido, pero no expresado, como sujeto del verbo subordinado.* 8. Siento que no tengamos sellos. (Siento no tener sellos.) 9. Quiero que Vd. vaya a buscarlos. 10. Deseo que Vd. lleve las cartas al correo. 11. Temo que Vd. no llegue a tiempo. 12. Espero que Vd. pueda hacerlo.

D. 1. Bring me five postal cards. 2. I desire you to bring me also ten postage stamps. 3. The postal cards cost two cents each (one). 4. The postage stamps cost five cents each (one). 5. Have you sent the postal money order? 6. I am glad that you have sent it. 7. Your father wishes you to post [1] this letter. 8. Please post it at once. 9. We hope that you will buy some Spanish books (**libros en español**). 10. And we hope (that) you will read them. 11. I fear (that) you may not read them all. 12. Do you believe (that) Ferdinand has read *Don Quixote?* 13. No, sir; I do not believe (that) he has read it. 14. He doesn't say (that) he has read it. 15. And I believe (that) he has not done so (**lo**).

E. 1. When does the mail for Cuba (**para Cuba**) leave? 2. It leaves every third day (**cada tres días**) at half-past four in the afternoon. 3. Will you (**¿Quiere Vd.**) post this letter? 4. If you have the time, please register it. 5. I prefer that you should register all my letters. 6. Is the post office near? — Yes, sir; it is very near. 7. Good! I am glad (that) it is near. 8. But this letter hasn't [any] stamp! 9. That is true. Please buy me five postage stamps. 10. Put one stamp on this envelope and bring me the others (**los demás**). 11. I have many other [2] letters to write. 12. What is the postage of a letter to a foreign country? 13. The postage of a

[1] *To post* = **echar al correo** or **echar en el buzón.**
[2] See XXXII, Exercises, D. 12.

letter is five cents and that (el) of a postal card two cents. 14. Have you written to your mother this week? 15. No, sir; I have not written to her this week. 16. I am very sorry that you have not written to her. 17. I fear that you may not be able to write to her to-day. 18. I desire you to write if you can (puede) do so. 19. But I doubt that you will have the time. 20. It is a pity that you do not write to your family every Sunday (todos los domingos).

RESUMEN GRAMATICAL

155. El radical del presente de subjuntivo. — 1. El presente de subjuntivo tiene, por regla general, el mismo radical que la primera persona singular del presente de indicativo.

2. Las excepciones de esta regla general son las de los seis verbos cuya primera persona singular del presente de indicativo no termina en −o.

3. Los verbos **poder** y **querer** se conjugan en el presente de subjuntivo como los verbos de la segunda conjugación que cambian su raíz.

156. Subjuntivo en cláusulas substantivadas. — 1. Se requiere el subjuntivo después de expresiones de sentimiento o emoción, tales como **temer, esperar, alegrarse de, sentir, ser lástima,** etc.

a. En español se usa la preposición delante de la cláusula substantivada pero se suprime en inglés.

2. Se emplea el subjuntivo después de expresiones de negación o duda, tales como **dudar** y **negar.**

157. Expresiones que implican ideas de creer o decir, tales como **creer, decir, estar seguro de,** rigen, por regla general, al modo indicativo; pero cuando son negativas o interrogativas, pueden expresar duda o negación y en este caso rigen al subjuntivo.

a. Del mismo modo, las expresiones **no dudo, no niego,** etc., pueden regir al modo indicativo para expresar un hecho.

b. Adviértase que el presente de subjuntivo en español puede indicar o bien tiempo presente o futuro, y que se traduce algunas veces al inglés por el presente o el futuro de indicativo.

LESSON XXXIV

158. **Subjunctive in Substantive Clauses,** Continued. —
1. The subjunctive is required after such impersonal expressions as **es preciso,** *it is necessary;* **importa,** *it is important;* **conviene,**[1] *it is proper;* **es posible,** *it is possible,* and the like.

Es preciso que él diga la verdad.	It is necessary for him to (that he should) tell the truth.
Importa que lleguemos temprano.	It is important for us to (that we should) arrive early.
No es posible que yo lo haga.	It is not possible for me to do it.

2. After most of these expressions the infinitive is used, as in English, if it does not have a definite subject, and it may be used if, in Spanish, its logical subject is an unstressed personal pronoun object of the principal verb.

Importa llegar temprano.	It is important to arrive early.
Nos importa llegar temprano.	It is important for us to arrive early.
No es posible hacerlo.	It is not possible to do it.
No me es posible hacerlo.	It is not possible for me to do it.

159. **Imperfect (or Past) Subjunctive.** — Spanish has two imperfect tenses of the subjunctive mood. These tenses may be formed for all verbs, both regular and irregular, by adding the following endings to the stem of the preterite indicative, third person:

I $\left\{ \begin{array}{l} \text{1. –ase, –ases, –ase, –ásemos, –aseis, –asen} \\ \text{2. –ara, –aras, –ara, –áramos, –arais, –aran} \end{array} \right.$

II *and* III. $\left\{ \begin{array}{l} \text{1. –iese, –ieses, –iese, –iésemos, –ieseis, –iesen} \\ \text{2. –iera, –ieras, –iera, –iéramos, –ierais, –ieran} \end{array} \right.$

[1] **Convenir** is inflected like **venir** (§264).

Pret. Ind. 3d Pers. Pl.	Past Subjunctive Hablar
habl-aron,	1. habl-ase, –ases, –ase, –ásemos, –aseis, –asen 2. habl-ara, –aras, –ara, –áramos, –arais, –aran

Aprender

aprend-ieron,	1. aprend-iese, –ieses, –iese, –iésemos, –ieseis, –iesen 2. aprend-iera, –ieras, –iera, –iéramos, –ierais, –ieran

Vivir

viv-ieron,	1. viv-iese, –ieses, –iese, –iésemos, –ieseis, –iesen 2. viv-iera, –ieras, –iera, –iéramos, –ierais, –ieran

Pedir

pid-ieron,	1. pid-iese, –ieses, –iese, –iésemos, –ieseis, –iesen 2. pid-iera, –ieras, –iera, –iéramos, –ierais, –ieran

Tener

tuv-ieron,	1. tuv-iese, –ieses, –iese, –iésemos, –ieseis, –iesen 2. tuv-iera, –ieras, –iera, –iéramos, –ierais, –ieran

a. In subordinate clauses either form may be used, but the form in –ra is more common in Spanish America.

b. Note the absence of i in **fueron**, etc., and in **dijeron**, etc.

160. Use of the Imperfect Subjunctive. — 1. If the principal verb of a sentence is past or conditional, the subordinate subjunctive verb is usually in the imperfect tense.

Yo quería que Vd. fuera feliz.	I wished you to be (that you might be) happy.
Temíamos que él no llegara temprano.	We feared that he would not arrive early.
Negó que fuese verdad.	He denied that it was true.
No sería posible que Pablo lo hiciera.	It would not be possible for Paul to do it.
But (§153), Yo quería ser feliz.	I wished to be happy.
Temíamos no llegar temprano.	We feared that we should not arrive early.
No sería posible hacerlo.	It would not be possible to do it.

2. The present perfect or the imperfect subjunctive is used after the present tense if the time of the subordinate verb is logically past.

Siento que Vd. haya estado enfermo.	I am sorry that you have been ill.
Dudo que fuese feliz.	I doubt that he was happy.

EXERCISES

acudir, to come (to), go (to)
la **aguja,** needle
aun, even; **aún,** yet
el **botón,** button
la **cajita,**[1] little box
calzarse, to put on one's shoes (boots)
castigar, to punish
cumplir, to fulfil
el **dedal,** thimble
descoser, to rip
la **gorra,** cap
el **hilo,** thread, linen
Juanito,[2] Johnny

llorar, to weep, cry
la **mamá,** mamma, mother
la **manga,** sleeve
remendar (ie), to mend
rogar (ue), to request, ask
romper, to break, tear
la **ropa,** clothes
roto, -a, broken, torn
subir a, to go up to, climb
las **tijeras,** scissors; **unas tijeras,** a pair of scissors
el **traje,** suit (*of clothes*)
usar, to use, wear
el **vestido,** dress

dejó de llorar, he stopped crying; **ayer cumplió ocho años,** he was eight years old yesterday.

A. 1. Juanito se rompe siempre la ropa. 2. Cuando se rompió la chaqueta al subir a un árbol, acudió a su mamá y le rogó que le remendara en seguida la chaqueta. 3. La mamá halló roto un bolsillo y descosida una manga. 4. Ella buscó una aguja e (*and*) hilo, el dedal, las tijeras y la cajita de botones, y remendó la chaqueta. 5. Para castigar a Juanito, la madre no le permitió llevar más aquel día su traje nuevo. 6. Juanito tuvo que ponerse una chaqueta usada, pantalones rotos y una gorra vieja. 7. Ayer cumplió Juanito ocho años, pero es todavía muy (*very much of a*) niño. 8. No puede

---

[1] Diminutive of **caja,** *box.*   [2] Diminutive of **Juan.**

lavarse, vestirse ni calzarse. 9. Esta mañana rogó a su
mamá que le pusiera la blusa y los zapatos. 10. Llora
cuando su mamá le lava la cara y las manos con agua y
jabón. 11. Llora cuando ella le peina y cepilla el pelo (los
cabellos). 12. Y llora aun más cuando ella le cepilla los
dientes con polvos.

B. *Contéstese.* 1. ¿Quién se rompe siempre la ropa?
2. ¿Qué se rompió al subir a un árbol? 3. ¿A quién acudió?
4. ¿Qué le rogó a su mamá? 5. ¿Qué halló roto la mamá?
6. ¿Qué halló descosido la mamá? 7. ¿Qué buscó ella
para remendar la chaqueta? 8. ¿Cómo castigó a Juanito?
9. ¿Qué tuvo que ponerse Juanito? 10. ¿Cuántos años cumplió Juanito ayer? 11. ¿Puede lavarse, vestirse y calzarse?
12. ¿Qué le rogó a su mamá esta mañana? 13. ¿Cuándo
llora él?

C. 1. *¿Cuáles son las dos formas del imperfecto de subjuntivo de estar, haber, decir, hacer, ir, venir? 2. ¿Cuáles
son las dos formas del pluscuamperfecto de subjuntivo (úsense
como verbos auxiliares* hubiese, –eses, *etc., y* hubiera, –eras,
etc.) de los verbos hablar, aprender, vivir?

D. *Repítase, con el verbo principal en el imperfecto de indicativo.* 1. Importa que lleguemos temprano. (Importaba
que llegáramos temprano.) 2. Nos importa llegar temprano.
(Nos importaba llegar temprano.) 3. No es posible que yo
lo haga. 4. No me es posible hacerlo. 5. ¿Quiere Vd. que
yo lleve las cartas al correo? 6. Deseo que Vd. certifique las
cartas. 7. Apenas puedo creer que haya tiempo. 8. No
estoy seguro de que Vd. pueda hacerlo. 9. ¿Cree Vd. que
sea posible?

*Repítase, con el verbo principal en el presente de indicativo, y
después en el futuro de indicativo.* 10. Prohibí que Vd. entrase
en esa casa. (Prohibo que Vd. entre, *etc.* Prohibiré que Vd.
entre, *etc.*) 11. Era preciso que dijera la verdad. 12. Vd.

140 FIRST SPANISH COURSE

negó que fuese verdad. 13. No sería posible que yo lo hiciera. 14. Yo quería ser feliz. 15. El dudó que tuviésemos tiempo. 16. Ellos sentían muchísimo que estuviéramos enfermos.

E. 1. It was not possible for me to go to the post office. 2. It was necessary that you should post the letter. 3. It was important that you should arrive early. 4. We feared that you could not do it. 5. Do you believe that he has put stamps on the envelopes? 6. No, sir; I can scarcely believe that he has done so. 7. I doubt that he has bought [any] stamps. 8. Did Johnnie tear his coat? 9. Yes, sir; and he asked his mother to mend it. 10. Did she mend it? 11. I doubt that she has mended it yet. 12. Did she permit him to wear (llevar) his new suit? 13. No, sir; she told him to put-on his old suit. 14. Did Johnnie cry? 15. Yes, sir; he cried a long time (mucho tiempo) and his mother punished him. 16. Did he stop crying when his mother punished him? 17. No, sir; he cried even more.

F. 1. Annie (Anita [1]) is the daughter of Mr. and Mrs. Enríquez. 2. She was five years old last Monday. 3. She is a handsome dark-complexioned-little-girl (trigueñita [2]). 4. But she cries when her mother washes her face with water and soap. 5. And she cries even more when her mother brushes her teeth. 6. Yesterday Annie tore her new dress. 7. She went weeping to her mother and asked her to mend it. 8. Her mother told her to go and get the needle and thread. 9. While she was mending the dress she asked: [3] How did you (tú) tear your dress? 10. Annie answered: I tore it while climbing (al subir a) a tree. 11. To (Para) punish Annie her mother told her to wear an old dress. 12. She forbade her (le) to climb (§152) the tree [any] more. 13. She said that it was necessary that she should stop climbing trees (§103, 1). 14. And that it was too bad that she had torn (hubiera roto) her new dress. 15. Annie was very sorry that she had done so (lo). 16. She told her mother that she would not climb the tree again (otra vez). 17. The mother kissed Annie and the child stopped crying.

[1] Diminutive of Ana, *Anna*.
[2] Diminutive of trigueña.
[3] Rogar or preguntar?

RESUMEN GRAMATICAL

158. Subjuntivo en cláusulas substantivadas. — 1. Se usa el subjuntivo después de expresiones impersonales tales como **es preciso, importa, conviene, es posible,** etc.

2. Después de la mayor parte de estas expresiones, se usa el infinitivo como en inglés si carece de sujeto determinado, y también puede usarse si el sujeto lógico es un pronombre personal no acentuado complemento del verbo principal.

159. Imperfecto (o pasado) de subjuntivo. — El español tiene dos tiempos imperfectos en el subjuntivo. Estos tiempos pueden formarse en todos los verbos, tanto regulares como irregulares, añadiendo las siguientes terminaciones al radical de la tercera persona del pretérito (pasado absoluto) de indicativo: . . .

a. En las cláusulas subordinadas puede usarse cualquiera de las dos formas, pero en la América española prefieren la forma en –**ra.**

b. Nótese la falta de **i** en **fueron,** etc., y en **dijeron,** etc.

160. Uso del imperfecto de subjuntivo. — 1. Si el verbo principal de una frase está en tiempo pasado o condicional, el verbo subordinado generalmente está en el imperfecto de subjuntivo.

2. El presente perfecto o el imperfecto de subjuntivo se emplean después del presente si el tiempo de la acción indicada por el verbo subordinado es lógicamente pasado.

LESSON XXXV

161. Subjunctive in Adjectival Clauses — The subjunctive is used in adjectival clauses [1] (introduced by a relative pronoun):

1. After a negative.

No encontré a nadie que hablase español.	I did not find anyone who spoke Spanish.

[1] A clause that modifies a noun or pronoun is called an adjectival clause.

2. If the relative pronoun has an indefinite antecedent.

Yo buscaba un hombre que hablase español.	I was looking for a man (= any man) who spoke Spanish.
But, Yo conocía a un hombre que hablaba español.	I knew a man (= some definite man) who spoke Spanish.
Prometió dar un premio al alumno que escribiera el mejor tema.	He promised to give a prize to the student (= any student) who should write the best theme.
But, Dió un premio al que escribió el mejor tema.	He gave a prize to the one (= some definite one) who wrote the best theme.
Todo viajero que tome este tren habrá de comprar un billete de primera clase.	Every passenger (whoever he may be) who shall take this train will have to buy a first-class ticket.

3. In clauses containing *whoever, whatever, however.*

Quienquiera que sea.	Whoever he may be.
Sea lo que sea.	Whatever it may be.
Por bueno que sea.	However good it may be.

162. The present indicative of **caer,** *to fall,* **oír,** *to hear,* **salir,** *to go out,* and **valer,** *to be worth,* is:

	SINGULAR	PLURAL		SINGULAR	PLURAL
Caer:	caigo	caemos	Salir:	salgo	salimos
	caes	caéis		sales	salís
	cae	caen		sale	salen
Oír:	oigo	oímos	Valer:	valgo	valemos
	oyes	oís		vales	valéis
	oye	oyen		vale	valen

What is the present subjunctive of these verbs? (see §155)

163. The future indicative of **salir** and **valer** is:

Salir: saldr-é, –ás, –á, –emos, –éis, –án
Valer: valdr-é, –ás, –á, –emos, –éis, –án

What is the conditional tense of these verbs?

164. The imperative of **oír, salir,** and **valer** is:

Oír: oye, oíd
Salir: sal, salid
Valer: val, valed

All other forms of the above verbs are regular. Note, however, the orthography of **caer** and **oír** (§ 114, 2, and § 126, 4).

EXERCISES

el **algodón,** cotton
la **cabritilla,** kid
la **camisa,** shirt
la **cantidad,** amount, quantity
   cargar, to charge
la **cosa,** thing
el **cuello,** neck, collar
la **cuenta,** account, bill
   desatar, to untie
la **docena,** dozen
   gastar, to spend
   mostrar (ue), to show

pagar, to pay
el **pañuelo,** handkerchief
el **paquete,** package
el **par,** pair
la **pechera,** bosom (*of a shirt*)
la **pieza,** piece, article
el **puño,** fist, cuff
la **seda,** silk
el **surtido,** supply, stock
   vender, to sell
   vistoso, –a, bright-colored,
    showy

de moda, in fashion, fashionable; **al contado,** for cash; **al fiado, on** credit; **de color,** colored

A. 1. Hoy gasté más de (*than*) cincuenta pesos. 2. Fuí a una tienda y compré a (*of*) un dependiente un par de guantes de cabritilla que me costaron dos pesos. 3. También compré una docena de pañuelos de hilo que valían treinta y cinco centavos cada uno. 4. Le pregunté al dependiente: ¿Tiene Vd. camisas del número quince que tengan la pechera y los puños de hilo? 5. Él me contestó: Sí, señor; ¿las quiere Vd. blancas o de color? 6. Le respondí: Las prefiero blancas. 7. Compré media docena de camisas y una docena de cuellos. 8. Después me dijo el dependiente: ¿Necesita Vd. corbatas? 9. Tenemos el surtido más completo que hay en la ciudad. 10. Le contesté: Tenga Vd. la bondad de mostrarme (*o*, enseñarme) algunas de seda.

11. Deseo dos o tres que no sean muy vistosas. 12. Él me
contestó: No tenemos corbatas de color que no sean vistosas.
13. Este invierno las corbatas vistosas están de moda.
14. No encontré ninguna corbata que me gustase. 15. Pero
compré diez pares de calcetines y alguna ropa interior.
16. Cuando hube escogido estas piezas, le dije al dependiente
que me las cargara en cuenta. 17. Me contestó que vendía
siempre al contado y no al fiado. 18. Pagué la cuenta y
rogué al dependiente que me lo mandase todo a casa.
19. Por la tarde recibí los paquetes. 20. Los desaté y encontré todas las cosas que había comprado.

B. *Contéstese.* 1. ¿Cuántos pesos gastó Vd. hoy?
2. ¿Cuánto costaron los guantes de cabritilla que Vd. compró? 3. ¿Cuánto valían los pañuelos de hilo? 4. ¿Prefiere
Vd. los pañuelos de hilo a los (*those*) de algodón? 5. ¿Prefiere Vd. las camisas blancas a las de color? 6. ¿Prefiere
Vd. las camisas con pechera de hilo o con pechera de seda?
7. ¿Cuántos cuellos compró Vd.? 8. ¿Le gustan a Vd. las
corbatas vistosas? 9. ¿Están de moda? 10. ¿Qué color
le gusta a Vd. más? 11. ¿Prefiere Vd. comprar al fiado o al
contado? 12. Cuando Vd. compra un traje (un vestido),
¿desea Vd. que el dependiente se lo cargue en cuenta? 13. O
¿prefiere Vd. pagar la cuenta desde luego? 14. ¿Pagó Vd.
la cuenta de hoy?

C. *Repítase, con el verbo principal en el presente de indicativo.*
1. Yo buscaba una corbata que no fuese vistosa. (Yo busco
una corbata que no sea vistosa.) 2. No encontré ninguna
que me gustara. 3. No tenían corbatas de color que no
fueran vistosas. 4. Sí, señor; tenían corbatas que no eran
vistosas. 5. Yo encontré una que me gustaba. 6. Buscá-
bamos pañuelos que no fueran de algodón. 7. Por buenos
que fuesen, no nos gustaban los (*those*) de algodón. 8. ¿No
tenían camisas que costasen menos? 9. No, señor; no

encontré ninguna que costara menos.   10. Sí, señor; yo
encontré una docena que costaban menos.   11. ¿Encontró
Vd. un dependiente que hablase inglés?   12. No encontré
ninguno que hablara inglés.   13. Yo encontré a uno que
hablaba bien el inglés.

D. 1. We are looking for a boy who speaks Spanish.   2. Do
you know a boy who speaks Spanish?   3. I *do* know (**Sí conozco**)
one who speaks Spanish very well.   4. He promised to give a dollar
to the student who should write the best exercise, whoever he
might be.   5. And he gave the dollar to the one who wrote the
best exercise.   6. However good it might be, an exercise would
not be worth a dollar.   7. We desire you to hear all that (**todo lo
que**) he may say.   8. It is necessary that you should hear it.   9. We
heard all that he said.   10. We are looking for silk handkerchiefs
(**pañuelos de seda**) that cost twenty-five cents each (one).   11. Have
you any that cost that amount?   12. No, sir; but I have some that
cost thirty cents each (one).   13. I do not see any (**ninguno**) that
I like.   14. I have some that you will like (*fut. ind.*).   15. They are
of white silk.

E. 1. What did you buy to-day at Rodríguez's shop?   2. I
bought a ready-made suit (**un traje hecho**) and some underclothes.
3. The suit cost me twenty dollars and the underclothes ten dollars.
4. Did you not buy shirts and collars too?   5. No, sir; I didn't
find any (**ninguno**) that I liked.   6. I looked for some colored
shirts without cuffs, but I could not find them.   7. Do you know
why white shirts (§103, 1) cost more than colored ones (**las de
color**)?   8. White shirts are of better linen (**de hilo de mejor
clase**), are they not (**¿no es verdad?**)?   9. I asked the clerk if he
had some red silk ties (= ties of red silk) that were not very
bright-colored.   10. He told me that bright-colored ties are in
fashion this year.   11. I bought one dozen white handkerchiefs that
cost me ten cents each (one).   12. I do not know whether they
are (**si son**) of cotton or of linen.   13. If they cost ten cents each
(one), I do not believe that they are of linen.   14. You will have to
pay twenty or twenty-five cents for (**por**) each one if they are (of)
linen.   15. Did you buy the articles (**cosas**) for cash or on credit?

16. I told the clerk to charge them on account. 17. He answered that they didn't sell on credit. 18. He said (that) they always sold for cash. 19. I paid the bill and received the things this afternoon.

RESUMEN GRAMATICAL

161. Se usa el **subjuntivo en cláusulas adjetivadas** (introducidas por un pronombre relativo):

1. Después de una expresión negativa.

2. Siempre que el pronombre relativo tenga un antecedente indeterminado.

3. Con las expresiones **quienquiera, como quiera,** etc.

LESSON XXXVI

165. Subjunctive in Adverbial Clauses. — The subjunctive is used in adverbial clauses: [1]

1. After the temporal conjunctions **cuando,** *when,* **antes que,** *before,* **hasta que,** *until,* **luego que,** *as soon as,* **mientras (que),** *as long as, while,* and the like, if future time is implied.

Cuando venga a verme, le recibiré cordialmente.	When he comes to see me, I shall receive him cordially.
No lo venda Vd. antes que yo lo vea.	Do not sell it before I see it.
Dijo que esperaría hasta que llegara el tren.	He said that he would wait until the train arrived (*or,* should arrive).

a. If future time is not implied, the indicative is used: **cuando viene a verme, siempre le recibo cordialmente,** *when he comes to see me, I always receive him cordially;* **cuando vino a verme, le recibí cordialmente,** *when he came to see me, I received him cordially.*

2. After **para que,** *in order that,* **de modo (manera) que,** *so as, so that,* **con tal que** or **siempre que,** *provided that,* **a menos que,** *unless,* **aunque,** *although, even if,* **dado que,** *granted*

---

[1] A clause that modifies a verb is called an adverbial clause.

that, and the like, if the subordinate verb does not state
something as an accomplished fact.

Le dí papel, pluma y tinta para que escribiese la carta.	I gave him paper, pen and ink in ·order that he should write the letter.
Me escribió que compraría la casa con tal que yo hiciese las reparaciones necesarias.	He wrote me that he would buy the house provided (that) I should make the necessary repairs.
No aprenderé esta lección aunque estudie toda la noche.	I shall not learn this lesson even if (although) I study all night.

a. After **aunque, de modo que,** and the like, the indicative is used
to state something as an accomplished fact: **no aprendí la lección aunque estudié toda la noche,** *I did not learn the lesson although I studied
all night.*

166. Conditional Clauses. — 1. The imperfect subjunctive is used in a conditional clause (or if-clause) to imply
that the statement is either contrary to fact in the present
or doubtful in the future.

Si yo tuviese (o tuviera) dinero, lo compraría desde luego.	If I had money, I should buy it immediately.

(This implies: **No tengo dinero.**)

Si yo tuviese (o tuviera) dinero mañana, lo com- praría.	If I should have money to-morrow, I should buy it.

(This implies: **Es dudoso** (*doubtful*) **que tenga dinero mañana.**)

2. In the conclusional clause of such a sentence the conditional tense or, less often, the imperfect subjunctive in **-ra**
is used, but not the imperfect subjunctive in **-se.**

Si yo tuviera, o tuviese, dinero, lo compraría (o lo comprara).	If I had money, I should buy it.

EXERCISES

la **bota,** high shoe, boot (= high
   shoe)
el **calzado,** footwear
el **chanclo,** rubber overshoe, golosh [1]
el **dinero,** money
el **fieltro,** felt
el **frac,** evening coat, " dress "
   coat
el **hongo,** "derby" hat, "bowler" [2]
lastimar, to hurt
la **llave,** key
la **medida,** measure
el **objeto,** object

la **paja,** straw
la **plumafuente,**[3] fountain **pen**
el **portamonedas,** purse
las **reparaciones,** repairs
el **sastre,** tailor
la **sastrería,** tailor shop
la **sombrerería,** hat shop, hatter's
el **sombrerero,** hatter, dealer in
   hats
la **suela,** sole (*of a shoe*) [4]
la **zapatería,** shoe store
el **zapatero,** shoemaker
la **zapatilla,** slipper [5]

la **bota de montar,** riding boot; el **sombrero de ala ancha,** broad-
brimmed hat; el **traje de etiqueta,** evening clothes, " dress " suit; me
mandé hacer un traje, I had, *or* I ordered, a suit made; **me sienta** (o
me cae) bien, it fits me well

A. 1. Entré en una sastrería.   2. Me mandé hacer un
traje, y el sastre me tomó la medida.   3. Me preguntó el
sastre si quería levita o americana (saco).   4. Me dijo
que la levita estaba más de moda.   5. Yo le contesté que
prefería la americana (el saco) aunque estuviera más de
moda la levita.   6. También me mandé hacer un traje de
etiqueta, frac y pantalón negros y chaleco blanco.   7. No
compro nunca los trajes hechos.   8. No me sientan (caen)
bien.   9. Yo necesito muchos bolsillos.   10. Llevo en ellos
muchos objetos: el reloj, el portamonedas, las llaves, un
pañuelo, un cortaplumas y un lápiz o una plumafuente.

---

[1] In most Spanish-American countries called **zapato** (o **zapatón) de goma,**
or **zapato de hule** (as in Mexico).

[2] Also called **bombín** (as in Mexico).

[3] Also **pluma de fuente,** or **pluma estilográfica** (as in Spain).

[4] The sole of the foot is **la planta del pie.**

[5] Moorish slippers, without counter, are **babuchas.**

11. Después fuí a una zapatería donde había un buen surtido de toda clase de calzado. 12. Compré al dependiente un par de botas, dos pares de zapatos y un par de zapatillas. 13. También compré un par de chanclos (zapatos de goma) que me pondré cuando llueva. 14. Mandé poner medias suelas a un par de zapatos viejos. 15. No me gustan las botas de montar porque me lastiman los pies. 16. Pero le dije al dependiente que compraría un par de botas de montar con tal que no me lastimaran los pies. 17. No las compré hoy, pero las compraré cuando vuelva otra vez, siempre que tenga dinero. 18. Fuí también a una sombrerería. 19. Compré al sombrerero un hongo y un sombrero de fieltro. 20. Compraré un sombrero de paja de ala ancha cuando llegue el verano.

B. 1. ¿En dónde entró Vd.? 2. Cuando Vd. mandó hacer un traje, ¿qué le tomó el sastre? 3. ¿Qué le preguntó a Vd. el sastre? 4. ¿Cuál estaba más de moda, la levita o la americana (el saco)? 5. ¿Cuál prefería Vd. aunque no estuviera de moda? 6. ¿Cuáles son las prendas (*parts*) de un traje de etiqueta? 7. ¿Por qué no le gustan a Vd. los trajes hechos? 8. ¿Qué lleva Vd. en los bolsillos? 9. ¿En dónde venden el calzado? 10. ¿Quién vende el calzado? 11. ¿Qué clase de calzado compró Vd.? 12–13. En el invierno (En el verano) ¿prefiere Vd. las botas a los zapatos? 14. ¿Cuándo se pondrá Vd. los chanclos (zapatos de goma)? 15. ¿Qué mandó Vd. poner a un par de zapatos viejos? 16. ¿Por qué no le gustan a Vd. las botas de montar? 17. ¿Comprará Vd. un par con tal que no le lastimen los pies? 18. ¿En dónde venden los sombreros? 19. ¿Quién vende los sombreros? 20. ¿Prefiere Vd. el hongo al sombrero de fieltro? 21. ¿Cuándo comprará Vd. un sombrero de paja? 22. ¿Quiere Vd. que sea de ala ancha?

C. *Léase* A., *usando la tercera persona de los verbos en lugar de la primera.*

D. 1. When (¿A qué hora) will the train arrive? 2. I shall wait until the train arrives. 3. I shall leave (Partiré) when the train arrives. 4. The train arrived at three o'clock. 5. I waited until the train should arrive. 6. I left when the train arrived. 7–8. He asks (He asked) him not to sell the piano before Mary sees (saw) it. 9. He sold it before Mary saw (viera) it. 10. We shall speak so as not to offend anyone. 11. We spoke so that we did not offend anyone. 12. I shall buy the house provided you make the repairs. 13. Will you (¿Quiere Vd.) make them? 14. They said (that) they would learn the lesson even if they studied all night. 15. But they did not learn the lesson although they did study all night. 16. If ready-made suits fitted him well, he would buy one. 17. If he had the money, he would have a good suit made. 18. If straw hats were in fashion, I should buy one. 19. If it were (hiciera *or* hiciese) cold, you would prefer a felt hat, would you not? 20. Should you wear (¿Usaría Vd.) riding boots if they did not hurt your feet? 21. If I rode on horseback, I should wear riding boots.

E. 1. Mr. (§103, 2) Martínez is a (§74) tailor and he has the best tailor shop in (the) town. 2. When I wish a suit that will fit (§161, 2) me well, I go to his tailor shop. 3. His suits cost more than ready-made suits (§103, 1), but they are much better. 4. When (the) autumn comes (*úsese* llegar), I shall have a woolen suit made. 5. Unless the suit fits me well, I shan't accept it. 6. And I want a suit that has a-lot-of (muchos) pockets. 7. In one vest (waistcoat) pocket (= one pocket of the vest) I carry my (el) watch and in another my (el) penknife. 8. I carry my (las) keys in a trousers pocket. 9. There are many kinds of men's suits: those with (los de) frock coat, with (de) evening coat, sack coat, jacket, etc. (etcétera). 10. In the morning I use [a] sack coat and I use [a] frock coat in the afternoon; but at night a (el) " dress " coat is more suitable (propio). 11. Mr. González bought this morning a pair of high shoes (boots). 12. He told the shoemaker to put half soles on (a) the old shoes (botas). 13. In (the) summer he prefers low shoes and in (the) winter he prefers high shoes (boots). 14. As soon as the rainy season (la estación de lluvias) begins, he will buy a pair of rubber overshoes (goloshes).

15. I hope (that) he will buy (**comprará**) them before the rains (**las lluvias**) begin. 16. Shall you wear a straw hat when summer comes? 17. Do you like a broad-brimmed hat? 18. In (the) winter you prefer a felt hat, do you not? 19. Although a (**el**) "derby" may be more fashionable, I shall wear a felt hat this winter. 20. I shall buy it of (**al**) Mr. Herrera, because he's the best hatter in (**de la**) town.

RESUMEN GRAMATICAL

165. Subjuntivo en cláusulas adverbiales. — Se emplea el subjuntivo:

1. Después de las conjunciones temporales **cuando, antes que, hasta que, luego que, mientras (que),** etc., siempre que se implique tiempo futuro.

a. Pero si las expresiones anteriores no implican tiempo futuro, se usa el indicativo.

2. Después de **para que, de modo (manera) que, con tal que, siempre que, a menos que, aunque, dado que,** etc., siempre que el verbo subordinado no exprese algo ya sucedido.

a. Después de **aunque, de modo que,** y otras conjunciones semejantes, se usa el indicativo para expresar algo como un hecho ya sucedido.

166. Cláusulas condicionales. —1. El imperfecto de subjuntivo se usa en cláusulas condicionales para indicar que la expresión es contraria a la verdad en el presente o dudosa en el futuro.

2. En las cláusulas terminales de tales frases se usan el condicional o, con menos frecuencia, el imperfecto de subjuntivo en **ra,** pero nunca el imperfecto de subjuntivo en –**se.**

LESSON XXXVII

167.   Use of Ojalá (que) with the Subjunctive

¡Ojalá (que) [1] viva mil años!	Oh, that he may (*or*, I hope he will) live a thousand years!
¡Ojalá (que) viviese (o viviera) mil años!	Oh, that he might (*or*, I wish he would) live a thousand years!
¡Ojalá (que) yo pudiera hacerlo!	I wish I could do it!

168.   Softened Statement

1. Yo quisiera vender la casa.	I should like (*or*, I should be glad) to sell the house.
Yo quisiera que Vd. la comprase (o comprara).	I wish you would buy it.
Vd. debiera hacer las reparaciones.	You ought to (*or*, should) make the repairs.

a. These are milder expressions, and therefore more commonly used, than the following:

Quiero vender la casa.	I want to sell the house.
Quiero que Vd. la compre.	I wish you to buy it.
Vd. debe hacer las reparaciones.	You must make the repairs.

2. The conditional is also thus used.

Me gustaría mucho hacerlo.	I should be very glad to do so.
Ella preferiría pasearse en coche.	She would prefer to go driving.

169.   *Will* and *Should*

Will (= *am, art, is,* etc., *willing*) is expressed by **quier-o, -es, -e,** etc.

Should (= *ought to*) is expressed by **debier-a, -as,** etc.

¿Quiere Vd. venderla?	Will you sell it?
¿Debiera (o debería) yo hacerlo?	Should I do it?

[1] **Que** is often omitted after **ojalá.**

170. Future (or Hypothetical) Subjunctive. — This tense may be formed for all verbs by adding the following endings to the stem of the preterite indicative, third person:

I: –are, –ares, –are, –áremos, –areis, –aren
II *and* III: –iere, –ieres, –iere, –iéremos, –iereis, –ieren

Pret. Ind. 3d Pers. Pl.	Future Subjunctive
Hablar: habl-aron;	habl-are, –ares, –are, –áremos, –areis, –aren
Pedir: pid-ieron;	pid-iere, –ieres, –iere, –iéremos, –iereis, –ieren
Estar: estuv-ieron;	estuv-iere, –ieres, –iere, –iéremos, –iereis, –ieren

Note that the imperfect subjunctive tenses are also formed from the stem of the preterite, third person.

171. Use of the Future Subjunctive. — The future subjunctive denotes a condition or hypothesis. In the spoken Spanish of to-day it is rarely used except in proverbs, legal expressions, etc. Its place is regularly taken by the present subjunctive, or by the present indicative if used with **si,** *if*.

Donde fueres, haz como vieres.	Wherever you go, do as you see. (*cf.* " When in Rome, do as the Romans do.")
Si algún accionista pidiere (o pide) que la reunión se difiera, decidirá la mayoría.	If any shareholder asks that the meeting be postponed, the majority shall decide.

172.   Traer, *to bring*

Present Indicative		Preterite Indicative	
SINGULAR	PLURAL	SINGULAR	PLURAL
traigo	traemos	traje	trajimos
traes	traéis	trajiste	trajisteis
trae	traen	trajo	trajeron [1]

Other forms of the indicative, and the imperative, are regular. What are the four subjunctive tenses of **traer**?

[1] Since **i** is omitted from **trajeron** (the ending is –**eron** instead of –**ieron**), it is also omitted from **trajese, trajera,** and **trajere.** See also **dijeron** (from **decir**): **dijese, dijera, dijere** (§277).

173. –uir Verbs. — These verbs add **y** to the stem vowel **u** except before an inflectional ending that begins with **i** or **y**.

Huir, *to flee*

Present Indicative		Imperative	
SINGULAR	PLURAL	SINGULAR	PLURAL
huyo	huimos		
huyes	huis	huye	huid
huye	huyen		

a. In **huyó** and **huyeron** the **y** is a part of the inflectional ending (§114, 2).

What are the four subjunctive tenses of **huir**?

b. Like **huir** are inflected **construir,** *to build, construct,* **instruir,** *to instruct,* etc.

EXERCISES

aficionado, –a (a), fond (of)
el almidón, starch
almidonar, to starch
la caballeriza, stable
el coche, carriage
encoger(se), to shrink
la espuela, spur [1]
hervir (ie), to boil
el jinete, horseman
el kilómetro, kilometer (= ⅝ mile)
el lavandero, laundryman; la lavandera, laundress
ligero, –a, light, fast

manso, –a, gentle, tame
marcar, to mark
la milla, mile
pasearse, to walk, drive, *or* ride for pleasure
planchar, to iron
el precio, price
la raza, race, breed
la silla, chair, saddle
subido, –a, high
tibio, –a, lukewarm
el tiro, pull; **caballo de tiro,** driving horse

hacer advertencias, to give directions; **dar un paseo,** to take a walk, ride, *etc.*

A. 1. Cuando el lavandero (la lavandera) venga por la ropa, yo quisiera que Vd. le hiciera las siguientes advertencias. 2. Me gustaría que estuvieran bien almidonados los cuellos, los puños y las pecheras de las camisas. 3. Pero la ropa

[1] Spurs with a single sharp point are called **los acicates.**

LA QUINTA DE LOS MOLINOS

Formerly a country residence of the Spanish Governors of Cuba,
the grounds are now used for expositions.

UNA EXHIBICIÓN DE GANADO

Judging highly bred cattle at an annual exhibition in South America.

interior la[1] quisiera sin almidón. 4. La ropa de lana debiera lavarse con agua tibia y no ponerse en agua hirviendo, porque se encoge. 5. La ropa de hilo y de algodón puede lavarse con agua caliente. 6. También quisiera todas las piezas bien planchadas. 7. Toda la ropa está marcada.

B. 1. ¿No quisiera Vd. venir a la caballeriza a ver nuestros caballos? 2. — Con mucho gusto. Soy aficionado a los caballos de silla (saddle horses). 3. — Tenemos también hermosos caballos de tiro. 4. — Sé que todos los caballos de Vds. son de buena raza. 5. — Sí, señor; mi padre paga precios subidos por ellos. 6. Mi hermana tiene un caballo muy manso. 7. Ella monta a caballo casi todos los días, si hace (it is) buen tiempo. 8. — ¡Ojalá que la mía hiciera lo mismo! 9. Pero prefiere pasearse en coche o en automóvil. 10. Yo tengo un caballo muy ligero que puede correr veinte kilómetros por hora (an hour). 11. Prefiero este caballo a todos los demás.

C. Contéstese. 1. ¿Quién vendrá por la ropa? 2. ¿Qué advertencias quiere Vd. que yo le haga?

D. Contéstese. 1. ¿Es Vd. aficionado (–a) a los caballos? 2. ¿Le gusta a Vd. montar a caballo? 3. ¿Son de buena raza los caballos de Vds.? 4. ¿Pagó su señor padre precios subidos por ellos? 5. ¿Cuáles costaron más, los caballos de silla o los (caballos) de tiro? 6. ¿Cuáles son más hermosos? 7. ¿Tiene la hermana de Vd. un caballo manso? 8. ¿Prefiere montar a caballo o pasearse en automóvil? 9. ¿Tiene Vd. un caballo ligero? 10. ¿Cuántos kilómetros (¿Cuántas millas) puede correr por hora?

E. 1. We should like to sell the house. 2. We wish you (Vds.) would buy the house. 3. We should like to sell it. 4. We should like you to buy it (or, We wish you would buy it). 5. Will you

---

[1] Note the personal pronoun la used here because the noun object (f.) precedes the verb.

buy it? 6. I *should* study more. 7. I must study more. 8. I have [got] to study more. 9. I should study more if I had the time. 10. Bring me a glass of water. 11. Please bring it at once. 12. I wish you would bring it now. 13. The house is built of brick(s). 14. I wish my house to be built [1] of stone. 15. Should you like your house to be built [1] of wood (**madera**)? 16. Please have (= order) a new suit made. 17. The suit (that) you are (**está**) wearing does not fit you well. 18. If the price of woolen suits (§103, 1) were not so (**tan**) high, I should have one made.

F. 1. Please tell the laundryman to come for the clothes [on] (the) Mondays. 2. And tell him to bring the clean clothes on Wednesdays or Thursdays. 3. When he comes, I wish you would give him the following directions. 4. The woolen underclothes should not be put [1] in boiling water, because they shrink. 5. But I should like [2] the linen and cotton clothes to be washed [1] in hot water. 6. Tell him also that I should like the cuffs and collars of the shirts well starched. 7. But I should prefer less starch in the shirt bosoms. 8. And I don't want any starch in the underclothes. 9. I think (**Creo que**) all the pieces are well marked.

G. 1. Have you a very fast saddle horse? 2. I should like to take a ride (**pasearme a caballo**) this afternoon. 3. Will you not come with us? We are going to take a drive in a (**pasearnos en**) motor car. 4. No, thank you; I should prefer the exercise of riding (§88, 3) on horseback. 5. But I should want a saddle horse: I shouldn't want to take a ride on a driving horse. 6. I wish you would choose a gentle horse, because I am not [a] good horseman. 7. I should like a good saddle, but I shouldn't want spurs. 8. I never put on spurs when I ride on horseback. 9. Should you like a fast horse? 10. Yes, sir; I should prefer a fast horse, provided it is gentle.

[1] Use reflexive construction.

[2] Note that *I should like* may mean either *I should wish* (**yo quisiera**) or *it would please me* (**me gustaría**).

RESUMEN GRAMATICAL

168. — 1. Quisiera, debiera, etc., son expresiones más suaves y por lo mismo más usadas que quiero, debo, etc.

2. También se usa el condicional en este sentido.

170. Futuro (o hipotético) de subjuntivo. — Este tiempo se forma en todos los verbos añadiendo al radical de la tercera persona del pretérito (pasado absoluto) de indicativo las siguientes terminaciones: . . .

171. Uso del futuro de subjuntivo. — El futuro de subjuntivo indica una condición o hipótesis. En el español hablado hoy en día, rara vez se emplea esta forma excepto en proverbios, expresiones legales, etc. Se substituye en el lenguaje corriente por el presente de subjuntivo, o por el presente de indicativo si se usa con la conjunción condicional **si.**

173. Verbos en –uir. — Los verbos en –uir añaden a la vocal radical **u** una **y,** excepto delante de las terminaciones que empiecen por **i** o por **y.**

a. La **y** de **huyó** y **huyeron** forma parte de la terminación.

b. Se conjugan como **huir** los verbos **construir, instruir,** etc.

LESSON XXXVIII

In this Lesson and in those that follow there is a review of rules of grammar given in preceding Lessons, with the more important exceptions to the rules.

NOUNS

174. Gender of Nouns. — Nouns ending in –o are usually masculine, and those ending in –a are usually feminine.

Exceptions. — 1. The name of a male being is masculine, even if the noun ends in –a.

    el cura, parish priest   **el artista,** artist, *m.*

2. **La mano,** *hand,* is feminine, and **el día,** *day,* is masculine.

3. **El mapa,** *map*, and some words of Greek origin ending in –ma or –ta, like **el poema,** *poem*, and **el planeta,** *planet*, are masculine.[1]

175. Number of Nouns. — A noun ending in a vowel adds –s, and a noun ending in a consonant adds –es, to form the plural.

Exceptions. — 1. A noun that ends in a stressed vowel or diphthong adds –es to form the plural.

> **rubí,** ruby; **rubíes,** rubies   **rey,** king; **reyes,** kings

a. But, **mamá,** *mamma,* **papá,** *papa,* and all nouns ending in stressed –e, add only –s: **papá, papás; café,** *coffee,* **cafés,** *coffees;* **pie,** *foot,* **pies,** *feet.*

2. Nouns ending in unstressed –es or –is have the same form in the plural as in the singular.

> **lunes,** Monday, Mondays   **crisis,** crisis, crises

3. Family names generally remain unchanged in the plural.

> **Martínez, los Martínez**   **García, los García**

176. Dative of Separation. — In Spanish, verbs meaning *to take from, ask of,* and the like, take the dative of the person.

> **Pido un favor a mi padre.**   I ask a favor of my father.
> **Lo compró al señor García.**   He bought it of Mr. García.

Note also: **le pido un favor,** *I ask a favor of him;* **se lo compró,** *he bought it from him.*

177. An English noun used as an adjective is generally expressed in Spanish by a noun preceded by **de** or **para.**

> **Un reloj de oro.**   A gold watch.
> **Una taza para te.**   A teacup (**una taza de te** is *a cup of tea*).

178. Study the inflection of regular verbs of the first conjugation. (§237).

[1] Thus **el clima,** *climate,* **el idioma,** *language,* **el diploma,** *diploma,* **el programa,** *program,* **el telegrama,** *telegram,* **el tema,** *theme, written exercise,* **el cometa,** *comet* (but **la cometa,** *kite*), etc.

EXERCISES

agitado, −a, rough, agitated
agradable, pleasant, agreeable
el billete, ticket,[1] note
el buque, boat
el camarote, stateroom
la cubierta, deck
desaparecer, to disappear
la distancia, distance
la litera, berth[2]
el mar,[3] sea
marearse, to get seasick

el marinero, sailor
el muelle, wharf, dock
el oficial, officer
la ola, wave
el pasajero, passenger
la tormenta, storm
tranquilo, −a, calm, tranquil
la travesía, passage
el vapor, steam; steamboat,
steamship[4]

a bordo de, aboard; en punto, promptly, exactly; ¿qué distancia
hay de . . . ? what is the distance from . . . ? how far is it from . . . ?

A. 1. ¿Cuándo sale el vapor para Buenos Aires? 2. — Todos los días a las nueve de la mañana. 3. — ¿Hay camarotes
de primera clase? 4. — Sí, señor; hay camarotes de primera
clase y de segunda. 5. — Déme Vd. un billete (o boleto)
de primera clase. 6. Quisiera un camarote sobre cubierta
en que no haya más de (than) dos literas (o camas). 7. — Sí,
señor; aquí tiene Vd. su billete. 8. — ¿Qué distancia hay
de Montevideo a Buenos Aires? 9. — Hay cerca de doscientos (200) kilómetros. 10. — Vamos a bordo. Ya son las
ocho y media. 11. ¿Cuántos pasajeros hay a bordo?
12. — Me dijo uno de los oficiales que habrá más de dos-
cientas personas a bordo sin contar los marineros. 13. — Espero que sea agradable la travesía. 14. — Yo temo una
tormenta. Si el mar está agitado, me mareo. 15. — Pero,
hombre, ¿no ve Vd. que el mar está tranquilo? Las olas ya
desaparecieron.[5] 16. Vamos a decir adiós a nuestros amigos

[1] In several Spanish-American countries *ticket* is boleto, and *ticket agent*
is boletero. [2] Or la cama. [3] Also la mar.

[4] One also says buque de vapor for *steamboat.*

[5] Note the preterite used with ya with the force of the English present
perfect.

del (*on the*) muelle antes que salga el buque. 17. — ¡Bueno!
Yo veo a los señores de García y a los señores de González
en el muelle. 18. ¡Buen viaje! — ¡Feliz viaje! — ¡Adiós! —
¡Adiós!

B. *Contéstese.* 1–4. (*Úsense, como preguntas orales*, A. 1, 3,
8 *y* 11.) 5. ¿Preferiría Vd. un camarote bajo (*below*) cubierta
o sobre cubierta? 6. ¿Cuántas literas (*o* camas) quisiera
Vd. en el camarote? 7. ¿Cuándo se marea Vd.? 8. ¿Está
el mar tranquilo o agitado? 9. ¿Ya desaparecieron las olas?
10. ¿Cree Vd. que sea agradable la travesía? 11. ¿Quiénes
han venido al muelle para despedirse de Vds.? 12. ¿Le
gusta a Vd. la vida (*life*) a bordo de un buque? 13. ¿Quisiera
Vd. ser marinero? 14. ¿Preferiría Vd. ser pasajero?

C. *Úsese el artículo determinado correspondiente a los siguientes
nombres en ambos números, singular y plural:* libro (*por ejemplo,*
el libro, los libros), pluma, mano, día, agua, artista (*m.*),
artista (*f.*), hombre, mujer, hermano, hermana, carta, planeta,
papá, mamá, idioma, hacha, cuchara, cura, pie, inglés, martes,
canapé (*m.*: *sofa*), sinopsis (*f.*: *synopsis*), rey, señor Ortiz,
señor Heredia, rubí, frac (§114), luz, reloj, café, alma, aguja,
americana, española.

D. 1. I asked [1] the man when (a qué hora) the train would
arrive. 2. I asked the man for a ticket. 3. I asked him to give
me the ticket at once. 4. Did he buy the gold watch from Mr.
Olmedo? 5. Yes, sir; he bought it from him. 6. Did you buy
Charles' horse? 7. Did you buy this horse from Charles? 8. Did
you take (*úsese* **quitar**) it from your sister? 9. No, ma'am; I
didn't take it from her. 10. Please bring me a coffee cup.
11. Please bring me a cup of coffee. 12. And bring me also a glass
of cold water.

E. 1. To-day we leave for Buenos Aires. 2. — How far is
Buenos Aires from Montevideo? (*véase* A. 8) 3. — It is (**Hay**) two

[1] Distinguish between **preguntar,** and **pedir** or **rogar.**

hundred kilometers more or less (más o menos). 4. — Is the steamship that you will take (tomará) large or small? 5. — It is not very large, but it is fast. 6. — Have you already bought your tickets? 7. — Yes, sir; I have bought two tickets from the agent (agente o boletero), one for me and the other for my brother. 8. — I am glad that your brother is going also to Buenos Aires. 9. Where is your stateroom? — We have a stateroom on deck with two berths. 10. It is small, but it is very comfortable. 11. — Do you get seasick if the sea is rough? 12. — When the sea is rough I always get seasick, but my brother never gets seasick. 13. — When shall you go aboard the boat? 14. — I should go aboard now if I could. 15. I shall ask an officer if I may (puedo) go aboard now. 16. I shall ask him to let me go aboard at once. 17. But before going (§88, 3) aboard I should like to take leave of my friends on the wharf. 18. I see the parish priest and his old mother. 19. Do you believe (that) they have come to say goodbye to us? 20. — No, sir; they have come to take leave of Mr. and Mrs. Núñez. 21. — Do you fear a storm? — No, sir; to-day there will not be [a] storm. 22. The waves have already disappeared and the sea is calm. 23. One of the sailors told me that there will be many passengers on the ship. 24. Yes, sir; I believe (that) there will be more than two hundred persons on board, without counting the officers and the sailors.

RESUMEN GRAMATICAL

174. Género de los nombres (o substantivos). — Los nombres que en singular terminan en –o son, por regla general, masculinos; y los que terminan en –a son generalmente femeninos.

Excepciones. — 1. El nombre de hombre o animal macho es masculino aunque termine en –a.

2. **Mano** es femenino, y **día** es masculino.

3. **El mapa** y algunas palabras de origen griego que terminan en –ma o –ta son masculinos.

175. Número de los nombres. — Los nombres que terminan en vocal forman el plural añadiendo una –s, y los que terminan en consonante añadiendo –es.

Excepciones. — 1. El nombre que termina en vocal acentuada (o diptongo acentuado) forma el plural añadiendo –es.

a. Las palabras **papá** y **mamá**, y todos los nombres que terminen en –é acentuada, forman su plural añadiendo solamente –s.

2. Los nombres que terminan en –es o –is sin el acento tienen en el plural la misma forma que en el singular.

3. Los nombres patronímicos, por regla general, no varían en el plural.

176. Dativo de separación. — En español los verbos **quitar, pedir,** etc., rigen al dativo de la persona.

177. El nombre inglés usado en calidad de adjetivo se traduce al español mediante un nombre precedido de las preposiciones **de** o **para.**

LESSON XXXIX

ADJECTIVES

179. Apocopation of Adjectives. — 1. **Bueno,** *good,* **malo,** *bad,* **uno,** *one, an,* or *a,* **alguno,** *some,* **ninguno,** *no, none,* **primero,** *first,* and **tercero,** *third,* lose the final –o of the masculine singular when they precede their noun.

2. **Grande,** *great,* **santo,** *Saint,* and **ciento,** *one hundred,* generally lose the final syllable before the word they modify:

Una gran ciudad, a great city.	**Cien pesos,** one hundred dollars.
San Pablo, Saint Paul.	But, **Ciento dos pesos,** one hundred and two dollars.

a. **Santa** does not lose its final syllable: **Santa Isabel,** *Saint Elizabeth.*

180. Position of Adjectives. — To the rule that Spanish descriptive adjectives usually follow their noun, there are these exceptions:

1. A descriptive adjective usually precedes its noun if it does not distinguish one object from another but merely

names a quality characteristic of the object It is then often used in a figurative sense.

Compare:

La casa blanca.	The white house.
La blanca nieve.	The white snow.
Una voz ronca.	A hoarse voice.
El ronco trueno.	The hoarse thunder.

2. A few adjectives have one meaning before, and another after their noun.

Un gran hombre.	A great man.
Un hombre grande.	A big man.
Una pobre mujer.	A poor woman.
Una mujer pobre.	A poor (poverty-stricken) woman.
Mi caro amigo.	My dear friend.
Un caballo caro.	A dear (expensive) horse.
Varios papeles.	Several papers.
Papeles varios.	Miscellaneous papers.

181. Agreement of Adjectives. — To the rule that an adjective agrees in number with its noun, there are the following apparent exceptions:

1. If an adjective modifies several singular nouns, the plural form of the adjective is used (see §38).

2. Sometimes a plural noun is modified by several singular adjectives. This occurs when each adjective modifies only one of the individuals denoted by the noun.

Los volúmenes primero y segundo.	The first and second volumes.

(For other rules for adjectives, see: **Inflection,** — §§35, 36, 99; **Position,** — §34; **Agreement,** — §37, 38.)

182. Comparison of Adjectives. — Most Spanish adjectives form their comparative of superiority by prefixing **más,** *more,* to the positive, and their superlative by prefixing the definite article or a possessive adjective to the comparative.

Este hombre es rico.	This man is rich.
Este hombre es más rico que aquél.	This man is richer than that one.
Estos hombres son los más ricos del mundo.	These men are the richest in the world.
Juan es mi amigo más íntimo.	John is my most intimate friend.

a. When there is no real comparison, *most* may be expressed by **muy,** or the suffix –**ísimo: es muy útil,** or **es utilísimo,** *it is most useful.*

183. Study the regular verbs of the second and third conjugations (§237).

EXERCISES

además, moreover, besides
allí, there
atravesar (ie), to cross (over)
barato, –a, cheap
el **baúl,** trunk
el **cochecama,**[1] sleeping car
el **cochecomedor,** dining car
la **comodidad,** convenience
el **conocido,** acquaintance
el **cuero,** leather
el **departamento,**[2] compartment
el **dril,** duck (cloth)

expreso, express [3]
el **ferrocarril,** railway
hasta, till, to
la **lona,** canvas
la **maleta,** valise, (hand)bag
meter en, to put in *or* into
la **pampa,** prairie, plain
sacar, to take out, get (*a ticket*)
la **sierra,** mountain range, mountains
el **tranvía,** street car, tramway
viajar, to travel

el billete sencillo, one-way ticket; **el billete de ida y vuelta,**[4] round-trip ticket; **mañana por la mañana,** to-morrow morning; **pasado mañana,** the day after to-morrow; **por supuesto,** of course; **está haciendo** (o **arreglando**) **el baúl,** he is packing his trunk; **hay de todo,** there is everything; **hace mucho calor,** it is very warm; **resulta más barato,** it is cheaper;[5] **tengo ganas de,** I long to; **¿qué le parece a Vd.?** what is your opinion? what do you think (about it)? **si le parece a Vd.,** if you think best (approve).

A. 1. ¿A qué hora sale el tren para Santiago de Chile? 2. — El tren expreso (*o* rápido) sale a las nueve y diez de

---

[1] Also **el coche dormitorio, el "Pullman"** (as in Mexico), or **el "sleeping."**

[2] Or **compartimiento.**

[3] Or **rápido.**

[4] Literally, *of going and returning.*

[5] Literally, *it results cheaper.*

la mañana. 3. — ¿Qué le parece a Vd.? ¿Tomamos ese tren mañana por la mañana? 4. — No, señor; mañana no podré partir. 5. Tengo que comprar varias cosas y hacer (arreglar) el baúl. 6. Además, tengo que despedirme de varios amigos y conocidos. 7. — ¡Bueno! Partiremos pasado mañana si le parece a Vd. 8. — ¿Qué traje debe llevar uno en el tren, de lana o de dril, y qué zapatos, de cuero o de lona? 9. — Lleve Vd. traje de lana y zapatos de cuero, por supuesto. 10. El primer día hará mucho calor cuando estemos atravesando las pampas. 11. Pero cuando atravesemos la sierra, hará más frío que en el Labrador. 12. — ¿Podremos meter las maletas en los departamentos? 13. Sí; con tal que no sean muy grandes. 14 — ¿Lleva ese tren cochecama y (coche)comedor[1]? 15. — Sí; hay de todo. El tren expreso tiene todas las comodidades que podamos apetecer. 16. — ¿Qué le parece a Vd.? ¿Sería más conveniente (*better*) sacar billete sencillo (de ida nada más), o de ida y vuelta? 17. — Si Vd. piensa volver a Buenos Aires, le aconsejo que compre billete (*o* boleto) de ida y vuelta. 18. Resulta más barato que dos billetes sencillos. 19. Yo sacaré un billete sencillo hasta Santiago. 20. De Santiago paso a Valparaíso y de allí voy por (*by*) mar a los Estados Unidos. 21. Cuesta menos venir por mar desde Valparaíso a los Estados Unidos que desde Buenos Aires. 22. Además, hace mucho tiempo que tengo ganas de ver a Lima y el canal de Panamá. 23. — ¡Bueno! Mañana a las ocho y media tomaremos el tranvía para ir a la estación del ferrocarril.

B. *Contéstese.* 1–6. (*Repítanse, como preguntas orales*, A. 1, 3, 8, 12, 14, 16.) 7. ¿De quiénes tiene Vd. que despedirse antes de partir? 8. ¿A dónde va Vd. por ferrocarril? 9. Cuando Vd. parta de Santiago de Chile, ¿ a dónde irá a tomar el vapor? 10. De Valparaíso ¿a dónde irá Vd. por vapor? 11. ¿Qué ciudad tiene Vd. ganas de ver?

---

[1] Here **comedor** alone would be sufficient.

12. ¿Hace mucho tiempo que Vd. piensa visitar a Lima?
13. ¿Qué otro lugar (*place*) tiene Vd. ganas de ver?
14. ¿Tomará Vd. un automóvil para ir a la estación del ferrocarril? 15. ¿Preferiría Vd. tomar el tranvía? 16. Si Vd. prefiere el tranvía, dígame por qué lo prefiere. 17. ¿Cuál es la tarifa (*fare*) del tranvía? (*Respuesta:* La tarifa del tranvía es de cinco centavos.)

C. *Repítase, omitiendo los nombres.* 1. ¿Tiene Vd. algún amigo? (¿Tiene Vd. alguno?) 2. Tengo un amigo. 3. No tengo ningún amigo. 4–6. Tenemos el primer (el tercer, el último) volumen. 7. Él tiene cien pesos. 8. Vd. tiene un buen caballo (Vd. tiene uno bueno).

D. *Póngase en los tres grados de comparación:* aplicado, perezosa, cansados, baratas, fuerte, inteligentes.

E. *Formúlense frases que contengan* (1) *un nombre modificado por* rojo, –a; azul (*blue*); mal(o), –a; gran(de); más fácil; (2) *dos o más nombres modificados por* blancos, –as; negros, –as; pobres; caros, –as; más pobres; más caros, –as; utilísimos, –as; varios, –as.

F. 1. We shall leave Buenos Aires for Santiago de Chile the day after to-morrow. 2. The express train leaves at half-past ten in the morning. 3. Before departing we must take leave of all our friends and of some acquaintances. 4. My father will get our tickets to-morrow if they will permit him [to do] so (si se lo permiten). 5. We shall take a carriage or a motor car to (para) go to the railway station. 6. The street (tram) car would be cheaper, of course. 7. But we have a lot (un montón) of parcels and hand-bags to carry with us. 8. I should prefer to pay more and take an automobile (motor car). 9. We must buy many things before we pack (§153) our trunks. 10. I wish I could wear (Quisiera poder llevar) a duck suit and canvas shoes while we are crossing the plains. 11. It will be very warm all (the) day on the train. 12. But there will be much dust, and the suit would soon be soiled (sucio). 13. When we cross the mountains between (entre) Argentina and

Chile, it will be very cold. 14. It is cold all (the) summer in the mountains. 15. I shall wear a woolen suit and leather shoes on the train. 16. We shall travel in the sleeping car, although it is (es) dearer. 17. There will be fewer people (menos gente) and more conveniences. 18. I am glad that the train carries a dining car (lleve comedor). 19. When I travel on the train, I like to take (hacer) three meals daily. 20. I have [a] good appetite, but my poor father can not eat much. 21. My father will not get round-trip tickets, because we shall not return to Buenos Aires this year. 22. After spending (pasar) two or three weeks in Santiago, we shall leave for Lima. 23. For a long time we have wished to see (el) Cuzco in the mountains of (del) Perú. 24. And, of course, we shall be glad to see the Panama Canal. 25. Then we shall go to New York (Nueva York) or to San Francisco.

RESUMEN GRAMATICAL

179. Adjetivos apocopados. — 1. **Bueno, malo, uno, alguno, ninguno, primero** y **tercero** pierden la –o del masculino singular cuando preceden al nombre.

2. **Grande, santo** y **ciento** pierden la sílaba final cuando preceden al nombre que modifican.

a. Se exceptúa **santa** de la regla anterior.

180. Colocación de los adjetivos. — En español los adjetivos descriptivos (o calificativos) siguen al nombre que modifican, con estas excepciones:

1. El adjetivo descriptivo, por regla general, precede al nombre si simplemente señala una cualidad inherente al objeto, sin tratar de distinguirlo de otro. Dicho adjetivo tiene muchas veces un sentido figurado.

2. Algunos adjetivos varían de significado según precedan o sigan al nombre.

181. Concordancia de los adjetivos. — A la regla que dice que el adjetivo debe concertar en género y número con el nombre tenemos estas excepciones aparentes:

1. Si el adjetivo se refiere a varios nombres en singular, se pone en plural.

2. Algunas veces un nombre en plural va modificado por varios adjetivos en singular. Esto acontece solamente cuando cada adjetivo modifica a uno de los individuos expresados por el nombre.

182. Grados de comparación de los adjetivos. — Casi todos los adjetivos españoles forman su comparativo de superioridad anteponiendo **más** al positivo, y su superlativo anteponiendo el artículo determinado o un adjetivo posesivo al comparativo.

a. Cuando no se trata de verdadera comparación, la palabra *most* se traduce por **muy** o mediante la terminación **–ísimo.**

LESSON XL

184. Comparison of Adjectives, continued. — The following adjectives are compared irregularly:

bueno, mejor, el mejor, good, better, the best.
malo, peor, el peor, bad, worse, the worst.

grande { **más grande, el más grande,** large, larger, the largest.
{ **mayor, el mayor,** large, larger *or* older, the largest *or* oldest.

pequeño { **más pequeño, el más pequeño,** small, smaller, the smallest.
{ **menor, el menor,** small, smaller *or* younger, the smallest *or* youngest

mucho, más, much, more *or* most.
poco, menos, little (few), less (fewer) *or* least (fewest).

a. **Mayor** means *larger* and **menor,** *smaller,* in quantitative expressions such as **en mayor (menor) cantidad,** *in larger (smaller) quantity.*
When applied to persons, **mayor** means *older,* and **menor,** *younger.*
b. *Most,* used with a noun or pronoun, is generally expressed by **la mayor parte (de): la mayor parte de mis libros,** *most of my books.*

185. Spanish adverbs are compared like Spanish adjectives.

aprisa, más aprisa, (lo) más aprisa, fast, faster, (the) fastest.

a. The article is used with a superlative adverb only when the adverb is followed by **posible** or a like expression: **Pablo es quien más estudia,** *Paul is the one who studies most;* **llegué lo más pronto posible,** *I came as soon as possible.*

186. The following adverbs are compared irregularly:

bien, mejor, (lo) mejor, well, better, (the) best.
mal, peor, (lo) peor, badly, worse, (the) worst.
mucho, más, (lo) más, much (a great deal), more, (the) most.
poco, menos, (lo) menos, little, less, (the) least.

187. Correlative *the . . . the,* followed by comparatives, is usually expressed in Spanish by **cuanto . . . (tanto).** **Tanto** is often omitted.

Cuanto más gana, (tanto) más gasta.	The more he earns, the more he spends.
Cuanto menos tiene, menos quiere.	The less he has, the less he wants.

a. The . . . the may also be expressed by **mientras . . . —,** with which **tanto** is never used: **mientras más gana, más gasta,** *the more he earns, the more he spends.*

188. Than. — 1. *Than* is usually expressed by **que.**

Juan es más alto que María.	John is taller than Mary.

2. Before a numeral, *more than* and *less than* are expressed by **más de** and **menos de.**

Hemos gastado más de cien pesos.	We have spent more than one hundred dollars.
Ella tiene menos de diez años.	She is less than ten years old.

3. Before a clause (containing a verb), *than* is usually **de lo que;** but *than* is **del que** (or, **de la que, de los que, de las que**) when the noun object of the principal verb is understood after **del** (or, **de la, de los, de las**).

Hace más frío de lo que Vd. cree.	It is colder than (what) you think.
Tenemos más libros de los que teníamos.	We have more books than (the books which) we used to have.

186. Study the inflection of the radical-changing verbs of the first class (§§ 244–245), including **errar** and **oler** (§ 247), and **jugar** (§ 249).

EXERCISES

anoche, last night
asustar, to frighten
bajar(se), to descend, alight, get out
el barrio, part (*of a city*), suburb
bastante, enough; **bastante bueno,** good enough
centígrado, –a, centigrade
cuarenta, forty
derecho, –a, *adj.*, straight, right; *adv.*, straight ahead
desagradable, unpleasant, disagreeable
desde, since (*in time*)
doblar, to turn (*a corner, etc.*)

equivaler, to be equivalent
la esquina, corner
izquierdo, –a, left
luego, soon, then
la neblina, fog
nevar (ie), to snow
la nieve, snow
relampaguear, to lighten
el sol, sun
soportar, to endure, support
tanto, so much, as much
la temperatura, temperature
el termómetro, thermometer
tronar (ue), to thunder
el viento, wind

seguir derecho, to go straight ahead; la casa de huéspedes, boarding house; hace buen (mal) tiempo, the weather is good (bad); hace viento, it is windy; no más . . . que, only

A. 1. ¿Me hace Vd. el favor de indicarme un buen hotel? 2. — Con mucho gusto. En mi opinión, el mejor es el Hotel A. que da a la Puerta del Sol en la esquina de la calle de B. 3. Para ir al Hotel A., toma Vd. el tranvía que pasa por aquí y baja Vd. en la Puerta del Sol. 4. O si prefiere ir a pie, Vd. sigue derecho hasta llegar a la iglesia. 5. Y luego dobla (la esquina de) la primera calle a su derecha (a su izquierda [1]). 6. Si Vd. busca una casa de huéspedes, hallará las mejores en C., el barrio más de moda de la población. 7. Yo viví muchos años en la casa número 18 de la calle de D., a poca distancia de la Puerta del Sol. 8. Me gusta mucho Madrid, pero no me gusta su clima. 9. En el verano hace mucho calor y en el invierno mucho frío. 10. No puedo soportar los calores [2] del verano ni los fríos del invierno. 11. Más me

---

[1] **Mano** is understood.

[2] Note the plural forms when used in this sense.

EL PALACIO REAL, MADRID

General view of the Royal Palace, one of the most imposing edifices of the Spanish capital.

LA BIBLIOTECA DEL ESCORIAL
A view of the library of the Escorial. This famous old monastery
was built during the reign of Philip the Second in the
sixteenth century.

gusta el clima de Málaga, donde no hace ni frío ni calor.
12. En mi opinión, la primavera es la mejor estación del
año en España. 13. Hay menos neblina que en el otoño
y no llueve tanto. 14. El invierno de Nueva York es también malísimo. 15. Ayer hizo un tiempo bastante bueno.
16. Pero anoche no hizo más que relampaguear, tronar y
llover toda la noche. 17. Hoy hace mal tiempo. Nieva
desde la mañana, y ahora hace tanto viento que no puedo
salir a la calle. 18. El viento y la nieve son muy desagra-
dables. 19. Mañana el termómetro centígrado marcará
(*will show*) diez y ocho grados bajo cero. 20. Diez y ocho
grados centígrados bajo cero equivalen aproximadamente
(*approximately*) a cero Fahrenheit.

B. 1. En su opinión ¿cuál es el mejor hotel de la población? 2. ¿A qué plaza da? 3. ¿Puedo tomar el tranvía
para ir a ese hotel? 4. ¿En dónde he de bajar? 5. Si
prefiero ir a pie, ¿qué dirección debo tomar? 6. ¿Dónde
podría hallar una buena casa de huéspedes? 7. ¿Cuál es
el número de la casa en que vivió Vd. tantos años? 8. ¿Está
cerca de la Puerta del Sol? 9–10. ¿Sabe Vd. por qué no
me gusta (por qué me gusta) el clima de Madrid (Málaga)?
11. ¿Cuál es la mejor estación del año en España? 12. ¿Por
qué? 13. ¿Hizo buen tiempo ayer? 14. ¿Relampagueó
anoche? 15. ¿Le asustan a Vd. los relámpagos (*lightning*)?
16. ¿También tronó? 17. ¿Le asustan a Vd. los truenos
(*thunder*)? 18. ¿Y llovió después? 19. Cuanto más relampagueó y tronó, (tanto) más llovió, ¿verdad? 20. ¿Le
gusta a Vd. la lluvia? 21. ¿Está nevando hoy? 22. Pues
(*Well then*), hoy hace más frío de lo que hacía ayer, ¿verdad? 23. ¿Le gusta a Vd. la nieve? 24. ¿Cuántos grados
bajo cero (o sobre cero) marca ahora el termómetro?
25–26. ¿A qué temperatura Fahrenheit (centígrada) hierve
el agua? [1]

[1] 212 ° (100) °.

27. ¿A qué temperatura Fahrenheit (centígrada) se congela (*freezes*) el agua? [1]   28. Conque (*So that*) nueve grados Fahrenheit equivalen a cinco grados centígrados, ¿no es verdad?

C. *Dense los tres grados de comparación de los adjetivos* grande, fuerte, malo, hermosa, buena, ricos, y pequeñas; *y de los adverbios* bien, pronto, y mal.

D. 1. Most men are lazy. 2. This is the most interesting (**interesante**) lesson of all. 3. And it is the most useful. 4. Charles is taller than Anna. 5. She is older than he. 6. But he is larger than she. 7. She is more than twenty years old. 8. It is colder than I thought. 9. It is warmer than it was yesterday. 10. The colder it is, the more I like it. 11. The more it thunders, the more it rains. 12. The more I have, the more I want. 13. The less you study, the less you will know. 14. The earlier he comes (**llegue**), the better. 15. The faster she wrote, the more mistakes she made. 16. John has fewer friends than he had (**tenía**) last year. 17. Mary has more friends (*f.*) than she used to have. 18. We receive more letters than we received last summer. 19. We received more than ten this morning.

E. 1. Do you prefer a boarding house to a hotel? 2. Yes, sir; I prefer a boarding house because it is less dear. 3. And in my opinion the cooking (**la cocina**) is better in a good boarding house. 4. Do you believe that Mrs. Hernández's boarding house is the best in (**de la**) town? 5. It is one of the best; but I do not say (that) it is the best of all. 6. As a rule, the more you pay, the better the cooking is (= is the cooking). 7. Please direct me to Mrs. Hernández's boarding house. 8. With great pleasure. You go straight ahead until you come (*úsese* **llegar**) to the church that is on the corner of Preciados Street. 9. Then you turn the corner and follow Preciados Street until you come to a large house that is on the corner of M. Street. 10. The number of the house is 25. 11. You will find the boarding house (that) you are looking for on the main floor of this house. 12. The rooms (**las habitaciones**)

---

[1] 32 ° (cero).

and the bed linen (**la ropa de cama**) are clean, and the cooking
is good. 13. Thank you very much!   (¡**Muchísimas gracias!**)
Can I take the street car to go to that (**esa**) house? 14. Yes, sir;
the street car passes near the house. 15. You get out at (**en**) the
corner of M. Street. 16. In (the) summer it is warm in Madrid,
but I believe (that) it is still (**aun**) warmer in New York. 17. The
heat does not trouble (*úsese* **molestar**) me so much as the thunder
and lightning during the electric storms. 18. But I like the rains
in (the) summer, because after raining there is less dust (**polvo**).
19. Last night it lightened and thundered and rained all (the)
night. 20. I should prefer (the) snow, as (**pues**) it doesn't lighten
and thunder when it snows. 21. This morning the thermometer
showed a temperature of thirty degrees centigrade. 22. It is
warmer than it was last summer. 23. The warmer it is, the more
I like it.

RESUMEN GRAMATICAL

184. Grados de comparación de los adjetivos, continuación. —
Bueno, malo, grande, pequeño, mucho y **poco** forman su comparativo de una manera irregular.

a. **Mayor** significa " más grande " y **menor** " más pequeño " tra-
tándose de expresiones de cantidad. Cuando se aplican a personas, el
mayor significa el " de mayor edad " y el **menor** el " de menor edad."

b. *Most,* usado con un nombre o pronombre, se traduce al español
por **la mayor parte (de).**

185. En español los adverbios forman su comparativo del
mismo modo que los adjetivos.

a. El artículo se usa con el adverbio en grado superlativo solamente
cuando el adverbio va seguido de la palabra **posible** u otra expresión
semejante.

186. Bien, mal, mucho y **poco** forman su comparativo de una
manera irregular.

187. El correlativo *the . . . the* seguido de un comparativo se
traduce por **cuanto . . . (tanto). Tanto** se omite generalmente.

a. *The . . . the* puede expresarse también por **mientras . . . —.**

188. *Than.*—1. *Than* se traduce generalmente por **que.**

2. Las expresiones *more than* y *less than* antepuestas a un adjetivo numeral se traducen por **más de** y **menos de.**

3. Ante una cláusula (que contenga verbo), *than* es generalmente **de lo que;** pero *than* es **del que** (o, **de la que, de los que, de las que**) cuando el nombre que es el complemento del verbo principal se sobrentiende detrás de **del** (o, **de la, de los, de las**).

LESSON XLI

PERSONAL PRONOUNS

190. The Spanish personal pronouns used as the subject or object of verbs are:

SINGULAR

SUBJECT	DIRECT OBJECT	INDIRECT OBJECT
yo, I	**me,** me	**me,** to me
tú, thou	**te,** thee	**te,** to thee
m. **él,** he, it	**le** or **lo,**[1] him, it	
f. **ella,** she, it	**la,** her, it	**le** { to him, to her / to it (**la,** to her) }
n. **ello,** it	**lo,** it	

PLURAL

SUBJECT	DIRECT OBJECT	INDIRECT OBJECT
nosotros, –as, we	**nos,** us	**nos,** to us
vosotros, –as, ye	**os,** you	**os,** to you
ellos, –as, they	*m.* **los** } them / *f.* **las**	**les,** to them (**las,** to them, *f.*)

a. **Ello** is rarely used as the subject of a verb, except in the expression **ello es que . . .,** *the fact is that.* . . . English *it,* as subject, is usually not expressed at all in Spanish. As direct object, *it* is **lo** (*m.*) or **la** (*f.*) when it refers to a definite thing, and **lo** (*n.*) when it refers to a statement or idea.

Relampaguea, llueve, nieva.	It lightens, rains, snows.
Hallé el libro: lo hallé.	I found the book: I found it.

[1] See §79, footnote.

Vendí la casa: la vendí.	I sold the house: I sold it.
No lo creemos.	We do not believe it.

b. The feminine dative forms **la,** *to her,* and **las,** *to them,* are often used, but their use is not sanctioned by the Spanish Academy.

See also §§42, 51, 75–77, 79, 80.

191.   Usted, −es

SINGULAR

SUBJECT	DIRECT OBJECT	INDIRECT OBJECT
usted, you	*m.* le or lo ⎫ you *f.* la ⎭	le ⎫ to you le (la) ⎭

PLURAL

SUBJECT	DIRECT OBJECT	INDIRECT OBJECT
ustedes, you	*m.* los ⎫ you *f.* las ⎭	les ⎫ to you les (las) ⎭

a. **Usted** and **ustedes** are of the second person in meaning, but they require the verb in the third person.

192. Se, *himself, herself, oneself, itself, yourself; themselves, yourselves* (see §77).

1. **Se,** with a singular verb, sometimes has the force of English *one, people,* etc., used as indefinite pronouns.

Se dice.	One says.
Se cree que es verdad.	People believe that it is true.

2. Some intransitive verbs may be used as reflexives, with change of meaning.

ir, to go	**dormir,** to sleep
irse, to go away	**dormirse,** to fall asleep

193. Study the inflection of the radical-changing verbs of the second and third classes (§§250–251).

EXERCISES

el **aceite,** oil
el **ascensor,** lift, elevator [1]
el **azúcar,** sugar
el **bizcocho,** biscuit [2]
la **carne de carnero,** mutton
la **cucharita,** teaspoon
descansar, to rest
el **despacho,** office
el **fósforo,** match [3]
fresco, –a, fresh
el **guisante,** pea [4]

el **jarro,** jug, "pitcher"
la **lechuga,** lettuce
la **nuez,** (English) walnut
la **pasta de guayaba,** guava marmalade
la **pimienta,** pepper
la **sal,** salt
el **servicio,** service
el **vinagre,** vinegar
el **vino tinto,** red wine

en buen orden, in good order; **en primer lugar,** in the first place; **tengo (mucha) hambre,** I am (very) hungry; **tengo (mucha) sed,** I am (very) thirsty; **tengo (mucho) sueño,** I am (very) sleepy; **tengo cuidado,** I am careful; **¡tenga Vd. cuidado!** be careful! look out! **pierda Vd. cuidado,** do not worry

A. 1. Después de pasearnos a pie toda la tarde teníamos mucha hambre. 2. Entramos en un hotel y nos dirigimos al comedor. 3. El mozo (camarero) vino y nos dió la lista. 4. Mientras leíamos la lista, el mozo puso sobre la mesa un mantel limpio, servilletas, platos, vasos, cuchillos, tenedores, cucharas para sopa, cucharitas, sal, pimienta, azúcar, aceite y vinagre. 5. En primer lugar pedimos los platos siguientes: sopa, pescado y ensalada de lechuga. 6. Después pedimos carne de carnero asada, papas (patatas) y guisantes. 7. Por regla general, prefiero la carne de vaca (de res) a la carne de carnero. 8. Pero hoy no había más que carne de carnero. 9. El mozo (camarero) nos trajo pan y vino tinto sin pedirlo nosotros (*without our ordering*). 10. Para mí (*For my part*) lo más difícil es escoger los pos-

---

[1] Or **el elevador** (as in Mexico).   [2] Or **galleta.**
[3] The little wax matches, so common in Latin countries, are generally called **cerillas** in Spanish (but are called **cerillos** in Mexico).
[4] Or **chícharo** (as in Mexico and some other Spanish-American countries).

tres.   11. Hoy pedí pasta de guayaba, bizcochos, queso,
nueces y café. 12. Después de la comida pagamos la cuenta
y dimos una propina al mozo. 13. Fuimos al despacho y
pedimos un cuarto. 14. Estábamos cansados y queríamos
descansar. 15. Pedimos un cuarto grande y cómodo con
ventanas que dieran a la plaza, con dos buenas camas, con
sus sábanas blancas y limpias, almohadas de pluma y frazadas (mantas) de lana. 16. Subimos al tercer piso en el ascensor y entramos en el cuarto. 17. El criado lo había puesto
todo en buen orden. 18. Nos trajo una vela y fósforos, un
jarro de agua fresca y vasos. 19. Se dice que la comida, las
habitaciones y el servicio de este hotel son excelentes.

B. *Contéstese.* 1. ¿Por qué tenían Vds. mucha hambre?
2. ¿En dónde entraron Vds. y a dónde se dirigieron?
3. ¿Dónde se sentaron Vds.? 4. ¿Qué les dió el mozo?
5. ¿Qué puso él sobre la mesa? 6. ¿Qué pidieron Vds. en
primer lugar? 7. ¿Qué pidieron Vds. después? 8. ¿Prefiere
Vd. la carne de carnero a la carne de vaca (de res)? 9. ¿Qué
cosas les trajo el mozo sin pedirlo Vds.? 10. ¿Qué postres
pidieron Vds.? 11. Después de pagar la cuenta, ¿qué le
dieron Vds. al mozo? 12. ¿A dónde fueron Vds. en seguida?
13. ¿Qué clase de cuarto pidieron Vds.? 14. ¿En qué subie-
ron Vds. al tercer piso? 15. ¿Qué les trajo el mozo? 16. ¿Se
dice que son excelentes la comida, las habitaciones y el servicio de este hotel?

C. 1. It is true. 2. It is raining. 3. I don't believe it. 4. I
doubt it. 5. Did you buy the horse? — I bought it. 6. Did you
sell the bicycle (**la bicicleta**)? — I sold it. 7. It is said to be (**que
es**) true. 8. Spanish is spoken here. 9. The house is warmed with
steam. 10. Coal is burned in the furnace. 11. We went to bed
at ten o'clock. 12. We got up at seven o'clock.

D. *Tradúzcase cada frase cuatro veces, usando* (1) **tú,** (2) **usted,**
(3) **vosotros, –as,** *y* (4) **ustedes,** *o los pronombres complementarios*

correspondientes. 1. You (*m.*) are tired. 2. You (*f.*) are ill. 3. He saw you (*m.*) yesterday. 4. I saw you (*f.*) this morning. 5. We told you the truth. 6. We gave you a present. 7. You fell asleep. 8. Did you go away?

E. 1. I am very tired and I am very hungry. 2. We have walked about (**por la**) town all (**the**) day. 3. It is said that they serve excellent meals in the restaurant of this hotel. 4. Should you like to dine here, or should you prefer to go to another restaurant? 5. — No, sir; I am tired of walking about town, and I should prefer to dine here. 6. Waiter! — I am coming (*véase XVIII*, D. 2 y 3), sir. What do the gentlemen wish? 7. — Bring me soup and fish, and let (§148) the soup be hot. 8. — Wouldn't the gentlemen wish salad? To-day we have a good lettuce salad. 9. — Bring us salad after the fish, and bring us oil and vinegar. 10. I like a lot of oil on (**en**) the salad, but I don't like pepper. 11. — Do the gentlemen wish beef or mutton? — Bring us beef and fried (**fritas**) potatoes. 12. — Very well! (**¡Está bien!**), sir; soup, fish, lettuce salad, roast beef, and fried potatoes. 13. Do the gentlemen wish red wine or white wine? 14. — I like (the) red wine, but my friend prefers (the) white. 15. Waiter! Please bring me another napkin: this [one] is torn. 16. — Here is (**Aquí tiene Vd.**) another, sir. Do the gentlemen wish dessert? 17. — Bring us a small cup (**una tacita**) [1] of coffee, and cheese and biscuits. 18. As (**De**) [a] tip how much shall we give the waiter? 19. — The dinner will cost two dollars. Let us give him twenty cents. 20. Let us go to the hotel office (= the office of the hotel) and ask for a room. 21. — On the second floor we have a large room, with two beds, that faces the square. 22. — Is there [an] elevator in this hotel? — No, sir; I am sorry to say (that) there isn't any elevator. 23. I could give you a good room on the first floor if you would prefer it. 24. — Very well! Let's go to bed: I am very sleepy. 25. Please send (**mandar**) to the room a jug of water and glasses. 26. — Very well, sir, and I shall also send some matches and a candle. 27. Good night, sirs. May (§150, *b:* *úsese* **que**) you sleep well.

[1] Diminutive of **taza.**

RESUMEN GRAMATICAL

190. Pronombres personales. — Los pronombres personales españoles usados como sujeto o complemento son los siguientes: . . .

a. **Ello** rara vez se usa como sujeto del verbo, excepto en la expresión **ello es que.** El *it* inglés, como sujeto, casi nunca se traduce al español. Como complemento directo, *it* equivale a lo (para el masculino) y **la** (para el femenino) cuando se refiere a una cosa determinada y concreta, y **lo** (para el neutro) cuando se refiere a una expresión o idea.

b. Las formas femeninas del dativo **la** y **las** se usan a menudo; pero su uso no está sancionado por la Real Academia.

191. Usted, –es: . . .

a. **Usted** y **ustedes** son, por su significado, de la segunda persona, pero piden el verbo en la tercera persona.

192. 1. **Se,** usado con un verbo en singular, equivale frecuentemente a *one, people,* etc., en inglés, usados como pronombres indefinidos.

2. Algunos verbos intransitivos pueden usarse como reflexivos, cambiando entonces de significado.

LESSON XLII

194. Personal Pronouns, continued. — Spanish object-pronouns usually precede their verb.

But an object-pronoun follows its verb and is attached to it when the verb is an infinitive, a present participle, or an affirmative imperative (or subjunctive used imperatively). See §§88, 2; 143; 85, 1 and 2.

a. If the sentence or clause begins with the verb, the object-pronoun may follow, but this rarely occurs in colloquial Spanish:

> **pláceme, dice el juez,** *it pleases me, says the judge.*

195. Reflexive **se,** whether direct or indirect object, always precedes another object-pronoun.

> **Se me figura.**   It seems to me.

See also § 80, 2.

196. Prepositional Forms of the Personal Pronouns. — When personal pronouns are governed by a preposition, the following forms are used:

1.
Singular	Plural
mí, me	nosotros, -as, us
ti, thee	vosotros, -as, you
m. él, him, it	
f. ella, her, it	ellos, -as, them
n. ello, it	

2. **Usted, -es,** *you,* and **sí,** *himself, herself,* etc., are also used with prepositions.

a. With me is **conmigo**; *with thee* is **contigo**; and *with himself, herself,* etc., is **consigo.**[1]

See also §§81–82.

197. If English *myself, thyself, himself,* etc., are emphatic, they are to be expressed in Spanish by the reflexive pronoun in the prepositional form, modified by **mismo** (–a, –os, –as).

Me engaño a mí mismo (–a).	1 deceive myself.
Ella se burla de sí misma.	She makes fun of herself.

198. In the plural a reflexive verb may become reciprocal. Usually no distinction of form is made in Spanish between reflexive and reciprocal verbs; thus, **nos engañamos** may mean *we deceive ourselves,* or *we deceive each other* or *one another.* But a reciprocal verb may be made explicit by the use of **el uno al** (**del**) **otro, unos a** (**de**) **otros,** etc.

Se engañan el uno al otro.	They deceive each other.
Se burlan unas de otras.	They make fun of one another.

199. The definite article is required before a noun used in apposition with a personal pronoun.

Nosotros los alumnos deseamos una vacación.	We students desire a vacation.
Ustedes las señoras nunca murmuran unas de otras.	You women never gossip about one another.

[1] Latin *mecum, tecum,* and *secum* became *migo, tigo,* and *sigo* in Old Spanish, and later the preposition *con* was prefixed.

200. Study the inflection of the inceptive and the –uir verbs (§§255, 256).

EXERCISES

el **acróbata,** acrobat

el **actor,** actor; la **actriz,** actress

el **anuncio,** advertisement

el **artista,** la **artista,** artist

el **cinematógrafo** (el "**cine**"), motion pictures ("movies")

la **comedia,** comedy, play

desocupado, –a, unoccupied

divertirse (ie), to enjoy oneself

la **entrada,** entrance, admission

estrenar, to perform *or* give (*a play, etc.*) for the first time

la **fila,** row

la **función,** performance

la **galería,**[1] balcony (*in theater*), gallery

la **butaca (de patio),** seat in "orchestra" *or* "pit"

ocupado, –a, occupied

el **palco,** box

el **periódico,** (news)paper

quedar, to remain

el **sainete,** farce

el **telón,** curtain (*of theater*)

la **tragedia,** tragedy

la **zarzuela,** operetta, musical comedy

el **teatro de variedades,** vaudeville theater; **¡ya lo creo!** I should say so! **no tardará en volver,** it will not be long before he returns; **se hace tarde,** it is getting late

A. 1. ¿Qué le parece a Vd.? ¿Vamos al teatro o a la ópera esta noche? 2. — Sí, señor; yo quisiera ir al teatro a divertirme. 3. — Carlos, tráigame el periódico de la mañana: quiero leer los anuncios de los teatros. 4. Si Vd. quiere divertirse, lo mejor será que no vaya a ver ninguna tragedia. 5. — No, señor; vamos a ver una comedia o un sainete, o una zarzuela si le gusta a Vd. la música. 6. — ¿Qué le parece? Vamos a un teatro de variedades donde haya acróbatas. 7. — No, señor; entre nosotros prefiero el cinematógrafo (el "cine") al teatro de variedades. 8. — ¡Bueno! Aquí tengo el anuncio de una función en el Teatro de Calderón. 9. Esta noche se estrena una nueva comedia de los hermanos Álvarez Quintero. 10. Si le parece a Vd., iremos, ¿eh? 11. — ¿Sabe Vd. cuánto cuesta la entrada? 12. — Butaca con entrada cuesta dos pesos; asiento en la galería (el

[1] Or **anfiteatro** (as in Madrid).

anfiteatro) con entrada, un peso. 13. Un asiento de palco
costaría más, por supuesto. 14. No somos bastante ricos
para ir a palco. 15. — ¿Y a qué hora se levanta el telón?
— A las ocho en punto. 16. — ¿Y hay buenos actores
(o artistas)? — ¡Ya lo creo! los mejores del país. 17. — ¡Está
bien! Vamos a tomar los billetes, porque ya son las siete y
cuarto. 18. Yo preferiría una butaca de la primera fila si
no están todas ocupadas. 19. — Temo que no quede
desocupada ninguna butaca de la primera fila, pero vere-
mos. 20. — Y después del teatro iremos al Café Real a
cenar, si le parece. 21. ¡Vamos! ¡Apresúrese Vd., que
(for) se hace tarde! No tardará en levantarse el telón.

B. *Contéstese.* 1. ¿Le gusta a Vd. ir al teatro? 2. ¿A qué
teatro quisiera Vd. ir? 3. ¿En dónde se pueden leer los
anuncios del teatro? 4. ¿Qué quiere Vd. ver, tragedia,
sainete, o zarzuela? 5. ¿Por qué? 6. ¿Le gusta a Vd. ir
al teatro de variedades? 7. ¿Por qué? 8. ¿Le gusta a Vd
el cinematógrafo (el "cine")? 9. ¿Por qué? 10. ¿Habrá
función esta noche en el Teatro de Calderón? 11. ¿Se estrena
una nueva comedia? 12. ¿Quiénes son los autores (*authors*)
de la comedia? 13. ¿Cuánto cuesta la entrada? 14. ¿A
qué hora se levanta el telón? 15. ¿Hay buenos actores (o
artistas)? 16. ¿En dónde preferiría Vd. sentarse? 17. ¿Cree
Vd. que queden desocupadas algunas butacas de la primera
fila? 18. Después del teatro, ¿a dónde iremos? 19. ¿A qué?
20. ¿Se hace tarde? 21. ¿Tardará en levantarse el telón?

C. 1. Give it to Ferdinand. 2. Give it to him. 3. Do not
give it to Ferdinand. 4. Do not give it to him. 5. Give it to *me*.
6. Do not give it to *me*. 7. Tell the truth to *me*. 8. Do not tell
it to *her*. 9. Bring me a napkin. 10. I shall bring it to you at
once. 11. Do not bring me a torn napkin. 12. He likes it. 13. She
does not like it. 14. I wish to do so (lo). 15. You are (está) doing
so now. 16. He presented himself to me. 17. Does it seem (*úsese
figurarse*) to you that it is possible? 18. Come with me. 19. I

can't go with you (*2a pers. fam.*). 20. Have you a letter for me?
21. I haven't any letter for you (*2a pers. fam.*). 22. John deceives
himself. 23. Charles makes fun of himself. 24. They deceive each
other. 25. They make fun of each other. 26. You students ought
to study more. 27. Men should never gossip about one another.
28. I agree to (**Convengo en**) it. 29. I insist upon (**Insisto en**) it.

D. 1. Have you read the advertisements of the theaters in the
afternoon paper? 2. — I have read all [of] them in the morning
paper. 3. At (**En**) the Calderon Theater a new tragedy by Jacinto
Benavente is given for the first time to-night. Should you like to
see it? 4. — No, sir; I want to enjoy myself, and I should prefer
a comedy or a farce. 5. — Well (**Pues**) a musical comedy is given
(**se representa**) to-night at the Lyric (**Lírico**) Theater. We'll go
there, if you think best. 6. — *I* don't like the music of musical
comedies. I prefer [grand] opera. 7. — All right! Let's go and
(**a**) see a farce by the Álvarez Quintero brothers. I enjoy greatly
(**Me divierto muchísimo con**) their comedies and farces. 8. — Will
there be [a] performance to-night? — I should say so! There is
[a] performance every night (**todas las noches**). 9. — Should
you like to take a box? — No, sir; we aren't rich enough to take
a box. 10. Let's take an orchestra seat or a seat in the first row of
the balcony. 11. — How much does a seat in the first row [to-
gether] with admission cost? 12. — As a rule it costs a dollar, but
it is dearer to-night. 13. According to the advertisement, it will
cost a dollar and [a] half to-night. 14. — And when (**a qué hora**)
does the curtain rise? — Promptly at half-past eight. 15. — Then
(**Pues**) we must hurry. It will not be long before the performance
begins. 16. Yesterday I went to a vaudeville theater. The performance was wretched (**malísima**). 17. There was a Spanish
actress who sang very well, and a Japanese (**japonés**) acrobat
who did well enough. 18. But the rest (**lo demás**) of the performance was not good. 19. To (**Para**) tell the truth, between us,
I prefer motion pictures to a vaudeville performance (= a performance of vaudeville). 20. All right! Let's hurry, for it's
getting late, and I want a seat in the first row. 21. We haven't
taken tickets yet. I fear that all the best seats may already be

occupied. 22. Let's catch (*úsese* **tomar**) the street (tram) car that is coming up the street.

RESUMEN GRAMATICAL

194. Pronombres personales, continuación. — En español los pronombres complementarios preceden generalmente al verbo.

Pero el pronombre complementario sigue al verbo y va unido a él si está en infinitivo, participio presente, o imperativo (o subjuntivo usado con el carácter de imperativo) afirmativo.

a. Si la frase o cláusula empieza con el verbo, el pronombre complementario puede seguirle, pero esto ocurre rara vez en el lenguaje usual.

195. El reflexivo **se,** ya sea como complemento directo o indirecto, siempre precede a los otros pronombres complementarios.

196. Formas de los pronombres personales con preposición. — Cuando los pronombres personales van regidos por una preposición se usan las siguientes formas: 1. **mí, ti, él, ella, ello, nosotros –as, vosotros –as, ellos –as.**

2. **Usted** y **sí** también se usan con preposiciones.

a. Cuando **con** se usa con **mí, ti,** o **sí,** la preposición y el pronombre se unen formando una sola palabra, y la combinación termina con la sílaba **–go.**

197. Si las expresiones inglesas *myself, thyself, himself,* etc., son enfáticas, deben traducirse al español mediante el pronombre reflexivo con preposición, modificado por **mismo** (–a, –os, –as).

198. En el plural un verbo reflexivo puede volverse recíproco. Por regla general, en español no se hace distinción de forma entre los verbos recíprocos y reflexivos; así, por ejemplo, **nos engañamos** puede significar "nos engañamos a nosotros mismos" o "nos engañamos el uno al otro." Pero un verbo recíproco puede hacerse explícito mediante las expresiones **el uno al (del) otro, unos a (de) otros,** etc.

199. El artículo determinado se requiere ante un nombre usado en aposición con un pronombre personal.

LESSON XLIII

201.   Definite Article

	MASCULINE	FEMININE	NEUTER
Sing.	el	la (el)	lo
Pl.	los	las	

1. The feminine **el** is used only immediately before a noun beginning with stressed **a–** or **ha–** (§96).

2. Neuter **lo** is used with neuter adjectives that have the force of abstract nouns (§98); with neuter pronouns (**lo mismo,** *the same,* **lo cual,** *which,* etc.); with adverbs (**por lo menos,** *at least,* **lo más aprisa posible,** *as fast as possible*); and in such idiomatic expressions as **sabemos lo buena que es,** *we know how good she is.*

202. The definite article is required: 1. With an adjective of nationality used to denote a language, except after **hablar** or **en** (§100); with a noun used in a general sense to denote all of the thing or kind it names (§103, 1); with a proper noun modified by a title or a descriptive adjective, except in direct address (§103, 2); instead of a possessive adjective, when speaking of parts of the body or articles of clothing, etc. (§107); with expressions of time modified by **próximo, pasado,** and the like (§123).

2. With some names of countries. These include all geographic names modified by an adjective, such as **los Estados Unidos,** *the United States,* and also some others including the following:

      el **Brasil,** *Brazil*   el **Japón,** *Japan*
      el **Canadá,** *Canada*   el **Perú,** *Peru*
      el **Ecuador,** *Ecuador*

a. Names of cities, as a rule, do not take the article, but to this rule, **la Habana,** *Havana,* and a few others are exceptions.

And the article may be used:

3. To modify an infinitive or a subject clause.

El hablar demasiado es un vicio.	To talk too much is a vice.
Me enfada el que Vd. no quiera hacerlo.	It angers me that you are not willing to do it.

4. To express measure.

Diez centavos la docena.	Ten cents a dozen.
A peso el metro.	(At) a dollar a meter.

203. Study the changes in spelling that occur in the inflection of verbs (§§ 239–243).

EXERCISES

amarillo, –a, yellow	lindo, –a, pretty
la avena, oats	el maíz, maize, Indian corn
claro, –a, clear, bright	la manzana, apple
el corral, yard	la naranja, orange
detrás de, behind	el nido, nest
en frente de, before	el pájaro, bird
la gallina, hen	la pera, pear
el grano, grain	el pez, (*living*) fish
la hacienda, large farm, plantation	el plátano, banana
la huerta, garden [1]	el trigo, wheat
el huevo, egg	las verduras, fresh vegetables
la legumbre, vegetable	vigilar, to watch over, guard

echar de menos, to miss (*a person or thing*); poco faltó para que se cayera, he almost fell; poner huevos, to lay eggs; ¿qué ha sido de él? what has become of him?

A. 1. No nos gusta la vida de la ciudad durante la estación de los calores. 2. Nuestra familia tiene una hacienda a quince kilómetros de la ciudad y allí pasamos el verano todos los años. 3. Nos divertimos más en el campo que en la ciudad. 4. Tenemos caballos de silla y nos paseamos a caballo casi todos los días. 5. Mi hermana no

---

[1] In some countries, as in Mexico, a *vegetable garden* is called **hortaliza. Jardín** usually means *flower garden.*

tiene caballo, porque no le gusta montar. 6. La primera
vez que montó a caballo poco faltó para que se cayera, y
no ha querido montar después. 7. A poca distancia de la
casa hay muchos peces en un hermoso lago de agua fresca
y clara. 8. Nos divertimos mucho pescando en este lago.
9. En un jardín en frente de la casa tenemos lindas flores
blancas, amarillas, azules y rojas. 10. Detrás de la casa
hay una huerta en la cual (*in which*) se cultivan muchas
clases de frutas y legumbres (verduras). 11. En mi opinión,
las manzanas y las peras son las mejores frutas. 12. Siento
mucho que en este clima no se produzcan frutas tropicales como la naranja, el plátano y la guayaba. 13. En un
corral hay gallinas blancas a las cuales echamos grano.
Ponen muchos huevos. 14. Los pájaros hacen su nido en
un árbol muy grande que está cerca de la casa. 15. Los
labradores, que cultivan los campos, se levantan temprano y
trabajan todo el día. 16. Cultivan varias clases de cereales,
como el trigo, el maíz y la avena. 17. El año pasado
teníamos un hermoso perro que vigilaba la casa. 18. El
pobrecito (*poor thing*) murió, y ahora le echamos de menos.
19. En la hacienda hay vacas Jersey que nos dan leche.
20. En el verano la vida del campo es muy agradable.
21. Pero cuando llegue el otoño, tendremos ganas de volver
a la ciudad.

B. *Contéstese.* 1–2. ¿Qué vida le gusta más a Vd. durante
la estación de los calores (de los fríos), la (*that*) del campo
o la de la ciudad? 3. ¿A qué distancia de la ciudad tiene
su familia la hacienda? 4. ¿Se pasea Vd. a caballo? 5. ¿Por
qué no quiere montar a caballo su hermana? 6. ¿Dónde se
divierten Vds. pescando? 7–8. ¿Dónde está el jardín (la
huerta)? 9–10. ¿Qué se cultiva en el jardín (en la huerta)?
11. En su opinión ¿qué frutas son las mejores? 12. ¿Por
qué no se pueden producir allí las frutas tropicales?
13. ¿Qué frutas tropicales? 14. ¿En dónde están las galli-

nas? 15. ¿Qué ponen? 16. ¿Dónde hacen los pájaros su nido? 17. ¿A qué hora se levantan los labradores? 18. ¿Trabajan mucho? 19. ¿Qué cereales cultivan? 20. ¿Quién vigilaba la casa el año pasado? 21. ¿Qué ha sido de él? 22. ¿Lo echan Vds. de menos? 23. ¿Qué raza de vacas tienen Vds.? 24. ¿Dan leche? 25. ¿Cuándo tendrán Vds. ganas de volver a la ciudad?

C. 1. Avoid (**Evitad**) the bad (*n.*) and seek the good. 2. Men do not comprehend (**no comprenden**) the infinite. 3. We shall do the same. 4. I prefer mine (*n.*) to yours. 5. Write as fast as possible. 6. Study at least two hours. 7. I know how good she is. 8. We know how ill you are. 9. We are studying Spanish. 10. Spanish is not difficult. 11. Do you speak Spanish? 12. This letter is written in Spanish. 13. Women love flowers. 14. Horses are strong. 15. Dogs are useful. 16. Gold is worth more than iron. 17. Mr. Pérez left yesterday. 18. Good day, Mr. Martínez. 19. Captain (*úsese* **capitán**) Treviño is a Mexican. 20. I took off my gloves. 21. I washed my hands. 22. The children washed their faces. 23. John has lost his hat. 24. We arrived last month. 25. We shall leave next Friday. 26. Is Argentina a richer country than Mexico? 27. Mexico has more inhabitants (**habitantes**) than Argentina. 28. He was born in Spain. 29. His wife was born in Perú. 30. Havana is the largest city in (**de**) Cuba. 31. To eat too much is a vice. 32. Oranges cost thirty cents a dozen. 33. This cloth (**paño**) is sold at two dollars a meter.

D. 1. My father has a large-farm (at) fifty kilometers from Boston. 2. We spend all our summer vacations (= vacations of the summer) on (**en**) the farm, because it is cooler there. 3. My brothers like to ride on horseback every day. 4. *I* do not (like it). The first time (that) I rode on horseback I almost fell [off]. 5. Since then (**entonces**) I have not ridden (**no monto**) on horseback. I prefer to ride on (**en**) [a] bicycle. 6. I used to have a dog that I loved dearly (**tiernamente**), but the poor thing died a year ago. 7. At night he used to guard the house, and during the day (**de día**) he followed me everywhere (**por todas partes**). 8. There

is a large lake near the farm where we go fishing (**a pescar**). 9. The
waters of the lake are cool and clear. 10. We have a lot of horses
and cows. 11. The Jersey cows are the best we have. 12. They
give better milk than the other cows give. 13. The farm laborers
have to work early and late in order to cultivate the fields.
14. They grow (= cultivate) many kinds of cereals, such as (**tales
como**) oats, wheat, and Indian corn. 15. We have a garden for
(**jardín para**) flowers before the house, and behind the house a garden for vegetables. 16. In the flower garden beautiful (*úsese* **bello**)
flowers of every color (**de todos los colores**) are grown. 17. There
are large flowers and little [ones]. Some are red and white, and
others are blue or yellow. 18. My mother prefers tropical fruits,
such as bananas and oranges, to northern fruits (**las frutas del
norte**). 19. But my father thinks that apples and pears are the
best fruits in the (**del**) world. 20. My little sister loves birds.
21. In a large tree before the house the birds make their nests.
22. We climb the (**al**) tree to look at the eggs, but we do not take
them away from (**no se los quitamos a**) the birds. 23. Our hens
lay many eggs and we take them from the hens and eat them up
(**nos los comemos**). 24. We shall be glad to return to (the) town
when September comes (*úsese* **llegar**).

RESUMEN GRAMATICAL

201. El artículo determinado. — 1. La forma femenina el sólo
se usa inmediatamente delante de un nombre que empieza por **a-**
o **ha-** acentuada.

2. La forma neutra **lo** se usa con adjetivos neutros usados como
nombres abstractos; con pronombres neutros; con adverbios; y
en algunas expresiones idiomáticas.

202. El artículo determinado se requiere: 1. Con un adjetivo de
nacionalidad cuando denota idioma, excepto después de **hablar** o **en;**
con un nombre usado en sentido general para denotar toda la cosa
o especie que nombra; con un nombre propio modificado por un
título o un adjetivo descriptivo, si aquél no está en vocativo; en
lugar del adjetivo posesivo cuando se refiere a las diferentes
partes del cuerpo humano o a las prendas de vestir, etc.; con
expresiones de tiempo modificadas por **próximo, pasado,** etc.

2. Con los nombres de algunos países. Entre ellos se cuentan todos los nombres geográficos modificados por un adjetivo, así como los **Estados Unidos,** y también los siguientes: · · ·

a. Los nombres de ciudades, por regla general, no llevan el artículo; sin embargo, **la Habana** y algunos otros son excepciones de esta regla.

El artículo puede usarse :

3. Para modificar a un infinitivo o una cláusula sujeto de verbo.

4. Para expresar medida.

LESSON XLIV

204. Omission of the Definite Article. — The definite article is omitted in Spanish, though required in English:

1. Usually before a noun in apposition.

    Santiago, capital de Chile.   Santiago, the capital of Chile.

2. Before a numeral modifying a title.

    Carlos Quinto.   Charles the Fifth.
    Alfonso Trece.   Alfonso the Thirteenth.

205. Omission of the Indefinite Article. — It is regularly omitted:

1. Before an unqualified noun in the predicate (§74).

2. Before a noun in apposition.

    Lima, ciudad del Perú.   Lima, a city of Perú.

3. Before **cierto,** *a certain,* **otro,** *another,* **ciento,** *a hundred,* **mil,** *a thousand;* and after **tal,** *such a.*

4. In many idioms, such as:

    Nunca lleva chaleco.   He never wears a waistcoat (vest).
    No dice palabra.   He doesn't say a word.
    ¡Qué lástima!   What a pity!

POSSESSIVES

206. Possessive Adjectives. — Study §§52–55.

207.   Possessive Pronouns

SINGULAR

el mío (la mía, lo mío, los míos, las mías), mine
el tuyo (la tuya, lo tuyo, los tuyos, las tuyas), thine
el suyo (la suya, lo suyo, los suyos, las suyas), his, hers, its, yours

PLURAL

el nuestro (la nuestra, lo nuestro, los nuestros, las nuestras), ours
el vuestro (la vuestra, lo vuestro, los vuestros, las vuestras), yours
el suyo (la suya, lo suyo, los suyos, las suyas), theirs, yours

Prefiero la casa de Vd. a la mía.	I prefer your house to mine.
La de Vd. es más grande que la mía.	Yours is larger than mine.

The possessive pronouns require the definite article in Spanish though not in English.

a. But the definite article is used with a possessive in the predicate only in a question beginning with *which*, or in answer to such a question. Compare:

¿De quién es este libro? — Es mío.	Whose book is this? — It is mine.
¿Qué libro es el de Vd.? — Éste es el mío.	Which book is yours? — This one is mine.
¿Cuál de las plumas es la mía? — Ésta es la de Vd.	Which pen is mine? — This is yours.

208. The definite article may be used with **de él, de ella,** etc., instead of **suyo,** etc., to make the meaning clear or emphatic (see also §83).

Tengo el libro de él: no tengo el de ella.	I have his book: I haven't hers.
Prefiere la casa de Vd. a la de ellos.	He prefers your house to theirs.

209. Study the inflection of **haber** (§257), **ser** (§259), and **ir** (§ 261).

EXERCISES

agradecer, to be grateful for;
 agradecido, -a, grateful
anhelar, to long for
atento, -a, devoted, courteous
el **borrón,** blot
el **cariño,** affection
el **compromiso,** engagement
 corriente, present (month), instant
 dentro de, within
 Enrique, Henry
 estimable, esteemed
 evitar, to avoid, help (=avoid)
 histórico, -a, historic(al)

la **molestia,** trouble
el **monumento,** monument, imposing public building
la **oportunidad,** opportunity
 permanecer, to remain
 prestar, to lend, show
 pues, well, for
 querido, -a, dear, beloved
el **respeto,** respect; **respetos,** regards
 saludar, to salute
el **servidor,** la **servidora,** servant
 subscribir, to subscribe, sign

Muy señor mío, My dear Sir; **su apreciable carta,** your favor; **no hay novedad,** all is well; **sin novedad,** without accident, as usual; **me hallo mejor,** I am better; **está de vuelta,** he has returned, he is back; **¿qué tal sigue Vd.?** how are you getting on? **da la una,** it is striking one; **dan las dos (tres,** *etc.***),** it is striking two (three, *etc.*); **no sirve para nada,** it is good for nothing; **su atento y seguro servidor,** your devoted and faithful servant [1]

A. 1.   Hotel Grande, Granada
                                    15 de Junio de 1918 [2]
Querido Pablo:

Hoy llegué a Granada sin novedad, y pienso permanecer aquí ocho días.   La verdad es que estaba cansado cuando llegué, pero ya me hallo mejor.   He oído decir que Granada tiene muchos monumentos históricos y deseo verlos todos. Hágame Vd. el favor de decir al señor Velázquez que estaré de vuelta dentro de quince días.   Bien sé que le doy a Vd. mucha molestia, pero no puedo evitarlo.   ¿Qué tal sigue

---

[1] This may be translated: *very sincerely yours.*
[2] **Mil novecientos diez y ocho.**

Vd.? Espero que ya se halle mejor. Ahora no puedo escribir más, pues tengo un compromiso a las dos y media, y ya dieron las dos. Dispense Vd. el borrón. ¡Esta pluma-fuente (pluma estilográfica) no sirve para nada!

Le saluda con cariño su amigo
Enrique.

2.   Calle de San Cristóbal, 55,[1] Barcelona
10 de Marzo de 1918

Sr. D.[2] Tomás Hidalgo y Rivera,
Calle del Arenal, 35,
     Madrid.

Muy señor mío y amigo:

Acabo de recibir su apreciable carta del 8 del corriente y me apresuro a contestarla. Mucho agradezco todo lo que (*that which*) Vd. ha hecho por (*for*) mi hijo durante su enfermedad.

Deseamos que cuente con que (*be assured of the fact that*) Vd. y todos los suyos (*all your family*) tienen en esta ciudad amigos muy agradecidos que anhelan la oportunidad de corresponder a los buenos servicios que Vd. ha tenido la bondad de prestar a nuestro querido hijo.

Con mi familia presento mis respetos a su estimable señora esposa, y me subscribo de Vd. muy atento y seguro servidor y amigo,

Carlos Pereda y Galdós.

B. *Contéstese.* 1. ¿A dónde llegó Enrique? 2. ¿Cómo llegó? 3. ¿Cuánto tiempo pensaba permanecer allí? 4. ¿Cómo estaba cuando llegó? 5. ¿Cómo se sentía cuando escribió la carta? 6. ¿Qué había oído decir? 7. ¿Qué le rogó a Pablo que dijera al señor Velázquez? 8. ¿Qué sabía

---

[1] In letter heads the number of the house is usually placed after the name of the street.

[2] Sr. D. = **Señor Don.**

Enrique que le daba a Pablo? 9. ¿Por qué no pudo Enrique escribir más? 10. ¿Qué hora dió? 11. ¿Por qué le pidió Enrique a Pablo que le dispensara? 12. ¿Qué cosa no servía para nada? 13. ¿Cómo acabó Enrique la carta?

14. ¿Dónde estaba Carlos Pereda y Galdós cuando escribió la carta a Tomás Hidalgo y Rivera? 15. ¿Cuál es la fecha de esa carta? 16. ¿Cuál es la dirección del señor Hidalgo? 17. ¿Qué acabó de recibir el señor Pereda? 18. ¿Qué se apresuró a hacer? 19. ¿Qué le agradeció al señor Hidalgo? 20. ¿Con qué deseaba que contase el señor Hidalgo? 21. ¿Qué le presentó al señor Hidalgo? 22. ¿Cómo se subscribió?

C. 1–3. He lives in Lima (Bogotá, Caracas), the capital of Perú (Colombia, Venezuela). 4. Alfonso the Thirteenth is king of Spain. 5. My father is a physician. 6. My uncle is a lawyer. 7. Both (Los dos) are Americans. 8. Mr. Carducci is a tailor. 9. His brother is a carpenter (carpintero). 10. Both are Italians. 11. They used to live in Pisa, a city of Italy. 12. A certain friend of mine (amigo mío) told me so (lo). 13. Another friend of mine denied it. 14. He did not believe such a story. 15. That man never wears a necktie. 16. What a pity that he does not dress (úsese vestirse) better! 17. Present my regards to your people (a los suyos). 18. He presented his regards to my people.

Tradúzcanse las siguientes frases, y repítanse después omitiendo los nombres. 19. He has his books. 20. She has her books. 21. Have you your books? 22. We have our books. 23. He read her letter. 24. She read his letter. 25. Did you read their letters? 26. I prefer my house to yours. 27. Do you prefer your house to mine? 28. Which house [1] is yours? 29. Whose house is that one (aquélla)?

D. 1.   Hotel Grande, Granada.
                                 April 25, 1918.

Dear Charles:

Granada is more interesting than Seville (Sevilla). It is not so large, but it has the Alhambra which is the most interesting his-

---

[1] Note that *which house* is qué casa, while *which* alone is cuál.

torical monument in Spain. It was built by the Moors (**moros**) many centuries ago.

I was very tired and nearly ill when I arrived yesterday, but I am better now. How are you getting on? I hope that you are feeling much better. Tell Mr. Pérez that I shall be back in a week. I can't stay longer (**más tiempo**) this time (**vez**), but I hope to return next year. It has struck half-past three and I have an engagement at four o'clock.

Yours affectionately (*véase* A. 1),
Ferdinand.

2.   33 San Cristóbal Street, Barcelona.
May 5, 1918.

Mr. Henry Valera Ortiz,
50 Arenal Street,
Madrid.

Dear Sir:

We have just received your favors of the 2nd and 3rd instant and we make haste to answer them. We are very grateful to you and your wife (**estimable señora**) for all that (**lo que**) you (**Vds.**) have done for our daughter during her illness, and we hope that we shall-be-able (§153) some day to repay you [for] the many good services that you have had the kindness to show our beloved daughter.

We present our respects to you (**Vd.**) and all your family, and we are very sincerely yours,

Paul Martínez Tamayo.
Anna Herrera de Martínez.

RESUMEN GRAMATICAL

204. Supresión del artículo determinado. — El artículo determinado, aunque necesario en inglés, se suprime en español:

1. Generalmente ante el nombre en aposición.
2. Ante el adjetivo numeral que modifica a un título.

196 FIRST SPANISH COURSE

205. Supresión del artículo indeterminado. — Generalmente se suprime:

1. Ante el nombre no calificado que sirve de predicado (atributo).
2. Ante el nombre en aposición.
3. Ante las voces **cierto, otro, ciento, mil**; y después de **tal.**
4. En diversas expresiones idiomáticas, tales como: . . .

207. Pronombres posesivos. — Obsérvese que en español los pronombres posesivos requieren el artículo determinado y no lo requieren en inglés.

a. Pero el artículo determinado se usa con el posesivo como predicado (atributo) solamente en las preguntas que empiezan por **cuál** o **qué** (*adj.*) o en la contestación a estas preguntas.

208. El artículo determinado puede usarse con **de él, de ella,** etc., en vez de **suyo,** etc., para dar mayor claridad o énfasis a la expresión.

LESSON XLV

210. Demonstratives. — Study §§59–62.

a. That of, the one of, etc., are usually expressed by **el (la, lo, los, las) de.**

La pluma de acero y la de oro.	The steel pen and the gold one (*lit.*, The pen of steel and that of gold).
Lo de ayer.	The affair of yesterday.

211. Relative Pronouns

que, who (whom), which, that
el cual (la cual, lo cual, los cuales, las cuales) }
el que (la que, lo que, los que, las que) } who (whom), which
quien (–es), who (whom)
cuanto (–a, –os, –as), all who, all that
cuyo (–a, –os, –as), whose

212. Uses of the Relative Pronouns. — 1. **Que,** the most common of the Spanish relative pronouns, is invariable. It is used as subject or object of a verb, and it may refer to persons or things. After a preposition, *whom* is **quien** (–es).

El alumno que partió hoy.	The student (*m.*) who (that) left to-day.
La alumna que ví esta mañana.	The student (*f.*) whom (that) I saw this morning.
Los alumnos de quienes hablábamos.	The students of whom we were speaking.

2. **El cual** (**la cual,** etc.), **el que** (**la que,** etc.), or **quien** (–es), may be used to avoid ambiguity. **El cual** and **el que** indicate the gender and number of the antecedent. **Quien** makes clear that the antecedent is a person and indicates the number.

He escrito al hijo de doña Francisca, el cual estudia para médico.	I have written to Doña Francisca's son who is studying to be a physician.
Ayer ví al dueño de la casa, quien está en la ciudad.	Yesterday I saw the owner of the house, who is in town.

3. *He who, she who, the one who,* etc., are expressed by **el que, la que,** etc., or by **quien** (–es).

El que desea mucho siempre es pobre.	He who desires much is always poor.
Estos muchachos son los que Vd. buscaba.	These boys are the ones that you were looking for.
Quien calla, otorga.	He who is silent gives assent.
No tengo a quien dirigirme.	I haven't any one to whom to apply.

4. Neuter *that which* or *what* (= *that which*), referring to a statement or idea, is **lo que,** and neuter *which* is commonly **lo cual.**

¿Sabe Vd. lo que quiere?	Do you know what he wants?
Prometió estudiar más, lo cual agradó mucho a su padre.	He promised to study more, which greatly pleased his father.

5. A Spanish relative pronoun can not be omitted, nor can it precede its preposition, as in English. Compare *the man we were talking about* with **el hombre de quien hablábamos.**

213. Study the inflection of **tener** (§258), **estar** (§260), and **andar** (§262).

EXERCISES

afectísimo, –a (afmo, –a), most affectionate(ly)	**ofrecer,** to offer
agradar, to please	**pedir (i) prestado,** to ask the loan of, borrow
apurado, –a, without money	el **placer,** pleasure
la **culpa,** fault, guilt	**privar,** to deprive (of)
el **dueño,** owner	**procurar,** to attempt, try
la **falta,** lack	**prometer,** to promise
el **guía,** guide	**tomar prestado,** to borrow

me hace falta, I lack, I need; **no puedo menos de hacerlo,** I can't help doing it; **si Vd. tiene inconveniente en hacerlo,** if you have any objection to doing it; **¿qué hay de nuevo?** what is the news? **lo logré,** I succeeded (in doing so); **no es mía la culpa,** it is not my fault; **Vd. tiene la culpa,** it is your fault; **no deje Vd. de hacerlo,** do not fail to do so; **no hay nada de particular,** there is nothing unusual

A. 1.   Calle de Preciados, 112, Matanzas, Cuba

8 de Enero de 1918

Querido Juan:

Me hace falta dinero. ¿Puede Vd. enviarme un giro postal de cincuenta pesos oro? Si me presta esta suma, prometo pagársela el primero del mes que viene. No me agrada pedir prestado el dinero que necesito, pero esta vez no puedo menos de hacerlo. Siento muchísimo molestar a Vd. y si tiene inconveniente en prestármelo, no lo haga. No es mía la culpa de hallarme apurado (sin dinero) en esta población. Se lo explicaré a Vd. cuando le vea. He procurado tomar prestado aquí el dinero que me falta, pero no lo logré. La verdad es que no tengo a quien dirigirme. ¿Qué hay de nuevo en la Habana? Aquí no hay nada de particular. No deje Vd. de escribirme.

> Suyo afmo,
> Felipe.

2.   Calle de Francos, 85

Señor Don Carlos Tamayo y Baus,
       Puerta del Sol, 10.

Muy señor mío:

Tendríamos gran placer en que nos hiciese Vd. el honor de comer con nosotros mañana por la noche. Espero que no tenga Vd. ningún otro compromiso que nos prive de su compañía en esta ocasión.

Mi marido tendrá el gusto de hacerle una visita hoy para saludarle y para ofrecerse a acompañarle (*accompany you*) mañana cuando venga a nuestra casa.

> Quedo de Vd. S. S.,
> Q. S. M. B.,[1]
> Mercedes García de Núñez.

A 21 de diciembre de 1918.

B. *Contéstese.* 1. ¿A quién escribió Felipe? 2. ¿Cuál es la fecha de su carta? 3. ¿Qué le hacía falta a Felipe? 4. ¿Cuánto dinero quería que le enviase Juan? 5. ¿Cuándo prometió pagárselo? 6. ¿Le agradaba a Felipe pedir prestado el dinero que necesitaba? 7. ¿No pudo menos de hacerlo? 8. ¿Tenía Felipe la culpa de hallarse apurado (sin dinero)? 9. ¿Cuándo se lo explicaría a su amigo? 10. ¿Dónde procuró tomar prestado el dinero que le faltaba? 11. ¿Lo logró?

---

[1] S. S. Q. S. M. B. here is to be read **segura servidora que su mano besa.** This very formal expression is now little used except in invitations, announcements, etc. When a man thus addresses a woman, the corresponding formal expression is S. S. Q. S. P. (pies) B. Instead of de Vd. S. S. Q. S. M. (P.) B., one also finds S. S. S. Q. B. S. M. (P.) = su seguro servidor que besa su mano (sus pies). In ordinary social and commercial correspondence, it is now customary to omit Q. B. S. M., or to use in its place Q. E. S. M. = que estrecha su mano, *who clasps your hand.*

12. ¿Por qué no?   13. ¿Había algo (*anything*) de particular en Matanzas?   14. ¿Dónde está Matanzas?

15. ¿A quién escribió la señora doña Mercedes García de Núñez?   16. ¿Cuál es el nombre de bautismo (de pila) de esta señora?   17–18. ¿Cuál es el apellido de su padre (de su marido)?   19. ¿En qué tendrían gran placer la señora y su marido?   20. ¿Para cuándo invitó ella al señor Tamayo a comer con ellos?   21. ¿Para qué tendría el marido el gusto de hacer una visita al señor Tamayo?   22. ¿Cuál es la fecha de la invitación?

C. 1. The lady who arrived yesterday.   2. The lady to whom I was speaking.   3. The young lady whom I saw this morning. 4. The book that he borrowed from me (**me pidió prestado**).   5. The man that borrowed the book.   6. The book of which we were speaking.   7. The house he bought.   8. The house in which he lives.   9. I have written to Mr. Herrera's daughter who is in New York.   10. I have written also to Mrs. Martínez's son who is in Havana.   11. Do you know a book which is (§161, 2) more interesting than this [one]?   12. Do you know the author of this book, who is [a] great poet in my opinion?   13–14. This boy (This girl) is the one who told me so.   15–16. These men (These women) are the ones who took it (**se lo llevaron**).   17. What do you want? 18. Tell me what you want.   19. I believe you don't know what you want.   20. What did he buy?   21. He will (**quiere**) not tell me what he bought.   22. He is working harder (**más**), which pleases me greatly (**mucho**).   23. He told us the truth, which (*n.*) surprised (**sorprendió**) us.

D. 1.   Calle de San Fernando, 15, Buenos Aires.
                                      May 5, 1918.

Dear Ferdinand:

Will you send me a postal money order for (**de**) seventy-five dollars?   I am without money.   I have spent the last dollar that I had.   I tried to borrow some money from (**a**) an acquaintance, but he would (**quería**) not lend it to me.   I haven't [any] friends in this town.   If you will lend me that (**esa**) amount, I promise to pay it back (= pay it to you) the first of next month. If you have any objection to lending me so (**tan**) large an amount (= an amount so large), send me fifty dollars.

I am sorry to trouble you, but it isn't my fault that I am without money. I haven't any one here to whom to apply. I tried to find some friend, but I didn't succeed. What's the news in Montevideo? I hope you and all your people are well. There is nothing unusual here. Do not fail to write me as soon as possible, because I need money.

Most affectionately yours,

Paul.

2. Mrs. Mary Herrera de López,
    Puerta del Sol, 15.

Dear Madam (**Muy señora mía**):

We should be greatly pleased if (*véase* A. 2) you would do us the honor of dining with us Thursday night (**el jueves por la noche**). We hope that you have no engagement that will deprive us of your company. (The) dinner will be served at seven o'clock. My husband will have the pleasure of sending you (**de mandar a Vd.**) our motor car, at the hour mentioned (**señalada**), to bring you to our house.   I am very sincerely yours (*véase* A. 2),

Anna Rodríguez de Ulloa.

January 12, 1918.

RESUMEN GRAMATICAL

210. Demostrativos: . . .

a. That of, the one of, etc., se expresan generalmente por **el** (**la, lo, los, las**) **de.**

212. Uso de los pronombres relativos. — 1. **Que,** el más común de los pronombres relativos españoles, es invariable. Se usa como sujeto o complemento verbal, pudiendo referirse a personas o cosas. Después de una preposición, *whom* es **quien** (**-es**).

2. Para evitar la ambigüedad en las expresiones se hace uso de **el cual** (**la cual,** etc.), **el que** (**la que,** etc.), o **quien** (**-es**). **El cual** y **el que** indican el género y el número del antecedente. **Quien** indica que el antecedente es una persona e indica su número.

3. *He who, she who, the one who,* etc., se traducen por **el que, la que,** etc., o por **quien (–es).**

4. Las expresiones neutras *that which* o *what* (= *that which*) que hacen referencia a una manifestación o idea se traducen por **lo que,** y el neutro *which* es comúnmente **lo cual.**

5. El pronombre relativo español no puede omitirse, ni puede preceder a su preposición, como en inglés.

LESSON XLVI

214. Interrogative Pronouns

quién (–es), who (whom)   cuál (–es), which
de quién (–es), whose   cuánto (–a, –os, –as), how much
qué, what (which)   (many)

All except **quién (–es)** may be used as pronominal adjectives.

a. In questions, *which* used as an attributive (or adherent) adjective is **qué**: ¿**qué libro quiere Vd.?** *which book do you wish?*

b. In exclamations, *what* (*a*) or *how* is **qué**: ¡**qué bonita niña!** *what a pretty girl!* ¡**qué pálida estás!** *how pale you are!*

215. Indefinite Pronouns and Pronominal Adjectives

alguien { some one, somebody / any one, anybody

alguno (–a, –os, –as), some, any, a few

alguna cosa } something, anything
algo

uno (–a, –os, –as), one, some

cada (*adj., invar.*), each, every

cada uno (–a), each one

ambos (–as) } both
los (las) dos

los (las) demás, the rest

cualquiera (cualesquiera), any (one) at all, whatever

nadie, no one, nobody

ninguno (–a, –os, –as). none, no

ninguna cosa }
cosa alguna } nothing
nada }

mucho (–a, –os, –as), much, many

poco (–a, –os, –as), little, few

todo (–a, –os, –as), all, every; (*n.*) everything

mismo (–a, –os, –as), same, self

otro (–a, –os, –as), other, another

tanto (–a, –os, –as), as (so) much (many)

tal, such, such a

quienquiera (quienesquiera), whoever

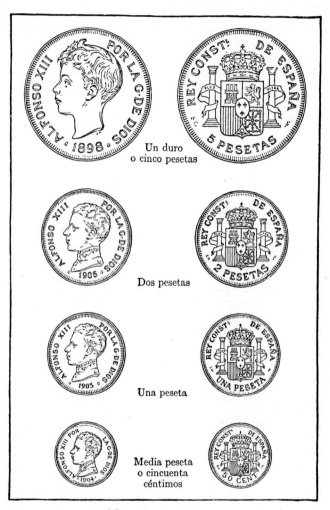

Un duro
o cinco pesetas

Dos pesetas

Una peseta

Media peseta
o cincuenta
céntimos

MONEDAS ESPAÑOLAS

Examples of Spanish currency struck in the early years of the
reign of Alfonso XIII.

Anverso   Reverso

Peso mexicano

Anverso   Reverso

50 Centavos de Argentina

Anverso   Reverso

Peso chileno

MONEDAS HISPANOAMERICANAS

Más vale algo que nada.	Something is better than nothing.
Todo hombre debe cumplir con su deber.	Every man should do his duty.
Todos los muchachos jugaban a la pelota.	All the boys were playing ball.
Va al teatro todas las noches (cada noche).	He goes to the theater every (each) night.
Cada dos horas sale un tren.	A train leaves every two hours.
Nos quiere a los dos.	He likes us both.
Murió el mismo día.	He died the same day.
Él mismo me lo dijo.	He told me so himself.
Quisiéramos otros dos.	We should like two others.
Hay tantos hombres como mujeres.	There are as many men as women.
Nunca pasé tal noche.	I never passed such a night.

a. An unemphatic *some* or *any* is usually not expressed in Spanish.

¿Quiere Vd. uvas?	Do you want some grapes?
¿Tiene Vd. peras? — No tengo.	Have you any pears? — I haven't any.

b. *A little* (denoting quantity) is **un poco de: ¿puede Vd. prestarme un poco de dinero?** *can you lend me a little money?*

c. **Cualquiera (cualesquiera)** may lose the final –a when it precedes the noun it modifies.

Cualquier hombre es bueno para eso.	Any man is good (enough) for that.
But, Para eso cualquiera es bueno.	For that any one (at all) is good.

d. Review §113.

216. Study the inflection of **poner** (§265), **saber** (§268), **caber** (§269), and **poder** (§270).

EXERCISES

adjunto, –a, *adj.*, adjunto, *adv.*, enclosed, herewith

asistir, to be present (at), attend

bonito, –a, pretty

casarse con, to marry, get married

la ceremonia, ceremony

el enlace, union, marriage

enojarse, to get angry; enojado, –a (con), angry (with)

fijamente, with certainty

Francisco, Francis

la noticia, news (item); las noticias, news

participar, to announce

reexpedir (i), to forward

religioso, –a, religious

remitir, to remit, send

resfriarse, to catch cold

simpático, –a, charming, pleasant

suplicar, to beg

la tardanza, delay

el templo, temple, church

verificarse, to be held *or* performed

¿cuándo tuvo Vd. noticias de él? when did you hear from him last? a los pocos años de estar aquí, after being here a few years; ¿qué hay? what's the matter? ¿qué tiene Vd.? what's the matter with you? no tengo nada, there's nothing the matter with me; de vez en cuando, from time to time; tuvo lugar, it took place; si mal no me acuerdo, if I remember rightly; guarda cama, he stays in bed; tengo miedo, I am frightened; se me olvidó, I forgot.

A. 1.   México,[1] 5 de Julio de 1918.

Querido Carlos:

¿Cuándo tuvo Vd. noticias de Pedro? A los pocos días de estar en México recibí una carta de él, pero no ha vuelto a escribirme después. ¿Qué tendrá que no quiere escribirme? ¿Cree Vd. que esté enojado conmigo? Yo le escribo de vez en cuando, pero no contesta a mis cartas.

¿Ha oído Vd. que Francisco se casó con la hija de los señores de Montoya? La ceremonia religiosa se verificó en

[1] Within Mexico itself, the word " México " usually means the city of Mexico. The country as a whole is usually spoken of as la República Mexicana, but officially it is called los Estados Unidos Mexicanos. The official spelling is México and mexicano, but the pronunciation is always Méjico and mejicano.

el templo de Santa Teresa el 15 de abril. La ceremonia civil [1] tuvo lugar la mañana del mismo día, si mal no me acuerdo. Yo no pude asistir por (*on account of*) haberme resfriado. Tuve que guardar cama ocho días. Doña Julia, la esposa de Francisco, es bonita y simpática; y, lo que es de mayor importancia, su padre es rico. Adjunta [2] le remito a Vd. la invitación que recibí de los señores de Montoya.

Como no sé fijamente su dirección, me permito remitir esta carta a casa de su padre, quien la reexpedirá si Vd. no está ahí (*there*). Le ruego perdone [3] la tardanza con que correspondo a su carta.

Créame siempre su buen amigo,

Juan.

2.   Felipe Montoya y Carranza
          y María Galdós de Montoya
        tienen el honor de participar a Vd.
           el próximo enlace de su hija
                  Julia
               con el Señor
               Don Francisco
              Tamayo y Baus

y le suplican se sirva (*to be kind enough*) asistir a la ceremonia religiosa que se verificará en el Templo de Santa Teresa el día 15 del presente a las 11 de la mañana.

México, abril de 1918.

B. *Contéstese.* 1. ¿A quién escribió Juan? 2. ¿Dónde estaba cuando escribió la carta? 3. ¿Cuál es la fecha de la carta? 4. ¿De quién quería noticias? 5. ¿Cuándo recibió

---

[1] In most countries a civil ceremony is requisite to make a marriage legal.

[2] Instead of **adjunta, adjunto** may here be used adverbially.

[3] After **rogar, suplicar,** and the like, the conjunction **que** may be omitted as here.

Juan una carta de Pedro? 6. ¿Ha vuelto Pedro a escribirle después? 7. ¿Sabía Juan lo que tenía Pedro? 8. ¿Temía que Pedro estuviera enojado con él? 9. ¿Cuándo le escribía? 10.' ¿Contestaba Pedro a las cartas de Juan? 11. ¿Con quién se casó Francisco? 12. ¿En dónde se verificó la ceremonia religiosa? 13. ¿Cuándo se verificó? 14. ¿Cuándo tuvo lugar la ceremonia civil? 15. ¿Pudo asistir Juan a las ceremonias? 16. ¿Por qué no? 17. ¿Cuánto tiempo tuvo que guardar cama? 18. ¿Es bonita o fea (*homely*) la esposa de Francisco? 19. ¿Es rico o pobre el padre de ella? 20. ¿Qué cosa le remitió Juan a su amigo? 21. ¿A casa de quién remitió Juan la carta? 22. ¿Que le rogó a su amigo que perdonase? 23. ¿Cómo se subscribió Juan?

24. ¿Quiénes son los padres de doña Julia? 25. ¿Qué tenían el honor de participar a Juan? 26. ¿Qué le suplicaron que se sirviera hacer?

C. 1. What a pretty girl! 2. But how pale she is! 3. What a handsome horse you have! 4. How gentle he is! 5. Whose horse have you? 6–7. Some one (No one) told me so. 8. Have you any friends in Guadalajara? 9. I haven't any friends there (**allá**). 10. I do not know any one there. 11. Have you anything that is (§161, 2) better than this (*n.*)? 12. I haven't anything better. 13. Have you any apples to-day? 14. No, ma'am; we haven't any to-day. 15. We have neither apples nor pears. 16. Every man ought to get married. 17. All men ought to work. 18. They ought to work every day except Sundays. 19. I believe everything (§212, 5) he says (**dice**). 20–21. A train leaves every hour (every two hours). 22. A little (**pequeño**) boy asked me for a little money. 23. I gave him a few (**unos pocos**) cents. 24. He likes us both. 25. He doesn't like either one of us (**No nos quiere ni a uno ni a otro**). 26–27. Did you buy another (the other) house? 28. They received many other (**otras muchas**) invitations. 29. She told him so herself. 30. Mr. Hidalgo arrived the same day. 31. He ought not to do such a thing. 32. I never passed such a day.

MÉXICO Y LA AMÉRICA CENTRAL

ESCALA DE KILÓMETROS
0   100   200   300   400   500   600

ESCALA DE MILLAS INGLESAS
0   100   200   300   400   500   600   1000

ESTADOS MEXICANOS

1. Baja California (Terr.)
2. Sonora
3. Chihuahua
4. Coahuila
5. Nuevo León
6. Tamaulipas
7. Sinaloa
8. Durango
9. Tepic (Terr.)
10. Zacatecas
11. Aguas Calientes
12. San Luis Potosí
13. Jalisco
14. Guanajuato
15. Querétaro
16. Hidalgo
17. Colima
18. Michoacán
19. México
20. Distrito Federal
21. Tlaxcala
22. Guerrero
23. Morelos
24. Puebla
25. Veracruz
26. Oaxaca
27. Chiapas
28. Tabasco
29. Campeche
30. Yucatán
31. Quintana Roo (Terr.)

SUFFOLK, BOSTON

ISLAS REVILLA GIGEDO

OCÉANO ATLÁNTICO

GOLFO DE MÉXICO

MAR CARIBE

AMÉRICA CENTRAL

ISTMO DE TEHUANTEPEC

GUATEMALA

SAN SALVADOR

HONDURAS

NICARAGUA

COSTA RICA

PANAMÁ

TRÓPICO DE CÁNCER

Longitud Oeste de Greenwich

33. Whatever amount he may offer me, I shall accept it. 34. I should be very glad to (**Tendría mucho placer en**) accept any amount (at all). 35. Are there as many women as men here? 36. There are not so many men as women.

D. 1.   Guadalajara, México.
                                          June 12, 1918.

Dear Philip:

Do you know that Paul Palacio married the daughter of Mr. and Mrs. Hidalgo last month? The religious ceremony was performed in the church of Saint Anne, May 5, at 10 o'clock in (**de**) the morning, if I remember rightly. The civil ceremony took place the same day. As I was ill, I couldn't go (= attend). I caught cold and had to stay in bed several days. Paul's wife is pretty, and her friends say that she is very charming. I hope to have the pleasure of knowing her soon. I send you herewith the invitation that the Hidalgos were good enough to (**tuvieron la bondad de**) send (**enviar**) me. I forgot to tell you that the lady's father is exceedingly-rich (**riquísimo**).

When did you hear from Ferdinand last? He doesn't write to me [any] more. After having been here a few months I wrote to him, but he didn't answer my letter. Do you think (*úsese* **creer**) he is angry with me? I haven't done anything that could offend him, so far as I know (**que yo sepa**). Can you tell me what is the matter with him (**lo que tiene**)?

I have [got] to send this letter to your father's house, as I don't know your address. Pardon the delay with which I answer your letter. Don't fail to write me all the news of Guanajuato. Nothing has happened here (**Aquí no hay novedad**), except Paul's marriage (**la boda**).

                          Believe me ever your cordial friend (*véase* A. 1),
                                                    Charles.

2. *Escríbase, siguiendo el modelo de* A. 2. Mr. and Mrs. Henry Hidalgo y Bazán [1] have the honor of announcing the approaching marriage of their daughter Mercedes to Mr. Paul Palacio Valdés,

---

[1] The lady's maiden name was María Ortiz.

and they beg you to be kind enough to be present at the religious ceremony which will be performed in the church of Saint Anne the fifth day of next month at 10 o'clock in the morning.

Guadalajara, April, 1918.

RESUMEN GRAMATICAL

214. **Pronombres interrogativos:** ... Todos excepto **quién** (–es) pueden usarse como adjetivos pronominales.

a. En las interrogaciones, el adjetivo *which*, antepuesto al nombre que modifica, se traduce por la palabra **qué**.

b. En las exclamaciones, las palabras *what* o *how* se traducen por la palabra **qué**.

215. Algunos pronombres indeterminados y adjetivos pronominales: ...

a. Por regla general si *some* o *any* no son enfáticos, no se expresan en español.

b. *A little*, denotando cantidad, es **un poco de**.

c. **Cualquiera** (**cualesquiera**), cuando precede al nombre que modifica, puede perder la –a final.

LESSON XLVII

217.   Cardinal Numerals

1	un(o), –a	11	once
2	dos	12	doce
3	tres	13	trece
4	cuatro	14	catorce
5	cinco	15	quince
6	seis	16	diez y seis [1]
7	siete	17	diez y siete
8	ocho	18	diez y ocho
9	nueve	19	diez y nueve
10	diez	20	veinte

[1] Or dieciséis, diecisiete, etc.

21	veintiun(o), –a [1]	80	ochenta
22	veintidós	90	noventa
23	veintitrés	100	cien(to)
24	veinticuatro	200	doscientos, –as
25	veinticinco	300	trescientos, –as
26	veintiséis	400	cuatrocientos, –as
27	veintisiete	500	quinientos, –as
28	veintiocho	600	seiscientos, –as
29	veintinueve	700	setecientos, –as
30	treinta	800	ochocientos, –as
31	treinta y un(o), –a	900	novecientos, –as
40	cuarenta	1000	mil
50	cincuenta	2000	dos mil
60	sesenta	1,000,000	un millón
70	setenta	2,000,000	dos millones

a. For the apocopation of **uno** and **ciento**, see §179. Note also the use of **un** and **una** in such expressions as **veintiún días**, *twenty-one days*, **veintiuna semanas**, *twenty-one weeks*.

b. For the omission of **un** before **cien(to)** and **mil**, see §205, 3. But note **veintiún mil**, 21,000; etc.

c. **Millón** is a masculine noun; its plural is **millones** It requires the preposition **de** before the word it multiplies: **un millón de pesos**, *a million dollars*.

d. In compound numbers, **y**, *and*, is placed before the last numeral, provided the numeral that immediately precedes is less than 100. Thus: **ciento noventa y cinco**, 195; but **doscientos cinco**, 205.

e. Counting by hundreds is not carried above nine hundred in Spanish; beginning with ten hundred, **mil** is used: **mil novecientos diez y siete**, 1917.

218.   Ordinal Numerals

1st	primer(o), –a, –os, –as [2]	6th	sexto, –a, –os, –as
2nd	segundo, –a, –os, –as	7th	séptimo, –a, –os, –as
3rd	tercer(o), –a, –os, –as	8th	octavo, –a, –os, –as
4th	cuarto, –a, –os, –as	9th	noveno, –a, –os, –as
5th	quinto, –a, –os, –as	10th	décimo, –a, –os, –as

[1] Also written **veinte y uno, veinte y dos**, etc., but not pronounced thus, **Veintiún** requires the accent mark.

[2] These may be abbreviated to 1º (1er), 1ª, 1os, 1as; etc.

a. For the apocopation of **primero** and **tercero,** see §179, 1.

b. The Spanish ordinals above **décimo** are little used. Their place is usually taken by the cardinals.

Alfonso Trece.	Alfonso the Thirteenth.
El capítulo cincuenta.	The fiftieth chapter.

219. Fractions

$\frac{1}{2} \begin{cases} \text{medio, -a} \\ \text{la mitad} \end{cases}$ $\qquad \frac{1}{3} \begin{cases} \text{un tercio} \\ \text{la tercera parte} \end{cases}$

$\frac{3}{4}$, **tres cuartos;** $\frac{1}{5}$, **un quinto** (or **la quinta parte**); $\frac{1}{10}$, **un décimo** (or **la décima parte**); etc.

From $\frac{1}{11}$ to $\frac{1}{99}$, fractional numerals are commonly formed by adding **-avo** to the cardinal after dropping a final vowel, except the **-e** of **-siete** and **-nueve**: $\frac{1}{11}$, **un onzavo;** $\frac{2}{12}$, **dos dozavos;** $\frac{5}{20}$, **cinco veintavos;** etc.; but $\frac{1}{17}$, **un diecisieteavo;** $\frac{1}{29}$, **un veintinueveavo.**

$\frac{1}{100}$ is la **centésima** (parte); $\frac{1}{1000}$, la **milésima** (parte) [1]

a. *Half* (*a half, one half, half a*) as substantive, is expressed by **la mitad;** as adjective, by **medio (-a).**

La mitad de mis bienes.	One half of my goods.
Trabajó medio día.	He worked a half day.

220. Arithmetical Signs

+, más o y	**×, (multiplicado) por**
−, menos	**:, dividido por**

=, es (igual a), son (iguales a).

$2 + 3 = 5$, **dos más (o y) tres son cinco.**
$5 − 3 = 2$, **cinco menos tres son (o es igual a) dos.**
$3 \times 3 = 9$, **tres (multiplicado) por tres son nueve.**
$9 : 3 = 3$, **nueve dividido por tres son tres.**

221. Study the inflection of **venir** (§264), **hacer** (§266), and **querer** (§271).

[1] One may also say **una tercera parte, dos quintas partes, una milésima (parte),** etc.

EXERCISES

alrededor de, around, about	el mercado, market
el céntimo, centime	la moneda, coin
la compra, purchase	multiplicar, to multiply
chico, –a, small, little	el níquel, nickel (*metal*)
desde, since, from	la onza, ounce
dividir, to divide	la plata, silver
el dólar, dollar (*of U. S. A.*)	el " real," (*in Spain*) " nickel ";
duro, –a, hard; el duro, dollar	(*in Mexico, etc.*) " shilling "
(*of Spain*)	*or* " bit "
estadounidense,[1] of the United	la tierra, earth, land
States	la unidad, unity
gordo, –a, stout, fat	el valor, value; courage
hispanoamericano, –a, Span-	variar (§243), to vary
ish-American	

da una vuelta, it makes a turn, revolves; el sol sale, the sun rises;
el sol se pone, the sun sets; por todo, altogether; ¿a cómo se vende?
how is it sold? what is it sold at? hace sol (luna), the sun (moon) is
shining (also hay luna)

A. 1. El año es el espacio de tiempo en que la tierra da
una vuelta completa alrededor del sol. 2. El año se divide
en 4 estaciones, en 12 meses, en 52 semanas, y en 365 días.
3. El mes tiene poco más de 4 semanas. 4. La semana es
el espacio de 7 días, de los cuales el primero es el lunes y el
último el domingo. 5. El día se divide en 24 horas; la hora
se divide en 60 minutos; y el minuto se divide en 60 segundos. 6. En el verano el sol sale temprano y se pone tarde.
7. En el invierno sale tarde y se pone temprano.

B. 1. La unidad monetaria de España es la peseta, que
vale poco menos de 20 centavos norteamericanos (estadounidenses). 2. La peseta se divide en 100 céntimos. 3. La
moneda de plata de 5 pesetas se llama popularmente "duro";

[1] Estadounidense (or estadunidense) is a new word that has not met
with general acceptance. In Spain and in South America the *Americans* of
the United States are usually called norteamericanos or yanquis.

25 céntimos son un " real." 4. A veces la moneda de cobre de 10 céntimos se llama vulgarmente " perra gorda " (o " perro gordo "), y la de 5 céntimos " perra chica " (o " perro chico ").[1]

5. El peso es la unidad monetaria de la Argentina, Chile, Cuba, México y algunos otros países hispanoamericanos. 6. El peso se divide en 100 centavos. 7. El valor del peso varía desde 40 centavos norteamericanos (estadounidenses) hasta 50 centavos. 8. En México la moneda de 25 centavos se llama también popularmente " dos reales."

C. *Contéstese.* 1. ¿Qué es el año? 2. ¿En cuántas estaciones se divide el año? 3. ¿Cuáles son? 4. ¿En cuántos meses se divide el año? 5. ¿Cuáles son? 6–7. ¿En cuántas semanas (¿En cuántos días) se divide el año? 8. ¿Cuántas semanas tiene el mes? 9. ¿Qué es la semana? 10–11. ¿Cuál es el primer (el último) día de la semana? 12. ¿Cuáles son los días de la semana? 13. ¿En cuántas horas se divide el día? 14. ¿En cuántos minutos se divide la hora? 15. ¿En cuántos segundos se divide el minuto? 16–17. ¿Sale el sol y se pone tarde o temprano en el verano (en el invierno)? 18–19. ¿Cuál es la unidad monetaria de España (de México)? 20–21. ¿En qué se divide la peseta (el peso)? 22–26. ¿Cómo se llama también la moneda de plata de 5 pesetas; (la moneda de cobre de 10 céntimos; la moneda de cobre de 5 céntimos; la moneda de plata de 25 centavos)? 27–28. ¿Cuál es el valor en centavos norteamericanos (estadounidenses) de la peseta española?

D. *Contéstese.* 1. ¿Cuál es la suma (*sum*) de $23.25 y $35.50?[2] 2. Si de $95.35 quito $33.15, ¿cuánto queda? 3. Si

---

[1] Because the image of a lion on the coin is humorously assumed to resemble a dog.

[2] In these problems read $ as " **peso** " or " **pesos.**" In some countries the $ is sometimes placed after the number: thus, 15$ = 15 **pesos.**

multiplico $21.75 por 7, ¿cuál es el producto? 4. Si divido $84.20 por 4, ¿cuál es el resultado? 5. Una persona ha hecho 3 compras, y ha gastado sucesivamente $14, $34 y $68. ¿Cuánto ha gastado por todo? 6. Un niño nació el 5 de febrero de 1910. ¿Cuándo cumplió 5 años? 7. Si Juan tenía $10 y gastó $6.60, ¿cuánto dinero le queda? 8. Si Vd. pagó $18 por 8 metros y medio de un género de seda, ¿a cómo se vendía el metro? 9–19. Si damos a una peseta española el valor de 20 centavos norteamericanos (estadounidenses), ¿cuánto vale en moneda norteamericana (estadounidense): Ptas.: 28.15; 15.10; 35.75; 93.35; 118.60; 175.70; 225.25; 280.20; 350.75; 500.35; 1,000? (Por ejemplo, 28 pesetas con 15 céntimos valen 5 pesos y 63 centavos norteamericanos [estadounidenses]).[1]

E. *Léase o escríbase en español.* 21; 32; 43; 54; 65; 76; 87; 98; 123; 234; 345; 456; 567; 678; 789; 1,240; 2,357; 5,962; 15,749; 100,154; 1,000,000; 2,100,150; el año 1492; el año 1808; el año 1892; el año 1917; el año 1919; el año 1920; la página 35; el capítulo 175; Carlos V.; Luis 14; el volumen 8; Alfonso 12; 1/2; 2/3; 1/4; 2/5; 5/8; 9/10; 1/50; 5/75; 9/100; 25/1000; $3 + 5 = 8$; $8 - 2 = 6$; $3 \times 15 = 45$; $48:16 = 3$.

F. 1. A (El) year is divided into four seasons, namely (a saber): spring, summer, autumn (o " fall "), and winter. 2. Summer is the warm season (*véase* XXVI, B. 4), and winter is the cold season. 3. It is cold in winter because the days are short (cortos) and there is not much sunshine. 4. The days are short because the sun rises late and sets early. 5. It is warm in summer because the days are long and there is much sunshine. 6. A (El) year is divided into twelve months, namely: January, February, March, April, May,

---

[1] The abbreviation of peseta is pta. Note the use of con before the number of céntimos. The easiest method of reducing pesetas to dollars is to multiply the number of pesetas by two, and move the decimal point one digit to the left.

June, July, August, September, October, November, December.
7. Some months are longer than the others (**los demás**). 8. For
instance (**Por ejemplo**), January has thirty-one days while (**en
tanto que**) February, as a rule, has only (**no tiene más que**) twenty-
eight days. 9. February has only four weeks, while January has
nearly four weeks and a half. 10. The days of the week are Monday, Tuesday, Wednesday, Thursday, Friday, Saturday, Sunday.
11. In Spain and in the Spanish-American countries Monday is
the first day of the week and Sunday is the last day. 12. Sunday
is the day of rest, and the others are work days (= days of work).
13. An (**La**) hour is divided into sixty minutes, and a (**el**) minute
is divided into sixty seconds

G. 1. The monetary unit of Spain is different from (**diferente de**)
that (§210, *a*) of the Spanish-American countries. 2. For instance, in Argentina and in Mexico, the monetary unit is the dollar,
which is divided into one hundred cents, while in Spain it is the
peseta, which is divided into one hundred centimes. 3. The Spanish
silver " **duro** " has approximately the same weight as (**que**) the
Mexican dollar. 4. A Spanish " **real**, " as a rule, is worth less
than a Mexican " **real**," because the Mexican " **real** " is of silver.
5. In Spain there are copper coins of one centime, and of five
and ten centimes. 6. In Spanish America the smallest coin, as
a rule, is that of one cent.

RESUMEN GRAMATICAL

217. Numerales cardinales: . . .

a. Para el apócope de **uno** y **ciento,** véase el §179. Obsérvese el
uso de **un** y **una** en expresiones como **veintiún días** y **veintiuna
semanas.**

b. Para la supresión de **un** ante las palabras **cien(to)** y **mil,** véase
el §205, 3. Obsérvese sin embargo **veintiún mil.**

c. **Millón** es nombre masculino: su plural es **millones.** Requiere
la preposición **de** ante el nombre que multiplica.

d. En números compuestos, **y** se coloca ante el último numeral,
con tal que el número que le preceda sea menor de **ciento.**

e. En español sólo se cuenta por **cientos** hasta **900;** de **1,000** en
adelante se emplea **mil.**

218. Numerales ordinales: . . .

a. Para el apócope de **primero** y **tercero,** véase el §179, 1.

b. En español se hace poco uso de los ordinales después de **décimo.** En su lugar se usan los cardinales.

219. Números quebrados: — Desde 1/11 hasta 1/99 se forman los números quebrados añadiendo **–avo** al número cardinal después de suprimir la vocal final excepto la **–e** de **–siete** y **–nueve.**

a. Half (a half, one half, half a) como substantivo se traduce por la **mitad;** como adjetivo, por **medio (–a).**

220. Signos aritméticos: . . .

LESSON XLVIII

ADVERBS

222. — 1. **Aquí, acá,** *here, hither;* **ahí,** *there* (near the person addressed); **allí, allá,** *there, thither* (more remote).

Aquí and **allí** denote a more specific and limited place than do **acá** and **allá.**

Ven acá.	Come here.
Ven aquí.	Come right here.

2. **Mucho,** *much, a great deal;* **muy,** *very.*

Ha estudiado mucho.	He has studied much (a great deal).
Está muy enferma.	She is very ill.

a. **Muy,** not **mucho,** is used *before* a past participle not occurring in a perfect tense: **le estaré muy agradecido,** *I shall be much obliged to him.*

b. Very, when standing alone, is **mucho,** as **muy** can never stand alone: **¿es interesante el libro?** — **sí, mucho;** *is the book interesting?* — *yes, very.*

3. Both **si**, *if*, and **sí**, *yes*, may be used as intensive adverbs.

¡Si no lo creo!	Indeed I don't believe it!
¡Si partió esta mañana!	Why, he left this morning!
Ahora sí lo creo.	Now I *do* believe it.
Eso sí que es bueno.	That is indeed good.

4. **Ya**, *already, now, in due time, indeed;* **ya no**, *no longer, no more.*

Ya acabé.	I have already finished.
Ya entendemos.	Now we understand.
Ya volverá.	He will return in due time.
¡Ya lo creo!	I should say so!
Ya no tengo dinero.	I have no more money.

5. **–mente.** — In Spanish, adverbs may be formed from many descriptive adjectives by adding **–mente** to the feminine singular of the adjective, as **correctamente** (from **correcto**), *correctly*, **fácilmente** (from **fácil**), *easily*, etc.

a. When several adverbs in **–mente** modify the same word, **–mente** is omitted from all but the last: **hable Vd. clara y distintamente**, *speak clearly and distinctly.*

223. Agreement of Subject and Verb. — A verb agrees with its subject in number and person.

Yo soy, *I am;* **tú eres,** *you are;* **Vd. y Juan son,** *you and John are;* etc.

a. When subjects are of different persons, the verb is in the first person plural if any of the subjects is of the first person; and it is in the second person plural if the subjects are of the second and third persons.

Tú y yo somos.	You and I are.
Él y yo somos.	He and I are.
Tú y él sois.	You and he are.

224. Study the inflection of **dar** (§263), **valer** (§273), **salir** (§274), and **ver** (§279).

EXERCISES

la **altura,** height
la **anchura,** width, breadth
el **área,** *f.,* are
  árido, –a, arid, dry; los **áridos,**
    dry objects
  ascender (ie) a, to amount to
la **caja,** box
el **comercio,** commerce, business
el **cuadrado,** square; **cuadrado,**
  –a, square
  espeso, –a, dense
el **gramo,** gramme
el **grueso,** bulk, thickness; **grueso,**
  –a, bulky, thick

la **hectárea,** hectare
  hondo, –a, deep
la **libra,** pound
el **litro,** liter
la **longitud,** length
  medir (i), to measure
la **pesa,** weight (*with which to*
  weigh objects)
  pesar, to weigh
la **profundidad,** depth
  servirse (i) de, to use
el **suelo,** ground, floor
la **superficie,** surface
el **tamaño,** size

¿**Cuál es la longitud** (la anchura, la altura, la profundidad, el grueso)?
what is the length (width, height, depth, thickness)? **es de un metro,**
o **tiene un metro, de largo** (ancho, alto, hondo, grueso), o **de longi-**
tud (anchura, etc.), it is one meter long (wide, high, deep, thick); **dos**
veces más grande que, twice as large as; ¿**cuánto cabe en esta caja?**
how much does this box hold (contain)? **es decir,** that is to say

A. 1. España y todos los países hispanoamericanos han
adoptado el sistema métrico de pesas y medidas, que es
más fácil que el sistema inglés por (*on account of*) ser decimal.
2. Por ejemplo, 10 centímetros hacen un decímetro y 10 decí-
metros hacen un metro, que es la unidad de longitud. 3. Para
medir las grandes distancias se emplea el kilómetro, que es
igual a mil metros o aproximadamente 5/8 de una milla
inglesa. 4. Los terrenos se miden por áreas (el área es un
cuadrado de 10 metros de lado) o por hectáreas (= 100
áreas, o aproximadamente 2 1/2 "*acres*" ingleses).

5. La unidad de capacidad para líquidos es el litro, que
tiene el volumen de un decímetro cúbico, y es igual a poco
más de un "*quart*" inglés. 6. Por regla general, en los
países españoles los áridos se pesan y no se miden.

7. La unidad de peso del sistema métrico decimal es el gramo, que es igual al peso de un centímetro cúbico de agua destilada (*distilled*). 8. Un gramo es equivalente aproximadamente a 15 granos ingleses. 9. En el comercio la pesa más usual es el "kilo" o kilogramo, que tiene mil gramos, y equivale a poco más de dos libras inglesas.[1]

B. 1. ¿Cuál es el tamaño de este cuarto? 2. — El suelo es un cuadrado de 5 metros de lado. 3. — Es decir, ¿la superficie del suelo asciende a 25 metros cuadrados? 4. — Sí, señor. — ¿Y cuál es la altura de las paredes? 5. — Tienen 3 metros de altura. El techo, por supuesto, tiene la misma superficie que el suelo.

6. ¿Tiene Vd. una caja grande en que quepan todos mis libros? Tengo unos 100 libros, poco más o menos. 7. — Aquí tengo una. El tamaño de esta caja es de un metro de largo, 75 centímetros de ancho y 50 centímetros de hondo. ¿Cree Vd. que sea bastante grande? 8. — No, señor; necesito una caja dos veces más grande que ésa. 9. — No tengo otra más grande. Los libros de Vd. deben de [2] ser muy grandes. 10. — Ya lo creo. La mayor parte de los volúmenes son gruesos.

C. *Contéstese.* 1. ¿Qué sistema de pesas y medidas han adoptado España y los países hispanoamericanos? 2–4. ¿Cuál es la unidad de longitud (de capacidad para líquidos, de peso) en el sistema métrico decimal? 5. ¿Cuál es más largo, el metro o la vara inglesa? 6. ¿Cuántas pulgadas inglesas tiene un metro? 7. ¿Qué medida se emplea para medir las grandes distancias? 8. ¿Cuál es más largo, el kilómetro o la milla inglesa? 9. ¿A qué fracción (*fraction*) de milla

---

[1] Several old names of weights and measures are still occasionally heard in Spanish-speaking countries, viz.: **legua,** *league* (about 3 miles, or 5 kilometers); **milla,** *mile;* **vara,** *yard* (32 inches); **pie,** *foot;* **pulgada,** *inch;* **tonelada,** *ton;* **quintal,** *hundredweight;* **arroba,** *25 pounds;* **libra,** *pound;* etc.

[2] See **deber de** in General Vocabulary.

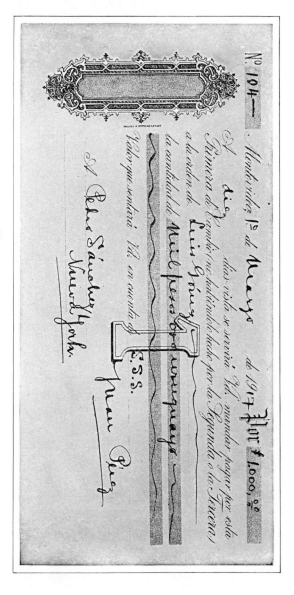

UNA LETRA DE CAMBIO

A bill of exchange or draft, the value of which will be charged to the account of Juan Pérez. Sometimes — but not in the present instance — a second or third copy is sent, to be used if the first is lost in the mails.

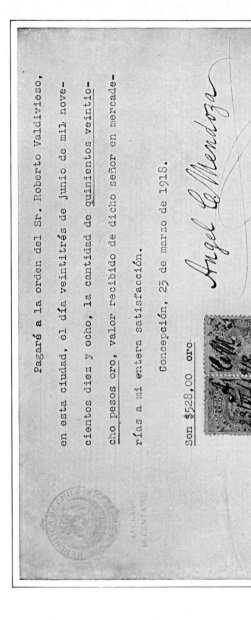

Un PAGARÉ

A typical promissory note.

equivale el kilómetro? 10. ¿Qué medida se emplea para medir los terrenos? 11. ¿A cuántos " *acres* " equivale la hectárea? 12. ¿Cuál es el volumen de un litro? 13. ¿A qué medida inglesa es aproximadamente igual? 14. En España ¿se miden o se pesan los áridos? 15. El peso del gramo ¿a qué volumen de agua destilada es igual? 16. ¿A cuántos granos ingleses equivale aproximadamente el gramo? 17. ¿Cuál es la pesa más usual de que se sirven en el comercio? 18. ¿A cuántas libras inglesas es aproximadamente igual?

D. *Fórmense adverbios de los siguientes adjetivos descriptivos:* afectuoso, agradable, amargo, aproximado, atento, ciego, claro, cómodo, completo, cordial, débil, fuerte, igual, real, triste.

E. 1–3. What is the length (width, depth) of this box? 4–6. It is one meter long (wide, deep). 7–9. What is the length (width, height) of this room? 10–12. It is 3 meters long (wide, high). 13. What is the thickness of this woolen goods? 14. It is one centimeter thick. 15. What is the thickness of this board (**tabla**)? 16. It is 3 centimeters thick. 17. What is the distance from Havana to Santiago de Cuba? 18. It is (**Hay**) about 1,000 kilometers. 19. How far is it from New York to Cádiz? 20. It is about 6,000 kilometers. 21. How far is it from Boston to San Francisco in a straight line (**en línea recta**)? 22. It is about 5,000 kilometers. 23. How far is it from Philadelphia to Chicago? 24. It is about 1,500 kilometers. 25. If the floor of a room is four meters square, how many square meters are there? 26. *Contéstese a la pregunta anterior.*

F. 1. He is not here. 2. Come here. 3. Come right-here (**aquí**). 4. She is not there. 5. There (**Allá**) in Havana it is warmer than here (**acá**). 6. Is she very ill? 7. Yes; very. 8. Why, I saw her this morning! 9. Indeed I don't believe it. 10. I also have seen her to-day. 11. Now I do believe it. 12. I don't (**Yo sí que no**). 13. Have you already finished? 14. I have already finished. 15. When will he return? 16. It will not be long before he returns. 17. He will return in due time. 18. I should say so! 19. Now we

understand each other. 20. Will you lend me a dollar? 21. I can't;
I haven't any more money. 22. John and I study a great deal.
23. You and John do not study much.

G. 1. Has Mr. Morales a plantation in Cuba? 2. — I should
say so! He bought five hundred hectares of fertile land (**terrenos**)
for which (**los cuales**) he paid only fifty dollars gold a hectare.
He intends to grow tobacco (**sembrar tabaco**). 3. — How many
acres are five hundred hectares equal to (*dígase:* To how many
acres, etc.)? 4. — You have only to (**No tiene Vd. que hacer más
que**) multiply the number of hectares by two and a half and you
will have the number of acres. Do you understand (it)? 5. — I
didn't understand (it), but now I do (**ahora sí lo entiendo**). 6. It
is easy, if one (**uno**) knows (**sabe**) the rule! 7. Do they use the
metric system in Cuba? 8. — Yes, sir; they use it in all the
Spanish-American countries. 9. — What is the size (**tamaño**) of
Mr. Morales's house? — It is twenty-five meters long by ten meters
wide. 10. — What is the height? 11. — There are only two
stories, but the ceilings of the rooms are high. 12. It is-probably-
about (§122) eight meters high and it has a flat roof. 13. — How
far is it from his plantation to Havana? 14. — It is about (**Es cosa
de**) one hundred kilometers in a straight line. 15. — How many
miles are one hundred kilometers equal to? 16. — About sixty.
To reduce (**Para reducir**) the kilometers to miles, we multiply the
number of kilometers by six and strike off (**quitamos**) the last digit
(**dígito**) of the product. 17. The result is not exact (**exacto**),
but it does pretty well (**sirve bastante bien**). 18. — In Cuba are
liquids bought and sold by liters? — Yes, sir. 19. — Is wheat sold
by bushels (**fanegas**) or by kilograms? — By kilograms. 20. In
the western (**occidentales**) states of the United States that formed
part of Mexico before 1848 all grains are sold still by (the) weight,
as, for instance, in Colorado and California.

RESUMEN GRAMATICAL

222. Adverbios. — 1. **Aquí, acá; ahí; allí, allá.**

Aquí y allí señalan un lugar más determinado y circunscrito que
el que señalan **acá** o **allá.**

2. **Mucho** significa, *much, a great deal;* **muy** significa *very.*

a. Se usa **muy,** y no **mucho,** ante un participio pasado, si éste no forma parte de un tiempo perfecto.

b. Very, cuando va solo, equivale a **mucho,** ya que **muy** no puede nunca ir solo.

3. Tanto **si** como **sí** se usan como adverbios intensivos.

4. **Ya** significa *now, in due time, indeed;* **ya no** significa *no longer, no more.*

5. **–mente.** En español se pueden formar adverbios de muchos adjetivos descriptivos, añadiendo la terminación **–mente** al femenino singular del adjetivo.

a. Cuando varios adverbios en **–mente** modifican al mismo nombre, la terminación **–mente** se omite en todos menos en el último.

223. Concordancia de sujeto y verbo. — El verbo concierta con el sujeto en número y persona.

a. Cuando los sujetos son de distintas personas, el verbo se pone en la primera persona plural si alguno de los sujetos es de la primera persona; y se pone en la segunda persona plural si los sujetos son de la segunda y tercera persona.

LESSON XLIX

PREPOSITIONS AND CONJUNCTIONS

225. The Prepositions Por and Para. — *For* is expressed by **por** or **para.** If *for* means *for the sake of, on account of,* or *in exchange for,* it is expressed by **por;** if it denotes purpose or destination, it is expressed by **para.**

Yo daría la vida por ella.	I would give my life for her.
Le castigó por haber dicho una mentira.	He punished him for having told a lie.
Pagamos doscientos pesos por el caballo.	We paid two hundred dollars for the horse.
Le envié por el médico.	I sent him for the physician.
Tengo un paquete para Vd.	I have a package for you.
Mañana parto para la Habana.	To-morrow I leave for Havana.

a. **Por** also means *through, by, " per."*

El ladrón entró por la ventana.	The thief entered through the window.
Me cogió por la mano.	He caught me by the hand.
Me pagan cinco mil pesos por año.	They pay me five thousand dollars a year (per year).
Ganamos seis por ciento por año.	We earn six per cent per annum.

b. Before an infinitive, *to,* meaning *for the sake of, in exchange for,* is **por,** and meaning *in order to* is **para**

Pugnando por entrar.	Fighting to enter.
Lo hizo para engañarme.	He did it to deceive me.

226. Conjunctions. —1. Y, or **e** before initial **i–** or **hi–** (not before **hie–**), *and.* **O,** or **u** before initial **o–** or **ho–,** *or.*

Padre y madre, father and mother.	**Padre e hijo,** father and son.
Cinco o seis, five or six.	**Siete u ocho,** seven or eight.

But, **helechos y hiedra,** ferns and ivy.

2. **Pero, mas, sino,** *but.* **Pero** and **mas** are synonyms, but **pero** is the more common. **Sino** is used after a negative statement that is offset by an affirmative statement.

Él lo dice, pero (o mas) yo no lo creo.	He says so, but I do not believe it.
No voy a Caracas sino a Bogotá.	I am not going to Caracas, but to Bogotá.

3. **Donde** (interrogatively, **dónde**) *where,* is often made more explicit by prefixing **a, en,** or **de.**

La casa en donde vive.	The house in which he lives.
¿A dónde va Vd. ?	Where are you going?
¿De dónde viene él?	Where does he come from?

227. Word Order. —1. When a verb precedes both its subject and a noun object or predicate adjective, the sub-

ject is placed before the object or predicate adjective if the
subject be the shorter, but if it be longer it follows.

¿Compró la casa su señor padre?	Did your father buy the house?
¿Compró su padre todas estas casas?	Did your father buy all these houses?
¿Es fácil la lección de castellano?	Is the Spanish lesson easy?
¿Es la lección fácil o difícil?	Is the lesson easy or difficult?

2. In a subordinate clause, the subject often follows the
verb if there be no noun object.

Esperaremos hasta que llegue el tren.	We shall wait until the train arrives.

228. Study the inflection of **asir** (§272), **caer** (§275),
and **oír** (§276).

EXERCISES

abonar, to credit
acusar, to acknowledge
el apartado (de correos), post-office box [1]
arrojar, to throw, cast
el cantar, song, poem
la conformidad, approval
el cheque, check, draft
detallar, to itemize
la espera, expectation
el extracto, summary, statement
la factura, bill
grato, –a, pleasing, kind

el importe, amount
la librería, bookstore
manifestar (ie), to advise (of) inform (of)
la orden, order
particular, especial, private
próximo pasado, last (month)
el recibo, receipt, reception
reiterar, to repeat
la remesa, remittance
respecto de, with regard to
retirar, to retire, take out
el saldo, balance

en rústica, in paper covers, unbound; Muy señores míos, Dear
Sirs; sírvase Vd., please; arroja un saldo a mi favor, there is (shown)
a balance in my favor

[1] Casilla, in Chile and some other Spanish-American countries.

A. 1.　　　Librería General de Luis Contreras [1]
　　　　Correos: Apartado 55　Teléfono 1695 [2]
　　　　　Madrid, 10 de Junio de 1917.

Sr. D. Felipe Heredia.

Muy señor mío:

Contesto a su grata (carta) de fecha 20 de mayo ppdo. (= próximo pasado) para manifestarle que el precio de la obra de Rodríguez Marín, *Quijote*, publicado en la Colección de " Clásicos castellanos," es de 3 ptas. en rústica cada tomo, siendo ocho la obra completa (*the complete work being eight*). Respecto de la edición crítica del mismo autor, están ya publicados 5 tomos [3] y el que falta, para completar los 6 de que se compondrá dicha obra, se publicará dentro de este año.

En espera de sus gratas y nuevas órdenes, se reitera de Vd. atento y seguro servidor,

　　　　　　　　　　　Q. E. S. M.
　　　　　　　　　　　　Luis Contreras.

2.　Muy señores míos:

Tengo el gusto de acusar a Vds. recibo de su apreciable carta de fecha 10 del actual, a la cual me apresuro a contestar. Sírvanse Vds. enviarme por correo las obras que siguen, todas encuadernadas:

Poem of The Cid, edición de Archer M. Huntington.
Cantar de Mío Cid, edición de Ramón Menéndez Pidal.
Don Quijote, edición crítica de Rodríguez Marín.

　　　　De Vds. atento y seguro servidor,

　　　　　　　　　　　　Felipe Heredia.

[1] This may be freely translated *Lewis Contreras, Publisher and Bookseller. A publishing house* is usually called **una casa editorial (o editora)**. *A publisher* is **un editor;** *an editor* of a review or newspaper is **un redactor**.

[2] When telephoning, this is generally read either **mil seiscientos noventa y cinco** or **diez y seis nueve cinco**.

[3] For the distinction between **volumen** and **tomo** see *volume* in the English-Spanish Vocabulary.

3. Muy señor mío:

Tengo el gusto de acusar a Vd. recibo de su grata de fecha 25 de abril último, de la cual retiré cheque a m/o (= mi orden) por ptas.: 125.50, que he abonado en su cuenta particular.

Por contra (*Against you*) cargo en la misma (cuenta) ptas.: 36.25, importe de las obras detalladas en la factura adjunta, remitidas en cinco paquetes certificados.

Se repite a las órdenes de Vd. atto y s. s. (= atento y seguro servidor),

Luis Contreras.

4. Muy señor mío:

Tengo el gusto de remitir a Vd. con la presente (carta) el extracto de su cuenta cerrada el 30 de julio de 1916.

Como Vd. observará, arroja en la indicada fecha un saldo a mi favor de ptas.: 136.45, que le cargo en cuenta nueva, rogándole me manifieste su conformidad si lo halla exacto.

Con este motivo se reitera de Vd. atento servidor,

Luis Contreras.

B. *Contéstese.* 1. ¿Cuál es el número del apartado de correos (el número de la casilla) de Luis Contreras? 2. ¿Cuál es el número de su teléfono? 3. ¿A quién escribe él en su carta fechada (*dated*) el 10 de junio de 1917? 4. ¿Qué manifiesta al señor Heredia? 5. Si cada tomo del *Quijote* cuesta 3 pesetas en rústica, ¿costará más encuadernado? 6. ¿De cuántos tomos se compondrá la edición crítica del *Quijote?* 7. ¿Cuántos tomos están ya publicados? 8. ¿Es más barata la edición de "Clásicos castellanos"? 9. ¿Cuántos tomos hay en esta edición? 10. Si el precio de cada tomo es de 3 pesetas, ¿cuánto cuestan los ocho tomos? 11. ¿Cuánto valen en moneda norteamericana (estadounidense) 24 pesetas españolas? 12. ¿Cómo se dice en castellano: *I have pleasure in acknowledging the receipt of your kind letter?* 13. ¿Cómo se dice: *Please send me by mail?* 14. *I have credited five pesetas to your account.* 15. *I charge five pesetas to your account.* 16. ¿Cómo se dice: *Dear Sir, Dear Sirs, Dear Madam,* etc. (etcétera)? 17. ¿Cómo se dice: *Yours truly, Sincerely yours, Affectionately yours,* etc.?

C. 1. He paid 100 dollars for that horse. 2. He bought it for his son. 3. I have a letter for you. 4. It was written by Mr. González. 5. I will give you (**Le doy a Vd.**) my watch for your bicycle. 6. I paid $35 for the bicycle. 7. I bought it for my brother. 8. To-morrow I leave for Santiago de Chile. 9. I am going for (**por**) six months. 10. I shall go by steamer. 11. He entered through the door. 12. He caught me by the arm (**brazo**). 13. I fought (**Yo peleé**) for my (**la**) life. 14. He went out through the window. 15. They earn eight per cent. 16. They pay him three dollars a day. 17. Mother and daughter, father and son, all were ill. 18. The father and his son died. 19. There are nine or ten volumes. 20. There are ten or eleven. 21. Was it (¿**Era**) [a] woman or [a] man? 22. Was it Mary or Anna? 23. Was it Henry or Octavius (**Octavio**)? 24. He is not a Spaniard but a Frenchman. 25. But he has studied the Spanish and English languages. 26. He is not going to Buenos Aires but to Montevideo. 27. He talks of nothing but (of) Montevideo. 28. Where do they live? 29. The house in which they live is near the post office. 30. Where do they come from? 31. Where are they going? 32. We are waiting until the train arrives. 33. You will wait as-long-as (**mientras**) life lasts. 34. Is the book interesting? 35. Is the Spanish exercise difficult? 36. Is the exercise easy or difficult? 37. Did John sell all his horses? 38. Did your brother buy a horse? 39. Did Mary write an interesting letter? 40. Did Mary's sister write a letter?

D. 1. Lewis Contreras, Publisher and Bookseller,
Post-office Box 55,
Madrid, Spain.

Dear Sir:

I have pleasure in acknowledging the receipt of your kind letter of the 10th inst., in which you advise me that the critical edition of the complete works of Calderón de la Barca costs ten pesetas each volume (**tomo**) unbound, or twelve pesetas and sixty centimes bound. Please send me by mail this edition, bound, and also the following books:

Lope de Vega, *Selected Works*

Tirso de Molina, *Complete Works*

Please send me with the bill a (**el**) statement of my account, and I shall send you a check to balance (**saldar**) it.

Very truly yours,

Philip Heredia.

2. Dear Sir

I have pleasure in sending you herewith a (**el**) statement of your account brought-up-to (**cerrada**) June 30, 1919.

1918.		Debit (**Debe**)	Credit (**Heber**)
July 1st (**Julio 1°**)	Balance in (**a**) my favor	139.55	
Dec. (**Dbre.**) 5	My bill	33.30	
1919.			
March 24	Your (**Su**) remittance .		100.00
June 30	Balance in my favor .		72.85
		172.85	172.85
		72.85	

As you will observe, there is a balance in my favor of 72.85 pesetas which I charge to you on a new account, begging you to advise me if you do not find it correct (**exacto**).

Very sincerely yours,

Luis Contreras.

RESUMEN GRAMATICAL

225. Las preposiciones *por* y *para.* — *For* puede traducirse mediante **por** o **para**. Si la voz inglesa *for* significa *for the sake of, on account of* o *in exchange for*, se traduce mediante **por**; si significa propósito o destino, se traduce por **para**.

a. **Por** también significa *through, by, " per."*

b. Delante de un infinitivo, la preposición inglesa *to* se expresa en español mediante **por** cuando significa *for the sake of* o *in exchange for*, y mediante **para** cuando significa *in order to*.

226. Conjunciones. — 1. **Y, e** ante **i–** o **hi–** iniciales (**y,** y no **e,** se usa ante **hie–**); **o, u** ante **o–** u **ho–** iniciales.

2. **Pero, mas, sino,** significan *but.* **Pero** y **mas** son sinónimos; se usa **pero** con más frecuencia. **Sino** se usa después de una expresión negativa, contradicha por una expresión afirmativa.

3. **Donde** (en forma interrogativa **dónde**) se hace a menudo más explícita mediante las preposiciones antepuestas **a, en** y **de.**

227. Orden de las palabras. — 1. Cuando el verbo precede al sujeto, y también al substantivo complementario o al adjetivo predicado (atributo), el sujeto precede a cualquiera de éstos dos con tal que sea más corto, pero le sigue si es más largo.

2. En cláusulas subordinadas el sujeto sigue muchas veces al verbo con tal que no haya ningún substantivo complementario.

LESSON L

AUGMENTATIVES AND DIMINUTIVES

229. There are many augmentative and diminutive suffixes in Spanish, which occur commonly in colloquial language. The foreigner should use them with the greatest caution. It is generally safe to use **–ito** (**–cito, –ecito**), but it is best to avoid the other suffixes until one has become familiar with their use. The suffixes are attached to the stem of a word after it has dropped a final unstressed vowel. A few of the more common suffixes are given below.

230. Augmentative Suffixes. — **–ón** (**–ona**) and **–azo** (**–a**) denote largeness, with or without grotesqueness. Feminine nouns usually become masculine upon adding the suffix **–ón,** unless sex is indicated.

Aquel **hombrón** es montañés.	That big man is a mountaineer.
Aquella **mujeraza** es su hermana.	That large woman is his sister.
Tráigame Vd. un **cucharón.**	Bring me a large spoon.

231 Diminutive Suffixes

–ito, –a (–cito, –a; –ecito, –a) denotes smallness, and may also express affection or pity.

–illo, –a (–cillo, –a; –ecillo, –a) denotes smallness, and may also express indifference or ridicule.

–uelo, –a (–zuelo, –a; –ezuelo, –a) denotes smallness, and may also express ridicule or scorn.

¿Cómo está su hijita, señora?	How is your (dear) little daughter, madam?
Mi hermanito se llama Juanito.	My little brother's name is Johnny.
Tenemos una casita de campo.	We have a cottage in the country.
En la jaula hay varios pajarillos.	In the cage there are several tiny birds.
No fué más que un descuidillo.	It was only a little slip.

a. The longer forms (–cito, –cillo, –zuelo, etc.) are used only with words of more than one syllable ending in –n or –r.

En la casita de su muñequita hay tres silloncitos.	In her dollie's little house there are three little armchairs.
Ese jovencito es un autorcillo de ninguna importancia.	That youth is a petty author of no importance.

b. The still longer forms (–ecito, –ecillo, –ezuelo, etc.) are used with monosyllables, with words ending in –e, and with those that have the radical diphthong ie or ue.

¡Qué bella florecita!	What a beautiful little flower!
Venció a varios reyezuelos.	He conquered several petty kings.
¡Madrecita mía!	My dear little mother!
La pobrecita está muy enferma.	The poor little girl is very ill.
Cada pueblecito tiene su plazuela.	Every small town has its little public square.

c. All the diminutives are most commonly used with nouns; but they are also used with adjectives, participles, and adverbs to denote smallness of quality or degree.

Estamos un poquillo cansaditos.	We are just a little tired.
Ya estamos cerquita.	Now we are quite near.
Ahorita llegamos.	We shall arrive very soon.

232. Study the inflection of **decir** (§267), **traer** (§277), and **conducir** (§278).

EXERCISES

anticipado, –a, in advance
asegurar, to assure, insure
el **banco,** bank
el **banquero,** banker
el **cajero,** cashier
  cobrar, to collect (*a bill*), cash (*a check*)
el **descuento,** discount
  efectuar, to effect, make
  endosar, to endorse
el **envío,** shipment
  exigir, to demand, insist on
la **expedición,** sending, shipping

la **firma,** signature
  firmar, to sign
los **impresos,** printed matter
la **letra de cambio,** bill of exchange
la **madera,** wood
  otorgar, to grant
el **pago,** payment
el **pedido,** order (*of goods*)
el **plazo,** time limit
el **prospecto,** announcement
  reducido, low (*price*)
  suelto, loose, single

hacer efectivo, to cash (*a check*); **perdone Vd.,** pardon me; **a vuelta de correo,** by return mail; **franco de porte,** postage prepaid

A. 1. Voy al Primer Banco Nacional a sacar $50 (a cobrar un cheque de $50). 2. — ¿Conoce Vd. al banquero? 3. — No, señor; pero conozco al cajero. 4. Sírvase Vd. hacerme efectivo este cheque. 5. — Se le olvidó a Vd. endosar el cheque. 6. — Perdone Vd. 7. — Escriba Vd.: "Páguese a la orden del Primer Banco Nacional," y ponga su firma aquí. 8. — Está bien. Ya lo firmé. 9. — ¿Quiere Vd. billetes de banco u oro? 10. — Prefiero los billetes de banco. 11. — Ahí los tiene Vd. — Muchas gracias.

B. 1. Muy señor mío:

Deseo tenga Vd. la bondad de remitirme a vuelta de correo el *Prospecto* y otros impresos de esa universidad.

Soy de Vd. atento seguro servidor.

2. Muy señor mío:

Adjunto le remito a Vd. en giro postal $5.00 importe de un año de subscripción a *La Esfera*, que le ruego me envíe a esta dirección.

Créame de Vd. atento seguro servidor.

Precios de subscripción, franco de porte.

Por mes, $0.50
Por año, $5.00
Número suelto, $0.10

3. Muy señores míos:

Sírvanse Vds. remitirme su catálogo y lista de precios. Espero que me concedan los precios más reducidos.

Dándoles las gracias anticipadas, soy de Vds. S. S.

4. Muy señor mío:

Tengo el gusto de remitir a Vd. por este mismo correo nuestro último catálogo. Todos los artículos mencionados en él están hechos de los mejores materiales.

Le concedemos a Vd. un descuento del 5 % (por ciento) en caso de pago al contado, o un descuento del 3 % si el pago se efectúa a 30 días desde la expedición del envío. Si Vd. exige un plazo de 3 meses, no podemos otorgar ningún descuento de los precios corrientes.

Podemos asegurar a Vd. que haremos cuanto sea posible para servir sus pedidos a su entera satisfacción. El importe de ellos puede ser enviado en letra de cambio, cheque o giro postal.

En espera de sus gratas órdenes, quedo de Vd. atto. y s. s. q. e. s. m.,[1]

Juan Rodríguez.

5. Muy señores míos:

Tengo el gusto de acusar a Vds. recibo de su apreciable carta y el catálogo de su casa.

Sírvanse Vds. enviarme los artículos detallados en la lista que les remito adjunta. Al recibo de su factura les remitiremos el importe en cheque sobre Nueva York. Rogamos

---

[1] Some business houses prefer the small letters here to capitals.

a Vds. se sirvan hacer embalar (*have packed*) bien los artículos en cajas de madera.

Se reitera de Vds. atento y seguro servidor.

C. *Contéstese.* 1. ¿A dónde fué Vd. a sacar dinero (a cobrar un cheque)? 2. ¿Conocía Vd. al banquero? 3. ¿Qué le dijo Vd. al cajero? 4. ¿Qué se le olvidó a Vd. hacer? 5. ¿Qué le dijo a Vd. el cajero que escribiera? 6. ¿Tuvo Vd. que firmar el cheque? 7. ¿Prefirió Vd. los billetes de banco al oro?

Para las respuestas a las siguientes preguntas véase B. 4, *suponiendo que el señor Rodríguez le escribió a Vd. la carta.* 8. ¿Qué le remitió a Vd. por correo el señor Rodríguez? 9. ¿De qué materiales dijo que están hechos los artículos? 10–12. ¿Qué descuento le concede a Vd. en caso de pago al contado? (si el pago se efectúa a 30 días desde la expedición del envío? si Vd. exige un plazo de 3 meses?) 13. ¿Qué le aseguró a Vd.? 14. ¿Cómo puede remitirse el importe de los pedidos? 15. ¿Cómo se subscribió el señor Rodríguez?

D. *Las palabras en letra bastardilla deben traducirse por diminutivos o aumentativos.* 1. *Johnny* was crying. 2. His mother spoke to him. 3. *Little-son*, what is the matter with you? (**¿qué tienes?**). 4. Alas! (**!Ay!**) *dear-little-mother*, he answered. 5. Last week the *little-bird* (–ito) died. 6. Now the *kitten* is dead. 7. And the *little-child* kept on crying (**siguió llorando**). 8. My *little-sister's* name is *Mary* (**Mariquita**). 9. She has a *little-house*. 10. In the *little-house* there are *little-chairs* and a *little-table*. 11. In a *little cage* there are several *tiny-birds* (–illos). 12. A *dollie* lives in the *little-house*. 13. In a *little-garden* there are many *tiny-flowers*. 14. *Very-near* the *little-house* there is a yard. 15. In the yard there are a *little-horse*, a *little-dog*, and some *tiny-hens*. 16. In this yard a *teaspoon* would seem a *large-spoon*. 17. Any (**Cualquier**) man would seem a *big-man*. 18. Any (**Cualquiera**) woman sould seem a *large-woman*.

E. 1. I must go to the bank and (a) draw some money. 2. I spent my last dollar this morning. 3. — Do you know the cashier?

4. — No, I do not (**No le conozco**), or rather (**o mejor dicho**) he doesn't know *me*.   5. Will you come with me (**acompañarme**) to the bank to identify me (**para identificarme**)?   6. I shall be greatly (**sumamente**) obliged to you.   7. This is the First National Bank.   8. I should like to cash this check.   9. — Very well, sir.   10. But you forgot to endorse it.   11. Please write on the back (**al dorso**) " Pay (= Let it be paid) to the order of the First National Bank," and sign it here.   12. Thank you.   Do you wish gold or paper money (= bank notes)?   13. — Please give me paper money.   14. I am not used to (**No estoy acostumbrado a**) carrying gold coins in my pocket, and I fear I may lose (§153) them.

F. 1. Sir:

Enclosed I am sending you $3.00 for a year's subscription to ——.   Please send it to this address.   For a long time I have been buying (§115) single copies in the street, but I prefer to receive it at my residence (**en mi domicilio**).

Very truly yours.

2. Dear Sir:

I am sending you (*escríbase:* I have the honor of sending you) herewith our catalogue and price list.   I can assure you that we shall do everything in our power to fill your orders to your entire satisfaction.   We offer (*úsese* **conceder**) you the lowest prices in this market (**de esta plaza**).   Moreover, we can offer you a discount of 6 per cent. if you pay cash (= in case of cash payment), or 3 per cent. if the payment is made in 30 days from time of shipping the goods (= from the sending of the shipment).   If you insist on more than 30 days' time (= on a time limit of more than 30 days), we can not grant any discount from current prices.

Hoping that we may have your kind orders, I am very sincerely yours.

RESUMEN GRAMATICAL

229. Aumentativos y diminutivos. — Hay muchos sufijos en español para formar los aumentativos y diminutivos, sobre todo en el lenguaje corriente.   El extranjero debe emplearlos con la mayor cautela.   Lo más seguro es usar el sufijo **–ito** (**–cito, –ecito**), y evitar los otros hasta estar familiarizado con su uso.

Los sufijos se añaden al radical de la palabra después de haber quitado a ésta la vocal final no acentuada.

230. Sufijos aumentativos: –ón (–ona) y –azo (–a) aumentan simplemente la idea del positivo, con o sin idea de monstruosidad. Los nombres femeninos se vuelven masculinos al añadirles el sufijo –ón, salvo el caso de indicarse el sexo.

231. Sufijos diminutivos: –ito, –illo y –uelo expresan idea de pequeñez, y pueden significar al mismo tiempo: –ito, sentimientos de cariño o conmiseración; –illo, indiferencia o menosprecio; –uelo, menosprecio o burla.

a. Los sufijos más largos (–cito, –cillo, –zuelo, etc.) se usan con voces de más de una sílaba que terminan en –n o –r.

b. Las formas aun más largas (–ecito, –ecillo, –ezuelo, etc.) se usan con monosílabos, con palabras que terminan en –e, y con aquellas que tienen el diptongo radical **ie** o **ue.**

c. Todos los diminutivos se usan principalmente con nombres; pero también se usan con adjetivos, participios y adverbios, para expresar pequeñez de calidad o grado.

TOPICAL CHARTS AND DIRECT-
METHOD EXERCISES

A WORD TO THE TEACHER

It is the opinion of many progressive teachers that a word or an expression is fixed more firmly in the student's memory, if, when the student utters the word or expression, he looks at the object designated or at its image. Similarly, if the word or expression denotes action, such as **yo tomo un lápiz, yo abro el libro, yo cierro el libro,** etc., the memory may be aided if the student acts the part.

Accordingly, when doing orally the following Direct-Method Exercises, it is suggested that, whenever a student gives the Spanish name of an object, he should either hold in his hand or point at any object that is available, or that he should point at the image of the object in the illustrated charts. And when a student says **yo, usted, el profesor (la profesora), el alumno (la alumna),** etc., he may indicate the person to whom he refers.

If the instructor so desires, the students may sit in pairs so that one student can verify the accuracy of the other student's work or correct him if he makes a mistake.

If the instructor wishes to devote some time to oral work before beginning the lessons proper, the Classroom Expressions may be used as Direct-Method material with the aid of objects in the classroom and the first illustrated chart.

At the end of the Direct-Method Exercises based on the charts will be found lists containing the Spanish names of the objects in the charts.

The charts may be studied and the Direct-Method Exercises may be practised quite independently of the Grammar Lessons, and in whatever order the instructor may choose. The charts and exercises, however, have been arranged in the order that coördinates best with the Lessons. References to the corresponding Lessons are given at the head of each exercise. The numbers in parenthesis refer to advanced Lessons that take up again the same topic. When the class comes to these advanced Lessons, the corresponding chart might well be reviewed.

EXPRESIONES DE LA CLASE

1. 1 (uno), 2 (dos), 3 (tres), 4 (cuatro), 5 (cinco), 6 (seis), 7 (siete), 8 (ocho), 9 (nueve), 10 (diez), 11 (once), 12 (doce), 13 (trece), 14 (catorce), 15 (quince), 16 (diez y seis), 17 (diez y siete), 18 (diez y ocho), 19 (diez y nueve), 20 (veinte), 21 (veintiuno), 22(veintidós), 23 (veintitrés), 24 (veinticuatro), 25 (veinticinco), 26 (veintiséis), 27 (veintisiete), 28 (veintiocho), 29 (veintinueve), 30 (treinta), 31 (treinta y uno), 40 (cuarenta), 50 (cincuenta).

2. a (*a*), b (*be*), c (*ce*), ch (*che*), d (*de*), e (*e*), f (*efe*), g (*ge*), h (*hache*), i (*i*), j (*jota*), k (*ka*), l (*ele*), ll (*elle*), m (*eme*), n (*ene*), ñ (*eñe*), o (*o*), p (*pe*), q (*cu*), r (*ere*), rr (*erre*), s (*ese*), t (*te*), u (*u*), v (*ve*, or *u ve*), w (*doble v*), x (*equis*), y (*i griega*), z (*zeta*).

3. Buenos días, Juan (María). Buenos días, clase. — Buenos días, señor (señora, señorita).

4. ¿ Cómo está usted ? (¿ Cómo están ustedes ?) — Muy bien, gracias. ¿ Cómo está usted ?

5. Preste usted (Presten ustedes) atención.

6. ¿ Qué es esto ? (*Respuesta:* Es un lápiz. Es una pluma . . .)

7. ¿ Qué tiene usted ? — Yo tengo un libro.
   ¿ Qué tienen ustedes ? — Nosotros (Nosotras) tenemos papel.

8. ¿ Qué tengo yo ? — Usted tiene un puntero.
   ¿ Qué tenemos ? — Ustedes tienen tiza.

9. ¿ Qué tomo yo ? — Usted toma un libro.
   ¿ Qué toma usted ? — Yo tomo un lápiz.

10. ¿ De qué color es el libro ? — El libro es rojo (verde, amarillo, blanco, negro).
    ¿ Cómo es el libro ? — Es rojo (verde, etc.).

11. ¿ De qué tamaño es la pluma ? — La pluma es grande (mediana, pequeña).
   ¿ Cómo es la pluma ? — Es grande, (etc.).

12. ¿ De qué forma es esto ? — Es redondo, (cuadrado).
   ¿ Cómo es esto ? — Es redondo, (etc.).

13. ¿ Cómo se llama esto en español ?
   ¿ Cómo se dice en español ?

14. Responda usted (Respondan ustedes) en español.

15. Dígame usted (Díganme ustedes) la palabra.

16. Hable usted (Hablen ustedes) español.

17. Pronuncie usted (Pronuncien ustedes) distintamente.

18. Clase, ¿ es correcto ?

19. Levánte(n)se usted(es).

20. Pase(n), o Vaya(n), usted(es) a la pizarra.

21. Tome(n) usted(es) la tiza.

22. Escriba(n) usted(es) *lápiz, libro,* . . .

23. No es correcto.

24. ¿ Cuál es la forma correcta ?
   ¿ Sabe usted cuál es la forma correcta ?

25. Sí, señor (señora, señorita), yo sé cual es.
   No, señor (señora, señorita), yo no sé cual es.

26. Substituya(n) usted(es) la **a** por una **o**.

27. Borre(n) usted(es) las palabras, o la frase.

28. Siénte(n)se usted(es).

29. Vuelva(n) usted(es) a la pizarra.

30. Tome usted el libro (la gramática, el libro de lectura).
   Tomen ustedes los libros (las gramáticas, etc.).

31. Abra(n) usted(es) el (los) libro(s).

32. Lea(n) usted(es) la lección.

33. Lea(n) usted(es) en alta voz.

34. Cierre(n) usted(es) el (los) libro(s).

35. Abra(n) usted(es) el (los) cuaderno(s).

36. Lea(n) usted(es) los ejercicios.

37. Continúe(n), o Siga(n), usted(es) leyendo (escribiendo).

38. ¿ Qué lección tenemos para hoy ?

39. Es la primera (1ª) lección, la segunda (2ª) lección, la tercera (3ª) lección, la cuarta (4ª) lección, la quinta (5ª) lección, la sexta (6ª) lección, la séptima (7ª) lección, la octava (8ª) lección, la novena (9ª) lección, la décima (10ª) lección, la lección once (11), la lección doce (12), la lección trece (13), la lección catorce (14).

40. Para mañana estudien ustedes la primera (1ª) lección, la segunda (2ª) lección, . . . la lección once (11).

41. Lea(n) usted(es) la primera (1ª) página, la segunda (2ª) página, la tercera (3ª) página, . . . la página doce (12), la página trece (13), . . . la página veinte (20).

42. Lea(n) usted(es) la primera (1ª) línea, la segunda (2ª) línea, . . . la línea quince (15), la línea diez y seis (16).

43. Lea(n) usted(es) desde la segunda (2ª) línea de la página doce (12) hasta la décima (10ª) línea de la página trece (13).

44. Estudien ustedes la primera (1ª) parte de la lección.

45. Escriba(n) usted(es) el primer (1) párrafo, el segundo (2°) párrafo, el tercer (3) párrafo, . . . el párrafo once (11), el párrafo doce (12).

46. Estudien ustedes toda la lección.

47. Aprendan ustedes de memoria todas las palabras y todas las reglas.

48. Conjuguen ustedes los verbos.

49. Repasen ustedes la primera (1ª) lección.

50. ¡ Adiós ! ¡ Hasta mañana !

La Sala de Clase

I. LA SALA DE CLASE

1. ¿ Qué es el número uno, dos, etc. (etcétera) de la ilustración ? (*Respuesta:* Es un lápiz, es papel, etc.) 2. ¿ Qué número tiene la carta, etc. ? (*Respuesta:* La carta tiene el número cuatro, etc.) 3. Yo tengo papel y un lápiz. Yo escribo en papel con lápiz. 4. Usted tiene papel y un lápiz. Usted escribe en papel con lápiz. 5. Juan tiene, etc. 6. Nosotros tenemos, etc. 7. Ustedes tienen, etc. 8. Juan y María tienen, etc. 9. Yo tengo una pluma y tinta. Yo escribo los ejercicios en el cuaderno con pluma y tinta. 10. Usted, etc. 11. El alumno, etc. 12. Nosotros, etc. 13. Ustedes, etc. 14. Los alumnos, etc. 15. Yo paso a la pizarra. Yo tomo la tiza y escribo los ejercicios en la pizarra. Yo tomo el borrador y borro los ejercicios. 16. Usted pasa, etc. 17. María, etc. 18. Nosotros, etc. 19. Ustedes, etc. 20. Los alumnos, etc. 21. Yo tomo tiza blanca y escribo los ejercicios en la pizarra. Yo subrayo las faltas (los errores) con tiza roja. Yo señalo las faltas (los errores) con el puntero. 22. Usted, etc. 23. Pablo, etc. 24. Nosotros, etc. 25. Ustedes, etc. 26. Los alumnos, etc. 27–50. ¿ Tengo yo papel y un lápiz ? — Sí, usted tiene papel y un lápiz. (*o* No, usted no tiene papel y un lápiz). — ¿ Escribo yo en papel con lápiz ? — Sí (No), usted (no) escribe en papel con lápiz.

De este modo pueden repetirse en forma interrogativa los números 3–26 de los ejercicios anteriores, con las respuestas afirmativas o negativas que corresponden.

51. En la clase hay libros, lápices, etc. 52. ¿ Cuántos alumnos (profesores, asientos, ventanas, etc.) hay en la clase ?

LA FAMILIA

II. LA FAMILIA

1. ¿ Qué es el número uno, dos, etc., de la ilustración ?
2. ¿ Qué número tiene el abuelo, etc. ?
3. Yo tengo un abuelo, una abuela, un padre y una madre.
4. Usted tiene, etc.
5. José (*Joseph*), etc.
6. Nosotros, etc.
7. Ustedes, etc.
8. José y Ana (*Anna*), etc.
9. El abuelo y la abuela (Los abuelos) tienen un hijo.
10. El padre y la madre (Los padres) tienen un hijo y una hija (hijos).
11. El hijo y la hija (Los hijos) tienen un padre y una madre (padres).
12. El hijo y la hija (Los hijos) son hermanos.
13. Los hijos tienen un perro y un gato.
14. (*Un alumno dice*) ¿ Es éste el abuelo ? — (*Otro alumno responde*) Sí, éste es el abuelo, *o* No, éste no es el abuelo.
15. ¿ Es ésta la abuela ? — Sí (No), ésta es (no es) la abuela. Etc.
16. ¿ Es éste el abuelo de usted ? — No, éste no es mi abuelo.
17. ¿ Es ésta la abuela de usted ? — No, ésta no es mi abuela. Etc.
18. ¿ Es éste mi abuelo ? — No, éste no es su abuelo, *o* el abuelo de usted.
19. ¿ Es ésta mi abuela ? — No, ésta no es su abuela. Etc.
20. ¿ Es éste el abuelo de aquél alumno ? — No, éste no es su abuelo, o el abuelo de él. Etc.
21. ¿ Cuántas personas hay en esta familia ?
22. ¿ Quiénes son ?

243

La Sala (de Recibo)

III. LA SALA (DE RECIBO)

LECCIONES XII (XXX)

1. ¿ Qué es el número uno, dos, etc., de la ilustración ?
2. ¿ Qué número tiene el piano, el sillón, etc. ?
3. ¿ Cuántos muebles hay en esta sala ?
4. ¿ Cuáles son ?
5. ¿ Cuántas puertas y cuántas ventanas hay ?
6. ¿ Dónde está el cuadro (el reloj, la alfombra, la cortina, el candelero, etc.) ? (*Respuestas:* El cuadro está en la pared; etc.)
7. ¿ Dónde están los libros ?
8. ¿ Cuántas sillas (¿ Cuántos sillones, ¿ Cuántas mesas) hay en la sala ?
9. ¿ Qué muebles hay en la sala de la casa de Vd. ?
10. (*Un alumno pregunta:*) ¿ Qué es esto ? — (*Otro alumno responde:*) Es una mesa, etc.
11. (*Un alumno pregunta:*) ¿ Abro (*infin.*, **abrir**) yo la ventana ? — (*Otro alumno responde:*) Sí, Vd. abre la ventana, *o* Vd. no abre la ventana. — ¿ Abre Vd. la ventana ? — Yo (no) abro la ventana. — ¿ Abre Julio, etc. ? ¿ Abrimos nosotros, etc. ? ¿ Abren Vds., etc. ? ¿ Abren los alumnos, etc. ?
12. ¿ Cierro yo, etc., la puerta ? — Vd. cierra, etc.
13. ¿ Toco yo, etc., el piano ? — Vd. toca, etc.
14. ¿ Leo yo, etc., algún libro ? — Vd. lee, etc.

EL DORMITORIO (LA ALCOBA)

IV. EL DORMITORIO (*LA ALCOBA*)

1. ¿ Qué es el número uno, dos, etc.?

2. ¿ Qué número tiene la cómoda, la silla, etc.?

3–5. ¿ Qué objetos (cosas) hay sobre la cama?... sobre el escritorio?... sobre el lavabo?

6–7. ¿ Cuál de los muebles está más cerca de la ventana? ... de la cama?

8–13. En mi dormitorio (*o* alcoba) tengo una buena cama con fundas de almohadas y sábanas limpias y blancas, y mantas (frazadas) de lana, un tocador con un buen espejo, una cómoda con varias gavetas, y una pequeña silla. En su dormitorio (*o* alcoba) Vd. tiene, etc. En su dormitorio (*o* alcoba) Pablo tiene, etc. En nuestro dormitorio, etc. En su dormitorio, etc.

14. Sobre mi escritorio (... el escritorio de Vd., etc.) hay papel blanco para escribir, tinta en un tintero, una pluma, y una lámpara eléctrica.

15. Sobre mi lavabo (... el lavabo de Vd., etc.) hay un jarro de agua, una palangana (*o* jofaina), una jabonera con jabón, un cepillo de dientes, un vaso para agua, y en el toallero hay varias toallas.

Preguntas y respuestas:

16. ¿ Dónde duermo yo? — Vd. duerme en la cama.
¿ Dónde duerme Vd.? Yo duermo en la cama.
¿ Dónde ... él, nosotros, Vds., ellos? (*Respuestas*)

17. ¿ A qué hora me levanto yo?... Vd., mi hermano, nosotros, Vds., mis padres? (*Respuestas*)

18. ¿ A qué hora me acuesto yo?... Vd., mi tío, nosotros, Vds., mis tíos? (*Respuestas*)

La Cocina

V. LA COCINA

1. ¿ Qué es el número uno, dos, etc. ?
2. ¿ Qué número tiene la cacerola, la olla, etc. ?
3. ¿ Cuáles son los muebles de la cocina ?
4. ¿ Qué es la batería de cocina ?   (*o* ¿ Qué son los trastos de cocina ?)
5. ¿ Quién prepara las comidas ?
6. ¿ En qué se asa la carne ?
7. ¿ En qué se cuece la carne ?
8. ¿ En qué se cuece el pan ?
9. ¿ Qué friega la cocinera ?
10. ¿ En esta cocina hay cocina económica (estufa), o hay fogón ?
11. ¿ Le gusta a Vd. cocinar ?
12. ¿ Le gusta a Vd. fregar las ollas y las cazuelas ?
13. ¿ Cómo prepara las comidas la cocinera ?
14. ¿ Le gustan a Vd. las comidas que prepara la cocinera ?
15. En la casa de Vds. ¿ quién prepara las comidas ?
16. ¿ A qué hora se levantan Vds. ?
17–19. ¿ A qué hora se desayunan (almuerzan, comen) Vds. ?
20. ¿ A qué hora se acuestan Vds. ?

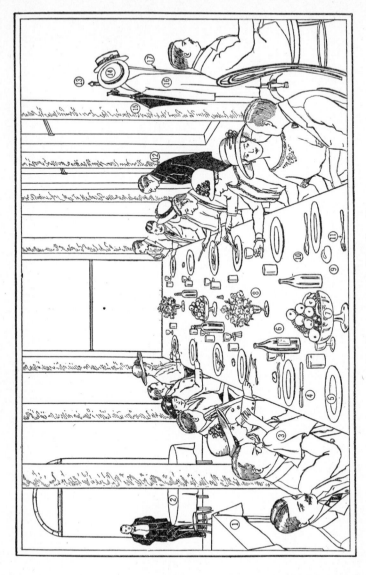

El Restaurant (El Café)

VI. EL RESTAURANT (*EL CAFÉ*)

LECCIONES XVII–XVIII (XLI)

1. ¿ Qué es el número uno, dos, etc. ?
2. ¿ Qué número tiene el cuchillo, el tenedor, etc. ?
3. ¿ Cuáles son los muebles del restaurant (*o* del café) ?
4. ¿ Qué cosas hay en la percha ?
5. ¿ Qué cosas hay sobre la mesa ?
6. ¿ Quién sirve ?
7. ¿ Qué tiene él en la mano ?

8–11. ¿ Qué empleo yo para tomar agua (sopa, café, vino) ?

12. Yo entro en un restaurant, me siento a una mesa, leo la lista, pido sopa, después pido carne, papas (patatas) y pan, después pido queso y frutas, no tomo café sino agua, y al fin me levanto de la mesa. Vd. entra, etc. Mi padre entra, etc. Nosotros entramos, etc. Vds. entran, etc. Mis padres entran, etc.

13–15. Cuando entra en el restaurant, ¿ dónde se sienta Vd. ? (. . . ¿ qué lee Vd., . . . ¿ qué pide Vd. ?)

16. ¿ Qué dice Vd. al mozo (camarero, *o* mesero) ?
17. ¿ Prefiere Vd. comer en casa o en un restaurant ?
18. ¿ Tiene Vd. buen apetito ?

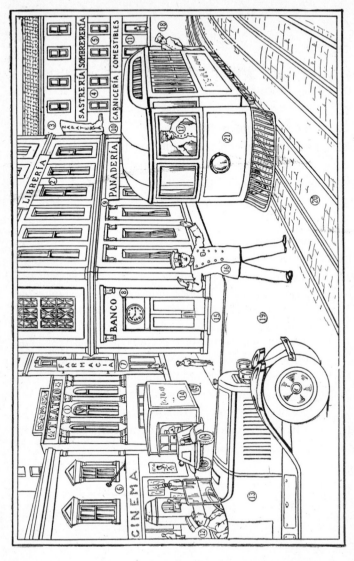

LA CALLE

VII. LA CALLE

LECCIONES XX (XXXII, XL)

1. ¿ Qué es el número uno, dos, etc. ?
2. ¿ Qué número tiene el automóvil, la acera, etc. ?
3. ¿ Cuántas personas hay en la calle ?
4. ¿ Está llena de hombres y mujeres la calle ?
5. ¿ Qué cosas hay en la calle ?
6. ¿ Qué tiendas se ven desde la calle ?
7. ¿ Quién conduce el tranvía (o carro eléctrico) ?
8. ¿ Quién cobra los billetes ?
9. ¿ Quién guía el automóvil ?
10–15. Si quiero comprar un sombrero (zapatos, libros, medicamentos o drogas, pan, carne), ¿ en dónde entro ?
16–21. ¿ Qué se vende en la sombrerería ? . . . en la zapatería ? . . . en la librería ? . . . en la farmacia (o botica) ? . . . en la panadería ? . . . en la carnicería ?
22–27. ¿ Quién vende o hace libros ? . . . carne ? . . . sombreros ? . . . panes ? . . . zapatos ? . . . medicamentos (o drogas) ?
28–29. ¿ Quién trabaja en la sastrería ?   ¿ Qué hace ?
30. Si necesita de dinero, ¿ a dónde se dirige Vd. ?
31. Si quiere ver una comedia, ¿ a dónde se dirige Vd. ?
32. ¿ Qué hace Vd. antes de salir a la calle ?
33. ¿ Cómo pasa Vd. el día ?
34. ¿ A qué hora vuelve Vd. a casa ?

EL CAMPO

VIII. EL CAMPO

LECCIONES XVI, XXV–XXVI, (XLIII)

1. ¿ Qué es el número uno, dos, etc. ?

2. ¿ Qué número tiene la carreta, la carretilla, etc. ?

3–6. ¿ Qué animales o cosas se ven en la carretera (o el camino) ? . . . en el jardín ? . . . en el huerto ? . . . en el prado ?

7. ¿ Qué se cultiva en el huerto ?

8. ¿ Cuáles son los instrumentos de agricultura ?

9. ¿ Cuáles sirven para remover (stir) la tierra ?

10. ¿ Cuál sirve para segar (mow) ?

11. ¿ Qué sirve para transportar los cereales, etc. ?

12. ¿ Cuáles son las legumbres y verduras ?

13. ¿ Cuál de ellas es la más grande ?

14–16. ¿ Qué color tiene la lechuga ? . . . el rábano ? . . . el nabo ?

17. ¿ Cuáles son las legumbres que tienen vainas (pods) ?

18. ¿ Qué legumbres prefiere Vd. ?

19. ¿ Le gusta a Vd. cultivar la tierra ?

20–21. ¿ En el campo nos levantaremos (nos acostaremos) temprano o tarde ?

22. Si hace buen tiempo, ¿ en dónde pescaremos ?

23–24. ¿ Les gusta a Vds. pasar el verano en el campo ? ¿ Por qué ?

25–26. ¿ Prefieren Vds. pasar el invierno en la población (la ciudad) ? ¿ Por qué ?

La Casa

IX. LA CASA

1–2. ¿ Qué es el número uno, dos, etc. de la casa norteamericana ? . . . de la casa española ?

3–4. ¿ Qué número tiene (A) el sótano, la chimenea, etc., (B) el zaguán, el patio, etc. ?

5. ¿ De qué están construídas las paredes de la casa norteamericana ?

6. ¿ Con qué está cubierto el techo ?

7. ¿ Tiene jardín y huerto ?

8. ¿ Qué hay en el sótano ?

9. ¿ Tiene la casa balcones ?

10. ¿ Qué clase de techo tiene esta casa española ?

11. ¿ Dónde están los balcones ?

12. ¿ Dónde está el patio ?

13. ¿ Qué hay en el patio ?

14. ¿ Cómo entramos al patio ?

15. ¿ Qué hay en cada lado de la puerta ?

16. ¿ Cuántos pisos tiene la casa ?

17. En la casa norteamericana ¿ dónde está el calorífero central ?

18. ¿ Dónde está la sala ?

19. ¿ Dónde están los dormitorios (cuartos de dormir) ?

20–21. Hágase una descripción de la casa norteamericana, . . . de la casa española.

22. ¿ Cuál prefiere Vd. ?

23. ¿ Por qué ?

PRENDAS DE VESTIR Y PARTES DEL CUERPO HUMANO

X. PRENDAS DE VESTIR Y PARTES DEL CUERPO HUMANO

1–3. ¿ Qué es el número uno, dos, etc., de *A* (*B*, *C*) ?

4–6. ¿ Qué número tiene (*A*) la corbata, etc., (*B*) el guante, etc., (*C*) el brazo, etc. ?

7–9. ¿ Cuál es la prenda de vestir que cubre la cabeza ? . . . la mano ? . . . el pie ?

10. ¿ Cuáles son las tres partes del traje del hombre ?

11–13. ¿ Cuántos bolsillos hay en la americana (el saco) ? . . . en el chaleco ? . . . en los pantalones ?

14. ¿ Hay bolsillos en la chaqueta de la mujer ?

15. ¿ Cuáles son más largos, los calcetines o las medias ?

16. ¿ Cuáles son más altos, los zapatos o los botines ?

17–18. ¿ Qué significa la palabra *cuello ?* . . . la palabra *puño ?*

19. ¿ Cuántos dedos tiene el hombre ?

20–22. ¿ Cuál es el órgano de la vista ? . . . del oído ? . . . del olfato ?

23. ¿ Cuál es el órgano principal del gusto ?

24. ¿ Cuáles son los órganos principales del tacto ?

25–29. ¿ Qué sirve para oír ? . . . para ver ? . . . para sentir el sabor de una cosa ? . . . para percibir los olores ? . . . para tocar ?

30–34. Hablando de los cinco sentidos, ¿ para qué sirve la nariz ? . . . el oído ? . . . la lengua ? ¿ Para qué sirven los ojos ? . . . los dedos ?

35–36. ¿ Cuáles son los órganos de la respiración ? . . . de la digestión ?

Los Animales

XI. LOS ANIMALES

LECCIÓN XXXVII

1. ¿ Qué es el número uno, dos, etc. ?
2. ¿ Qué número tiene el perro, la gallina, etc. ?
3. De estos animales cuadrúpedos ¿ cuáles son domésticos ?
4. ¿ Cuáles son salvajes ?
5. ¿ Cuáles trabajan por los hombres ?
6. ¿ Cuáles son más útiles ?
7. De estas aves ¿ cuáles son domésticas ?
8. ¿ Cuáles son salvajes ?
9. ¿ Cuáles son las más útiles ?
10. De estos animales ¿ cuál es el más grande ?
11. ¿ Cuál es el más pequeño ?
12. ¿ Cuál es el amigo más fiel del hombre ?
13. ¿ Cuáles comen hierbas ?
14. ¿ Cuáles comen carne ?
15. ¿ Cuáles tienen alas ?
16. ¿ Cuáles vuelan ?
17. ¿ Qué animal prefiere Vd. ?
18. ¿ Qué animal teme Vd. más ?
19–25. ¿ Cómo se llama la cría de la yegua ? . . . de la vaca ?
. . . de la oveja ? . . . de la cabra ? . . . de la gata ?
. . de la perra ? . . . de la gallina ?

A. El Vapor　　*B.* El Tren

XII. EL VAPOR Y EL TREN

LECCIONES XXXVIII–XXXIX

1–2. ¿ Qué es el número uno, dos, etc. de *A*, . . . de *B* ?

3–4. ¿ Qué número tiene (*A*) la popa, la proa, etc. ? . . .
(*B*) el baúl, la maleta, etc. ?

A. 1. ¿ Cuántos palos tiene este vapor ?

2. ¿ Cuántas chimeneas tiene ?

3. ¿ Dónde está el ancla, en la proa o en la popa ?

4. ¿ Dónde está el pabellón ?

5. ¿ De qué nación es este vapor ?

6. ¿ Qué es una portilla ?

7. ¿ Para qué sirve la plancha ?

8. ¿ Qué hace el camarero ?

B. 1. ¿ Cuántos coches hay en este tren ?

2. ¿ Cuáles son ?

3. ¿ Dónde lleva el tren los baúles ?

4. ¿ Dónde lleva el correo ?

5. ¿ Quién cobra los billetes (*o* los boletos) ?

6. ¿ En dónde se compran (se sacan) los billetes (los boletos) ?

7. ¿ En dónde se guardan los equipajes (los baúles, las maletas, etc.) ?

8. ¿ Para qué sirve el mozo ?

9. ¿ Cuántos viajeros hay en la estación ?

10. ¿ Qué hacen los viajeros cuando el empleado grita: « Señores viajeros al tren » ?

11. ¿ Cuál es la diferencia entre un pasajero y un viajero ?

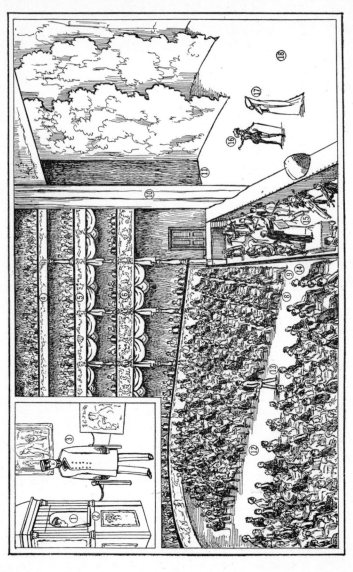

LA SALA DE TEATRO

XIII. EL TEATRO

1. ¿ Qué es el número uno, dos, etc. ?
2. ¿ Qué número tiene el actor, el acomodador, etc. ?
3. ¿ Que forma tiene la sala de teatro ?
4. ¿ Cuál es la parte de enfrente ?
5. ¿ Qué se levanta alrededor de la sala ?
6. ¿ Cómo se llaman los asientos que hay enfrente ?
7. ¿ Dónde están los músicos (o ¿ Dónde está la orquesta ?) ?
8. ¿ Qué clases de espectáculos o piezas dramáticas se representan en un teatro ?
9. ¿ Cuál prefiere Vd. ?
10-11. ¿ A qué hora empieza la función de tarde ? ... la función de noche ?
12. ¿ En dónde compramos (sacamos) los billetes (los boletos) ?
13. ¿ Quién los despacha ?
14. ¿ Quién nos acompaña y designa nuestros asientos ?
15. ¿ Qué se levanta antes de empezar la función ?
16. ¿ Cuál prefiere Vd., el teatro de variedades o el cinematógrafo (el « cine », o el « cinema ») ?
17. ¿ Por qué ?
18. Cuando va al teatro, ¿ en dónde prefiere Vd. sentarse ?
19. ¿ Por qué ?
20. Después del teatro ¿ a dónde va Vd. ?
21. ¿ Le gustaría a Vd. ser actor (actriz) ?
22. ¿ Por qué ?
23. ¿ Ha representado Vd. un papel en alguna obra dramática ?

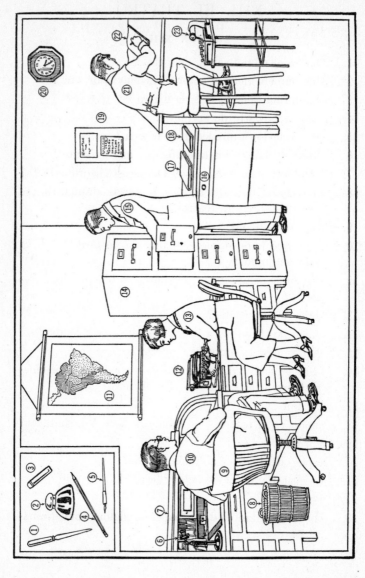

LA OFICINA

XIV. UNA OFICINA (*UN DESPACHO*)

1. ¿ Qué es el número uno, dos, etc. ?
2. ¿ Qué número tiene el teléfono, la cesta, etc. ?
3. ¿ Cuáles son los muebles de la oficina (del despacho) ?
4. ¿ Qué clase de silla tiene el jefe de la oficina ?
5. ¿ Cuántas sillas hay en la oficina ?
6. ¿ Cuántos escritorios y cuántas mesas hay ?
7. ¿ Qué cosas hay en el escritorio del jefe ? .
8. ¿ Quiénes son los empleados de la oficina ?
9. ¿ Qué libros tiene el tenedor de libros ?
10. ¿ Cuáles son las dos máquinas de la oficina ?
11. ¿ En qué cosa se halla la tinta ?
12. ¿ Con qué cosa se corta papel ?
13. ¿ Con qué cosa se seca la tinta ?
14. ¿ En qué cosa se escriben las cartas ?
15. ¿ Para qué sirve el teléfono ?
16. ¿ En qué se guardan los documentos ?
17. ¿ Están ocupados todos los empleados de la oficina ?
18. ¿ Qué hora es en el reloj de la oficina ?
19. ¿ Qué está haciendo el jefe de la oficina ?
20. ¿ Qué está haciendo la estenógrafa ?
21. ¿ A qué hora empiezan a trabajar los empleados ?
22. ¿ A qué hora termina el trabajo ?
23. ¿ Le gustaría a Vd. ser un empleado de esta oficina ?
    ¿ Por qué ?

VOCABULARIO

I. La Sala de Clase

1. El lápiz. 2. El papel. 3. El tintero. 4. La carta.
5. La pluma. 6. La pizarra (o el pizarrón). 7. La ventana.
8. El profesor. 9. La silla. 10. Los libros. 11. La mesa.
12. La cesta para papeles. 13. El pupitre. 14. El alumno.
15. El cuaderno. 16. La alumna. 17. El asiento. 18. La
tiza. 19. El puntero. 20. El sobre. 21. El borrador.
22. La regla.

II. La Familia

1. La ventana. 2. La madre. 3. El padre. 4. La silla.
5. La mesa. 6. El abuelo. 7. La abuela. 8. La hija.
9. El hijo. 10. El perro. 11. El gato.

III. La Sala (de Recibo)

1. La luz eléctrica. 2. La ventana. 3. La cortina.
4. La pared. 5. La puerta. 6. El candelero. 7. El
cuadro. 8. El reloj. 9. El piano. 10. El estante de
libros. 11. El manto de chimenea. 12. La chimenea.
13. El sillón. 14. La alfombra. 15. La silla. 16. El sofá.
17. El libro. 18. La mesa. 19. El suelo.

IV. El Dormitorio (*La Alcoba*)

1. La manta (frazada). 2. La cama. 3. La almohada.
4. La funda de almohada. 5. La sábana. 6. El tocador.
7. El espejo. 8. La luz eléctrica. 9. El jarro. 10. La
palangana (jofaina). 11. El lavabo. 12. La jabonera.
13. El toallero. 14. La toalla. 15. El cepillo de dientes.
16. La silla. 17. La gaveta. 18. La cómoda. 19. El

cuadro. 20. La lámpara. 21. El escritorio. 22. El tintero. 23. La pluma. 24. El papel.

V. La Cocina

1. La cafetera. 2. La cacerola. 3. La cocina económica (la estufa). 4. El horno. 5. El delantal. 6. La cocinera. 7. La tetera. 8. La olla. 9. La botella de leche. 10. La cazuela. 11. El tenedor. 12. El cuchillo. 13. El vaso.

VI. El Restaurant (*El Café*)

1. El mantel. 2. La mesa. 3. La servilleta. 4. El cuchillo. 5. El plato. 6. La botella. 7. Las frutas. 8. Las flores. 9. El pan (el panecillo). 10. La cuchara. 11. El tenedor. 12. El mozo (camarero, mesero). 13. La percha. 14. El sombrero de paja. 15. El paraguas. 16. El sobretodo (el gabán). 17. El bastón.

VII. La Calle

Las palabras en paréntesis angulares se refieren a las cosas que se hacen o se venden, y a las personas que las hacen o venden.

1. El teatro. 2. La librería [el librero, el libro]. 3. La zapatería [el zapatero, el zapato] 4. La sastrería [el sastre, el traje]. 5. La sombrerería [el sombrerero, el sombrero]. 6. El teatro cinematógrafo (el «cinema», el «cine»). 7. La farmacia *o* botica [el farmacéutico *o* boticario, las drogas *y* los medicamentos *o* remedios]. 8. El banco. 9. La panadería [el panadero, el pan]. 10. La carnicería [el carnicero, la carne]. 11. La tienda de comestibles. 12. El conductor (el chófer). 13. El automóvil. 14. El camión. 15. La acera (la vereda, la banqueta). 16. El policía (el guardia). 17. El conductor.

18. El cobrador. 19. El pavimento. 20. La vía del tranvía (del carro eléctrico). 21. El tranvía (el carro eléctrico).

VIII. El Campo

1. La pala. 2. La carretilla. 3. La guadaña. 4. La horquilla. 5. El rastrillo. 6. El arado. 7. La azada. 8. El pozo. 9. Los caballos. 10. El prado. 11. Las vacas. 12. El campo labrado. 13. El huerto (de legumbres y árboles frutales). 14. La carretera (el camino). 15. La casa. 16. El garage. 17. Los árboles. 18. La carreta. 19. El carro. 20. El seto vivo. 21. El jardín (de flores). 22. Las gallinas. 23. El estanque y los patos. 24. La papa (patata). 25. El guisante. 26. La remolacha (el betabel). 27. La zanahoria. 28. La col (el repollo). 29. El rábano. 30. El nabo. 31. La judía (el frijol). 32. La lechuga. 33. El tomate.

IX. La Casa

A. 1. El techo. 2. La chimenea. 3. La pared. 4. La puerta. 5. La ventana. 6. El sótano. 7. El césped. 8. El árbol. 9. Las flores. 10. La acera. 11. La calle.

B. 1. La azotea. 2. La pared. 3. La acera (la vereda, la banqueta). 4. La puerta. 5. El zaguán. 6. El patio. 7. La ventana. 8. El balcón. 9. La tienda.

X. Prendas de Vestir y Partes del Cuerpo Humano

A. 1. El sombrero. 2. El cuello. 3. La americana (el saco). 4. La manga. 5. El botón. 6. La corbata. 7. La camisa. 8. El chaleco. 9. El pañuelo. 10. El puño. 11. El bolsillo. 12. Los pantalones. 13. Los guantes. 14. El botín. 15. El calcetín.

B. 1. El quitasol. 2. El sombrero. 3. La cinta. 4. La pluma. 5. El pendiente (para la oreja). 6. La gargantilla.

7. La manga. 8. La chaqueta. 9. La corbata. 10. El puño. 11. El guante. 12. El cinturón. 13. La blusa. 14. Las faldas. 15. La media. 16. La hebilla. 17. El zapato.

C. 1. La barbilla. 2. El ojo. 3. La frente. 4. La cabellera (los cabellos). 5. La sien. 6. La nariz. 7. La boca. 8. La oreja. 9. La cabeza. 10. El labio. 11. El cuello. 12. La mejilla. 13. La quijada. 14. El hombro. 15. El pecho (contiene los pulmones y el corazón). 16. El brazo. 17. El abdomen (contiene el estómago, el hígado, los riñones y los intestinos). 18. La mano. 19. La cadera. 20. Los dedos de la mano. 21. El muslo. 22. La rodilla. 23. La pierna. 24. El pie. 25. Los dedos del pie.

XI. Los Animales

Las palabras en paréntesis angulares se refieren a la cría del animal.

1. El perro [el cachorro]. 2. El gato [el gatito]. 3. El caballo, la yegua [el potrillo]. 4. El burro. 5. La vaca [el ternero]. 6. El carnero, la oveja [el cordero]. 7. La cabra [el cabrito]. 8. El puerco (el cerdo, el marrano, el cochino, el chancho en la Argentina). 9. El conejo. 10. El gallo. 11. La gallina [el pollito]. 12. El pavo. 13. El ganso. 14. El pato. 15. La paloma. 16. El águila (*fem.*). 17. El elefante. 18. El león. 19. El tigre. 20. El oso. 21. El lobo. 22. El ciervo. 23. La zorra. 24. El mono. 25. La rata. 26. El ratón.

XII. A. El Vapór

1. El pabellón nacional. 2. El palo. 3. La chimenea. 4. La popa. 5. La cubierta. 6. El ancla (*fem.*). 7. Los pasajeros. 8. La plancha. 9. El camarero. 10. La maleta. 11. La portilla. 12. La proa. 13. El muelle. 14. Los baúles (equipajes).

B. El Tren

1. La sala de espera. 2. Los viajeros. 3. El despacho de billetes (boletos). 4. Los coches o los vagones (de primera clase, de segunda clase, de tercera clase, el cochecama, el cochecomedor). 5. El interventor (el conductor). 6. El vagón (coche) correo. 7. El vagón de equipajes (el furgón). 8. El ténder (carro de carbón). 9. La vía. 10. La máquina. 11. La maleta. 12. El mozo (de equipajes). 13. El baúl. 14. El despacho de equipajes. 15. El andén.

XIII. La Sala de Teatro

1. El expendedor de billetes (el boletero). 2. La taquilla (boletería). 3. El portero. 4–5. Las galerías. 6. Los palcos. 7. La segunda fila. 8. La primera fila. 9. El telón. 10. Los bastidores. 11. Las butacas (las lunetas). 12. El acomodador. 13. El espectador. 14. Los músicos. 15. El actor (el artista). 16. La actriz (la artista). 17. La escena.

XIV. La Oficina (*El Despacho*)

1. El cortapapel. 2. El tintero. 3. El raspador. 4. El lápiz. 5. La pluma. 6. El teléfono. 7. El escritorio. 8. La cesta para papeles. 9. La silla giratoria. 10. El jefe de la oficina (está dictando una carta). 11. El mapa. 12. La máquina de escribir. 13. La estenógrafa (está escribiendo al dictado). 14. El archivo. 15. El escribiente. 16. La mesa. 17. El libro diario. 18. El libro de caja. 19. El calendario. 20. El reloj. 21. El tenedor de libros. 22. El libro mayor. 23. La máquina para sumar.

ALTERNATIVE EXERCISES

ALTERNATIVE EXERCISES

I

¿ Qué es esto?	What is this?
Es un libro.	It is a book.
¿ Qué tengo yo?	What have I?
Usted tiene una pluma.	You have a pen.
¿ Qué tiene usted?	What have you?
Yo tengo papel.	I have paper.

un puntero, a pointer; una regla, a ruler

Escríbase en español. 1. I have a pencil. 2. You have a pencil. 3. I have a book. 4. You have a book. 5. I have paper. 6. You have paper. 7. I have ink. 8. You have ink. 9. I have a pen and a pencil. 10. You have a book and a pencil. 11. I have a pen and ink. 12. You have a pencil and paper. 13. What have you? 14. I have a ruler. 15. What have I? 16. You have a pointer. 17. What is this? 18. It is a book.

II

¿ Qué es esto?	Es un lápiz, *etc.*
¿ Qué tomo yo?	What do I take?
Usted toma un libro.	You take a book.
¿ Qué toma usted?	What do you take?
Yo tomo un lápiz.	I take a pencil.
¿ Cómo se llama esto en español?	What is this called in Spanish?
Se llama *papel.*	It is called **papel.**
Hable usted español.	Speak Spanish.

una carta, a letter; un escritorio, a desk; un cuaderno, a notebook; un sobre, an envelope

275

Escríbase.   1. Have you a pencil?   2. I have a pencil.
3. Have you paper?   4. I have paper.   5. Do you write with
[a]¹ pencil?   6. I write with [a] pencil.   7. Do you write on
paper?   8. I write on paper.   9. Have I a pen and ink?   10. You
have a pen and ink.   11. Do I write on paper with pen and ink?
12. You write on paper with [a] pencil.   13. Do you write an
exercise with [a] pencil?   14. I write an exercise with pen and
ink.   15. What do I take?   16. You take a notebook.   17. What
do you take?   18. I take a letter.   19. What is this called in
Spanish?   20. It is called **escritorio.**   21. John (**Juan**), speak
Spanish.

III

Pase usted a la pizarra.	Go to the (black)board.
Escriba usted *libro.*	Write **libro.**
No es correcto.	It is not correct.
¿ Cuál es la forma correcta?	What is the correct form?
Siéntese usted.	Take your seat.

el borrador, the eraser; **la silla,** the chair; **la puerta,** the
door; **la ventana,** the window

1. Who teaches the lessons?   2. The teacher teaches the lessons.
3. Who studies the lessons?   4. The student (*masc.*) studies the
lessons.   5. Who writes the exercises?   6. The student (*fem.*)
writes the exercises with pen and ink.   7. Who corrects (**corrige**)
the exercises?   8. The teacher corrects the exercises.   9. Does
the student write the exercises on the blackboard?   10. Yes, sir
(ma'am); the student (*fem.*) writes the exercises on the blackboard with chalk.   11. I write the exercises on paper with [a]
pencil.   12. John (**Juan**) writes the exercises with pen and ink.
13. The student (*masc.*) studies the lessons and writes the exercises.
14. The teacher teaches the lessons and corrects the exercises.
15. Mary, go to the board and write the exercises.   16. It is not
correct.   17. What is the correct form?   18. Take your seat.
19. John, go to the board and write **borrador.**   20. That (**Eso**)
is correct.

¹ A word in square brackets [ ] is to be omitted in the translation.

IV

¿ Es rojo el libro ?	Sí, señora; el libro es rojo.
¿ Cómo (How) es el libro?	El libro es rojo.
Abra usted el libro.	Open the book.
Lea usted la lección.	Read the lesson.
Cierre usted el libro.	Close the book.

1. Is the lesson difficult? 2. Yes, sir; the lesson is very difficult. 3. Are all the lessons difficult? 4. Some (**Algunas**) lessons are very easy. 5. Do you write all the exercises? 6. I write all the exercises with pen and ink. 7. Is the house white or black? 8. The house is white. 9. Are all the houses white? 10. Some houses are red. 11. Is the pencil black or red? 12. The pencil is black. 13. Are all the pencils black? 14. Some (**Algunos**) pencils are red. 15. Do you study all the lessons? 16. I study all the lessons and write all the exercises. 17. Are you (*masc.*) a hard worker? 18. All the students (*masc. pl.*) are hard workers. 19. All the students study the lessons a great deal (*véase* A, 9). 20. The teacher teaches all the lessons and corrects all the exercises. 21. John, what have you? 22. I have a pencil. 23. What sort of pencil is it? (= How is the pencil?) 24. The pencil is black. 25. Mary, open the book and read the lesson. 26. Close the book and take your seat.

V

Abra(n) usted(es) el (los) libro(s).	Open the book(s).
Lea(n) usted(es) la segunda frase de la lección.	Read the second sentence of the lesson.
Cierre(n) usted(es) el (los) libro(s).	Close the book(s).
Pase(n) usted(es) a la pizarra.	Go to the board.
Escriba(n) usted(es) los ejercicios.	Write the exercises.
Borre(n) usted(es) los ejercicios.	Erase the exercises.
Siénte(n)se usted(es).	Take your seats.

1. Are the chalk and the ink black ? (= Are black the chalk . . . ?)
2. The chalk is white and the ink is black.   3. Are the paper and
the pencil white?   4. The paper is white and the pencil is black.
5. The chalk and the paper are white.   6. The ink and the pencil
are not white.   7. Do you write letters with [a] pencil?   8. No,
sir; I write letters on white paper with [a] pen and black ink.
9. What are you writing? — I am writing a letter.   10. Do you
write the address on the envelope?   11. Yes, ma'am; I write
the address on the envelope with pen and ink.   12. Do you write
letters in English and in Spanish?   13. I write many letters in
English, but (pero) I do not write letters in Spanish.   14. Are
the lessons and the exercises easy?   15. The lessons are not easy;
the exercises are difficult.   16. Do you study all the lessons?
17. Yes, sir; I study all the lessons, but I do not write all the
exercises.   18. Are there many students and many teachers in
the school?   19. There are many students, but there are not
many teachers.   20. Class (Clase), open (*pl.*: abran ustedes)
the books.   21. Joseph (José), read the first sentence of the
exercises.   22. Anna (Ana), read the second sentence.   23. Close
(*pl.*) the books and go to the blackboard.   24. Write the exercises on the blackboard.   25. Erase the exercises and take your
seats.

VI

Pase(n) usted(es) a la pizarra.	Go to the board.
Tome(n) usted(es) la tiza.	Take the chalk.
Escriba(n) usted(es) la frase.	Write the sentence.
Corrija(n) usted(es) los errores.	Correct the mistakes.
Tome(n) usted(es) el borrador.	Take the eraser.
Borre(n) usted(es) los ejer-cicios.	Erase the exercises.
Siénte(n)se usted(es).	Take your seat(s).

1. The classroom has one (una) door and many windows.
2. The door is high and wide.   3. The teacher has a desk and a
chair.   4. There are many seats for the students in the classroom.   5. There is a blackboard on which (que) the students
write the exercises with white chalk.   6. The teacher corrects

the exercises with red chalk. 7. The students open (**abren**) the books and read (**leen**) the lesson. 8. They have to study the lessons a-great-deal (study a-great-deal the lessons) in-order-to read (**leer**) well. 9. Do you write all the exercises on paper? 10. I write all the exercises on white paper with black ink. 11. Are the lessons easy or difficult? 12. Some lessons are easy and some are difficult. 13. Are all the students hard-workers? 14. Some students are hard-workers, but there are some who (**que**) do not study (**estudian**) the lessons. 15. Do you write letters in English or in Spanish? 16. I write some letters in Spanish, but I write the address in English. 17. The letters that I write in English are easy. 18. Class, go (*pl.*) to the blackboard. 19. Joseph, take the chalk and write the third sentence. 20. Anna, write the sixth sentence. 21. Correct (*pl.*) the mistakes. 22. Take the erasers and erase the exercises. 23. Take your seats and open the books.

VII

¡ Atención !	Attention !
Abra(n) usted(es) el (los) libro(s).	Open the book(s).
Lea(n) usted(es) la lección.	Read the lesson.
Lea(n) usted(es) en alta voz.	Read aloud.
Pronuncie(n) usted(es) distintamente.	Pronounce distinctly.
Estudien ustedes para mañana la octava lección.	Study for to-morrow the eighth lesson.
Repasen ustedes la séptima lección.	Review the seventh lesson.

1. Mary, have you John's book? 2. No, sir; but John has my (**mi**) book. 3. He studies all the lessons in my grammar. 4. John, have you Mary's grammar? 5. Yes, sir; I have her (**su**) book, but Mary is lazy and doesn't study the lessons. 6. Class, attention! 7. Go (*pl.*) to the blackboard and write the exercises. 8. Joseph (**José**), the exercises that (**que**) you write on the board are not difficult. 9. But you make (**comete**) many errors (**errores**). 10. You do not study the lessons. 11. Yes, sir; I study all the grammar lessons. 12. I read (**leo**) all the lessons in (**de**) the reader. 13. I study a-great-deal the

Spanish lesson, but I do not study the geography lesson. 14. Is (the) [1] Spanish spelling easy or difficult? 15. (The) Spanish spelling is easy, but (the) English spelling is difficult. 16. Anna (**Ana**), what are you studying now? 17. I am studying the grammar lesson in Mary's book. 18. And I am writing the exercises on Mary's paper. 19. Are you writing the exercises with Mary's pencil too? 20. No, sir; I have a pencil, but I haven't [any] paper. 21. Class, open (*pl.*) the books and read the lesson. 22. Read aloud and pronounce distinctly. 23. Study for to-morrow the fifth lesson and review the fourth. 24. Close your books and go to the board.

VIII

1. Attention! To-day (**Hoy**) we have a very difficult lesson. 2. Go (*pl.*) to the blackboard and write all the exercises. 3. John, you make many mistakes. Do you study the lessons? 4. Yes, ma'am; I study all the lessons, but this (**esta**) lesson is difficult. 5. If we do not write the exercises correctly (write correctly the exercises), you call-attention-to the mistakes. 6. You underline the mistakes with red chalk. 7. You explain all the difficulties, and then we erase the exercises with the eraser. 8. Do you (*pl.*) speak English and Spanish? 9. No, sir; we do not speak Spanish yet (**todavía**). 10. We are learning to (**a**) speak Spanish. 11. We study all the grammar lessons and we write all the exercises in our (**nuestros**) notebooks. 12. If we do not write the exercises correctly, the teacher (*fem.*) calls attention to the mistakes. 13. She underlines the mistakes with red ink, but she does not correct the mistakes. 14. Are there many difficulties in Spanish? 15. Yes, sir; but there are also many difficulties in English. 16. (The) English spelling is more (**más**) difficult than (**que**) (the) Spanish spelling. 17. But (the) English grammar is easier (= more easy) than (the) Spanish grammar. 18. In-order-to learn to speak Spanish, we must study much. 19. And we must talk Spanish with Spaniards (**españoles**) or Spanish Americans (**hispanoamericanos**).

[1] Words in parenthesis, if in the ordinary type, are to be translated.

IX

¿ Qué lección tenemos para hoy?	What lesson do we have for to-day?
Tenemos la segunda parte de la novena lección.	We have the second part of the ninth lesson.
Abran ustedes los libros y lean el texto.	Open the books and read the text.
Continúe(n), o Siga(n), leyendo.	Continue reading, or keep on reading.
Es suficiente, gracias.	That's sufficient (enough); thank you.
Para mañana estudien ustedes la siguiente lección.	For to-morrow study the next lesson.

1. My brother-and-sister are students in (de) a city school. 2. They are studying arithmetic, geography, spelling, English and Spanish. 3. My sister learns all the lessons, but my brother is lazy. 4. He studies very little. 5. But he plays the piano very well (*véase* B, 4). 6. He has taken many music lessons. 7. Our parents also have taken music lessons and they play the piano. 8. Our father desires (desea) [to] learn to speak Spanish. 9. He says (Dice) that he desires [to] live in Spain (España) or in (the) Argentina. 10. He has not learned to speak Spanish yet. 11. He says that (the) Spanish is very difficult. 12. Paul (Pablo), whose book have you? 13. I have Alice's (Alicia) grammar. 14. My sister has my book. 15. She says that she has lost (perdido) her book. 16. If all the students have lost their books, they can (pueden) not study the lessons. 17. I have lost all my books, but I have found Alice's grammar. 18. Is this book yours? 19. No, sir; it is John's. 20. My grammar is red. 21. Henry (Enrique), do you know (¿ sabe usted) what lesson we have for to-day? 22. No, sir; I don't know (yo no sé) what lesson we have. 23. I have not studied the lesson. 24. Alice (Alicia) says that we have the second part of the eighth lesson. 25. That (Eso) is not correct. 26. Anna, open the grammar and read the text of the lesson. 27. Continue reading and pronounce more (más) distinctly. 28. That is enough; thank you.

X

1. What is this? — [It] is John's arithmetic. 2. What is that? [which you have] — [It] is my reader. 3. What is that [over there]? — [It] is my sister's geography. 4. These books are of many colors (**colores**). 5. Some are red and some are green (**verdes**), but the paper is white. 6. That man [over there] is Henry's (**Enrique**) grandfather. 7. He is very old, and he is not strong. 8. Henry's grandmother is old also, but she is strong. 9. Henry lives with his grandparents in that white house. 10. The grandparents have two children. 11. One is Henry's father and the other (**otro**) is the sister of Henry's father. 12. Henry's mother is not living now. 13. His grandparents are rich. 14. My parents are not rich, and they have to work hard (**mucho**). 15. This house in which we live is small (**pequeña**). 16. This is a small house, but it is comfortable (**cómoda**). 17. That house [over there] is Paul's. 18. They are rich also. 19. I am going (**voy**) to study and learn a great deal and be rich too. 20. Class, is this book red? — Yes, sir; it is red. 21. What sort of book is it? (= How is the book?) — It is red. 22. Open your books and read the lesson. 23. Pronounce distinctly. 24. That is enough. 25. Close your books and go to the board. 26. Write the exercises. 27. Correct the mistakes. 28. Now (**Ahora**) erase the exercises and take your seats.

XI

Abra(n) usted(es) el (los) libro(s) de lectura.	Open the reader(s).
Lea(n) usted(es) la primera página de la lección.	Read the first page of the lesson.
Lea(n) usted(es) la segunda línea de la página once.	Read the second line of page eleven.
Lea(n) usted(es) el tercer párrafo.	Read the third paragraph.
Para mañana lean desde la quinta línea de la octava página hasta la línea quince de la página doce.	For to-morrow read from the fifth line of the eighth page to the fifteenth line of page twelve.

1. Ferdinand, have you many relatives (**parientes**)? 2. Yes, sir; I have many. 3. I have four grandparents, a father and a mother, and five brothers-and-sisters. 4. I have also six uncles-and-aunts and fifteen cousins. 5. You have many relatives, but if I count all my relatives I have sixteen. 6. Who lives in that white house? 7. Don José and Doña Ana his wife live in that small house. 8. It is a six-room house (*véase* B, 4). 9. There are three rooms on the ground floor, the living room, the dining room, and the kitchen. 10. On the upper floor there are three bedrooms and a bathroom. 11. [They] all sleep on the upper floor; they do not wish to sleep on the ground floor. 12. They have one servant (*fem.*), but she doesn't sleep in the house. 13. Don José and Doña Ana are old, but Doña Ana plays the piano very well. 14. She has taken many music lessons. 15. Don José is Spanish, and of course (**por supuesto**) he speaks Spanish. 16. Doña Ana is [a] Mexican (**mejicana**). 17. You know (**Usted sabe**) that the Mexicans speak Spanish also. 18. Yes, they speak Spanish in Mexico, Cuba, Porto (**Puerto**) Rico, Chile, (the) Argentina, and other Spanish-American countries (**países**). 19. Class, open (*pl.*) the readers. 20. Paul (**Pablo**), read the first paragraph of the lesson. 21. Read aloud and pronounce distinctly. 22. Sophia (**Sofía**), read from the tenth line of page twelve to the fifteenth line of page thirteen. 23. That is enough, thank you! 24. For to-morrow study the five following pages.

XII

1. My uncle Joseph (**José**) has a good eight-room house. 2. On the ground floor there are four rooms, a living room, a small library, a dining room, and a kitchen. 3. On the upper floor there are four bedrooms and two bathrooms. 4. One of the bedrooms is for (**para**) the maid. 5. There is electric light in all the house. 6. My uncle Joseph is not rich, but he has good furniture. 7. In the living room there are two tables, a piano, a sofa, chairs and armchairs, and many pictures. 8. My uncle-and-aunt receive their friends in the living room. 9. The furniture of the dining room is a table, a sideboard, and eight chairs. 10. There are not [any] pictures in the dining room. 11. In the library there

are a desk, a small table, two armchairs, some pictures, and many books.   12. When (**Cuando**) I look for my uncle, I can generally (**generalmente**) find him (**encontrarle**) in the library.   13. He reads a-great-deal, and he has books in English and in Spanish. 14. I intend to spend three months with my uncle-and-aunt. 15. I am very fond of my two cousins, John and Mary.   16. My father is the brother of my uncle Joseph and the uncle of John and Mary.   17. Now open (*pl.*) the readers and read the first page of the lesson.   18. Joseph, pronounce more distinctly. 19. You do not pronounce correctly the (**la**) Spanish **b**.   20. Now go (*pl.*) to the board.   21. John, write the eighth sentence of the exercises.   22. You make many mistakes.   23. Correct the mistakes.   24. Now take your seat.

XIII

Escriba(n) usted(es) los números uno y dos de los ejercicios.	Write numbers one and two of the exercises.
Substituya(n) usted(es) la *a* (la *b*, *etc.*) por una *o*.	Put an **o** in place of the **a**.
Está bien.	All right.
Para mañana aprendan de memoria todas las palabras y todas las reglas de la nueva lección.	For to-morrow learn by heart all the words and all the rules of the new lesson.
Conjuguen todos los verbos.	Conjugate all the verbs.

1. Is your friend a lawyer?   2. No, sir; he is a good physician. 3. His father is a lawyer.   4. Is he an Englishman or a Spaniard? 5. He says that he is a Spaniard, but he doesn't speak Spanish. 6. I believe (**Creo**) that he is an American (**americano**).   7. I am looking for my friend now, but he is not at home.   8. I believe that he is at my uncle's.   9. Your uncle is ill, is he not (= is it not true)?   10. He says that he is ill, but I believe that he is tired.   11. He works a great deal and he doesn't sleep well. 12. Have you a good bedroom?   13. Yes, sir; I have a good bed with sheets and pillowcases clean and white, and red blankets. 14. The other furniture of my bedroom is a small table, a desk,

two chairs, a dressing table (dresser) with a mirror, and a chest of drawers (chiffonier).   15. I have also four pictures on the walls. 16. You have a good bedroom. Do you sleep well?   17. Yes, I sleep very well if I am tired physically (**físicamente**).   18. If I have been at home all (the) day (**día,** *masc.*) and have read (**leído**) a great deal, I do not sleep well.   19. Paul, go to the board and write (the) number five of the exercises.   20. It is not correct. 21. Put an **e** in place of the **a,** and put a **b** in place of the **v.**   22. All right. Take your seat.   23. Class, for to-morrow learn (*pl.*) by heart all the new rules.   24. And conjugate the new verbs.

XIV

1. My brother and I get up (*1st pers. pl.*) at seven o'clock if our father calls (**llama**) us.   2. We have-breakfast at half-past seven or at a quarter to eight.   3. At half-past eight we go (**vamos**) to (the) school.   4. In (the) school we study algebra (**álgebra**), history (**historia**), chemistry (**química**), English and Spanish. 5. The teacher explains to-us all the difficulties.   6. At noon (= twelve o'clock) we return home and have-lunch with our parents.   7. My father works in an office (**oficina**), but he returns home for lunch (**para el almuerzo**).   8. We go to school at one o'clock and study till (**hasta**) three.   9. We have-dinner at half-past six o'clock.   10. My brother and I study one or two hours every night (= all the nights).   11. If I do not understand the lesson, he teaches me.   12. If I lose my book, my brother lends (**presta**) me (the) his.   13. Then we talk with our parents and with our friends, or we play the piano and sing (**cantamos**). 14. At ten o'clock I am tired and I go to bed.   15. I sleep eight or nine hours every night, and I study four hours every day. 16. Our house is warmed by steam.   17. In the basement we have a furnace in which coal is burned.   18. With the heat that is produced all the house is warmed.

XV

1. If I lose my book, I look-for (= seek) it in my room.   2. If I do not find it there (**allí**), I look for it in the living room.   3. If my brother loses his books, he looks for them in the dining room.

4. If he doesn't find them there, I lend (**presto**) him my books.
5. I lend him the books with much pleasure (**placer**), because
(**porque**) I do not like to study. 6. But I like the meals which our
cook prepares. 7. In our kitchen there is a range in which gas
(**gas**) is burned. 8. The cook has to work hard. 9. She prepares the meals and scours the kitchen utensils. 10. The bread
which she bakes in the oven is very good. 11. I like to eat bread
and butter with (**en**) all the meals. 12. The cook roasts the meat
in the oven or she boils it in a pot. 13. The meat that she cooks
tastes good. 14. She is a good cook and the kitchen is always
(**siempre**) clean. 15. She says that she likes to cook, but she
doesn't like to scour the pots and pans. 16. But she scours them
every day. 17. I like to return home from (the) school and have
lunch with my parents.

XVI

1. If my brother has my book, I ask him [for] it (**se lo pido**).
2. If I have his books, he asks me [for] them. 3. When I do not
understand the lesson, my brother explains it [to] me. 4. When
my brother does not understand the lessons, I explain them [to]
him. 5. My brother likes to study, but I do not (**a mí no me
gusta**). 6. I like to play the piano and sing, but my brother
does not. 7. If there is a letter for me, my brother gives it to
me. He doesn't read it. 8. If there are letters for him, I give
them to him. I do not read them. 9. It is said (**Se dice**) that
in Spain the cattle raisers, the planters and the farm laborers rise
at five or six o'clock. 10. They have breakfast at six or half-
past six, and they have dinner at noon. 11. At six or seven o'clock
they have supper. 12. The farm laborers go to bed very
early (**temprano**). 13. The inhabitants of the cities rise later
(**más tarde**) and have breakfast at eight or nine o'clock. 14. They
have lunch at twelve o'clock and they dine at eight or nine at
night. 15. Sometimes they have supper after the theater or the
opera. 16. For breakfast (**Para el desayuno**) my father takes
coffee and milk and bread and butter. 17. I do not like coffee,
but he likes [it].

XVII

1. Class, pay (*pl.*) attention. Open the books.   2. Mary, read the first page of the lesson.   3. I do not understand it. Repeat it.   4. Please read aloud and pronounce distinctly.   5. Joseph, Henry, and Paul, go to the board.   6. Write the first six (= six first) numbers of the exercises.   7. Write them correctly.   8. Please listen, Henry. That sentence has two errors.   9. In **travaje** put a **b** in place of the **v** and an **a** in place of the **e**.   10. All right, now erase (*pl.*) the exercises and take your seats.   11. For to-morrow, study the next lesson.   12. Learn by heart all the new words and all the new rules.   13. And conjugate all the new verbs.   14. Professor (**Señor profesor,** *o* **Señora profesora**), please explain this sentence.   15. It is very difficult and I don't understand it.   16. I have studied all the lesson and written all the exercises.   17. There are ten words in the lesson that I can't find.   18. John, you can find all the words in the vocabulary (**vocabulario**) or in the exercises of the previous lessons (**lecciones anteriores**).   19. Let us dine in this restaurant.   20. All right! Let us sit down at this table.   21. While we are reading the bill of fare, the waiter puts on the table a white (table) cloth.   22. Then he brings us napkins, knives, forks, and spoons, plates, and glasses.

XVIII

1. Don Fernando, won't you (**¿ no quiere usted**) dine with us?   2. No, thank you; I have just dined at home.   3. You prefer to dine at home, do you not?   4. Yes, we have a good cook, and the meals that she prepares are excellent (**excelentes**).   5. Won't you sit down and take a cup of coffee?   6. With much pleasure. I like to talk (**charlar**) with (the) friends.   7. Waiter, bring us the bill of fare.   8. I have [a] good appetite.   9. Let us read the bill of fare.   10. In the first place (**En primer lugar**) I am going to order (**pedir**) soup.   11. I like the soup that they serve in this restaurant.   12. Then I wish a good salad.   13. After the salad bring me fish, beef and fried (**fritas**) potatoes.   14. For (the) dessert I want cheese, fruit, and black coffee.   15. Bring me

also a bottle of red (**tinto**) wine.   16. Don't you like (the) white
wine?   17. No, I prefer (the) red wine.   18. Let us give (to)
the waiter a tip of twenty-five cents (**centavos**).   19. Waiter,
bring me a glass of water (**agua**).   20. Let us go home. It is
ten o'clock, and I am tired.   21. Generally I go to bed at half-
past ten o'clock.   22. Goodbye (**Adiós**), Don Fernando.

XIX

1. In what year (**año**) did Christopher Columbus discover the
New World?   2. He discovered America (**la América**) the twelfth
day of October, fourteen hundred and ninety-two.   3. The Spaniards conquered (*empléese* **conquistar**) Granada the same year.
4. Did Columbus make more than one voyage to (the) America?
5. Yes, sir; he made four voyages to the New World.   6. How
old was Columbus when he made the last (**último**) trip?   7. It
is said that he was then fifty-six years old.   8. (To) where did
he go (*empléese* **pasar**) when he returned to Spain?   9. He was
ill when he returned to Spain.   10. He went to Valladolid, where
he died a little later.   11. How old was your father when he died?
12. My father was fifty-eight years old when he died.   13. He
died very young (**joven**).   14. Did the illness last long (**mucho
tiempo**)?   15. He was ill when he returned from a trip.   16. He
died the next day.   17. What were you looking for when I came
in (= entered)?   18. I was looking for a book that I lost yesterday (**ayer**).   19. Did you find it?   20. No, sir; I looked for it
everywhere (**en todas partes**), but I did not find it.   21. Do you
know (**Sabe usted**) when I arrived (**llegué**)?[1]   22. It was ten
o'clock in the morning when you arrived.   23. Did the Arabs
live a long time in Spain?   24. The Arabs conquered Spain and
they lived there (**allí**) seven centuries.

XX

1. One can say (**Se puede decir**): " the water of the Tagus
(**Tajo**) is brown " (*empléese* **pardo**), or " the waters of the Tagus
are brown."   2. How does one say (¿ **Cómo se dice**) in Spanish:

[1] Note the **u** in **llegué**, to show that the **g** is " hard " before **e**.

" the axe is sharp " *(empléese* **afilado**), " the axes are sharp ? "
3. How does one write in Spanish: the water, the waters; the soup, the soups; the axe, the axes; the pencil, the pencils; the door, the doors?

4. When (= At what hour) did you get up this morning? 5. I got up at half-past six.   6. I took a bath, dressed, and ate breakfast.   7. Then I went out into the street.   8. The sky was clear (**despejado**) and the streets were full of students who were going (**iban**) to school.   9. I went to [the] house of a friend, who lives in Atocha Street, [at] number twenty-five.   10. Don José received me cordially and invited me to lunch with him. 11. I accepted the invitation with great (= much) pleasure. 12. The family is composed of Don José, his daughter Mary and his son John.   13. Don José's wife died two years ago. 14. After lunch I took leave of Don José and his children. 15. Then I went to the " movies " (**cínema,** *masc.*).   16. Afterwards (**Después**) I went to a restaurant and dined with a friend. 17. At ten o'clock I returned home.   18. I went to bed at eleven, and as I was very tired I went to sleep at once.

XXI

1. How does one say in Spanish: " a polite girl, a French girl ? " 2. How does one explain the difference (**diferencia**) that there is between (**entre**) the feminine forms (**formas**) of the two adjectives? 3. How does one write in Spanish: " an English grammar, a Spanish grammar " and " an English lesson, a Spanish lesson ? " 4. I believe that (the) English grammar is easier (= more easy) than (the) Spanish grammar.   5. But (the) English spelling is more difficult than (the) Spanish spelling.   6. (The) Spanish spelling is more phonetic than (the) English spelling.

7. When I lived in Madrid I used-to-give every day English lessons to the children of Don Fernando.   8. This gentleman and his wife Doña Alicia were Toledans (**toledanos**) and they spoke Spanish almost perfectly.   9. They pronounced all the words very distinctly.   10. Their children, Philip and Elizabeth, were dark-complexioned.   11. They were handsome and courteous.

12. They wished to learn English in order to speak with the English and the North Americans (**norteamericanos**). 13. They used to learn all the rules and write all the exercises. 14. After taking fifty lessons they could speak English fairly (**bastante**) well. 15. Their pronunciation (**pronunciación**) was almost correct. 16. Their greatest (**mayor**) difficulty was the pronunciation of the **b,** the **d,** and the **r.** 17. In (**Con el**) time they did learn to pronounce correctly these difficult sounds (**sonidos**).

XXII

1. My father said that iron and coal were more useful than gold. 2. But gold was worth (**valía**) more than iron or coal. 3. I preferred gold, because with that metal (**metal,** *masc.*) I could buy many useful things (**cosas**). 4. Do you like flowers? 5. Yes sir; I like flowers. 6. Do you buy flowers, or do you grow (cultivate) them? 7. I used to buy flowers for my mother almost every day. 8. My father said that flowers were more beautiful (**bellas**) than coal and iron, but coal and iron were more useful than flowers. 9. He said that he bought coal to warm the house, but he could not warm the house with flowers.

10. When we were in Córdoba we became acquainted with Mr. and Mrs. Heredia. 11. Don Pablo invited us to make them a visit. 12. We went to see them and they received us cordially. 13. A few (**Algunos**) days later Don Pablo came to see us. 14. His wife was ill and could not accompany (**acompañar**) him. 15. The maid handed me Don Pablo's visiting card. 16. On the card I read " Pablo Heredia y Sánchez." 17. I took the liberty (**Me tomé la libertad**) of asking Don Pablo the meaning of these names. 18. He explained to me that Pablo was his given (Christian) name. 19. Heredia was his father's family name and Sánchez was his mother's family name. 20. He told me that many Spaniards and Spanish Americans use the two family names. 21. He told me that his wife's given name and family names were María Fernández de Heredia. 22. He explained to me that in Spain and in (the) Spanish America married women keep generally the father's family name. 23. Their son was Julio Heredia y Fernández.

XXIII

1. To-day it is cold.   2. Yes, I am cold.   3. The water is
(está) cold.   4. Yesterday it (= *the weather*) was warm (calor).
5. Yes, I was warm (*empléese* tener calor).   6. The water was
warm (hot).   7. I like to drink warm water when I am cold.
8. When I am warm, I like to drink cold water.   9. Are you
hungry?   10. Yes, I am very (mucha) hungry, and it is time to
eat-dinner.   11. Before dining I wish to wash my face and hands.

12. This morning I woke up at seven o'clock.   13. I rose,
bathed, and cleaned my teeth with [a] brush and tooth powder.
14. I combed my hair, brushed my clothes and dressed.   15. I
made haste to dress because we have breakfast at half-past seven.
16. When I entered the dining room my mother already (ya) was
there.   17. I said: "Good morning, mamma."   18. She
answered: "Good morning, my son."   19. After breakfast I
put on my hat and went out into the street.   20. The sky was
cloudy, but it was not raining.   21. I went to school and returned
home at three o'clock.   22. My father returned home at six and
we dined at six-thirty.   23. My father was born in America, but
my mother was born in Mexico.

XXIV

1. My father died ten years ago.   2. He was fifty years old
when he died.   3. My mother, my sister and I have been living
in Buenos Aires for five years.   4. I haven't any brother.
5. How long (¿ Cuánto tiempo) have you been here?   6. I have
lived in Buenos Aires almost two years.   7. Do you like this city?
8. Yes, I do (like).   I have many friends in (the) Argentina.   9. My
cousin has been here six years and he speaks Spanish almost
perfectly.   10. You have lived in Madrid also.   11. Do you
notice (¿ Nota usted) any difference between the Spanish of Madrid
and that (el) of Buenos Aires?   12. Very little.   In Buenos Aires
the z (zeta) is pronounced like s (ese), and the ll (elle) like y
(i griega).   13. But I have heard (oído) this pronunciation (pronunciación) in some parts of Spain.   14. There is also some

difference between the English of England (**Inglaterra**) and that of America.

15. Joseph and Henry rose early, washed their faces and hands and began to dress.   16. First they put on their underclothes and their hose (socks).   17. Next they put on their shirts and their trousers, and they sat down on the bed to put on their shoes.   18. Finally (**Al fin**) they put on their collars (**cuello**) and neckties, their waistcoats (vests), and their (sack) coats. 19. As neither one had [a] watch, they looked at the clock while they were dressing.   20. They finished dressing at half-past seven and they went to the dining room where their parents were waiting for them.   21. The boys were very hungry and they began to eat with [a] good appetite.

XXV

1. January is the first month of the year and it has thirty-one days.   2. February is the second month and it has twenty-eight days.   3. There are four weeks in the month of February and four weeks and three days in the month of January.   4. The first of January is the first day of the year.   5. The thirty-first of December is the last day of the year.   6. There are twenty-four hours in a day.   7. There are seven days in a week and twelve months in a year.   8. The months of the year are January, February, March, April, May, June, July, August, September, October, November, and December.

9. We shall spend the summer in the country.   10. We shall leave (the) town the twentieth of June.   11. In the country we shall get up and go to bed early.   12. We shall have breakfast at seven o'clock and have dinner at twelve o'clock.   13. Nearly every day we shall ride on horseback or we shall fish in the lake. 14. If it rains we shall read books or write letters to our friends. 15. We shall return to (the) town September first.   16. Should you like to live in the country all (the) year?   17. No, I should prefer to live in the city in winter (**en el invierno**).   18. I should learn more in the city school.   19. My sister would take music lessons, and I should talk Spanish with my Spanish friends. 20. No, I should not like to live in the country in (the) winter.

XXVI

1. The seven days of the week are Sunday, Monday, Tuesday, Wednesday, Thursday, Friday, and Saturday.   2. The four seasons of the year are (the) spring, (the) summer, (the) autumn (*or* fall), and (the) winter.   3. In (the) spring the trees will put on leaves and the flowers will appear in our gardens.   4. (The) summer is the hot season (*véase* B, 4), and it is also vacation time. 5. In (the) summer we shall go to the country and we shall not have lessons to study.   6. It is for this reason (**por esto**) that I prefer (the) summer to (the) winter.   7. The autumn is the season of fruits.   8. In (the) autumn the new school year will begin. 9. We shall go to school every day in (**de**) the week except (the) Saturday and (the) Sunday.   10. In each week there will be five work days and two days of rest.   11. But I shall not rest (**descansaré**) [on] (the) Saturday.   12. In the morning I shall ride horseback and in the afternoon I shall fish in the lake. 13. At night I shall visit my friends or I shall read some book. 14. In (the) winter it will be cold and we shall not be able to fish. 15. What time is it? — It is probably about eleven o'clock.   16. It is time to go to bed.   17. I am tired and I shall go to sleep at once.   18. My father went to Toledo ten days ago.   19. He has been in Toledo for a week.   20. He will come to-morrow at seven o'clock.   21. I shall tell him that I have studied a great deal during (**durante**) his absence (**ausencia**).

XXVII

1. It is said that Don Felipe was killed by thieves.   2. He was dead when the police (**la policía**) arrived.   3. A window of his house was open and it is believed that the thief entered through (**por**) the window.   4. He was beloved of all.   5. How old was Don Felipe?   6. He was probably about fifty years old.   7. This morning I received a letter from Doña Mercedes, the widow (**viuda**) of Don Felipe.   8. The letter was written in Spanish.   9. She has lived in Salamanca twenty years, but she intends to spend the rest (**resto**) of her life (**vida**) in Madrid.

10. We have lived in our house for ten years. 11. It was built by a good architect. 12. The walls are built of brick and the roof is covered with slate. 13. It is an eight-room house. 14. On the first floor are the living room, the dining room, a small library, and the kitchen. 15. When we go up (by) the stairs to the upper floor, we find four bedrooms and two bathrooms. 16. There is a bedroom for the cook. 17. She is a good cook, and the meals that she prepares are excellent. 18. She says that she likes to cook the food, but she doesn't like to scour the pots and pans. 19. In the basement of the house there is a furnace in which coal is burned. 20. All the house is warmed by the heat that is produced in the furnace. 21. Our house is not large, but it is very comfortable.

XXVIII

1. I have a Spanish grammar and I have studied it every day. 2. My brother has a gold pen (= pen of gold), and with the pen he has written many letters to his friends. 3. My sisters have a piano and they have taken many music lessons. 4. We have many books, but we have not read them. 5. Mr. Morales is a Spaniard and he is now in Burgos. 6. He is very intelligent, but he is ill most (la mayor parte) of the time. 7. He is not lazy, but he is always tired. 8. Yesterday it was cold and I was cold all (the) day. 9. When it is cold I am cold, and when it is warm I am warm. 10. I believe that I too am ill.

11. We spent the winter in a Spanish house. 12. It was built of stone and had a flat roof. 13. There was a shop at each side of the passageway. 14. In the inner court there were a few trees and many beautiful flowers. 15. When it was hot we spent the day in the court. 16. On the ground floor were the kitchen and some rooms for the servants. 17. On the main floor were the living room, the dining room, the bathroom, and three bedrooms (alcobas). 18. The bedrooms faced a veranda that overlooked (dominaba) the court. 19. The house was lighted with candles or with oil lamps. 20. In (the) winter the house was warmed by the fire of the copper brasiers or the fireplaces. 21. The kitchen did not have a range, but there were several fogones in which charcoal was burned.

XXIX

1. Ferdinand, do you know the lesson? 2. No, sir; last night (**anoche**) I couldn't (*pret.*) study. I was ill. 3. Trinidad, do you know Mrs. Henríquez? 4. No, ma'am; I don't know her. 5. Diego, can you swim? 6. Yes, sir; I learned to swim last summer in the country. 7. My brother knows (how) to swim very well, but he is lame (**está cojo**) now and can't[1] swim. 8. Doña Julia, can your son read and write? 9. Yes, he can read and write very well. 10. My grandfather has lost his (**la**) sight. The poor (**pobre**) man is unhappy (**infeliz**) because he can't read.

11. (The) man has two eyes in order to see. 12. If he loses one eye, he can see with the other. 13. The eyes are the organs of (the) sight. 14. Joseph believes that hearing is more important than sight, but I should prefer sight to hearing. 15. Joseph is very fond of music, but I prefer flowers to music. 16. The nose is the organ of the sense of smell. 17. It serves to perceive the odors of flowers. 18. Joseph says that he doesn't like the perfume of flowers. 19. The principal organ of taste and of speech is the tongue. 20. Without a (**la**) tongue we could not speak and we should be mute. 21. Without eyes we could not see and we should be blind. 22. Without ears we could not hear and we should be deaf. 23. The fingers (**dedos**) are the principal organs of (the) touch (**tacto**). 24. I used to know a boy who was deaf and dumb. 25. The poor boy couldn't hear or (**ni**) speak. 26. I have heard (**He oído hablar**) of a lady who is deaf and blind. 27. The poor lady can't hear or see, but she has learned to speak.

XXX

1. What is Charles doing? 2. He is writing a letter. 3. Well (**Pues**), tell him that his father is waiting for him. 4. And what is Elizabeth doing? 5. She is studying. 6. Elizabeth studies all the time. 7. What is Diego doing? 8. He is reading. Diego reads every night. 9. What is Henry doing? 10. He is sleeping.

[1] **Saber** or **poder**?

11. I believe that Henry sleeps all (the) night and all (the) day too.   12. Is Mary ill? She is turning pale.   13. No, she is not ill, but she is very tired.   14. She is growing very rapidly (**rápidamente**).   15. Well, goodbye for a while. We shall see one-another (**nos**) to-morrow.

16. Yesterday I called on (*empléese* **hacer una visita a**) Mr. Fernández.   17. A servant opened the door [for] me and I inquired: " Is Mr. Fernández at home? "   18. The servant answered: " Yes, sir; he is at home. Whom shall I (am I to) announce? "   19. I took off my hat, overcoat, and gloves and entered the living room.   20. After a few moments Mr. Fernández came out and saluted me cordially.   21. He said to me: " How are you, sir? " and I replied: " Very well, thank you."   22. Mr. Fernández presented me to his wife, Doña Ana, and to his daughter, Caroline.   23. I bowed and said: " I am delighted to make your acquaintance, ladies."   24. Later [there] entered a friend of the family, Mr. Navarro.   25. Mr. Fernández presented me to Mr. Navarro.   26. He said: " Sir, I am very glad to know you."   27. I bowed and replied: " The pleasure is mine, sir."   28. When I took leave of the family, I bowed to Mrs. Fernández and her daughter and said: " At your feet, ladies."   29. To Mr. Fernández and Mr. Navarro I said: " I kiss your hands, sirs. May you all keep well."

XXXI

1. John, speak (*fam.*) Spanish. Don't speak English in the class.   2. Mary, write (*fam.*) the second sentence of the exercises. Write it correctly. Don't write the first sentence.   3. Now, erase (*fam.*) it. No, don't erase it yet. Let me read it.   4. Class, let us read the lesson in (**de**) the reader.   5. Caroline, read (*fam.*) the second part of page twenty-five.   6. Don't read the first part.   7. Pronounce (*fam.*) the (**la**) **b** correctly.   8. Don't pronounce it like the English **b**.   9–16. *Repítanse los números* 1 . . . 8, *empleando* **usted** *como sujeto de los verbos.*[1]

17. Anna, I am very ill this morning. Telephone (*fam.*) to Dr. Pidal.   18. — Very well. (After a few moments.) The doctor says he will come at once.   Here he comes in his car.   19. The

---

[1] Repeat numbers 1 . . . 8, using **usted** as subject of the verbs.

doctor enters, bows to Caroline and says to me: 20. Good day, my friend. Are you ill?   21. I answer: Yes, doctor; I have been ill for three days.   22. I have [a] headache and I haven't [any] appetite.   23. — Let me take your pulse and see your tongue.   24. You have a fever. You must stay in bed (**guardar cama**) a few days.   25. Take one of these pills every three hours.   26. Take also a teaspoonful of this medicine after each meal.   27. Eat little and drink (**beba**) a great deal of water.

XXXII

1. Joseph, close (*empléese* **usted**) the door.   2. Joseph, I want you to close the door.   3. — The teacher wants me to close the door.   4. I do not want to close the door.   5. — Close it.   6. I want you to close it.   7. Class, learn (*pl.*) all the rules.   8. I want you to learn all the rules of the new lesson.   9. — The teacher wants us to learn the rules.   10. We do not want to learn the rules.   11. — But I insist (**insisto en**) that you learn them. 12. Paul, return home.   13. — My father tells me to return home. 14. I do not want to return home now.   15. — I advise you to return home immediately (**inmediatamente**).   16. Ferdinand, do not close the window.   17. I forbid your closing it.   18. — He forbids my closing the window.   19. Well, I don't want to close it.

20. Let us go into the bookshop of Melchor Suárez.   21. My father wishes me to buy the poetical (**poéticas**) works of Rubén Darío.   22. He advises me to read them.   23. — Here is a good edition, well printed, well bound and illustrated.   24. It is a de luxe edition, in four volumes.   25. — What is this edition worth? 26. — It is worth twelve dollars.   27. — It is dear, but my father wishes me to buy an edition and I [will] take it. 28. — Don't you want to buy [some] other books?   29. We have the *Complete Works* of Juan Ruiz de Alarcón and the *Selected Works* of Lope de Vega.   30. — No, thank you. To-day I do not wish to buy [any] more books.   31. — Here is a copy of a new book written by Pío Baroja, which Fernando García has just published.   32. It is interesting and I believe (that) you would like [it].   33. It is not dear. It is worth one dollar.   34. — All right; I [will] take it. Please send it [for] me to [the] house.

XXXIII

1. I fear (that) you are ill.   2. — Yes, I am very ill.   3. — I am sorry that you are ill.   4. I am sorry to be ill.   5. John doesn't study much.   6. It is a pity that he doesn't study more.   7. John, I desire you to study the lessons.   8. I advise you to study them.   9. I doubt that you [will] pass the examinations (**exámenes**) if you don't study more.   10. I believe that you will not pass them.   11. Is Mary happy?   12. — I doubt that she is happy.   13. But she denies that she is unhappy (**infeliz**).

14. I have just written a letter to a friend who is in Mexico, but I haven't [any] stamps.   15. — Do you wish me to go [and] get [some] stamps?   16. — Yes, please go and get them.   17. Do you wish me to take the letter to the post office?   18. — Yes, take it to the post office.   The train (**El tren**) leaves in an hour and I fear that you may not arrive in time.   19. Put a stamp on the envelope and post the letter.   20. I am glad that the post office is near.   21. What (**¿ Cuál**) is the postage for (**de**) a letter to a foreign country?   22. The postage for (**de**) a letter to Mexico is two cents.   23. Please bring me some post(al) cards.   24. To-night I must write a letter to my mother.   25. It is a pity that I don't write [to] her more frequently (**con más frecuencia**).   26. She wishes me to write to her every day.

XXXIV

1. My father wished (*imperf.*) me to study more.   2. It was necessary, he said, that I should study a great deal.   3. He feared that I shouldn't pass the examinations.   4. He believed that I shouldn't pass them.   5. I did not wish to study more.   6. I believed that I should pass them and I did not study much.   7. — Did you pass the examinations?   — No, sir; I didn't pass them.   8. Now I am very sorry that I didn't study more.   9. But it was not possible for me to study every day.   10. My father advised me to study every day and all (the) day, but I couldn't do so (**hacerlo**).   11. But I am very sorry that I didn't pass the examinations.   12. My brother says that he is glad that he didn't pass them.

13. Yesterday, Joe (**Pepe**) climbed a tree and tore his coat.
14. He went to his sister and asked her to mend the coat.
15. Anna took her (**el**) thimble, a needle and thread, her box of buttons and her scissors, and mended the coat.   16. She found one sleeve ripped and two pockets torn.   17. Joe begged her not to tell (it) to his mother.   18. He feared that she would punish him.   19. While his sister was mending the coat, Joe put on a worn [-out] coat and an old cap.   20. Joe is very much of a child.
21. He doesn't cry when his mother washes his face, but he cries sometimes when she combs his hair.   22. — How old is Joe?
23. — I don't know exactly (**con certeza**).   24. He is probably six years old more or less (**menos**).   25. His mother is a widow.
26. His father died two years ago.   27. It is a pity that his father died so (**tan**) young.

XXXV

1. I do not know any one who speaks Spanish.   2. I am looking for a man who speaks Spanish.   3. — I know a man who speaks Spanish perfectly (= speaks perfectly the Spanish).   4. He told me that he didn't know any one who spoke Spanish.   5. He told me that he was looking for a man who spoke Spanish.   6. And I told him that I knew a man who spoke Spanish perfectly.

7. To-day I bought at Martínez's shop a hat, a ready-màde suit, and some underclothes.   8. The hat cost me five dollars, the underclothes cost fifteen dollars, and for (**por**) the suit I paid forty-five dollars.   9. I didn't buy shirts because I didn't find any (*sing.*) that I liked.   10. — Did you buy collars?   11. — Yes, I bought a dozen (of) white collars of the best linen (**mejor hilo**).
12. I wanted to buy also some silk ties (= ties of silk).   13. I told the clerk that I was looking for ties that were not bright-colored.   14. He told me that bright-colored ties are now in fashion.   15. Finally, I bought one that cost me two dollars.
16. — Did you buy handkerchiefs too?   17. — Yes, I bought a dozen handkerchiefs that cost me three dollars.   18. I believe that they are of linen, but it is possible (**puede ser**) that they may be of cotton.   19. I hope they are of linen.   20. When I bought these articles (**cosas**), I asked the clerk to send them [for] me to [the] house and charge them to me on account.   21. He

answered that he couldn't sell on credit.   22. He said that they
always sold (= sold always) for cash in that store.   23. I paid
the bill and the clerk sent (me) the articles to [the] house.

XXXVI

1. If I had the money I should buy a new suit.   2. But I shall
not buy a new suit because I haven't [got] the money.   3. If I
worked more I could (**podría**) earn (**ganar**) the money that I need
(**necesito**), but I do not like to work.   4. If I studied more, I
should pass the examinations.   5. If I passed the examinations,
my father would be very glad (**contento**).   6. My father is very
sorry that I do not study more.   7. The train will arrive at ten
o'clock P.M.   8. I shall wait until it arrives.   9. I shall not leave
before it arrives.   10. He said he would wait until the train arrived.
11. He said he would not leave before it arrived.

12. This morning I went into a shoe shop where I bought (me)
a pair of riding boots, which I shall put on when I ride on horseback.   13. I bought also a pair of rubber overshoes (galoshes)
that I shall put on when it rains.   14. I didn't buy [any] shoes,
but I had a pair of old shoes half-soled.   15. Afterwards I went to
a hat shop and bought from the hatter a straw hat which I shall
wear when summer comes (*úsese* **llegar**).   16. Finally, I went
to a tailor shop and ordered a suit made.   17. The tailor took my
measure and asked me whether (**si**) I wanted [a] frock coat or
[a] sack coat.   18. I told him that I wanted a sack coat even
if the frock coat were more fashionable.   19. I also (= Also I)
ordered a suit of evening clothes made, with [a] white waistcoat
(vest) and black trousers.   20. I never buy (the) ready-made
suits because they do not fit me well.   21. My brother prefers
(the) ready-made suits.   22. He told me that he wished to see
what (**lo que**) he was buying before he bought it.

XXXVII

1. I should like to sell this house.   2. You ought to make the
repairs before selling it.   3. Yes, I know I should make the repairs.
4. If I had the money, I should make them.   5. But I haven't

[got] the money, and I can't make them now.   6. I wish I could make them!   7. Will you dine with me?   8. — I should be very glad to do so, but I have [an] engagement (**compromiso**) to-night (**esta noche**).   9. Will you have lunch with me at one o'clock?   10. — Many thanks! I accept with great (= much) pleasure.   11. — Well (**Pues**), we shall see each other (**nos**) at one. Goodbye for a while.   12. I hope it won't rain!

13. I wish you would give the following instructions to the laundryman when he comes for the clothing.   14. I should like to have the cuffs and bosoms (fronts) of the shirts well starched (*véase* A, 2).   15. Tell him also that I should like [to have] the shirts well ironed.   16. And tell him that the woolen clothes should be washed in lukewarm water.   17. They would shrink if they were washed in hot water.   18. The linen and cotton clothes can be washed in boiling water.

19. We have [some] saddle horses of good breed.   20. Shouldn't you like to go to the stable to see them?   21. — With great pleasure; I am fond of saddle horses.   22. I have a saddle horse, and I ride on horseback nearly every day if the weather is fine.   23. The horse is gentle, but he is fast and can run more than twenty kilometers an hour.   24. Have you also [some] driving horses?   25. — No, we haven't any driving horses, but we have a (motor-) car.   26. We prefer to ride in [a] car.

XXXVIII

1. The church (**iglesia**), the parish priest, the painting (**pintura**), the artist (*masc.*), the grammar, the map, the hand, the soup, the water, the ruby, the Monday, the Frenchman, the teacup, the gold watch.   2. *Repítase el número uno en plural*.

3. To-morrow I shall leave (*úsese* **partir**) for Montevideo.   4. Do you know when the boat leaves?   5. — The boat leaves (from) Buenos Aires every day promptly at eight A.M., and arrives at Montevideo in the afternoon.   6. — Do you know how far it is from Buenos Aires to Montevideo?   7. — I do not know exactly, but it is two hundred kilometers more or less, or about (**cerca de**) one hundred and twenty English miles (**millas**).   8. — Is the

boat large? 9. — It is not very large, but there will be two
hundred passengers on board without counting the sailors.
10. — I hope (that) the sea is calm, because I get seasick if it is
rough. 11. — Do not worry. (¡ **Pierda cuidado !**) The waves
have disappeared and the sea is perfectly calm. 12. I believe that
the passage will be very pleasant. 13. — Well, before the boat
leaves, I should like to say goodbye to the friends who are on the
wharf. 14. I see Mr. and Mrs. Martínez and Joseph Pimentel.
15. Goodbye ! — Goodbye ! Pleasant journey !

XXXIX

1. Have you one hundred dollars? — Yes, I have one hundred.
2. Napoleon was [a] great man, but he was not a large man.
3. The poor woman! — Yes, she is a very poor woman. 4. We
live in a white house. 5. Mr. and Mrs. Heredia live in a red
house. 6. The white snow of the mountain range (**de la sierra**)
is beautiful (**bella**). 7. And the white moon of a summer night
(= a night of summer) is romantic (**romántica**). 8. In school we
are studying the French and Spanish languages. 9. We have
read the first and second volumes of *Don Quixote* (**Quijote**).
10. We have not yet read the works of Saint Theresa (**Teresa**) or
(**ni**) of Saint Isidore (**Isidoro**) of Seville (**Sevilla**).

11. To-morrow I shall leave El Paso, Texas (**Tejas**), for the
City of Mexico. 12. The express train leaves El Paso at ten P.M.,
and crosses a desert (**desierto**) during the night. 13. In this
Mexican desert it is very hot during the day. 14. But when we
arrive at Zacatecas we shall be at an altitude (**altura**) of seven
thousand (**mil**) feet above the level (**nivel**) of the sea. 15. From
Zacatecas to Mexico City the summer temperature (**temperatura**)
is pleasant. 16. Have you packed your trunk? 17. — Not
yet (= yet not), but I shall pack it this afternoon. 18. — Shall
you wear a linen (**hilo**) suit? 19. — I prefer a woolen suit because
it is never very warm in Mexico City. 20. — Does the train
carry [a] sleeping car and [a] dining car? 21. — Yes, the express
train has all the conveniences that we can desire, and the service
is excellent. 22. — Shall you get a one-way ticket or a round-

trip ticket?   23. — I shall get a one-way ticket because I intend
to go to Vera Cruz.   24. From there I shall go by sea to New
(**Nueva**) York.   25. Well, [goodbye] till to-morrow!   26. If the
weather permits, I shall accompany you to the railway station.

XL

1. Most of my books are in the library.   2. I have more books
than I had last year.   3. In fact (**efecto**), I have more than a
thousand.   4. I read many books, but my brother Julius is the
one who reads most in our family.   5. This book is most (**sumamente**) interesting.   6. It is the most interesting book that I
have read this year.   7. It is more interesting than the book
that you are reading.   8. Is the water cold this morning?   9. It
is colder than I thought (*úsese* **creer**).   10. The colder it is, the
more I like [it].   11. Does Mr. Hernández earn much?   12. Yes,
he earns very much (**muchísimo**).   13. But the more he earns
the less he possesses (**posee**), because he spends more than he
earns.

14. Please give me the address of (**indicarme**) a good boarding
house or an inexpensive (**económico**) hotel.   15. With great pleasure. In my opinion the best inexpensive hotel in (**de**) Madrid is
the Hotel de Londres which faces the Puerta del Sol, at the corner
of A. Street.   16. You can walk (= go afoot) if you wish.
17. You go straight ahead until you come (*infin.*) to the fourth
corner.   18. Then you turn the corner to the right and you find
yourself in the Puerta del Sol.   19. Or you can take the street
car (tramway) that passes by here and get off in the Puerta del
Sol.   20. If you prefer a boarding house, there is a good one
(**una**) near here in the house number 215 of this street.   21. I
have lived for ten years in this boarding house and the service is
excellent.   22. Thank you very much (= Many thanks), but I
should prefer the hotel because it is nearer to the theaters.   23. In
Madrid it is not cold in winter, and there is little snow.   24. But
it is very hot in summer, and sometimes it thunders and lightens
a great deal.   25. I prefer the climate of Cádiz, where it is neither
cold nor hot.

XLI

1. Bring (*2nd pers. sing.*) me the book. Don't bring me the book. Yes, bring it to me. No, don't bring it to me.   2. Give (*2nd pers. sing.*) him the pen. No, don't give him the pen. Yes, give it to him. Don't give it to him.   3. Lend (*úsese* **usted**) the pen to me. Don't lend the pen to John. Lend it to me. Don't lend it to him.   4. Tell (*úsese* **usted**) him (it), but don't tell her (it). I mean (**Digo**), tell her (it), but don't tell him (it).   5. It is said that Joseph's illness is serious (**grave**).   6. It is true, but the more ill he is the less he complains (**se queja**).   7. Generally he doesn't sleep well, but last night he fell asleep at nine o'clock and slept well all (the) night.   8. As a result (**Resulta que**) he feels better this morning.

9. We have walked about town all (the) day. I am tired and (am) hungry.   10. Here is an excellent restaurant. Will you dine here or do you prefer to go to the hotel?   11. — Let's dine here. Waiter! — I am coming (*véase* XVIII, D, 2 *y* 3). What do the gentlemen wish?   12. Bring us the bill of fare and please put another cloth on the table.   13. Yes, sir. Do the gentlemen wish soup?   14. Yes; bring us soup, fish, beef and fried potatoes.   15. Very well, sir. Do the gentlemen wish salad?   16. Yes, bring us lettuce salad, and a bottle of red wine.   17. Waiter, bring me another napkin. This [one] is torn. — Here you have another, sir.   18. — Do the gentlemen wish dessert?   19. — Yes, bring us fruit, cheese and biscuits.   20. Bring me a small cup of black coffee. My friend doesn't take coffee.   21. As (**De**) [a] tip, let us give the waiter twenty-five cents.   22. Let us go to the hotel. I am sleepy.   23. We have a large room that faces the square.   24. But it is on the third floor and there isn't [any] elevator (lift).   25. Call the boy (**mozo**) and tell him to bring us a jug (pitcher) of water and two glasses.   26. Let him bring also some matches and a candle.   27. After twelve o'clock there isn't [any] electric light in this hotel.

XLII

1. He doesn't tell me the truth. Tell me the truth. Don't tell me a lie (**mentira**). He doesn't want to tell me the truth.   2. They talk Spanish with me.   Do they talk Spanish with you (= thee, *2nd pers. sing.*)?   They don't talk Spanish with her.   3. I deceive myself. You (**Usted**) also deceive yourself. In fact [we] all deceive ourselves every day. And we deceive each other too.   4. Have you a letter for me? — No, I haven't any letter for you, but I have one for her.   5. Teacher, we students desire a vacation. — You students desire a vacation every day in (**de**) the year.

6. Let us go to the theater to-night.   7. I am tired of writing exercises and I should like to enjoy myself.   8. Joseph, bring me the evening paper.   I wish to read the advertisements (announcements) of the theaters and the motion pictures ("movies").   9. — Don't you want to go to the opera or to a musical comedy?   10. — No, I am not fond of music, and I should prefer to see a comedy or go to a vaudeville theater.   11. — Well (**Pues**), I have here the advertisement of a performance in the Teatro Real.   12. To-night a new comedy by (**de**) the Quinteros will be given for the first time, and the tickets cost one dollar.   13. — But I don't want a seat in the gallery.   14. I prefer an orchestra (**orquesta**) seat which costs two dollars.   15. — I should prefer a box seat, but we are not rich enough to occupy a box (*véase* A, 14).   16. — Well, we [have] (already) finished dinner. Let us go [and] get the tickets.   17. It is already eight o'clock, and the curtain rises at half-past eight, if I am not mistaken.   18. It will not be long before the performance begins, and I should like to have a seat in the first row or the second.   19. — I fear that all the seats of the first two (= two first) rows may already be occupied.   20. — Let us take the street car (tramway) that passes by here.   21. Last night I went to the Gran Teatro to see a farce.   22. The performance was wretched (**malísima**) and the farce was not interesting.   23. To tell the truth, I prefer (the) motion pictures ("movies") to the poor (**mala**) performance of a comedy.

XLIII

1. Do you speak Spanish? — No, but I am studying Spanish. In my opinion, Spanish is not more difficult than English. 2. Men are more intelligent than horses, but horses are stronger than men. 3. Man prefers the beautiful to the ugly, the good to the bad. 4. Iron is more useful than gold, but gold is worth more than iron. 5. Mr. García is a Spaniard, but his wife is a Mexican. Both speak Spanish almost perfectly. 6. Little Mary is very good. — Yes, we know how good she is. 7. Last week she went to school every day and to the " movies " every night. 8. The children rose early, washed their faces and their hands, brushed their hair, ate breakfast, and went to school. 9. Does your brother live in Mexico? — No, he is now in Peru, but he intends to spend the summer in Ecuador. 10. What are oranges worth? — Thirty-five cents a dozen. — And what are apples worth? — Five cents a pound. 11. Well, I [will] take one dozen oranges and five pounds of apples.

12. We have a plantation (at) forty kilometers from Mexico City, near the pyramids (las pirámides) of Teotihuacán, where we spend the summer every year. 13. When I am in the country I like to ride on horseback, but my sister doesn't (like). 14. One day she was riding on horseback and the horse almost fell. 15. That frightened my sister and she hasn't wanted to ride since. 16. My father is fond (aficionado a) of fishing (la pesca), and he goes fishing (va a la pesca) almost every day in a lake that is not far from the house. 17. In front of our house there is a flower-garden, and behind the house we have a large orchard-and-garden. 18. During the summer we have an abundance (abundancia) of tropical fruits [such] as the orange, the banana, the guava, etc. (etcétera). 19. I am sorry that northern (septentrionales) fruits such as the apple and the pear are not grown in this climate. 20. Near the house there is a very large tree that we climb sometimes, and in which (el cual) birds make their nests. 21. We have cows and goats (cabras) that give us milk. 22. It is said that goat milk (= the milk of the goat) is more healthful (saludable) than cow milk (la de la vaca). 23. Most of the farm laborers are Indian peones, and their favorite food (alimento predilecto) is the maize (Indian corn).

XLIV

1. Buenos Aires, the capital of (the) Argentina, is a beautiful city. It has more inhabitants than Madrid.   2. Cuzco (**El Cuzco**), a city of Peru, was the capital of the Incas (*masc.*). The city is situated at an altitude (**altura**) of twelve thousand feet above the level (**nivel**) of the sea.   3. The present (**actual**) king of Spain is Alphonso the Thirteenth. One of the most famous (**famosos**) kings of Spain was Alphonso the Tenth, called the Wise (**Sabio**). 4. Whose house is this? — It is Mr. Pidal's house. — It is larger than mine, but I prefer mine to his.   5. Whose book have you? — I have mine.   6. — Do you know where mine is? — No, sir; I haven't seen yours.   7. Have you his book or hers? — I have mine.

8.   Hotel Grande, Granada,
                                                      July 21, 19—.

Dear Joseph:

I was very tired when I arrived yesterday at Granada, but this morning I am better. Granada is a beautiful city and it possesses (**posee**) many historical monuments that I desire to see. The Alhambra is the most interesting palace (**palacio**) that I have seen in Spain. It was built by the Arabs many centuries ago. Please tell Mr. Morales that I intend to remain here a fortnight. If all is well, I shall return August 5. I can't stay longer (**más tiempo**) this time (**vez**), but I hope to return next summer.

                                   Yours affectionately (*véase* A, 1),
                                                               Paul.

9.   Calle de Preciados, 51, Madrid,
                                                  October 10, 19—.

Dear Sir and Friend:

To-day I received your kind letters (favors) of the 7th and 9th instant, and I make haste to answer them. My wife and I are very grateful for all that (**lo que**) you have done for our nephew during his illness. We are very fond (*úsese* **querer**) of Ferdinand and we learned (**supimos**) with true (**verdadero**) sorrow (**sentimiento**) that he was ill. We hope to have the opportunity of repaying you

[for] the good services that you have had the kindness to show our nephew. Please tell Ferdinand that I shall go to Córdoba day after to-morrow.

> I am very sincerely yours,
> Julio Martínez y Ortega.

XLV

1. This book is mine. This is mine.   2. That book [near you] is hers. That is hers.   3. That book [over there] is yours. That is yours.   4. I prefer this house to that of Mr. González.   5. My horse is faster than Mr. Pidal's (= that of Mr. Pidal).   6. Gold watches cost more than silver watches (= those of silver).   7. He who spends all that he earns is always poor.   8. He who is silent gives assent.

9.   Calle de Atocha, 110, Madrid,
                                        December 5, 19—.

Dear Henry:

I am exceedingly (**muchísimo**) sorry to trouble you, but I am without money. I was (*pret.*) ill last month and could not work. If you can lend me one hundred dollars I shall be very grateful, and I promise to pay you within (**dentro de**) a month. I do not like to borrow money, but this time I can't help it. If you have any objection to lending me the sum that I ask, don't do it. But the truth is (that) here I haven't any one to whom to apply. I went to the bank and tried to borrow some money, but I did not succeed. My illness was not serious, but I had to stay in bed (**guardar cama**) two weeks. I am better now and I expect to go to the office to-morrow. What is the news in Seville (**Sevilla**)? If all is well, I shall go to Seville during the summer vacation.

> Most affectionately yours,
> Frederick (**Federico**).

10.   Calle de Francos, 65.

Mr. Paul Henríquez y Navarro,
   Calle de Preciados, 125.
Dear Sir:

We should be greatly pleased if you would do us the honor of dining with us Wednesday night at seven o'clock. Mr. and

Mrs. Ortega, whom you know, will be present. I hope that you may have no other engagement that will deprive us of your company Wednesday night.

I am very sincerely yours, (*véase* A, 2),

Juan Núñez.

February 10, 19—.

XLVI

1. Have you any apples? — I haven't any. — Have you any brothers? — No, sir; I haven't any brothers. 2. Which book have you? — I have Mary's (= that of Mary). — Which [one] of these books do you like best (**más**)? — I like best the [one] that I am reading now. 3. Have you another saddle horse? — Yes, sir; I have several, but I prefer this [one] to the rest. 4. Anna, how pale you are! Are you ill? — No, sir; I am not ill, but I am very tired. 5. Every man should earn his living (**la vida**). He should work every day except Sunday, if he is well. 6. Every two hours a train leaves Madrid for Toledo. I go to Toledo every day. 7. Ferdinand is fond of (**quiere**) me and he is fond of you too. He is fond of both [of] us. 8. Do you believe all (that) he says? — Yes, sir; I believe all (that) he says, because he never lies. 9. He is a little (**pequeño**) boy. Do you want to give him a little money? — No, sir; I haven't any money.

10. Matanzas, Cuba.
June 15, 19—,

Dear Julius:

I am writing to tell you that Joseph Hernández married the daughter of Mr. and Mrs. Ortega last Wednesday, June 10. The civil ceremony was performed in the morning. The religious ceremony took place in the afternoon of the same day. Joseph's wife is charming, and her father is very rich. I caught cold and couldn't be present at the religious ceremony, which was performed in the church of Saint Anne.

I am sending you herewith the invitation that the Ortegas were good enough (**tuvieron la bondad de**) to send me. I have forgotten your address and I am sending (= I send) this letter to your brother's house. What is the news in Havana? I hope that you and all your family are enjoying (*úsese* **gozar de**) good health. I was ill last week, but I am better now. Frederick Navarro doesn't write [to] me [any] more. I have written him several letters since (**desde que**) I have been here, but he doesn't answer. Do you think (that) he is angry with me? I hope not (**que no**). If you see him, tell him to write to me. I forgot to tell you that next week I shall go hunting (**a la caza**), but I shall return to Matanzas within three days, if God wills (**quiere**) and the weather permits, as they say here.

> Cordially yours,
> Francis (Francisco).

XLVII

1. The first of January is the first day of the year, and the thirty-first of December is the last day of the year. 2. Has he a million dollars? — No, sir; he hasn't more than a thousand dollars. He has lost nine tenths of his little fortune (**fortuna**). 3. Have you one hundred dollars to (**para**) lend me? — I have one hundred more or less, but they are not for you. 4. Columbus discovered America [in] the year fourteen hundred and ninety-two. 5. The World War (**Guerra Mundial**) began [in] the year nineteen hundred and fourteen. 6. How many passengers are there aboard? — It is said that there are two hundred and twenty-five. — No, sir; there are two hundred and eight passengers. I counted them. 7. Did he lose one half of his goods? — No, sir; but he lost one fifth. — He told me that he lost only one twelfth.

8. A (The) year is divided into four seasons, namely (**a saber**) spring, which is the season of flowers; summer, the warm season; autumn (fall), the season of fruits; and winter, which is the cold season. In Europe (**Europa**) and in the United States the summer months are June, July, and August, but in South America (**la América del Sur**) the summer months are December, January, and February. In a year there are twelve months, fifty-two weeks, and three hundred and sixty-five days. The number of days in a month varies (**varía**) from twenty-eight to thirty-one. A week is the space of seven days. A day is divided into twenty-four hours. An hour is divided into sixty minutes and a minute is divided into

sixty seconds. There are many seconds in a year, are there not? In winter the sun rises late and sets early. In summer the sun rises early and sets late. As a result (**Resulta que**) the summer days are longer than the winter days.

9. The monetary unit of Spain is the **peseta.** The gold **peseta** has the same value as (**de**) the gold franc (**franco**), namely [a] little less than twenty American cents or ten English pence (**peniques,** *masc.*). The **peseta** is divided into one hundred centimes. The five **pesetas** coin is popularly called a **duro,** and a coin of twenty-five centimes is called a **real.** The **peso** is the monetary unit of the United States and of Mexico, Cuba, (the) Argentina, Chile, and other Spanish-American countries. The **peso** is divided into one hundred cents. The gold **peso** of Mexico, for instance (**por ejemplo**), has the value of a gold dollar (**dólar**) of the United States, but the silver **peso** is worth less and the paper **peso** is worth still (**aun**) less. In Spain and in most Spanish-American countries the value of the paper money varies from time to time (**de vez en cuando**).

XLVIII

1. John, come (*fam.*) here. I wish to speak with you. Come right here.   2. Are you (**usted**) very tired? — Yes, very. — Well, you have worked all day and I am much obliged [to] you.   3. Has your brother written all the exercises? — I hope so, but I believe not. Why he left this morning before breakfast and he hasn't returned yet! — He will return in due time. — I should say so!   4. I have already finished. Let's have-dinner. 5. Paul, read the first page of the lesson. Pronounce clearly and distinctly.   6. Are you and your brother students in (**de**) this school? — Yes, my brother and I are students in this school.

7. Most European (**europeos**) and Spanish-American countries have adopted the decimal system of weights and measures. I believe that England and the United States are the only (**únicos**) civilized (**civilizados**) countries in (**de**) the world that have not adopted it. In the decimal system the unit of weight is the gram, which is equal to the weight of a cubic centimeter of distilled water at the level of the sea. A (**El**) kilogram has one thousand grams,

and is equivalent to a little more than two English pounds. The liter has the volume of a cubic decimeter and is equivalent to a little more than our English " quart." Consequently (**Resulta que**) an English pint is approximately equivalent to a half liter and an English pound is approximately equivalent to a half kilogram. As a rule, in Spain and Spanish America, dry objects are not measured but (**sino**) are weighed. The unit of length is the meter, which is a little longer than an English yard. The meter can be divided into ten decimeters or one hundred centimeters. The kilometer, which is equal to one thousand meters, is used for measuring great distances. Ten kilometers are approximately equal to six English miles. For instance, fifty-five kilometers are approximately equal to thirty-three miles. Land (**Los terrenos**) is measured by ares (= ten meters square) or by hectares (one hundred ares). The hectare is approximately equal to two and a half English " acres." There is no (**No cabe**) doubt (of) that the decimal system of weights and measures is simpler (**más sencillo**) and more practical (**práctico**) than the English system, and I am surprised (**me extraña**) that England and its colonies (**colonias**) and the United States have not adopted it.

XLIX

1. Have you a letter for me? — No, ma'am, but I have a package for you. 2. To-morrow we are leaving for Santiago de Chile, and we shall remain there [for] three months. 3. Ferdinand fell in love with (**se enamoró de**) Mr. Garcia's daughter and he said that he would give his life for her. 4. As (**Como**) the thief went out through the window, Mr. Alonso caught him by the hand, but he couldn't hold (**sujetar**) him. The thief drew out a revolver (**revólver**) and killed Mr. Alonso. — Yes, I heard (**oí decir**) that Mr. Alonso was killed by a thief. The poor man! 5. Do you live in this house? — No, sir; I don't live in this house, but in the [one] across-the-street (**de enfrente**). 6. Are you ill? — I am not ill, but [I am] very tired. I have been working [for] twenty-four hours without rest.

7. Dear Sir:

I have pleasure in acknowledging the receipt of your kind letter of the fifteenth instant, and we shall send you by return mail **(por vuelta de correo)** the books which you order.

With best regards I remain

Very sincerely yours (*véase* A, 2),

Felipe Suárez.

8. Dear Sir:

I have pleasure in sending you herewith a **(el)** statement of your account brought-up-to **(cerrada)** June 30, 19—.

		Debit	Credit
1926		**(Debe)**	**(Haber)**
August 1st	Balance in **(a)** our favor	155.25	
November 5	Our bill......................	62.50	
1927			
January 24	Your **(Su)** remittance..........		100.00
March 30	Balance in our favor...........		117.75
		217.75	217.75

As you will observe, there is a balance in our favor of 117.75 **pesetas** which we charge to you on a new account, begging you to advise us if you do not find it correct **(exacto)**.

Trusting that we may be of further service to you, we remain

Very truly yours (*véase* A, 3),

Luis Herrera.

L

1. Now I must go to the bank to draw some money.   2. This morning I spent my last cent.   3. Do you know the cashier?   4. No, I don't know any one in the bank.   5. Will you come with me **(acompañarme)** to identify me **(para identificarme)**?   6. — With great pleasure. This is the Second National Bank.   7. — I should like to cash this check.   8. — Very well, sir. Please write on the back **(al dorso)** " Pay (= Let it be paid) to the order of the Second National Bank," and sign it here.   9. Do you wish silver or paper money (= bank notes) ?   10. — Please give me paper money. I am not used to **(No estoy acostumbrado a)** silver, and I fear I may lose (§ 153) it.

11. Dear Sir:

We have much pleasure in sending you herewith our catalogue and price list, and we assure you that we shall do everything in our power to fill your orders to your entire satisfaction. We can offer you a discount of 5 per cent if you pay cash (= in case of cash payment), or of 3 per cent if the payment is made in 30 days. We have the largest stock (**surtido**) in (**de**) this market (**plaza**), and our prices are low (**reducidos**).

Hoping that we may have your kind orders, I am very sincerely yours,   Felipe Heredía.

12. Dear Sirs:

I have pleasure in acknowledging the receipt of the catalogue of your house. Please send me the articles itemized in the following list. I hope you can send them by return mail. Please have the articles packed in wooden boxes. Send me your bill and I shall remit the amount in a check on New York.

I am yours very truly,
Felipe Pidal.

THE VERB

233. The Spanish verb system, being derived from that of Latin, shows flexional endings characteristic of mood, tense, person, and number:

habl-ar, to speak   **habl-amos,** we speak
habl-ando, speaking   **habl-aba,** I (he) was speaking,
habl-o, I speak   used to speak

The perfect tenses are compounded by adding to the auxiliary verb **haber,** *to have,* the invariable past participle of the main verb:

he hablado, I have spoken   **había hablado,** I (he) had spoken

234. The Spanish verb may be divided into five leading classes: (1) the regular verb, (2) the radical-changing verb, (3) the verb with inceptive endings, (4) the **–uir** verb, (5) the irregular verb.

235. The future of the indicative and the conditional of all verbs are based upon their infinitive form. This may suffer some modification in the case of irregular verbs:

$$\textbf{hablar,} \text{ to speak} \begin{cases} \textbf{hablar-é,} \text{ I shall speak} \\ \textbf{hablar-ía,} \text{ I should speak} \end{cases}$$

$$\textbf{decir,} \text{ to say} \begin{cases} \textbf{dir-án,} \text{ they will say} \\ \textbf{dir-ían,} \text{ they would say} \end{cases}$$

a. The endings of the future of the indicative and the conditional are derived from the present and the imperfect, respectively, of the indicative of **haber,** *to have* (cf. §116, footnote).

236. — 1. For regular verbs the stem may be found by cutting off the ending **–o** of the first person singular of the present indicative, or the ending **–ar, –er, –ir** of the infinitive:

habl-o, I speak	habl-ar, to speak
aprend-o, I learn	aprend-er, to learn
escrib-o, I write	escrib-ir, to write

In regular verbs this stem is the basis of all forms except those of the future of the indicative and of the conditional.

2. In the case of radical-changing and irregular verbs the stem of the third singular (or plural) of the preterite indicative is the same as that of the two imperfect (or past) subjunctives and of the future (or hypothetical) subjunctive:

Pedir, to ask: pid-ió (pid-ieron), he asked (they asked); *impf. subj.*, pid-iese, *etc.*, pid-iera, *etc.; fut. subj.*, pid-iere, *etc.*

Saber, to know: sup-o (sup-ieron), he knew (they knew); *impf. subj.*, sup-iese, *etc.*, sup-iera, *etc.; fut. subj.*, sup-iere, *etc.*

237. The Regular Verb. — There are three regular conjugations in Spanish characterized by the vowels of their infinitive endings, namely, –ar for the first conjugation, –er for the second, and –ir for the third. But, as a matter of fact, the endings of the second and third conjugations are the same except in the infinitive (and the infinitive stem of the future and conditional indicative), in the first and second persons plural of the present indicative, and in the second person plural of the imperative.

PARADIGMS

I	II	III
	INFINITIVE MOOD	
Present	**Present**	**Present**
habl-**ar**, *to speak*	aprend-**er**, *to learn*	viv-**ir**, *to live*

PARTICIPLES

Present (Gerund)	**Present (Gerund)**	**Present (Gerund)**
habl-**ando**, *speaking*	aprend-**iendo**, *learning*	viv-**iendo**, *living*
Past	**Past**	**Past**
habl-**ado**, *spoken*	aprend-**ido**, *learned*	viv-**ido**, *lived*

INDICATIVE MOOD

Present	**Present**	**Present**
I speak, do speak, am speaking; etc.	*I learn, do learn, am learning; etc.*	*I live, do live, am living; etc.*
habl-**o**	aprend-**o**	viv-**o**
habl-**as**	aprend-**es**	viv-**es**
habl-**a**	aprend-**e**	viv-**e**
habl-**amos**	aprend-**emos**	viv-**imos**
habl-**áis**	aprend-**éis**	viv-**ís**
habl-**an**	aprend-**en**	viv-**en**

Imperfect	**Imperfect** [1]	**Imperfect** [1]
I spoke, was speaking, used to speak; etc.	*I learned, was learning, used to learn; etc.*	*I lived, was living, used to live; etc.*
habl-**aba**	aprend-**ía**	viv-**ía**
habl-**abas**	aprend-**ías**	viv-**ías**
habl-**aba**	aprend-**ía**	viv-**ía**
habl-**ábamos**	aprend-**íamos**	viv-**íamos**
habl-**abais**	aprend-**íais**	viv-**íais**
habl-**aban**	aprend-**ían**	viv-**ían**

Preterite	**Preterite**	**Preterite**
I spoke, did speak; etc.	*I learned, did learn; etc.*	*I lived, did live; etc.*
habl-**é**	aprend-**í**	viv-**í**
habl-**aste**	aprend-**iste**	viv-**iste**
habl-**ó**	aprend-**ió**	viv-**ió**
habl-**amos**	aprend-**imos**	viv-**imos**
habl-**asteis**	aprend-**isteis**	viv-**isteis**
habl-**aron**	aprend-**ieron**	viv-**ieron**

[1] In the imperfect indicative of the second and third conjugations and also in the conditional of all three conjugations the accent remains on the same vowel throughout all the forms and is always written.

Future	Future	Future
I shall speak; etc.	*I shall learn; etc.*	*I shall live; etc.*
hablar-é	aprender-é	vivir-é
hablar-**ás**	aprender-**ás**	vivir-**ás**
hablar-**á**	aprender-**á**	vivir-**á**
hablar-**emos**	aprender-**emos**	vivir-**emos**
hablar-**éis**	aprender-**éis**	vivir-**éis**
hablar-**án**	aprender-**án**	vivir-**án**

Conditional	Conditional	Conditional
I should speak; etc.	*I should learn; etc.*	*I should live; etc.*
hablar-**ía**	aprender-**ía**	vivir-**ía**
hablar-**ías**	aprender-**ías**	vivir-**ías**
hablar-**ía**	aprender-**ía**	vivir-**ía**
hablar-**íamos**	aprender-**íamos**	vivir-**íamos**
hablar-**íais**	aprender-**íais**	vivir-**íais**
hablar-**ían**	aprender-**ían**	vivir-**ían**

IMPERATIVE MOOD

	speak	*learn*	*live*
Sing. 2	habl-**a**	aprend-**e**	viv-**e**
Pl. 2	habl-**ad**	aprend-**ed**	viv-**id**

SUBJUNCTIVE MOOD

Present	Present	Present
(that I may) speak,	*(that I may) learn,*	*(that I may) live,*
(let me) speak; etc.	*(let me) learn; etc.*	*(let me) live; etc.*
habl-**e**	aprend-**a**	viv-**a**
habl-**es**	aprend-**as**	viv-**as**
habl-**e**	aprend-**a**	viv-**a**
habl-**emos**	aprend-**amos**	viv-**amos**
habl-**éis**	aprend-**áis**	viv-**áis**
habl-**en**	aprend-**an**	viv-**an**

–se Imperfect	–se Imperfect	–se Imperfect
(that or if I might) speak; etc.	*(that or if I might) learn; etc.*	*(that or if I might) live; etc.*
habl-**ase**	aprend-**iese**	viv-**iese**
habl-**ases**	aprend-**ieses**	viv-**ieses**
habl-**ase**	aprend-**iese**	viv-**iese**
habl-**ásemos**	aprend-**iésemos**	viv-**iésemos**
habl-**aseis**	aprend-**ieseis**	viv-**ieseis**
habl-**asen**	aprend-**iesen**	viv-**iesen**

–ra Imperfect	–ra Imperfect	–ra Imperfect
I should speak, (that or if I might) speak; etc.	*I should learn, (that or if I might) learn; etc.*	*I should live, (that or if I might) live; etc.*
habl-**ara**	aprend-**iera**	viv-**iera**
habl-**aras**	aprend-**ieras**	viv-**ieras**
habl-**ara**	aprend-**iera**	viv-**iera**
habl-**áramos**	aprend-**iéramos**	viv-**iéramos**
habl-**arais**	aprend-**ierais**	viv-**ierais**
habl-**aran**	aprend-**ieran**	viv-**ieran**

Future (or Hypothetical)	Future (or Hypothetical)	Future (or Hypothetical)
I (may or shall) speak; etc.	*I (may or shall) learn; etc.*	*I (may or shall) live; etc.*
habl-**are**	aprend-**iere**	viv-**iere**
habl-**ares**	aprend-**ieres**	viv-**ieres**
habl-**are**	aprend-**iere**	viv-**iere**
habl-**áremos**	aprend-**iéremos**	viv-**iéremos**
habl-**areis**	aprend-**iereis**	viv-**iereis**
habl-**aren**	aprend-**ieren**	viv-**ieren**

PERFECT TENSES OF HABLAR

INFINITIVE	PARTICIPLE (GERUND)
to have spoken	*having spoken*
haber hablado	habiendo hablado

INDICATIVE

Present Perfect
I have spoken; etc.
he hablado
has hablado; *etc.*

Preterite Perfect
I had spoken; etc.
hube hablado
hubiste hablado; *etc.*

Pluperfect
I had spoken; etc.
había hablado; *etc.*

Future Perfect
I shall have spoken; etc.
habré hablado; *etc.*

Conditional Perfect
I should have spoken; etc.
habría hablado; *etc.*

SUBJUNCTIVE

Present Perfect
*(That I may) have
spoken; etc.*
haya hablado; *etc.*

–ra Pluperfect
*I should have spoken;
etc.*
hubiera hablado; *etc.*

–se Pluperfect
*(That I might) have
spoken; etc.*
hubiese hablado; *etc.*

**Future (or Hypo-
thetical) Perfect**
*I (may or shall) have
spoken; etc.*
hubiere hablado; *etc.*

a. The following tables of moods and tenses give (1) the English names and
(2) the Spanish names, to which preference is given in this book, and (3) the names
given in the *Gramática de la lengua castellana* (Madrid, 1913) published by the Royal
Spanish Academy.

	1	2	3
	INFINITIVE	INFINITIVO	INFINITIVO
hablar:	present	presente	presente
haber hablado:	perfect	perfecto	pretérito
	PARTICIPLES	PARTICIPIOS	
hablando:	present	presente	gerundio
hablado:	past	pasado	participio (pasivo)

	INDICATIVE	INDICATIVO	INDICATIVO
hablo:	present	presente	presente
hablaba:	imperfect	imperfecto	pretérito imperfecto
hablé:	preterite	pretérito	pretérito perfecto
hablaré:	future	futuro	futuro imperfecto
hablaría:	conditional	condicional	pretérito imperfecto (de subjuntivo)
he hablado:	present perfect	presente perfecto	pretérito perfecto
había hablado:	pluperfect	pluscuamperfecto	pretérito pluscuamperfecto
hube hablado:	preterite perfect	pretérito perfecto	pretérito perfecto
habré hablado:	future perfect	futuro perfecto	futuro perfecto
habría hablado:	conditional perfect	condicional perfecto	pretérito pluscuamperfecto (de subjuntivo)

habla:	IMPERATIVE	IMPERATIVO	IMPERATIVO
	SUBJUNCTIVE	SUBJUNTIVO	SUBJUNTIVO
hable:	present	presente	presente
hablase } *hablara*	imperfect	imperfecto	pretérito imperfecto
hablare:	future	futuro	futuro imperfecto
haya hablado:	present perfect	presente perfecto	pretérito perfecto
hubiese } *hubiera* *hablado:*	pluperfect	pluscuamperfecto	pretérito pluscuamperfecto
hubiere hablado:	future perfect	futuro perfecto	futuro perfecto

In the nomenclature of the Spanish Academy the three tenses *hablé, he hablado,* and *hube hablado* have the same name: **pretérito perfecto de indicativo.** Likewise *hablase, hablara,* and *hablaría* are called the **pretérito imperfecto de subjuntivo;** and *hubiese hablado, hubiera hablado,* and *habría hablado* are called the **pretérito pluscuamperfecto de subjuntivo.** Confusion of names may be avoided in part, as follows: *hablé,* **pretérito perfecto simple;** *he hablado,* **pretérito perfecto compuesto** (con *he, has,* etc.).

b. The tense names recommended in the *Report of the Joint Committee on Grammatical Nomenclature* (University of Chicago Press, 1913), which differ from those to which preference is given in this book, are: *hablaba,* **past descriptive;** *hablé,* **past absolute;** *hablaría,* **past future;** *había hablado,* **past perfect;** *hube hablado,* **2nd past perfect;** *habría hablado,* **past future perfect;** *hablase* or *hablara,* **past subjunctive.**

238. Compound Progressive Tenses. — The present participle of a principal verb may be combined with the auxiliary **estar** (never **ser**) to form a progressive construction.

estamos hablando, we are speaking

Certain verbs of motion or rest such as **ir,** *to go,* **quedar,** *to remain,* may appear instead of **estar** in this construction.

239. Changes in Spelling. — It is a regular tendency of Spanish verbs to preserve throughout their conjugation the consonantal *sound* at the end of the stem (found ordinarily by cutting off the infinitive ending –ar, –er, –ir). Hence, before certain vowels of the flexional suffix a change in spelling of the end of the stem is necessitated. This is so not only for regular verbs but for many others also.

240. Before flexional –e these changes occur:

1. Verbs in –c-ar change c to qu to keep the k sound ("hard" c sound):

Buscar, *to seek*

Pret. Indic., 1st Sing. } busqué

Pres. Subj.   busque   busques   busque   busquemos   busquéis   busquen

2. Verbs in –g-ar add to the g an unpronounced u to keep the "hard" g sound:

Pagar, *to pay*

Pret. Indic., 1st Sing. } pagué

Pres. Subj.   pague   pagues   pague   paguemos   paguéis   paguen

3. Verbs in –gu-ar take a diaeresis over the u to show that this u of the stem has always a pronounced value:

Averiguar, *to ascertain*

Pret. Indic., 1st Sing.	averigüé		
Pres. Subj.	averigüe	averigües	averigüe
	averigüemos	averigüéis	averigüen

4. Verbs in –z-ar change z to c, without involving any difference in sound:

Cazar, *to hunt*

Pret. Indic., 1st Sing. } cacé

Pres. Subj.   cace   caces   cace   cacemos   cacéis   cacen

N. B. It is to be noted that only seven forms of the verb inflexion are concerned in the four cases just mentioned.

241. Before flexional **o** or **a** the following changes occur:

1. Verbs in **–c-er** and **–c-ir** preceded by a consonant change **c** to **z**:

Vencer, *to conquer*

Pres. Indic., 1*st Sing.* venzo   *Pres. Subj.* venza, *etc.*

Zurcir, *to darn*

Pres. Indic., 1*st Sing.* zurzo   *Pres. Subj.* zurza, *etc.*

N. B. Most verbs in –cer or –cir preceded by a vowel belong to the class with inceptive endings. See §255.

2. All verbs in **–g-er** or **–g-ir**, regular or not, change **g** to **j**:

Coger, *to catch, gather*

Pres. Indic., 1*st Sing.* cojo   *Pres. Subj.* coja, *etc.*

Elegir, *to choose*

Pres. Indic., 1*st Sing.* elijo   *Pres. Subj.* elija, *etc.*

3. Verbs in **–qu-ir** change **qu** to **c**, as **qu** (denoting the **k** sound) is written in Spanish only before **e** or **i**:

Delinquir, *to be delinquent*

Pres. Indic., 1*st Sing.* delinco   *Pres. Subj.* delinca, *etc.*

4. Verbs in **–gu-ir** omit their unpronounced **u**, which is not needed to indicate a "hard" **g** before **o** or **a**:

Distinguir, *to distinguish*

Pres. Indic., 1*st. Sing.* distingo   *Pres. Subj.* distinga, *etc.*

N. B. It is to be noted that only seven forms of the verb inflexion are concerned in the four cases above.

242. Diphthongal ending **–ió** and **–ie– :**

1. Verbs of the second and third conjugations (regular or not), whose stem ends in a vowel, change the **i** of the

diphthongal endings –ió and –ie– to **y,** as unaccented **i** can-not stand between vowels in Spanish:

Cre-er, to believe; cre-yendo (*for* cre-iendo); cre-yó (*for* cre-ió); cre-yeron (*for* cre-ieron); cre-yese (*for* cre-iese), *etc.;* cre-yera (*for* cre-iera), *etc.;* cre-yere (*for* cre-iere), *etc.*

Conclu-ir, to conclude; conclu-yendo; conclu-yó; conclu-yeron; *etc.*

2. The **i** of the endings –ió and –ie– disappears after all verb stems ending in **ll** or **ñ** and after certain irregular preterite stems ending in **j:**

Bull-ir, to boil; bullendo; bulló; bulleron; bullese; *etc.; etc.*
Gruñ-ir, to grunt; gruñ-endo; gruñ-ó; gruñ-eron; *etc.; etc.*
Tra-er, to bring; traj-o; traj-eron; traj-ese; *etc.; etc.*

243. Verbs in –iar and –uar. A certain number of verbs in –iar and –uar (to be learned by practice) take a written accent on the **i** or **u** of the three persons of the singular and the third person plural of their present tenses (indicative, subjunctive, imperative):

Criar, to bring up: crío, crías, cría, crían
críe, críes, críe, críen
cría

Continuar, to continue: continúo, continúas, continúa, continúan
continúe, continúes, continúe, continúen
continúa

Among the commonest verbs with this peculiarity are **aliar,** *to ally,* **ataviar,** *to adorn,* **confiar,** *to confide,* **contrariar,** *to oppose, vex,* **desafiar,** *to challenge,* **desconfiar,** *to distrust,* **desvariar,** *to rave,* **desviar,** *to divert,* **enviar,** *to send,* **espiar,** *to spy,* **expiar,** *to expiate,* **fiar,** *to trust,* **guiar,** *to guide,* **inventariar,** *to take an inventory of,* **liar,** *to bind,* **porfiar,** *to persist,* **resfriar,** *to chill,* **telegrafiar,** *to telegraph,* **vaciar,** *to empty,* **variar,** *to vary;* **acentuar,** *to accentuate,* **atenuar,** *to attenuate,* **conceptuar,** *to conceive,* **efectuar,** *to effectuate,* **exceptuar,** *to except,* **graduar,** *to graduate,* **habituar,** *to habituate,* **insinuar,** *to insinuate,* **perpetuar,** *to perpetuate,* **puntuar,** *to punctuate,* **situar,** *to situate,* **valuar,** *to appraise.*

a. A considerable number of verbs do not take this accent; cf. **afiliar,** *to affiliate,* **afilio; anunciar,** *to announce,* **anuncio; apremiar,** *to* *press*, **apremio**; **cambiar,** *to change*, **cambio**; **diferenciar,** *to differentiate*, **diferencio**; **encomiar,** *to extol*, **encomio**; **estudiar,** *to study*, **estudio**; **iniciar,** *to initiate*, **inicio**; **lidiar,** *to fight*, **lidio**; **premiar,** *to reward*, **premio**; **presenciar,** *to witness*, **presencio**; **principiar,** *to begin*, **principio**; *etc.*

244. Radical-changing Verbs. — Under certain conditions some verbs change their radical (root) vowels **e** to **ie** or **i** and **o** to **ue** or **u**. The conditions are such as to make three classes thus represented:

I. If accented { the radical vowel **e** becomes **ie** / the radical vowel **o** becomes **ue**

II. If accented { the radical vowel **e** becomes **ie** / the radical vowel **o** becomes **ue**

If unaccented { the radical vowel **e** becomes **i** / the radical vowel **o** becomes **u** } { before a following –a–, –ie–, or –ió of the flexional ending

III. If accented the radical vowel **e** becomes **i**
If unaccented the radical vowel **e** becomes **i** before a following –a–, –ie–, or –ió of the flexional ending

245. Class I. — This comprises only first and second conjugation verbs. The change of accented **e** to **ie** and accented **o** to **ue** can occur in only nine forms, viz., all the singular and the third plural of the present indicative and present subjunctive and the second singular of the imperative; all other forms show the original **e** or **o**. The endings are regular. These verbs illustrate the class:

1. Cerrar, *to close*

Participles	cerrando	cerrado				
Pres. Indic.	cierro	cierras	cierra	cierran	*But*	cerramos cerráis
Pres. Subj.	cierre	cierres	cierre	cierren	*But*	cerremos cerréis
Imperat.		cierra			*But*	cerrad

Impf. Indic.	cerraba, *etc.*	*Fut. Indic.*	cerraré, *etc.*
Pret. Indic.	cerré, *etc.*	*Cond. Indic.*	cerraría, *etc.*
Impf. Subj.	{ cerrase, *etc.* / cerrara, *etc.*	*Fut.* or *Hyp. Subj.*	cerrare, *etc.*

2. Entender, *to understand*

Participles entendiendo entendido
Pres. Indic. entiendo entiendes entiende
                               entienden   *But* entendemos entendéis
Pres. Subj. entienda entiendas entienda
                               entiendan   *But* entendamos entendáis
Imperat.   entiende   *But*   entended

All other forms with the radical vowel **e** are perfectly regular as of the second conjugation.

3. Contar, *to count*

Participles   contando contado
Pres. Indic. cuento   cuentas cuenta cuentan *But* contamos contáis
Pres. Subj. cuente   cuentes cuente cuenten *But* contemos contéis
Imperat.   cuenta   *But*   contad

Impf. Indic. contaba, *etc.*   *Fut. Indic.*   contaré, *etc.*
Pret. Indic. conté, *etc.*   *Cond. Indic.*   contaría, *etc.*
Impf. Subj. $\begin{cases} \text{contase, } etc. \\ \text{contara, } etc. \end{cases}$ *Fut.* or *Hyp. Subj.* contare, *etc.*

4. Volver, *to return*

Participles volviendo vuelto
Pres. Indic. vuelvo   vuelves vuelve vuelven *But* volvemos volvéis
Pres. Subj. vuelva   vuelvas vuelva vuelvan *But* volvamos volváis
Imperat.   vuelve   *But*   volved

All other forms with the radical vowel **o** are perfectly regular as of the second conjugation.

N. B. The past participle of this verb and of other verbs in **–olver** is irregular. So **devolver,** *to give back,* **devuelto; envolver,** *to wrap up,* **envuelto; revolver,** *to stir,* **revuelto; solver,** *to loosen,* **suelto; absolver,** *to absolve,* **absuelto; disolver,** *to dissolve,* **disuelto; resolver,** *to resolve,* **resuelto;** *etc.* Most radical-changing verbs of this class have regular participles; thus **mover,** *to move;* **muevo,** *I move,* etc.; **movido.**

246. The changes in spelling of the end of the stem, already listed for regular verbs, occur here also; cf. §§239–241.

1. Before **e, c** becomes **qu:**

> **Revolcar,** to wallow: *Pret. Indic.*, 1*st Sing.* revolqué
> *Pres. Subj.* revuelque, *etc.*

2. Before **e, g** becomes **gu:**

> **Negar,** to deny: *Pret. Indic.*, 1*st Sing.* negué
> *Pres. Subj.* niegue, *etc.*

3. Before **e, z** becomes **c:**

> **Empezar,** to begin: *Pret. Indic.*, 1*st Sing.* empecé
> *Pres. Subj.* empiece, *etc.*

4. Before **o** or **a, c** becomes **z:**

> **Torcer,** to twist: *Pres. Indic.*, 1*st Sing.* tuerzo
> *Pres. Subj.* tuerza, *etc.*

5. After **g, ue** from **o** takes a diaeresis:

> **Degollar,** to behead: *Pres. Indic.* degüello degüellas, *etc.*
> *Pres. Subj.* degüelle, *etc.*
> *Imperat.* degüella

247. When initial, the stressed **e** and **o** of radical-changing verbs become **ye** and **hue** respectively, as Spanish does not write **ie** and **ue** at the beginning of words:

> 1. **Errar,** to err: *Pres. Indic.*   yerro yerras, *etc.*
> *Pres. Subj.*   yerre, *etc.*
> *Imperat.*   yerra
>
> 2. **Oler,** to smell: *Pres. Indic.*   huelo hueles, *etc.*
> *Pres. Subj.*   huela, *etc.*
> *Imperat.*   huele

a. In derivatives the change of **o** to **hue** occurs also; thus **desosar,** *to remove the bones from,* **deshueso,** *etc.;* **desovar,** *to spawn,* **deshuevan,** *etc.* (cf. **hueso,** *bone,* and **huevo,** *egg*).

248. Being based on second conjugation (–er) verbs, some derivatives of the third (–ir) conjugation have their stem-stressed forms treated as of this first radical-changing class. These are **concernir,** *to concern,*[1] and **discernir,** *to discern*

---

[1] **Concernir** has only third person forms in the finite tenses.

(cf. the simple verb **cerner**, *to sift*, **cierno**, *etc.*), **adquirir**, *to acquire*, and **inquirir**, *to inquire* (cf. the simple verb **querer**, *to wish*, **quiero**, *etc.*). **Adquirir** and **inquirir** have **i** in the unstressed stem everywhere.

1. Discernir, *to discern*

Pres. Indic.	discierno	disciernes	discierne		
			disciernen	*But* discernimos	discernís
Pres. Subj.	discierna	disciernas	discierna		
			disciernan	*But* discernamos	discernáis
Imperat.		discierne		*But*	discernid

2. Adquirir, *to acquire*

Pres. Indic.	adquiero	adquieres	adquiere		
			adquieren	*But* adquirimos	adquirís
Pres. Subj.	adquiera	adquieras	adquiera		
			adquieran	*But* adquiramos	adquiráis
Imperat.		adquiere		*But*	adquirid

249. Jugar, *to play,* had originally an **o** stem (cf. Latin *jocari*). The stem-stressed forms show **ue**, the others have **u**:

Pres. Indic.	juego	juegas	juega	juegan	*But* jugamos	jugáis
Pres. Subj.	juegue	juegues	juegue	jueguen	*But* juguemos	juguéis
Imperat.		juega			*But*	jugad

250. Class II. — This includes only verbs of the third conjugation with the radical vowel **e** or **o**. As in Class I, the **e** becomes **ie** and the **o** becomes **ue** when accented. Unaccented, the **e** becomes **i** and the **o** becomes **u** before an immediately following –a–, –ie–, or –ió of the flexional suffix; otherwise the unaccented **e** and **o** remain.

1. Sentir, *to feel*

Participles	sint-iendo	sentido			
Pres. Indic.	siento	sientes	siente		
			sienten	*But* sentimos	sentís
Pres. Subj.	sienta	sientas	sienta		
	sint-amos	sint-áis	sientan		
Imperat.		siente		*But*	sentid

Impf. Indic.	sentía, *etc. (reg.)*				
Pret. Indic.	sentí	sentiste	sint-ió	sentimos sentisteis	sint-ieron
-se Impf. Subj.	sint-iese	sint-ieses	sint-iese	sint-iésemos	sint-ieseis
	sint-iesen				
-ra Impf. Subj.	sint-iera, *etc.*				
Fut. or *Hyp. Subj.*	sint-iere, *etc.*				

2. Dormir, *to sleep*

Participles	durm-iendo	dormido	
Pres. Indic.	duermo	duermes	duerme
			duermen *But* dormimos dormís
Pres. Subj.	duerma	duermas	duerma
	durm-amos	durm-áis	duerman
Imperat.		duerme	*But* dormid
Impf. Indic.	dormía, *etc. (reg.)*		
Pret. Indic.	dormí	dormiste	durm-ió
	dormimos	dormisteis	durm-ieron
-se Impf. Subj.	durm-iese [1]	durm-ieses	durm-iese durm-iésemos
		durm-ieseis	durm-iesen
-ra Impf. Subj.	durm-iera, *etc.*		
Fut. or *Hyp. Subj.*	durm-iere, *etc.*		

a. The only simple **o** verbs in Class II are **dormir** and **morir,** *to die;* in the past participle **morir** has only the irregular form **muerto.** In perfect tenses this, if intransitive, means *died:* **el hombre ha muerto,** *the man has died;* if transitive with a *personal* object, it means *killed:* **han muerto al hombre,** *they have killed the man.* But in the perfect tenses of the reflexive verb **matado,** past participle of **matar,** *to kill,* must be used: **el hombre se ha matado,** *the man has killed himself.* With the verb *to be,* and equivalent verbs, **muerto** (–a, –os, –as) naturally means *dead:* **la mujer está muerta,** *the woman is dead.*

251. Class III. — As in Class II, so here only third conjugation verbs are concerned, and, furthermore, only those with the radical vowel **e.** This changes in precisely the same cases as in Class II, except that here the **e** becomes **i** both under the accent and when unaccented and followed by

[1] As to the stem of the imperfect and future forms of the subjunctive of radical-changing verbs, see §236, 2.

330 FIRST SPANISH COURSE

–a–, –ie–, or –ió. The original **e** maintains itself here in the cases in which it persists in Class II.

Pedir, *to ask*

Participles	pid-iendo		pedido

Pres. Indic. pido   pides   pide

                               piden   *But* pedimos pedís

Pres. Subj. pida   pidas   pida

             pidamos pidáis pidan

Imperat.   pide   *But*   pedid

Impf. Indic. pedía, *etc.* (*reg.*)

Pret. Indic. pedí   pediste   pid-ió   pedimos   pedisteis

                    pid-ieron

–se Impf. Subj. pid-iese   pid-ieses   pid-iese   pid-iésemos   pid-ieseis

                        pid-iesen

–ra Impf. Subj.   pid-iera, *etc.*

Fut. or

Hyp. Subj. } pid-iere, *etc.*

252. Changes in spelling of the end of the stem occur here in accordance with the rules previously stated (§241):

1. **g** (**i**, **e**) becomes **j** before **o** or **a**:

    Corregir, to correct: *Pres. Indic.*, 1*st Sing.* corrijo

                                   Pres. Subj. corrija, *etc.*

2. **gu** (**i**, **e**) drops the **u** before **o** or **a**:

    Seguir, to follow: *Pres. Indic.*, 1*st Sing.* sigo

                          Pres. Subj. siga, *etc.*

3. After **ñ**, –ie– and –ió lose their **i**:

    Ceñir, to gird: *Pres. Part.* ciñ-endo

                        Pret. Indic., 3*rd Sing.* ciñ-ó, 3*rd Pl.* ciñ-eron

                        –se Impf. Subj. ciñ-ese, *etc.*

                        –ra Impf. Subj. ciñ-era, *etc.*

                            Fut. or *Hyp. Subj.* ciñ-ere, *etc.*

253. Verbs in –eír are of Class III. In them the **i** of the stem ending and that of the –ie– and –ió in the flexional endings following coalesce:

Reír, to laugh: riendo (*for* ri-iendo); rió (*for* ri-ió); rieron (*for* ri-ieron); riese (*for* ri-iese), *etc.;* riera (*for* ri-iera), *etc.;* riere (*for* ri-iere), *etc.*

254. The verb **erguir,** *to erect,* may be conjugated as of either Class II or Class III with due attention to changes in spelling of the stem ending; thus **yergo** (cf. §247, 1) or **irgo, yergues** or **irgues,** *etc.*

N. B. Class I contains many verbs of the –ar and –er conjugations. Class II contains all verbs in –entir, –erir, and –ertir, as well as **hervir,** *to boil,* and its derivative **rehervir.** Class III contains all verbs in –ebir, –edir, –egir, –eguir, –eír, –emir, –enchir, –endir, –eñir, –estir, and –etir, as well as **servir,** *to serve,* and its derivative **deservir,** *to do a disservice.*

255. Verbs with Inceptive Endings. — Verbs in –cer and –cir, having a vowel before these infinitive endings, insert a **z** before the **c** in their present indicative and present subjunctive, wherever the verb ending begins with **o** or **a.** All the other forms are perfectly regular, and the –zc– or inceptive forms are only seven in number, viz., the first person singular of the present indicative and all six forms of the present subjunctive. There is no obvious inceptive meaning in the verbs of this class. While certain of them have relations to Latin inceptive verbs (cf. Spanish **conocer** and Latin *cognoscere*), others have no such connections.

1. Conocer, *to know*

Participles   conociendo   conocido

Pres. Indic., 1st Sing. } conozco (All other forms reg.)

Pres. Subj. conozca conozcas conozca conozcamos conozcáis conozcan

The rest of the verb regular as of the second conjugation

2. Lucir, *to shine*

Participles   luciendo   lucido

Pres. Indic., 1st Sing. } luzco (All other forms reg.)

Pres. Subj.   luzca   luzcas   luzca   luzcamos   luzcáis   luzcan

The rest of the verb regular as of the third conjugation

a. The **c** is simply changed to **z** in **mecer**, *to rock,* and its derivative **remecer,** which are regular verbs, and in **cocer,** *to boil,* and its derivatives **recocer,** *to boil again,* and **escocer,** *to smart,* which are radical-changing verbs of the first class. Hence the forms **mezo; meza,** *etc.;* **cuezo; cueza,** *etc.* The irregular verbs **hacer,** *to do, make,* and **decir,** *to say,* with their derivatives, have no inceptive endings, but irregular verbs in –**ucir** (**conducir,** *etc.*) have them (**conduzco,** *etc.*).

256. The –uir Verb. — This class comprises only verbs with a pronounced **u** (**huir, argüir,** *etc.,* but not **seguir** and the like). In their present forms (indicative, subjunctive, and imperative) they add **y** to the **u** of the stem (**hu-yo,** *etc.*), except where the flexional ending begins with **i.** All the other forms are regular. In accordance with the rule stated previously (cf. §242) an unaccented **i** between vowels will be written **y** in the third person of the preterite indicative, in all the forms of the two imperfects and the future of the subjunctive, and in the present participle (gerund):

Huir, *to flee*

Participles	hu-yendo	huído				
Pres. Indic.	huy-o	huy-es	huy-e	*But*	huimos	huis
			huy-en			
Pres. Subj.	huy-a	huy-as	huy-a			
	hu-yamos	huy-áis	huy-an			
Imperat.		huy-e		*But*		huid

Fut. Indic. huiré, *etc.* (*reg.*)
Cond. Indic. huiría, *etc.* (*reg.*)
Impf. Indic. huía, *etc.* (*reg.*)
Pret. Indic. huí huiste hu-yó huimos huisteis hu-yeron
–*se Impf. Subj.* hu-yese   hu-yeses, *etc.*
–*ra Impf. Subj.* hu-yera, *etc.*
Fut. or
Hyp. Subj. } hu-yere, *etc.*

N. B. Verbs in –**güir** retain the diaeresis only before a written **i: argüir,** *to argue,* **argüido, argüimos, argüía, argüí,** *etc.;* but **arguyendo, arguyo, arguyes, arguya,** *etc.*

IRREGULAR VERBS

257   Haber, *to have*

Participles
    hab-iendo hab-ido
Pres. Indic.

he	has	ha	hemos	hab-éis	han

Pres. Subj.

hay-a	hay-as	hay-a	hay-amos	hay-áis	hay-an

Imperat.   (he)   hab-ed

Fut. Indic.

habr-é	habr-ás	habr-á	habr-emos	habr-éis	habr-án

Cond. Indic.

habr-ía	habr-ías	habr-ía	habr-íamos	habr-íais	habr-ían

Impf. Indic.

hab-ía	hab-ías	hab-ía	hab-íamos, *etc.* (*reg.*)

Pret. Indic.

hub-e	hub-iste	hub-o	hub-imos	hub-isteis	hub-ieron

-se Impf. Subj.
    hub-iese hub-ieses hub-iese hub-iésemos, *etc.*

-ra Impf. Subj.
    hub-iera hub-ieras, *etc.*

Fut. or Hyp. Subj.
    hub-iere hub-ieres, *etc.*

a. The indicative future and conditional have a contract infinitive basis. It is not absolutely certain that **he** is a part of **haber;** it occurs most often with the adverb **aquí,** *here;* **he aquí,** *behold.* **Haber** is also the impersonal verb (*there*) *to be,* and as such it employs only the third singular of its finite forms. In the impersonal use the third singular present indicative (and only this one form) appends the otherwise obsolete adverb **y,** *here, there:* **hay,** *there is* (*are*).

Note that **haber** has in the first and third singular of the preterite indicative so-called "strong" forms, i.e., forms stressing the stem and not the flexional ending. This is a marked characteristic also of the irregular verbs **tener, estar, andar, querer, poder, caber, saber, hacer, venir, poner, traer, decir,** and the derivatives in **–ducir (aducir, conducir, deducir,** *etc.*).

258. Tener, *to have, hold*

Participles
 ten-iendo ten-ido

Pres. Indic.
 teng-o tien-es tien-e ten-emos ten-éis tien-en

Pres. Subj.
 teng-a teng-as teng-a teng-amos teng-áis teng-an

Imperat.
 ten   ten-ed

Fut. Indic.
 tendr-é tendr-ás tendr-á tendr-emos tendr-éis tendr-án

Cond. Indic.
 tendr-ía tendr-ías tendr-ía tendr-íamos tendr-íais tendr-ían

Impf. Indic.
 ten-ía ten-ías (*reg.*)

Pret. Indic.
 tuv-e tuv-iste tuv-o tuv-imos tuv-isteis tuv-ieron

–se Impf. Subj.
 tuv-iese tuv-ieses tuv-iese tuv-iésemos, *etc.*

–ra Impf. Subj.
 tuv-iera   tuv-ieras, *etc.*

Fut. or Hyp. Subj.
 tuv-iere tuv-ieres, *etc.*

a. The indicative future and conditional have a contract infinitive basis with a phonetically developed **d: tendr–**; for the same phenomenon, cf. also **venir, poner, salir,** and **valer.** Certain present forms show radical-changing peculiarities. Like **venir, poner, valer, salir, hacer,** and **decir, tener** has no flexional ending in the imperative singular.

259. Ser, *to be*

Participles	s-iendo	s-ido				
Pres. Indic.	soy	eres	es	somos	sois	son
Pres. Subj.	se-a	se-as	se-a	se-amos	se-áis	se-an
Imperat.		sé			sed	
Fut. Indic.	ser-é	ser-ás	ser-á	ser-emos	ser-éis	ser-án
Cond. Indic.	ser-ía	ser-ías	ser-ía	ser-íamos	ser-íais	ser-ían
Impf. Indic.	era	eras	era	éramos	erais	eran
Pret. Indic.	fu-í	fu-iste	fu-é	fu-imos	fu-isteis	fu-eron
–se Impf. Subj.	fu-ese	fu-eses	fu-ese	fu-ésemos, *etc.*		
–ra Impf. Subj.	fu-era	fu-eras, *etc.*				
Fut. or Hyp. Subj.	fu-ere	fu-eres, *etc.*				

260. Estar, *to be*

Participles	est-ando	est-ado				
Pres. Indic.	est-oy	est-ás	est-á	est-amos	est-áis	est-án
Pres. Subj.	est-é	est-és	est-é	est-emos	est-éis	est-én
Imperat.		est-á			est-ad	
Fut. Indic.	estar-é	estar-ás	estar-á	estar-emos, etc. (reg.)		
Cond. Indic.	estar-ía	estar-ías, etc. (reg.)				
Impf. Indic.	est-aba	est-abas	est-aba	est-ábamos, etc. (reg.)		
Pret. Indic.	estuv-e	estuv-iste	estuv-o	estuv-imos	estuv-isteis	
						estuv-ieron

−se Impf. Subj. estuv-iese estuv-ieses estuv-iese estuv-iésemos, *etc.*
−ra Impf. Subj. estuv-iera estuv-ieras, *etc.*

Fut. or
Hyp. Subj. } estuv-iere estuv-ieres, *etc.*

a. This is the Latin *stare*, whose sense has weakened from *stand* to *be.* It is regular, as of the first conjugation, in its present tenses and in the future, conditional, and imperfect of the indicative except for the **y** added in **estoy.** This **y** is found also in **soy** from **ser, voy** from **ir,** and **doy** from **dar.** Note the frequency of the written accent in the present tenses.

261. Ir, *to go*

Participles	yendo	ido				
Pres. Indic.	voy	vas	va	vamos	vais	van
Pres. Subj.	vay-a	vay-as	vay-a	vay-amos	vay-áis	vay-an
Imperat.		ve		(vamos)	id	
Fut. Indic.	ir-é	ir-ás, etc. (reg.)				
Cond. Indic.	ir-ía	ir-ías, etc. (reg.)				
Impf. Indic.	iba	ibas	iba	íbamos	ibais	iban
Pret. Indic.	fu-í	fu-iste, etc. (as for **ser**)				
−se Impf. Subj.	fu-ese	fu-eses, etc. (as for **ser**)				
−ra Impf. Subj.	fu-era	fu-eras, etc. (as for **ser**)				

Fut. or
Hyp. Subj. } fu-ere fu-eres, *etc.* (as for **ser**)

a. This verb is very irregular; its forms are related to those of three different Latin verbs, *ire, vadere,* and *esse.* It is obvious that it borrows from **ser** the forms of its preterite indicative and its two imperfects and future of the subjunctive. The grammars usually register for it a first plural of the imperative, **vamos**, *let us go* (also used as an interjection, *come now*, etc.), which is strictly speaking an older form of the first plural of the present subjunctive. **Vayamos** is restricted to the purely subjunctive use in clauses that are clearly subordinate; **vamos** occurs only in clauses that are independent or apparently so.

262. Andar, *to go, walk*

Participles	and-ando	and-ado			
Pres. Indic.	and-o	and-as, *etc.* (*reg.*)			
Pres. Subj.	and-e	and-es, *etc.* (*reg.*)			
Imperat.		anda, *etc.* (*reg.*)			
Fut. Indic.	andar-é	andar-ás, *etc.* (*reg.*)			
Cond. Indic.	andar-ía, *etc.* (*reg.*)				
Impf. Indic.	and-aba, *etc.* (*reg.*)				
Pret. Indic.	anduv-e	anduv-iste	anduv-o	anduv-imos	anduv-isteis
					anduv-ieron

–se Impf. Subj.	anduv-iese	anduv-ieses, *etc.*	
–ra Impf. Subj.	anduv-iera	anduv-ieras, *etc.*	
Fut. or *Hyp. Subj.*	anduv-iere	anduv-ieres, *etc.*	

a. This verb is perfectly regular as of the first conjugation in its infinitive, participles, present tenses, and future, conditional, and imperfect of the indicative. With the stem **anduv–** it is of the second or third regular conjugation in the preterite indicative and the three subjunctive tenses that follow it.

263. Dar, *to give, strike*

Participles	d-ando	d-ado				
Pres. Indic	d-oy	d-as	d-a	d-amos, *etc.*		
Pres. Subj.	d-é	d-es	d-é	d-emos, *etc.*		
Imperat.		d-a			d-ad (*reg.*)	
Fut. Indic.	dar-é	dar-ás, *etc.* (*reg.*)				
Cond. Indic.	dar-ía	dar-ías, *etc.* (*reg.*)				
Impf. Indic.	d-aba	d-abas, *etc.* (*reg*).				
Pret. Indic.	d-i	d-iste	d-ió	d-imos	d-isteis	d-ieron
–se Impf. Subj.	d-iese	d-ieses	d-iese	d-iésemos, *etc.*		
–ra Impf. Subj	d-iera	d-ieras, *etc.*				
Fut. or *Hyp. Subj.*	d-iere	d-ieres, *etc.*				

a. With the stem **d–**, this verb is regular as of the first conjugation (save for the **y** of **doy**) in its infinitive, participles, present tenses, and future, conditional, and imperfect of the indicative; and it is regular as of the second or third conjugation in the preterite indicative and the three subjunctive tenses that follow it.

264.   **Venir,** *to come*

Participles
    vin-iendo ven-ido
Pres. Indic.
    veng-o   vien-es   vien-e   ven-imos   ven-ís   vien-en
Pres. Subj.
    veng-a   veng-as   veng-a   veng-amos   veng-áis   veng-an
Imperat.   ven   ven-id
Fut. Indic.
    vendr-é   vendr-ás vendr-á vendr-emos vendr-éis vendr-án
Cond. Indic.
    vendr-ía   vendr-ías vendr-ía, *etc.*
Impf. Indic.
    ven-ía   ven-ías, *etc.* (*reg.*)
Pret. Indic.
    vin-e   vin-iste vin-o   vin-imos   vin-isteis vin-ieron
–se Impf. Subj.
    vin-iese   vin-ieses, *etc.*
–ra Impf. Subj.
    vin-iera   vin-ieras, *etc.*
Fut. or Hyp. Subj.
    vin-iere   vin-ieres, *etc.*

a. This is one of several irregular verbs which add **g** or **ig** to the verb stem in the first singular of the present indicative and in all six forms of the present subjunctive; the others are **tener, poner, asir, salir,** and **valer,** which add g, and **caer, oír,** and **traer,** which add –ig. In part **venir** is, like **tener,** of the radical-changing class.

265.   **Poner,** *to put*

Participles
    pon-iendo   puesto
Pres. Indic.
    pong-o   pon-es   pon-e   pon-emos   pon-éis   pon-en
Pres. Subj.
    pong-a   pong-as pong-a   pong-amos pong-áis pong-an

Imperat.   pon   pon-ed
   Fut. Indic.

| pondr-é | pondr-ás | pondr-á | pondr-emos | pondr-éis | pondr-án |

Cond. Indic.

pondr-ía pondr-ías, *etc.*

Impf. Indic.

pon-ía pon-ías, *etc.* (*reg.*)

Pret. Indic.

| pus-e | pus-iste | pus-o | pus-imos | pus-isteis | pus-ieron |

-se Impf. Subj.

pus-iese pus-ieses, *etc.*

-ra Impf. Subj.

pus-iera pus-ieras, *etc.*

Fut. or *Hyp. Subj.*

pus-iere pus-ieres, *etc.*

a. The past participle, the preterite indicative, and the imperfects and future of the subjunctive have irregular formations.

266.   Hacer, *to do, make*

Participles

hac-iendo   hecho

Pres. Indic.

| hag-o | hac-es | hac-e | hac-emos | hac-éis | hac-en |

Pres. Subj.

| hag-a | hag-as | hag-a | hag-amos | hag-áis | hag-an |

Imperat.   haz   hac-ed

Fut. Indic.

| har-é | har-ás | har-á | har-emos | har-éis | har-án |

Cond. Indic.

har-ía har-ías, *etc.*

Impf. Indic.

hac-ía hac-ías, *etc.* (*reg.*)

Pret. Indic.

| hic-e | hic-iste | hiz-o | hic-imos | hic-isteis | hic-ieron |

-se Impf. Subj.

hic-iese hic-ieses, *etc.*

-ra Impf. Subj.

hic-iera hic-ieras, *etc.*

Fut. or *Hyp. Subj.*

hic-iere hic-ieres, *etc.*

a. This verb, like **decir,** has many irregularities; notable are the formation of the past participle, the –g– in certain of the present forms, the contract infinitive basis, **har–,** of the future and conditional of the indicative, and the preterite stem **hic–, hiz–.**

267.   Decir, *to say*

Participles	dic-iendo	dicho
Pres. Indic.	dig-o	dic-es	dic-e	dec-imos	dec-ís	dic-en
Pres. Subj.	dig-a	dig-as	dig-a	dig-amos	dig-áis	dig-an
Imperat.	•	di			dec-id	
Fut. Indic.	dir-é	dir-ás	dir-á	dir-emos	dir-éis	dir-án
Cond. Indic.	dir-ía	dir-ías, *etc.*				
Impf. Indic.	dec-ía	dec-ías, *etc.* (*reg.*)				
Pret. Indic.	dij-e	dij-iste	dij-o	dij-imos	dij-isteis	dij-eron
–se Impf. Subj.	dij-ese	dij-eses, *etc.*				
–ra Impf. Subj.	dij-era	dij-eras, *etc.*				
Fut. or *Hyp. Subj.*	dij-ere	dij-eres, *etc.*				

a. Leading peculiarities are the irregular past participle, a –g– stem and radical-changing forms in the present tenses, the contract infinitive basis of the indicative future and conditional, and the preterite stem **dij–** with the loss of **i** in the diphthongal endings after it (**dijeron, dijese,** *etc.*).

268.   Saber, *to know*

Participles	sab-iendo	sab-ido
Pres. Indic.	sé	sab-es	sab-e	sab-emos	sab-éis	sab-en
Pres. Subj.	sep-a	sep-as	sep-a	sep-amos	sep-áis	sep-an
Imperat.		sab-e			sab-ed	
Fut. Indic.	sabr-é	sabr-ás	sabr-á	sabr-emos	sabr-éis	sabr-án
Cond. Indic.	sabr-ía	sabr-ías, *etc.*				
Impf. Indic.	sab-ía	sab-ías, *etc.* (*reg.*)				
Pret. Indic.	sup-e	sup-iste	sup-o	sup-imos	sup-isteis	sup-ieron
–se Impf. Subj.	sup-iese	sup-ieses, *etc.*				
–ra Impf. Subj.	sup-iera	sup-ieras, *etc.*				
Fut. or *Hyp. Subj.*	sup-iere	sup-ieres, *etc.*				

269. Caber, *to be contained, fit*

Participles

cab-iendo   cab-ido

Pres. Indic.

quep-o   cab-es   cab-e   cab-emos   cab-éis   cab-en

Pres. Subj.

quep-a   quep-as   quep-a   quep-amos   quep-áis   quep-an

Imperat   cab-e   cab-ed

Fut. Indic.

cabr-é   cabr-ás   cabr-á   cabr-emos   càbr-éis   cabr-án

Cond. Indic.

cabr-ía   cabr-ías, *etc.*

Impf. Indic.

cab-ía   cab-ías, *etc.* (*reg.*)

Pret. Indic.

cup-e   cup-iste cup-o   cup-imos   cup-isteis   cup-ieron

–se *Impf. Subj.*

cup-iese   cup-ieses, *etc.*

–ra *Impf. Subj.*

cup-iera   cup-ieras, *etc.*

Fut. or Hyp. Subj.

cup-iere   cup-ieres, *etc.*

a. **Saber** and **caber** are exactly alike in their peculiarities, except that **saber** has a reduced form **sé** (instead of **sepo**) in the present indicative, first singular, where **caber** has **quepo**. The interchange of –p– and –b– in the present stem, the contract infinitive basis for the indicative future and conditional, and the irregular preterite stem, **sup–**, **cup–**, are to be noted.

270. Poder, *to be able*

Participles

pud-iendo   pod-ido

Pres. Indic.

pued-o   pued-es   pued-e   pod-emos   pod-éis   pued-en

Pres. Subj.

pued-a   pued-as   pued-a   pod-amos   pod-áis   pued-an

Imperat. (*None*)

Fut. Indic.

podr-é   podr-ás   podr-á   podr-emos   podr-éis   podr-án

Cond. Indic.

    podr-ía   podr-ías, *etc.*

Impf. Indic.

    pod-ía   pod-ías, *etc. (reg.)*

Pret. Indic.

    pud-e   pud-iste   pud-o   pud-imos   pud-isteis   pud-ieron

–se Impf. Subj.

    pud-iese   pud-ieses, *etc.*

–ra Impf. Subj.

    pud-iera   pud-ieras, *etc.*

Fut. or Hyp. Subj.

    pud-iere   pud-ieres, *etc.*

a. **Poder** has certain features of the radical-changing verb and a contract stem in the future and conditional of the indicative. Its preterite stem is **pud–**. Its sense precludes its having a real imperative.

271.   **Querer,** *to wish, be fond of*

Participles

    quer-iendo   quer-ido

Pres. Indic.

    quier-o   quier-es   quier-e   quer-emos   quer-éis   quier-en

Pres. Subj.

    quier-a   quier-as   quier-a   quer-amos   quer-áis   quier-an

Imperat.   quier-e   quer-ed

Fut. Indic.

    querr-é   querr-ás   querr-á   querr-emos   querr-éis   querr-án

Cond. Indic.

    querr-ía   querr-ías, *etc.*

Impf. Indic.

    quer-ía   quer-ías, *etc. (reg.)*

Pret. Indic.

    quis-e   quis-iste   quis-o   quis-imos   quis-isteis   quis-ieron

–se Impf. Subj.

    quis-iese   quis-ieses, *etc.*

–ra Impf. Subj.

    quis-iera   quis-ieras, *etc.*

Fut. or Hyp. Subj.

    quis-iere   quis-ieres, *etc.*

a. **Querer** has features of the radical-changing verb, a contract infinitive in the future and conditional of the indicative, and a preterite stem **quis–**.

272. Asir, *to grasp*

Participles	as-iendo	as-ido				
Pres. Indic.	asg-o	as-es	as-e	as-imos	as-ís	as-en
Pres. Subj.	asg-a	asg-as	asg-a	asg-amos	asg-áis	asg-an

All the other forms are perfectly regular as of the third conjugation.

273. Valer, *to be worth*

Participles	val-iendo	val-ido				
Pres. Indic	valg-o	val-es	val-e	val-emos	val-éis	val-en
Pres. Subj.	valg-a	valg-as	valg-a	valg-amos	valg-áis	valg-an
Imperat.		val *or* vale			val-ed	
Fut. Indic.	valdr-é	valdr-ás	valdr-á	valdr-emos	valdr-éis	valdr-án
Cond. Indic.	valdr-ía	valdr-ías, *etc.*				
Impf. Indic.	val-ía	val-ías, *etc.* (*reg.*)				
Pret. Indic.	(*reg.*)					
–se Impf. Subj.	(*reg.*)					
–ra Impf. Subj.	(*reg.*)					
Fut. or *Hyp. Subj.*	(*reg.*)					

274. Salir, *to go out, come out*

Participles	sal-iendo	sal-ido				
Pres. Indic.	salg-o	sal-es	sal-e	sal-imos	sal-ís	sal-en
Pres. Subj.	salg-a	salg-as	salg-a	salg-amos	salg-áis	salg-an
Imperat.		sal			sal-id	

The other forms follow the model of **valer.**

275. Caer, *to fall*

Participles	ca-yendo	ca-ído				
Pres. Indic.	caig-o	ca-es	ca-e	ca-emos	ca-éis	ca-en
Pres. Subj.	caig-a	caig-as	caig-a	caig-amos	caig-áis	caig-an
Imperat.		ca-e			ca-ed	

The other forms are regular; they show the change of unaccented **i** between vowels to **y,** as in **cayó, cayeron, cayese,** *etc.*

a. The noticeable peculiarity here, as in the case of the two verbs following, is the addition of –**ig**– to the present stem for the 1st singular of the present indicative and for all of the present subjunctive.

276. Oír, *to hear*

Participles	o-yendo	o-ído				
Pres. Indic.	oig-o	oy-es	oy-e	o-ímos	o-ís	oy-en
Pres. Subj.	oig-a	oig-as	oig-a	oig-amos	oig-áis	oig-an
Imperat.		oy-e			o-íd	

The other forms are regular; they show the change of unaccented **i** between vowels to **y**, as in **oyó, oyeron, oyese,** *etc.*

a. Note the three present stems: **oig–** before **–o** and **–a**; **oy–** before **–e**; and **o–** before **–i**.

277. Traer, *to bring*

Participles

tra-yendo tra-ído

Pres. Indic.

traig-o	tra-es	tra-e	tra-emos	tra-éis	tra-en

Pres. Subj.

traig-a	traig-as	traig-a	traig-amos	traig-áis	traig-an

Imperat.	tra-e			tra-ed	
Fut. Indic.	(reg.)				
Cond. Indic.	(reg.)				
Impf. Indic.	(reg.)				

Pret. Indic.

traj-e	traj-iste	traj-o	traj-imos	traj-isteis	traj-eron

–se Impf. Subj.

traj-ese	traj-eses	traj-ese	traj-ésemos	traj-eseis	traj-esen

–ra Impf. Subj.

traj-era	traj-eras	traj-era	traj-éramos	traj-erais	traj-eran

Fut. or Hyp. Subj.

traj-ere	traj-eres	traj-ere	traj-éremos	traj-ereis	traj-eren

a. **Traer** and verbs in **–ducir** have a preterite stem in **–j–** after which the **–i–** of a diphthongal ending is lost.

278. Conducir, *to conduct*

Participles	conduc-iendo	conduc-ido	
Pres. Indic.	conduzc-o	conduc-es	conduc-e
	conduc-imos	conduc-ís	conduc-en
Pres. Subj.	conduzc-a	conduzc-as	conduzc-a
	conduzc-amos	conduzc-áis	conduzc-an

Imperat. conduc-e
         conduc-id

Fut. Indic. (reg.)			
Cond. Indic. (reg.)			
Impf. Indic. (reg.)			
Pret. Indic. conduj-e	conduj-iste	conduj-o	
conduj-imos	conduj-isteis	conduj-eron	
-se Impf. Subj. conduj-ese	conduj-eses	conduj-ese	
conduj-ésemos	conduj-eseis	conduj-esen	
-ra Impf. Subj. conduj-era	conduj-eras	conduj-era	
conduj-éramos	conduj-erais	conduj-eran	
Fut. or conduj-ere	conduj-eres	conduj-ere	
Hyp. Subj. conduj-éremos	conduj-ereis	conduj-eren	

a. Like **conducir** are conjugated the other derivatives in **–ducir**: **aducir, deducir, inducir, producir, reducir, seducir**; in the present tenses they show inceptive endings.

279. Ver, *to see*

Participles v-iendo	visto				
Pres. Indic. ve-o	v-es	v-e	v-emos	v-eis	v-en
Pres. Subj. ve-a	ve-as	ve-a	ve-amos	ve-áis	ve-an
Imperat.	v-e			v-ed	
Fut. Indic. ver-é	ver-ás, *etc.*				
Cond. Indic. ver-ía	ver-ías, *etc.*				
Pret. Indic. v-i	v-iste	v-ió	v-imos	v-isteis	v-ieron
-se Impf. Subj. v-iese	v-ieses, *etc.*				
-ra Impf. Subj. v-iera	v-ieras, *etc.*				
Fut. or v-iere	v-ieres, *etc.*				
Hyp. Subj.					

a. The full stem **ve–** of the present is reduced to **v–** before **–e,** as in **v-er, v-es,** etc.; the preterite stem is **v–**.

The derivatives in **–ver**, e.g., **antever, prever,** are conjugated as above.

Proveer, *to provide,* has the full stem **prove–** throughout and is regular in its conjugation. It has, however, both **proveído** and **provisto** as the past participle.

280. Irregular Past Participles. — Four verbs of the third conjugation, — **abrir,** *to open,* **cubrir,** *to cover,* **escribir,** *to write,* and **imprimir,** *to print, impress,* — have only irregular past participles; these are **abierto, cubierto, escrito,** and **impreso.** Otherwise these verbs are entirely regular. Two second conjugation verbs, **prender,** *to catch, arrest,* and **romper,** *to break, tear,* are perfectly regular throughout, but they have irregular past participles beside the regular ones; the irregular forms, **preso** and **roto,** are preferred for the perfect tenses and in the literal sense.

281. Defective Verbs. — The verbs **placer,** *to please,* and **yacer,** *to lie,* are now used chiefly in the third person forms, **place, yace,** etc. Perhaps the commonest form of **placer** is the imperfect subjunctive **pluguiera,** employed especially in **¡pluguiera a Dios!** *would to God;* **yacer** figures in tombstone inscriptions, **aquí yace** (**yacen**), *here lies* (*lie*), and occasionally in other uses in higher style. The radical-changing verb **concernir,** *to concern,* occurs only in the forms of the third singular and plural of the various tenses. The radical-changing verb **soler,** *to be accustomed,* is used frequently only in the forms of the indicative present and imperfect, as follows:

suelo	sueles	suele	solemos	soléis	suelen
solía	solías	solía	solíamos	solíais	solían

The following list embraces radical-changing, –**uir,** and **irregular** verbs. The verbs with inceptive endings (–**cer** or –**cir** preceded by a vowel) are not included: they simply follow the models given in §255. In the case of derivatives, reference is made to the conjugation of the simple verbs, which they follow. Radical-changing verbs are indicated by (**ie**), (**ue**), or (**i**) placed after the verb. The numbers refer to paragraphs.

abnegar (**ie**), to renounce: 240, 2; 246, 2

abrir, to open: *p.p. irr.,* 280

absolver (**ue**), to absolve: *p.p. irr.,* 245, 4

abstenerse, to abstain: *irr.,* 258

abstraer, to abstract: *irr.,* 277

abuñolar (**ue**), to make fritter-shaped: *cf.* **abuñuelar,** *reg.*

acertar (**ie**), to hit the mark

aclocarse (**ue**), to stretch out, brood: 240, 1; 246, 1

acordar (**ue**), to resolve, remind, tune; —**se** (**ue**), to remember

acostar (**ue**), to lay down; —**se** (**ue**), to lie down

acrecentar (**ie**), to increase

adestrar (**ie**), to guide: *also* **adiestrar,** *reg.*

adherir (**ie**), to adhere

adormir (**ue**), to make drowsy

adquirir (**ie**), to acquire: 248, 2

aducir, to adduce: *irr.,* 278; 255, *a;* 242, 2

advertir (**ie**), to observe, advise

afollar (**ue**), to blow with bellows

aforar (**ue**), to give a charter: **aforar,** to gauge, *reg.*

agorar (**ue**), to divine, prognosticate: 246, 5

alebrarse (**ie**), to squat, cower

alentar (**ie**), to breathe, encourage

aliquebrar (**ie**), to break the wings

almorzar (**ue**), to breakfast: 240, 4; 246, 3

alongar (**ue**), to lengthen: 240, 2; 246, 2

amoblar (**ue**), to furnish: *also* **amueblar,** *reg.*

amolar (**ue**), to whet

amover (**ue**), to remove, dismiss

andar, to go, walk: *irr.,* 262

antedecir, to foretell: *irr.,* 267

anteponer, to put before, prefer: *irr.,* 265

antever, to foresee: *irr.,* 279

apacentar (**ie**), to graze

apercollar (**ue**), to collar, snatch

apernar (**ie**), to seize by the legs

aplacer, to please: *irr.,* 281

apostar (ue), to bet, post: apostar, to post troops, *reg.*

apretar (ie), to squeeze, press

aprobar (ue), to approve

argüir, to argue: 256

arrendar (ie), to rent, hire

arrepentirse (ie), to repent

ascender (ie), to ascend

asentar (ie), to seat, set down

asentir (ie), to assent, acquiesce

aserrar (ie), to saw

asir, to seize, grasp: *irr.*, 272

asolar (ue), to level to ground, raze

asoldar (ue), to hire

asonar (ue), to assonate, be in assonance

asosegar: *see* sosegar

atender (ie), to attend, mind

atenerse, to abide, hold: *irr*, 258

atentar (ie), to try: atentar, to attempt a crime, *reg.*

aterrar (ie), to fell: aterrar, to terrify, *reg.*

atestar (ie), to cram, stuff: atestar, to attest, *reg.*

atraer, to attract: *irr.*, 277; 242, 2

atravesar (ie), to cross

atribuir, to attribute: 256

atronar (ue), to make a thundering din, stun

avenir, to reconcile: *irr.*, 264

aventar (ie), to fan, winnow

avergonzar (ue), to shame: 240, 4; 246, 3; 246, 5

azolar (ue), to shape with the adze

bendecir, to bless: *irr.*, 267; 242, 2

bruñir, to burnish: 242, 2

bullir, to boil: 242, 2

caber, to be contained, find room: *irr.*, 269

caer, to fall: *irr.*, 275

calentar (ie), to warm

cegar (ie), to blind: 240, 2; 246, 2

ceñir (i), to gird: 242, 2; 252, 3

cerner (ie), to sift; bud

cerrar (ie), to close

cimentar (ie), to found, establish

circuir, to encircle: 256

clocar (ue), to cluck: 240, 1; 246, 1

cocer (ue), to boil, bake: 255, *a.*

coextenderse (ie), to be coextensive

colar (ue), to strain, filter

colegir (i), to collect: 241, 2; 252, 1

colgar (ue), to hang up: 240, 2; 246, 2

comedirse (i), to behave

comenzar (ie), to commence: 240, 4; 246, 3

competir (i), to compete

complacer, to please, content: *irr.*, 281

componer, to compose: *irr.*, 265

comprobar (ue), to verify, confirm

concebir (i), to conceive

concernir (ie), to concern: 248, 1, footnote 1; 281

concertar (ie), to concert, regulate

concluir, to conclude: 256; 242, 1

concordar (ue), to accord, agree

condescender (ie), to condescend

condolerse (ue), to condole

conducir, to conduct: *irr.*, 278; 255, *a*; 242, 2

conferir (ie), to confer

confesar (ie), to confess

confluir, to join: 256

conmover (ue), to move, affect

conseguir (i), to obtain, attain: 241, 4; 252, 2

consentir (ie), to consent

consolar (ue), to console

consonar (ue), to be in consonance, rhyme

constituir, to constitute: 256

constreñir (i), to compel, constrain: 242, 2; 252, 3

construir, to construct: 256

contar (ue), to count, tell

contender (ie), to contend

contener, to contain: irr., 258

contorcerse (ue), to be distorted, writhe: 241, 1

contradecir, to contradict: irr., 267; 242, 2; 255, a.

contraer, to contract: irr., 277; 242, 2

contrahacer, to counterfeit: irr., 266; 255, a.

contraponer, to oppose, compare: irr., 265

contravenir, to contravene: irr., 264

contribuir, to contribute: 256

controvertir (ie), to controvert

convenir, to agree, fit: irr., 264

convertir (ie), to convert

corregir (i), to correct: 241, 2; 252, 1

costar (ue), to cost

creer, to believe: 242, 1

cubrir, to cover: p.p. irr., 280

dar, to give: irr., 263

decaer, to decay: irr., 275

decentar (ie), to begin to use

decir, to say: irr., 267; 255, a; 242, 2

deducir, to deduce: irr., 278; 255, a; 242, 2

defender (ie), to defend

deferir (ie), to defer

degollar (ue), to behead, cut the throat: 246, 5

demoler (ue), to demolish

demostrar (ue), to demonstrate

denegar (ie), to deny: 240, 2; 246, 2

denostar (ue), to insult

dentar (ie), to tooth, indent; to teethe

deponer, to depose, depone: irr., 265

derrengar (ie), to sprain the hip, cripple: 240, 2; 246, 2

derretir (i), to melt

derrocar (ue), to pull down, demolish: 240, 1; 246, 1

derruir, to cast down, destroy: 256

desacertar (ie), to blunder, err

desacordar (ue), to make discordant; —se (ue), to forget

desaferrar (ie), to loosen, unfurl

desalentar (ie), to put out of breath, discourage

desamoblar (ue), to unfurnish, remove furniture: also desamueblar, reg.

desandar, to retrace steps, undo: irr., 262

desapretar (ie), to slacken, loosen

desaprobar (ue), to disapprove

desarrendarse (ie), to shake off the bridle

desasentar (ie), to disagree, displease; —se (ie), to get up desasir, to let go, release hold: *irr.*, 272

desasosegar (ie), to disturb, disquiet: 240, 2; 246, 2

desatender (ie), to disregard, neglect

desatentar (ie), to perturb, perplex

desavenir, to discompose, disconcert: *irr.*, 264

descender (ie), to descend

desceñir (i), to ungird: 242, 2; 252, 3

descolgar (ue), to unhang, take down: 240, 2; 246, 2

descollar (ue), to stand forth, excel

descomedirse (i), to be disrespectful, behave ill

descomponer, to disconcert, decompose: *irr.*, 265

desconcertar (ie), to disconcert, confound

desconsentir (ie), to dissent

desconsolar (ue), to make disconsolate

descontar (ue), to discount

desconvenir, to disagree, be unlike: *irr.*, 264

descordar (ue), to remove cords

descornar (ue), to remove horns

descubrir, to uncover, discover: *p.p. irr.*, 280

desdar, to untwist: *irr.*, 263

desdecir, to gainsay: *irr.*, 267; 242, 2

desdentar (ie), to remove teeth

desempedrar (ie), to unpave

desencerrar (ie), to release from confinement

desencordar (ue), to remove strings, loosen

desengrosar (ue), to make lean

desentenderse (ie), to disregard, feign not to notice

desenterrar (ie), to disinter

desenvolver (ue), to unfold, unravel: *p.p. irr.*, 245, 4

deservir (i), to neglect duty, do a disservice

desflocar (ue), to remove flocks (*of wool*): 240, 1; 246, 1

desgobernar (ie), to derange the government, misgovern

deshacer, to undo, destroy: *irr.*, 266; 255, *a*

deshelar (ie), to thaw

desherbar (ie), to pluck out herbs

desherrar, to uniron, remove horseshoes

desleír (i), to dilute: 253

deslendrar (ie), to remove nits (*from hair*)

desmajolar (ue), to uproot vines

desmedirse (i), to go beyond bounds, be unreasonable

desmembrar (ie), to dismember

desmentir (ie), to belie

desnegar (ie), to retract denial: 240, 2; 246, 2

desnevar (ie), to melt away (*of snow*)

desobstruir, to remove obstruction: 256

desoír, not to heed, feign not to hear: *irr.*, 276

desolar (ue), to make desolate

desoldar (ue), to unsolder

desollar (ue), to flay

desosar (ue), to remove bones: 247, *a*

desovar (ue), to spawn: 247, *a*

despedir (i), to dismiss; —se (i), to take leave

despernar (ie), to remove legs, cripple

despertar (ie), to awaken

despezar (ie), to arrange (stones) at intervals, taper at the end: 240, 4; 246, 3

desplacer, to displease: 281

desplegar (ie), to unfold, unfurl: 240, 2; 246, 2

despoblar (ue), to depopulate

desproveer, to leave unprovided, deprive of supplies: 279, a; 242, 1

desteñir (i), to discolor, fade: 242, 2; 252, 3

desterrar (ie), to exile

destituir, to deprive, remove from office: 256

destorcer (ue), to untwist: 241, 1; 246, 4

destrocar (ue), to return a bartered object: 240, 1; 246, 1

destruir, to destroy: 256

desventar (ie), to vent, let out air

desvergonzarse (ue), to be shameless or impudent: 240, 4; 246, 3; 246, 5

detener, to detain: irr., 258

detraer, to detract: irr., 277; 242, 2

devolver (ue), to give back: p.p. irr., 245, 4

diferir (ie), to defer, delay, differ

digerir (ie), to digest

diluir, to dilute: 256

discernir (ie), to discern: 248, 1

disconvenir: see desconvenir

discordar (ue), to disagree, be discordant

disentir (ie), to dissent

disminuir, to diminish: 256

disolver (ue), to dissolve: p.p. irr., 245, 4

disonar (ue), to be in dissonance

dispertar: see despertar

displacer, to displease: irr., 281

disponer, to dispose: irr., 265

distender (ie), to distend

distraer, to distract: irr., 277; 242, 2

distribuir, to distribute: 256

divertir (ie), to divert

dolar (ue), to plane, smooth (wood, etc.)

doler (ue), to pain, grieve

dormir (ue), to sleep

educir, to educe, bring out: irr., 278; 255, a; 242, 2

elegir (i), to elect: 241, 2; 252, 1

embestir (i), to invest, attack

emparentar (ie), to be related by marriage

empedrar (ie), to pave

empeller, to urge, push: 242, 2

empezar (ie), to begin: 240, 4; 246, 3

emporcar (ue), to sully, befoul: 240, 1; 246, 1

encender (ie), to light, kindle

encentar (ie), to begin to use for first time

encerrar (ie), to shut up, confine

enclocar (ue), to cluck: 240, 1; 246, 1

encomendar (ie), to commend

encontrar (ue), to meet, find

encorar (ue), to cover with leather, renew the skin

encordar (ue), to string (musical instruments), lash

encovar (ue), to put into a cave *or* cellar, lock up

encubertar (ie), to cover over

endentar (ie), to mortise in

engorar (ue), to lay addled eggs: 246, 5

engreír (i), to elate, puff up: 253

engrosar (ue), to fatten, strengthen

enhestar (ie), to erect, set upright

enmelar (ie), to honey, sweeten

enmendar (ie), to amend, correct

enrodar (ue), to break on the wheel

ensangrentar (ie), to cover with blood

entender (ie), to hear, understand

enterrar (ie), to inter

entortar (ue), to make crooked; to deprive of one eye

entredecir, to interdict: *irr.*, 267; 242, 2; 255, *a*

entremorir (ue), to pine away: *p.p. irr.*, 250, *a*

entreoír, to hear indistinctly: *irr.*, 276

entrepernar (ie), to put the legs in between (*something else*)

entreponer, to interpose: *irr.*, 265

entretener, to delay, entertain: *irr.*, 258

entrever, to see imperfectly, catch a glimpse of: *irr.*, 279

envolver (ue), to involve, wrap up, complicate: *p.p. irr.*, 245, 4

equivaler, to equal, be equivalent: *irr.*, 273

erguir (ie *or* i), to erect: 254; 241, 4

errar (ye–), to err, wander: 247, 1

escarmentar (ie), to give warning example, learn by experience

escocer (ue), to smart: 255, *a*; 241, 1; 246, 4

escribir, to write: *p.p. irr.*, 280

esforzar (ue), to strengthen; —se (ue), to attempt: 240, 4; 246, 3

estar, to be: *irr.*, 260

estatuir, to establish: 256

estregar (ie), to rub, scour, grind: 240, 2; 246, 2

estreñir (i), to bind, restrain: 242, 2

excluir, to exclude: 256

expedir (i), to expedite, despatch

exponer, to expose: *irr.*, 265

extender (ie), to extend

extraer, to extract: *irr.*, 277; 242, 2

ferrar (ie), to put on iron points, *etc.*

fluir, to flow: 256

follar (ue), to blow with bellows

forzar (ue), to force: 240, 4; 246, 3

fregar (ie), to rub, scour: 240, 2; 246, 2

freír (i), to fry: 253

gemir (i), to groan, moan

gobernar (ie), to govern

gruir, to cry like cranes: 256

gruñir, to grunt: 242, 2; 252, 3

haber, to have: *irr.*, 257

hacendar (ie), to transfer property

hacer, to do, make: *irr.*, 266; 255, *a* (*thus derivatives in* —**facer**)

heder (ie), to have a stench, stink

helar (ie), to freeze
henchir (i), to stuff, cram
hender (ie), to cleave, split
herbar (ie), to dress skins
herir (ie), to wound
hervir (ie), to boil, bubble
herrar (ie), to shoe (*horses*), brand (*cattle*)
holgar (ue), to rest, cease working: 240, 2; 246, 2
hollar (ue), to trample on, tread on
huir, to flee: 256

imbuir, to imbue: 256
impedir (i), to impede
imponer, to impose: *irr.*, 265
imprimir, to print: *p.p. irr.*, 280
improbar (ue), to disapprove, censure
incensar (ie), to perfume, incense
incluir, to include: 256
indisponer, to indispose, disincline: *irr.*, 265
inducir, to induce: *irr.*, 278; 255, *a*; 242, 2
inferir (ie), to infer
infernar (ie), to damn, vex
influir, to influence: 256
ingerir (ie), to graft, insert
inquirir (ie), to inquire: 248, 2
instituir, to institute: 256
instruir, to instruct: 256
interdecir, to indict: *irr.*, 267; 242, 2
interponer, to interpose: *irr.*, 265
intervenir, to intervene: *irr.*, 264
introducir, to introduce: *irr.*, 278; 255, *a*; 242, 2
invernar (ie), to winter

invertir (ie), to invert, spend, invest
investir (i), to invest, gird
ir, to go: *irr.*, 261

jugar (ue), to play: 249

leer, to read: 242, 1
llover (ue), to rain

maldecir, to curse: *irr.*, 267; 242, 2
malherir (ie), to wound seriously
malsonar (ue), to make cacophony
maltraer, to maltreat: *irr.*, 277; 242, 2
manifestar (ie), to manifest
mantener, to maintain: *irr.*, 258
mecer, to rock, lull, mix: 255, *a*
medir (i), to measure
melar (ie), to boil to honey, deposit honey (*of bees*)
mentar (ie), to mention
mentir (ie), to lie
merendar (ie), to lunch
moblar (ue), to furnish: *also* mueblar, *reg.*
moler (ue), to grind
morder (ue), to bite
morir (ue), to die: *p.p. irr.*, 250, *a*
mostrar (ue), to show
mover (ue), to move

negar (ie), to deny: 240, 2; 246, 2
nevar (ie), to snow, *impers.*

obstruir, to obstruct: 256
obtener, to obtain: *irr.*, 258
oír, to hear: *irr.*, 276
oler (hue–), to smell, have an odor: 247, 2
oponer, to oppose: *irr.*, 265

pedir (i), to ask

pensar (ie), to think, mean, believe

perder (ie), to lose, spoil, destroy

perniquebrar (ie), to break the legs

perseguir (i), to pursue, persecute: 241, 4; 252, 2

pervertir (ie), to pervert

placer, to please: *irr.*, 281

plañir, to lament, bewail: 242, 2; 252, 3

plegar (ie), to fold: 240, 2; 246, 2

poblar (ue), to found, people, fill

poder, to be able; can: *irr.*, 270

poner, to put: *irr.*, 265

poseer, to possess: 242, 1

posponer, to place after, postpone: *irr.*, 265

predecir, to predict: *irr.*, 267; 242, 2

predisponer, to predispose: *irr.*, 265

preferir (ie), to prefer

prender, to arrest, catch: 280

preponer, to put before, prefer: *irr.*, 265

presentir (ie), to forebode, foresee

presuponer, to presuppose: *irr.*, 265

prevalerse, to prevail: *irr.*, 273

prevenir, to forestall, prevent: *irr.*, 264

prever, to foresee: *irr.*, 279

probar (ue), to prove, try, taste

producir, to produce: *irr.*, 278; 255, *a*; 242, 2

proferir (ie), to utter, pronounce

promover (ue), to promote

proponer, to propose: *irr.*, 265

proseguir (i), to pursue, prosecute: 241, 4; 252, 2

prostituir, to prostitute: 256

proveer, to provide: 242, 1; 279, *a*

provenir, to proceed: *irr.*, 264

quebrar (ie), to break

querer, to wish, like: *irr.*, 271

reapretar (ie), to squeeze again

rebendecir, to bless again: *irr.*, 267; 255, *a*; 242, 2

recaer, to fall back, relapse: *irr.*, 275

recalentar (ie), to heat again

recentar (ie), to leaven

recluir, to shut up, seclude: 256

recocer (ue), to boil again: 255, *a*; 246, 4

recolar (ue), to strain again

recomendar (ie), to recommend

recomponer, to recompose, mend: *irr.*, 265

reconducir, to renew lease *or* contract: *irr.*, 278; 255, *a*; 242, 2

reconstruir, to reconstruct: 256

recontar (ue), to recount

reconvenir, to accuse, rebuke: *irr.*, 264

recordar (ue), to remind

recostar (ue), to lean against, recline

redargüir, to reargue: 256

reducir, to reduce: *irr.*, 278; 255, *a*; 242, 2

reelegir (i), to reëlect: 241, 2; 252, 1

referir (ie), to relate, refer

refluir, to flow back: 256

reforzar (ue), to strengthen, fortify: 240, 4; 246, 3

refregar (ie), to rub over again: 240, 2; 246, 2

refreír, to fry again: 253

regar (ie), to water: 240, 2; 246 2

regir (i), to rule, direct: 241, 2; 252, 1

regoldar (ue), to belch, eruct: 246, 5

rehacer, to make again, mend: *irr.*, 266; 255, *a*

rehenchir (i), to fill again, restuff

reherir (ie), to wound again

reherrar (ie), to shoe (*horses*) again

rehervir (ie), to reboil

rehollar (ue), to trample under foot

rehuir, to withdraw, deny: 256

reír, to laugh: 253

remendar (ie), to repair, patch

rementir (ie), to lie again

remoler (ue), to grind again

remorder (ue), to bite repeatedly, cause remorse

remover (ue), to remove, alter

rendir (i), to subdue, render; —se (i), to surrender

renegar (ie), to deny, disown: 240, 2; 246, 2

renovar (ue), to renovate, renew

reñir (i), to quarrel, scold: 242, 2; 252, 3

repensar (ie), to think over again

repetir (i), to repeat, recite

replegar (ie), to refold, double again: 240, 2; 246, 2

repoblar (ue), to repopulate

reponer, to put back, replace: *irr.*, 265

reprobar (ue), to reject, condemn

reproducir, to reproduce: *irr.*, 278; 255, *a*; 242, 2

requebrar (ie), to court, make love

requerir (ie), to investigate, require, request

resalir, to project, be prominent: *irr.*, 274

resegar (ie), to reap again: 240, 2; 246, 2

resembrar (ie), to sow again

resentirse (ie), to begin to give way, resent

resolver (ue), to resolve: *p.p. irr.*, 245, 4

resollar (ue), to respire

resonar (ue), to resound

resquebrar (ie), to crack, split, burst

restituir, to restore, reëstablish: 256

restregar (ie), to scrub: 240, 2; 246, 2

retemblar (ie), to shake, tremble much, brandish

retener, to retain: *irr.*, 258

retentar (ie), to threaten (with a relapse)

reteñir (i), to dye over again: 242, 2; 252, 3

retorcer (ue), to twist, contort: 241, 1; 246, 4

retostar (ue), to toast again, scorch well

retraer, to retract: *irr.*, 277; 242, 2

retribuir, to make retribution, recompense: 256

retronar (ue), to thunder again

retrotraer, to make retroactive: *irr.*, 277; 242, 2

revenirse, to be consumed gradually, sour, ferment: *irr.*, 264

reventar (ie), to burst

rever, to see again, review, revise: *irr.*, 279

reverter (ie), to revert

revestir (i), to put on vestments

revolar (ue), to fly again

revolcarse (ue), to wallow: 240, 1; 246, 1

revolver (ue), to stir, revolve: *p.p. irr.*, 245, 4

rodar (ue), to roll

rogar (ue), to entreat, ask: 240, 2; 246, 2; *derivatives* (abrogar, derogar) *reg.*

romper, to break: *p.p. irr.*, 280

saber, to know: *irr.*, 268

salir, to go out, come out: *irr.*, 274

salpimentar (ie), to season with pepper and salt   [of vine

sarmentar (ie), to gather prunings

satisfacer, to satisfy: *irr.*, 266; 255, *a*

segar (ie), to reap: 240, 2; 246, 2

seguir (i), to follow: 241, 4; 252, 2

sembrar (ie), to sow

sementar (ie), to sow

sentar (ie), to seat, set, suit

sentir (ie), to feel, regret

ser, to be: *irr.*, 259

serrar (ie), to saw

servir (i), to serve

sobre(e)ntenderse (ie), to be understood

sobreponer, to put above, add: *irr.*, 265

sobresalir, to rise above, surpass: *irr.*, 274

sobresembrar (ie), to sow over again

sobresolar (ue), to pave again, put on new sole

sobrevenir, to happen, supervene: *irr.*, 264

sobreverterse (ie), to overflow

sobrevestir (i), to put on an outer coat

sofreír (i), to fry slightly: 253

solar (ue), to floor, pave, sole

soldar (ue), to solder, mend

soler (ue), to be wont *or* accustomed: 281

soltar (ue), to untie, loosen

solver (ue), to loosen: *p.p. irr.*, 245, 4

sonar (ue), to sound

sonreír (i), to smile: 253

sonrodarse (ue), to stick in the mud

soñar (ue), to dream

sorregar (ie), to change channels: 240, 2; 246, 2

sosegar (ie), to appease, rest: 240, 2; 246, 2

sostener, to sustain: *irr.*, 258

soterrar (ie), to put underground, bury

subarrendar (ie), to take a sublease, subrent

subentender (ie), to subintend

subseguir (i), to be next in sequence: 241, 4; 252, 2

substituir: *see* sustituir

substraer: *see* sustraer

subtender (ie), to subtend

subvenir, to aid, give a subvention: *irr.*, 264

subvertir (ie), to subvert

sugerir (ie), to suggest

superponer, to superimpose: *irr.*, 265

supervenir, to supervene: *irr.*, 264

suponer, to suppose: *irr.*, 265
sustituir, to substitute: 256
sustraer, to subtract: *irr.*, 277;
242, 2

tañer, to ring, peal, touch: 242, 2
temblar (ie), to tremble
tender (ie), to stretch
tener, to have, hold: *irr.*, 258
tentar (ie), to feel, try
teñir (i), to tinge, dye, stain: 242,
2; 252, 3
torcer (ue), to twist, bend: 241, 1;
246, 4
tostar (ue), to toast
traducir, to translate: *irr.*, 278;
255, *a*; 242, 2
traer, to bring: *irr.*, 277; 242, 2
transcender: *see* trascender
transferir (ie), to transfer
transfregar: *see* trasfregar
transponer: *see* trasponer
trascender (ie), to transcend
trascolar (ue), to filter through
trascordarse (ue), to forget
trasegar (ie), to upset, decant:
240, 2; 246, 2
trasfregar (ie), to rub: 240, 2;
246, 2
trasoír, to misunderstand, hear
imperfectly: *irr.*, 276
trasoñar (ue), to dream

trasponer, to transpose, go beyond; —se, to set (*of sun*):
irr., 265
trastrocar (ue), to change about,
invert order: 240, 1; 246, 1
trasverter (ie), to overflow
trasvolar (ue), to fly across *or*
beyond
travesar (ie), to cross
trocar (ue), to exchange, barter:
240, 1; 246, 1
tronar (ue), to thunder
tropezar (ie), to stumble: 240, 4;
246, 3

valer, to be worth: *irr.*, 273
venir, to come: *irr.*, 264
ventar (ie), to blow
ver, to see: *irr.*, 279
verter (ie), to pour, shed
vestir (i), to dress, clothe
volar (ue), to fly, rise, blow up
volcar (ue), to overturn: 240, 1;
246, 1
volver (ue), to return, come back:
p.p. irr., 245, 4

yacer, to lie: *irr.*, 281
yuxtaponer, to put in juxtaposi-
tion: *irr.*, 265

za(m)bullirse, to dive: 242, 2
zaherir (ie), to reproach, censure

Taking a Direct Infinitive Object, or Requiring a Preposition Before a Subordinate Infinitive.

If the principal verb is followed by a direct infinitive object, without the interposition of a preposition, this fact is indicated by a dash (–) placed after the principal verb, thus: **querer –,** *to wish to.*

If a preposition is required before the subordinate infinitive, the preposition is given after the principal verb, thus: **empezar a,** *to begin to;* **tratar de,** *to try to.*

If the gerund may be used instead of a subordinate infinitive, this fact is indicated thus: **continuar a** *or ger.*

After many verbs in the list, the infinitive is used only when the principal and the subordinate verbs have the same subject. This is true of verbs of *affirming, denying, believing, doubting, knowing,* etc. (**afirmar, asegurar, confesar, creer, dudar, negar, reconocer, saber, sostener,** etc.), verbs of *willing* or *wishing* (**anhelar, desear, querer,** etc.), and verbs that express *feeling* or *emotion* (**alegrarse de, sentir, temer,** etc.).

The following list does not include verbs and expressions with which an infinitive is used only as subject of the sentence, such as **importar** (e.g., **me importa hacerlo**), **ocurrir** (e.g., **se me ocurre hacerlo**), **ser fácil, necesario,** etc. (e.g., **es fácil hacerlo**), **tocar** (e.g., **me toca hacerlo**), **valer más** (e.g., **vale más hacerlo**), etc. Nor is reference made to the use of an infinitive subject with such verbs as **convenir** (e.g., **me conviene hacerlo**), **gustar** (e.g., **me gusta hacerlo**), etc.

abandonar (se) a, to give (oneself) up to

abstenerse de, to refrain from

acabar de, to finish, have just; — **por,** to end by

acceder a, to accede, agree to

acomodarse a, to conform to

aconsejar –, to advise to

acordarse de, to remember

acostumbrar –, to be used to; **—(se) a,** to make (become) used to

acudir a, to go, come, hasten to

acusar de, to accuse of

adherir(se) a, to stick to

afanarse por, to exert oneself to

aficionarse a, to become addicted to

afirmar –, to affirm, declare

afligirse de, to lament

agraviarse de, to be grieved at

ajustarse a, to agree to

alcanzar a, to reach, attain to,

alegrarse de, to be glad to

amenazar –, to threaten to; — con, to threaten with

anhelar –, to long to

animar a, to encourage to

aplicarse a, to apply oneself to

aprender a, to learn to

apresurar(se) a, to hurry, hasten to

aprovecharse de, to profit by

apurarse por, to exert oneself to

arrepentirse de, to repent of

arriesgar con, to risk by

asegurar –, to assure, claim to

aspirar a, to aspire to

asustarse de, to be terrified at

atreverse a, to dare to

autorizar a, to authorize to

aventurarse a, to venture to

avergonzarse de, to be ashamed of

ayudar a, to aid, help to

bastar con, to be enough, suffice to

cansar(se) de, to tire, make (grow) weary of

celebrar –, to be glad to

cesar de, to cease to

comenzar a, to begin, commence to

complacerse en, to take pleasure in

comprometer(se) a, to engage (oneself), agree to

condenar a, to condemn to

condescender a, to condescend to

conducir a, to lead, conduct to

confesar –, to confess

confiar en, to trust, hope to

conformarse a, to conform, agree to

consagrar(se) a, to devote (oneself) to

conseguir –, to succeed in

consentir en, to consent to

consistir en, to consist in

conspirar a, to conspire to

consumirse en, to be consumed in

contar con, to count on

contentarse con, to content oneself with; — de, to be satisfied to

continuar a or ger., to continue (to)

contribuir a, to contribute to

convenir(se) – en or a, to agree to

convidar a, to invite to

correr a, to run to

creer –, to believe, think

dar a, to give to; —se a, to give oneself up to

deber –, should, ought to; — de, ought to (supposition)

decidir(se) – or a, to decide, determine to

declarar –, to declare

dedicar(se) a, to dedicate (oneself) to

dejar –, to let, allow, permit to; — de, to leave off, cease to

deleitarse en, to take delight in

desafiar a, to challenge to

descender a, to descend to

descuidar de, to neglect to

desdeñar(se) – or de, to disdain to

desear –, to desire to

desesperar(se) de, to despair of

desistir de, to desist from

destinar a, to destine to

detenerse a, to stop to

determinarse a, to determine to

dignarse – or de, to deign to

disculpar(se) de, to excuse oneself for

dispensar de, to excuse from

disponer(se) a, to get ready, prepare to

disuadir de, to dissuade from

divertirse en, con or ger., to amuse oneself by or with

dudar –, to doubt; — en, to hesitate to

echar(se) a, to begin to

elegir –, to choose to

empeñarse en, to insist on

empezar a, to begin to

encargarse de, to undertake to

enseñar a, to teach to

entrar a, to enter on, begin to

entretener(se) a or ger., to entertain oneself by or with

enviar a, to send to

equivocarse en, to be mistaken in

escuchar –, to listen to

esforzar(se) a, en, or por, to attempt, endeavor to

esmerarse en, to take pains in

esperar –, to hope to

estar para, to be about to; — por, to be inclined to

evitar –, to avoid

excitar a, to excite to

excusar(se) de, to excuse (oneself) from

exhortar a, to exhort to

exponer(se) a, to expose (oneself) to

fastidiar(se) de, to weary, be weary of

fatigar(se) de, to tire, be tired of

felicitar(se) de, to congratulate (oneself) on

fijarse en, to pay attention to

fingir –, to pretend to

forzar a, to force to

gozar(se) de, to enjoy; —(se) en, or ger., to take pleasure in

guardarse de, to guard against

haber de, to have to

habituar(se) a, to accustom one(self) to

hacer –, to make, have; — por, to try to

hartarse de, to be sated with

humillar(se) a, to humiliate (oneself) to

imaginarse –, to imagine

impedir –, to prevent, hinder

impeler a, to impel to

incitar a, to incite to

inclinar a, to induce to; —se a, to be inclined to

incomodarse de, to be annoyed at; — por, to put oneself out to

indignarse de, to be indignant at

inducir a, to induce to

insistir en, to insist on

inspirar a, to inspire to

intentar –, to try, attempt

invitar a, to invite to

ir a, to go to

jactarse de, to boast of

jurar –, to swear to

justificar(se) de, to justify (oneself) for

librar de, to free from

limitar(se) a, to limit (oneself) to

lograr –, to succeed in

llegar a, to come to, succeed in

mandar –, to command, have; **—
a,** to send to
matarse por, to try hard to
meditar en, to meditate upon
merecer –, to deserve to
meterse a, to undertake to
mezclarse en, to take part in
mirar –, to look at, watch
morirse por, to be dying to

necesitar –, to need, want to
negar –, to deny; **—se a,** to decline, refuse to

obligar(se) a, to oblige (oneself) to
obstinarse en, to persist in
ocupar(se) en, to busy (oneself)
with
odiar –, to hate to
ofrecer(se) –, to offer, promise to;
—(se) a, to offer to
oír –, to hear
olvidar –, to forget to; **—(se) de,**
to forget
oponerse a, to be opposed to
ordenar –, to order to

pararse a, to stop to
parecer –, to seem to
particularizarse en, to specialize in
pasar a, to proceed, pass to
pensar –, to intend to; **— en,** to
think of
permitir –, to permit to
perseverar en, to persevere in
persistir en, to persist in
persuadir(se) a, to persuade (oneself) to
poder –, can, may, to be able to
poner a, to put to; **—se a,** to
begin to

preciarse de, to boast of
preferir –, to prefer to
preparar(se) a, to prepare, make
ready to
presumir –, to presume to
pretender –, to claim, try to
principiar a, to begin to
privar(se) de, to deprive, be de-
prived of
probar a, to try to
proceder a, to proceed to
procurar –, to try to
prohibir –, to forbid
prometer –, to promise to
proponer –, to propose, purpose to
provocar a, to provoke to
pugnar por, to strive, struggle to

quedar(se) a, to remain to; **— en,**
to agree to; **— por,** to remain
to (be . . .)
quejarse de, to complain of
querer –, to wish to

rabiar por, to be crazy to
recelarse –, to fear
recomendar –, to recommend to
reconocer –, to acknowledge, confess to
recordar –, to remember
recrear(se) en *or* **ger.,** to divert
(oneself) by
reducir(se) a, to bring (oneself) to
rehusar(se) – *or* **a,** to refuse to
renunciar a, to renounce
resignarse a, to resign oneself,
submit to
resistirse a, to resist
resolver(se), a to resolve, decide
to
reventar por, to be bursting to

saber –, to know how, be able to, can

salir a, to go (*or* come) out to

sentarse a, to sit down to

sentir –, to regret, be sorry to

ser de, to be

servirse –, to please, be so kind as to

sobresalir en, to excel in

soler –, to be wont, used to

soltar a, to start to

someter(se) a, to submit (oneself) to

soñar con, to dream of

sospechar de, to suspect of

sostener –, to maintain, affirm

subir a, to go up to

sugerir -, to suggest

tardar en, to delay, be long in

temer –, to fear to

terminar en, to end by

tornar a, to return to; to . . . again

tratar de, to try to

urgir a, to urge to

vacilar en, to hesitate to

valerse de, to avail oneself of

venir a, to come to; — de, to come from, have just

ver –, to see

volar a, to fly to

volver a, to return to; to . . . again

GENERAL VOCABULARY

SPANISH-ENGLISH

A

a, to, at; from.

el **abogado,** lawyer, attorney.

abonar, to credit.

a bordo (de), aboard.

abril *m.*, April.

abrir §280, to open.

el **abuelo,** la —**a,** grandfather, grandmother; los **abuelos,** grandparents.

acá, here.

acabar, to finish; **ya acabé, I** have finished, I'm done; **se acabó,** it's finished *or* done; **acaba (acababa) de hablar,** he has (had) just spoken; **acabó de hablar,** he finished speaking.

el **aceite,** oil.

aceptar, to accept.

acertadamente, accurately.

aclarar, to make clear.

la **acogida,** reception.

acompañar, to accompany, go with, come with.

aconsejar, to advise.

acontecer, to happen.

acordarse (ue) de, to remember; **si mal no me acuerdo,** if I remember rightly.

acostar (ue), to lay down, put to bed; —**se,** to lie down, go to bed.

acostumbrado, —**a,** (a), used (to).

el **acróbata,** la —, acrobat.

la **actriz,** actress.

actual, present, instant.

acudir, to come (to), go (to), hasten to.

acusar, to acknowledge.

el **acusativo,** accusative.

además, moreover, besides; — **de,** besides, in addition to.

adentro, within, inside.

adiós, goodbye, farewell.

el **adjetivo,** adjective.

adjunto, - a *adj.*, **adjunto** *adv.*, enclosed, herewith.

la **admiración,** exclamation, admiration, wonder; **signo de** —, exclamation mark.

adoptar, to adopt.

adquerir (ie), to acquire.

el **adverbio,** adverb.

las **advertencias,** instructions.

advertir (ie), to note; **adviértase,** note.

afectísimo, most affectionate(ly).

afectuosamente, affectionately.

aficionado, –a (a), fond (of).

afmo: *see* **afectísimo.**

el **agente,** agent.

agitado, –a, agitated, rough (*as the sea*).

agitar, to shake, wave.

agosto *m.*, August.

agradable, pleasant, agreeable.

agradecer, to be grateful for; **agradecido,** –a, grateful, obliged.

agregar, to add.

el **agua** *f.*, water.

aguardar, to await, wait for.

la **aguja,** needle.

ahí, there (*near the person addressed*).

ahora, now.

el **aire,** air.

el **ala** *f.,* wing, brim (*of hat*).

la **alcoba,** (alcove) bedroom.

alegrarse (de), to be glad (of).

algo, something, anything; *adv.,* somewhat.

el **algodón,** cotton.

alguien, someone, somebody, anyone, anybody.

alguno, –a, some, any; *pl.,* some, any, a few; **alguna cosa,** something, anything.

el **alma** *f.,* soul.

el **almidón,** starch.

la **almohada,** pillow.

almorzar (ue), to lunch.

el **almuerzo,** lunch, (late) breakfast.

alto, –a, high, tall, loud.

la **altura,** height.

alumbrar, to light.

el **alumno,** la —a, pupil, student.

allá, there.

allí, there.

amar, to love.

amargo, –a, bitter.

amarillo, –a, yellow.

ambos, –as, both.

la **americana,** morning *or* business coat, "sack" coat.

americano, –a, American.

el **amigo,** la –a, friend.

Ana, Anna.

análogo, –a, analogous, similar.

la **anana** (*in Span. Am.,* el **ananá** o el **ananás**), pineapple.

ancho, –a, wide, broad.

la **anchura,** width, breadth.

andar §262, to go.

el **anfiteatro,** balcony (*in theater*).

anoche, last night.

ante, before (*in place*).

anteponer §265, to place before.

antepuesto, –a, placed before.

anterior, preceding.

antes, before (*in time*); — **de** *prep.,* — **que** *conj.,* before.

anticipado, –a, in advance.

anunciar §243, to announce.

el **anuncio,** advertisement.

añadir, to add.

el **año,** year; **Año nuevo,** New Year's Day.

el **aparador,** sideboard.

aparecer, to appear.

el **apartado (de correos),** post-office box.

el **apellido,** surname, family name.

apenas, scarcely, hardly.

apetecer, to have an appetite for, long for, want.

el **apetito,** appetite.

aplicado, –a, industrious, diligent; **es** —, he is a hard worker.

apocopar, to shorten.

apreciable: su — carta, your favor.

aprender, to learn.

apresurarse (a), to make haste (to).

aprisa, fast.

aproximadamente, approximately.

apurado, –a, without money.

aquí, here.

el **árabe,** la —, Arab.

el **árbol,** tree.

el **área** *f.,* are (= *100 square meters*).

argentino, –a, Argentine.

árido, –a, arid, dry; los —s, dry articles, dry objects (*as grain which is sold by measure*).

la **aritmética,** arithmetic.

el **aroma,** perfume, aroma.

el **arquitecto,** architect.

arreglar, to arrange, pack (a trunk).

la arroba, 25 pounds.

arrojar, to throw, cast; arroja un saldo a mi favor, there is a balance in my favor.

el artículo, article.

el artista, la —, artist.

asar, to roast.

ascender (ie) a, to amount to.

el ascensor, lift, elevator.

asegurar, to assure, insure.

así, thus; — como, as well as.

el asiento, seat.

asistir, to be present (at), attend.

asustar, to frighten.

la atención, attention.

atento, -a, devoted, courteous.

atravesar (ie), to cross, pass through.

aumentar, to increase.

aun, even; aún, still, yet.

aunque, although, even if.

el automóvil, motor car, automobile.

el autor, la —a, author.

la avena, oats.

ayer, yesterday.

la azotea, flat roof.

el azúcar, sugar.

azul, blue.

la azumbre, two quarts.

B

bajar(se), to alight, descend.

bajo, -a, low.

el balcón, balcony.

el banco, bench, bank.

el banquero, banker.

bañarse, to bathe, take a bath.

el baño, bath, bathtub.

barato, -a, cheap.

el barrio, ward, part (of a city).

bastante adj., enough; adv., enough, rather.

bastardilla: la letra —, italics.

la batería de cocina, cooking utensils.

el baúl, trunk.

el bautismo, baptism; nombre de —, given or Christian name.

besar, to kiss.

la biblioteca, library.

la bicicleta, bicycle.

bien, well; o bien . . . o, either . . . or.

el billete, ticket, note; — de ida y vuelta, round-trip ticket; — sencillo, one-way ticket.

el bizcocho, biscuit, "cracker."

blanco, -a, white.

la blusa, blouse.

la boda, marriage.

el boletero (Span. Am.), ticket agent.

el boleto (Span. Am.), ticket.

la bolsa, purse, pocket.

el bolsillo, pocket.

la bondad, kindness, goodness.

bonito, -a, pretty.

borrar, to erase.

el borrón, blot.

la bota, boot, high shoe; — de montar, riding boot.

la botella, bottle.

el botón, button.

el brasero, brazier.

el Brasil, Brazil.

el brazo, arm.

breve, short.

bueno, -a, good; estar —, to be well.

el buque, boat, vessel.

burlarse de, to make fun of, mock.

buscar, to seek, look for; ir a —, to go and get.

la butaca, easy chair, seat (in "orchestra" or "dress circle" of theater).

el buzón, letter box.

C

la **caballeriza**, stable.

el **caballero**, gentleman, sir.

el **caballo**, horse; — **de silla**, riding *or* saddle horse.

el **cabello**, los —s, hair (*of the head*).

caber §269, to be contained; **¿cuánto cabe en la caja?** how much does the box hold?

la **cabeza**, head.

la **cabritilla**, kid.

cada, each; — **uno**, each one; — **dos días**, every two days.

caer §275, to fall, fit.

el **café**, coffee; — **con leche**, coffee and milk.

la **caja**, box.

la **cajita**, little box.

el **calcetín**, sock, half-hose.

calentar (ie), to warm, heat.

la **calidad**, quality.

caliente, warm, hot.

calificar, to qualify, modify.

calificativo, –a, qualifying.

el **calor**, warmth, heat.

el **calorífero**, heater, furnace.

calvo, –a, bald.

el **calzado**, footwear.

calzar, to put on *or* wear (*shoes*); —se, to put on one's shoes.

el **calzón**, knee-breeches.

la **calle**, street.

la **cama**, bed, berth.

el **camarero**, steward, waiter.

el **camarote**, stateroom.

cambiar (**de**), to change.

el **cambio**, change; **en** —, on the other hand.

la **camisa**, shirt.

el **campo**, country (*as distinguished from the city*); los —s, fields.

el **Canadá**, Canada.

cansado, –a, tired.

el **cantar**, song, poem.

cantar, to sing, crow.

la **cantidad**, amount, quantity.

el **cantor**, la —a, singer.

la **capacidad**, capacity.

el **capitán**, captain.

el **capítulo**, chapter.

la **cara**, face.

el **carácter**, character, force.

el **carbón**: — **de piedra**, coal; — **de leña**, charcoal.

carecer de, to lack.

cargar, to charge, load.

el **cariño**, affection; **hacer** —s, to pet.

Carlos, Charles.

la **carne**, meat, flesh; — **de vaca** (**de res**), beef.

el **carnero**, sheep; **carne de** —, mutton.

caro, –a, dear, expensive.

Carolina, Caroline.

el **carpintero**, carpenter.

la **carta**, letter.

la **casa**, house; — **de correos**, post office; — **de huéspedes**, boarding-house; **a** —, home; **en** —, at home.

casado, –a, married.

casarse con, to marry.

casi, almost.

la **casilla** = el **apartado**.

el **caso**, case.

castellano, –a, Castilian, Spanish.

castigar, to punish.

Castilla, *f.*, Castile.

el **catálogo**, catalogue.

la **cazuela**, pan.

celebrar, to rejoice at, be glad of, celebrate.

la **cena**, supper.

cenar, to sup, have supper.

el **centavo**, cent.

el **centímetro**, centimeter.

el **céntimo,** centime (*100* —s = *1* peseta).

el **centro,** center.

cepillar, to brush.

el **cepillo,** brush; — **de dientes,** toothbrush.

cerca *adv.,* near; — **de** *prep.,* near, nearly, about.

la **ceremonia,** ceremony.

la **cerilla,** wax match.

cerrar (ie), to close, shut, bring (*an account*) up to.

certificar, to register (*a letter, package, etc.*).

ciego, –a, blind.

el **cielo,** sky.

el **cinematógrafo** ("**cine**"), moving pictures, "movies."

circunscrito, –a, limited, circumscribed.

citar, to quote, mention.

la **ciudad,** city, (large) town.

la **claridad,** clearness.

claro, –a, clear, bright.

la **clase,** class, kind, classroom; — **de español,** Spanish class.

clásico, –a, classic.

la **cláusula,** clause.

el **clima,** climate.

cobrar, to collect (*a bill*), cash (*a check*).

el **cobre,** copper.

cocer (ue), to bake, boil (*food*).

la **cocina,** kitchen, cooking; — **económica,** modern iron kitchen range.

el **cocinero,** la —**a,** cook.

el **coche,** carriage, coach; — **cama** (— **dormitorio**), sleeping car; — **comedor,** dining car; **ir (pasearse) en** —, to drive.

coger, to catch.

la **colección,** collection.

la **colocación,** position.

colocar, to place.

Colón, Columbus.

el **color,** color.

la **comedia,** play, comedy.

el **comedor,** dining room.

comer, to eat, dine; **dar de** —, to feed.

el **comercio,** commerce, business.

el **cometa,** comet.

la **comida,** (prepared) food, meal, dinner.

las **comillas,** quotation marks.

como, as, about; **¿cómo?** how?

la **cómoda,** chest of drawers, "chiffonier."

la **comodidad,** convenience.

cómodo, –a, comfortable, convenient.

la **compañía,** company.

la **comparación,** comparison.

el **compartimiento,** compartment.

complementario, –a, (*used as*) object.

el **complemento,** complement, object.

completar, to complete.

completo, –a, complete.

componer §265, to compose; —**se de,** to be composed of.

la **compra,** purchase.

comprar, to buy.

comprender, to comprehend, include.

el **compromiso,** engagement.

compuesto, –a (*p.p. of* **componer**), compound.

con, with.

conceder, to give, offer.

concertar (ie), to agree.

la **concordancia,** agreement.

concordar (ue), to agree.

concreto, –a, concrete.

la **conformidad,** conformity, approval.

congelarse, to freeze.

la **conjugación,** conjugation.

conmigo, with me.

conocer, to know, be acquainted with, make the acquaintance of, meet.

el **conocido,** la —a, acquaintance.

conservar, to retain, keep.

consigo, with himself, herself, *etc.*

consistir en, to consist of.

la **consonante,** consonant.

constante, consistent, regularly recurring.

la **construcción,** order (*of words in a sentence*).

construir, to build, make, construe, use (with).

contado: al —, for cash.

contar (ue), to count; — **con,** to count on, be assured (*that*).

contestar, to answer.

el **contexto,** context.

contigo, with thee.

la **continuación,** continuation.

continuar §243, to continue.

contra, against; **por —,** against you (your account).

contradicho, -a, contradicted, offset.

contrario, contrary; **al —, por el —,** on the contrary, on the other hand.

conveniente, suitable, well.

convenir §264, to be proper.

la **corbata,** cravat, (neck)tie.

cordialmente, cordially.

el **corral,** yard.

correctamente, correctly.

corregir (i), to correct.

el **correo,** mail; **casa de —s,** post office.

correr, to run. [office.

corresponder, to correspond, repay.

corriente, current, present (month), instant, usual, of every day.

el **cortaplumas,** (pen)knife.

cortar, to cut.

la **Corte,** Court.

cortés, polite, courteous.

corto, -a, short.

la **cosa,** thing, matter; — **de,** a matter of, about.

costar (ue), to cost.

crecer, to grow.

el **crédito,** credit.

creer, to believe, think; **¡ya lo creo!** I should say so! [ant.

el **criado,** la —a, (domestic) serv-

la **crisis,** crisis.

Cristóbal, Christopher.

crítico, -a, critical.

el **cuaderno,** notebook, exercise book.

el **cuadrado,** square; **cuadrado,** -a, square.

el **cuadro,** picture.

cual, which; **el (la, lo) —, los (las) —es,** who (whom), which; **cuál** *interrog.,* which.

la **cualidad,** quality.

cual(es)quier(a), any(one) at all, whatever.

cuando, when; **cuándo** *interrog.,* when.

cuanto, -a, all who, all that; **en — a,** with regard to; **cuánto,** -a *interrog.,* how much (many).

la **cuarta** (= ¼ **vara**), 8 inches.

el **cuartillo,** pint.

el **cuarto,** room; — **de baño,** bathroom.

cúbico, -a, cubic.

la **cubierta,** deck (*of a ship*).

cubierto, *p.p. of* **cubrir.**

cubrir §280, to cover.

la **cuchara,** spoon.

la **cucharadita,** teaspoonful.

la **cucharita,** teaspoon.

el **cuchillo,** knife.

el **cuello,** neck, collar.

la **cuenta,** account, bill; **a —,** on account.

el **cuero,** hide, leather.

el **cuidado,** care; **tengo —,** I am careful; **¡tenga Vd. —!** look out! **pierda Vd. —,** do not worry.

la **culpa,** fault; **no es mía la —,** it is not my fault; **Vd. tiene la —,** it is your fault.

cultivar, to cultivate, grow.

cumplir, to fulfil; **— ocho años,** to be eight years old.

el **cura,** parish priest.

el **curso,** school *or* college year.

cuyo, –a, whose.

Ch

el **chaleco,** waistcoat, vest.

el **chanclo,** rubber overshoe, "golosh."

la **chaqueta,** boy's coat, jacket.

el **cheque,** check, draft.

chico, –a, small, little.

el **chícharo** (*Span. Am.*), pea.

chileno, –a, Chilean.

la **chimenea,** fireplace.

el **chocolate,** chocolate.

D

da, gives.

dado que, granted that.

dar §263, to give; **— a,** to face; **da la una (dan las dos),** it is striking one (two); **— de comer,** to feed; **— a conocer,** to make known.

el **dativo,** dative.

de, of, from, by, than.

debajo de, below, under.

deber, to owe, must; **debiera,** should, ought to; **debe,** debit; **— de,** must (*according to opinion*); **esto se debe a que,** this is due to the fact that.

débil, weak.

el **decímetro,** decimeter.

decir §267, to say, tell; **querer —,** to mean.

el **dedal,** thimble.

deducir, to deduce.

definido, –a, definite.

dejar, to let, allow; **— de,** to stop; **no — de,** not to fail to.

delante de, before.

demás, rest, others; **por lo —,** otherwise.

demostrativo, –a, demonstrative.

el **departamento,** department, compartment.

el **dependiente,** clerk.

derecho, –a *adj.,* straight, right; **derecho** *adv.,* straight (ahead).

desagradable, unpleasant, disagreeable.

desaparecer, to disappear.

desatar, to untie.

desayunar, to breakfast.

el **desayuno,** (early) breakfast.

descansar, to rest.

el **descanso,** rest.

descoser, to rip.

descubrir §280, to discover.

el **descuento,** discount.

desde, since, from; **— que,** from the time when, since; **— luego,** at once.

desear, to desire.

el **deseo,** desire, wish.

la **desinencia,** ending.

desocupado, –a, unoccupied.

el **despacho,** office.

despedirse (i), to take leave.

despertarse (ie), to wake up, awaken.

después, afterwards, since; **— de, — que,** after.

detallar, to itemize.

detrás de, behind.

el día, day; **buenos —s,** good day, good morning; **al —,** daily.

diario, -a, daily.

diciembre *m.,* December.

dicho (*p.p. of* **decir**), said; **mejor —,** rather.

el diente, tooth.

la dieta, diet.

diferente, different.

difícil, difficult, hard.

la dificultad, difficulty.

el dígito, digit.

el dinero, money.

el diploma, diploma.

la dirección, direction, address.

el director, la —a, director, principal.

dirigir, to direct, address; **—se (a),** to make one's way (to), go (to).

dispensar, to give, grant, excuse.

la distancia, distance.

distinto, -a, several, distinct.

divertir (ie), to amuse; **—se,** to enjoy oneself; **—se con,** to enjoy.

dividir, to divide.

doblar, to double, turn (*a corner*).

la docena, dozen.

el dólar, dollar (*of U. S. A.*).

el dolor, pain, sorrow; **— de cabeza,** headache.

el domicilio, residence.

el domingo, Sunday.

don (doña), Mr. (Mrs.).

donde, where; **dónde** *interrog.,* where.

dormir, to sleep; **—se,** to go to sleep.

el dormitorio, bedroom.

el dorso, back (*of check*).

dos, two; **los —,** both.

la dosis, dose.

el dril, duck (cloth).

la duda, doubt.

dudar, to doubt.

el dueño, owner.

durante, during.

durar, to last, endure.

duro, -a, hard; **el duro,** dollar (*in gold or silver*).

E

e, and.

echar, to throw, cast, put, pour; **— en el buzón, al correo,** to post; **una gallina está echada,** a hen is sitting.

la edición, edition.

el edificio, building.

editorial, publishing.

efectivo: hacer —, to cash (*a check for someone*).

efectuar §243, to effect, make.

la ejecución, execution, progress.

ejecutar, to execute, fill (*an order*).

el ejemplar, copy (*of a book, etc.*).

el ejemplo, example, instance.

el ejercicio, exercise.

eléctrico, -a, electric.

embalar, to pack.

Emilia, Emily.

empaquetar, to pack.

empezar (ie), to begin.

emplear, to use, employ.

el empleo, employment, use.

en, in, into, on.

enclítico, -a, enclitic, attached to a preceding word.

encoger(se), to shrink.

encontrar (ue), to meet, encounter.

encuadernar, to bind.

endosar, to endorse.

el enemigo, la —a, enemy.

enero, *m.,* January.

enfadarse, to get angry.

enfático, -a, emphatic.

la **enfermedad,** illness.
 enfermo, –a, ill, sick; **el enfermo, la —a,** the patient.
 enfrente de, in front of, before.
 engañar, to deceive.
 enjugar, to wipe, dry.
el **enlace,** union, marriage.
 enojarse, to get angry; **enojado con,** angry with.
 Enrique, Henry.
la **ensalada,** salad.
 en seguida: *see* **seguida.**
 enseñar, to teach, show.
 entender (ie), to understand.
 entero, –a, entire.
 entonces, then.
la **entrada,** entrance, admission.
 entrar en (o a), to enter (into), go (into), come (into).
 entre, between, among.
 entregar, to hand, deliver.
 enviar §243, to send.
el **envío,** shipment (*of goods*).
 equivalente, equivalent.
 equivaler §273, to be equivalent.
 equivocarse, to be mistaken.
 errar (ye–) §247, 1, to err.
la **escalera,** stairs, stairway.
 escoger, to choose, select.
 escribir §280, to write.
 escrito (*irr. p.p. of* **escribir**), written.
el **escritorio,** writing desk.
 escuchar, to listen.
la **escuela,** school.
el **espacio,** space.
 España *f.,* Spain.
el **español, la —a,** Spaniard; Spanish woman; **español, —ola,** Spanish.
el **espejo,** mirror, looking-glass.
la **espera,** expectation.
 esperar, to hope, wait.
 espeso, –a, thick.
el **esposo, la —a,** husband, wife.

la **espuela,** spur.
la **esquina,** corner; **las cuatro —s,** (*game of*) puss-in-a-corner.
la **estación,** season, station.
el **estado,** state; **Estados Unidos,** United States.
 estad(o)unidense, of the United States, American.
la **estampilla,** stamp.
 estar §260, to be.
el **este,** east.
 estimable, esteemed.
 estrechar, to press, clasp.
 estrenar, to perform *or* give (*a play, etc.*) for the first time.
el **estribor,** starboard (= *right*).
 estudiar §243, to study.
la **estufa,** stove.
 etc. = **etcétera.**
la **etiqueta,** etiquette; **traje de —,** evening clothes, "dress" suit.
 evitar, to avoid.
 exacto, –a, exact, correct.
 excelente, excellent.
 excepto, except.
 exceptuar §243, to except.
 excusar, to excuse.
 exigir, to demand, insist on.
la **expedición,** sending, shipping.
 explicar, to explain.
 expreso, –a, express.
el **extracto,** extract, summary.

F

 fácil, easy.
la **factura,** bill.
la **falta,** lack, mistake; **me hace —,** I lack, need.
 faltar, to lack; **le falta,** he lacks; **poco faltó para que se cayera,** he almost fell.
la **familia,** family.
la **fanega,** $1\frac{1}{2}$ bushels; **— de tierra,** $1\frac{2}{3}$ acres.
 febrero *m.,* February.

la **fecha,** date.

fechar, to date.

Felipe, Philip.

feliz, happy.

femenino, -a, feminine.

feo, -a, homely, ugly.

Fernando, Ferdinand.

el **ferrocarril,** railway.

la **fiebre,** fever.

el **fieltro,** felt.

figurarse, to seem, appear.

fijamente, with certainty.

la **fila,** row.

la **firma,** signature.

firmar, to sign.

flexible, soft, flexible.

la **flor,** flower.

el **fogón,** fireplace

fonético, -a, phonetic.

formular, to formulate.

el **fósforo,** match.

el **frac,** evening coat, "dress" coat.

el **francés,** la **francesa,** Frenchman, French woman; **francés, -esa,** French.

Francisco, Francis; —a, Frances.

franco (-a) de porte, postage prepaid.

la **frase,** phrase, sentence.

la **frazada,** blanket.

fregar (ie), to scour (*pots, etc.*), scrub (*floors*).

el **frente,** front; la —, forehead.

fresco, -a, fresh, cool.

el **frío,** cold; **tengo —,** I am cold; **hace —,** it is cold; **frío, -a,** cold.

frito, -a (*irr. p.p. of* **freír**), fried.

la(s) **fruta(s),** fruit.

fuerte, strong.

la **función,** performance.

funda (de almohada), (pillow) case.

futuro, -a, future.

G

la **galería,** gallery, balcony, veranda.

la **gallina,** hen.

el **ganadero,** cattle raiser, stockman.

ganar, to earn, win.

ganas: tengo — de, I long to.

el **gas,** gas.

gastar, to spend, use up, take.

el **gatito,** la —a, kitten.

el **género,** gender, goods.

el **genitivo,** genitive.

la **gente,** people.

la **geografía,** geography.

girar, to revolve.

el **giro,** order, draft; — **postal,** post-office money order.

gordo, -a, stout, fat.

la **gorra,** cap.

gracias, thanks, thank you.

el **grado,** degree.

gráfico, -a, graphic, written.

la **gramática,** grammar.

el **gramo,** gramme.

grande, large, big, great.

el **grano,** grain.

grato, -a, pleasing, kind.

griego, -a, Greek.

el **grueso,** bulk, thickness; **grueso, -a,** bulky, thick.

el **guante,** glove.

guardar, to keep; — **cama,** to stay in bed.

la **guayaba,** guava.

la **guerra,** war.

el **guía,** guide.

el **guisante,** pea.

guisar, to cook.

gustar, to please; **me gusta,** I like.

el **gusto,** taste, pleasure; **tener buen —,** to have (a) good taste.

H

la Habana, Havana.

haber §257, to have, there . . . be; **hay,** there is (are); **hay que,** one must; ¿qué **hay?** what is the matter?

la habitación, suite of rooms, room.

el habitante, inhabitant.

hablar, to speak.

el hacendado, planter, farmer.

hacer §266, to do, make; — **frío (calor),** to be cold, (warm); — **el baúl,** to pack the trunk; — **ejercicio,** to take exercise; **hace ocho días,** a week ago; **hágame Vd. el favor de,** please.

la hacienda, large farm, plantation.

el hacha *f.*, axe.

hallar, to find; **me hallo mejor,** I am better.

el hambre *f.*, hunger; **tengo** —, I am hungry.

hasta, till, to; — **que,** until.

hay: *see* **haber.**

la hectárea, hectare (= *about 2½ acres*).

el hecho, act, fact.

el hermano, la —a, brother, sister.

hermoso, –a, handsome.

hervir (ie), to boil.

el hierro, iron.

el hijo, la —a, son, daughter; los **hijos,** children (= *sons and daughters*).

el hilo, thread; (fine) linen.

hipotético, –a, hypothetic.

hispanoamericano, –a, Spanish-American.

la historia, history, story.

histórico, –a, historic(al).

hizo, *pret. of* **hacer.**

la hoja, leaf.

el hombre, man.

hondo, –a, deep.

el hongo, "derby" hat, "bowler."

la hora, hour; ¿qué — **es?** what time (o'clock) is it? **es — de,** it is time to (for).

el horno, oven.

hoy, to-day.

la huerta, garden.

el huésped, la **huéspeda,** guest; **casa de** —**es,** boarding house.

el huevo, egg.

huir, to flee.

el hule (*Mex.*), rubber.

I

identificar, to identify.

el idioma, language.

la iglesia, church.

igual, equal.

igualmente, equally.

ilustrar, to illustrate.

el imperativo, imperative.

imperfecto, –a, imperfect.

implicar, to imply, denote.

la importancia, importance.

importante, important.

importar, to be important, amount to.

el importe, amount, cost.

los impresos, printed matter.

inclinarse, to bow, be inclined.

incluir, to include.

el inconveniente, impropriety; **si Vd. tiene — en hacerlo,** if you have any objection to doing so.

indefinido, –a, indefinite.

indicar, to point out, indicate.

el indicativo, indicative.

indio, –a, Indian.

el individuo, individual, member.

el infinitivo, infinitive.

infinito, –a, infinite.

la inflexión, inflection.

Inglaterra *f.*, England.

el inglés, la inglesa, Englishman,
　Englishwoman; inglés, –esa,
　English.
inmortal, immortal.
instruir, to instruct.
inteligente, intelligent.
interesante, interesting.
interrogativo, –a, interrogative.
íntimo, –a, intimate.
invertido, –a, inverted.
el invierno, winter.
la invitación, invitation.
invitar, to invite.
ir §261, to go; — creciendo,
　to be growing.
Isabel, Elizabeth, Isabel.
Italia f., Italy.
italiano, –a, Italian.
izquierdo, –a, left.

J

el jabón, soap.
el Japón, Japan.
el jardín, flower garden.
el jarro, jug, "pitcher."
Juan, John.
Juanito, Johnny.
el jueves, Thursday.
jugar §249, to play; — a la
　pelota, to play ball.
julio m., July.
junio m., June.
juntar, to join.
la juventud, youth.

K

el kilo: see kilogramo.
el kilogramo, kilogramme (=
　1,000 grammes or about 2
　pounds).
el kilómetro, kilometer (= ⅝ Eng-
　lish mile).

L

el labrador, (small) farmer, farm
　laborer, farm "hand."

labrar, to till.
el lado, side.
el ladrillo, brick.
el lago, lake.
la lámpara, lamp.
la lana, wool; de —, woolen.
el lápiz, pencil.
largo, –a, long.
la lástima, pity; es (una) —, it is
　a pity, it is too bad.
lastimar, to hurt.
el lavandero, la —a, laundry-
　man, laundress.
lavar, to wash.
la lección, lesson.
la lectura, reading.
la leche, milk.
la lechuga, lettuce.
leer, to read.
la legua, league (= about 3 miles
　or 5 kilometers).
la legumbre, vegetable.
la lengua, tongue, language.
la leña, firewood.
León m., Leon (ancient king-
　dom, now a part of the king-
　dom of Spain).
la letra de cambio, bill of ex-
　change.
levantar, to raise; —se, to
　rise, get up.
la levita, coat.
la libra, pound.
la librería, bookstore; — gen-
　eral, publisher(s) and book-
　seller(s).
el libro, book; — de lectura,
　reading book, reader.
ligero, –a, light; swift.
limpiar, to clean.
limpio, –a, clean.
lindo, –a, pretty.
la línea, line; en — recta, in a
　straight line.
líquido, –a, liquid.
la lista, list, bill of fare.

la **litera,** berth.

la **literatura,** literature.

el **litro,** liter (*a little more than a quart*).

lograr, to succeed (in).

la **lona,** canvas.

la **longitud,** length.

luego, soon, then; — **que,** as soon as; **hasta** —, farewell for a while; **desde** —, at once.

el **lugar,** place, position; **tener** —, to take place.

Luis, Lewis, Louis.

el **lujo,** luxury; **de** —, de luxe, elegant.

la **lumbre,** fire.

la **luna,** moon; **hay (hace)** —, the moon is shining.

el **lunes,** Monday.

la **luz,** light.

Ll

llamar, to call, knock, ring (*the door bell*); **me llamo,** my name is; **¿cómo se llama Vd.?** what is your name?

la **llave,** key.

llegar, to arrive, come.

lleno, -a, full.

llevar, to carry, bring, wear.

llorar, to weep, cry.

llover (ue), to rain.

M

macho, male.

la **madera,** wood (*for manufacture, building, etc.*).

la **madre,** mother.

el **maíz,** maize, Indian corn.

mal, badly

la **maleta,** valise, (hand)bag.

malo, -a, bad, poor (= *bad*); **estar** —, to be ill.

la **mamá,** mamma, mother.

mandar, to command, order, send; — **hacer alguna cosa,** to have something done.

el **mando,** command.

la **manera,** manner; **de** — **que,** so as, so that.

la **manga,** sleeve.

la **manifestación,** statement.

manifestar (ie), to manifest, inform, advise.

la **mano,** hand.

manso, -a, gentle, tame.

la **manta,** blanket.

la **manteca,** lard, butter (*in Spain*).

el **mantel,** tablecloth.

la **mantequilla,** butter (*in Span. Am.*), sweetened butter-cake (*in Spain*).

la **manzana,** apple.

la **mañana,** morning; **por la** —, in the morning; *adv.*, to-morrow; **pasado** —, the day after to-morrow.

el **mapa,** map.

el **mar,** *or* la —, sea.

marcar, to mark.

marearse, to become seasick.

María, Mary.

el **marido,** husband.

el **marinero,** sailor.

el **martes,** Tuesday.

marzo *m.,* March.

mas, but.

más, more, most, plus; **no** — **que,** only, no more than.

masculino, -a, masculine.

el **material,** material.

mayo *m.,* May.

mayor, greater, greatest; older, oldest (*of persons*).

la **mayoría,** majority; — **de,** most.

la **mayúscula,** capital letter.

la **media,** stocking, hose

mediante, by means of.

la **medicina,** medicine.

el **médico,** physician, doctor

la **medida,** measure.

medio, -a, half.

medir (i), to measure.

mejor, better, best.

mencionar, to mention.

menor, less, least; younger, youngest (*of persons*).

menos, less, least, minus; **a —
que,** unless; **al —, por lo —,**
at least.

menudo: a —, often.

el **mercado,** market.

el **mes,** month.

la **mesa,** table, desk.

meter (en), to put (in *or* into).

métrico, -a, metric.

México (*or* **Méjico**) *m.,* Mexico, City of Mexico.

el **miedo,** fear; **tengo —,** I am frightened.

mientras: — que, while, as long as.

el **miércoles,** Wednesday.

la **milla,** mile.

la **minúscula,** small letter, lower-case letter.

el **minuto,** minute.

mirar, to look at.

mismo, -a, same, self.

la **mitad,** half, middle.

m/o = mi orden.

la **moda,** fashion; **de —,** in fashion, fashionable.

el **modo,** manner, mode, mood, way; **de — que,** so as, so that; **de dos —s,** in two ways.

molestar, to trouble.

la **molestia,** trouble.

el **momento,** moment; **en este —,** at this moment.

la **moneda,** coin.

monetario, -a, monetary.

montar, to ride; **— a caballo,** to ride on horseback; **— en bicicleta,** to ride a bicycle.

el **montón,** heap, pile.

el **monumento,** monument, imposing public building.

morir (ue), to die.

el **moro,** Moor.

mortal, mortal.

mostrar (ue), to show.

el **motivo,** motive, object.

el **mozo,** servant-boy, waiter.

el **muchacho,** la **—a,** boy, girl; los **—s,** children.

muchísimo, -a *adj.,* **muchísimo** *adv.,* very much.

mucho, -a, much (many), "a lot of"; **—** *adv.,* much, a great deal, very; **trabaja —,** he works hard; **me agrada —,** it pleases me greatly.

mudo, -a, dumb, mute.

el **mueble,** piece of furniture; los **—s,** furniture.

el **muelle,** wharf, dock, pier.

la **mujer,** woman.

multiplicar, to multiply.

el **mundo,** world.

murmurar, to gossip.

la **música,** music.

la **mutación,** change.

muy, very; **— . . . para,** too **. . .** to.

N

nacer, to be born.

nada, nothing; **no . . . —,** not . . . anything.

nadar, to swim.

nadie, no one, nobody; **no . . . —,** not . . . anyone, not . . . anybody.

la **naranja,** orange.

la **nariz,** nose.

la **neblina,** fog.

necesario, -a, necessary.

necesitar (de), to need.

la **negación,** negation.

negar (ie), to deny.

negativo, –a, negative.
negro, –a, black.
nevar (ie), to snow.
ni, nor; ni . . . ni, neither . . . nor.
el nido, nest.
la nieve, snow.
ninguno, –a, no, none; no . . . —, not . . . any.
el niño, la —a, small boy, small girl; child; muy —, very much of a child.
el níquel, nickel (*metal*).
no, no, not.
la noche, night, evening (*after dark*); de —, at night; por (en) la —, in the evening, at night; esta —, to-night.
el nombre, name, noun.
norteamericano, –a, (North) American.
la noticia, news (item); las —s, news; ¿cuándo tuvo Vd. —s de él? when did you hear from him last?
la novedad, novelty, news; no hay —, all is well; sin —, without accident, all right.
noviembre *m.*, November.
nublado, –a, cloudy, overcast.
nuevo, –a, new; ¿qué hay de —? what is the news?
la nuez, (English) walnut.
el número, number.
nunca, never.

O

o, or; o . . . o, o bien . . . o, either . . . or.
el objeto, object.
la obra, work (*of literature, music, art, etc.*).
observar, to observe.
la ocasión, occasion, opportunity.
occidental, western.
octubre *m.*, October.

ocupado, –a, occupied, busy.
ocho, eight; — días, a week.
el oeste, west.
ofender, to offend.
el oficial, officer.
ofrecer, to offer.
el oído, (inner) ear, hearing.
oír §276, to hear.
ojalá, would that, I wish he (she, *etc.*) would.
el ojo, eye.
la ola, wave.
oler (hue–) §247, 2, to smell.
el olfato, sense of smell.
el olor, odor, smell.
olvidar, to forget; se me olvidó, I forgot.
la olla, pot.
omitir, to omit.
la onza, ounce.
la ópera, opera.
la oportunidad, opportunity.
la oración, prayer, sentence.
el orden, order (= *arrangement*); la —, order (*for goods; or a religious or military order*), command.
la oreja, ear.
el órgano, organ.
el oro, gold.
la ortografía, spelling, orthography.
ortográfico, –a, orthographic.
la oruga, caterpillar.
el otoño, autumn.
otorgar, to grant.
otro, –a, other, another.
la oveja, ewe, sheep.

P

Pablo, Paul.
el padre, father; los —s, parents.
pagar, to pay.
la página, page.
el pago, payment.
el país, country.

la **paja,** straw.

el **pájaro,** bird.

la **palabra,** word, speech.

el **palco,** box (*in theater*).

pálido, -a, pale.

la **pampa,** plain, prairie.

el **pan,** bread.

el **pantalón,** trousers.

el **paño,** cloth.

el **pañuelo,** handkerchief.

la **papa** (*Span. Am.*), potato.

el **papá,** papa, father.

el **papel,** paper.

el **paquete,** package, parcel.

el **par,** pair.

para, for, in order to, to; — **que,** in order that.

el **parangón,** comparison.

parar, to stop.

parecer, to appear, seem; ¿**qué le parece a Vd.?** what do you think about it? **si le parece a Vd.,** if you think best.

la **pared,** wall.

la **parte,** part; **la mayor —,** most; **a, en, por todas —s,** everywhere.

participar, to announce.

el **participio,** participle.

particular, especial, private.

partir (**de**), to leave, depart (from), crack, split.

pasado, -a, past, last (= *past*).

el **pasajero,** la **—a,** passenger.

pasar, to pass, come in, go (*to the blackboard*), spend (*time*).

pasearse, to walk, drive, *or* ride for pleasure, stroll.

pasivo, -a, passive; **en —a,** in the passive (voice).

la **pasta,** dough; **— de guayaba,** guava marmalade.

la **pata,** foot (*of an animal*), paw.

la **patata** (*in Spain*), potato.

el **patio,** (inner) courtyard, pit (*of theater*).

patronímico, -a: nombre —o, family name.

la **paz,** peace.

la **pechera,** (shirt) bosom, front.

el **pedido,** order (*of goods*).

pedir (i), to ask (for), request, order.

Pedro, Peter.

peinar, to comb.

el **pelo,** hair.

pensar (ie), to think, intend.

pequeño, -a, little, small.

percibir, to perceive, collect.

el **perdón,** pardon.

perdonar, to pardon, forgive.

perezoso, -a, indolent, lazy.

perfectamente, perfectly.

perfecto, -a, perfect.

el **periódico,** (news)paper.

permanecer, to remain.

permitir, to permit, let.

pero, but.

el **perro,** la **—a,** dog.

la **persona,** person.

la **pesa,** weight (*with which to weigh objects*).

pesar, to weigh.

el **pescado,** fish (*after being caught*).

pescar, to fish.

el **peso,** weight, dollar.

el **petróleo,** coal oil, petroleum, "kerosene."

el **pez,** (living) fish.

el **piano,** piano.

el **pie,** foot, leg (*of chair, etc.*); **ir a —,** to go afoot, walk.

la **piedra,** stone.

la **pieza,** piece, room.

la **pila,** baptismal font; **el nombre de —,** Christian *or* given name.

la **píldora,** pill.

la **pimienta,** pepper.

el **piso,** story, floor; — **alto,** upper story; — **bajo,** ground floor.

la **pizarra,** slate, (*slate*) blackboard.

el **placer,** pleasure.

planchar, to iron.

el **planeta,** planet.

la **planta,** plant, sole (*of foot*).

la **plata,** silver.

el **plátano,** banana.

el **plato,** plate, dish.

la **plaza,** public square, market place.

el **plazo,** time limit.

la **pluma,** feather, pen; — **estilográfica,** fountain pen.

la **plumafuente,** fountain pen.

el **pluscuamperfecto,** pluperfect.

pobre, poor.

poco, -a, little, (*pl.*) few; **un —** **de dinero,** a little money; **—o** *adv.,* little.

poder §270, to be able, can, **no puedo menos de hacerlo,** I can't help doing it.

el **poema,** poem.

la **poesía,** poetry, poem.

el **polvo,** dust; **—s dentífricos,** *o* **—s para los dientes,** toothpowder.

ponderal, of weight.

poner §265, to put, put on, set, lay (eggs); **—se,** to become, turn.

popularmente, popularly.

por, for, by, through, "per"; ¿**— qué?** why?

porque, because, for.

el **portamonedas,** purse, pocketbook.

el **porte,** transportation, postage.

poseer, to possess.

posesivo, -a, possessive.

posible, possible.

pospuesto, -a, placed after.

los **postres,** dessert.

ppdo = **próximo pasado** (*see* **próximo**).

preceder, to precede.

el **precio,** price.

preciso, -a, necessary.

preferir (ie), to prefer.

la **pregunta,** question.

preguntar, to ask (*a question*).

el **premio,** prize.

la **prenda de vestir,** article of clothing.

preparar, to prepare.

la **preposición,** preposition.

presentar, to present, offer.

presente, present; **con la —** (**carta**), herewith.

el **presidente,** president.

prestar, to lend, afford, show: **pedir (i) prestado,** to ask the loan of, borrow; **tomar prestado,** to borrow; **— atención,** to pay attention.

el **pretérito,** preterite.

la **primavera,** spring.

el **primo,** la **—a,** cousin; **primo hermano,** first cousin.

principal, main, principal.

principiar §243, to begin.

privar, to deprive (of).

la **probabilidad,** probability.

procurar, to attempt, try.

producir, to produce, create.

el **producto,** product.

el **profesor,** la **—a,** teacher, professor.

la **profundidad,** depth.

el **programa,** program.

prohibir, to forbid, prohibit.

prometer, to promise.

el **pronombre,** pronoun.

pronto, soon.

la **propina,** tip, gratuity.

propio, -a, proper, own; **— de,** peculiar to.

prosódico, -a: **acento —o,** vocal stress.

próximo, –a, next, approaching; — pasado, last (month).

publicar, to publish.

la puerta, door.

pues, well, as, well then, for.

la pulgada, inch.

el pulso, pulse.

el punto, point, period; — de admiración, exclamation mark; — de interrogación, interrogation mark; de —, promptly, exactly.

el puño, fist; cuff (*of sleeve*).

puro, –a, pure.

Q

Q. B. S. M. (P.), o Q. S. M. (P.) B. = que besa su mano (sus pies), o que su mano (sus pies) besa.

Q. E. S. M. = que estrecha su mano.

que *conj.*, that, for, than; con—, so that, so then.

que *rel. pron.*, that, who (whom), which; el (la, lo, los, las) —, who (whom), which.

¿qué? what? ¿a —? ¿para —? ¿por —? why? ¡—! what, what a, how!

quebrar (ie), to break; número quebrado, fraction.

quedar(se), to remain; —se con alguna cosa, to keep something.

quemar, to burn.

querer §271, to wish, want; — a, to be fond of, like (*a person*); yo quisiera, I should like to, I should be glad to; — decir, to mean.

querido, –a, dear, beloved.

el queso, cheese.

quien, –es, quién, –es *interrog.*, who (whom); de quién, whose.

quien(es)quiera, who(m)ever, who(m)soever.

quince, fifteen; — días, a fortnight, two weeks.

el quintal, hundredweight.

quitar, to take off, take away, strike off.

R

el radical, stem (*of a word*).

la raíz, root.

rápido, –a, rapid, express (train).

la raya, dash.

la raza, race, breed.

el real, "nickel" (*in Spain* = 25 *céntimos*), shilling, "bit" (*in Mexico, etc.* = 12½ *centavos*).

real, royal.

recibir, to receive.

el recibo, receipt, reception.

recitar, to recite.

el recuerdo, reminder, souvenir; los —s, regards.

reducido, –a, low (*price*).

reducir, to reduce.

reexpedir, to forward; a —, to be forwarded, please forward.

referirse, to refer.

reflexivo, –a, reflexive.

el régimen, government.

regir (i), to govern, take.

la regla, rule; por — general, as a rule.

regular, regular, ordinary, "fair."

reiterar, to reiterate, repeat.

el relámpago, flash of lightning; los —s, lightning.

relampaguear, to lighten.

religioso, –a, religious.

el reloj, clock, watch; — de mesa, de pared, clock; — de bolsillo, watch.

remediar §243, to help, remedy.

remedio, remedy, medicine.

el **remendar (ie)**, to mend.
la **remesa**, remittance.
remitir, to remit, send.
reparar, to repair.
repasar, to review.
repetir (i), to repeat.
requerir (ie), to require.
la **res**, quadruped, (*Span. Am.*) cattle.
el **resfriado**, cold (*disease*).
resfriarse, to catch cold.
el **respaldo**, back.
respecto de, with regard to.
el **respeto**, respect; los —s, regards.
responder, to answer.
la **respuesta**, answer.
el **restaurant**, restaurant.
el **resto**, rest, remainder.
el **resultado**, result.
resultar, to result, become; **resulta más barato**, it is cheaper.
el **resumen**, summary, résumé.
retirar, to retire, take out.
la **reverencia**, bow.
rico, –a, rich.
el **río**, river.
rogar (ue), to request.
rojo, –a, red.
romance, Romance (*derived from Latin*).
romper, to break, tear.
la **ropa**, clothes; — **interior**, underclothes; — **de cama**, bed linen.
roto, –a, torn.
el **rubí**, ruby.
rústico, –a, rustic; **en o a la rústica**, unbound, paper-covered.

S

S. S. S. = su seguro servidor o su segura servidora, your faithful servant.

el **sábado**, Saturday.
la **sábana**, sheet.
saber §268, to know, know how to, can; **a** —, namely, to wit; **que yo sepa**, so far as I know.
sabroso, –a, savory; **ser** —, to taste good.
sacar, to take out, draw (out), get (*a ticket*), get (out), hatch.
el **saco**, morning *or* business coat, "sack" coat.
el **sainete**, farce.
la **sal**, salt.
la **sala**, room, drawing room; — **de recibo**, reception room.
saldar, to balance, settle (*an account*).
el **saldo**, balance (*of account*).
salir §274, to go out, come out, leave, rise (*as the sun*); — **a la calle**, to go out into the street.
saltar, to jump (out), skip.
saludar, to salute, bow to.
salvo, except.
santo, –a, holy, saint.
el **sastre**, tailor.
la **sastrería**, tailor shop, "tailor's."
la **satisfacción**, satisfaction.
sea (*pres. subj. of* ser): ya — ... o, whether it be ... or.
secar, to dry.
seco, –a, dry.
la **sed**, thirst; **tengo** —, I am thirsty.
la **seda**, silk.
la **seguida**, continuation; **en** —, next, then, immediately.
seguir (i), to follow, continue, go on; — **derecho**, to go straight ahead; **¿qué tal sigue Vd.?** how are you getting on?

según, according to.
segundo, -a, second.
seguro, -a, sure; **su — servidor,** your faithful servant.
el **sello,** stamp; **— de correo, — postal,** postage stamp.
la **semana,** week.
sentar (ie), to seat, set, fit; **—se,** to seat oneself, be seated, sit, sit down.
el **sentido,** sense.
sentir (ie), to feel, regret; **me siento débil,** I feel weak.
señalar, to point out, call attention to, show, indicate.
el **señor,** gentleman, sir, Mr.; Señor, Lord; la **—a,** lady, madam, Mrs.; los **—es,** gentlemen, sirs, gentlemen and ladies, Mr. and Mrs.; **muy — mío,** my dear sir; **su —a madre de Vd.,** your mother.
el **señorito,** young gentleman, sir, Master; la **señorita,** young lady, madam, Miss.
septiembre *m.,* September.
ser §259, to be; el **—,** being.
el **servicio,** service.
el **servidor,** la **—ora,** servant.
la **servilleta,** napkin.
servir (i), to serve; **sirve bastante bien,** it does pretty well; **no sirve para nada,** it is good for nothing; **—se,** to be pleased (*to do something*); **sírvase Vd.,** please; **—se de,** to use; **— de,** to serve as.
Sevilla, *f.,* Seville.
si, if, why, indeed.
sí, yes, indeed.
siempre, always; **— que,** whenever, provided that.
la **sierra,** mountain range, mountains.
el **siglo,** century.

el **significado,** meaning, significance.
el **signo,** sign, mark.
siguiente, following, next.
la **sílaba,** syllable.
la **silla,** chair, saddle.
el **sillón,** armchair.
simpático, -a, likable, pleasant, charming.
simple, single, simple.
sin, without; **— embargo,** nevertheless.
sino, but; **no . . . —,** only.
la **sinopsis,** synopsis, résumé.
el **sitio,** site, place.
el **sobre,** envelope.
sobre *prep.,* on, upon.
sobrentenderse, to be understood (*not expressed*).
el **sobrino,** la **—a,** nephew, niece.
el **sol,** sun, sunshine; **hace —,** the sun is shining.
solo, —a, alone.
sólo, only.
la **sombrerería,** hat shop, hatter's.
el **sombrerero,** hatter, dealer in hats.
el **sombrero,** hat.
el **sonido,** sound.
la **sopa,** soup.
soportar, to endure, support.
sordo, -a, deaf.
sorprender, to surprise.
el **sótano,** basement.
subido, -a, high.
subir, to go up, come up, ascend, climb.
el **subjuntivo,** subjunctive.
subordinado, -a, subordinate, dependent.
subrayar, to underline.
subscribir, to subscribe, sign.
la **subscripción,** subscription.
substantivado, -a, substantive.
substituir, to replace.

suceder, to happen; — **con,** to be true of.

sucesivamente, successively.

sucio, -a, dirty.

la **suela,** sole (*of a shoe*).

el **suelo,** ground, floor.

suelto, -a, loose, single.

sufrir, to suffer, undergo.

el **sujeto,** subject.

la **suma,** sum.

sumamente, greatly, exceedingly.

la **superficie,** surface.

suplicar, to beg (*a favor*).

suponer §265, to suppose, assume.

la **supresión,** suppression, omission.

supuesto: por —, of course.

el **sur,** south.

el **surtido,** supply, stock.

T

el **tabaco,** tobacco.

la **tabla,** board, plank.

la **tablilla,** tablet, shingle.

tal, such, such a; **con — que,** provided that; **¿qué tal (sigue)?** how are you (getting on)?

el **tamaño,** size.

también, also, too.

tampoco, neither, nor; **no (ni) . . . —,** not (nor) . . . either.

tan, so.

tanto(s), as (so) much (many); **en — que,** while; **otro —,** the same thing; **tanto . . . como,** both . . . as.

la **tardanza,** delay.

tardar, to delay; **no tardará en volver,** it will not be long before he returns.

la **tarde,** afternoon; **por o en la —,** in the afternoon; *adv.,* late.

la **tarifa,** scale of prices, fare.

la **tarjeta,** card; — **postal,** post(al) card; — **de visita,** visiting card.

la **taza,** cup.

el **te,** tea.

el **teatro,** theater.

el **techo,** roof, ceiling.

el **tejamaní o tejamanil** (*Span. Am.*), (wooden) shingle.

telefonear, to telephone.

el **teléfono,** telephone.

el **telegrama,** telegram.

el **telón,** curtain (*of theater*).

el **tema,** theme, written exercise, composition.

temer, to fear.

la **temperatura,** temperature.

el **templo,** temple, church.

temprano, early.

el **tenedor,** fork.

tener §258, to have; — **que,** to have to, must; **tengo frío (calor, sueño,** *etc.*), I am cold (warm, sleepy, *etc.*); **¿qué tiene Vd.?** what is the matter with you? **no tengo nada,** there is nothing the matter with me.

Teresa, Theresa.

la **terminación,** ending.

terminar, to end, terminate.

el **término,** term, expression.

el **termómetro,** thermometer.

el **terreno,** land.

tibio, -a, lukewarm.

el **tiempo,** time, tense, weather; **mucho —,** a long time.

la **tienda,** shop, store. [of scissors.

las **tijeras,** scissors; **unas —,** a pair

la **tinta,** ink.

tinto, -a, red (*of wine*).

el **tío, la —a,** uncle, aunt.

el **tiro,** throw, pull; **caballo de —,** driving horse, draught horse.

la **tiza,** chalk.

la **toalla,** towel.

el **tocador,** dressing-table, "dresser."

tocar, to touch, play (*a musical instrument*).

todavía, yet, still.

todo, -a, all, every; *n.*, everything; —**s los días,** every day; **por** —, altogether.

tomar, to take.

el **tomo,** volume.

la **tonelada,** ton.

la **tormenta,** storm.

trabajar, to work.

el **trabajo,** work.

traducir §278, to translate.

traer §277, to bring.

la **tragedia,** tragedy.

traidor, -ora, treacherous.

el **traje,** suit (*of clothes*).

tranquilo, -a, calm, tranquil.

el **tranvía,** street car, tramway.

tratar de, to try (to), refer (to).

la **travesía,** passage.

el **tren,** train.

el **trigo,** wheat.

trigueño, -a, dark-complexioned.

triste, sad, gloomy.

tronar (ue), to thunder.

el **trueno,** thunder.

U

u, or.

último, -a, last (*in a series*).

la **unidad,** unity.

unir, to join, unite.

la **universidad,** university.

uno, -a, one; —**s,** some.

usar, to use, wear, wear out.

útil, useful.

V

la **vaca,** cow; **carne de** —, beef.

las **vacaciones,** vacation(s).

valer §273, to be worth.

el **valor,** worth, courage.

vamos (*pres. indic. and imperat. of* ir), we go, let us go.

el **vapor,** steam, steamboat.

la **vara,** yard (= *32 inches*).

variable, variable, changeable.

la **variación,** change, variation.

variar § 243, to vary; — **de,** to change, vary in.

la **variedad,** variety; **teatro de** —**es,** vaudeville theater.

varios, -as, several.

el **vaso,** (drinking-)glass.

el **vecino, la** —**a,** neighbor.

la **vela,** candle, sail.

vender, to sell.

venir §264, to come; **la semana que viene,** next week.

la **ventana,** window.

ver §279, to see; **véase,** see.

el **verano,** summer.

verbigracia (*Lat.*), for instance.

el **verbo,** verb.

la **verdad,** truth; **¿no es verdad?** o **¿verdad?** isn't it so? **¡en verdad que estoy cansado!** my, but I'm tired!

verdadero, -a, true.

verde, green.

la **verdura,** fresh (*green*) vegetable.

verificarse, to be held, occur.

el **vestido,** dress; **los** —**s,** clothes.

vestirse (i), to dress (*oneself*).

la **vez,** time; **una** —, once; **dos veces,** twice; **tres veces,** three times; **a veces, algunas veces,** sometimes; **en** — **de,** instead of; **otra** —, again; **de** — **en cuando,** from time to time; **hacer las veces de,** to serve as; **rara** —, rarely.

el **viaje,** trip, voyage; **de** —, traveling.

el **viajero, la** —**a,** traveler, passenger (*on train*).

la **vida,** life.

viejo, –a, old.

el **viento,** wind.

el **viernes,** Friday.

vigilar, to watch over, guard.

el **vigor,** vigor.

el **vinagre,** vinegar.

el **vino,** wine.

la **visita,** visit.

visitar, to visit, call on.

la **vista,** sight.

vistoso, –a, bright, showy.

vivir, to live.

el **vocablo,** word.

el **vocabulario,** vocabulary.

la **vocal,** vowel.

el **volumen,** volume.

volver (ue) §245, 4, to turn, return; — a hacer alguna cosa, to do something again; —se, to become.

la **voz,** voice, word.

la **vuelta,** turn, return; **está de —,** he has returned, he is back; **a — de correo,** by return mail; **dar la —,** to turn; **dar una —,** to make a turn, revolve.

vulgarmente, vulgarly.

Y

y, and.

ya, already, now, in due time, indeed; **ya . . . no,** no . . . longer, no . . . more; **ya que,** since.

Z

el **zaguán,** vestibule, passageway.

la **zapatería,** shoe shop, shoe store.

el **zapatero,** shoemaker, dealer in shoes.

la **zapatilla,** slipper.

el **zapato,** shoe; **— de goma (hule),** rubber overshoe, "golosh."

la **zarzuela,** operetta, musical comedy.

GENERAL VOCABULARY
ENGLISH–SPANISH

A
able: be —, poder (ue).
aboard, a bordo (de).
about, cerca de, como, cosa de.
abundant, abundante; **be —,** abundar.
accept, aceptar.
accompany, acompañar.
according to, según.
account, cuenta.
accusative, acusativo.
acknowledge, acusar.
acquaintance, conocido, –a; **make the — of,** conocer.
acquainted: be — with, conocer.
acre: 1⅔ —s, fanega de tierra.
acrobat, el *o* la acróbata.
actress, la actriz.
add, añadir.
address, la dirección.
adjective, adjetivo.
admiration, la admiración.
admission, entrada.
adopt, adoptar.
adoration, la adoración.
advance: in —, anticipado, –a.
adverb, adverbio.
advertisement, anuncio.
advise, aconsejar.
affection, cariño.
affectionately, afectuosamente; **most —,** afectísimo, –a.
afford, prestar.
afraid: be —, tener miedo.
after, después de, después que.
afternoon, la tarde; **in the —,** en *o* por la tarde.

afterwards, después.
again, otra vez; **do something —,** volver (ue) a hacer alguna cosa.
against, contra.
aged, anciano, –a.
agent, el agente; **ticket —,** agente de billetes, boletero (*Span. Am.*).
agitated, agitado, –a.
ago: a week —, hace ocho días.
agree, concertar (ie).
agreeable, agradable.
agreement, concordancia.
air, el aire.
alcove, alcoba.
alight, bajar(se).
all, todo, –a; **— is well,** no hay novedad; **— who,** **— that,** cuanto, –a.
allow, dejar, permitir.
almost, casi; **he — fell,** poco faltó para que se cayera.
alone, solo, –a.
already, ya.
also, también.
although, aunque.
altogether, por todo.
always, siempre.
American, americano, –a; (*of U. S. A.*) norteamericano, –a, estadounidense, yanqui.
among, entre.
amount, el importe, la cantidad; **— to,** ascender (ie) a, importar.
amuse, divertir (ie).
and, y, e (*before i– or hi–*).
angry (with), enojado, –a (con); **become —,** enojarse, enfadarse.

Anna, Ana.

announce, anunciar, participar.

another, otro, –a.

answer *v.*, contestar, responder; *noun*, respuesta.

any, alguno (algún), –a; — **one,** alguien; — **one (at all),** cual(es)quiera.

anybody, alguien.

anything, algo, alguna cosa; **not** —, no . . . nada.

appear, aparecer, parecer, figurarse; **it —s to me,** me parece, se me figura.

appetite, apetito; **have an — for,** apetecer.

apple, manzana.

approaching, próximo, –a.

approval, la conformidad.

approximately, aproximadamente.

April, abril *m.*

Arab, el *o* la árabe.

architect, arquitecto.

are (= *100 square meters*), área.

Argentine, argentino, –a.

arid, árido, –a.

arise, levantarse.

arithmetic, aritmética.

arm, brazo.

armchair, el sillón.

aroma, el aroma.

arrange, arreglar.

arrive, llegar.

article, artículo; — **of clothing,** prenda de vestir; — **of food,** el manjar.

artist, el *o* la artista.

as, como, tan, pues; — . . . —, tan . . . como.

ascend, subir.

ask (*a favor*), pedir (i), rogar (ue); — (*a question*), preguntar; — **the loan of,** pedir prestado.

assure, asegurar; **be —d (that),** contar (ue) con (que).

at, a, en.

attempt, procurar.

attend, asistir.

attention, la atención.

attorney, abogado.

August, agosto.

aunt, tía.

author, el autor, la autora.

automobile, el automóvil.

autumn, otoño.

avoid, evitar.

await, aguardar.

awaken, despertarse (ie).

axe, el hacha, *f.*

B

back (*of chair*), respaldo, (*of check*) dorso; **be back,** estar de vuelta.

bad, malo, –a; **it is too —,** es (una) lástima.

badly, mal.

baggage, el equipaje; — **room,** sala de equipaje.

bake, cocer (ue).

balance (*of account*), saldo; **there is a — in my favor,** arroja un saldo a mi favor; — (*an account*), *v.*, saldar.

balcony (*before a window*), el balcón; (*in theater*) galería *o* anfiteatro.

bald, calvo, –a.

banana, plátano.

bank, banco.

banker, banquero.

basement, sótano, subterráneo.

bath, baño; — **tub,** baño, bañadera (*Arg.*), tina de baño (*Mex.*); **take a —,** bañarse; —**room,** cuarto de baño.

bathe, bañarse.

be, estar §260, ser §259.

because, porque.

become, ponerse §265.

bed, cama; —**room,** *see* **bedroom.**

bedroom, dormitorio, alcoba (*Spain*), recámara (*Mex.*).

beef, la carne de vaca (*o* de res).
before *prep.* (*position*), ante, delante de, en frente de; (*time*) antes de; *conj.*, antes que.
beg (*a favor*), suplicar, pedir.
begin, empezar (ie), principiar.
behind, detrás de.
believe, creer.
beloved, querido, -a, amado, -a.
below, debajo de.
berth, litera, cama.
besides, además (de).
best, mejor.
better, mejor; **I am —,** me hallo mejor.
between, entre.
bicycle, bicicleta.
big, grande.
bill, cuenta, factura; **— of exchange,** letra de cambio; **— of fare,** lista (de platos).
bind, encuadernar.
bird, pájaro.
biscuit, bizcocho, galleta (*Span. Am.*).
bitter, amargo, -a.
black, negro, -a.
blackboard, pizarra, el pizarrón.
blanket, frazada, manta (*Spain*).
blind, ciego, -a.
blot, el borrón.
blouse, blusa.
blue, azul.
board, tabla.
boarding-house, casa de huéspedes.
boat, el buque.
boil, hervir (ie); **—** (*food*) cocer (ue).
book, libro.
bookstore, librería.
boot, bota; **riding —,** bota de montar.
born: be —, nacer.
borrow, pedir (i) prestado, tomar prestado.

both, ambos, -as, los *o* las dos.
bottle, botella.
bow, reverencia; *v.*, inclinarse; **— to,** saludar a
box, caja; **little —,** cajita; (*in theater*), palco.
boy, muchacho; **little —,** niño; **—'s coat,** chaqueta.
brazier, brasero.
Brazil, el Brasil.
bread, el pan.
breadth, anchura.
break *v.*, quebrar (ie).
breakfast, (*early*) desayuno, (*late*) almuerzo; *v.*, desayunarse, almorzar (ue).
breed, raza.
brick, ladrillo.
bright, claro, -a, vistoso, -a; **bright-colored,** vistoso, -a.
bring, traer §277, llevar.
broad, ancho, -a.
brother, hermano; **—s and sisters,** hermanos.
brush, cepillo; *v.*, cepillar *o* acepillar.
build, construir.
building, edificio.
bulk, grueso.
bulky, grueso, -a.
burn, quemar.
bushel: 1½ —s, fanega.
business, negocio, comercio.
busy, ocupado, -a.
but, mas, pero, sino, no . . . sino.
butter, mantequilla (*Span. Am.*), manteca de vaca (*Spain*).
buy, comprar.
by, por, de.

C

call *v.*, llamar; **— on,** visitar.
calm, tranquilo, -a.
can *v.*, poder §270, (= *know how*) saber §268.
Canada, el Canadá.

candle, vela.
canvas, lona.
cap, gorra.
capacity, la capacidad.
captain, el capitán.
card, tarjeta; **post(al) —,** tarjeta postal; **visiting —,** tarjeta de visita.
care, cuidado; **take — of,** cuidar; **take —,** tenga Vd. cuidado; **in — of,** a (en) casa de; **— for,** cuidar.
careful: be —, tener cuidado.
Caroline, Carolina.
carpenter, carpintero.
carriage, el coche.
carry, llevar.
case, caso.
cash: for —, al contado; *v.*, cobrar, hacer efectivo.
cast *v.*, arrojar, echar.
Castile, Castilla.
Castilian, castellano, –a.
catalogue, catálogo.
catch *v.*, coger; **— cold,** resfriarse.
caterpillar, oruga.
cattleraiser, ganadero.
ceiling, techo.
celebrate, celebrar.
cent, centavo.
center, centro.
centime *(100 —s = 1 peseta),* céntimo.
centimeter, centímetro.
century, siglo.
ceremony, ceremonia.
certainty: with —, fijamente.
chair, silla.
chalk, tiza, yeso, el gis *(Mex.).*
change, cambio, la variación.
changeable, variable.
chapter, capítulo.
charcoal, el carbón (de leña).
charge *v.*, cargar.
Charles, Carlos.
charming, simpático, –a.

chase, caza.
cheap, barato, –a.
check, el cheque.
cheese, queso.
chest of drawers, cómoda.
chiffonnier, cómoda.
child, niño, –a; **very much of a —,** muy niño, –a; **children** (= *sons and daughters*), hijos.
Chilean, chileno, –a.
chin, barba.
chocolate, el chocolate.
choose, escoger.
Christian, cristiano, –a; **— name,** el nombre de bautismo *o* de pila.
Christopher, Cristóbal.
church, iglesia, templo.
city, la poblacion, la ciudad.
clasp *(someone's hand)* *v.*, estrechar.
class, la clase; **—room,** la clase; **Spanish —,** clase de español.
classic, clásico, –a.
clause, cláusula.
clean *v.*, limpiar; *adj.*, limpio, –a.
clear, claro, –a.
clerk, el dependiente.
climate, el clima.
climb *v.*, subir.
clock, el reloj (de pared).
close *v.*, cerrar (ie).
cloth, paño.
clothes, ropa.
cloudy, nublado, –a.
coach, el coche.
coal, el carbón de piedra; **— oil,** petróleo.
coat: frock —, levita; **morning** or **business —,** americana, saco; **evening** or **dress —,** el frac; **boy's —,** chaqueta.
coffee, el café.
coin, moneda.
cold, *(a disease)* resfriado; *adj.*, frío, –a; **be –,** tener frío; **it is —,** hace frío.

collar, cuello.
collect, cobrar, percibir.
collection, la colección.
color, el color.
Columbus, Colón.
comb v., peinar.
come, venir §264; — in, pasar;
— into, entrar en; — out,
salir; — up, subir; — with,
acompañar.
comedy, comedia; musical —, zarzuela.
comfortable, cómodo, -a.
command v., mandar.
commerce, comercio.
common: be —, abundar.
company, compañía.
comparison, la comparación.
compartment, compartimiento, departamento.
complete v., completar; adj., completo, -a.
compose, componer §265.
composition, el tema.
comprehend, comprender.
conditional, condicional.
conformity, la conformidad.
conjugation, la conjugación.
consist (of), consistir (en).
contain, contener §258; be —ed,
caber § 269.
context, contexto.
continuation, la continuación, seguida.
continue, continuar, seguir (i).
contrary, contrario, -a; on the —,
al contrario, por el contrario.
convenience, la comodidad.
convenient, cómodo, -a.
cook, cocinero, -a; v., guisar, cocinar.
cooking, cocina.
cool, fresco, -a.
copper, el cobre.
copy (of a book, etc.), el ejemplar.
cordially, cordialmente.

corner, esquina.
correct, exacto, -a, correcto, -a.
correctly, correctamente.
correspond, corresponder.
cost v., costar (ue).
cotton, el algodón.
count v., contar (ue); — on, contar con.
country, el país; (as distinguished
from the city) campo.
courage, el valor.
course: of —, por supuesto.
court, la corte; (inner) — yard,
patio.
courteous, cortés.
cousin, primo, -a; first —, primo
hermano, prima hermana.
cover v., cubrir (p.p. cubierto).
cow, vaca.
crack v., partir.
"cracker," galleta.
cravat, corbata.
create, producir.
credit, crédito; v., abonar
crisis, la crisis.
critical, crítico, -a.
cross v., atravesar.
crow v., cantar.
cry v., llorar.
cubic, cúbico, -a.
cuff (of sleeve), puño.
cultivate, cultivar.
cup, taza.
current, corriente.
curtain (of theater), el telón.

D

daily adj., diario, -a; adv., al día,
por día.
dark, obscuro, -a; — -complex-
ioned, trigueño, -a.
dash, raya.
date, fecha; v., fechar.
dative, dativo.
daughter, hija.
day, el día; good — ! ¡buenos días!

deaf, sordo, –a.
dear, caro, –a, querido, –a; my —
Sir, muy señor mío.
debit, debe.
deceive, engañar.
December, diciembre m.
decimeter, decímetro.
deck (of a ship), cubierta.
deep, hondo, –a.
definite, determinado, –a, definido, –a
degree, grado.
delay, tardanza; v., tardar (en).
deliver, entregar.
demand v., exigir.
demonstrative, demostrativo, –a.
deny, negar (ie).
depart (from), partir (de).
dependent, subordinado, –a.
deprive (of), privar.
depth, la profundidad.
" derby " (hat), hongo.
descend, bajar(se).
desire v., desear.
desk, escritorio, mesa.
dessert, los postres.
die, morir (ue).
diet, dieta.
different, diferente.
difficult, difícil.
difficulty, la dificultad.
digit, dígito.
diligent, aplicado, –a.
dine, comer.
dining car, el cochecomedor.
dining room, el comedor.
dinner, comida (principal); have
—, comer.
diploma, el diploma.
direct v., dirigir.
direction, la dirección; –s, advertencias.
director, el director, la directora.
dirty, sucio, –a.
disagreeable, desagradable.
disappear, desaparecer.

discount, descuento.
discover, descubrir.
dish, plato.
distance, distancia.
divide, dividir.
do, hacer §266; it does pretty well,
sirve bastante bien.
dock, el muelle.
doctor, médico.
dog, perro, –a.
dollar, duro (Spain), peso (Span.
Am.); (of U. S. A.) el dólar.
domestic servant, criado, –a.
door, puerta.
dose, la dosis.
double v., doblar.
doubt, duda; v., dudar.
dough, pasta.
dozen, docena.
draft, giro, el cheque.
draught horse, caballo de tiro.
draw (out), sacar.
dress, vestido; — coat, el frac;
— suit, el traje de etiqueta;
v., vestir (i); — oneself, vestirse (i).
dressing table, "dresser," el tocador.
drive v., ir o pasearse en coche o
automóvil.
driving horse, caballo de tiro.
dry, seco, –a, árido, –a; v., secar.
duck (cloth), el dril.
dumb, mudo, –a.
during, durante.
dust, polvo.

E

each, cada; — one, cada uno.
ear, oreja; inner —, oído.
early adj., temprano, –a; adv.,
temprano.
earn, ganar.
east, el este.
easy, fácil.
eat, comer.

edition, la edición.
effect *v.*, efectuar.
egg, huevo.
either . . . or, o . . . o.
electric, eléctrico, –a.
elegant, de lujo, elegante.
elevator, el ascensor, el elevador (*Mex.*).
Elizabeth, Isabel.
Emily, Emilia.
employment, empleo.
enclosed *adj.*, adjunto, –a; *adv.*, adjunto.
encounter *v.*, encontrar (ue).
end *v.*, terminar.
endorse, endosar.
endure, durar, soportar.
enemy, enemigo, –a.
engagement, compromiso.
England, Inglaterra.
English, inglés, –esa.
Englishman, inglés; Englishwoman, inglesa.
enjoy, divertirse (ie) con; — oneself, divertirse.
enough, bastante.
enter (into), entrar (en *o* a).
entire, entero, –a, íntegro, –a.
entrance, entrada.
envelope, el sobre.
equal, igual.
equally, igualmente.
equivalent, equivalente; be —, equivaler §273.
erase, borrar.
eraser, el borrador, cepillo.
err, errar (ye–).
error, el error.
especial, particular.
esteemed: highly —, estimable, estimado, –a.
etc., etc. (= et cetera).
etiquette, etiqueta.
even, aun; — if, aunque.
evening (*before dark*), la tarde; (*after dark*) la noche; in the —,

por *o* en la noche; — coat, el frac; — clothes, el traje de etiqueta.
every (one), todo, –a; — day, todos los días; — two days, cada dos días.
everybody, todo el mundo.
everything, todo.
everywhere, a, en, por todas partes.
exact, exacto, –a.
exactly (*of time*), al punto.
example, ejemplo.
exceedingly, sumamente.
excellent, excelente.
except, excepto.
exclamation mark, signo de admiración.
excuse *v.*, dispensar, excusar, perdonar.
execute, ejecutar.
exercise, ejercicio; — book, cuaderno; take —, hacer ejercicio; written —, el tema.
expectation, espera.
expensive, caro, –a.
explain, explicar.
express, expreso, –a; — train, el tren expreso *o* rápido.
extract, extracto.
eye, ojo.

F

face, cara; *v.*, dar a.
fail: not — to, no dejar de.
fair (*as price, etc.*), regular.
faithful, fiel; your — servant, S. S. S. (= su seguro servidor).
fall *v.*, caer §275.
family, familia; — name, apellido.
far, lejos; how — is it? ¿cuánto
farce, el sainete. [hay?
fare, tarifa. [hasta luego.
farewell, adiós; — for a while,
farm: large —, hacienda; — hand, — laborer, labrador, –ora.

farmer, el agricultor, hacendado.

fashion, moda; **be in —,** estar de moda.

fashionable, de moda.

fast, aprisa.

fat, gordo, –a.

father, padre, papá.

fault, culpa; **it is not my —,** no es mía la culpa; **it is your —,** Vd. tiene la culpa.

favor, el favor; **your —** (= *letter*), su apreciable carta.

fear, miedo; *v.,* temer, tener miedo.

feather, pluma.

February, febrero.

feed, dar de comer.

feel, sentir (ie); **I — weak,** me siento débil.

felt, fieltro.

feminine, femenino, –a.

Ferdinand, Fernando.

fever, la fiebre.

few, a —, pocos, –as, unos (–as) cuantos (–as).

field, campo.

fill, llenar; **—** (*an order*), ejecutar.

find, hallar, encontrar.

finish *v.,* acabar; **I have —ed,** ya acabé; **it's —ed,** se acabó; **he —ed speaking,** acabó de hablar.

fire, fuego, la lumbre; **—place,** chimenea, (*for cooking*) el fogón; **—wood,** leña.

fish (*living*), el pez; (*after being caught*) pescado.

fist, puño.

fit *v.,* caer §275, sentar (ie).

flee, huir.

flesh, la carne.

flexible, flexible.

floor, piso, suelo; **ground —,** piso bajo.

flower, la flor.

fog, neblina.

follow, seguir (i); **—ing,** siguiente.

fond (of), aficionado, –a (a); **be — of** (*a person*), querer (a) §271.

food (*prepared*), comida.

foot, el pie, (*of an animal*) pata.

for, para, por; *conj.,* porque, que, pues.

forbid, prohibir.

forehead, la frente.

forget, olvidar; **I forgot,** se me olvidó.

fork, el tenedor.

fortnight, quince días.

forward *v.,* reexpedir (i); **please —, to be —ed,** a reexpedir.

fountain pen: *see* **pen.**

fraction, número quebrado.

Frances, Francisca.

Francis, Francisco.

freeze, helar (ie), congelarse.

French, francés, –esa.

Frenchman, francés; **Frenchwoman,** francesa.

fresh, fresco, –a; **— water** (*distinguished from salt water*), agua dulce.

Friday, el viernes.

fried, frito, –a.

friend, amigo, –a.

frighten, asustar.

frightened: to be —, asustarse, tener miedo.

from, de, desde.

front, el frente; **in — of,** en frente de.

fruit, fruta(s).

fulfil, cumplir.

full, lleno, –a.

fun: make — of, burlarse de.

furnace, horno; **central —** (*to warm a building*), calorífero *o* estufa central, caldera (= *boiler*).

furniture, los muebles; **piece of —,** el mueble.

future, futuro, –a.

G

gallery, galería.

garden, huerta, jardín.

gas, el gas.

gender, género.

genitive, genitivo.

gentle, manso, –a.

gentleman, caballero, señor; **young —,** señorito; **gentlemen and ladies,** señores.

get, conseguir (i), obtener §258; **—** (= *take out*), sacar; **how are you —ting on?** ¿qué tal sigue Vd.? **— out** (*of train, etc.*), bajar(se); **— up,** levantarse; **go and —,** ir a buscar.

girl, muchacha; **little —,** niña.

give, dar §263, conceder, dispensar; **—** (*a play*), *see* **perform; given name,** el nombre de bautismo *o* de pila.

glad, contento, –a; **be —** (**of**), alegrarse (de), celebrar; **I should be — to,** quisiera.

glass (= *drinking- —*), vaso.

gloomy, triste.

glove, el guante.

go, andar §262, ir §261, dirigirse; **— afoot,** ir a pie; **— in** or **into,** entrar en; **— on,** continuar, seguir (i); **— out,** salir §274; **— out into the street,** salir a la calle; **— up,** subir; **— with,** acompañar a; **— and get,** ir a buscar; **— to bed,** acostarse (ue); **let us —,** vamos.

gold, oro.

golosh, chanclo.

good, bueno, –a; **he (it,** *etc.*) **is — for nothing,** no sirve para nada.

goodbye, adiós.

goodness, la bondad.

goods, género(s).

gossip *v.,* murmurar, referir chismes.

grain, grano.

grammar, gramática.

gramme, gramo.

grandfather, abuelo.

grandmother, abuela.

grandparents, abuelos.

grant *v.,* conceder, otorgar, dispensar; **—ed that,** dado que.

grateful, agradecido, –a; **be — for,** agradecer.

great, grande; **a — deal,** mucho; **—er,** más grande, mayor.

greatly, sumamente.

green, verde.

ground, suelo.

grow, crecer; **be —ing,** ir creciendo; *trans.,* cultivar, producir.

guard *v.,* vigilar.

guava, guayaba.

guest, huésped, –eda.

guide, el *o* la guía.

H

hair (*of the head*), cabellos (*pl.*), pelo.

half *adj.,* medio, –a; *noun,* la mitad; **— -hose,** el calcetín.

hand, la mano; **on the other —,** por el contrario; **— bag,** maleta; *v.,* entregar.

handkerchief, pañuelo.

handsome, hermoso, –a.

happy, feliz.

hard, duro, –a, difícil; **"— up,"** apurado, –a; **he works —,** trabaja mucho.

hardly, apenas.

haste: make — (to), apresurarse (a).

hat, sombrero.

hatch *v.,* sacar.

hatter, sombrerero; **—'s** (= *hat shop*), sombrerería.

Havana, la Habana.

have, haber §257, tener §258; **— to** (= *must*), tener que; **—**

something made or **done**, mandar hacer alguna cosa.

head, cabeza; **—ache,** el dolor de cabeza.

hear, oír §276; **when did you — from him?** ¿cuándo tuvo Vd. noticias de él?

hearing, oído.

heat, el calor.

hectare, hectárea (= *about 2½ acres*).

height, altura.

help *v.*, ayudar, remediar, evitar; **I can't — doing it,** no puedo menos de hacerlo.

hen, gallina; **a — is sitting,** una gallina está echada.

Henry, Enrique.

here, aquí, acá. [presente (carta).

herewith, adjunto (–a), con la

hide, cuero.

high, alto, –a; (*in price*)subido, –a.

historic(al), histórico, –a.

history, historia.

hold *v.*, caber § 269; **how much does the box —?** ¿cuánto cabe en la caja? **be held,** verificarse.

holy, santo, –a.

home, casa, a casa; **at —,** en casa.

homely, feo, –a.

hope *v.*, esperar.

horse, caballo.

horseman, el jinete.

hose, media.

hot, caliente.

hotel, el hotel.

hour, hora.

house, casa.

how, como; *interrog.*, cómo; **— much (many),** cuánto, –a (–os, –as); **— pretty!** ¡qué bonito, –a!

hundredweight, el quintal.

hunger, el hambre (*f.*).

hungry: be —, tener hambre.

hunting, caza; **go —,** ir a caza.

hurt *v.*, lastimar.

husband, esposo, marido.

hypothetic, hipotético, –a.

I

identify, identificar.

if, si.

ill, enfermo, –a; **be —,** estar malo, –a.

illness, la enfermedad.

illustrate, ilustrar.

immortal, inmortal.

imperative, imperativo, –a.

imperfect, imperfecto, –a.

importance, importancia.

important, importante; **be —,** importar.

imposing: — public building, monumento.

in, en.

inch, pulgada.

include, comprender, incluir.

indeed, sí, si, ya.

indefinite, indeterminado, –a, indefinido, –a.

Indian, indio, –a; **— corn,** el maíz.

indicate, indicar.

indicative, indicativo.

indolent, perezoso, –a.

industrious, aplicado, –a.

infinite, infinito, –a.

infinitive, infinitivo.

inflection, la inflexión.

inform, manifestar (ie).

inhabit, habitar.

inhabitant, el *o* la habitante.

ink, tinta.

inn, el hotel.

inside, adentro.

insist (on), exigir.

instance, ejemplo.

instant *adj.*, actual, corriente.

instead of, en vez de.

instruct, instruir.

instructions, advertencias.

insure, asegurar.

intelligent, inteligente.

intend, pensar (ie).
interesting, interesante.
interrogative, interrogativo, –a.
intimate, íntimo, –a.
into, en.
inverted, invertido, –a.
invitation, la invitación.
invite, invitar.
iron, hierro; v., planchar.
Italian, italiano, –a.
Italy, Italia.
itemize, detallar.

J

jacket, chaqueta.
January, enero.
Japan, el Japón.
John, Juan.
Johnny, Juanito.
join, juntar.
joke, broma.
jug, jarro.
July, julio.
jump (out), saltar.
just: I have — done it, acabo de hacerlo; he had — spoken, acababa de hablar.

K

keep, guardar, conservar; — on, seguir (i); — something, quedarse con alguna cosa.
kerosene, petróleo.
key, la llave.
kid, cabritilla.
kilo, see kilogramme.
kilogramme, kilogramo.
kilometer, kilómetro.
kind, la clase, la especie; adj., bondadoso, –a, grato, –a.
kindness, la bondad.
kiss v., besar.
kitchen, cocina; (modern iron) — range or stove, cocina económica.
kitten, gatito, –a.

knee-breeches, los calzones, los pantalones cortos.
knife, cuchillo.
knock v., llamar.
know, saber §268, conocer; so far as I —, que yo sepa; — how (to), saber.

L

lack, falta; v., faltar; I —, me falta, me hace falta.
lady, señora; young —, señorita.
lake, lago.
lamp, lámpara.
language, lengua, el idioma.
lard, manteca (de cerdo).
large, grande.
last v., durar; adj., (of a series) último, –a; — month, el (mes) próximo pasado.
late adv., tarde.
laundress, lavandera.
laundryman, lavandero.
lawyer, abogado.
lay (eggs), poner §265; — down, poner, acostar (ue).
lazy, perezoso, –a, flojo, –a.
leaf, hoja.
league, legua (= about 3 miles, or 5 kilometers).
learn, aprender.
least, menor; at —, al menos, por lo menos.
leather, cuero.
leave, dejar, intrans. partir; to take —, despedirse.
lecture, conferencia; — room, sala de conferencias, aula.
left, izquierdo, –a.
leg, pierna, (of chair, etc.) el pie.
lend, prestar.
length, la longitud.
less adj., menor; adv., menos.
lesson, la lección.
let, dejar, permitir; — us go, vamos.

letter, carta; — box, el buzón; — carrier, cartero.
lettuce, lechuga.
Lewis, Luis.
library, biblioteca.
lie v., mentir (ie); — down, acostarse (ue).
life, vida.
lift, el ascensor, el elevador (Mex.).
light, la luz; v., alumbrar; adj., ligero, –a.
lighten, relampaguear.
lightning, relámpago(s).
likable, simpático, –a.
like v., gustar (de); I —, me gusta; I should —, me gustaría, quisiera.
line, línea; in a straight —, en línea recta.
linen, hilo; bed —, ropa de cama.
liquid, líquido; adj., líquido, –a.
list, lista.
listen, escuchar.
liter, litro.
literature, literatura.
little, poco, –a; a — money, un poco de dinero; (= small) pequeño, –a, chico, –a.
live, vivir.
load v., cargar.
long, largo, –a; be — (= delay), tardar en; it will not be — before he returns, no tardará en volver; adv., as — as, mientras (que); no —er, ya no.
look (at), mirar; — for, buscar; — out! ¡tenga Vd. cuidado!
looking-glass, espejo.
loose, suelto, –a.
Lord, Señor.
lose, perder (ie).   [tón de.
lot: a — of, muchos, –as, un mon-
loud, alto, –a.
Louis, Luis.
love v., amar.
low, bajo, –a; (price) reducido, –a.

luggage, el equipaje.
lukewarm, tibio, –a.
lunch, almuerzo; v., almorzar (ue)
luxe: de —, de lujo.
luxury, lujo.

M

madam, señora; my dear —, muy señora mía.
mail, correo.
main, principal.
maize, el maíz.
make, hacer §266, construir, efectuar; — one's way, dirigirse a.
mamma, mamá.
man, el hombre.
manifest, manifestar (ie).
manner, manera, modo.
map, el mapa.
March, marzo.
mark, signo; exclamation —, punto de admiración; interrogation —, punto de interrogación; v., marcar, señalar.
market, mercado; — place, plaza.
marmalade, pasta.
marriage, boda, el enlace.
married, casado, –a.
marry, casar, casarse con.
Mary, María.
masculine, masculino, –a.
Master, (el) señorito.   [(Mex.).]
match, fósforo, cerilla o cerillo
material, el material.
matter: what is the —? ¿qué hay? what is the — with you? ¿qué tiene Vd.? nothing is the — with me, no tengo nada.
May, mayo.
meal, comida.
meaning, significado.
measure, medida; v., medir (i).
meat, la carne.
medicine, medicina, remedio.
meet, v., encontrar (ue), conocer.
mend, remendar (ie).

mention v., mencionar.

metric, métrico, –a.

mexican, mejicano, –a.

Mexico, México o Méjico; City of —, México, Ciudad de México.

middle, medio, la mitad; adj., me-mile, milla.   [dio, –a.

milk, la leche.

minus, menos.

minute, minuto.

mirror, espejo.

Miss, (la) señorita, doña.

mistake, el error.

mistaken: be —, equivocarse, es-tar equivocado, –a.

mock v., burlarse de.

mode, modo.

moment, momento; at this —, en este momento.

Monday, el lunes.

monetary, monetario, –a.

money, dinero; post-office — order, giro postal; without —, apurado, –a, sin dinero.

month, el mes; last —, el (mes) próximo pasado.

monument, monumento.

mood, modo.

moon, luna; the — is shining, hace (hay) luna.

Moor, moro, –a.

more, más; no —, ya no.

moreover, además (de).

morning, mañana; in the —, por o en la mañana; good —! ¡buenos días!

mortal, mortal.

most, más, la mayor parte (de).

mother, madre; your —, su señora madre de Vd.

motion pictures, cinematógrafo, el "cine" o el "cinema."

motive, motivo.

motor car, el automóvil.

mountains or mountain range, sierra.

move v., mover (ue).

moving pictures ("movies"), ci-nematógrafo.

Mr., (el) señor; (before given names) don; — and Mrs. García, el señor García y su señora es-posa, los señores de García.

Mrs., (la) señora, (before given names) doña.

much, mucho, –a; very —, muchí-simo, –a; so —, tanto, –a; adv., multiply, multiplicar.   [mucho.

music, música.

must, deber, tener que; (according to opinion) deber de; one —, hay que.

mute, mudo, –a.

mutton, la carne de carnero.

N

name, el nombre; given or Chris-tian —, nombre de bautismo o de pila; family —, apellido.

namely, a saber.

napkin, servilleta.

near, cerca; prep., cerca de.

nearly, casi.

necessary, necesario, –a; preciso, –a.

neck, cuello; —tie, corbata.

need v., necesitar (de); I —, ne-cesito (de), me hace falta.

needle, aguja.

negation, la negación.

negative, negativo, –a.

neighbor, vecino, –a.

neither, tampoco; — . . . nor, ni . . . ni.

nephew, sobrino.

nest, nido.

never, nunca, jamás.

new, nuevo, –a.

news, noticias; — item, noticia; what is the —? ¿qué hay de nuevo?

newspaper, periódico.

next, próximo, –a, siguiente; *adv.*, en seguida.

nickel, el níquel; (*money*) el real (*Spain*), medio real (*Mexico, Cuba, etc.*).

niece, sobrina.

night, la noche; **last** —, anoche; **to**—, esta noche.

no, no.

no, no one, none, ninguno (ningún), –a.

nobody, nadie.

nor, ni.

nose, la nariz.

not, no; — **anyone,** — **anybody,** no . . . nadie, ninguno (ningún), –a.

notebook, cuaderno.

nothing, nada, no . . . nada; — **is the matter with me,** no tengo nada; **be good for** —, no servir para nada.

noun, el nombre, substantivo.

novelty, la novedad.

November, noviembre *m.*

now, ahora, ya.

number, número.

numeral, el numeral.

O

oats, avena.

object, objeto, motivo.

objection: if you have any — **to doing so,** si Vd. tiene inconveniente en hacerlo.

obliged (= *grateful*), agradecido, –a.

observe, observar.

occasion, la ocasión.

occupied, ocupado, –a.

occur, verificarse.

October, octubre *m.*

odor, el olor.

of, de.

offend, ofender.

offer *v.*, ofrecer, conceder, presentar.

office, despacho.

officer, el oficial.

often, a menudo, muchas veces.

oil, el aceite.   [*persons*), mayor

old, viejo, –a, anciano, –a; —**er** (*of*

omission, la omisión, la supresión.

on, en, sobre.

once, una vez; **at** —, desde luego.

only, sólo, solamente, sino, no más que.

open *v.*, abrir; *adj.*, abierto, –a.

opera, ópera; **comic** —, zarzuela.

opportunity, la oportunidad, la ocasión.

or, o, u (*before* o– *or* ho–).

orange, naranja.

order (= *arrangement*), el orden; (*religious or military*) la orden; (*for merchandise*) pedido, la orden; **in** — **to,** para; **in** — **that,** para que; *v.*, pedir (i), mandar.

ordinary, regular.

organ, órgano.

orthographic, ortográfico, –a.

orthography, ortografía.

other, otro, –a; **the** —**s,** los *o* las demás, el resto.

ought to, deber; **he** — —, debiera.

ounce, onza.

oven, horno.

overcast (*with clouds*), nublado, –a.

overcoat, sobretodo, el gabán.

owner, dueño.

P

pack *v.*, empaquetar, embalar; — **a trunk,** hacer *o* arreglar un baúl.

package, el paquete.

page, página.

pain, el dolor.

pair, el par; **a** — **of scissors, unas** tijeras.

pale, pálido, –a.

pan, cazuela.

papa, el papá.

paper, el papel.

parcel, el paquete.
pardon, el perdón.
pardon v., perdonar.
parents, los padres.
parish priest, el cura.
part, la parte.
participle, participio.
pass v., pasar.
passage, travesía.
passenger, pasajero, -a, (on train) viajero, -a.
passive, pasivo, -a.
past, pasado, -a.
patient, enfermo, -a.
Paul, Pablo.
paw, pata.
pay v., pagar; — attention, prestar atención.
payment, pago.
pea, el guisante, chícharo (Span. Am.)
pen, pluma; fountain —, pluma estilográfica, la plumafuente o la pluma de fuente (in most of Span. Am.).
pencil, el lápiz.
penknife, el cortaplumas.
people, pueblo, la gente.
pepper, pimienta.
"per," por.
perceive, percibir.
perfect, perfecto, -a.
perfectly, perfectamente.
perform: — (a play, etc.) for the first time, estrenar.
performance, la función.
perfume, el aroma, el perfume.
period (in punctuation), punto.
permit v., permitir.
person, persona.
Peter, Pedro.
petroleum, petróleo.
Philip, Felipe.
phonetic, fonético, -a.
physician, médico.
piano, piano.

picture, cuadro.
piece, pieza, (= fragment) pedazo.
pier, el muelle.
pill, píldora.
pillow, almohada; —case, funda (de almohada).
pineapple, (in Spain) anana, (in Span. Am.) el ananá o el ananás.
pipe, tubo; steam —, tubo de vapor.
pitcher (= jug), jarro.
pity: it is a —, es (una) lástima.
place, el lugar, sitio; take —, verificarse, tener lugar; v., colocar.
plain, pampa.
planet, el planeta.
plank, tabla.
plant, planta.
plantation, hacienda.
planter, hacendado.
plate, plato.
play v., jugar (ue); — ball, jugar a la pelota; (on a musical instrument) tocar.
pleasant, agradable, simpático, -a.
please, gustar, agradar; it —s me greatly, me agrada o gusta mucho; (= be kind enough to) hágame Vd. el favor de, sírvase Vd.
pleasing, grato, -a.
pleasure, gusto, el placer.
pluperfect, pluscuamperfecto.
plus, más.
pocket, bolsillo, bolsa (Mex.).
pocketbook, el portamonedas.
poem, poesía, el cantar, el poema.
point, punto; — out, señalar, indicar.
polite, cortés.
poor, pobre.
popularly, popularmente.
port (= left), el babor.
position, la colocación, la posición.
possessive, posesivo, -a.

possible, posible.

post *v.*, echar al correo *o* en el buzón.

postage, el porte; — stamp, sello *o* estampilla de correo, sello *o* estampilla postal; — prepaid, franco de porte.

postman, cartero.

post office, correo, casa de correos; — box, apartado *o* casilla (de correos).

pot, olla.

potato, patata (*Spain*), papa (*Span. Am.*); sweet —, batata, el camote (*Mex.*), boniato (*Cuba*).

pound, libra; 25 —s, arroba.

pour *v.*, echar.

powder, polvo; tooth—, polvos dentífricos.

prairie, pampa.

prefer, preferir (ie).

prepare, preparar.

preposition, la preposición.

present *n.*, regalo; *v.*, presentar; *adj.*, presente, actual; — month, el corriente, el actual; be — (at), asistir (a).

president, el presidente.

press *v.*, estrechar.

preterite, pretérito.

pretty, bonito, -a, lindo, -a; *adv.*, bastante.

price, precio.

principal, director, -ora; *adj.*, principal.

print *v.*, imprimir; —ed matter, los impresos.

private, particular.

prize, premio.

probability, la probabilidad.

produce, *v.*, producir.

product, producto.

professor, profesor, -ora, catedrático (*in university*).

program, el programa.

prohibit, prohibir.

promise *v.*, prometer.

promptly, al punto.

pronoun, el pronombre.

proper: be —, convenir §264.

provided that, siempre que, con tal que.

public, público, -a; — square, plaza.

publish, publicar.

publisher, el editor; —(s) and bookdealer(s), librería general.

publishing house, casa editorial.

pull, tiro.

pulse, pulso.

punish, castigar.

purchase, compra.

pure, puro, -a.

purse, bolsa, el portamonedas.

put, poner §265; — (in or into), meter (en); — on (*shoes*), calzar; — on one's shoes, calzarse.

Q

quotation marks, comillas.

R

race, raza.

railway, el ferrocarril.

rain *v.*, llover (ue) ; *n.*, lluvia.

raise, levantar.

range (= *modern cooking* —), cocina económica, *also* estufa (*Mex.*).

rather, más bien, mejor dicho, bastante.

read, leer.

reader (= *reading book*), libro de lectura.

reading, lectura; — book, libro de lectura.

receipt, recibo.

receive, recibir.

reception, recibo; — room, sala (de recibo).

recite, recitar.

red, rojo, -a, (of wine) tinto, -a.
reduce, reducir.
reflexive, reflexivo, -a.
regard: in — to, cuanto a; with —
to, respecto de; —s, recuerdos,
respetos.
register (a letter, package, etc.),
certificar.
regret v., sentir (ie).
regular, regular.
reiterate, reiterar.
rejoice at, alegrarse de, celebrar.
religious, religioso, -a.
remain, quedar(se), permanecer.
remedy, remedio; v., remediar.
remember, acordarse (ue) de; if I
— rightly, si mal no me acuerdo.
reminder, recuerdo.
remit, remitir.
remittance, remesa.
repair v., reparar, hacer las reparaciones; —s, las reparaciones.
repay, corresponder.
repeat, repetir (i), reiterar.
reply v., contestar, corresponder.
request v., pedir (i), rogar (ue),
suplicar.
residence, domicilio.
respect, respeto; with or in — to,
(con) respecto de.
rest, resto, lo (los, las) demás;
(= repose) descanso; v., descansar.
restaurant, el restaurant.
result, resultado.
résumé, la sinopsis.
retire, retirar(se).
return, vuelta; by — mail, a vuelta
de correo; v., volver (ue); he has
—ed, está de vuelta; (= give
back) devolver (ue).
review v., repasar.
revolve, girar.
rich, rico, -a.
ride v., montar; — on horseback,
montar a caballo; — a bicycle,

montar en bicicleta; — for
pleasure, pasearse.
right, derecho, -a.
ring (the doorbell), llamar.
rip v., descoser.
rise v., levantarse; (the sun) salir.
river, río.
roast v., asar.
Romance, romance (= derived from
Latin).
roof, techo; flat —, azotea.
room, cuarto, pieza, la habitación;
class—, la clase.
root, la raíz.
rough (as the sea), agitado, -a.
row, fila.
royal, real.
rubber overshoe, chanclo (Spain),
zapato de goma (South Am.),
zapato de hule (Mex.).
ruby, el rubí.
rule, regla; as a —, por regla general.
run v., correr.
rustic, rústico, -a.

S

sack coat, americana (Spain), saco
(Span. Am.).
sad, triste.
saddle, silla; — -horse, caballo de
silla.
said, dicho, -a.
sail, vela.
sailor, marinero.
saint, santo, -a.
salad, ensalada.
salt, la sal.
salute v., saludar.
same, mismo, -a.
satisfaction, la satisfacción.
Saturday, sábado.
savory, sabroso, -a.
say, decir §267; I should — so,
ya lo creo.

scarcely, apenas.

school, escuela; — year, curso.

scissors, tijeras; a pair of —, unas tijeras.

scrub (*floors, kettles, etc.*), fregar (ie).

sea, el *o* la mar.

seasick, mareado, –a; become —, marearse.

season, la estación.

seat, asiento; (*in theater*) butaca; *v.*, sentar (ie); — oneself, be —ed, sentarse.

see, ver § 279.

seek, buscar.

seem, figurarse, parecer; it —s to me, se me figura, me parece.

select, escoger.

self, mismo, –a.

sell, vender.

send, enviar, mandar, remitir.

sending, la expedición.

sentence, la frase, la oración.

September, septiembre *m.*

servant, criado, –a, servidor, –ora; — -boy, mozo.

serve, servir (i).

service, servicio.

set *v.*, poner § 265, sentar (ie).

settle (*an account*), saldar.

several, varios, –as.

Seville, Sevilla.

shake, agitar.

sheep, carnero, oveja.

sheet, sábana.

shilling, el real (*Span. Am.*).

shingle, el tejamaní *o* tejamanil, tablilla (de madera).

shipment (*of goods*), envío.

shipping, la expedición.

shirt, camisa; — bosom, pechera.

shoe, zapato; high —, bota; — dealer, —maker, zapatero; — shop, — store, zapatería

shop, tienda.

short, corto, –a.

should (= *ought to*), deber; he —, él debiera.

show *v.*, mostrar (ue), enseñar, marcar.

showy, vistoso, –a.

shrink, encoger(se).

shut, cerrar (ie).

sick, enfermo, –a.

side, lado.

sideboard, el aparador.

sight, vista.

sign *v.*, firmar(se), subscribir(se).

signature, firma.

significance, significado.

silk, seda.

silver, plata.

since, desde, después.

sing, cantar.

single, simple, suelto, –a.

singular, singular.

sir, señor, caballero; my dear —, muy señor mío.

sister, hermana.

sit (down), sentarse (ie).

site, sitio.

size, tamaño.

skip, saltar.

sky, cielo.

slate, pizarra.

sleep, sueño; *v.*, dormir (ue); go to —, fall a—, dormirse (ue).

sleeping: — car, el cochecama, el coche dormitorio, el "sleeping," el pulmán (*Mex.*); — room, cuarto de dormir.

sleepy: be —, tener sueño.

sleeve, manga.

slipper, zapatilla.

small, chico, –a, pequeño, –a.

smell (*sense of*), olfato, (= *odor*) el olor; *v.*, oler (hue–).

snow, la nieve; *v.*, nevar (ie).

so, así, tan; — as, — that, de manera (modo) que; — much (many), tanto, –a, (tantos, –as); — that (= then), conque; isn't it —? ¿no es verdad? **he did** —, lo hizo.

soap, el jabón.

sock, el calcetín.

sofa, el sofá.

sole, (*of foot*) planta, (*of a shoe*) suela.

some, alguno (algún), –a; *pl.*, algunos, –as, unos, –as.

somebody, alguien.

some one, alguien.

something, algo, alguna cosa.

sometimes, a veces, algunas veces.

somewhat, algo.

son, hijo; —**s and daughters,** hijos.

song, la canción, el cantar.

soon, pronto; **as** — **as,** luego que; **no** —**er,** apenas.

sorrow, el dolor.

soul, el alma *f.*

soup, sopa.

south, el sur.

souvenir, recuerdo.

space, espacio.

Spain, España.

Spaniard, español, –ola.

Spanish, español, –ola, castellano, –a; — **-American,** hispano-americano, –a; — **class,** la clase de español; —**woman,** española.

speak, hablar.

speech, palabra.

spelling, ortografía.

spend, gastar, (*time*) pasar.

split *v.*, partir.

spoon, cuchara.

spring, primavera.

spur, espuela, (*pointed*) el acicate.

square, cuadrado; *adj.*, cuadrado, –a.

stable, caballeriza.

stairs, stairway, escalera.

stamp, sello, estampilla.

starboard (= *right*), el estribor.

starch, el almidón.

state, estado.

stateroom, el camarote.

station, la estación.

stay *v.*, quedar(se), permanecer; — **in bed,** guardar cama.

steam, el vapor.

steamboat, el vapor.

stem (*of a word*), el radical.

still, aún, todavía.

sting, el aguijón.

stocking, media.

stockman, ganadero.

stone, piedra.

stop *v.*, parar, dejar de.

store (= *shop*), tienda.

storm, tormenta, el temporal.

story, cuento, historia; piso; **upper** —, piso alto.

stout, gordo, –a.

stove: cooking —, cocina económica, estufa (*Mex.*).

straight, derecho, –a; **go** — **ahead,** seguir (i) derecho.

straw, paja.

street, la calle; — **car,** el tranvía.

strike (*as a clock*) *v.*, dar; **it is striking one, two,** da la una, dan las dos; — **off,** quitar.

stroll *v.*, pasearse.

strong, fuerte; — **coffee,** el café cargado.

student, alumno, –a, el *o* la estudiante.

study *v.*, estudiar.

subject, sujeto.

subjunctive, subjuntivo.

subordinate, subordinado, –a.

subscribe, subscribir(se).

subscription, la subscripción.

substantive *adj.*, substantivado, –a.

succeed (**in**), lograr.

successively, sucesivamente.

such, such a, tal.

sugar, el *o* la azúcar.

suit (*of clothes*), el traje.

suitable, propio, –a.

sum, suma.

summary, extracto.

summer, verano.

sun, el sol; —shine, sol; the — is shining, hace sol.

Sunday, domingo.

sup, cenar.

supper, cena; have —, cenar.

support v., soportar, mantener §258.

sure, seguro, –a.

surface, la superficie.

surname, apellido.

surprise v., sorprender.

sweet, dulce.

swift, ligero, –a.

swim v., nadar.

synopsis, la sinopsis.

T

table, mesa; — cloth, el mantel.

tailor, el sastre; — shop, "tailor's," sastrería.

take, tomar; — leave, despedirse (i); — away, — off, quitar, retirar; — out, sacar.

tall, alto, –a.

tame, manso, –a.

taste, gusto, el sabor; v., — good, ser sabroso, tener buen sabor.

tea, el te; —spoon, cucharita; — spoonful, cucharadita.

teach, enseñar.

teacher, maestro, –a, profesor, –ora.

tear v., romper, rasgar.

telegram, el telegrama.

telephone, teléfono; v., telefonear.

tell, decir §267.

temperature, temperatura.

temple, templo.

tense, tiempo.

term, término.

terminate, terminar.

than, que, de.

thanks! thank you! ¡gracias!

that rel., que; dem., ese, –a, –o; aquel, aquella, aquello; conj., que, (= in order that) para que.

that one, ése, –a; aquél, aquélla.

theater, teatro.

theme, el tema.

then, entonces, luego.

there, allí, allá; (near the person addressed) ahí; — is (are), hay.

Theresa, Teresa.

thermometer, termómetro.

thick, grueso, –a, espeso, –a.

thickness, grueso.

thimble, el dedal.

thing, cosa.

think, pensar (ie), creer; what do you — about it? ¿qué le parece a Vd.? if you — best, si le parece a Vd.

thirst, la sed.

thirsty: be —, tener sed.

this, este, –a, –o; — one, éste, –a.

thread, hilo.

through, por.

throw, tiro; v., arrojar, tirar, echar.

thunder, trueno(s); v., tronar (ue).

Thursday, el jueves.

ticket, el billete, boleto (Span. Am.); round-trip —, billete (boleto) de ida y vuelta.

till v., labrar; prep., hasta.

time, tiempo, la vez; a long —, mucho tiempo; three —s, tres veces; — limit, plazo; from — to —, de vez en cuando; what — (o'clock) is it? ¿qué hora es? it is — to (for), es hora de.

tip, propina.

tired, cansado, –a.

to, a, hasta.

tobacco, tabaco.

to-day, hoy.

to-morrow, mañana; the day after —, pasado mañana.

ton, tonelada.

tongue, lengua.

too, demasiado; — **much (many),** demasiado, -a (-os, -as); **too . . . to,** muy . . . para; (= *also*) también.

tooth, el diente; **molar** —, muela; —**brush,** cepillo de dientes *o* cepillo para los dientes; —**powder,** polvos dentífricos *o* polvos para los dientes; —**ache,** el dolor de muelas.

torn, roto, -a.

touch *v.*, tocar.

towel, toalla.

town, pueblo, la población.

tragedy, tragedia.

train, el tren.

tramway, el tranvía.

tranquil, tranquilo, -a.

translate, traducir §278.

traveler, viajero, -a.

treacherous, traidor, -ora.

tree, el árbol.

trick, broma; **play** —s, dar bromas.

trip, el viaje.

tropical, tropical.

trouble, molestia; *v.*, molestar.

trousers, los pantalones (*also* el pantalón).

true, cierto, -a; **it is** —, es verdad; **isn't it** —? ¿no es verdad?

trunk, el baúl.

truth, la verdad.

try, procurar, tratar de.

Tuesday, el martes.

turn *v.*, volver (ue), doblar (*la esquina, página, etc.*); (= *become*) ponerse §265.

U

ugly, feo, -a.

unbound, en *o* a la rústica.

uncle, tío.

under, debajo de.

underclothes, ropa interior.

underline, subrayar.

understand, entender (ie).

union, el enlace, la unión.

unite, unir.

United States, Estados Unidos; **of the** — —, estad(o)unidense.

unity, la unidad.

university, la universidad.

unless, a menos que.

unoccupied, desocupado, -a.

unpleasant, desagradable.

untie, desatar.

until, hasta que.

upon, en, sobre.

upper, superior; — **story,** piso alto.

use, empleo, uso.

use *v.*, servirse (i) de, usar, emplear; **be** —**d to,** estar acostumbrado a.

useful, útil.

utensil, utensilio, trasto.

V

vacation(s), las vacaciones.

valise, maleta.

variable, variable.

variation, la variación.

variety, la variedad.

vary, variar.

vaudeville theater, teatro de variedades.

vegetables, verduras, las legumbres.

veranda, galería.

verb, verbo.

very, muy, mucho.

vessel, el buque.

vest, chaleco.

vestibule, el zaguán.

vigor, el vigor.

vinegar, el vinagre.

visit, visita; *v.*, visitar.

vocabulary, vocabulario.

voice, la voz.

volume, el volumen, tomo (= *part of a work, several* **tomos** *being sometimes bound in one* **volumen**).

voyage, el viaje.
vulgarly, vulgarmente.

W

waistcoat, chaleco.
wait (for), aguardar, esperar.
waiter, mozo, camarero, mesero (*Mex.*).
wake up, despertarse (ie).
walk *v.,* ir a pie, (*for pleasure*) pasearse.
wall, la pared, muro.
walnut: English —, la nuez.
want *v.,* querer §271.
ward (= *part of a city*), barrio.
warm, calentar (ie); *adj.,* caliente; **I am —,** tengo calor; **it is —** (*of the weather*), hace calor.
warmth, el calor.
wash *v.,* lavar.
watch, el reloj, reloj de bolsillo; *v.,* **— over,** vigilar.
water, el agua *f.*
watery, aguanoso, –a.
wave, ola.
wax, cera; **— match,** cerilla, cerillo (*Mex.*).
way, camino; **make one's — (to),** dirigirse (a).
weak, débil.
wear *v.,* llevar, usar; **— out,** usar.
weather, tiempo.
Wednesday, el miércoles.
week, semana; **one —,** ocho días; **two —s,** quince días; **next —,** la semana que viene.
weep, llorar.
weigh, pesar.
weight, peso, (*with which to weigh*) pesa; **of —,** ponderal.
well, bien, pues; **— then,** pues; **be —,** estar bueno, –a.
west, el oeste.
western, occidental.
wharf, el muelle.

what (a), ¡qué!, (= *that which*) lo que; *interrog.,* qué, (= *which*) cuál.
wheat, trigo.
when, cuando; *interrog.,* cuándo, a qué hora.
where, donde; *interrog.,* dónde.
which, que; el, la *o* lo cual; el, la *o* lo que; *interrog.,* cuál, qué.
while, mientras (que), en tanto que.
white, blanco, –a.
who, que; el *o* la cual; el *o* la que; quien; *interrog.,* quién.
whoever, quien(es)quiera.
whom *rel.,* que, quien, el cual, *etc.*; el que, *etc.*; *interrog.,* quién.
whose *rel.,* cuyo, –a, de quien; *interrog.,* de quién.
whosoever, quien(es)quiera.
why, por qué, a qué, para qué; *exclam.,* si.
wide, ancho, –a.
width, anchura.
wife, esposa.
will *v.,* querer §271.
wind, viento.
window, ventana.
wine, vino.
wing, ala.
winter, invierno.
wipe, secar, enjugar.
wish *v.,* desear, querer §271; **I — he would do it,** yo quisiera, *o* ojalá, que él lo hiciera.
wit: to —, a saber.
with, con; **— me,** conmigo; **— himself, herself,** *etc.,* consigo; **— thee (you),** contigo.
within, adentro.
without, sin; **— accident,** sin novedad; **— money,** apurado, –a, sin dinero.
woman, mujer.
wood, (*for manufacture, building, etc.*) madera, (*for fuel*) leña.

wool, lana.
woolen, de lana.
word, palabra.
work, trabajo, (*of literature, music, art, e'c.*) obra; *v.,* trabajar.
worker: he is a hard —, es muy aplicado.
world, mundo.
worry: do not —, pierda Vd. cuidado.
worship, la adoración.
worth, el valor; **be** —, valer §273.
would that, ojalá (que).
write, escribir.

written, escrito, –a, *irr. p.p. of* escribir; — **exercise,** el tema.

Y

yard, el corral; vara (= *32 inches*).
year, año; **New Year's Day,** Año nuevo; **school** —, curso; **be eight** —**s old,** cumplir ocho años.
yellow, amarillo, –a.
yes, sí.
yesterday, ayer.
yet, aún, todavía; **not** —, todavía no.
young, joven; —**er,** —**est** (*of persons*), menor.
youth, la juventud.

INDEX

The numbers refer to sections unless otherwise indicated